T0181806

Lecture Notes in Artificial Intelligence 11683

Subseries of Lecture Notes in Computer Science

More information about this series at http://www.springer.com/series/1244

Ngoc Thanh Nguyen · Richard Chbeir ·
Ernesto Exposito · Philippe Aniorté ·
Bogdan Trawiński (Eds.)

Computational Collective Intelligence

11th International Conference, ICCCI 2019
Hendaye, France, September 4–6, 2019
Proceedings, Part I

 Springer

Editors
Ngoc Thanh Nguyen 🆔
Ton Duc Thang University
Ho Chi Minh City, Vietnam

Wrocław University of Science
and Technology
Wrocław, Poland

Ernesto Exposito 🆔
University of Pau and Pays de l'Adour
Pau, France

Bogdan Trawiński 🆔
Wrocław University of Science
and Technology
Wrocław, Poland

Richard Chbeir 🆔
University of Pau and Pays de l'Adour
Pau, France

Philippe Aniorté 🆔
University of Pau and Pays de l'Adour
Pau, France

ISSN 0302-9743   ISSN 1611-3349   (electronic)
Lecture Notes in Artificial Intelligence
ISBN 978-3-030-28376-6   ISBN 978-3-030-28377-3   (eBook)
https://doi.org/10.1007/978-3-030-28377-3

LNCS Sublibrary: SL7 – Artificial Intelligence

This Springer imprint is published by the registered company Springer Nature Switzerland AG
The registered company address is: Gewerbestrasse 11, 6330 Cham, Switzerland

Preface

This volume contains the proceedings of the 11th International Conference on Computational Collective Intelligence (ICCCI 2019), held in Hendaye, France, September 4–6, 2019. The conference was co-organized by the French SIGAPP Chapter (ACM Special Interest Group on Applied Computing), the LIUPPA (Laboratoire d'Informatique de l'Université de Pau et des Pays de l'Adour), France, and the Wrocław University of Science and Technology, Poland. The conference was run under the patronage of the IEEE SMC Technical Committee on Computational Collective Intelligence.

Following the successes of the First ICCCI (2009) held in Wrocław, Poland, the Second ICCCI (2010) in Kaohsiung, Taiwan, the Third ICCCI (2011) in Gdynia, Poland, the 4th ICCCI (2012) in Ho Chi Minh City, Vietnam, the 5th ICCCI (2013) in Craiova, Romania, the 6th ICCCI (2014) in Seoul, South Korea, the 7th ICCCI (2015) in Madrid, Spain, the 8th ICCCI (2016) in Halkidiki, Greece, the 9th ICCCI (2017) in Nicosia, Cyprus, and the 10th ICCCI (2018) in Bristol, UK, this conference continued to provide an internationally respected forum for scientific research in the computer-based methods of collective intelligence and their applications.

Computational collective intelligence (CCI) is most often understood as a sub-field of artificial intelligence (AI) dealing with soft computing methods that facilitate group decisions or processing knowledge among autonomous units acting in distributed environments. Methodological, theoretical, and practical aspects of CCI are considered as the form of intelligence that emerges from the collaboration and competition of many individuals (artificial and/or natural). The application of multiple computational intelligence technologies such as fuzzy systems, evolutionary computation, neural systems, consensus theory, etc., can support human and other collective intelligence, and create new forms of CCI in natural and/or artificial systems. Three subfields of the application of computational intelligence technologies to support various forms of collective intelligence are of special interest but are not exclusive: the Semantic Web (as an advanced tool for increasing collective intelligence), social network analysis (as the field targeted at the emergence of new forms of CCI), and multi-agent systems (as a computational and modeling paradigm especially tailored to capture the nature of CCI emergence in populations of autonomous individuals).

The ICCCI 2019 conference featured a number of keynote talks and oral presentations, closely aligned to the theme of the conference. The conference attracted a substantial number of researchers and practitioners from all over the world, who submitted their papers for the main track and four special sessions.

The main track, covering the methodology and applications of CCI, included: knowledge engineering and Semantic Web, social networks and recommender systems, text processing and information retrieval, data mining methods and applications, computer vision techniques, decision support and control systems, as well as innovations in intelligent systems. The special sessions, covering some specific topics of particular interest, included: cooperative strategies for decision making and optimization, intelligent modeling and simulation approaches for real world systems, computational collective intelligence and natural language processing, machine learning in real-world data, distributed collective intelligence for smart manufacturing, collective intelligence for science and technology, intelligent management information systems, intelligent sustainable smart cities, new trends and challenges in education: the University 4.0, intelligent processing of multimedia in web systems, as well as big data streaming, applications and security.

We received more than 200 submissions from 41 countries all over the world. Each paper was reviewed by two to four members of the international Program Committee (PC) of either the main track or one of the special sessions. Finally, we selected 117 best papers for oral presentation and publication in two volumes of the *Lecture Notes in Artificial Intelligence* series.

We would like to express our thanks to the keynote speakers: Eneko Agirre from University of the Basque Country, Spain, Costin Bădică from University of Craiova, Romania, Piotr Jędrzejowicz from Gdynia Maritime University, Poland, and Nicolas Spyratos from Paris-Sud (Paris-Saclay) University, France, for their world-class plenary speeches.

Many people contributed toward the success of the conference. First, we would like to recognize the work of the PC co-chairs and special sessions organizers for taking good care of the organization of the reviewing process, an essential stage in ensuring the high quality of the accepted papers. The workshop and special session chairs deserve a special mention for the evaluation of the proposals and the organization and coordination of the work of seven special sessions. In addition, we would like to thank the PC members, of the main track and of the special sessions, for performing their reviewing work with diligence. We thank the local Organizing Committee chairs, publicity chair, Web chair, and technical support chair for their fantastic work before and during the conference. Finally, we cordially thank all the authors, presenters, and delegates for their valuable contribution to this successful event. The conference would not have been possible without their support.

Our special thanks are also due to Springer for publishing the proceedings and sponsoring awards, and to all the other sponsors for their kind support.

It is our pleasure to announce that the ICCCI conference series continues to have a close cooperation with the Springer journal *Transactions on Computational Collective Intelligence*, and the IEEE SMC Technical Committee on Transactions on Computational Collective Intelligence.

Finally, we hope that ICCCI 2019 contributed significantly to the academic excellence of the field and will lead to the even greater success of ICCCI events in the future.

September 2019

Ngoc Thanh Nguyen
Richard Chbeir
Ernesto Exposito
Philippe Aniorté
Bogdan Trawiński

Organization

Organizing Committee

Honorary Chairs

Mohamad Amara — President of University of Pau and Pays de l'Adour, France

Cezary Madryas — Rector of Wrocław University of Science and Technology, Poland

General Chairs

Richard Chbeir — University of Pau and Pays de l'Adour, France

Ngoc Thanh Nguyen — Wrocław University of Science and Technology, Poland

General Vice-chair

Philippe Aniorté — University of Pau and Pays de l'Adour, France

Program Chairs

Ernesto Exposito — University of Pau and Pays de l'Adour, France

Nick Bassiliades — Aristotle University of Thessaloniki, Greece

Costin Bădică — University of Craiova, Romania

Gottfried Vossen — University of Münster, Germany

Edward Szczerbicki — University of Newcastle, Australia

Organizing Chair

Khouloud Salameh — American University of Ras Al Khaimah, UAE

Steering Committee

Ngoc Thanh Nguyen — Wrocław University of Science and Technology, Poland

Shyi-Ming Chen — National Taiwan University of Science and Technology, Taiwan

Toyoaki Nishida — Kyoto University, Japan

Geun-Sik Jo — Inha University, South Korea

Kiem Hoang — University of Information Technology, VNU-HCM, Vietnam

Ryszard Kowalczyk — Swinburne University of Technology, Australia

Lakhmi C. Jain — University of South Australia, Australia

Janusz Kacprzyk	Polish Academy of Sciences, Poland
Manuel Núñez	Universidad Complutense de Madrid, Spain
Yannis Manolopolos	Aristotle University of Thessaloniki, Greece
Piotr Jędrzejowicz	Gdynia Maritime University, Poland
Dosam Hwang	Yeungnam University, South Korea

Special Session Chairs

| Bogdan Trawiński | Wrocław University of Science and Technology, Poland |
| Joe Tekli | Lebanese American University, Lebanon |

Doctoral Track Chair

| Khouloud Salameh | American University of Ras Al Khaimah, UAE |

Publicity Chairs

| Philippe Arnould | University of Pau and Pays de l'Adour, France |
| Marek Krótkiewicz | Wrocław University of Science and Technology, Poland |

Webmaster

| Elio Mansour | University of Pau and Pays de l'Adour, France |

Local Organizing Committee

Elio Mansour	University of Pau and Pays de l'Adour, France
Lara Kallab	University of Pau and Pays de l'Adour, France
Karam Bou Chaaya	University of Pau and Pays de l'Adour, France
Marcin Jodłowiec	Wrocław University of Science and Technology, Poland
Bernadetta Maleszka	Wrocław University of Science and Technology, Poland
Marcin Maleszka	Wrocław University of Science and Technology, Poland
Krystian Wojtkiewicz	Wrocław University of Science and Technology, Poland

Keynote Speakers

Eneko Agirre	University of the Basque Country, Spain
Costin Bădică	University of Craiova, Romania
Piotr Jędrzejowicz	Gdynia Maritime University, Poland
Nicolas Spyratos	Paris-Sud (Paris-Saclay) University, France

Special Session Organizers

BiSAS 2019 – Special Session on Big Data Streaming, Applications and Security

Raja Chiky	ISEP Paris, France
Farid Meziane	Salford University, UK

CCINLP 2019 – Special Session on Computational Collective Intelligence and Natural Language Processing

Ismaïl Biskri	University of Québec à Trois-Rivières, Canada
Adel Jebali	Concordia University, Canada

CIST 2019 – Special Session on Collective Intelligence for Science and Technology

Habiba Drias	Laboratory of Research in Artificial Intelligence, USTHB, Algiers, Algeria
Sadok Ben Yahia	Tallinn University of Technology, Estonia
Abdellatif El-Afia	University Mohammed V in Rabat, ENSIAS, Morocco
Nadjet Kamel	University Ferhat Abbas Setif 1, Algeria

CSDMO 2019 – Special Session on Cooperative Strategies for Decision Making and Optimization

Dariusz Barbucha	Gdynia Maritime University, Poland
Ireneusz Czarnowski	Gdynia Maritime University, Poland
Piotr Jędrzejowicz	Gdynia Maritime University, Poland

DCISM 2019 – Distributed Collective Intelligence for Smart Manufacturing

Marcin Fojcik	Western Norway University of Applied Sciences, Norway
Rafał Cupek	Silesian University of Technology, Poland
Adam Ziębiński	Silesian University of Technology, Poland
Knut Øvsthus	Western Norway University of Applied Sciences, Norway

IMIS 2019 – Special Session on Intelligent Management Information Systems

Marcin Hernes	Wrocław University of Economics, Poland
Artur Rot	Wrocław University of Economics, Poland

IMSARWS 2019 – Special Session on Intelligent Modeling and Simulation Approaches for Real World Systems

Doina Logofătu	Frankfurt University of Applied Sciences, Germany
Costin Bădică	University of Craiova, Romania
Florin Leon	Gheorghe Asachi Technical University of Iaşi, Romania

ISSC 2019 – Special Session on Intelligent Sustainable Smart Cities

Libuše Svobodová	University of Hradec Kralove, Czech Republic
Ali Selamat	Universiti Teknology Malaysia, Malaysia
Petra Marešová	University of Hradec Kralove, Czech Republic
Arkadiusz Kawa	Poznan University of Economics and Business, Poland
Bartłomiej Pierański	Poznan University of Economics and Business, Poland
Miroslava Mikušová	University of Zilina, Slovakia

MLRWD 2019 – Special Session on Machine Learning in Real-World Data

Krzysztof Kania	University of Economics in Katowice, Poland
Jan Kozak	University of Economics in Katowice, Poland
Przemysław Juszczuk	University of Economics in Katowice, Poland
Barbara Probierz	University of Economics in Katowice, Poland

UNI4.0 2019 Special Session on New Trends and Challenges in Education: The University 4.0

Ernesto Exposito	University of Pau and Pays de l'Adour, France
Philippe Aniorté	University of Pau and Pays de l'Adour, France
Laurent Gallon	University of Pau and Pays de l'Adour, France

WEBSYS 2019 – Intelligent Processing of Multimedia in Web Systems

Kazimierz Choroś	Wrocław University of Science and Technology, Poland
Maria Trocan	Institut Supérieur d'électronique de Paris, France

Program Committee

Muhammad Abulaish	South Asian University, India
Waseem Ahmad	Toi Ohomai Institute of Technology, New Zealand
Sharat Akhoury	University of Cape Town, South Africa
Jacky Akoka	Conservatoire National des Arts et Métiers, France
Ana Almeida	GECAD-ISEP-IPP, Portugal
Orcan Alpar	University of Hradec Kralove, Czech Republic
Bashar Al-Shboul	University of Jordan, Jordan
Adel Alti	University of Setif, Algeria
Vardis Dimitrios Anezakis	Democritus University of Thrace, Greece
Taha Arbaoui	University of Technology of Troyes, France
Philippe Arnoult	University of Pau and Pays de l'Adour, France
Mehmet Emin Aydin	University of the West of England, Bristol, UK
Thierry Badard	Laval University, Canada
Amelia Badica	University of Craiova, Romania
Costin Badica	University of Craiova, Romania
Dariusz Barbucha	Gdynia Maritime University, Poland
Khalid Benali	University of Lorraine, France

Morad Benyoucef	University of Ottawa, Canada
Leon Bobrowski	Białystok University of Technology, Poland
Mariusz Boryczka	University of Silesia, Poland
Urszula Boryczka	University of Silesia, Poland
Abdelhamid Bouchachia	Bournemouth University, UK
Peter Brida	University of Zilina, Slovakia
Krisztian Buza	Budapest University of Technology and Economics, Hungary
Aleksander Byrski	AGH University of Science and Technology, Poland
Jose Luis Calvo-Rolle	University of A Coruña, Spain
David Camacho	Universidad Autonoma de Madrid, Spain
Alberto Cano	Virginia Commonwealth University, USA
Frantisek Capkovic	Institute of Informatics, Slovak Academy of Sciences, Slovakia
Stefano A. Cerri	University of Montpellier, France
Richard Chbeir	University of Pau and Pays de l'Adour, France
Shyi-Ming Chen	National Taiwan University of Science and Technology, Taiwan
Raja Chiky	Institut Supérieur d'électronique de Paris, France
Sung-Bae Cho	Yonsei University, South Korea
Amine Chohra	Paris-East University, France
Kazimierz Choroś	Wrocław University of Science and Technology, Poland
Christophe Claramunt	Naval Academy Research Institute, France
Mihaela Colhon	University of Craiova, Romania
Jose Alfredo Ferreira Costa	Universidade Federal do Rio Grande do Norte, Brazil
Nadine Cullot	University of Burgundy, France
Rafał Cupek	Silesian University of Technology, Poland
Ireneusz Czarnowski	Gdynia Maritime University, Poland
Paul Davidsson	Malmo University, Sweden
Camelia Delcea	Bucharest University of Economic Studies, Romania
Tien V. Do	Budapest University of Technology and Economics, Hungary
Habiba Drias	University of Science and Technology Houari Boumedienne, Algeria
Mohamed El Yafrani	Aalborg University, Denmark
Nadia Essoussi	University of Tunis, Tunisia
Marcin Fojcik	Western Norway University of Applied Sciences, Norway
Anna Formica	IASI-CNR, Italy
Naoki Fukuta	Shizuoka University, Japan
Mohamed Gaber	Birmingham City University, UK
Laurent Gallon	University of Pau and Pays de l'Adour, France
Faiez Gargouri	University of Sfax, Tunisia
Mauro Gaspari	University of Bologna, Italy
K. M. George	Oklahoma State University, USA

Janusz Getta	University of Wollongong, Australia
Daniela Gifu	University Alexandru Ioan Cuza of Iasi, Romania
Fethullah Göçer	Galatasaray University, Turkey
Daniela Godoy	ISISTAN Research Institute, Argentina
Manuel Grana	University of Basque Country, Spain
Michael Granitzer	University of Passau, Germany
Patrizia Grifoni	IRPPS-CNR, Italy
Foteini Grivokostopoulou	University of Patras, Greece
William Grosky	University of Michigan, USA
Kenji Hatano	Doshisha University, Japan
Marcin Hernes	Wrocław University of Economics, Poland
Huu Hanh Hoang	Hue University, Vietnam
Tzung-Pei Hong	National University of Kaohsiung, Taiwan
Mong-Fong Horng	National Kaohsiung University of Applied Sciences, Taiwan
Frédéric Hubert	Laval University, Canada
Maciej Huk	Wrocław University of Science and Technology, Poland
Zbigniew Huzar	Wrocław University of Science and Technology, Poland
Dosam Hwang	Yeungnam University, South Korea
Lazaros Iliadis	Democritus University of Thrace, Greece
Mirjana Ivanovic	University of Novi Sad, Serbia
Indu Jain	Jiwaji University, India
Jarosław Jankowski	West Pomeranian University of Technology, Poland
Joanna Jędrzejowicz	University of Gdansk, Poland
Piotr Jędrzejowicz	Gdynia Maritime University, Poland
Gordan Jezic	University of Zagreb, Croatia
Geun Sik Jo	Inha University, South Korea
Kang-Hyun Jo	University of Ulsan, South Korea
Christophe Jouis	Université de la Sorbonne Nouvelle Paris 3, France
Jason Jung	Chung-Ang University, South Korea
Przemysław Juszczuk	University of Economics in Katowice, Poland
Tomasz Kajdanowicz	Wrocław University of Science and Technology, Poland
Petros Kefalas	University of Sheffield, Greece
Rafał Kern	Wrocław University of Science and Technology, Poland
Marek Kisiel-Dorohinicki	AGH University of Science and Technology, Poland
Attila Kiss	Eotvos Lorand University, Hungary
Marek Kopel	Wrocław University of Science and Technology, Poland
Leszek Koszałka	Wrocław University of Science and Technology, Poland

Leszek Kotulski	AGH University of Science and Technology, Poland
Abderrafiaa Koukam	Université de Technologie de Belfort-Montbéliard, France
Ivan Koychev	University of Sofia St. Kliment Ohridski, Bulgaria
Jan Kozak	University of Economics in Katowice, Poland
Adrianna Kozierkiewicz	Wrocław University of Science and Technology, Poland
Bartosz Krawczyk	Virginia Commonwealth University, USA
Ondrej Krejcar	University of Hradec Kralove, Czech Republic
Dalia Kriksciuniene	Vilnius University, Lithuania
Dariusz Król	Wrocław University of Science and Technology, Poland
Marek Krótkiewicz	Wrocław University of Science and Technology, Poland
Jan Kubicek	VSB - Technical University of Ostrava, Czech Republic
Elżbieta Kukla	Wrocław University of Science and Technology, Poland
Julita Kulbacka	Wrocław Medical University, Poland
Marek Kulbacki	Polish-Japanese Academy of Information Technology, Poland
Piotr Kulczycki	Polish Academy of Science, Systems Research Institute, Poland
Kazuhiro Kuwabara	Ritsumeikan University, Japan
Halina Kwaśnicka	Wrocław University of Science and Technology, Poland
Imene Lahyani	University of Sfax, Tunisia
Mark Last	Ben-Gurion University of the Negev, Israel
Anne Laurent	University of Montpellier, France
Hoai An Le Thi	University of Lorraine, France
Sylvain Lefebvre	Toyota ITC, France
Philippe Lemoisson	French Agricultural Research Centre for International Development (CIRAD), France
Florin Leon	Gheorghe Asachi Technical University of Iasi, Romania
Doina Logofatu	Frankfurt University of Applied Sciences, Germany
Edwin Lughofer	Johannes Kepler University Linz, Austria
Juraj Machaj	University of Zilina, Slovakia
Bernadetta Maleszka	Wrocław University of Science and Technology, Poland
Marcin Maleszka	Wrocław University of Science and Technology, Poland
Yannis Manolopoulos	Aristotle University of Thessaloniki, Greece
Yi Mei	Victoria University of Wellington, New Zealand
Adam Meissner	Poznań University of Technology, Poland
Héctor Menéndez	University College London, UK

Mercedes Merayo	Universidad Complutense de Madrid, Spain
Jacek Mercik	WSB University in Wrocław, Poland
Radosław Michalski	Wrocław University of Science and Technology, Poland
Peter Mikulecky	University of Hradec Kralove, Czech Republic
Miroslava Mikušová	University of Zilina, Slovakia
Jean-Luc Minel	Université Paris Ouest Nanterre La Défense, France
Javier Montero	Universidad Complutense de Madrid, Spain
Ahmed Moussa	Universite Abdelmalek Essaadi, Morocco
Manuel Munier	University of Pau and Pays de l'Adour, France
Grzegorz J. Nalepa	AGH University of Science and Technology, Poland
Laurent Nana	University of Brest, France
Fulufhelo Nelwamondo	Council for Scientific and Industrial Research, South Africa
Filippo Neri	University of Napoli Federico II, Italy
Linh Anh Nguyen	University of Warsaw, Poland
Loan T. T. Nguyen	Nguyen Tat Thanh University, Vietnam
Adam Niewiadomski	Łódź University of Technology, Poland
Adel Noureddine	University of Pau and Pays de l'Adour, France
Agnieszka Nowak-Brzezińska	University of Silesia, Poland
Alberto Núñez	Universidad Complutense de Madrid, Spain
Manuel Núñez	Universidad Complutense de Madrid, Spain
Tarkko Oksala	Aalto University, Finland
Mieczyslaw Owoc	Wrocław University of Economics, Poland
Marcin Paprzycki	Systems Research Institute, Polish Academy of Sciences, Poland
Batista Paulo	Universidade de Evora, Portugal
Marek Penhaker	VSB - Technical University of Ostrava, Czech Republic
Isidoros Perikos	University of Patras, Greece
Marcin Pietranik	Wrocław University of Science and Technology, Poland
Elias Pimenidis	University of the West of England, Bristol, UK
Nikolaos Polatidis	University of Brighton, UK
Hiram Ponce Espinosa	Universidad Panamericana, Brazil
Piotr Porwik	University of Silesia, Poland
Radu-Emil Precup	Politehnica University of Timisoara, Romania
Paulo Quaresma	Universidade de Evora, Portugal
David Ramsey	Wrocław University of Science and Technology, Poland
Mohammad Rashedur Rahman	North South University, Bangladesh
Ewa Ratajczak-Ropel	Gdynia Maritime University, Poland
Tomasz M. Rutkowski	University of Tokyo, Japan
Virgilijus Sakalauskas	Vilnius University, Lithuania

Imad Saleh	Université Paris 8, France
Maria Luisa Sapino	Universitá di Torino, Italy
Lionel Seinturier	University of Lille, France
Ali Selamat	Universiti Teknologi Malaysia, Malaysia
Nicolas Seydoux	LAAS-CNRS/IRIT, France
Andrzej Siemiński	Wrocław University of Science and Technology, Poland
Dragan Simic	University of Novi Sad, Serbia
Vladimir Sobeslav	University of Hradec Kralove, Czech Republic
Stanimir Stoyanov	University of Plovdiv Paisii Hilendarski, Bulgaria
Libuše Svobodová	University of Hradec Kralove, Czech Republic
Martin Tabakov	Wrocław University of Science and Technology, Poland
Muhammad Atif Tahir	National University of Computer and Emerging Sciences, Pakistan
Yasufumi Takama	Tokyo Metropolitan University, Japan
Joe Tekli	Lebanese American University, Lebanon
Zbigniew Telec	Wrocław University of Science and Technology, Poland
Agma Traina	University of São Paulo, Brazil
Caetano Traina	University of São Paulo, Brazil
Diana Trandabat	University Alexandru Ioan Cuza of Iasi, Romania
Bogdan Trawiński	Wrocław University of Science and Technology, Poland
Jan Treur	Vrije Universiteit Amsterdam, The Netherlands
Maria Trocan	Institut Superieur délectronique de Paris, France
Krzysztof Trojanowski	Cardinal Stefan Wyszyński University in Warsaw, Poland
Chrisa Tsinaraki	European Commission - Joint Research Center, Italy
Ualsher Tukeyev	al-Farabi Kazakh National University, Kazakhstan
Olgierd Unold	Wrocław University of Science and Technology, Poland
Natalie Van Der Wal	Vrije Universiteit Amsterdam, The Netherlands
Genoveva Vargas Solar	CNRS-LIG-LAFMIA, France
Bay Vo	Ho Chi Minh City University of Technology, Vietnam
Izabela Wierzbowska	Gdynia Maritime University, Poland
Adam Wojciechowski	Łódź University of Technology, Poland
Krystian Wojtkiewicz	Wrocław University of Science and Technology, Poland
Charles Yaacoub	Holy Spirit University of Kaslik, Lebanon
Farouk Yalaoui	University of Technology of Troyes, France
Sławomir Zadrożny	Systems Research Institute, Polish Academy of Sciences, Poland
Drago Zagar	University of Osijek, Croatia
Danuta Zakrzewska	Łódź University of Technology, Poland
Constantin-Bala Zamfirescu	Lucian Blaga University of Sibiu, Romania

Katerina Zdravkova	University St Cyril and Methodius, Macedonia
Aleksander Zgrzywa	Wrocław University of Science and Technology, Poland
Adam Ziębiński	Silesian University of Technology, Poland

Special Session Program Committees

BiSAS 2019 – Special Session on Big Data Streaming, Applications and Security

Raja Chiky	ISEP, France
Yousra Chabchoub	ISEP, France
Zakia Kazi-Aoul	ISEP, France
Mohamed Sellami	Telecom Sud Paris, France
Aliou Boly	UCAD, Senegal
Alzennyr Da Silva	EDF, France
Elisabeth Metais	CNAM, France
Farid Meziane	University of Salford, UK
Rosanna Verde	University Campania, Italy
Jacques Demerjian	Lebanese University, Lebanon
Jacques Abou Abdou	Notre Dame University - Louaize, Lebanon
Abdellah Idrissi	Mohammed V University In Rabat, Morocco
Rokia Missaoui	Université Du Quebec En Outaouais, Canada
Sana Belguith	University of Salford, UK
Saraee Mo	University of Salford, UK
Tooska Dergahi	University of Salford, UK

CCINLP 2019 – Special Session on Computational Collective Intelligence and Natural Language Processing

Ismaïl Biskri	Université du Québec à Trois-Rivières, Canada
Mounir Zrigui	Université de Monastir, Tunisia
Anca Pascu	Université de Bretagne Occidentale, France
Éric Poirier	Université du Québec à Trois-Rivières, Canada
Fatiha Sadat	Université du Québec à Montréal, Canada
Adel Jebali	Concordia University, Canada
Eva Hajiova	Charles University, Prague, Czech Republic
Khaled Shaalan	British University, Dubai, UAE
Vladislav Kubon	Charles University, Czech Republic
Louis Rompré	Cascades, Canada
Rim Faiz	IHEC, Tunisia

CIST 2019 – Special Session on Collective Intelligence for Science and Technology

Sadok Ben Yahia	Tallinn University of Technology, Estonia
Hadda Cherroun	University of Laghouat, Algeria
Raddouane Chiheb	University Mohammed V in Rabat – ENSIAS, Morocco
Gayo Diallo	University of Bordeaux, France

Dirk Draheim	Tallinn University of Technology, Estonia
Habiba Drias	USTHB Algiers, Algeria
Abdelatif El Afia	University Mohammed V in Rabat – ENSIAS, Morocco
Maria Gini	University of Minnesota, USA
Fadratul Hafinaz	University of Sains, Malaysia
Chihab Hannachi	University of Toulouse 1, France
Said Jabbour	University of Artois, France
Imed Kacem	University of Lorraine, France
Nadjet Kamel	University Ferhat Abbas Sétif 1, Algeria
Saroj Kaushik	Indian Institute of Technology Delhi, India
Samir Kechid	USTHB Algiers, Algeria
Ilyes Khennak	USTHB Algiers, Algeria
Amira Mouakher	University of Bourgogne, France
Alexander Norta	Tallinn University of Technology, Estonia
Mourad Oussalah	Nantes University, France
Houari Sahraoui	University of Montreal, Canada
Lakhdar Sais	University of Artois, France
Djelloul Ziadi	University of Rouen, France
Djaafar Zouache	UBBA, Algeria

CSDMO 2019 – Special Session on Cooperative Strategies for Decision Making and Optimization

Dariusz Barbucha	Gdynia Maritime University, Poland
Amine Chohra	Paris East University, France
Ireneusz Czarnowski	Gdynia Maritime University, Poland
Joanna Jędrzejowicz	Gdansk University, Poland
Piotr Jędrzejowicz	Gdynia Maritime University, Poland
Edyta Kucharska	AGH University of Science and Technology, Poland
Antonio D. Masegosa	University of Deusto, Spain
Jacek Mercik	WSB University in Wroclaw, Poland
Javier Montero	Complutense University, Spain
Ewa Ratajczak-Ropel	Gdynia Maritime University, Poland
Iza Wierzbowska	Gdynia Maritime University, Poland
Mahdi Zargayouna	IFSTTAR, France

DCISM 2019 – Distributed Collective Intelligence for Smart Manufacturing

Markus Bregulla	Ingolstadt University of Applied Sciences, Germany
Rafał Cupek	Silesian University of Technology, Poland
Marcin Fojcik	Western Norway University of Applied Sciences, Poland
Jörg Franke	Friedrich-Alexander-University of Erlangen-Nürnberg, Germany
Dariusz Frejlichowski	West Pomeranian University of Technology, Poland
Damian Grzechca	Silesian University of Technology, Poland

Maciej Huk	Wroclaw University of Science and Technology, Poland
Dariusz Mrozek	Silesian University of Technology, Poland
Agnieszka Nowak-Brzezińska	University of Silesia, Poland
Krzysztof Tokarz	Silesian University of Technology, Poland
Olav Sande	Western Norway University of Applied Sciences, Norway
Knut Øvsthus	Western Norway University of Applied Sciences, Norway
Alexey Vinel	Western Norway University of Applied Sciences, Norway
Adam Ziębiński	Silesian University of Technology, Poland

IMIS 2019 – Special Session on Intelligent Management Information Systems

Eunika Mercier-Laurent	Jean Moulin Lyon 3 University, France
Małgorzata Pańkowska	University of Economics in Katowice, Poland
Mieczysław Owoc	Wrocław University of Economics, Poland
Bogdan Franczyk	University of Leipzig, Germany
Kazimierz Perechuda	Wrocław University of Economics, Poland
Jan Stępniewski	Université Paris 13, France
Helena Dudycz	Wrocław University of Economics, Poland
Jerzy Korczak	International University of Logistics and Transport in Wrocław, Poland
Andrzej Bytniewski	Wrocław University of Economics, Poland
Marcin Fojcik	Western Norway University of Applied Sciences, Norway
Monika Eisenbardt	Wrocław University of Economics, Poland
Dorota Jelonek	Czestochowa University of Technology, Poland
Paweł Weichbroth	WSB University in Gdańsk, Poland
Jadwiga Sobieska-Karpińska	The Witelon State University of Applied Sciences in Legnica, Poland
Krzysztof Hauke	Wrocław University of Economics, Poland
Daria Hołodnik	Opole University of Technology, Poland
Krzysztof Nowosielski	Wrocław University of Economics, Poland
Zdzisław Kes	Wrocław University of Economics, Poland

IMSARWS 2019 – Special Session on Intelligent Modeling and Simulation Approaches for Real World Systems

Alabbas Alhaj Ali	Frankfurt University of Applied Sciences, Germany
Costin Bădică	University of Craiova, Romania
Petru Cașcaval	Gheorghe Asachi Technical University of Iași, Romania

Gia Thuan Lam	Vietnamese-German University, Vietnam
Florin Leon	Gheorghe Asachi Technical University of Iaşi, Romania
Doina Logofătu	Frankfurt University of Applied Sciences, Germany
Fitore Muharemi	Frankfurt University of Applied Sciences, Germany
Minh Nguyen	Frankfurt University of Applied Sciences, Germany
Julian Szymański	Gdańsk University of Technology, Poland
Pawel Sitek	Kielce University of Technology, Poland
Daniel Stamate	Goldsmiths, University of London, UK

ISSC 2019 – Special Session on Intelligent Sustainable Smart Cities

Costin Bădică	University of Craiova, Romania
Peter Bracinik	University of Zilina, Slovakia
Peter Brida	University of Zilina, Czech Republic
Davor Dujak	University of Osijek, Croatia
Martina Hedvičáková	University of Hradec Kralove, Czech Republic
Marek Hoger	University of Zilina, Slovakia
Jiří Horák	Technical University of Ostrava, Czech Republic
Petra Marešová	University of Hradec Kralove, Czech Republic
Hana Mohelska	University of Hradec Kralove, Czech Republic
Arkadiusz Kawa	Poznan University of Economics and Business, Poland
Waldemar Koczkodaj	Laurentian University, Canada
Ondrej Krejcar	University of Hradec Kralove, Czech Republic
Martina Látková	University of Zilina, Slovakia
Juraj Machaj	University of Zilina, Slovakia
Miroslava Mikušová	University of Zilina, Slovakia
Dorota Bednarska-Olejniczak	Wroclaw University of Economics, Poland
Jaroslaw Olejniczak	Wroclaw University of Economics, Poland
Paweł Piątkowski	Poznan University of Technology, Poland
Bartłomiej Pierański	Poznan University of Economics and Business, Poland
Peter Poor	University of West Bohemia, Czech Republic
Petra Poulová	University of Hradec Kralove, Czech Republic
Michal Regula	University of Zilina, Slovakia
Marek Roch	University of Zilina, Slovakia
Carlos Andres Romano	Polytechnic University of Valencia, Spain
Ali Selamat	Universiti Teknologi Malaysia, Malaysia
Marcela Sokolová	University of Hradec Kralove, Czech Republic
Libuše Svobodová	University of Hradec Kralove, Czech Republic
Emese Tokarčíková	University of Zilina, Slovakia
Hana Tomášková	University of Hradec Kralove, Czech Republic
Marek Vokoun	Institute of Technology and Business in Ceske Budejovice, Czech Republic

MLRWD 2019 – Special Session on Machine Learning in Real-World Data

Franciszek Białas	University of Economics in Katowice, Poland
Grzegorz Dziczkowski	University of Economics in Katowice, Poland
Marcin Grzegorzek	University of Lübeck, Germany
Ignacy Kaliszewski	Systems Research Institute, Polish Academy of Sciences, Poland
Krzysztof Kania	University of Economics in Katowice, Poland
Jan Kozak	University of Economics in Katowice, Poland
Przemysław Juszczuk	University of Economics in Katowice, Poland
Janusz Miroforidis	Systems Research Institute, Polish Academy of Sciences, Poland
Agnieszka Nowak-Brzezińska	University of Silesia, Poland
Dmitry Podkopaev	Systems Research Institute, Polish Academy of Sciences, Poland
Małgorzata Przybyła-Kasperek	University of Economics in Katowice, Poland
Tomasz Staś	University of Economics in Katowice, Poland
Magdalena Tkacz	University of Silesia, Poland
Bogna Zacny	University of Economics in Katowice, Poland

UNI4.0 2019 – Special Session on New Trends and Challenges in Education: The University 4.0

Archundia Etelvina	BUAP, Mexico
Bouassida Ismail	ReDCAD, Tunisia
Diop Codé	Activeeon, France
Gomez-Montalvo	Jorge R. UADY, Mexico
Lamolle Myriam	Laboratoire LIASD - Université Paris 8, France
Mezghani Emna	Orange Labs, France
Noureddine Adel	UPPA, France
Perez González Héctor	UASLP, Mexico
Rodriguez Laura	UPAEP, Mexico

WEBSYS 2019 – Intelligent Processing of Multimedia in Web Systems

František Čapkovič	Academy of Sciences, Slovakia
Patricia Conde-Céspedes	Institut Supérieur d'électronique de Paris, France
Jarosław Jankowski	West Pomeranian University of Technology, Poland
Ondřej Krejcar	University of Hradec Kralove, Czech Republic
Alin Moldoveanu	Politehnica University of Bucharest, Romania
Tarkko Oksala	Helsinki University of Technology, Finland
Aleš Procházka	Institute of Chemical Technology, Czech Republic
Andrzej Siemiński	Wrocław University of Science and Technology, Poland
Aleksander Zgrzywa	Wrocław University of Science and Technology, Poland

Contents – Part I

Text Processing and Information Retrieval

Data Mining Methods and Applications

Computer Vision Techniques

Decision Support and Control Systems

Cooperative Strategies for Decision Making and Optimization

Intelligent Modeling and Simulation Approaches for Real World Systems

Innovations in Intelligent Systems

Contents – Part II

Distributed Collective Intelligence for Smart Manufacturing

Collective Intelligence for Science and Technology

Intelligent Management Information Systems

Intelligent Sustainable Smart Cities

New Trends and Challenges in Education: The University 4.0

Intelligent Processing of Multimedia in Web Systems

Big Data Streaming, Applications and Security

Knowledge Engineering and Semantic Web

VWA: ViewpointS Web Application to Assess Collective Knowledge Building

Philippe Lemoisson[1,2(✉)], Clarel M. H. Rakotondrahaja[3,4],
Aroniaina Safidy Précieux Andriamialison[4], Harish A. Sankar[5],
and Stefano A. Cerri[6,7]

[1] CIRAD, UMR TETIS, 34398 Montpellier, France
philippe.lemoisson@cirad.fr
[2] TETIS, Univ Montpellier, AgroParisTech, CIRAD, CNRS, IRSTEA,
Montpellier, France
[3] Ecole Doctorale de Modélisation Informatique, University of Fianarantsoa,
Fianarantsoa, Madagascar
[4] Etech Research Lab, Arkeup Group, Antananarivo, Madagascar
{c.rakotondrahaja,aroniaina}@etechconsulting-mg.com
[5] Department of Computer Engineering, National Institute of Technology,
Kurukshetra, India
harishsa85@gmail.com
[6] LIRMM, University of Montpellier & CNRS, Montpellier, France
[7] FBK: Fondazione Bruno Kessler, Trento, Italy
scerri@fbk.eu

Abstract. Collective intelligence is one major outcome of the digital revolution, but this outcome is hardly evaluated. By implementing a topological knowledge graph (KG) in the metaphor of a brain, the ViewpointS approach attempts to trace and assess the dynamics of collaborative knowledge building. Our approach relies on a bipartite graph of resources (agents, documents, topics) and time stamped "viewpoints" emitted by human or artificial agents. These viewpoints are typed (logical, mining, subjective). User agents feed the graph with resources and viewpoints and exploit maps where resources are linked by "synapses" aggregating the viewpoints. They reversely emit feedback viewpoints which tighten or loosen the synapses along the knowledge paths. Shared knowledge is continuously elicited against the individual "systems of values" along the agents' exploitation/feedback loops. This selection process implements a rudimentary form of collective intelligence, which we assess through innovative metrics.

In this paper, we present the exploitation/feedback loops in detail. We expose the mechanism underlying the reinforcement along the knowledge paths and introduce a new measure called Multi Paths Proximity inspired from the parallel neural circuits in the brain. Then we present the Web prototype VWA implementing the ViewpointS approach and set a small experiment assessing collective knowledge building on top of the exploitation/feedback loops.

© Springer Nature Switzerland AG 2019
N. T. Nguyen et al. (Eds.): ICCCI 2019, LNAI 11683, pp. 3–15, 2019.
https://doi.org/10.1007/978-3-030-28377-3_1

Keywords: Collective intelligence · Knowledge graph · Knowledge map · Knowledge paths · Knowledge assessment · Reinforcement · Serendipitous learning · Unsupervised learning

1   Introduction

The so-called digital revolution has been progressively changing our lives in depth since the turn of the millennium, bringing in the hope of a collective intelligence [1]; the World Wide Web together with the internauts has often been compared to a collective brain.

Our previous work implements a topological numeric space where "knowledge shared within a community of agents is continuously elicited against the systems of values of the agents in a selection process." The goal of our approach is twofold: (i) to exploit the metaphor of the brain [2] for improving the collective construction of knowledge and (ii) to better exploit our digital traces in order to refine the understanding of our learning processes. We adopted a tripartite model 'resource/agent'–'resource'–'resource' called ViewpointS by storing and exploiting 'declarations by agents that two resources are close'. Assessing knowledge may seem a hazardous enterprise in such a context characterized by weak semantics. Whereas standard measurements exist in the case of explicit information retrieval, as listed in [3], none of those apply to serendipity: assessing informal learning remains an open issue despite the great deal of research work reviewed in [4]. Our approach is topology driven within the numeric space; it relies on a metric distance which opens the way both for "learning close to what we already know" in agreement with the principle of the "zones of proximal development" [5, 6] and for assessing knowledge acquisition.

This paper is a step forward in deepening the brain metaphor exposed by Edelman in [7]; we implement a feedback mechanism underlying the reinforcement along the knowledge paths and design a new metric taking into account the multiplicity of the knowledge paths.

We start in Sect. 2 by recalling the ViewpointS paradigm, presenting the feedback mechanism and defining a new metric called Multi Paths Distance. In Sect. 3 we briefly present the ViewpointS Web Application implementing the approach. In Sect. 4 we demonstrate the assessment of collective knowledge building through a small experiment using the feedback mechanism. Section 5 starts with a discussion about the results and then presents short term perspectives.

2   The ViewpointS Paradigm

The ViewpointS paradigm previously presented in [8–10] builds up upon trust towards 'peers', would they be humans, databases or mining algorithms. A community of human agents combines in a fully transparent and trackable way their own knowledge and feelings with declarations extracted from the Web. This happens in one single numeric space where:

(i)   Inferences of the semantic Web (e.g. "Marguerite Yourcenar was born in 1903") as well as 'objective' declarations of the users (e.g. "I was born in Paris") provide the *Logical viewpoints*;

(ii) Statistical recommendations due to mining algorithms provide the *Mining viewpoints* (e.g. "https://www.aps.org/publications/apsnews/200207/history.cfm is related to 'serendipity'");

(iii) Spontaneous opinions, feelings and feedbacks of the community of agents provide the *Subjective viewpoints* (e.g. "I like this book"; "I think John is the person to contact if you are interested in 'Serendipity'").

The formalism adopted in the ViewpointS paradigm is briefly recalled in Sect. 2.1; for more details the reader might refer to [8, 9]. The feedback mechanism is presented in Sect. 2.2. The metrics governing the exploration of knowledge are presented in Sect. 2.3.

2.1   Interconnected Observation/Action Loops in a Numeric Knowledge Space

In the ViewpointS paradigm, agents, documents and topics constitute the *knowledge resources*; those are interlinked via the *viewpoints*. The *viewpoint* $(r_1, \{r_2, r_3\}, \theta, \tau)$ stands for: 'agent r_1' (human or artificial) declares at time 'τ' that 'r_2' and 'r_3' are connected in the paradigm θ (*Logical* versus *Mining* versus *Subjective*).

We call Knowledge Graph the bipartite graph consisting of *knowledge resources* and *viewpoints* imported or emitted by the users themselves or by artificial agents. Given two *knowledge resources*, the aggregation of all the *viewpoints* interlinking them is called a *synapse*; it can be quantified and interpreted in terms of proximity by choosing a *perspective*. This is illustrated in Fig. 1.

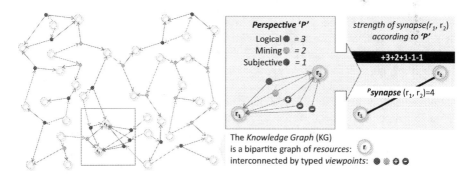

Fig. 1.   The bipartite graph of resources and viewpoints is exploited by the user after choosing a perspective ruling the aggregation of viewpoints

The left part of Fig. 1 shows the bipartite graph of resources and viewpoints. When zooming on the two resources r_1 and r_2, we see that five viewpoints (emitted by five distinct agents) interconnect them. These five viewpoints are colored according to their types: blue = *Logical*, green = *Mining* and red = *Subjective*. *Subjective* viewpoints have a polarity: in the example, one is 'positive' (declaring proximity according to the subjectivity of the emitter) whereas two are 'negative' (denying proximity).

By choosing a *perspective*, any agent can tune the rules aggregating the qualitative *viewpoints* into quantitative *synapses* according to his own preferences with respect to the extraction of the knowledge available on the graph. These rules can integrate any type of IF-THEN predicate filtering the time-stamp, the emitter or the type of the *viewpoints*. In the examples of this paper, choosing the perspective simply consists in tuning the respective weights of the *Logical*, *Mining* and *Subjective viewpoints*, e.g. in Fig. 1 the chosen *perspective* 'P' consists in attributing the weights 3, 2 and 1 respectively for the *Logical*, *Mining* and *Subjective*. As a result, $^P synapse (r_1, r_2) = +3 + 2 + 1 - 1 - 1 = 4$, which is interpreted as "the proximity between r_1 and r_2 is '4'" OR "r_1 and r_2 are at distance $\frac{1}{4}$".

Given a *perspective* 'P', we call ^{P}KM (*knowledge map* according to 'P') the following undirected labelled graph:

- the nodes of ^{P}KM are the *resources* of KG;
- the edges of ^{P}KM are the positive $^P synapses$ labelled by their values.

The shared semantics emerge from the dynamics of the intricate observation/action loops among the community of agents interacting with the KG through the ^{P}KM. Agents choose a *perspective*, browse the *knowledge map* ^{P}KM and exploit the shared knowledge issued from the *viewpoints* of the whole community (observation), and reversely update the *knowledge graph* KG by adding new *viewpoints* expressing their feedback (action). Intertwining exploitation of shared resources and feedback on their links enhances collaborative knowledge building; this has been analyzed in [11] and illustrated in [12]. In the ViewpointS paradigm, the shared knowledge is continuously elicited against the individual systems of values of the members of the community in a selection process.

2.2   Reinforcing Versus Weakening Knowledge Paths in the Loops

Subjective viewpoints have a polarity. Positive (resp. negative) *viewpoints* are used for declaring (resp. denying) proximity between *resources*. Through *subjective viewpoints*, an agent may create direct connections: (i) between him/her and a given *resource*, e.g. "like/dislike" OR (ii) between two given *resources*, e.g. "match/mismatch".

A complementary mechanism involves a special category of *subjective viewpoints* called *feedback viewpoints*; it is illustrated in this paper. *Feedback viewpoints* allow agents to strengthen OR weaken the shortest path[1] between two distant *resources*, by distributing fragments of a subjective viewpoint along the shortest path in the metaphor of the reinforcement of synapses in our neural circuits. We illustrate this by an imaginary use case based on the following KG:

- *documents* have been connected via *Mining viewpoints* to *topics*, e.g. 'saying92' has been connected to 'topic-A';
- *human agents* (*Marguerite Yourcenar, Voltaire…*) have been connected via *Logical viewpoints* to *topics* (topic-G, topic-S …);
- by transitivity, the *agents* are connected to the *documents* by paths where the proximities are computable.

---

[1] The computation of the shortest path distance bounded by 'b' is explained in Sect. 2.3.

Three human agents (HA_1, HA_2 and HA_3) exploit the knowledge through the perspective P_0 where the weights of the *Logical, Mining* and *Subjective viewpoints* are all equal to '1'; the corresponding knowledge map is denoted ^{P0}KM. They react to the proximities by emitting the *Subjective feedback viewpoints* illustrated in Fig. 2.

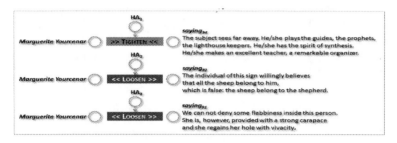

Fig. 2. The human agents HA_1, HA_2 and HA_3 update the proximities between *Marguerite Yourcenar* and *saying94, saying92* and *saying91* respectively.

Figure 3A below illustrates the initial state of ^{P0}KM. The *Subjective feedback viewpoints* yield the final state illustrated in Fig. 3B.

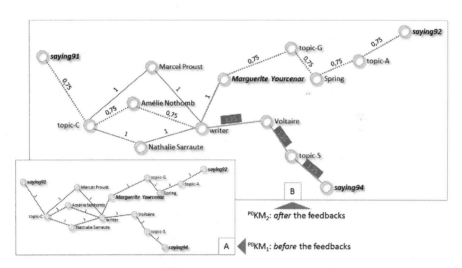

Fig. 3. Evolution A → B of the ^{P0}KM as a consequence of the TIGHTENING and LOOSENING; the labels are the strengths of the synapses (Color figure online)

- The shortest path between *Marguerite Yourcenar* and *saying94* counts 'n = 4' edges and goes through 'writer', 'Voltaire' and 'topic-S'. HA_1 TIGHTENS the path through a *positive feedback viewpoint* by adding a subjective viewpoint of '+1/(n = 4)' on each edge; each corresponding $^P synapse$ evolves from '1' (grey lines in image A) to '1,25' (green lines in image B).

- The shortest path between *Marguerite Yourcenar* and *saying₉₁* counts '4' edges and goes through 'topic-G', 'spring' and 'topic-A'. HA_2 LOOSENS the path through a *negative feedback viewpoint* by adding a subjective viewpoint of '−1/4' on each edge; each corresponding $^P synapse$ evolves from '1' (grey lines in A) to '0,75' (red dotted lines in B).

- The shortest path between *Marguerite Yourcenar* and *saying₉₁* counts '4' edges and goes through 'writer', 'Amélie Nothomb' and 'topic-C'. HA_3 LOOSENS the path through a *negative feedback viewpoint* by adding in the KG a subjective viewpoint of '−1/4' on each edge; each corresponding $^P synapse$ evolves from '1' (grey lines in A) to '0,75' (red dotted lines in B).

2.3   The Metrics Sustaining the Exploitation of Knowledge

In our previous work [9], the metric in use was the "shortest path distance bounded by 'b'", denoted $^b SPD$, an adaptation of Dijkstra's algorithm with acceptable complexity[2] which: (i) scans all the paths respecting the threshold 'b' between two given resources and (ii) computes the shortest path. Given a $^P KM$, the length of an edge $r_i - r_j$ is defined as $1/^P synapse$ (r_i, r_j); the length of a path $r_i - \ldots - r_j \ldots - r_k$ is the sum of the edges' lengths. $^b SPD(r_i, r_j)$ returns 'NA' if no path of length $<= b$ link r_i to r_j; it returns $d <= b$ otherwise. $^b SPD$ has been illustrated in the imaginary case developed in [8].

In this paper, we wish to consider multiple parallel paths when computing proximities in $^P KM$. We characterize an "equivalent synapse" expressing a proximity between two given resources by taking into account all the possible paths; we call it "multi paths proximity bounded by 'b'" and denote it $^b MPP$. The computation of $^b MPP$ requires two preliminary definitions:

- we call $^b Neighbours(r_0)$ the set of resources r_x such that $^b SPD(r_0, r_x)$ is available;
- we call $^b Paths(r_0, r_x)$ the set of all paths $(r_0, \ldots, r_x)$ of length $<= b$ between r_0 and resources belonging to $^b Neighbours(r_0)$.

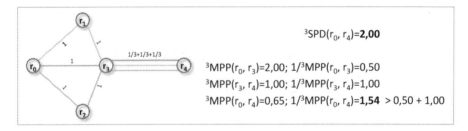

$$^3 SPD(r_0, r_4) = \mathbf{2,00}$$

$$^3 MPP(r_0, r_3) = 2,00; \quad 1/^3 MPP(r_0, r_3) = 0,50$$
$$^3 MPP(r_3, r_4) = 1,00; \quad 1/^3 MPP(r_3, r_4) = 1,00$$
$$^3 MPP(r_0, r_4) = 0,65; \quad 1/^3 MPP(r_0, r_4) = \mathbf{1,54} > 0,50 + 1,00$$

Fig. 4. Computation of $^3 MPP(r_0, r_4)$. The label "1/3 + 1/3 + 1/3" between r_3 and r_4 indicates that *synapse*(r_3, r_4) participates to three paths linking r_3 to r_4, each of these paths using a channel capacity of 1/3 of the strength of the synapse.

---

[2] The worst case complexity of Dijkstra's algorithm is O $(N_W^2 \ N_R^2)$, where N_W is the number of viewpoints in KG and N_R is the number of resources in KG. In $^b SPD$, the worst case complexity is practically never reached because of the bound 'b'.

The computation of ^{b}MPP (r_1, r_2) illustrated in Fig. 4 obeys four rules:

- rule 1: given 'b', we restrict the computation to the following subgraph of KG: ^{b}Paths(r_1, r_2);
- rule 2: when 'n' paths of ^{b}Paths(r_1, r_2) share a ^{P}synapse, we consider a channel capacity 'cc = ^{P}synapse/n' for each path, and a pseudo-length 'L_{edge} = 1/cc' for this edge in each path;
- rule 3: for each path$_i$ between r_1 and r_2, we consider the pseudo-length $LL(path_i) = \sum_{edges\ in\ path} L_{edge}(path_i))$;
- rule 4: ^{b}MPP $(r_1, r_2) = \sum_{i=1,\ n} 1/LL(path_i)$.

$1/^b$MPP$(r_0,\ r_0) = 0$. $1/^b$MPP satisfies the symmetry condition: $1/^b$MPP$(r_1, r_2) = 1/^b$MPP(r_2, r_1). However $1/^b$MPP DOES NOT satisfy the triangle inequality: $1/^b$MPP $(r_0, r_4) > 1/^b$MPP$(r_0, r_3) + 1/^b$MPP(r_3, r_4). It is NOT a metric distance.

3   VWA, the ViewpointS Web Application

The ViewpointS Web Application (VWA) has been implemented in the Spring Web MVC framework providing Model-View-Controller (MVC) architecture; the KG is stored in a Postgresql database exploited through a Java API. Once logged in, any user can create *resources* and emit *viewpoints* shared by the community.

The web based graphical user interface presents 7 significant zones marked in red in Fig. 5 below.

Zone 1 lists the menu commands:

- New resource: Knowledge graphs (KGs) are populated with different classes of *resources*: "artificial agent", "human agent", "numeric document", "physical document", or "topic". Every resource class has a distinct color when appearing in the draw area (*Zone 3*). Only in case of a Numeric document, an additional option of attaching (uploading) an URL is presented. All resources are identified based on their name. It must be noted that the set of *resources* is shared by all the KGs; on the contrary, each *viewpoints* belongs to one and only one KG.
- New Logical Viewpoint: Two resources are to be selected before a logical viewpoint can be emitted (by the current user) to interconnect them. A radio-button (containing '+' sign) is preselected.
- New Subjective Viewpoint: Similar to the previous option, two resources are to be mentioned. Four radio buttons allow the user to tune the polarity and strength of the emitted viewpoint. Choosing '−', '0', '+' and '++' signs create a 'negative', 'neutral', 'positive' and 'double positive' *viewpoint* respectively.
- New Feedback: A feedback between two resources can either be positive (TIGHTEN) or negative (LOOSEN) as depicted by the '−' and '+' signs respectively[3].

---

[3] In either case, the result is the emission of a series of fragmented viewpoints along the shortest path between the two resources, as explained in Sect. 2.2.

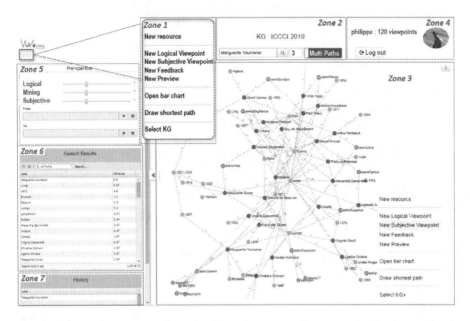

Fig. 5. The graphical user interface of VWA as it appears after user authentication and log in (Color figure online)

- New Preview: A *resource* 'x' can be connected to a Numeric document that will appear on right click on 'x' in the draw area. Nota: preview viewpoints do not contribute to the *synapses*.
- Open bar chart: This function calculates all the proximities (according to the metrics selected in zone 2) between (i) a given *resource* 'x' and (ii) a vector 'Z' of selected *resources* playing the role of referential. The result is a bar chart drawing the Z-profile of 'x'.
- Draw shortest path: Operates on two resources selected from "Search results" *(Zone 6)* and/or "History" *(Zone 7)*. The shortest path between them according to the current *perspective* is computed and drawn in the draw area *(Zone 3)*.
- Select KG: A list of knowledge graphs (created by the administrator) is provided to the user.

Zone 2 is the area for activating a search, on the basis of the parameters defined in the *perspective (Zone 5)*. The results are shown graphically in the draw area *(Zone 3)* and also listed in "search results" *(Zone 6)*. The search is conducted on the basis of resource name (auto completion is available). The neighborhood radius ('b' for [b]SPD and [b]MPP as mentioned in Sect. 2.2) tunes the depth of the search. A toggle between "shortest-path" and "multi-paths" metrics is available[4].

Zone 3 is the draw area where the neighborhood of the target in [P]KM is edited with *resources* interlinked by *'synapses'* with labels corresponding to their weights.

---

[4] These metrics have been described in Sect. 2.2.

The target of the search is circled in red. The graph can be resized and reshaped with simple mouse drag operations. Right clicking on a resource circled in green shows its preview in a tiny dialogue box. They can be further elaborated with a left click. The edition is cumulative until a change of *perspective* or a "clean visu" (up-right button)

Zone 4 is self-explanatory as shown in the Fig. 5. The picture of the agent and the number of viewpoints emitted by the agent are displayed. The logout button is also present in this zone.

Zone 5 is the perspective pane that monitors the aggregation of viewpoints into *synapses* as explained in Sect. 2.1. In the current state of the prototype, only simple tuning of perspectives is available: the *synapses* of the knowledge graph can be revaluated according to the three sliders corresponding to the *viewpoints* types (*Logical, Mining* and *Subjective*). Besides, *viewpoints* can be filtered according to time 'τ'.

Zone 6 contains the search results. These results are ranked according to their proximities from the selected resource. Double clicking on a resource can select the resource and copy it in the search area.

Zone 7 keeps track of every resource that has been successfully searched and selected.

The ViewpointS Web Application (VWA) is regularly enriched with new functionalities; a demo version, where the sessions are not persistent, is available at url: viewpoints.cirad.fr/vwademo.

4   Assessing Collective Knowledge

In order to assess the collective knowledge with the metrics presented in Sect. 2.3, we have set a toy experiment where three VWA users express knowledge about a panel of writers. The knowledge graph (KG) is initially populated by *Logical viewpoints* and *Mining viewpoints*; the three VWA users express their own opinions about the writers by adding subjective *feedback* viewpoints. Then we use the metrics presented in Sect. 2.3 to measure the reinforcement versus weakening of the knowledge paths.

4.1   Settings

The following *resources* initially populate the KG:

- 'HA_1', 'HA_2' and 'HA_3': human agents sources of the *Subjective* knowledge in VWA; other "human agents", e.g. 'Marguerite Yourcenar'
- 'AUTHORS DATABASE': artificial agent source of the *Logical* knowledge
- 'ASTROLOGICAL STATISTICS': artificial agent source of the *Mining* knowledge
- a few "topics": 'solar year', 'spring', 'astroCancer', 'astroSagittarius', ...
- numeric documents called "sayings" that the users may read by right-clicking on them in the KM, e.g. 'saying$_{81}$: The person does not look into her past: she dives into it, she bathes there. She does not make plans for the future; she makes plans for the past.'

The following *viewpoints* initially populate the KG:

- Logical *viewpoints* emitted by 'AUTHORS DATABASE' interlink the writers, their astrological signs and the seasons of the solar year, e.g. 'Marguerite Yourcenar LINKEDTo astroGemini'
- *Mining viewpoints* emitted by 'ASTROLOGICAL STATISTICS' interlink the sayings and the astrological signs, e.g. 'saying$_{81}$ LINKEDTo astroGemini'.

The three users 'HA$_1$', 'HA$_2$' and 'HA$_3$' are invited to browse the knowledge graph under the *perspective* P$_1$ illustrated in Fig. 6. They benefit in real time from the contributions of the others BUT are deprived from the *Mining viewpoints*, i.e. they are not influenced by the knowledge of 'ASTROLOGICAL STATISTICS'. During this browsing, they are invited to express in feedback their own opinions about the proximities between the "sayings" and the writers by exclusively using the TIGHTEN and LOOSEN facilities exposed in Sect. 2.2.

4.2   Results

The first result is a proof of concept: we have implemented the mechanism described in Sect. 2.2 and proven the reinforcement versus weakening of some knowledge paths: Fig. 6 (directly issued from VWA) is a perfect match of Fig. 3 (drawn at design phase) through the following translations: topic-A → astroAries; topic-C → astroCancer; topic-G → astroGemini; topic-S → astroSagittarius. After the experiment, the probability to reach *saying$_{94}$* from *Marguerite Yourcenar* when browsing along the paths has become stronger than the probability to reach *saying$_{91}$* or *saying$_{92}$*; in other words, the communities of agents have collectively declared that *saying$_{94}$* fits her better than by the two other sayings.

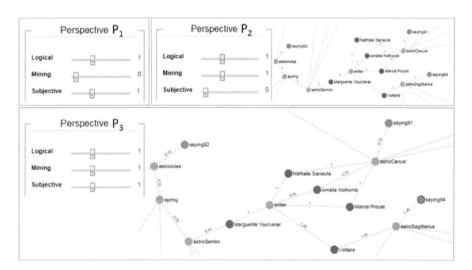

Fig. 6. *Perspectives* and corresponding *knowledge maps*: P$_1$ considers *Logical+Subjective viewpoints*, P$_2$ considers *Logical+Mining* and P$_3$ considers *Logical+Mining+Subjective*

The results presented in Fig. 7 illustrate a search where the target is 'Marguerite Yourcenar'.

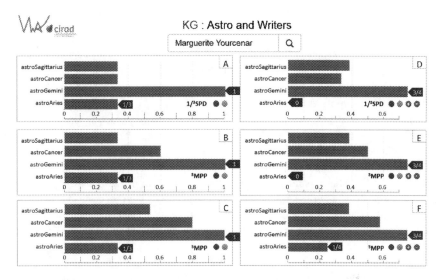

Fig. 7. Impact of the feedbacks on the "astrological profile" of Marguerite Yourcenar (M. Y.); the bar charts reflect proximities according to two distinct perspectives, 'WITH subjective viewpoints' in the right diagrams) and various metrics (1/SPD versus MPP) (Color figure online)

By comparing left to right we assess the reinforcement mechanism. The left diagrams A, B, C give proximities according to *perspective* P_2: WITHOUT subjective viewpoints (only blue and green viewpoints), i.e. with all viewpoints BEFORE the feedback by the users. The right diagrams D, E, F give proximities according to *perspective* P_3: WITH the subjective viewpoints, i.e. with all viewpoints INCLUDING the feedback by the users (blue, green, red+ and red− viewpoints).

By comparing up to down, we compare the metrics: A&D use the shortest path proximity $1/^3$SPD; B&C use the multi paths proximity ^{3}MPP; E&F use the multi paths proximity ^{5}MPP.

The measures displayed in the six diagrams open to the following comments:

- given a *perspective* (either P_2 or P_3), proximities computed by MPP are equal or bigger than proximities computed by 1/SPD: the proximities in 'B' are bigger than in 'A'; the proximities in 'E' are bigger than in 'D'.
- ^{b}MPP increases when 'b' increases: the proximities in 'C' are bigger than in 'B'; the proximities in 'F' are bigger than in 'E'.
- both TIGHTEN and LOOSEN operate independently from the metric or the bound 'b' chosen: by comparing successively A&D, B&C and E&F, we can see that the respective proximity between: (i) 'M. Y.' and 'astroAries' decreases, (ii) 'M. Y.' and 'astroGemini' decreases, (iii) 'M. Y.' and 'astroCancer' decreases, (iv) 'M. Y.' and 'astroSagittarius' increases.

5 Discussion

In this paper, we have put the focus on the exploitation/feedback loops of a community of agents sharing knowledge resources. We have provided features and metrics aimed at aggregating individual viewpoints into measurable proximities and presented the ViewpointS Web Application (VWA), working online.

We have proved the concept of a feedback mechanism impacting the topology of the knowledge graph in the metaphor of a collective brain by setting an experiment where users were specifically required to feedback. We have described and operated a new measure called "multi paths proximity (MPP)". MPP does not respect the triangle inequality. MPP yields greater proximities than 1/SPD and these proximities increase with the bound 'b' reflecting the depth of the search. We have opened the way to the assessment of collective knowledge: (i) perspective-dependent knowledge paths appear through Knowledge Maps and (ii) these paths are strengthened or weakened depending on the dynamics of the interactions.

Our next step will consist in setting a more ambitious real-life experiment in order to better analyze MPP in comparison with 1/SPD, especially by comparing their respective stabilities along the dynamics of the interactions, and better explicit the benefits driven from the brain metaphor in assessing collective knowledge.

References

1. Gruber, T.: Collective knowledge systems: where the Social Web meets the Semantic Web. Web. Semant. Sci. Serv. Agents World Wide Web **6**(1), 4–13 (2008)
2. Cerri, S.A., Lemoisson, P.: Tracing and enhancing serendipitous learning with ViewpointS. In: Frasson, C., Kostopoulos, G. (eds.) Brain Function Assessment in Learning. LNCS (LNAI), vol. 10512, pp. 36–47. Springer, Cham (2017). https://doi.org/10.1007/978-3-319-67615-9_3
3. Qin, T., Liu, T.-Y., Xu, J., Li, H.: LETOR: a benchmark collection for research on learning to rank for information retrieval. Inf. Retr. **13**(4), 346–374 (2010)
4. Sefton-Green, J.: Literature Review in Informal Learning with Technology Outside School. A NESTA Futurelab Series - report 7 (2004)
5. Piaget, J.: Development and learning. In: Piaget Rediscovered (1964)
6. Vygotsky, L.S.: Mind in Society: The Development of Higher Psychological Processes. Harvard University Press, Cambridge (1980)
7. Edelman, G.M.: Neural Darwinism: The Theory of Neuronal Group Selection. Basic Books, New York (1989)
8. Lemoisson, P., Cerri, S.A.: ViewpointS: towards a collective brain. In: Nguyen, N.T., Pimenidis, E., Khan, Z., Trawiński, B. (eds.) ICCCI 2018. LNCS (LNAI), vol. 11055, pp. 3–12. Springer, Cham (2018). https://doi.org/10.1007/978-3-319-98443-8_1
9. Lemoisson, P., Surroca, G., Jonquet, C., Cerri, S.A.: ViewPointS: capturing formal data and informal contributions into an evolutionary knowledge graph. Int. J. Knowl. Learn. **12**(2), 119–145 (2018)

10. Lemoisson, P., Surroca, G., Jonquet, C., Méric, L., Cerri, S.A.: ViewPointS: bridging the gap between explicit knowledge of the semantic Web and implicit knowledge of the social web. Semant. Web J. Special Issue

11. Laurillard, D.: A conversational framework for individual learning applied to the 'learning organisation' and the 'learning society'. Syst. Res. Behav. Sci. **16**(2), 113–122 (1999)

12. Lemoisson, P., Passouant, M.: Un cadre pour la construction collaborative de connaissances lors de la conception d'un observatoire des pratiques territoriales. Cah. Agric. **21**(1), 11–17 (2012)

Bisimulations for Fuzzy Description Logics with Involutive Negation Under the Gödel Semantics

Linh Anh Nguyen[1,2(✉)] and Ngoc Thanh Nguyen[3]

[1] Division of Knowledge and System Engineering for ICT, Faculty of Information
Technology, Ton Duc Thang University, Ho Chi Minh City, Vietnam
nguyenanhlinh@tdtu.edu.vn
[2] Institute of Informatics, University of Warsaw, Banacha 2, 02-097 Warsaw, Poland
nguyen@mimuw.edu.pl
[3] Department of Information Systems,
Faculty of Computer Science and Management,
Wroclaw University of Science and Technology, Wroclaw, Poland
Ngoc-Thanh.Nguyen@pwr.edu.pl

Abstract. We define and study crisp bisimulation and strong bisimilarity for fuzzy description logics (DLs) with involutive negation under the Gödel semantics. The considered logics are fuzzy extensions of the DL $\mathcal{ALC}_{reg}$ with involutive negation and additional features among inverse roles, nominals, (qualified or unqualified) number restrictions, the universal role and local reflexivity of a role. We give results on invariance of concepts under crisp bisimulations as well as conditional invariance of TBoxes and ABoxes under strong bisimilarity in the mentioned fuzzy DLs. We also provide a theorem on the Hennessy-Milner property of crisp bisimulations in those logics. Furthermore, we also present our results on minimizing fuzzy interpretations by using strong bisimilarity.

1 Introduction

Description logics (DLs) are variants of modal logics used to represent knowledge and reason about individuals by using concepts, axioms and assertions, which are built from concept names (unary predicates), role names (binary predicates) and individual names by using concept/role constructors. A concept is interpreted as a set of individuals, and a role as a binary relation between individuals. Axioms for all individuals are grouped into a TBox (terminological box), and assertions about named individuals are grouped into an ABox (assertional box). DLs found a logical basis for the Web Ontology Language (OWL), a layer of the Semantic Web, which has influence also on other areas, including knowledge integration.

To deal with imprecise or vague knowledge, fuzzy extensions of logical formalisms can be used. The most popular families of fuzzy operators are the ones named Gödel, Lukasiewicz, Product and Zadeh. In the Gödel family, the conjunction (resp. disjunction) of two fuzzy values is defined to be their minimum (resp. maximum), implication is defined by using a t-norm-based residuum,

© Springer Nature Switzerland AG 2019
N. T. Nguyen et al. (Eds.): ICCCI 2019, LNAI 11683, pp. 16–30, 2019.
https://doi.org/10.1007/978-3-030-28377-3_2

with $(p \to q) \overset{\text{def}}{=}$ (if $p \leq q$ then 1 else q). The Gödel negation is defined by $\neg p \overset{\text{def}}{=} (p \to 0)$. It is non-involutive, as $\neg\neg p \neq p$ for $0 < p < 1$. Involutive negation, denoted in this paper by $\dot{\neg}$ and defined by $\dot{\neg}p \overset{\text{def}}{=} 1 - p$, is used for the Zadeh family of fuzzy operators.

Fuzzy DLs have been studied for two decades and still have challenging research problems [2,4]. Each family of fuzzy operators can be used to specify a semantics of fuzzy DLs (see, e.g., [3]). Fuzzy DLs under the Zadeh semantics were introduced and studied first, but after Hájek's work [13], fuzzy DLs under the other semantics have attracted more attention [2,4].

Indiscernibility in modal and description logics is characterized by bisimilarity. The bisimilarity relation of an interpretation $\mathcal{I}$ (w.r.t. to a logic L) is the largest bisimulation between $\mathcal{I}$ and itself (w.r.t. L). The notions of bisimulation were first introduced for modal logic and state transition systems [14,18,20]. They have been exploited in concept learning for DL-based information systems (see, e.g., [17,19]).

In [11] Fan introduced fuzzy bisimulations for the fuzzy monomodal logic K under the Gödel semantics and its extension with converse. She also introduced crisp bisimulations for the fuzzy logics that extend those two logics with involutive negation. She provided results on invariance of formulas and the Hennessy-Milner property for those fuzzy (resp. crisp) bisimulations, which are proved for the class of image-finite (resp. degree-finite) of Kripke models. The work [11] is related to bisimulation/bisimilarity defined for Heyting-valued modal languages [10], fuzzy automata [6] and fuzzy transition systems [5].

Inspired by the results of [11], Ha *et al.* [12] defined fuzzy Φ-bisimulations in a uniform way for the class of fuzzy DLs $\mathcal{L}_\Phi$ under the Gödel semantics, where $\mathcal{L}$ extends the DL $\mathcal{ALC}_{reg}$ with fuzzy truth values and $\mathcal{L}_\Phi$ extends $\mathcal{L}$ with the features from $\Phi \subseteq \{I, O, U, Q, \texttt{Self}\}$, which stand for inverse roles, nominals, the universal role, qualified number restrictions and local reflexivity of a role, respectively.[1] A fuzzy Φ-bisimulation between fuzzy interpretations $\mathcal{I}$ and $\mathcal{I}'$ is a function $Z : \Delta^{\mathcal{I}} \times \Delta^{\mathcal{I}'} \to [0,1]$ satisfying certain conditions, where $\Delta^{\mathcal{I}}$ and $\Delta^{\mathcal{I}'}$ are the domains of $\mathcal{I}$ and $\mathcal{I}'$. If there exists a fuzzy Φ-bisimulation Z between $\mathcal{I}$ and $\mathcal{I}'$ such that $Z(a^{\mathcal{I}}, a^{\mathcal{I}'}) = 1$ for all named individuals a, then $\mathcal{I}$ and $\mathcal{I}'$ are said to be Φ-bisimilar. Ha *et al.* provided results on invariance of concepts and the Hennessy-Milner property for fuzzy Φ-bisimulations, using restrictions weaker than image-finiteness for the considered fuzzy interpretations. They also provided results on invariance of concepts and conditional invariance of TBoxes and ABoxes under Φ-bisimilarity between witnessed (fuzzy) interpretations.

Inspired by the results of [11,12], in this paper we define and study *crisp Φ-bisimulations* in a uniform way for the class of fuzzy DLs $\mathcal{L}_{(\Phi,\dot{\neg})}$ under the Gödel semantics, where $\mathcal{L}_{(\Phi,\dot{\neg})}$ extends $\mathcal{L}_\Phi$ with involutive negation, and $\Phi \subseteq \{I, O, U, \texttt{Self}, Q_n, N_n \mid n \in \mathbb{N}\setminus\{0\}\}$, with Q_n (resp. N_n) standing for qualified (resp. unqualified) number restrictions that use n as the bound. Following the

---

[1] In [12], Φ-bisimulation and Φ-bisimilarity are named $\mathcal{L}_\Phi$-bisimulation and $\mathcal{L}_\Phi$-bisimilarity, respectively. Here, we simplify the terms.

approach of [11], we define the notion of crisp Φ-bisimulation by using the same conditions of fuzzy Φ-bisimulation with an additional condition that the range of Z is $\{0, 1\}$ (instead of $[0, 1]$), but we simplify the presentation by treating Z as a binary relation and reformulating the conditions to make them more natural. If there exists a crisp Φ-bisimulation Z between fuzzy interpretations $\mathcal{I}$ and $\mathcal{I}'$ such that $Z(a^{\mathcal{I}}, a^{\mathcal{I}'}) = 1$ for all named individuals a, then $\mathcal{I}$ and $\mathcal{I}'$ are said to be *strongly Φ-bisimilar*. Based on [11,12], defining crisp Φ-bisimulation and strong Φ-bisimilarity for $\Phi \subseteq \{I, O, Q, U, \mathtt{Self}\}$ is a simple task. What is new is that we consider the features Q_n and N_n instead of Q and our results on crisp Φ-bisimulation and strong Φ-bisimilarity are formulated and proved w.r.t. $\mathcal{L}_{(\Phi, \doteq)}$ instead of $\mathcal{L}_\Phi$. The results are about invariance of concepts, conditional invariance of fuzzy TBoxes/ABoxes and the Hennessy-Milner property. For the formulation, we identify a tight sublanguage $\mathcal{L}^0_{(\Phi, \triangle)}$ of $\mathcal{L}_{(\Phi, \doteq)}$ and introduce a sophisticated notion of modal saturatedness w.r.t. $\mathcal{L}^0_{(\Phi, \triangle)}$ in order to make the Hennessy-Milner property of crisp Φ-bisimulations as strong as possible.

Note that the notions of crisp bisimulation and strong bisimilarity studied in this paper are different from the notion of strong bisimulation in the concurrency theory, as the latter is the one where internal actions are treated just as external actions (in contrast to weak bisimulation where internal actions are partially abstracted).

Let $\dot\sim_{\Phi, \mathcal{I}}$ denote the largest crisp Φ-bisimulation between a fuzzy interpretation $\mathcal{I}$ and itself. It is an equivalence relation, called the strong Φ-bisimilarity relation of $\mathcal{I}$. As a novel result, we also introduce the quotient fuzzy interpretation of $\mathcal{I}$ w.r.t. $\dot\sim_{\Phi, \mathcal{I}}$ for the case when $\Phi \subseteq \{I, O, U\}$ and prove that under some light assumptions it is a minimum fuzzy interpretation equivalent to $\mathcal{I}$ w.r.t. some aspects like validity of fuzzy axioms/assertions of $\mathcal{L}_{(\Phi, \doteq)}$.

As related work, apart from the works [5,6,10–12] discussed or mentioned earlier, another notable one is [15]. In this latter work, Nguyen studied bisimilarity for fuzzy DLs under the Zadeh semantics. As stated in [15], this semantics for fuzzy DLs is essentially different from the Gödel semantics. Nguyen justified that both fuzzy bisimulation and crisp bisimulation for fuzzy DLs under the Zadeh semantics seem undefinable. To define bisimilarity for such logics, he used cut-based simulations.

The rest of the paper is structured as follows. In Sect. 2, we formally define the fuzzy DLs studied in this paper. In Sect. 3, we define crisp Φ-bisimulations between fuzzy interpretations and present fundamental results about them. In Sect. 4, we present our results on minimizing fuzzy interpretations by using strong Φ-bisimilarity. Conclusions are given in Sect. 5. Due to the lack of space, proofs of our results are provided only in [16].

2   Preliminaries

This section provides necessary definitions. It is based on [3,8,12,15].

By Φ we denote a set of symbols among I, O, U, $\mathtt{Self}$, Q_n and N_n (with $n \in \mathbb{N} \setminus \{0\}$), which stand for inverse roles, nominals, the universal role, local reflexivity of a role, qualified number restrictions and unqualified number restrictions, respectively, with n being the bound used in the number restriction. We first define the syntax of concepts and roles in the fuzzy DL $\mathcal{L}_{(\Phi,\dot\neg)}$, where $\mathcal{L}$ extends the DL $\mathcal{ALC}_{reg}$ with fuzzy truth values and $\mathcal{L}_{(\Phi,\dot\neg)}$ extends $\mathcal{L}$ with involutive negation (denoted by $\dot\neg$) and the features from Φ. The non-involutive (Gödel) negation is denoted by $\neg$.

Our logic language uses a set $\mathbf{C}$ of *concept names*, a set $\mathbf{R}$ of role names, and a set $\mathbf{I}$ of individual names. A *basic role* w.r.t. Φ is either a role name or the inverse r^- of a role name r (when $I \in \Phi$).

Roles and *concepts* of $\mathcal{L}_{(\Phi,\dot\neg)}$ are defined as follows:

- if $r \in \mathbf{R}$, then r is a role of $\mathcal{L}_{(\Phi,\dot\neg)}$,
- if R, S are roles of $\mathcal{L}_{(\Phi,\dot\neg)}$ and C is a concept of $\mathcal{L}_{(\Phi,\dot\neg)}$, then $R \sqcup S$, $R \circ S$, R^* and $C?$ are roles of $\mathcal{L}_{(\Phi,\dot\neg)}$,
- if $I \in \Phi$ and R is a role of $\mathcal{L}_{(\Phi,\dot\neg)}$, then R^- is a role of $\mathcal{L}_{(\Phi,\dot\neg)}$,
- if $U \in \Phi$, then U is a role of $\mathcal{L}_{(\Phi,\dot\neg)}$, called the *universal role* (we assume that $U \notin \mathbf{R}$),
- if $p \in [0,1]$, then p is a concept of $\mathcal{L}_{(\Phi,\dot\neg)}$,
- if $A \in \mathbf{C}$, then A is a concept of $\mathcal{L}_{(\Phi,\dot\neg)}$,
- if C, D are concepts of $\mathcal{L}_{(\Phi,\dot\neg)}$ and R is a role of $\mathcal{L}_{(\Phi,\dot\neg)}$, then:
  - $C \sqcap D$, $C \to D$, $\neg C$, $\dot\neg C$, $C \sqcup D$, $\forall R.C$, $\exists R.C$ are concepts of $\mathcal{L}_{(\Phi,\dot\neg)}$,
  - if $O \in \Phi$ and $a \in \mathbf{I}$, then $\{a\}$ is a concept of $\mathcal{L}_{(\Phi,\dot\neg)}$,
  - if $\mathtt{Self} \in \Phi$ and $r \in \mathbf{R}$, then $\exists r.\mathtt{Self}$ is a concept of $\mathcal{L}_{(\Phi,\dot\neg)}$,
  - if $Q_n \in \Phi$ and R is a basic role w.r.t. Φ, then $\geq n\, R.C$ and $< n\, R.C$ are concepts of $\mathcal{L}_{(\Phi,\dot\neg)}$,
  - if $N_n \in \Phi$ and R is a basic role w.r.t. Φ, then $\geq n\, R$ and $< n\, R$ are concepts of $\mathcal{L}_{(\Phi,\dot\neg)}$.

The concept 0 stands for $\perp$, and 1 for $\top$. We will use $\triangle$ as an abbreviation for $\neg\dot\neg$. By $\mathcal{L}^0_{(\Phi,\triangle)}$ we denote the largest sublanguage of $\mathcal{L}_{(\Phi,\dot\neg)}$ that:

- disallows the role constructors $R \sqcup S$, $R \circ S$, R^*, $C?$ and the concept constructors $C \sqcup D$, $\forall R.C$, $< n\, R.C$, $< n\, R$,
- uses $\neg$ and $\dot\neg$ only in the form $\neg\dot\neg C$ (i.e., $\triangle C$).

We use letters A and B to denote concept names, which are *atomic concepts*, C and D to denote arbitrary concepts, r and s to denote role names, which are *atomic roles*, R and S to denote arbitrary roles, a and b to denote individual names.

Fuzzy operators of the Gödel family are defined as follows (for $x, y \in [0,1]$):

$$x \otimes y = \min\{x, y\}$$
$$x \oplus y = \max\{x, y\}$$
$$\ominus x = (\text{if } x = 0 \text{ then } 1 \text{ else } 0)$$
$$(x \Rightarrow y) = (\text{if } x \leq y \text{ then } 1 \text{ else } y)$$
$$(x \Leftrightarrow y) = (x \Rightarrow y) \otimes (y \Rightarrow x).$$

Note that $(x \Leftrightarrow y) = 1$ if $x = y$, and $(x \Leftrightarrow y) = \min\{x, y\}$ otherwise. For a finite set $\Gamma = \{p_1, \ldots, p_n\} \subset [0, 1]$ with $n \geq 0$, we define:

$$\otimes \Gamma = p_1 \otimes \cdots \otimes p_n \otimes 1$$
$$\oplus \Gamma = p_1 \oplus \cdots \oplus p_n \oplus 0.$$

Definition 1. A *fuzzy interpretation* is a pair $\mathcal{I} = \langle \Delta^{\mathcal{I}}, \cdot^{\mathcal{I}} \rangle$ consisting of the *domain* $\Delta^{\mathcal{I}}$, which is a non-empty set, and the *interpretation function* $\cdot^{\mathcal{I}}$, which maps every individual name a to an element $a^{\mathcal{I}} \in \Delta^{\mathcal{I}}$, every concept name A to a function $A^{\mathcal{I}} : \Delta^{\mathcal{I}} \to [0, 1]$, and every role name r to a function $r^{\mathcal{I}} : \Delta^{\mathcal{I}} \times \Delta^{\mathcal{I}} \to [0, 1]$. The function $\cdot^{\mathcal{I}}$ is extended to complex roles and concepts as follows (cf. [3]), where the extrema are taken in the complete lattice $[0, 1]$:

$$U^{\mathcal{I}}(x, y) = 1$$
$$(R^-)^{\mathcal{I}}(x, y) = R^{\mathcal{I}}(y, x)$$
$$(C?)^{\mathcal{I}}(x, y) = (\text{if } x = y \text{ then } C^{\mathcal{I}}(x) \text{ else } 0)$$
$$(R \sqcup S)^{\mathcal{I}}(x, y) = R^{\mathcal{I}}(x, y) \oplus S^{\mathcal{I}}(x, y)$$
$$(R \circ S)^{\mathcal{I}}(x, y) = \sup\{R^{\mathcal{I}}(x, z) \otimes S^{\mathcal{I}}(z, y) \mid z \in \Delta^{\mathcal{I}}\}$$
$$(R^*)^{\mathcal{I}}(x, y) = \sup\{\otimes\{R^{\mathcal{I}}(x_i, x_{i+1}) \mid 0 \leq i < n\} \mid$$
$$n \geq 0, \ x_0, \ldots, x_n \in \Delta^{\mathcal{I}}, \ x_0 = x, \ x_n = y\}$$
$$p^{\mathcal{I}}(x) = p$$
$$\{a\}^{\mathcal{I}}(x) = (\text{if } x = a^{\mathcal{I}} \text{ then } 1 \text{ else } 0)$$
$$(\neg C)^{\mathcal{I}}(x) = \ominus C^{\mathcal{I}}(x) = (\text{if } C^{\mathcal{I}}(x) = 0 \text{ then } 1 \text{ else } 0)$$
$$(\dot\neg C)^{\mathcal{I}}(x) = 1 - C^{\mathcal{I}}(x)$$
$$(C \sqcap D)^{\mathcal{I}}(x) = C^{\mathcal{I}}(x) \otimes D^{\mathcal{I}}(x)$$
$$(C \sqcup D)^{\mathcal{I}}(x) = C^{\mathcal{I}}(x) \oplus D^{\mathcal{I}}(x)$$
$$(C \to D)^{\mathcal{I}}(x) = (C^{\mathcal{I}}(x) \Rightarrow D^{\mathcal{I}}(x))$$
$$(\exists r.\mathsf{Self})^{\mathcal{I}}(x) = r^{\mathcal{I}}(x, x)$$
$$(\exists R.C)^{\mathcal{I}}(x) = \sup\{R^{\mathcal{I}}(x, y) \otimes C^{\mathcal{I}}(y) \mid y \in \Delta^{\mathcal{I}}\}$$
$$(\forall R.C)^{\mathcal{I}}(x) = \inf\{R^{\mathcal{I}}(x, y) \Rightarrow C^{\mathcal{I}}(y) \mid y \in \Delta^{\mathcal{I}}\}$$
$$(\geq n\, R.C)^{\mathcal{I}}(x) = \sup\{\otimes\{R^{\mathcal{I}}(x, y_i) \otimes C^{\mathcal{I}}(y_i) \mid 1 \leq i \leq n\} \mid$$
$$y_1, \ldots, y_n \in \Delta^{\mathcal{I}}, \ y_i \neq y_j \text{ if } i \neq j\}$$
$$(< n\, R.C)^{\mathcal{I}}(x) = \inf\{(\otimes\{R^{\mathcal{I}}(x, y_i) \otimes C^{\mathcal{I}}(y_i) \mid 1 \leq i \leq n\} \Rightarrow$$
$$\oplus\{y_j = y_k \mid 1 \leq j < k \leq n\}) \mid y_1, \ldots, y_n \in \Delta^{\mathcal{I}}\}$$
$$(\geq n\, R)^{\mathcal{I}}(x) = (\geq n\, R.1)^{\mathcal{I}}(x)$$
$$(< n\, R)^{\mathcal{I}}(x) = (< n\, R.1)^{\mathcal{I}}(x).$$

∎

Observe that $(\triangle C)^{\mathcal{I}} = (\neg\dot\neg C)^{\mathcal{I}} = (\text{if } C^{\mathcal{I}} = 1 \text{ then } 1 \text{ else } 0)$. The projection operator $\triangle : [0, 1] \to \{0, 1\}$ specified as $\triangle p = (\text{if } p = 1 \text{ then } 1 \text{ else } 0)$ was introduced by Baaz [1] and called the Baaz Delta in [11].

Example 1. Let $\mathbf{C} = \{A\}$, $\mathbf{R} = \{r\}$ and $\mathbf{I} = \emptyset$. Consider the fuzzy interpretation $\mathcal{I}$ specified and illustrated below:

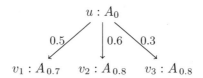

- $\Delta^{\mathcal{I}} = \{u, v_1, v_2, v_3\}$,
- $A^{\mathcal{I}}(u) = 0$, $A^{\mathcal{I}}(v_1) = 0.7$, $A^{\mathcal{I}}(v_2) = A^{\mathcal{I}}(v_3) = 0.8$,
- $r^{\mathcal{I}}(u, v_1) = 0.5$, $r^{\mathcal{I}}(u, v_2) = 0.6$, $r^{\mathcal{I}}(u, v_3) = 0.3$, and $r^{\mathcal{I}}(x, y) = 0$ for the other pairs $\langle x, y \rangle$.

We have that:

- $(\exists r.A)^{\mathcal{I}}(u) = 0.6$ and $(\forall r.A)^{\mathcal{I}}(u) = 1$,
- $(\forall r.\neg A)^{\mathcal{I}}(u) = 0$ and $(\exists r.\neg A)^{\mathcal{I}}(u) = 0$,
- $(\forall r.\mathbin{\dot\neg} A)^{\mathcal{I}}(u) = 0.2$ and $(\exists r.\mathbin{\dot\neg} A)^{\mathcal{I}}(u) = 0.3$,
- $(\geq 2\,r.A)^{\mathcal{I}}(u) = 0.5$ and $(< 2\,r.A)^{\mathcal{I}}(u) = 0$,
- for $C = \exists(r \sqcup r^-)^*.A$: $C^{\mathcal{I}}(v_1) = 0.7$ and $C^{\mathcal{I}}(v_2) = C^{\mathcal{I}}(v_3) = 0.8$,
- for $C = \forall(r \sqcup r^-)^*.A$ and $1 \leq i \leq 3$: $C^{\mathcal{I}}(v_i) = 0$. ∎

A fuzzy interpretation $\mathcal{I}$ is *witnessed w.r.t.* $\mathcal{L}_{(\varPhi, \mathbin{\dot\neg})}$ (cf. [13]) if any infinite set under the infimum (resp. supremum) operator in Definition 1 has the smallest (resp. biggest) element. The notion of being *witnessed w.r.t.* $\mathcal{L}^0_{(\varPhi, \triangle)}$ is defined similarly under the assumption that only roles and concepts of $\mathcal{L}^0_{(\varPhi, \triangle)}$ are allowed. A fuzzy interpretation $\mathcal{I}$ is *finite* if $\Delta^{\mathcal{I}}$, $\mathbf{C}$, $\mathbf{R}$ and $\mathbf{I}$ are finite, and is *image-finite* w.r.t. $\varPhi$ if, for every $x \in \Delta^{\mathcal{I}}$ and every basic role R w.r.t. $\varPhi$, $\{y \in \Delta^{\mathcal{I}} \mid R^{\mathcal{I}}(x, y) > 0\}$ is finite. Observe that every finite fuzzy interpretation is witnessed w.r.t. $\mathcal{L}_{(\varPhi, \mathbin{\dot\neg})}$ and, if $U \notin \varPhi$, then every image-finite fuzzy interpretation w.r.t. $\varPhi$ is witnessed w.r.t. $\mathcal{L}^0_{(\varPhi, \triangle)}$.

A *fuzzy assertion* in $\mathcal{L}_{(\varPhi, \mathbin{\dot\neg})}$ is an expression of the form $C(a) \bowtie p$, $R(a, b) \bowtie p$, $a \doteq b$ or $a \not\doteq b$, where C is a concept of $\mathcal{L}_{(\varPhi, \mathbin{\dot\neg})}$, $p \in [0, 1]$, R is a role of $\mathcal{L}_{(\varPhi, \mathbin{\dot\neg})}$ and $\bowtie \in \{\geq, >, \leq, <\}$. A *fuzzy ABox* in $\mathcal{L}_{(\varPhi, \mathbin{\dot\neg})}$ is a finite set of fuzzy assertions in $\mathcal{L}_{(\varPhi, \mathbin{\dot\neg})}$.

A *fuzzy GCI* (general concept inclusion) in $\mathcal{L}_{(\varPhi, \mathbin{\dot\neg})}$ is an expression of the form $(C \sqsubseteq D) \triangleright p$, where C and D are concepts of $\mathcal{L}_{(\varPhi, \mathbin{\dot\neg})}$, $\triangleright \in \{\geq, >\}$ and $p \in (0, 1]$. A *fuzzy TBox* in $\mathcal{L}_{(\varPhi, \mathbin{\dot\neg})}$ is a finite set of fuzzy GCIs in $\mathcal{L}_{(\varPhi, \mathbin{\dot\neg})}$.

Given a fuzzy interpretation $\mathcal{I}$ and a fuzzy assertion or GCI φ, we say that $\mathcal{I}$ *validates* φ, denoted by $\mathcal{I} \models \varphi$, if:

- case $\varphi = (C(a) \bowtie p)$: $C^{\mathcal{I}}(a^{\mathcal{I}}) \bowtie p$,
- case $\varphi = (R(a, b) \bowtie p)$: $R^{\mathcal{I}}(a^{\mathcal{I}}, b^{\mathcal{I}}) \bowtie p$,
- case $\varphi = (a \doteq b)$: $a^{\mathcal{I}} = b^{\mathcal{I}}$,
- case $\varphi = (a \not\doteq b)$: $a^{\mathcal{I}} \neq b^{\mathcal{I}}$,

– case $\varphi = (C \sqsubseteq D) \rhd p : (C \to D)^{\mathcal{I}}(x) \rhd p$ for all $x \in \Delta^{\mathcal{I}}$.

A fuzzy interpretation $\mathcal{I}$ is a *model* of a fuzzy ABox $\mathcal{A}$, denoted by $\mathcal{I} \models \mathcal{A}$, if $\mathcal{I} \models \varphi$ for all $\varphi \in \mathcal{A}$. Similarly, $\mathcal{I}$ is a model of a fuzzy TBox $\mathcal{T}$, denoted by $\mathcal{I} \models \mathcal{T}$, if $\mathcal{I} \models \varphi$ for all $\varphi \in \mathcal{T}$.

3   Bisimulations Between Fuzzy Interpretations

In this section, we first define (crisp) bisimulations for fuzzy DLs with involutive negation under the Gödel semantics, as well as strong bisimilarity relations based on such bisimulations. After that we present fundamental results about them.

Definition 2. Let $\Phi \subseteq \{I, O, U, \mathtt{Self}, Q_n, N_n \mid n \in \mathbb{N} \setminus \{0\}\}$ and let $\mathcal{I}$, $\mathcal{I}'$ be fuzzy interpretations. A non-empty relation $Z \subseteq \Delta^{\mathcal{I}} \times \Delta^{\mathcal{I}'}$ is called a *(crisp) Φ-bisimulation* (under the Gödel semantics) between $\mathcal{I}$ and $\mathcal{I}'$ if the following conditions hold for every $x, y \in \Delta^{\mathcal{I}}$, $x', y' \in \Delta^{\mathcal{I}'}$, $A \in \mathbf{C}$, $a \in \mathbf{I}$, $r \in \mathbf{R}$ and every basic role R w.r.t. Φ, where $\to$, $\leftrightarrow$ and $\wedge$ are the usual (crisp) logical connectives:

$$Z(x, x') \to A^{\mathcal{I}}(x) = A^{\mathcal{I}'}(x') \tag{1}$$

$$[Z(x, x') \wedge R^{\mathcal{I}}(x, y) > 0] \to \exists y' \in \Delta^{\mathcal{I}'} [Z(y, y') \wedge R^{\mathcal{I}}(x, y) \leq R^{\mathcal{I}'}(x', y')] \tag{2}$$

$$[Z(x, x') \wedge R^{\mathcal{I}'}(x', y') > 0] \to \exists y \in \Delta^{\mathcal{I}} [Z(y, y') \wedge R^{\mathcal{I}'}(x', y') \leq R^{\mathcal{I}}(x, y)]; \tag{3}$$

if $O \in \Phi$, then

$$Z(x, x') \to (x = a^{\mathcal{I}} \leftrightarrow x' = a^{\mathcal{I}'}); \tag{4}$$

if $U \in \Phi$, then

$$\forall y \in \Delta^{\mathcal{I}} \, \exists y' \in \Delta^{\mathcal{I}'} \, Z(y, y') \tag{5}$$

$$\forall y' \in \Delta^{\mathcal{I}'} \, \exists y \in \Delta^{\mathcal{I}} \, Z(y, y'); \tag{6}$$

if $\mathtt{Self} \in \Phi$, then

$$Z(x, x') \to r^{\mathcal{I}}(x, x) = r^{\mathcal{I}'}(x', x'); \tag{7}$$

if $Q_n \in \Phi$, then

> if $Z(x, x')$ holds and $y_1, \ldots, y_n$ are pairwise distinct elements of $\Delta^{\mathcal{I}}$ such that $R^{\mathcal{I}}(x, y_j) > 0$ for all $1 \leq j \leq n$, then there exist pairwise distinct elements $y'_1, \ldots, y'_n$ of $\Delta^{\mathcal{I}'}$ such that, for every $1 \leq i \leq n$, there exists $1 \leq j \leq n$ such that $Z(y_j, y'_i)$ holds and $R^{\mathcal{I}}(x, y_j) \leq R^{\mathcal{I}'}(x', y'_i)$, $\tag{8}$

> if $Z(x, x')$ holds and $y'_1, \ldots, y'_n$ are pairwise distinct elements of $\Delta^{\mathcal{I}'}$ such that $R^{\mathcal{I}'}(x', y'_j) > 0$ for all $1 \leq j \leq n$, then there exist pairwise distinct elements $y_1, \ldots, y_n$ of $\Delta^{\mathcal{I}}$ such that, for every $1 \leq i \leq n$, there exists $1 \leq j \leq n$ such that $Z(y_i, y'_j)$ holds and $R^{\mathcal{I}'}(x', y'_j) \leq R^{\mathcal{I}}(x, y_i)$; $\tag{9}$

if $N_n \in \Phi$, then

> if $Z(x, x')$ holds and $y_1, \ldots, y_n$ are pairwise distinct elements of $\Delta^{\mathcal{I}}$
> such that $R^{\mathcal{I}}(x, y_j) > 0$ for all $1 \leq j \leq n$, then there exist pairwise
> distinct elements $y'_1, \ldots, y'_n$ of $\Delta^{\mathcal{I}'}$ such that, for every $1 \leq i \leq n$,
> there exists $1 \leq j \leq n$ such that $R^{\mathcal{I}}(x, y_j) \leq R^{\mathcal{I}'}(x', y'_i)$, $\qquad$ (10)

> if $Z(x, x')$ holds and $y'_1, \ldots, y'_n$ are pairwise distinct elements of $\Delta^{\mathcal{I}'}$
> such that $R^{\mathcal{I}'}(x', y'_j) > 0$ for all $1 \leq j \leq n$, then there exist pairwise
> distinct elements $y_1, \ldots, y_n$ of $\Delta^{\mathcal{I}}$ such that, for every $1 \leq i \leq n$,
> there exists $1 \leq j \leq n$ such that $R^{\mathcal{I}'}(x', y'_j) \leq R^{\mathcal{I}}(x, y_i)$. $\qquad$ (11)

For example, if $\Phi = \{I, N_2\}$, then only Conditions (1)–(3), (10) and (11)
with $n = 2$ are essential. $\qquad\blacksquare$

Let $\mathcal{I}$ and $\mathcal{I}'$ be fuzzy interpretations. For $x \in \Delta^{\mathcal{I}}$ and $x' \in \Delta^{\mathcal{I}'}$, we write
$x \sim_\Phi x'$ to denote that there exists a Φ-bisimulation Z between $\mathcal{I}$ and $\mathcal{I}'$
such that $Z(x, x')$ holds. If $x \sim_\Phi x'$, then we say that x and x' are *strongly*
Φ-bisimilar. If $\mathbf{I} \neq \emptyset$ and there exists a Φ-bisimulation Z between $\mathcal{I}$ and $\mathcal{I}'$
such that $Z(a^{\mathcal{I}}, a^{\mathcal{I}'})$ holds for all $a \in \mathbf{I}$, then we say that $\mathcal{I}$ and $\mathcal{I}'$ are *strongly*
Φ-bisimilar and write $\mathcal{I} \sim_\Phi \mathcal{I}'$.

Example 2. Let $\mathbf{C} = \{A\}$, $\mathbf{R} = \{r\}$ and $\mathbf{I} = \{a\}$. Consider the fuzzy interpretations $\mathcal{I}$ and $\mathcal{I}'$ illustrated below and specified analogously as in Example 1, with
$a^{\mathcal{I}} = u$ and $a^{\mathcal{I}'} = u'$:

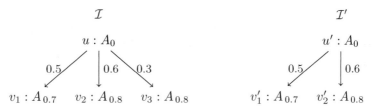

Let $Z = \{\langle u, u'\rangle, \langle v_1, v'_1\rangle, \langle v_2, v'_2\rangle, \langle v_3, v'_2\rangle\}$. It can be checked that, for any
$\Phi \subseteq \{O, U, \texttt{Self}, Q_n, N_n \mid n \in \mathbb{N} \setminus \{0, 3\}\}$, Z is a Φ-bisimulation between $\mathcal{I}$
and $\mathcal{I}'$, and these fuzzy interpretations are strongly Φ-bisimilar. If $I \in \Phi$, then
$v_3 \not\sim_\Phi v'_2$, and hence $u \not\sim_\Phi u'$. If $\{Q_3, N_3\} \cap \Phi \neq \emptyset$, then clearly $u \not\sim_\Phi u'$.
Therefore, if $\{I, Q_3, N_3\} \cap \Phi \neq \emptyset$, then $\mathcal{I}$ and $\mathcal{I}'$ are not strongly Φ-bisimilar. $\blacksquare$

Proposition 1. *Let $\mathcal{I}$, $\mathcal{I}'$ and $\mathcal{I}''$ be fuzzy interpretations.*

1. *The relation $\{\langle x, x\rangle \mid x \in \Delta^{\mathcal{I}}\}$ is a Φ-bisimulation between $\mathcal{I}$ and itself.*
2. *If Z is a Φ-bisimulation between $\mathcal{I}$ and $\mathcal{I}'$, then Z^{-1} is a Φ-bisimulation between $\mathcal{I}'$ and $\mathcal{I}$.*
3. *If Z_1 is a Φ-bisimulation between $\mathcal{I}$ and $\mathcal{I}'$, and Z_2 is a Φ-bisimulation between $\mathcal{I}'$ and $\mathcal{I}''$, then $Z_1 \circ Z_2$ is a Φ-bisimulation between $\mathcal{I}$ and $\mathcal{I}''$.*
4. *If $\mathcal{Z}$ is a set of Φ-bisimulations between $\mathcal{I}$ and $\mathcal{I}'$, then $\bigcup \mathcal{Z}$ is also a Φ-bisimulation between $\mathcal{I}$ and $\mathcal{I}'$.*

3.1   Invariance Results

In this subsection, we present results on invariance of concepts, fuzzy TBoxes and fuzzy ABoxes under strong Φ-bisimilarity between fuzzy interpretations.

Lemma 1. *Let $\mathcal{I}$ and $\mathcal{I}'$ be fuzzy interpretations that are witnessed w.r.t. $\mathcal{L}_{(\Phi,\dot{\neg})}$ and Z a Φ-bisimulation between $\mathcal{I}$ and $\mathcal{I}'$. Then, the following properties hold for every concept C of $\mathcal{L}_{(\Phi,\dot{\neg})}$, every role R of $\mathcal{L}_{(\Phi,\dot{\neg})}$, every $x \in \Delta^{\mathcal{I}}$ and every $x' \in \Delta^{\mathcal{I}'}$:*

$$Z(x,x') \to C^{\mathcal{I}}(x) = C^{\mathcal{I}'}(x') \tag{12}$$

$$[Z(x,x') \wedge R^{\mathcal{I}}(x,y) > 0] \to \exists y' \in \Delta^{\mathcal{I}'} [Z(y,y') \wedge R^{\mathcal{I}}(x,y) \leq R^{\mathcal{I}'}(x',y')] \tag{13}$$

$$[Z(x,x') \wedge R^{\mathcal{I}'}(x',y') > 0] \to \exists y \in \Delta^{\mathcal{I}} [Z(y,y') \wedge R^{\mathcal{I}'}(x',y') \leq R^{\mathcal{I}}(x,y)]. \tag{14}$$

The following lemma differs from Lemma 1 in that $\mathcal{L}^0_{(\Phi,\triangle)}$ is used instead of $\mathcal{L}_{(\Phi,\dot{\neg})}$. When R is a role of $\mathcal{L}^0_{(\Phi,\triangle)}$, the assertions (13) and (14) are the same as Conditions (2) and (3), respectively.

Lemma 2. *Let $\mathcal{I}$ and $\mathcal{I}'$ be fuzzy interpretations that are witnessed w.r.t. $\mathcal{L}^0_{(\Phi,\triangle)}$ and Z a Φ-bisimulation between $\mathcal{I}$ and $\mathcal{I}'$. Then, for every concept C of $\mathcal{L}^0_{(\Phi,\triangle)}$, every $x \in \Delta^{\mathcal{I}}$ and every $x' \in \Delta^{\mathcal{I}'}$,*

$$Z(x,x') \to C^{\mathcal{I}}(x) = C^{\mathcal{I}'}(x').$$

A concept C of $\mathcal{L}_{(\Phi,\dot{\neg})}$ is said to be *invariant under strong Φ-bisimilarity* (between witnessed interpretations) if, for any interpretations $\mathcal{I}$ and $\mathcal{I}'$ that are witnessed w.r.t. $\mathcal{L}_{(\Phi,\dot{\neg})}$ and any $x \in \Delta^{\mathcal{I}}$ and $x' \in \Delta^{\mathcal{I}'}$, if $x \sim_{\Phi} x'$, then $C^{\mathcal{I}}(x) = C^{\mathcal{I}'}(x')$.

Theorem 1. *All concepts of $\mathcal{L}_{(\Phi,\dot{\neg})}$ are invariant under strong Φ-bisimilarity.*

A fuzzy TBox $\mathcal{T}$ is said to be *invariant under strong Φ-bisimilarity* (between witnessed interpretations) if, for every interpretations $\mathcal{I}$ and $\mathcal{I}'$ that are witnessed w.r.t. $\mathcal{L}_{(\Phi,\dot{\neg})}$ and strongly Φ-bisimilar to each other, $\mathcal{I} \models \mathcal{T}$ iff $\mathcal{I}' \models \mathcal{T}$. The notion of invariance of fuzzy ABoxes under strong Φ-bisimilarity (between witnessed interpretations) is defined similarly.

Theorem 2. *If $U \in \Phi$, then all fuzzy TBoxes in $\mathcal{L}_{(\Phi,\dot{\neg})}$ are invariant under strong Φ-bisimilarity.*

A fuzzy interpretation $\mathcal{I}$ is *connected* w.r.t. Φ if, for every $x \in \Delta^{\mathcal{I}}$, there exists $a \in \mathbf{I}$, $x_0, \ldots, x_n \in \Delta^{\mathcal{I}}$ and basic roles $R_1, \ldots, R_n$ w.r.t. Φ such that $x_0 = a^{\mathcal{I}}$, $x_n = x$ and $R_i^{\mathcal{I}}(x_{i-1}, x_i) > 0$ for all $1 \leq i \leq n$. Our notion of connectedness is an adaptation of the one in [9] and the notion of being unreachable-objects-free [8]. The following theorem concerns invariance of fuzzy TBoxes without requiring $U \in \Phi$.

Theorem 3. *Let $\mathcal{T}$ be a fuzzy TBox in $\mathcal{L}_{(\Phi,\dot{\neg})}$ and $\mathcal{I}$, $\mathcal{I}'$ interpretations that are witnessed w.r.t. $\mathcal{L}_{(\Phi,\dot{\neg})}$ and strongly Φ-bisimilar to each other. If $\mathcal{I}$ and $\mathcal{I}'$ are connected w.r.t. Φ, then $\mathcal{I} \models \mathcal{T}$ iff $\mathcal{I}' \models \mathcal{T}$.*

The following theorem concerns invariance of fuzzy ABoxes.

Theorem 4. *Let $\mathcal{A}$ be a fuzzy ABox in $\mathcal{L}_{(\Phi,\dot{\neg})}$. If $O \in \Phi$ or $\mathcal{A}$ consists of only fuzzy assertions of the form $C(a) \bowtie p$, then $\mathcal{A}$ is invariant under strong Φ-bisimilarity.*

3.2   The Hennessy-Milner Property

In this subsection, we present a theorem about the Hennessy-Milner property of Φ-bisimulations between fuzzy interpretations. It is formulated for the class of fuzzy interpretations that are witnessed and modally saturated w.r.t. $\mathcal{L}^0_{(\Phi,\triangle)}$, which is more general than the class of image-finite fuzzy interpretations.

Definition 3. A fuzzy interpretation $\mathcal{I}$ is said to be *modally saturated* w.r.t. $\mathcal{L}^0_{(\Phi,\triangle)}$ (and the Gödel semantics) if the following conditions hold:

- for every $p \in (0,1]$, every $x \in \Delta^{\mathcal{I}}$, every basic role R w.r.t. Φ and every infinite set Γ of concepts in $\mathcal{L}^0_{(\Phi,\triangle)}$, if for every finite subset Λ of Γ there exists $y \in \Delta^{\mathcal{I}}$ such that $R^{\mathcal{I}}(x,y) \otimes C^{\mathcal{I}}(y) \geq p$ for all $C \in \Lambda$, then there exists $y \in \Delta^{\mathcal{I}}$ such that $R^{\mathcal{I}}(x,y) \geq p$ and $C^{\mathcal{I}}(y) > 0$ for all $C \in \Gamma$;
- if $Q_n \in \Phi$, then for every $p \in (0,1]$, every $x \in \Delta^{\mathcal{I}}$, every basic role R w.r.t. Φ and every infinite set Γ of concepts in $\mathcal{L}^0_{(\Phi,\triangle)}$, if for every finite subset Λ of Γ there exist n pairwise distinct $y_1, \ldots, y_n \in \Delta^{\mathcal{I}}$ such that $R^{\mathcal{I}}(x,y_i) \otimes C^{\mathcal{I}}(y_i) \geq p$ for all $1 \leq i \leq n$ and $C \in \Lambda$, then there exist n pairwise distinct $y_1, \ldots, y_n \in \Delta^{\mathcal{I}}$ such that $R^{\mathcal{I}}(x,y_i) \geq p$ and $C^{\mathcal{I}}(y_i) > 0$ for all $1 \leq i \leq n$ and $C \in \Gamma$;
- if $U \in \Phi$, then for every infinite set Γ of concepts in $\mathcal{L}^0_{(\Phi,\triangle)}$, if for every finite subset Λ of Γ there exists $y \in \Delta^{\mathcal{I}}$ such that $C^{\mathcal{I}}(y) = 1$ for all $C \in \Lambda$, then there exists $y \in \Delta^{\mathcal{I}}$ such that $C^{\mathcal{I}}(y) > 0$ for all $C \in \Gamma$.   ∎

The following claims can easily be checked:

- every finite fuzzy interpretation is modally saturated w.r.t. $\mathcal{L}^0_{(\Phi,\triangle)}$,
- if $U \notin \Phi$, then every image-finite fuzzy interpretation w.r.t. Φ is modally saturated w.r.t. $\mathcal{L}^0_{(\Phi,\triangle)}$.

Theorem 5. *Let $\mathcal{I}$ and $\mathcal{I}'$ be fuzzy interpretations that are witnessed and modally saturated w.r.t. $\mathcal{L}^0_{(\Phi,\triangle)}$. Then, the relation*

$$Z = \{\langle x, x'\rangle \in \Delta^{\mathcal{I}} \times \Delta^{\mathcal{I}'} \mid C^{\mathcal{I}}(x) = C^{\mathcal{I}'}(x') \text{ for all concepts } C \text{ of } \mathcal{L}^0_{(\Phi,\triangle)}\}$$

is the largest Φ-bisimulation between $\mathcal{I}$ and $\mathcal{I}'$.

Given fuzzy interpretations $\mathcal{I}$, $\mathcal{I}'$ and $x \in \Delta^{\mathcal{I}}$, $x' \in \Delta^{\mathcal{I}'}$, we write $x \equiv_{(\Phi, \dot{\neg})} x'$ to denote that $C^{\mathcal{I}}(x) = C^{\mathcal{I}'}(x')$ for all concepts C of $\mathcal{L}_{(\Phi, \dot{\neg})}$. Similarly, we write $x \equiv^0_{(\Phi, \triangle)} x'$ to denote that $C^{\mathcal{I}}(x) = C^{\mathcal{I}'}(x')$ for all concepts C of $\mathcal{L}^0_{(\Phi, \triangle)}$.

Corollary 1. *Let $\mathcal{I}$, $\mathcal{I}'$ be fuzzy interpretations and let $x \in \Delta^{\mathcal{I}}$, $x' \in \Delta^{\mathcal{I}'}$.*

1. If $\mathcal{I}$ and $\mathcal{I}'$ are witnessed and modally saturated w.r.t. $\mathcal{L}^0_{(\Phi, \triangle)}$, then

$$x \sim_{\Phi}^{\cdot} x' \quad \textit{iff} \quad x \equiv^0_{(\Phi, \triangle)} x'.$$

2. If $\mathcal{I}$ and $\mathcal{I}'$ are image-finite w.r.t. Φ and $U \notin \Phi$, then

$$x \sim_{\Phi}^{\cdot} x' \quad \textit{iff} \quad x \equiv^0_{(\Phi, \triangle)} x'.$$

3. If $\mathcal{I}$ and $\mathcal{I}'$ are witnessed w.r.t. $\mathcal{L}_{(\Phi, \dot{\neg})}$ and modally saturated w.r.t. $\mathcal{L}^0_{(\Phi, \triangle)}$, then

$$x \equiv_{(\Phi, \dot{\neg})} x' \quad \textit{iff} \quad x \sim_{\Phi}^{\cdot} x' \quad \textit{iff} \quad x \equiv^0_{(\Phi, \triangle)} x'.$$

Corollary 2. *Suppose $\mathbf{I} \neq \emptyset$ and let $\mathcal{I}$ and $\mathcal{I}'$ be fuzzy interpretations that are witnessed w.r.t. $\mathcal{L}_{(\Phi, \dot{\neg})}$ and modally saturated w.r.t. $\mathcal{L}^0_{(\Phi, \triangle)}$. Then, $\mathcal{I}$ and $\mathcal{I}'$ are strongly Φ-bisimilar iff $a^{\mathcal{I}} \equiv^0_{(\Phi, \triangle)} a^{\mathcal{I}'}$ for all $a \in \mathbf{I}$.*

4 Minimizing Fuzzy Interpretations

In this section, as an application of strong Φ-bisimilarity, we study the problem of minimizing a finite fuzzy interpretation while preserving certain properties.

Given a fuzzy interpretation $\mathcal{I}$, by $\sim_{\Phi, \mathcal{I}}^{\cdot}$ we denote the binary relation on $\Delta^{\mathcal{I}}$ such that, for $x, x' \in \Delta^{\mathcal{I}}$, $x \sim_{\Phi, \mathcal{I}}^{\cdot} x'$ iff $x \sim_{\Phi}^{\cdot} x'$. We call it the *strong Φ-bisimilarity relation of $\mathcal{I}$*. By Proposition 1, $\sim_{\Phi, \mathcal{I}}^{\cdot}$ is an equivalence relation and the largest Φ-bisimulation between $\mathcal{I}$ and itself.

Definition 4. *Given a fuzzy interpretation $\mathcal{I}$ and $\Phi \subseteq \{I, O, U\}$, the quotient fuzzy interpretation $\mathcal{I}/_{\sim_{\Phi}}$ of $\mathcal{I}$ w.r.t. the equivalence relation $\sim_{\Phi, \mathcal{I}}^{\cdot}$ is specified as follows:[2]*

- $\Delta^{\mathcal{I}/_{\sim_{\Phi}}} = \{[x]_{\sim_{\Phi, \mathcal{I}}} \mid x \in \Delta^{\mathcal{I}}\}$, where $[x]_{\sim_{\Phi, \mathcal{I}}}$ is the equivalence class of x w.r.t. $\sim_{\Phi, \mathcal{I}}^{\cdot}$,
- $a^{\mathcal{I}/_{\sim_{\Phi}}} = [a^{\mathcal{I}}]_{\sim_{\Phi, \mathcal{I}}}$ for $a \in \mathbf{I}$,
- $A^{\mathcal{I}/_{\sim_{\Phi}}}([x]_{\sim_{\Phi, \mathcal{I}}}) = A^{\mathcal{I}}(x)$ for $A \in \mathbf{C}$ and $x \in \Delta^{\mathcal{I}}$,
- $r^{\mathcal{I}/_{\sim_{\Phi}}}([x]_{\sim_{\Phi, \mathcal{I}}}, [y]_{\sim_{\Phi, \mathcal{I}}}) = \sup\{r^{\mathcal{I}}(x, y') \mid y' \in [y]_{\sim_{\Phi, \mathcal{I}}}\}$ for $r \in \mathbf{R}$ and $x, y \in \Delta^{\mathcal{I}}$. $\blacksquare$

To justify that Definition 4 is well specified, we need to show that:

---

[2] Formally, the quotient fuzzy interpretation of $\mathcal{I}$ w.r.t. the equivalence relation $\sim_{\Phi, \mathcal{I}}^{\cdot}$ should be denoted by $\mathcal{I}/_{\sim_{\Phi, \mathcal{I}}}$. We use $\mathcal{I}/_{\sim_{\Phi}}$ instead to simplify the notation.

1. For every $A \in \mathbf{C}$, $x \in \Delta^{\mathcal{I}}$ and $x' \in [x]_{\dot{\sim}_{\Phi,\mathcal{I}}}$, $A^{\mathcal{I}}(x) = A^{\mathcal{I}}(x')$.
2. For every $r \in \mathbf{R}$, $x, y \in \Delta^{\mathcal{I}}$ and $x' \in [x]_{\dot{\sim}_{\Phi,\mathcal{I}}}$,

$$\sup\{r^{\mathcal{I}}(x,y') \mid y' \in [y]_{\dot{\sim}_{\Phi,\mathcal{I}}}\} = \sup\{r^{\mathcal{I}}(x',y') \mid y' \in [y]_{\dot{\sim}_{\Phi,\mathcal{I}}}\}.$$

Let Z be $\dot{\sim}_{\Phi,\mathcal{I}}$. Then, the first assertion follows from Condition (1) and the assumption that $Z(x, x')$ holds. The second one follows from Conditions (2), (3) and the assumption that $Z(x, x')$ holds.

Example 3. Let $\mathbf{C} = \{A\}$, $\mathbf{R} = \{r\}$ and $\mathbf{I} = \{a\}$. Consider the fuzzy interpretation $\mathcal{I}$ illustrated below and specified similarly as in Example 1, with $a^{\mathcal{I}} = u$:

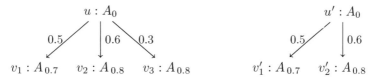

- Case $\Phi \subseteq \{U\}$: We have

$$\dot{\sim}_{\Phi,\mathcal{I}} = \{\langle x, x\rangle \mid x \in \Delta^{\mathcal{I}}\} \cup \{\langle u, u'\rangle, \langle u', u\rangle, \langle v_1, v_1'\rangle, \langle v_1', v_1\rangle\} \cup$$
$$\{\langle x, x'\rangle \mid x, x' \in \{v_2, v_3, v_2'\}\}$$

and $\mathcal{I}/_{\dot{\sim}_{\Phi}}$ has the following form, with $a^{\mathcal{I}/_{\dot{\sim}_{\Phi}}} = \{u, u'\}$:

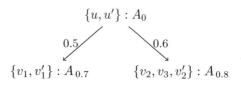

- Case $\{O\} \subseteq \Phi \subseteq \{O, U\}$: We have

$$\dot{\sim}_{\Phi,\mathcal{I}} = \{\langle x, x\rangle \mid x \in \Delta^{\mathcal{I}}\} \cup \{\langle v_1, v_1'\rangle, \langle v_1', v_1\rangle\} \cup \{\langle x, x'\rangle \mid x, x' \in \{v_2, v_3, v_2'\}\}$$

and $\mathcal{I}/_{\dot{\sim}_{\Phi}}$ has the following form, with $a^{\mathcal{I}/_{\dot{\sim}_{\Phi}}} = \{u\}$:

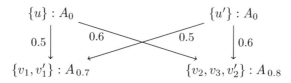

- Case $I \in \Phi$: We have $\dot{\sim}_{\Phi,\mathcal{I}} = \{\langle x, x\rangle \mid x \in \Delta^{\mathcal{I}}\}$ and $\mathcal{I}/_{\dot{\sim}_{\Phi}}$ has the same form as $\mathcal{I}$. ∎

Lemma 3. *Let $\Phi \subseteq \{I, O, U\}$, $\mathcal{I}$ be a fuzzy interpretation that is image-finite w.r.t. Φ, and $Z = \{\langle x, [x]_{\dot{\sim}_{\Phi,\mathcal{I}}}\rangle \mid x \in \Delta^{\mathcal{I}}\}$. Then, Z is a Φ-bisimulation between $\mathcal{I}$ and $\mathcal{I}/_{\dot{\sim}_{\Phi}}$. It is also a $(\Phi \cup \{U\})$-bisimulation between $\mathcal{I}$ and $\mathcal{I}/_{\dot{\sim}_{\Phi}}$.*

Corollary 3. *Suppose that* $\mathbf{I} \neq \emptyset$, $\Phi \subseteq \{I, O, U\}$ *and* $\mathcal{I}$ *is a fuzzy interpretation that is image-finite w.r.t.* Φ. *Then,* $\mathcal{I}$ *and* $\mathcal{I}/_{\sim_{\Phi}}$ *are both strongly* Φ-*bisimilar and strongly* $(\Phi \cup \{U\})$-*bisimilar.*

Corollary 4. *Let* $\Phi \subseteq \{I, O, U\}$, $\mathcal{I}$ *be a finite fuzzy interpretation,* $\mathcal{T}$ *a fuzzy TBox and* $\mathcal{A}$ *a fuzzy ABox in* $\mathcal{L}_{(\Phi, \dot{\neg})}$. *Then:*

1. $\mathcal{I} \models \mathcal{T}$ *iff* $\mathcal{I}/_{\sim_{\Phi}} \models \mathcal{T}$,
2. *if* $O \in \Phi$ *or* $\mathcal{A}$ *consists of only fuzzy assertions of the form* $C(a) \bowtie p$, *then* $\mathcal{I} \models \mathcal{A}$ *iff* $\mathcal{I}/_{\sim_{\Phi}} \models \mathcal{A}$.

In the following theorem, the term "minimum" is understood w.r.t. the size of the domain of the considered fuzzy interpretation.

Theorem 6. *Let* $\Phi \subseteq \{I, O, U\}$ *and let* $\mathcal{I}$ *be a finite fuzzy interpretation. Then:*

1. $\mathcal{I}/_{\sim_{\Phi}}$ *is a minimum fuzzy interpretation that validates the same set of fuzzy GCIs in* $\mathcal{L}_{(\Phi, \dot{\neg})}$ *as* $\mathcal{I}$,
2. *if* $\mathbf{I} \neq \emptyset$ *and either* $U \in \Phi$ *or* $\mathcal{I}$ *is connected w.r.t.* Φ, *then:*
   (a) $\mathcal{I}/_{\sim_{\Phi}}$ *is a minimum fuzzy interpretation strongly* Φ-*bisimilar to* $\mathcal{I}$,
   (b) $\mathcal{I}/_{\sim_{\Phi}}$ *is a minimum fuzzy interpretation that validates the same set of fuzzy assertions of the form* $C(a) \bowtie p$ *in* $\mathcal{L}_{(\Phi, \dot{\neg})}$ *as* $\mathcal{I}$.

In this section, we have studied minimizing finite fuzzy interpretations for the case when $\Phi \subseteq \{I, O, U\}$. In [7,8], Nguyen and Divroodi studied the problem of minimizing (traditional) interpretations also for the cases when the considered interpretation is infinite or $\Phi \cap \{Q, \mathtt{Self}\} \neq \emptyset$. For dealing with the case when $\Phi \cap \{Q, \mathtt{Self}\} \neq \emptyset$, they introduced the notion of QS-interpretation that allows "multi-edges" and keeps information about "self-edges" (where "edge" is understood as an instance of a role). Minimizing fuzzy interpretations can be extended for those cases using their approach. Here, we have restricted to finite (fuzzy) interpretations and the case when $\Phi \subseteq \{I, O, U\}$ to increase the readability.

5   Conclusions

We have defined crisp bisimulation and strong bisimilarity in a uniform way for a large class of fuzzy DLs with involutive negation under the Gödel semantics. We have given fundamental results about them, including the ones on invariance of concepts, conditional invariance of fuzzy TBoxes/ABoxes and the Hennessy-Milner property. Furthermore, we have provided results on minimizing fuzzy interpretations by using strong bisimilarity. Minimization is useful not only for saving memory but also for speeding up computations on the interpretation. Our study is a starting point for investigating bisimulation and bisimilarity for fuzzy DLs under other t-norm based semantics (e.g., Lukasiewicz and Product). As future work, we intend to apply strong bisimilarity to concept learning for DL-based information systems.

References

1. Baaz, M.: Infinite-valued Gödel logics with 0-1-projections and relativizations. In: Gödel'96: Logical Foundations of Mathematics, Computer Science and Physics– Kurt Gödel's Legacy, pp. 23–33 (1996)
2. Bobillo, F., Cerami, M., Esteva, F., García-Cerdaña, Á., Peñaloza, R., Straccia, U.: Fuzzy description logics. In: Handbook of Mathematical Fuzzy Logic, Volume 3, volume 58 of Studies in Logic, Mathematical Logic and Foundations, pp. 1105–1181. College Publications (2015)
3. Bobillo, F., Delgado, M., Gómez-Romero, J., Straccia, U.: Fuzzy description logics under Gödel semantics. Int. J. Approx. Reasoning **50**(3), 494–514 (2009)
4. Borgwardt, S., Peñaloza, R.: Fuzzy description logics – a survey. In: Moral, S., Pivert, O., Sánchez, D., Marín, N. (eds.) SUM 2017. LNCS (LNAI), vol. 10564, pp. 31–45. Springer, Cham (2017). https://doi.org/10.1007/978-3-319-67582-4_3
5. Cao, Y., Chen, G., Kerre, E.E.: Bisimulations for fuzzy-transition systems. IEEE Trans. Fuzzy Syst. **19**(3), 540–552 (2011)
6. Ćirić, M., Ignjatović, J., Damljanović, N., Bašic, M.: Bisimulations for fuzzy automata. Fuzzy Sets Syst. **186**(1), 100–139 (2012)
7. Divroodi, A.R.: Bisimulation equivalence in description logics and its applications. Ph.D. thesis, University of Warsaw (2015)
8. Divroodi, A.R., Nguyen, L.A.: On bisimulations for description logics. Inf. Sci. **295**, 465–493 (2015)
9. Divroodi, A.R., Nguyen, L.A.: On directed simulations in description logics. J. Log. Comput. **27**(7), 1955–1986 (2017)
10. Eleftheriou, P.E., Koutras, C.D., Nomikos, C.: Notions of bisimulation for Heyting-valued modal languages. J. Log. Comput. **22**(2), 213–235 (2012)
11. Fan, T.-F.: Fuzzy bisimulation for Gödel modal logic. IEEE Trans. Fuzzy Syst. **23**(6), 2387–2396 (2015)
12. Ha, Q.-T., Nguyen, L.A., Nguyen, T.H.K., Tran, T.-L.: Fuzzy bisimulations in fuzzy description logics under the Gödel semantics. In: Nguyen, H.S., Ha, Q.-T., Li, T., Przybyła-Kasperek, M. (eds.) IJCRS 2018. LNCS (LNAI), vol. 11103, pp. 559–571. Springer, Cham (2018). https://doi.org/10.1007/978-3-319-99368-3_44
13. Hájek, P.: Making fuzzy description logic more general. Fuzzy Sets Syst. **154**(1), 1–15 (2005)
14. Hennessy, M., Milner, R.: Algebraic laws for nondeterminism and concurrency. J. ACM **32**(1), 137–161 (1985)
15. Nguyen, L.A.: Bisimilarity in fuzzy description logics under the Zadeh semantics. IEEE Trans. Fuzzy Syst. **27**, 1151 (2018). https://doi.org/10.1109/TFUZZ.2018.2871004
16. Nguyen, L.A., Ha, Q.-T., Nguyen, N.-T., Nguyen, T.H.K., Tran, T.-L.: Bisimulation and bisimilarity for fuzzy description logics under the Gödel semantics (2019, Submitted)
17. Nguyen, L.A., Szałas, A.: Logic-based roughification. In: Skowron, A., Suraj, Z. (eds.) Rough Sets and Intelligent Systems - Professor Zdzisław Pawlak in Memoriam. ISRL, vol. 1, pp. 529–556. Springer, Heidelberg (2013). https://doi.org/10.1007/978-3-642-30344-9_19
18. Park, D.: Concurrency and automata on infinite sequences. In: Deussen, P. (ed.) GI-TCS 1981. LNCS, vol. 104, pp. 167–183. Springer, Heidelberg (1981). https://doi.org/10.1007/BFb0017309

19. Tran, T.-L., Nguyen, L.A., Hoang, T.-L.-G.: Bisimulation-based concept learning for information systems in description logics. Vietnam J. Comput. Sci. **2**(3), 149–167 (2015)
20. van Benthem, J.: Modal correspondence theory. Ph.D. thesis, Mathematisch Instituut & Instituut voor Grondslagenonderzoek, University of Amsterdam (1976)

The Collective-Based Approach to Knowledge Diffusion in Social Networks

Marcin Maleszka[(⊠)]

Faculty of Computer Science and Management,
Wroclaw University of Science and Technology, Wroclaw, Poland
`marcin.maleszka@pwr.edu.pl`

Abstract. In this paper we present our work towards creating a model of communication if collectives that is geared towards collective knowledge integration, based on sociological models of social influence. The model allows several different strategies of internalization of knowledge and of forgetting existing knowledge. We test the validity of the model in a general simulation in a multi-agent environment, based on properties of real world group communication derived from sociological literature.

Keywords: Collective knowledge · Knowledge integration ·
Multi-agent system · Knowledge diffusion

1 Introduction

The research in the knowledge diffusion area is a modern topic, which sees more and more practical applications in social network environments. Modeling the spread of gossip, or fake news, is an important topic with a lot of practical applications.

The classical models of knowledge diffusion are often derived directly from epidemic models, when the spread of information is analogous to the spread of some disease in a population. The basic models start from Susceptible-Infected ones [15] (ie. a person does not yet have the information and a person has the information, the chance of changing the group is often determined only by statistical probability), and range up to variants of Susceptible-Infected-Resistant-Susceptible model [8] (ie. after a person learns the information, he may discard it and for a *limited* time be resistant to receiving it again). The variants include additional states, like Exposed in SEIR [17] (ie. knowledge spread requires a social network user to be logged in) or Contacted in SCIR [5] (ie. user needs to read the message), and other parameters, like the emotional state considered in ESIS [19]. These models are statistical in nature and do not focus on modeling a single user, which is done e.g. in influence maximization models measuring node centrality [18] or assigning users to classes based on their leadership potential [4]. Yet other knowledge diffusion models focus on probability of sending out information [16] or of knowledge state change based on Markov Chains [21].

© Springer Nature Switzerland AG 2019
N. T. Nguyen et al. (Eds.): ICCCI 2019, LNAI 11683, pp. 31–40, 2019.
https://doi.org/10.1007/978-3-030-28377-3_3

In our research, we aim to develop an entirely new approach to knowledge diffusion, one based on collective intelligence research as applied on local and global level to social groups. We incorporate sociological research discussing knowledge internalization and persuasion to model the behavior of group members, introducing elements of consensus approach as needed. The communication of identical members of the collective leads to changing knowledge dynamics in the overall group. In essence, we model the collective not as a supervised entity (with some central agent conducting integration of knowledge), but as an unsupervised one.

In this paper we discuss the notions of modeling a collective that represents a Twitter-like social network with dynamic agent memory (an option to forget some information). This is further extension of research done in [11]. At this point the research and the model itself are focused on different aspects of the group than classical social network models and as such, it is incomparable in most aspects. In this place, we verify it against requirements stated in sociological literature for real-world groups.

This paper is organized as follows: Sect. 2 presents details on the sociological aspect of this research and computer science research used to expand upon it; Sect. 3 describes the model of the collective and Sect. 4 details the experiment showing its validity; finally the paper is concluded in Sect. 5 with more details on the expansion of the model planned in future works.

2   Related Works

Psychological and sociological literature gives examples of multiple theories of social influence. In most cases the theories are not conflicting, but rather focus on different aspects of real life phenomena. In our research, the approach used is mostly based on works by Kelman [9]. The author proposed to distinguish different variants of social influence that may be exerted upon a person and different possible reactions to that influence. In our work the notion of *resistance to induction* is especially important – it represents the reaction of a person to social influence and ranges from full to none (in our research called Discard and Substitute integration strategies). It was shown that the same approach is applicable in social network research [20].

Psychological research shows also that a person joining a group slowly changes their opinions and behavior to better fit the group (internalizes or complies to group rules), by simply gathering information about the inner workings of the group [10].

Alternatively one may consider *Social Judgment Theory*, as described in [3]. Each message that a person receives is compared with their current knowledge (opinion). If it is very different from personal opinion it will be rejected. Otherwise, it will influence the person, leading to them changing their opinion. Additionally, the more different the incoming knowledge, the larger will be the change of the personal one. The same approach is used to determine how discussions may lead to polarization of attitude of group members [2] – as the same message is repeated consistently, the opinion of the collective slowly changes to reflect it. It is one of the basis' we use for experimental evaluation in simulation environment.

As this non-computer-science research lacks mathematical descriptions on occurring processes, in our research we use consensus and voting approaches for determining specific values. The consensus approach is based on determining median solutions and stems from research done in [1] and was further expanded in [6,14]. Multiple works helped define classes of consensus functions and defined methods and criteria for integration of specific data structures or for specific problems. We also use the results from works describing asynchronous decentralized communication in multi-agent systems. Some research, where multiple communication channels with different connection structures are used [13], provide a good basis for describing a social network as a collective of agents.

3   The Model of the Collective

The model covered in this phase of our research is based on the concepts of communication in the Twitter social platform. In that social networks users usually communicate single declarative statements, due to initial limitation of message length. This often represents user knowledge, opinion or his current state. Besides the statements itself, the message may have some emotional content – called *sentiment* – representing the strength of person's feeling towards the issue. For example a single statement "watching movies" may be further enhanced by user sentiment "I love watching movies", "I like watching movies", "I hate watching movies", etc. Those short messages are in turn read by various recipients. Some of them are specific followers of that person, others follow all messages on some topic (usually defined by a category – *hashtag*). Depending on situation, not all messages will be read (e.g. due to watching too many categories/people and missing it among other messages) or a person may read the same message several times without realizing it is from the same person. Many messages are forwarded directly (retweeted) and some are commented upon (e.g. when opinions differ). The message exchange is very fast and topics covered in some categories change daily or even hourly. There are also more specific situations that may occur in this social network, but only this general part is covered by the model presented below.

The basic element of the model is a pair consisting of a declarative knowledge statement and its weight (sentiment). The statements are treated as general ones (A, *not* A), where negative ones are represented by negative weights. Each agent, representing a single person, may have multiple such pairs, up to the maximum number of statements allowed in the experiment. Initially, the size of personal knowledge base is limited. To avoid unnecessary growth of knowledge stored in each agent (and represent changing topics in real social network), periodically there is a chance that an agent will forget some statements. We denote the knowledge-weight pair describing the i-th knowledge statement, weighted by a-th agent as $<k_i, w_i^a>$. Possible weights are in range $[-W, W]$. The total number of knowledge statements in the model is K, and initially each agent knows only K_a statements. We assume that this covers all the statements in a single category. Positive or negative opinion is assigned to each initially known statement, but due to later influence weight may be also equal to 0. All statements are additionally labeled by the time moment they were first created. We consider 4 different strategies for forgetting knowledge statements:

- No forgetting – in this strategy all knowledge is kept and the amount of statements known to any agent can only increase with time.
- Random forgetting – in this strategy in regular intervals there is a chance that an agent will randomly forget one or more knowledge statements. The chance for selecting any specific statement is determined by uniform distribution. This strategy is used as a baseline.
- Random oldest forgetting – in this strategy in regular intervals there is a chance that an agent will randomly forget one or more knowledge statements. The chance for selecting any specific statement is determined by Poisson distribution with maximum in the area of oldest created. This is parallel to a person forgetting old knowledge.
- Random newest forgetting – in this strategy in regular intervals there is a chance that an agent will randomly forget one or more knowledge statements. The chance for selecting any specific statement is determined by Poisson distribution with maximum in the area of oldest created. This is parallel to a person having difficulty to acquire or memorize new knowledge.

The information about followers is stored not in the receivers, but in the sender (i.e. an agent stores the list of his followers). This does not change the structure of communication. Each agent a stores a list of f_a followers. Agents may send a message in any discrete time moment with probability P_c. A message consists of a single knowledge-weight pair. The number of receivers (representing people that *read* a message in real social network) is determined randomly with Poisson distribution, but at least one other agent will receive (read) it. The receivers are selected with uniform distribution from either the *followers* group (with P_f probability) or from the overall group. Any agent may occur multiple times on the receivers list, representing the situation where a person reads the same message multiple times.

Once an agent receives knowledge, it integrates the message with his internal knowledge according to one of predetermined strategies. In this version of the model all agents follow the same strategy (following a group of similar minded people). The integration strategies are as follows:

- Discard – agents ignore incoming messages and their state of knowledge does not change. These agents are static over the whole processing of the model (in simulations we only use this strategy for special situations).
- Substitute – agents always add incoming messages to their own knowledge. If they already had the received elements in their internal ontology, the sentiment value that was received is used. If the element itself is new to agents knowledge, it is added to the agents knowledge base as is.

– Extend – agents add incoming messages to their own knowledge, but if they
  already had some element in the ontology, the old sentiment value is used
  and the new one is discarded.
– Merge now – in this integration strategy the received knowledge immediately
  influences the knowledge and sentiment of the agent. If the received knowledge
  is new (previously unknown), it is added to the agents knowledge base, with
  the sentiment as received. If the knowledge was previously known, the new
  sentiment is calculated as the average of the old one and the received one.
– Merge later – the most complex strategy, incorporating several variants. In
  all of them, the agents store incoming messages and do not act on them. Only
  once a given number T of messages about the same knowledge statement are
  received, the new sentiment is calculated and the used remembered messages
  are discarded. If agent already had knowledge about the statement, the new
  value will be calculated out of all received and his opinion on the statement
  according to one of the variants, otherwise it will be determined only based on
  outside opinion. Each of the variants may be additionally treated as weighted
  or non-weighted one. The four variants used are:
  - Voting – the actual weight of the sentiment is disregarded. The number
    of positive and negative opinions is calculated and the winning vote will
    be given maximum weight W or $-W$. In case of a tie, the sentiment is
    neutral (0).
  - Average – the new sentiment is calculated simply as the average of own
    weight assigned to the knowledge and weights from received communi-
    cates.
  - Simplified median – the sentiment values from communicates and own
    knowledge are ordered from smallest to largest, without repetitions, and
    the middle one is selected. In case of even number of opinions, one of two
    middle elements is chosen randomly.
  - *Weighted* median – the approach is similar to the previous one, but rep-
    etitions may occur. In case of even number of values in final calculation,
    one of two middle elements is chosen randomly.

There are three distinct discrete time measures used in the model: one for
communication delays, one for agent memory (forgetting) and one for overall
model observation. The last one may be reduced to only observing the state of
the collective at the start of simulation and at the desired moment when the
simulation is finished. Otherwise, in a collective based on a real world group,
individual knowledge states may be observed at any time.

4   Evaluation of the Model

The psychological and sociological literature does not provide any mathematical measures that would allow determining the quality of models described as
collectives, but among others the research states that these groups are generally
unchanging, unless an external factor introduces some new concepts – in that
case, even if the concepts were opposed to group knowledge, the collective will

over time change to reflect it [2]. We have adopted and formalized this notion, to create a measure for changes occurring in the collective.

Definition 1. Drift of the collective C is the average change δ of collective opinion towards a single topic over time τ.

$$D_C = |\frac{\delta}{\tau}| \tag{1}$$

The measure of drift shows which collectives change more over time. We say that a collective is ϵ, τ-stable when it changes no more than ϵ over time τ (therefore $\delta \leq \epsilon$), otherwise we call it unstable. Based on sociological literature in our research we have assumed that the allowed drift should be no more than 10% of possible maximum change of the collective. Therefore we say that the model is *stable* if drift is withing these parameters, that is $D_C \leq |\frac{0.1*W*N}{\tau}|$. Following the literature we conduct a pair of experiments for the model (for each combination of strategies in the model): first we perform a simulation of a collective with identical members that should not change their opinion over time (stable collective); then we add a single agent following the discard strategy to the simulation – in that case the collective should become unstable.

We have prepared a simulation environment using JADE [7] agent framework, which is sufficient for this purpose, but should not be used in most practical applications of the model due to necessity of using a centralized approach with management agents. The parameters of the simulation were set up as follows:

- Total number of knowledge statements possible $K = 100$
- Maximum number of issues for each agent at initialization $K_A = 20$ (for every agent a, we have that $K_a \leq K_A$, with Poisson distribution)
- Maximum weight of an issue $W = 10$ (for readability, as $\epsilon = 1$)
- Total number of agents in simulation $N = 1000$
- Maximum number of followers for each agent $F = 10$ ($f_a \leq F$)
- Probability of communication in each tick $P_c = 20\%$
- Probability of communication to follower $P_f = 50\%$
- Number of receivers for each issue $R = 5$
- Size of message buffer for *Merge Later* strategy $T = 10$
- Number of ticks, length of simulation $\tau = 1000$
- Forgetting rate $M_r = \frac{K}{2}$ (up to half of total possible memory statements may be forgotten over the whole simulation by a single agent)

Most of the parameters were determined based on previous research and similar validity simulation using same methodology [11,12] and further tuned for this simulation. All combinations of integration and forgetting strategies described were tested. The results of simulations averaged over 100 runs are provided in Table 1 and illustrated in Figs. 1 and 2.

Considering only the integration strategies, like in our previous research, the results show that all strategies except *Substitute* and *Merge Later* in Median variant satisfy the requirement (parallel the sociological observations), with *Merge*

Table 1. The results of the experiment – drift value for all combinations of forgetting and integration strategies, two variants of experiment, averaged over 100 repetitions.

Forgetting	None	Random	Oldest	Newest
No influencers				
Substitute	2.33	1.19	1.52	0.74
Extend	0.01	0.45	0.28	0.05
Merge now	0.002	0.93	2.89	1.98
Merge later – maj. vote	1.05	0.44	0.68	0.28
Merge later – average	0.65	0.008	0.48	0.39
Merge later – s. median	1.66	1.85	0.69	1.60
Merge later – median	0.09	0.89	0.18	0.20
One influencer				
Substitute	10	10	10	10
Extend	1.13	2.36	1.77	1.63
Merge now	1.0	1.91	2.89	0.98
Merge later – maj. vote	4.81	4.56	3.11	3.49
Merge later – average	4.70	4.41	2.05	2.14
Merge later – s. median	3.86	4.48	3.0	2.83
Merge later – median	3.25	3.80	2.91	3.18

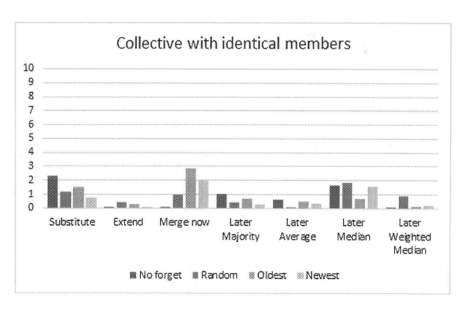

Fig. 1. Observed drift in different variants of the experiment – no influencer agents.

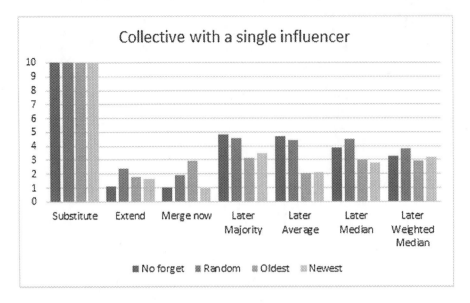

Fig. 2. Observed drift in different variants of the experiment – a single influencer agent introduced.

Now and *Merge Later* in Majority Vote variant strategies being borderline. The introduction of memory to the model, as different forgetting strategies, changes this behaviour:

– With *Random* forgetting, the same strategies as with no forgetting do not satisfy the sociological requirements, but as opposed to no forgetting approach, the *Substitute* strategy has smaller drift than the *Merge Later* Median variant.
– With *Oldest* forgetting, the *Substitute* and *Merge Now* integration strategies are not viable.
– The *Substitute* integration strategy becomes viable with the *Newest* forgetting strategy, but the agents in this combination could be described as very naive due to extreme change of opinion caused by influencers. The *Merge Now* and *Merge Later* Median variant integration strategies are not viable with this forgetting strategy. *Merge Now* strategy becomes more stable with an influencer introduced, which is directly opposite to the sociological research.
– In general terms, all forgetting strategies are comparable – in each case, exactly two integration strategies are not viable.
– The integration strategies that satisfy the sociological conditions in all forgetting strategies are *Extend* (agent is naive for new knowledge, otherwise skeptical) and *Merge Later* in Average and Weighted Median variants (agent gathers multiple opinions before changing his own).

These experiments cover most types of groups or individual people that may occur in real world collectives. We have determined which ones are the most viable in terms of sociological literature and will focus our future research on those specific combinations of strategies in the general model.

5 Conclusions

This paper introduced dynamic agent memory (in the form of forgetting knowledge) to a model of a Twitter-like social network. The model incorporates sociological research discussing knowledge internalization and persuasion as a basis for the behavior of group members, and is expanded with elements from consensus theory and collective intelligence area. While at this point the research is not comparable to classical knowledge diffusion models, it was tested in terms of sociological aspects of a similar group. In future works we aim for extensive testing in cooperation with sociologists to better tune the model to real-world groups of users. More future work can be also done to either enhance the practical application related to advertising (the *influencer* aspect) or move the model towards an influence maximization model of a social network (both tasks may be considered as identical with a change of focus in the research). In time the model will be expanded to cover different social networks (not only online ones), different knowledge structures and knowledge uncertainty. This will also allow application in other areas, like managing information flow in complex distributed systems.

Acknowledgments. This research is financially supported by Polish Ministry of Higher Education and Science.

References

1. Barthelemy, J.P., Janowitz, M.F.: A formal theory of consensus. SIAM J. Discrete Math. **4**, 305–322 (1991)
2. Brauer, M., Judd, C.M., Gliner, M.D.: The effects of repeated expressions on attitude polarization during group discussions. In: Levine, J.M., Moreland, R.L. (eds.) Small Groups, pp. 265–296. Psychology Press, New York (2006)
3. Cameron, K.A.: A practitioner's guide to persuasion: an overview of 15 selected persuasion theories, models and frameworks. Patient Educ. Couns. **74**, 309–317 (2009)
4. Chen, B., Tang, X., Yu, L., Liu, Y.: Identifying method for opinion leaders in social network based on competency model. J. Commun. **35**, 12–22 (2014)
5. Ding, X.J.: Research on propagation model of public opinion topics based on SCIR in microblogging. Comput. Eng. Appl. **51**, 20–26 (2015)
6. Dubois, D., Liu, W., Ma, J., Prade, H.: The basic principles of uncertain information fusion. An organised review of merging rules in different representation frameworks. Inf. Fus. **32**, 12–39 (2016)
7. Bellifemine, F., Poggi, A., Rimassa, G.: JADE-A FIPA-compliant agent framework. In: Proceedings of PAAM, vol. 99, no. 97–108 (1999)
8. Jin, Y., Wang, W., Xiao, S.: An SIRS model with a nonlinear incidence rate. Chaos Solitons Fractals **34**, 1482–1497 (2007)

9. Kelman, H.C.: Further thoughts on the processes of compliance, identification, and internalization. In: Tedeschi, J.T. (ed.) Social Power and Political Influence, pp. 125–171. Routledge (1974). Reprint (2017)
10. Kelman, H.C.: Interests, relationships, identities: three central issues for individuals and groups in negotiating their social environment. Annu. Rev. Psychol. **57**, 1–26 (2006). https://doi.org/10.1146/annurev.psych.57.102904.190156
11. Maleszka, M.: Application of collective knowledge diffusion in a social network environment. Enterp. Inf. Syst. (2018). https://doi.org/10.1080/17517575.2018.1526325
12. Maleszka, M.: Observing collective knowledge state during integration. Expert Syst. Appl. **42**(1), 332–340 (2017)
13. De Montjoye, Y.-A., Stopczynski, A., Shmueli, E., Pentland, A., Lehmann, S.: The strength of the strongest ties in collaborative problem solving. Sci. Rep. **4**, 5277 (2014)
14. Nguyen, N.T.: Advanced Methods for Inconsistent Knowledge Management, 1st edn. Springer, London (2007). https://doi.org/10.1007/978-1-84628-889-0
15. Pastorsatorras, R.: Epidemic spreading in scale-free networks. Phys. Rev. Lett. **86**, 3200–3203 (2001)
16. Saito, K., Nakano, R., Kimura, M.: Prediction of information diffusion probabilities for independent cascade model. In: Proceedings of the International Conference on Knowledge-Based and Intelligent Information and Engineering Systems, Zagreb, Croatia, 3–5 September 2008, pp. 67–75 (2008)
17. Wang, C., Yang, X.Y., Xu, K., Ma, J.F.: SEIR-based model for the information spreading over SNS. Tien Tzu Hsueh Pao/Acta Electron. Sin. **42**, 2325–2330 (2014)
18. Wang, C.X., Guan, X.H., Qin, T., Zhou, Y.D.: Modelling on opinion leader's influence in microblog message propagation and its application. J. Softw. **26**, 1473–1485 (2015)
19. Wang, Q., Lin, Z., Jin, Y., Cheng, S., Yang, T.: ESIS: emotion-based spreader-ignorant-stifler model for information diffusion. Knowl.-Based Syst. **81**, 46–55 (2015)
20. Zhou, T.: Understanding online community user participation: a social influence perspective. Internet Res. **21**(1), 67–81 (2011). https://doi.org/10.1108/10662241111104884
21. Zhu, T., Wang, B., Wu, B., Zhu, C.: Maximizing the spread of influence ranking in social networks. Inf. Sci. **278**, 535–544 (2014)

Visualizing a Linguistic Ontology
with Ling-Graph

Mariem Neji[1(✉)], Fatma Ghorbel[1,2], and Bilel Gargouri[1]

[1] MIRACL Laboratory, University of Sfax, Sfax, Tunisia
`maryam.fsegs@gmail.com`
[2] CEDRIC Laboratory, Conservatoire National des Arts et Mtiers, Paris, France

Abstract. We are proposing a semantic approach that aims to identify valid linguistic web services composition scenarios. It targets both
linguistic and software engineering experts. It is based on an OWL 2 multilingual ontology, named LingOnto which models and reasons about linguistic knowledge. However, users especially non-ontology experts have
difficulty to make sense of LingOnto as they do not understand OWL
2 syntax. Hence, we decide to visualize LingOnto to attempt this issue.
Nevertheless, the current ontology visualization tools overlook the importance of the understandability issues which are particularly problematic for non-ontology experts. In this paper, we propose a user-friendly
ontology visualization tool, called Ling-Graph. It targets both ontology
and non-ontology experts and addresses the understandability requirement. This tool is also applied to visualize the PersonLink ontology for
non-ontology experts and a large-scale ontology DBpedia for ontology
experts. Finally, we discuss the promising results derived from the evaluation of Ling-Graph.

Keywords: Linguistic ontology · Ontology visualization · Usability ·
Understandable visualization

1 Introduction

The **Ling**uistic **W**eb **S**ervices *(LingWS)* are a kind of web services related to
the linguistic information system [1]. Such services are used to compose other
LingWS(s) corresponding to well-known **N**atural **L**anguage **P**rocessing *(NLP)*
applications such as Text Summarization and Machine Translation.

In our previous work [2], we are proposing a semantic approach that aims
to identify valid LingWS(s) composition scenarios. It targets both linguistic and
software engineering experts. It is based on an OWL2 multilingual ontology,
called LingOnto which models and reasons about linguistic knowledge (i.e., linguistic data and linguistic processing). This approach consists of three steps.
The first step consists in generating, from LingOnto, a dynamic ontological view
that contains only components corresponding to the user's need. The second step
helps identify an initial composition scenario by selecting a sequence of linguistic
processing from the generated ontological view. This sequence is validated by a

© Springer Nature Switzerland AG 2019
N. T. Nguyen et al. (Eds.): ICCCI 2019, LNAI 11683, pp. 41–52, 2019.
https://doi.org/10.1007/978-3-030-28377-3_4

set of defined SWRL rules. We should mention that the composition scenario identified in this step represents a high level service process model. Finally, the third step helps discover LingWS(s) corresponding to each selected linguistic processing while proposing alternative scenarios once one or more LingWS(s) are not found.

LingOnto is the angular stone of identifying valid LingWS(s) composition scenarios. However, users especially non-ontology experts have difficulty to make sense it as they do not understand OWL 2 syntax. Hence, we decide to visualize this ontology as ontology visualizations facilitate its sense-making [3]. Nevertheless, the heterogeneity and the amount number of linguistic knowledge make the visualization hard to comprehend due to the visual clutter and information overload. Hence, there is a need for a user-friendly ontology visualization tool which offers an understandable visualization not only for ontology experts but also non-ontology experts.

Several ontology visualization tools have been proposed in the literature such as NavigOWL [4], BioOntoVis [5], OWLeasyViz [6] and Protégé VOWL [7]. Nevertheless, most of them target only ontology experts and overlook the importance of the understandability issues. For instance, VOM[1] and OWLGrEd [8] offer UML-based ontology visualization which require knowledge about UML. Thus, they are understandable only for expert users.

In this paper, we propose a user-friendly tool, called Ling-Graph for visualizing and navigating ontologies. Compared to related work, it is designed to be used by both ontology and non-ontology experts. It aims to offer an understandable visualization by alleviating the generated graph based on a "smart" search interaction technique.

The remainder of the paper is organized as follows. Section 2 presents some research works on the field of ontology visualization. Section 3 describes our Ling-Graph visualization tool. Section 4, includes an evaluation of Ling-Graph. Finally, in Sect. 5, we summarize our work and outline some future works.

2   Related Work

Quite a number of ontology visualization tools have been proposed in the last couple of decades. We classify them, according to the target users, into **"Ontology Expert"** and **"Non-Ontology Expert"** users-oriented ontology visualization tools. Table 1 summarizes some ontologies visualization tools.

Most of ontology visualization tools are designed to be used only by ontology expert users. According to [7], these generated visualizations "are hard to read for casual users". For instance, OWLGrEd, ezOWL and VOM reuse and adapt popular diagram type to visualize the ontology, such as UML class diagrams. A major drawback of these tools is that they require knowledge about UML. Thus, they are not understandable for non-expert users. GrOWL and SOVA

---

[1] (Visual Ontology Modeler) http://thematix.com/tools/vom.

Table 1. Ontologies visualization tools

Visualization tool	Classes	Object properties	DataType properties	Filter	Search	Zoom	Overview	Details on demand	Ontology	Plug-in for an ontology editor	Standalone application
Ontology visualization tools for ontology expert users											
Protégé browser [9]	*		*		*				OWL, RDF	*	
OWLViz[a]	*			*		*	*		OWL	*	
KC-Viz [10]	*			*	*				OWL, RDF	*	
OntoGraf[b]	*	*		*		*	*	*	OWL	*	
TGViz Tab [11]	*	*		*		*	*	*	OWL	*	
GrOWL [12]	*	*	*	*	*	*	*		OWL	*	
GLOW [13]	*	*	*			*	*		OWL	*	
ezOWL [14]	*	*	*			*	*		OWL	*	
OntoViz Tab [15]	*	*	*			*	*	*	OWL		
OntoSphere [16]	*	*				*	*	*	OWL, RDF		
Ontorama [17]	*	*	*				*	*	RDF		
Onto3DViz [18]	*	*	*	*			*	*	OWL		
NavigOWL	*	*			*	*	*		OWL, RDF	*	
CropCircles [19]	*	*				*	*	*	OWL, RDF	*	
OWLGrEd	*	*				*	*		OWL	*	
Knoocks [20]	*	*	*	*		*	*		OWL		
VOM	*	*				*	*	*	OWL		
Treebolic[c]	*	*				*	*	*	OWL, RDF	*	
JUNG[d]	*	*		*			*	*	OWL, RDF	*	
FlexViz [21]	*	*		*	*	*	*		OWL	*	
BioOntoVis	*	*	*	*	*	*		*	RDF		*
Ontology visualization tools for non-ontology expert users											
OWLeasyViz	*	*	*	*	*	*	*		OWL		
WebVOWL [22]	*	*	*	*	*	*	*	*	OWL, RDF		
ProtégéVOWL	*	*	*	*		*	*	*	OWL	*	
Memo Graph [23]	*	*	*	*		*	*	*	RDF		*

[a] http://protegewiki.stanford.edu/wiki/OWLViz.
[b] http://protegewiki.stanford.edu/wiki/OntoGraf.
[c] http://treebolic.sourceforge.net/.
[d] http://jung.sourceforge.net/doc/api.
http://protegewiki.stanford.edu/wiki/OWLPropViz.
http://protegewiki.stanford.edu/wiki/SOVA.

are intended to offer understandable visualizations by defining notations using different symbols, colors, and node shapes for each ontology key-element. However, the proposed notations contain many abbreviations and symbols from the Description Logic. As a consequence, these visualizations are not suitable for casual users. Then, OWLViz, OntoTrack, KC-Viz and OntoViz show only a specific element of the ontology. For instance, the OWLViz and KC-Viz visualize only the class hierarchy of ontology while shows only inheritance relationships between the graph nodes. This is different with TGViz Tab and NavigOWL which provide more understandable visualizations representing all the key elements of the ontology. However, these tools do not make a clear visual distinction between the different ontology key-elements (i.e., TBox and ABox). For instance, they use a plain node-link diagram where all the links and nodes look the same except for their color. This issue has a bad impact on the understandability of the generated visualization.

WebVOWL, ProtégéVOWL and Memo Graph targeting non-ontology expert users, aim to offer understandable visualizations by defining notations using different symbols, colors, and node shapes to each ontology key-element. However, WebVOWL, ProtégéVOWL use some technical words related to Semantic Web. On the other hand, Memo Graph is designed to be used by Alzheimer's disease patients.

Some tools present interaction techniques that help to enhance the understandability issues such as zoom, overview, filter, history and search. However, these interactions are rarely implemented.

Only few visualization tools are implemented as standalone applications, most are provided as plug-in for ontology editors like Protégé. This latter seems complicated for non-ontology expert users.

3   Our Ontology Visualisation Tool: Ling-Graph

Ling-Graph is a user-friendly ontology visualisation tool. It is designed to be used by both ontology and non-ontology experts. To aims to offer understandable visualizations, it visualizes ontology as graphs based on a force-directed method. It uses an easy to-understand wording. For instance, it does not use semantic web vocabulary. It offers a simple layout in which its interfaces is divided into three parts: the "Ling-Graph Viewer" displaying the visualization, the "Ling-Graph details" listing details about a selected graph node, and the "Ling-Graph search criteria" providing a set of search criteria. In order to make these three parts distinguishable, we use different color for each frame. It provides the seven interaction techniques detailed by Shneiderman [24], as well as other more advanced techniques such as "smart" search interaction technique. This latter aims to alleviate the generated graphs by extracting and visualizing a dynamic ontological view containing only components corresponding to the user's need. It is relied on a SPARQL patterns-based approach that takes the user's need materialized by a set of search criteria as input and generates the ontological view that match these criteria. Ling-Graph, is available for downloading[2].

---

[2] https://github.com/mariemNeji/Ling-Graph.

3.1 "Smart" Search Interaction Technique: Our SPARQL Patterns-Based Approach

Ling-Graph offers a "smart" search interaction technique based on a SPARQL patterns-based approach. It aims to extract and visualize a dynamic onto-logical view, from a given ontology, containing only components correspond-ing to the user's need. This need is materialized by a set of search criteria $C = (C_1, C_2, C_3, ..., C_n)$. For each search criterion $C_i (i \in [1, n])$, a set of prefer-ences $CP = (CP_{i/1}, CP_{i/2}, CP_{i/3}, ..., CP_{i/m})$ is associated.

We proposed a set of SPARQL patterns $P = (P_1, P_2, P_3, ..., P_k)$ that defines a combination of these criteria. A pattern $P_j (j \in [1, k])$ is a 3-tuple (G, SP, S) where :

- G = (G_n, G_e) is an oriented graph that describes the general structure of the pattern and represents a family of SPARQL queries. It contains a subset of nodes G_n, where each node refers to a search criterion C_i, and a subset of edges G_e where each edge refers to a relation between two search criteria.
- SP = $(SP_{j/1}, SP_{j/2}, SP_{j/3}, ..., SP_{j/n})$ is a set of n sub-patterns of P where $\forall SP_{j/i} = (SG, cardmin, cardmax) \in P_j$, then, we have SG as a subgraph of G and cardmin, cardmax are respectively the minimal and maximal car-dinalities of $SP_{j/i}$ where $0 \leq cardmin \leq cardmax$. The minimal cardinality is 0 and means that the user does not choose any preference of the criterion C_i defined by the "sub pattern" SP_i. The maximal cardinality of 1 means that the users selects just one preference of G_i and the maximal cardinality greater than 1 means that the user selects a set of preferences of C_i.
- S = $((SW_1, SW_2, SW_3, ..., SW_n), (W_1, W_2, W_3, ..., W_l))$ is a template of a descriptive sentence in which n substrings SW_i corresponds to the n sub-patterns of the pattern, l distinct substrings $W_k (k \in [1, (n-1)])$ corresponds to the pattern elements (*i.e. nodes and edges*).

The proposed patterns are modular since each of them P_j $(j \in [1, k])$ is composed of a set of "sub-patterns" SP = $(SP_{j/1}, SP_{j/2}, SP_{j/3}, ..., SP_{j/n})$. Each sub-pattern $SP_{j/i}$ defines a single criterion C_i and can be optional or repeat-able in the generated SPARQL query. Then, each SPARQL query pattern is instantiated into a SPARQL query graph.

3.2 Application of Ling-Graph on LingOnto

We test Ling-Graph on the LingOnto ontology that allows modeling and reason-ing about linguistic knowledge. The current version of this ontology includes 80 classes, 136 object properties and 326 SWRL rules.

Figure 1 shows a SPARQL pattern composed of four "sub-patterns" which define same criteria of LingOnto: $C_1=$ "treatments level", $C_2 =$ "language", $C_3 =$ "granularity level" and $C_4 =$ "dichotomy level". All the sub-patterns are optional and repeatable. In the descriptive sentence template, sub-patterns sentences are represented between square brackets and the sub-pattern identifier as an index. The pattern elements are underlined, with an index referring to the graph element. Then, this SPARQL query pattern is instantiated into a SPARQL query graph. For instance, the user expresses his need to develop an automatic summarization application which transforms the most significant sentences in an Arabic text. Consequently, the user selects the following preferences, $CP_{1/1}$ = morphological level, $CP_{2/1}$ = "Arabic", $CP_{3/1}$ ="SubclassOf concepts" and $CP_{4/1}$= "Linguistic processing". Subsequently, Ling-Graph applies the instantiation of the pattern as shown in Fig. 2. Figure 3 presents the generated SPARQL query graph and its associated ontological view.

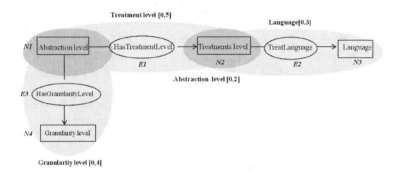

S = [Granularity level $C4$]Granularity level [of Abstraction level $C1$ [has a Treatment level $C2$]Treatments level [treat the language $C3$]Language] Abstraction level

Fig. 1. Example of a SPARQL query pattern.

S = SubClassOf Linguistic processing has a Morphological level treat the language Arabic

Fig. 2. Instantiation of the SPARQL query pattern shown in Fig. 1.

The generated template of the descriptive sentence allows the final SPARQL query to be built :
SELECT DISTINCT (?x)
WHERE {?x rdfs:subClassOf* :Morphological_Level_Processing.
FILTER {:Treat_Language_Arabic rdfs:domain ?x }}

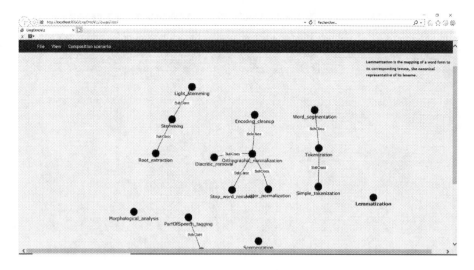

Fig. 3. Screenshot of the generated ontological view.

3.3   Other Applications of Ling-Graph

Ling-Graph is mainly proposed to be integrated in the prototype of our approach of constructing valid LingWS(s) composition scenarios. As consequential effects, it can be used by ontology and non-ontology expert users to offer understandable visualizations not only of small-scale inputs, but also for the large-scale ones thanks to the "smart" search interaction technique that allow alleviating the generated graph based on the user's need.

Integration of Ling-Graph in CAPTAIN MEMO for Non-ontology Experts. We integrated Ling-Graph into CAPTIN MEMO [25] to visualize PersonLink [26] which is a multicultural and multilingual OWL 2 ontology that allows storing, representing and reasoning about interpersonal relationships. It targets Alzheimer's disease patients (non-ontology experts). We set three search criteria: C_1 = "language", C_2 = "culture" and C_3 = "photo". Then, we successively selected the preference(s) associated with each criterion: $CP_{1/1}$ = "French", $CP_{2/1}$ = "France" and $CP_{3/1}$ = "yes", as shown in Fig. 4.

Visualization of a Large-Scale Ontology DBpedia. We aim to test the ability of our Ling-Graph in supporting scalability. It is tested on the well-known large-scale DBpedia[3] ontology which is a semantic knowledge base built from structured information and extracted from Wikipedia. To date, it covers 685 classes described by 2,795 datatype and object properties about 4,233,000 instances. All this knowledge is spread over several domains such as "Sport",

---

[3] http://dbpedia.org/.

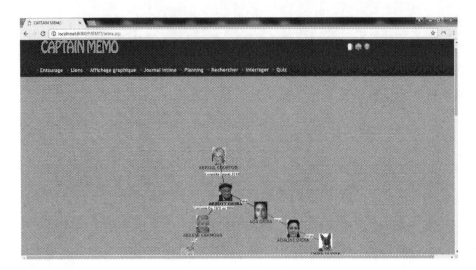

Fig. 4. Screenshot of Ling-Graph that it is used for visualizing PersonLink in CAPTAIN MEMO.

"Tourism", "City", etc. We set two search criteria: C_1 = "domain" and C_2 = "number of instance". Then, we successively selected the preference(s) associated with each criterion: $CP_{1/1}$= "sport", $CP_{2/1}$="30", as shown in Fig. 5.

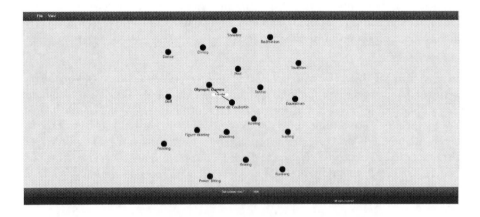

Fig. 5. Screenshot of Ling-Graph that it is used for visualizing DBpedia ontology.

4   Evaluation of Ling-Graph

We conduct a human-centred study to evaluate the usefulness and usability of Ling-Graph. We use the LingOnto ontology. 39 participants enter this study. They are ontology and non-ontology expert users. 24 from them are researcher members from the MIRACL laboratory (University of Sfax, Sfax-Tunisia). The other participants are linguistic experts. The participants are randomly allocated into three groups, labelled Gp_X, Gp_Y, and Gp_Z, where each group uses a specific ontology visualization tool to perform some ontological tasks. Members of the group Gp X use RDF Gravity. Members of group Gp_Y are use WebVOWL. Members of group Gp_Z use Ling-Graph. At the beginning of all sessions, the participants are told about the goal of the study. To avoid being against or in favour a particular ontology visualization tool, they are told that the purpose of the study was "to comparatively evaluate the usefulness of some ontology visualization tools".

4.1   Usability Evaluation

Each group fill out a questionnaire to describe their overall opinion towards the usability of the user interfaces of the tool that they use. We use the standard System Usability Scale (SUS) [27]. The SUS questionnaire is a ten-item attitude Likert scale to measure the usability of any system. Scores range on a scale from one (strongly agree) to five (strongly disagree). Table 2 shows the results of the SUS questionnaire.

Table 2. Usability evaluation's results

	RDF Gravity (Gp_X)	WebVOWL (Gp_Y)	Ling-Graph (Gp_Z)
SUS score	61,5	66,4	70,9

The evaluation confirm that Ling-Graph had the highest usability score. Hence, It is comparatively usable ontology visualization tool.

4.2   Usefulness Evaluation

We prepare four ontological tasks to evaluate the quantitatively Ling-Graph :

- Task 1: Which are the direct subclasses of the class "Lemmatization"?
- Task 2: Which are the subclasses of the classes "Semantic_level_processing" and "Lexical_level_processing"?
- Task 3: Which are the subclasses of the class "Morphological_level_processing" that have relations with the class "English_language"?
- Task 4: Which are the ranges classes of the classes "Linguistic_processing" and "Linguistic_data" that have relations with the class "Arabic_language"?

For each task, the participant is given a 5 min time slot to give the response. Within 5 min, the task would be recorded as "failed". Table 3 summarizes the results of this experiment.

Table 3. Usefulness evaluation's results.

	RDF Gravity (Gp_X)		WebVOWL (Gp_Y)		Ling-Graph (Gp_Z)	
	Mean (min:secs)	Number of "failed"	Mean (min:secs)	Number of "failed"	Mean (min:secs)	Number of "failed"
Task 1	00:17	4	00:12	3	00:07	0
Task 2	02:54	7	02:36	6	01:29	0
Task 3	03:07	9	03:21	8	01:21	0
Task 4	03:52	11	03:46	10	01:10	0
Overall mean and Total number of "failed"	02:18	31	02:39	27	01:02	0

All tasks that are performed with Ling-Graph are completed within the time limit, while 31 tasks, performed with RDF Gravity, and 27 tasks, performed with WebVOWL, are recorded as failed.

Ling-Graph has the fastest overall mean performance. Its overall mean time is about one minutes and sixteen seconds faster than RDF Gravity and one minute and thirty seven seconds faster than WebVOWL.

According to the two ascertainment, we confirm that Ling-Graph is, comparatively, a useful ontology visualization tool.

For all tasks, only few participants using RDF Gravity and WebVOWL complete successfully within the time limit. At beginning of the session, they apply filters to alleviate the initial dense graph and have a more readable one. The other participants fail to give the correct response.

For all tasks, Ling-Graph has the slowest mean time. RDF Gravity and WebVOWL have approximately the same mean time. The temporal gap is explained as RDF Gravity and WebVOWL does not have an advanced search interaction technique such as our "smart" search. Thus, the participants take more time to find the specific elements nodes corresponding to each task by visually scanning the visualization or using static search interaction technique which is key word search.

5   Conclusion

This paper presents a user-friendly tool, called Ling-Graph for visualizing and navigating ontologies. It is designed to be used by both ontology and non-ontology experts. It aims to offer an understandable visualization by alleviating the generated graph based on a "smart" search interaction technique.

This work is proposed mainly to be integrated in the context of an approach that aims to identify valid LingWS(s) scenarios which targets both linguistic and software engineering experts. This approach is based on a multilingual ontology, named LingOnto. However, users, especially non-ontology experts, have difficulty to make sense of LingOnto since they do not understand OWL 2 syntax. In fact, ontology visualization can help with sense-making of LingOnto. Thus, we reviewed same existing ontology visualization tools. This study shows that the majority of research studies, targets only ontology expert users and overlook the importance of understandability issues. Based on these requirements, we propose the Ling-Graph ontology visualization tool. It aims to offer an understandable visualisation to both ontology and non-ontology expert users. This tool is applied, as a standalone application, of a small scale ontology for non-ontology expert users (PersonLink) and a large-scale ontology (DBpedia). Finally, we discuss the promising results derived from the evaluation of Ling-Graph.

Future research will be devoted to ameliorate the actual version of the Ling-Graph. More specifically, we intend to evaluate the proposed search interaction technique using the recall and precision measures.

References

1. Baklouti, N., Gargiuri, B., Jmaiel, M.: Semantic-based approach to improve the description and the discovery of linguistic web services. In: Engineering Applications of Artificial Intelligence (2015)
2. Neji, M., Gargiuri, B., Jmaiel, M.: A semantic approach for constructing valid composition scenarios of linguistic web services. In: International Conference on Knowledge-Based and Intelligent Information Engineering Systems (2018)
3. Lanzenberger, M., Sampson, J., Rester, M.: Visualization in ontology tools. In: Proceedings of the International Conference on Complex, Intelligent and Software Intensive Systems, CISIS 2009, pp. 705–711 (2009)
4. Hussain, A., Latif, K., Tariq Rextin, A., Hayat, A., Alam, M.: Scalable visualization of semantic nets using power-law graph. In: Applied Mathematics and Information Sciences (2014)
5. Achich, N., Algergawy, A., Bouaziz, B., Konig-Ries, B.: BioOntoVis: an ontology visualization tool. In: International Conference on Knowledge Engineering and Knowledge Management (2018)
6. Catenazzi, N., et al.: User-friendly ontology editing and visualization tools: the OWLeasyViz approach. In: International Conference Information Visualisation (2013)
7. Lohmann, S., Negru, S., Haag, S., Ertl, T.: Visualizing ontologies with VOWL. Semantic Web 7(4), 399–419 (2016)
8. Bārzdiņš, J., Bārzdiņš, G., Čerāns, K., Liepiņš, R., Sproģis, A.: OWLGrEd: a UML style graphical notation and editor for OWL 2. In: OWL: Experiences and Directions Workshop (2010)
9. Noy, N.F., Fergerson, R.W., Musen, M.A.: The knowledge model of protégé-2000: combining interoperability and flexibility. In: Dieng, R., Corby, O. (eds.) EKAW 2000. LNCS (LNAI), vol. 1937, pp. 17–32. Springer, Heidelberg (2000). https://doi.org/10.1007/3-540-39967-4_2
10. Peroni, S., Motta, E., d'Aquin, M.: Identifying key concepts in an ontology, through the integration of cognitive principles with statistical and topological measures. In: Domingue, J., Anutariya, C. (eds.) ASWC 2008. LNCS, vol. 5367, pp. 242–256. Springer, Heidelberg (2008). https://doi.org/10.1007/978-3-540-89704-0_17
11. Harith, A.: TGVizTab: an ontology visualisation extension for protégé. In: Knowledge Capture (2003)
12. Krivov, S., Williams, R., Villa, F.: GrOWL: a tool for visualization and editing of OWL ontologies. In: Web Semantics: Science, Services and Agents on the World Wide Web (2007)

13. Hop, W., De Ridder, S., Hogenboom, F.: Using hierarchical edge bundles to visualize complex ontologies in glow. In: Annual ACM Symposium on Applied Computing (2012)
14. Chung, M., Oh, S., Cho, H., Cho, H.K.: Visualizing and authoring OWL in ezOWL. In: International Conference on Advanced Communication Technology (2005)
15. Singh, G., Prabhakar, T., Chatterjee, J., Patil, V., Ninomiya, S.: OntoViz: visualizing ontologies and thesauri using layout algorithms. In: The Fifth International Conference of the Asian Federation for Information Technology in Agriculture (2006)
16. Bosca, A., Bonino, D., Pellegrino, P.: OntoSphere3D: a multidimensional visualization tool for ontologies. In: The 17th International Conference on Database and Expert Systems Applications (2006)
17. Eklund, P., Nataliya, R., Green, S.: OntoRama: browsing RDF ontologies using a hyperbolic-style browser. In: The First International Symposium on Cyber Worlds (2002)
18. Guo, S.S., Chan, C.: A tool for ontology visualization in 3D graphics: Onto3DViz. In: The Canadian Conference on Electrical and Computer Engineering (2010)
19. Wang, T.D., Parsia, B.: CropCircles: topology sensitive visualization of OWL class hierarchies. In: Cruz, I., et al. (eds.) ISWC 2006. LNCS, vol. 4273, pp. 695–708. Springer, Heidelberg (2006). https://doi.org/10.1007/11926078_50
20. Kriglstein, S., Wallner, G.: Knoocks - a visualization approach for OWL lite ontologies. In: Complex, Intelligent and Software Intensive Systems (CISIS) (2010)
21. Falconer, S.M., Callendar, C., Storey, M.A.: FLEXVIZ: visualizing biomedical ontologies on the web. In: International Conference on Biomedical Ontology (2009)
22. Lohmann, S., Negru, S., Haag, F., Ertl, T.: Visualizing ontologies with VOWL. Semantic Web 7(4), 399–419 (2016)
23. Ghorbel, F., Ellouze, N., Métais, E., Hamdi, F., Gargouri, F., Herradi, N.: MEMO GRAPH: an ontology visualization tool for everyone. In: 20th International Conference on Knowledge-Based and Intelligent Information and Engineering Systems (KES-2016), pp. 265–274 (2016)
24. Shneiderman, B., Plaisant, C., Cohen, M., Jacobs, S.: Designing the User Interface: Strategies for Effective Human-Computer Interaction (2009)
25. Ghorbel, F., Ellouze, N., Métais, E., Gargouri, F., Hamdi, F., Herradi, N.: Designing and evaluating interfaces for the CAPTAIN MEMO memory prosthesis. In: International Conference on Advances in Computer-Human Interactions (2016)
26. Herradi, N., Hamdi, F., Métais, E., Ghorbel, F., Soukane, A.: PersonLink: an ontology representing family relationships for the CAPTAIN MEMO memory prosthesis. In: Jeusfeld, M.A., Karlapalem, K. (eds.) ER 2015. LNCS, vol. 9382, pp. 3–13. Springer, Cham (2015). https://doi.org/10.1007/978-3-319-25747-1_1
27. Brooke, J.: SUS: a retrospective. J. Usability Stud. 8, 29–40 (2013)

The Stable Model Semantics of Normal Fuzzy Linguistic Logic Programs

Van Hung Le[(⊠)]

Faculty of Information Technology, Hanoi University of Mining and Geology,
Duc Thang, Bac Tu Liem, Hanoi, Vietnam
levanhung@humg.edu.vn

Abstract. Fuzzy linguistic logic programming is a framework for representing and reasoning with linguistically-expressed human knowledge. It is well known that allowing the representation and the manipulation of negation is an important feature for many real-world applications. In this work, we extend the framework by allowing negation connectives to occur in rule bodies, resulting in normal fuzzy linguistic logic programs, and study the stable model semantics of such logic programs.

Keywords: Fuzzy logic programming · Stable model · Hedge algebra

1 Introduction

Humans mainly use words, which are essentially qualitative and vague, to describe real world phenomena, to reason, and to decide. Also, humans often express knowledge linguistically and hence make use of fuzzy predicates. Moreover, in linguistically-expressed human knowledge, various linguistic hedges are usually used simultaneously to express many levels of emphasis. Thus, it is necessary to have formalisms that can directly deal with linguistic terms and hedges since those systems can represent and reason with linguistically-expressed human knowledge to some extent.

Fuzzy linguistic logic programming (FLLP), introduced in [1], is a logic programming (LP) framework without negation for dealing with vagueness in linguistically-expressed human knowledge, where truth values of vague sentences are linguistic terms, and linguistic hedges can be utilized to state various levels of emphasis. In FLLP, every fact or rule is evaluated to some degree stated by a linguistic truth value, and hedges can be utilized as unary connectives in rule bodies. For instance, the statement "(A worker is good if he is *rather* skillful and *very* hard-working) is *highly true*" can be represented using the following rule:

$$good(X) \leftarrow \wedge(Rather\ skillful(X), Very\ hard\_working(X)).HighlyTrue$$

The framework can have a counterpart for most of the concepts and results of traditional definite LP [1,2]. The procedural semantics [1] and tabulation proof procedures [3] of FLLP can directly compute on linguistic terms to give answers

© Springer Nature Switzerland AG 2019
N. T. Nguyen et al. (Eds.): ICCCI 2019, LNAI 11683, pp. 53–65, 2019.
https://doi.org/10.1007/978-3-030-28377-3_5

to queries. Hence, in the presence of vagueness, FLLP can provide to human reasoning a computational approach.

It is well known that allowing the representation and the manipulation of *default negation* is an important feature for many real-world applications. In this paper, we extend FLLP by allowing negation connectives to occur in rule bodies, resulting in *normal fuzzy linguistic logic programs*, and present the stable model semantics of such programs.

The paper is organized as follows: Sect. 2 gives an overview of FLLP without negation while Sect. 3 presents FLLP with negation and its stable model semantics. Section 4 discusses related work and Sect. 5 gives several directions for future work and concludes the paper.

2 Preliminaries

2.1 Linguistic Truth Domains

In hedge algebra (HA) theory [4,5], values of the linguistic variable *Truth*, e.g., *Very True, Very Slightly False*, can be regarded as being generated from the set of primary terms $\mathcal{G} = \{False, True\}$ using hedges from a set $\mathcal{H} = \{Very, Slightly, \dots\}$ as unary operators. There is a natural ordering among such values, for instance, *Very False* $<$ *False*, where $x \leq y$ states that x represents a truth degree less than or equal to y. Hence, a set $\mathcal{X}$ of such values of *Truth* is a partially ordered set and can be characterized by an HA $\underline{X} = (\mathcal{X}, \mathcal{G}, \mathcal{H}, \leq)$.

Linguistic hedges either decrease or increase the meaning of terms, thus they can be considered as *order operations*, i.e., for all $h \in \mathcal{H}$ and for all $x \in \mathcal{X}$, we have either $hx \geq x$ or $hx \leq x$. We denote by $h \geq k$ if h modifies terms more than or equal to k, i.e., for all $x \in \mathcal{X}$, either $hx \leq kx \leq x$ or $x \leq kx \leq hx$. Note that $\mathcal{H}$ and $\mathcal{X}$ are disjoint, so the same notation $\leq$ can be used without confusion for the order relations on $\mathcal{H}$ and $\mathcal{X}$. Let V, R, H, S, A, M, c^+, and c^- stand respectively for *Very, Rather, Highly, Slightly, Approximately, More or less, True,* and *False*. We have $S > R$ ($h > k$ iff $h \geq k$ and $h \neq k$) since, e.g., $Sc^+ < Rc^+ < c^+$ and $c^- < Rc^- < Sc^-$, and $V > H$ since, e.g., $c^+ < Hc^+ < Vc^+$ and $Vc^- < Hc^- < c^-$.

$\mathcal{H}$ can be split into disjoint subsets $\mathcal{H}^+$ and $\mathcal{H}^-$ characterized by $\mathcal{H}^+ = \{h | hc^+ > c^+\} = \{h | hc^- < c^-\}$ and $\mathcal{H}^- = \{h | hc^+ < c^+\} = \{h | hc^- > c^-\}$. For instance, given the set $\mathcal{H} = \{V, H, A, M, R, S\}$, $\mathcal{H}$ can be divided into $\mathcal{H}^+ = \{V, H\}$ and $\mathcal{H}^- = \{A, M, R, S\}$. Two hedges in each of $\mathcal{H}^+$ and $\mathcal{H}^-$ might be comparable, e.g., V and H, or incomparable, e.g., A and M. An HA $\underline{X} = (\mathcal{X}, \mathcal{G}, \mathcal{H}, \leq)$ is called a *linear* HA (lin-HA) if both $\mathcal{H}^+$ and $\mathcal{H}^-$ are linearly ordered. For instance, the HA $\underline{X} = (\mathcal{X}, \mathcal{G}, \{V, H, R, S\}, \leq)$ is a lin-HA since $\mathcal{H}$ is split into $\mathcal{H}^+ = \{V, H\}$ with $V > H$ and $\mathcal{H}^- = \{R, S\}$ with $S > R$. For any lin-HA $\underline{X} = (\mathcal{X}, \mathcal{G}, \mathcal{H}, \leq)$, we have $\mathcal{X}$ is linearly ordered.

A *linguistic truth domain* (LTD) $\overline{X}$ taken from a lin-HA $\underline{X} = (\mathcal{X}, \mathcal{G}, \mathcal{H}, \leq)$ is the linearly ordered set $\overline{X} = \mathcal{X} \cup \{0, W, 1\}$, where 0 (*AbsolutelyFalse*), W (the *middle truth value*), and 1 (*AbsolutelyTrue*) are respectively the least, the neutral and the greatest elements of $\overline{X}$, and for all $x \in \{0, W, 1\}$ and for all

$h \in \mathcal{H}$, we have $hx = x$ [1,3]. To have well-defined Łukasiewicz operations, we consider only finitely many truth values. An *l-limit* HA, where l is a positive integer, is a lin-HA in which all terms have a length of at most $l+1$, i.e., at most l hedges. An LTD taken from an l-limit HA is finite.

Example 1. The 1-limit HA $\underline{X} = (\mathcal{X}, \{c^-, c^+\}, \{V, H, R, S\}, \leq)$ gives the LTD $\overline{X} = \{v_0 = 0, v_1 = Vc^-, v_2 = Hc^-, v_3 = c^-, v_4 = Rc^-, v_5 = Sc^-, v_6 = W, v_7 = Sc^+, v_8 = Rc^+, v_9 = c^+, v_{10} = Hc^+, v_{11} = Vc^+, v_{12} = 1\}$, in which truth values are listed in ascending order.

2.2 Truth Functions of Hedge Connectives

Let $I \notin \mathcal{H}$ be an artificial hedge, called the *identity*, defined by $\forall x \in \mathcal{X}, Ix = x$. I is the least element in each of $\mathcal{H}^+ \cup \{I\}$ and $\mathcal{H}^- \cup \{I\}$ [1,3]. An *extended order relation* $\leq_e$ on $\mathcal{H} \cup \{I\}$ is defined by: $\forall h, k \in \mathcal{H} \cup \{I\}$, $h \leq_e k$ if one of the following conditions is satisfied: (i) $h \in \mathcal{H}^-, k \in \mathcal{H}^+$; (ii) $h, k \in \mathcal{H}^+ \cup \{I\}$ and $h \leq k$; (iii) $h, k \in \mathcal{H}^- \cup \{I\}$ and $h \geq k$. We denote $h <_e k$ if $h \leq_e k$ and $h \neq k$.

Let $\underline{X} = (\mathcal{X}, \{c^+, c^-\}, \mathcal{H}, \leq)$ be a lin-HA. *Truth functions* $h^{\bullet} : \overline{X} \to \overline{X}$ of all hedges $h \in \mathcal{H} \cup \{I\}$ satisfy the following conditions [3,6,7]:

$$\forall x \in \{0, W, 1\}, h^{\bullet}(x) = x \tag{1}$$

$$\forall x \in \overline{X}, I^{\bullet}(x) = x \tag{2}$$

$$h^{\bullet}(hc^+) = c^+ \tag{3}$$

$$\text{if } x \geq y, h^{\bullet}(x) \geq h^{\bullet}(y) \tag{4}$$

$$\forall k \in \mathcal{H} \cup \{I\} \text{ such that } h \leq_e k, h^{\bullet}(x) \geq k^{\bullet}(x) \tag{5}$$

Truth functions of hedges are non-decreasing and preserve 0 and 1. Moreover, truth functions of all truth-stressing hedges $h \in \mathcal{H}^+$ are subdiagonal ($h^{\bullet}(x) \leq x$), and those of all truth-depressing hedges $h \in \mathcal{H}^-$ are superdiagonal ($h^{\bullet}(x) \geq x$). Condition (3) ensures that if the truth value of the sentence "Lucia is *young*" is *very true*, then that of the sentence "Lucia is *very young*" is *true* [8,9]. It is shown in [1] that truth functions of hedges always exist.

2.3 Operations on Linguistic Truth Domains

Gödel t-norm, its residuum, and Gödel t-conorm can be defined as [1,3]:

$$\mathcal{C}_G(v_i, v_j) = \min(v_i, v_j),$$

$$\leftarrow^{\bullet}_G (v_j, v_i) = \begin{cases} v_n & \text{if } i \leq j \\ v_j & \text{otherwise,} \end{cases}$$

$$\vee^{\bullet}_G(v_i, v_j) = \max(v_i, v_j).$$

Łukasiewicz t-norm, its residuum, and Łukasiewicz t-conorm can be defined on a finite LTD $\overline{X} = \{v_0, \ldots, v_n\}$ with $v_0 \leq v_1 \leq \cdots \leq v_n$ as [1,3]:

$$\mathcal{C}_L(v_i, v_j) = \begin{cases} v_{i+j-n} & \text{if } i+j-n > 0 \\ v_0 & \text{otherwise,} \end{cases}$$

$$\leftarrow^{\bullet}_L (v_j, v_i) = \begin{cases} v_n & \text{if } i \leq j \\ v_{n+j-i} & \text{otherwise,} \end{cases}$$

$$\vee^{\bullet}_L (v_i, v_j) = \begin{cases} v_{i+j} & \text{if } i+j < n \\ v_n & \text{otherwise.} \end{cases}$$

All the residua are non-decreasing in the first argument and non-increasing in the second, and all the other operations are non-decreasing in all arguments.

The negation is defined as follows [1]: given $x = \sigma c$, where σ is a string of hedges (including the empty one) and $c \in \{c^+, c^-\}$, then $y = -x$, if $y = \sigma c'$ and $\{c, c'\} = \{c^+, c^-\}$, e.g., $Vc^+ = -Vc^-$ and $Vc^- = -Vc^+$.

Each of the t-norms and its residuum satisfy the following properties [10]:

$$\mathcal{C}(b, r) \leq h \text{ iff } r \leq \leftarrow^{\bullet} (h, b) \tag{6}$$

$$(\forall b)(\forall h) \ \mathcal{C}(b, \leftarrow^{\bullet} (h, b)) \leq h \tag{7}$$

$$(\forall b)(\forall r) \ \leftarrow^{\bullet} (\mathcal{C}(b, r), b) \geq r \tag{8}$$

2.4   Fuzzy Linguistic Logic Programming Without Negation

The language is a many-sorted (or typed) predicate language without function symbols. Clauses in logic programs are without negation. The fact that function symbols do not appear in the language makes FLLP implementable. Without function symbols, Herbrand universes of all sorts of variables of a finite logic program are finite, and so is the Herbrand base (consisting of all ground atoms) of the program. This, together with a finite LTD, allows obtaining the least Herbrand model of a logic program by finitely iterating an immediate consequence operator from the least Herbrand interpretation. As usual the underlying language of a program P is assumed to be defined by constants (if no such constant exists, we add some constant a to form ground terms) and predicate symbols occurring in P.

Connectives consist of the following: $\wedge_G, \wedge_L$ (Gödel and Łukasiewicz conjunctions); $\vee_G, \vee_L$ (Gödel and Łukasiewicz disjunctions); $\leftarrow_G, \leftarrow_L$ (Gödel and Łukasiewicz implications); and hedges as unary connectives. For a connective c, its truth function is denoted by $c^{\bullet}$. Moreover, it is shown in [2] that linguistic aggregation operators can be used in rule bodies.

A *term* is either a constant or a variable. An *atom* (or *atomic formula*) is of the form $p(t_1, ..., t_n)$, where p is an n-ary predicate symbol, and $t_1, ..., t_n$ are terms. A *fact* is a graded atom $(A.a)$, where A is an atom called the logical part of the fact, and a is a truth value apart from 0. A *body formula* is defined inductively as follows: (i) an atom is a body formula; (ii) if B_1 and B_2 are body formulae, then so are $\wedge(B_1, B_2)$, $\vee(B_1, B_2)$, and hB_1, where h is a hedge connective. A *rule* is a graded implication $(A \leftarrow B.r)$, where A is an atom called *rule head*, B is a body formula called *rule body*, and r is a truth value apart from 0; $(A \leftarrow B)$ is called the *logical part* of the rule. In a graded formula $(\varphi.t)$, t is understood as a lower bound to the exact truth value of φ. A *fuzzy linguistic logic program* (*positive program*, for short) is a finite set of facts and rules, and there are no two facts (rules) having the same logical part, but different truth values. Thus, a program P can be represented as the following partial mapping:

$$P : Formulae \rightarrow \overline{X} \setminus \{0\},$$

where the domain of P, denoted $dom(P)$, is finite and composed only of logical parts of facts and rules. For each formula $(\varphi.t) \in P$, $P(\varphi) = t$.

Let P be a program, and $\overline{X}$ the LTD; a *fuzzy linguistic Herbrand interpretation* (interpretation, for short) f of P is a mapping from the Herbrand base B_P to $\overline{X}$, associating with each ground atom in B_P a truth value in $\overline{X}$.

The ordering $\leq$ in $\overline{X}$ is extended to interpretations pointwise as follows: for any interpretations f_1 and f_2 of a program P, $f_1 \sqsubseteq f_2$ iff $f_1(A) \leq f_2(A)$, $\forall A \in B_P$. Let $\otimes$ and $\oplus$ denote the meet (or infimum, greatest lower bound) and join (or supremum, least upper bound) operators, respectively; for all interpretations f_1 and f_2 of P and for all $A \in B_P$, we have: (i) $(f_1 \otimes f_2)(A) = f_1(A) \otimes f_2(A)$, and (ii) $(f_1 \oplus f_2)(A) = f_1(A) \oplus f_2(A)$.

Every interpretation f can be extended to all ground formulae, denoted $\overline{f}$, as follows: (i) $\overline{f}(A) = f(A)$, if A is a ground atom; (ii) $\overline{f}(c(B_1, B_2)) = c^\bullet(\overline{f}(B_1), \overline{f}(B_2))$, where B_1, B_2 are ground formulae, and c is a binary connective; and (iii) $\overline{f}(hB) = h^\bullet(\overline{f}(B))$, where B is a ground body formula, and h is a hedge. For non-ground formulae, since all variables in formulae are assumed to be universally quantified, the interpretation $\overline{f}$ is defined as

$$\overline{f}(\varphi) = \overline{f}(\forall\varphi) = \otimes\{\overline{f}(\varphi\vartheta) | \varphi\vartheta \text{ is a ground instance of } \varphi\},$$

where $\forall\varphi$ denotes the *universal closure* of φ, which is obtained from φ by adding a universal quantifier for every variable having a free occurrence in φ.

An interpretation f is an *Herbrand model* (model, for short) of a program P if for all formulae $\varphi \in dom(P)$, we have $\overline{f}(\varphi) \geq P(\varphi)$.

Theorem 1. *[2] Let P be a positive program.*

(i) Let $\mathcal{F}_P$ be the set of all interpretations of P. Then $\langle \mathcal{F}_P, \otimes, \oplus \rangle$ is a complete lattice.

(ii) Let F be a non-empty set of models of P. Then $\otimes F$ is a model of P.

(iii) $M_P = \otimes\{f | f \text{ is a model of } P\}$ is the least model of P.

Definition 1 (Immediate consequence operator). *Let P be a positive program. The operator T_P that maps from interpretations to interpretations is defined as follows: for any interpretation f and each ground atom $A \in B_P$,*

$$T_P(f)(A) = max\{\oplus\{\mathcal{C}_i(\overline{f}(B), r) : (A \leftarrow_i B.r) \text{ is a ground instance of a rule in } P\}, \oplus\{a : (A.a) \text{ is a ground instance of a fact in } P\}\}.$$

Since the Herbrand base B_P is finite, for each $A \in B_P$, there are a finite number of ground instances of rule heads and logical parts of facts which match A. Therefore, both $\oplus$ operators in the definition of T_P are, in deed, maxima. T_P is shown to be monotone and continuous [1].

The bottom-up iteration of T_P is defined as follows:

$$T_P^k(\bot) = \begin{cases} \bot & \text{if } k = 0 \\ T_P(T_P^{k-1}(\bot)) & \text{if } k \text{ is a successor ordinal} \\ \oplus\{T_P^n(\bot)|n < k\} & \text{if } k \text{ is a limit ordinal,} \end{cases}$$

where $\bot$ denotes the least interpretation, mapping every ground atom to 0.

The least model M_P is exactly the least fixpoint of T_P, denoted $lfp(T_P)$, and can be obtained by finitely bottom-up iterating T_P.

Theorem 2. *[1] Let P be a positive program. Then there exists a finite number α such that $n \geq \alpha$ implies $T_P^n(\bot) = lfp(T_P) = M_P$.*

3 Normal Fuzzy Linguistic Logic Programs

We extend FLLP with negation by allowing negative literals to occur in rule bodies, resulting in *normal fuzzy linguistic logic programs* (*normal programs*, for short). An *extended positive fuzzy linguistic logic program* (*extended positive program*, for short) is a (positive) fuzzy linguistic logic program in which elements of the truth domain can appear in the places of atoms in rule bodies, and the value of such an element under any interpretation of the program is itself.

The notions of an interpretation, a model and the immediate consequence operator of a normal or extended positive program can be defined similarly to those of a positive program.

Definition 2 (Stable model). *Let P be a normal program and I an interpretation of P. Let P^* denote a program consisting of all ground instances of rules and facts in P. I is a stable model of P iff $I = I'$, where the interpretation I' is obtained according to the Gelfond-Lifschitz transformation [11] as follows:*

(i) first, substitute (fix) in P^* all negative literals by their values w.r.t. I, which are computed as $\overline{I}(\neg A) = -I(A)$ for all ground atoms A. Let P^I denote the resulting extended positive program, called the reduct *of P w.r.t. I;*

(ii) then, compute the least model I' of P^I.

This approach defines a whole family of models of a normal program P, called the *stable model semantics* of P. In the subsequent proofs, it can be easily seen that when proving a model of P being a model of P^I or vice versa, since the fact parts of the programs have the same ground instances, we only need to deal with the rule parts. For each rule $(A \leftarrow B.r)$ in P, B can be denoted by $B[B_1, \ldots, B_m, \neg B_{m+1}, \ldots, \neg B_n]$, where $1 \leq m \leq n$ and $B_1, \ldots, B_n$ are all atoms appearing in B. Each ground instance of the rule in P^* is of the form $(A\vartheta \leftarrow B[B_1\vartheta, \ldots, B_m\vartheta, \neg B_{m+1}\vartheta, \ldots, \neg B_n\vartheta].r)$, and the corresponding one in

P^I can be denoted as $(A\vartheta \leftarrow B[B_1\vartheta, \ldots, B_m\vartheta, -I(B_{m+1}\vartheta), \ldots, -I(B_n\vartheta)].r)$, where every negative literal $\neg B_i\vartheta$, $m + 1 \le i \le n$, is replaced by its value under I. Let $\mathcal{B}$ be the expression obtained from B by replacing every connective apart from the negation with its truth function.

Theorem 3. *Any stable model of a normal program P is a model of P.*

Proof. Let $(A \leftarrow B[B_1, \ldots, B_m, \neg B_{m+1}, \ldots, \neg B_n].r)$ be any rule in P and I be a stable model of P. By definition, I is the least model of P^I, so for all ground instances $(A\vartheta \leftarrow B[B_1\vartheta, \ldots, B_m\vartheta, \neg B_{m+1}\vartheta, \ldots, \neg B_n\vartheta].r)$ in P^* of the rule and the corresponding one $(A\vartheta \leftarrow B[B_1\vartheta, \ldots, B_m\vartheta, -I(B_{m+1}\vartheta), \ldots, -I(B_n\vartheta)].r)$ in P^I, we have:

$$r \le \overline{I}(A\vartheta \leftarrow B[B_1\vartheta, \ldots, B_m\vartheta, -I(B_{m+1}\vartheta), \ldots, -I(B_n\vartheta)])$$
$$= \overline{I}(A\vartheta \leftarrow B[B_1\vartheta, \ldots, B_m\vartheta, \neg B_{m+1}\vartheta, \ldots, \neg B_n\vartheta])$$

Thus, for all ground instances $(A\vartheta \leftarrow B[B_1\vartheta, \ldots, B_m\vartheta, \neg B_{m+1}\vartheta, \ldots, \neg B_n\vartheta])$ of $(A \leftarrow B[B_1, \ldots, B_m, \neg B_{m+1}, \ldots, \neg B_n])$, we have:

$$r \le \otimes\{\overline{I}(A\vartheta \leftarrow B[B_1\vartheta, \ldots, B_m\vartheta, \neg B_{m+1}\vartheta, \ldots, \neg B_n\vartheta])\}$$
$$= \overline{I}(A \leftarrow B[B_1, \ldots, B_m, \neg B_{m+1}, \ldots, \neg B_n])$$

Hence, I is a model of the rule $(A \leftarrow B[B_1, \ldots, B_m, \neg B_{m+1}, \ldots, \neg B_n].r)$. Since the rule is arbitrary, I is a model of P. $\qquad\square$

A normal program may have several stable models as in the following example.

Example 2. Given the LTD in Example 1, consider the program P consisting of the following rules:

$$(good(X) \leftarrow_G \neg bad(X).Vc^+)$$
$$(bad(X) \leftarrow_G \neg good(X).Vc^+)$$

We will determine stable models of P. Let $I = \{(good(a), x), (bad(a), y)\}$ be an interpretation of P, where the constant a is added to form ground terms. The reduct P^I consists of the following rules:

$$(good(a) \leftarrow_G -y.Vc^+)$$
$$(bad(a) \leftarrow_G -x.Vc^+)$$

The least model of P^I is $M_{P^I} = \{(good(a), \mathcal{C}_G(-y, Vc^+)), (bad(a), \mathcal{C}_G(-x, Vc^+))\}$. Thus, I is a stable model of P iff $x = \mathcal{C}_G(-y, Vc^+) = \min(-y, Vc^+)$ and $y = \mathcal{C}_G(-x, Vc^+) = \min(-x, Vc^+)$. It can be seen that all $Vc^- \le x = -y \le Vc^+$ (so $Vc^- \le y = -x \le Vc^+$) satisfying the conditions. That is, we have 11 stable models $I = \{(good(a), x), (bad(a), -x)\}$ such that $v_1 = Vc^- \le x \le Vc^+ = v_{11}$.

Furthermore, we have the following result. Note that as shown in Example 2, a normal program may not have a least model, but may have several minimal models.

Theorem 4. *Any stable model of a normal program P is a minimal model of P.*

Proof. Let I be a stable model of P. By definition, I is the least model of P^I. We will prove that I is a minimal model of P. Suppose that there exists a model J of P such that $J \sqsubset I$. We will show that J is a model of P^I. Since I is the least model of P^I, we have $I \sqsubseteq J$, which is a contradiction to the hypothesis.

Let $(A \leftarrow B[B_1, \ldots, B_m, \neg B_{m+1}, \ldots, \neg B_n].r)$ be any rule in P. Each of its ground instances in P^* is of the form $(A\vartheta \leftarrow B[B_1\vartheta, \ldots, B_m\vartheta, \neg B_{m+1}\vartheta, \ldots, \neg B_n\vartheta].r)$, and the counterpart in P^I is $(A\vartheta \leftarrow B[B_1\vartheta, \ldots, B_m\vartheta, -I(B_{m+1}\vartheta), \ldots, -I(B_n\vartheta)].r)$. Since $J \sqsubset I$, we have, for all $m+1 \leq i \leq n$, $J(B_i\vartheta) \leq I(B_i\vartheta)$, hence $-J(B_i\vartheta) \geq -I(B_i\vartheta)$. J is a model of P, so we have:

$$
\begin{aligned}
r &\leq \overline{J}(A \leftarrow B[B_1, \ldots, B_m, \neg B_{m+1}, \ldots, \neg B_n]) \\
&\leq \overline{J}(A\vartheta \leftarrow B[B_1\vartheta, \ldots, B_m\vartheta, \neg B_{m+1}\vartheta, \ldots, \neg B_n\vartheta]) \\
&= \leftarrow^\bullet (J(A\vartheta), \mathcal{B}(J(B_1\vartheta), \ldots, J(B_m\vartheta), -J(B_{m+1}\vartheta), \ldots, -J(B_n\vartheta))) \\
&\leq \leftarrow^\bullet (J(A\vartheta), \mathcal{B}(J(B_1\vartheta), \ldots, J(B_m\vartheta), -I(B_{m+1}\vartheta), \ldots, -I(B_n\vartheta))) \\
&= \overline{J}(A\vartheta \leftarrow B[B_1\vartheta, \ldots, B_m\vartheta, -I(B_{m+1}\vartheta), \ldots, -I(B_n\vartheta)])
\end{aligned}
$$

The last inequality holds due to the fact that every truth function in $\mathcal{B}$ (apart from the negation) is non-decreasing, and $\leftarrow^\bullet$ is non-increasing in the second argument. Thus, J is a model of $(A\vartheta \leftarrow B[B_1\vartheta, \ldots, B_m\vartheta, -I(B_{m+1}\vartheta), \ldots, -I(B_n\vartheta)].r)$ in P^I. Since the rule in P is arbitrary, J is a model of P^I.   □

The notion of the immediate consequence operator T_P for a normal program P is defined analogously to the case of positive programs. Similar to the case of positive programs, a model of P is a pre-fixpoint of T_P and vice versa [12] as follows.

Theorem 5. *Let P be a normal program. Then an interpretation f is a model of P iff $T_P(f) \sqsubseteq f$.*

Proof. First, let f be a model of P; we prove that $T_P(f) \sqsubseteq f$. Let A be any ground atom; consider the following cases:

(i) If A is neither a ground instance of the logical part of a fact nor a ground instance of a rule head in P, then $T_P(f)(A) = 0 \leq f(A)$.

(ii) For each ground instance $(A.a)$ of a fact, say $(C.a)$, in P, since f is a model of P, and A is a ground instance of C, we have $a = P(C) \leq \overline{f}(C) \leq f(A)$. Hence, $f(A) \geq \oplus\{a|(A.a)$ is a ground instance of a fact in $P\}$.

(iii) For each ground instance $(A \leftarrow_i B.r)$, where $i \in \{G, L\}$, of a rule, say $(C.r)$, in P, we have: $\mathcal{C}_i(\overline{f}(B), r) = \mathcal{C}_i(\overline{f}(B), P(C)) \leq^{(*)} \mathcal{C}_i(\overline{f}(B), \overline{f}(A \leftarrow_i B)) = \mathcal{C}_i(\overline{f}(B), \leftarrow_i^{\bullet} (f(A), \overline{f}(B))) \leq^{(**)} f(A)$, where $(*)$ holds since $(A \leftarrow_i B)$ is a ground instance of C, and $(**)$ follows from (7). Therefore, $f(A) \geq \oplus\{\mathcal{C}_i(\overline{f}(B), r) | (A \leftarrow_i B.r)$ is a ground instance of a rule in $P\}$.

By definition, $T_P(f)(A) \leq f(A)$. Since A is arbitrary, we have $T_P(f) \sqsubseteq f$.

Finally, let us show that if $T_P(f) \sqsubseteq f$, then f is a model of P. Suppose there is an interpretation f such that $T_P(f) \sqsubseteq f$. Let C be any formula in $dom(P)$. There are two cases:

(i) $(C.c)$, where c is a truth value, is a fact in P. For each ground instance A of C, by the assumption $T_P(f) \sqsubseteq f$, we have $f(A) \geq T_P(f)(A) \geq \oplus\{a | (A.a)$ is a ground instance of a fact in $P\} \geq c = P(C)$. Therefore, $\overline{f}(C) = \otimes\{f(A) | A$ is a ground instance of $C\} \geq P(C)$.

(ii) $(C.c)$ is a rule in P. For each ground instance $A \leftarrow_j D$ of C, where $j \in \{G, L\}$, since $T_P(f) \sqsubseteq f$, we have $f(A) \geq T_P(f)(A) \geq \oplus\{\mathcal{C}_i(\overline{f}(B), r) | (A \leftarrow_i B.r)$ is a ground instance of a rule in $P\} \geq \mathcal{C}_j(\overline{f}(D), c) = \mathcal{C}_j(\overline{f}(D), P(C))$. Hence, $\overline{f}(A \leftarrow_j D) = \leftarrow_j^{\bullet} (f(A), \overline{f}(D)) \geq^{(*)} \leftarrow_j^{\bullet} (\mathcal{C}_j(\overline{f}(D), P(C)), \overline{f}(D)) \geq^{(**)} P(C)$, where $(*)$ holds since $\leftarrow_i^{\bullet}$ is non-decreasing in the first argument, and $(**)$ follows from (8). Consequently, $\overline{f}(C) = \otimes\{\overline{f}(A \leftarrow_j D) | (A \leftarrow_j D)$ is a ground instance of $C\} \geq P(C)$.

Since C is arbitrary, by definition, f is a model of P. $\square$

However, for a normal program P, T_P may not be monotone as in the following example, so it does not necessarily have a least fixpoint.

Example 3. Consider a normal program P consisting of the following rule:

$$(good(X) \leftarrow_G \neg bad(X).1)$$

Given an interpretation $I = \{(good(a), x), (bad(a), y)\}$, where x and y are truth values, $T_P(I) = \{(good(a), -y), (bad(a), 0)\}$. Clearly, $T_P(I)$ is not monotone.

Theorem 6. *Any stable model of a normal program P is a minimal fixpoint of T_P.*

Proof. First, we show that, for every interpretation I, $T_P(I)$ for P coincides with $T_{P^I}(I)$ for the extended positive program P^I. In Definition 1,

(i) The second $\oplus$ operator is obviously the same for both $T_P(I)$ and $T_{P^I}(I)$.
(ii) Concerning the first $\oplus$, let $(A \leftarrow B[B_1, \ldots, B_m, \neg B_{m+1}, \ldots, \neg B_n].r)$ be any rule in P. For each of its ground instances $(A\vartheta \leftarrow B[B_1\vartheta, \ldots, B_m\vartheta, \neg B_{m+1}\vartheta, \ldots, \neg B_n\vartheta].r)$ and the counterpart $(A\vartheta \leftarrow$

$B[B_1\vartheta, \ldots, B_m\vartheta, -I(B_{m+1}\vartheta), \ldots, -I(B_n\vartheta)].r)$ in P^I, we have the following:

$$\mathcal{C}(\overline{I}(B[B_1\vartheta, \ldots, B_m\vartheta, \neg B_{m+1}\vartheta, \ldots, \neg B_n\vartheta]), r)$$
$$= \mathcal{C}(\mathcal{B}(I(B_1\vartheta), \ldots, I(B_m\vartheta), \overline{I}(\neg B_{m+1}\vartheta), \ldots, \overline{I}(\neg B_n\vartheta)), r)$$
$$= \mathcal{C}(\mathcal{B}(I(B_1\vartheta), \ldots, I(B_m\vartheta), -I(B_{m+1}\vartheta), \ldots, -I(B_n\vartheta)), r)$$
$$= \mathcal{C}(\overline{I}(B[B_1\vartheta, \ldots, B_m\vartheta, -I(B_{m+1}\vartheta), \ldots, -I(B_n\vartheta)]), r)$$

By taking suprema for all the ground instances, we have:

$$\oplus\{\mathcal{C}(\overline{I}(B[B_1\vartheta, \ldots, B_m\vartheta, \neg B_{m+1}\vartheta, \ldots, \neg B_n\vartheta]), r)\}$$
$$= \oplus\{\mathcal{C}(\overline{I}(B[B_1\vartheta, \ldots, B_m\vartheta, -I(B_{m+1}\vartheta), \ldots, -I(B_n\vartheta)]), r)\}$$

Therefore, $T_P(I) = T_{P^I}(I)$ for every interpretation I.

Now, let M be a stable model of P. By definition, M is the least model of the extended positive program P^M. By Theorem 2, M is the least fixpoint of T_{P^M}, so $M = T_{P^M}(M) = T_P(M)$, i.e., M is a fixpoint of T_P. It remains to show that M is a minimal fixpoint of T_P. Assume that there is a fixpoint N of T_P such that $N \sqsubseteq M$. By Theorem 5, N is a model of P. Moreover, by Theorem 4, M is a minimal model of P, so we have $M = N$. □

As shown in the following example, for a normal program P, T_P may have many minimal fixpoints, which might not be obtained by the bottom-up iteration of T_P. Moreover, a minimal fixpoint of T_P may not be a stable model of P.

Example 4. Consider a normal program P consisting of the following rules:

$$(good(X) \leftarrow_G good(X).1)$$
$$(bad(X) \leftarrow_G \neg good(X).1)$$

First, we determine stable models of P. Let $I = \{(good(a), x), (bad(a), y)\}$, where x and y are truth values, be an interpretation of P. The reduct P^I is as follows:

$$(good(a) \leftarrow_G good(a).1)$$
$$(bad(a) \leftarrow_G -x.1)$$

The least model of P^I is $M_{P^I} = \{(good(a), 0), (bad(a), -x)\}$. Thus, I is a stable model of P iff $I = M_{P^I}$, i.e., $I = \{(good(a), 0), (bad(a), 1)\}$.

Finally, we determine the set of fixpoints of T_P. Given an interpretation $I = \{(good(a), x), (bad(a), y)\}$, we have $T_P(I) = \{(good(a), x), (bad(a), -x)\}$. Hence, I is a fixpoint of T_P iff $I = \{(good(a), x), (bad(a), -x)\}$, for all truth values x. It can be seen that all such fixpoints are minimal, but only the interpretation $\{(good(a), 0), (bad(a), 1)\}$ is a stable model.

4   Related Work

Of the various approaches to the management of negation in logic programming, the stable model semantics approach, introduced by Gelfond and Lifschitz [11], has become one of the most widely studied and commonly adopted proposal. There are several works on fuzzy logic programming with negation. The authors of [13] and [14] deal with normal *propositional* residuated logic programs and normal *propositional* multi-adjoint logic programs, respectively. In addition to studying the fixpoint characterization of the stable model semantics, they show that there exists a stable model for such finite programs if the truth domain is a convex compact set in an euclidean space and truth functions of all connectives except the implication are continuous. They also give sufficient conditions for the unicity of stable models for several particular truth domains. Nevertheless, the existence of stable models of normal fuzzy linguistic logic programs seems to be more complicated due to the fact that our truth domains are discrete.

Besides the stable model semantics, there are several other approaches to studying the semantics of normal programs as follows:

(i) define the *compromise semantics* [15] based on van Gelder's *alternating fixpoint approach* [16]. The *binary* immediate consequence operator $T_P(I, J)$ for a normal program P is an extension of the one for positive programs in which the interpretation I (resp., J) is used to assign meaning to positive literals (resp., negative literals); $T_P(I, J)$ is similar to the operator $\Psi_P(I, J)$ in [17,18]. T_P is continuous in the first argument and anti-monotone in the second. Then, the operator $S_P(J)$ is defined as the least fixpoint of $T_P(I, J)$, i.e., the least model of P^J, denoted $S_P(J) = T_P^\infty(\bot, J)$. Since S_P is anti-monotone, $S_P \circ S_P$ is monotone. It is known that S_P has two *extreme oscillation points* $S_P^\bot = (S_P \circ S_P)^\infty(\bot)$ and $S_P^\top = (S_P \circ S_P)^\infty(\top)$, where $\top$ is the greatest interpretation mapping every ground atom to 1, and $S_P^\bot \sqsubseteq S_P^\top$. As in [16], $S_P^\bot$ and $S_P^\top$ are an under-estimation and an over-estimation of the semantics of P, respectively. The *compromise semantics* of P is defined as a *partial* interpretation $CS(P) = S_P^\bot \cap S_P^\top$. This semantics coincides with the *well-founded semantics* for traditional Datalog programs with negation [19].

(ii) define different semantics, e.g., the stable model semantics and the well-founded semantics, of normal programs over bilattices [20], in which the truth domain is a complete lattice under the truth ordering as well as the knowledge ordering. For example, in *interval* bilattices, an element is greater than another under the knowledge ordering if the former is more precise than the latter. Following this idea, it can be seen that all linguistic truth values generated from x using hedges are greater than x in the knowledge ordering since they are more precise values than x; for instance, we have *True* $\leq_k$ *VeryTrue* $\leq_k$ *SlightlyVeryTrue*, where $\leq_k$ is the knowledge order relation. Thus, an LTD is also a poset under $\leq_k$. However, it is still not a complete lattice under $\leq_k$ since it does not have a top element and a bottom element.

5   Conclusion and Future Work

In this paper, we extend fuzzy linguistic logic programming with negation and present the stable model semantics of normal fuzzy linguistic logic programs, called *normal programs*. More precisely, a stable model of a normal program is obtained according to the usual Gelfond-Lifschitz transformation. We prove that a stable model of a normal program P is a minimal model of P and a minimal fixpoint of the intermediate consequence operator T_P. We also show that a normal program P can have multiple stable models and a minimal fixpoint of T_P may not be a stable model of P. For future work, we will study the conditions for the existence and unicity of stable models of normal programs and a method to compute such models.

Acknowledgment. This research is funded by Vietnam National Foundation for Science and Technology Development (NAFOSTED) under grant number 105.08-2018.09.

References

1. Le, V.H., Liu, F., Tran, D.K.: Fuzzy linguistic logic programming and its applications. Theor. Pract. Logic Programm. **9**(3), 309–341 (2009)
2. Le, V.H., Tran, D.K.: Further results on fuzzy linguistic logic programming. J. Comput. Sci. Cybern. **30**(2), 139–147 (2014)
3. Le, V.H., Liu, F.: Tabulation proof procedures for fuzzy linguistic logic programming. Int. J. Approximate Reasoning **63**, 62–88 (2015)
4. Nguyen, C.H., Wechler, W.: Hedge algebras: an algebraic approach to structure of sets of linguistic truth values. Fuzzy Sets Syst. **35**, 281–293 (1990)
5. Nguyen, C.H., Wechler, W.: Extended hedge algebras and their application to fuzzy logic. Fuzzy Sets Syst. **52**, 259–281 (1992)
6. Le, V.H., Tran, D.K.: Extending fuzzy logics with many hedges. Fuzzy Sets Syst. **345**, 126–138 (2018)
7. Le, V.H., Liu, F., Tran, D.K.: Mathematical fuzzy logic with many dual hedges. In: The Fifth Symposium on Information and Communication Technology (SoICT), pp. 7–13 (2014)
8. Zadeh, L.A.: A theory of approximate reasoning. In: Hayes, J.E., Michie, D., Mikulich, L.I., (eds.) Machine Intelligence, vol. 9, pp. 149–194. Wiley (1979)
9. Bellman, R.E., Zadeh, L.A.: Local and fuzzy logics. In: Fuzzy Sets, Fuzzy Logic, and Fuzzy Systems: Selected Papers by Lotfi A. Zadeh, pp. 283–335. World Scientific Publishing Co., Inc, River Edge (1996)
10. Hájek, P.: Metamathematics of Fuzzy Logic. Kluwer, Dordrecht (1998)
11. Gelfond, M., Lifschitz, V.: The stable model semantics for logic programming. In: Proceedings of the 5th International Conference on Logic Programming, pp. 1070–1080. MIT Press, Cambridge (1988)
12. Davey, B.A., Priestley, H.A.: Introduction to Lattices and Order. Cambridge University Press, Cambridge (2002)
13. Madrid, N., Ojeda-Aciego, M.: On the existence and unicity of stable models in normal residuated logic programs. Int. J. Comput. Math. **89**(3), 310–324 (2012)
14. Cornejo, M.E., Lobo, D., Medina, J.: Syntax and semantics of multi-adjoint normal logic programming. Fuzzy Sets Syst. **345**, 41–62 (2018)

15. Loyer, Y., Straccia, U.: The well-founded semantics in normal logic programs with uncertainty. In: Hu, Z., Rodríguez-Artalejo, M. (eds.) FLOPS 2002. LNCS, vol. 2441, pp. 152–166. Springer, Heidelberg (2002). https://doi.org/10.1007/3-540-45788-7_9

16. van Gelder, A.: The alternating fixpoint of logic programs with negation. In: PODS 1989: Proceedings of the 8th ACM SIGACT-SIGMOD-SIGART Symposium on Principles of Database Systems, pp. 1–10. ACM, New York (1989)

17. Fitting, M.: Fixpoint semantics for logic programming: a survey. Theor. Comput. Sci. **278**(1–2), 25–51 (2002)

18. Fitting, M.: The family of stable models. J. Logic Programm. **17**(2/3&4), 197–225 (1993)

19. van Gelder, A., Ross, K.A., Schlipf, J.S.: The well-founded semantics for general logic programs. J. ACM **38**(3), 619–649 (1991)

20. Fitting, M.: Bilattices and the semantics of logic programming. J. Logic Programm. **11**(2), 91–116 (1991)

Graph-Based Crowd Definition
for Assessing Wise Crowd Measures

Marcin Jodłowiec$^{(\boxtimes)}$, Marek Krótkiewicz$^{(\boxtimes)}$, Rafał Palak$^{(\boxtimes)}$,
and Krystian Wojtkiewicz$^{(\boxtimes)}$

Faculty of Computer Science and Management,
Wrocław University of Science and Technology, Wrocław, Poland
{marcin.jodlowiec,marek.krotkiewicz,rafal.palak,
krystian.wojtkiewicz}@pwr.edu.pl

Abstract. Research in the field of collective intelligence is currently focused mainly on determining ways to provide a more and more accurate prediction. However, the development of collective intelligence requires a more formal approach. Thus the natural next step is to introduce the formal model of collective. Many scientists seem to see this need, but available solutions usually focus on narrow specialization. The problems within the scope of collective intelligence field typically require complex models. Sometimes more than one model has to be used. This paper addresses both issues. Authors introduce graph-based meta-model of collective that intend to describe all collective's properties based on psychological knowledge, especially on Surowiecki's work. Moreover, we introduced the taxonomy of metrics that allow assessing the qualitative aspects of crowd's structure and dynamics.

Keywords: Collective modelling · Collective properties ·
Graph-based collective · Collective metric

1 Introduction

Collective intelligence is one of the emerging areas of science. One of the most popular approaches define it as "the capacity of human collectives to engage in intellectual cooperation in order to create, innovate and invent" [7] or "groups of individuals acting collectively in ways that seem intelligent" [9]. There are two critical common aspects of both definitions. First of them is that the action is performed by a group that we can name collective, while another is a common target. In this paper, authors focus on defining a way to understand what makes the collective an efficient tool in task such as prediction. It is not only theoretical divagation but also a very practical question. What makes jury good in a trial? What makes the team effective? How build a cabinet to provide best outcomes? These and many other issues are reflections of a theoretical question, how to assess the structure of the crowd, and what makes it wise? The authors are not the first to ask it, and not the first ones to answer it. The main research

© Springer Nature Switzerland AG 2019
N. T. Nguyen et al. (Eds.): ICCCI 2019, LNAI 11683, pp. 66–78, 2019.
https://doi.org/10.1007/978-3-030-28377-3_6

problem is thus the definition of a collective model, that allows precise definition of collective's structure. At the same time, this model should provide the means to describe the dynamics of crowd changes in time.

In this paper, authors introduce a framework for assessing collective properties using graph theory. Moreover, the taxonomy of metrics provides the ground for the unified analysis of collective structure and dynamics. The paper structure is as follows. In the next section, the related work presents state of the art in the field of the crowd and its features definition. Later, authors define the collective as a graph and, in Sect. 4, provide the taxonomy of collective's metrics available for calculation. The last section concludes the paper.

2   Related Works

There is no simple answer to a question "what exactly makes a crowd smart?" [11]. One of the most popular was given by Surowiecki. In his work he distinguishes the following conditions that need to be met for a crowd to consider it wise:

- the *diversity* of opinion – each person should have some private information, even if it is just an eccentric interpretation of the known facts,
- *independence* – people's opinions are not determined by the opinions of those around them,
- *decentralization* of opinion – people can specialize and draw on local knowledge,
- *aggregation* – some mechanism exists for turning private judgments into a collective decision [15]

It is worth mentioning that it is not the only well-known answer. Another, very popular one was proposed by Woolley et al. [17]. Authors distinguish there the following factors:

- average social *sensitivity* of group members
- *equality in the distribution* of conversational turn-taking
- *the proportion of females* in the group.

Authors in [1] conducted similar experiment and the results did not support the conclusions drawn by Woolley et al. Authors stated that group performance is strongly affected by individuals IQ. Besides that, the experiment did not show any correlations between group IQ and a number of females in the group. Also social sensitivity failed to emerge as a significant predictor of group-IQ. Due to the fact that the importance of Surowiecki rules was confirmed in many experiments, we decided to focus on them in this article.

One of the biggest drawbacks of Surowiecki theory is the fact that he did not formally define the factors or even the collective itself [12]. Nevertheless, few other authors tried to formalize a concept of collective. One of the most popular models is the one proposed by DeGroot [4]. In his work, he proposed the way to model the collective and how to reach the consensus. The DeGroot model uses connection between collective members to define collective. In his model, he assumed that each collective members have its own subjective distribution $F_1, F_2, ..., F_n$ about the unknown value of some parameter θ. The subjective distributions are developed from different levels of experience and different types of information among members. Authors assumed that typical collective members apprised by others subjective distribution will be forced to change the judgment. The exchange of information could be described by the equation:

$$F_{i_1} = \sum_{j=1}^{k} p_{i_j} F_j \qquad (1)$$

where $p_{i_1}, p_{i_2}, ..., p_{i_k}$ are weights chosen by individual i before he or she is informed about distributions of other members, $p_{i_j} \geq 0$ and $\sum_{j=1}^{k} p_{i_j} = 1$, F_{i_1} is revised subjective distribution, probably differ from F_i The revision process continues indefinitely or until the moment when further revision does not change any member's subjective distribution. It is worth notice that this model has very strong assumption: $p_{i_j} \geq 0$. It is not hard to imagine a collective where two collective members have no direct influence between each other. Another problem with this model is the fact that it only takes into account the social structure of the collective; the other factors distinguished by Surowiecki like diversity seems to be omitted in this model. The model described in [4] could be considered as a model with very narrow specialization, lack of possibility to fully collective is one of the highest drawbacks of this model. Its specialization could be considered a good thing, but this also makes it impossible to apply this model for different problems.

A similar approach was presented by Wagner [16]. In his work he defined matrix:

$$A = (a_{i_j}) \qquad (2)$$

where a_{i_j} represents individual i opinion as to the most appropriate value of variable j. This matrix is regarded as undergoing modification through repeated multiplication by $P = (p_{i_j})$ where p_{i_j} is numerical measure of power of individual j to influence the opinion of individual i and $\sum_{j=1}^{k} p_{i_j} = 1$. Wagner [16] model is very similar as DeGroot [4]. The set of weights in DeGroot [4] was changed to a matrix in Wagner [16], but the problems with this model are the same as it was in case of DeGroot [4]. Both models have a lot in common; it could be invisible on the first sight, but after deep analyze, more common features become more clear. Both models also share the same problems with their definitions. This situation also shows another need in the literature: the need for universal meta-model of a collective which could be extended by other models. This could make easier to compare two models such as DeGroot [4] and Wagner [16], it would also make it easier to use some of the ideas from one model in another.

Both models, namely DeGroot's [4] and Wagner's [16] are very popular. Many extensions were proposed based on them. One of the most popular was presented in [6]. This work is considered by many as an example of the formal model of the collective. Authors use graph concept to define collective. This is probably more intuitive way to represent the crowd structure, but it worth notice that DeGroot [4] and Wagner [16] models can be easily translated to graph-based models. Authors define set of agents as:

$$A = 1, 2, .., n \tag{3}$$

The agents are the nodes of a directed graph. The critical aspect of this model is matrix T which captured the interaction patterns, and the entry T_{ij} is the weight of trust that agent i places on the current belief of agent j in forming his or her belief. Collective members naively update their beliefs by repeatedly taking weighted averages of their neighbors' opinions. The update process is similar to Wagner [16]. Therefore deeper analysis of it for the purpose of this article is not necessary. The model tries to extend some concepts presented previously by DeGroot [4], but the changes are not outstanding in this model. Authors conduct an in-depth theoretical analysis of this model, describing its properties, for example: showing that trust coming into a finite group should not be concentrated. This model is very mature, but despite offering so many insights into crowd wisdom, it also omits some vital aspect of it. One aspect that seems to be overlooked in this model is the aspect of collective member and its description. The model focuses only on interactions in collective completely neglecting the most essential aspect of the collective – its members. This creates some restrictions where the model could be used and what aspects of a wise crowd can be modeled using such a model. Therefore, as it was in case of DeGroot [4] and Wagner, [16] diversity aspect of collective with this model could be hard to model.

Similarly to [6] a lot of authors tried to improve Wagner or DeGroot model or propose similar one with some small changes [2,5,8,10,14]. Due to the page limit and the fact, this works share the same problems as the original one, deeper analyze of them will be omitted in this paper.

In [3] authors proposed a collective model that focuses on knowledge transfer in collective. Each collective member is described by knowledge vector which evolves over time as agent receives information broadcasted by others, what could be described formally as:

$$V_i(t) = (V_{i,k}(t); k = 1, ..., K) \tag{4}$$

where $V_i(t)$ is knowledge endowment at time t of collective member i This approach assumes that knowledge could be transferred to any collective member that meet the following criteria:

- has a direct link to the broadcasting agent
- knowledge endowment of the collective member is not too dissimilar

Dissimilarity is defined as the relative distance between two collective members i and j in terms of knowledge:

$$\Delta(i, j) = \frac{||V_i - V_j||}{||V_i||} = \sum_k \left(\frac{V_{i,k} - V_{j,k}}{V_{i,k}} \right)^2 \tag{5}$$

Knowledge could be transferred if $\Delta(i, j) < \theta \in (0, 1)$. Knowledge is received and assimilated by any agent who can use it. For every knowledge category k, when i broadcasts, knowledge of j increases according to[1]:

$$V_{j,k}(t + 1) = V_{j,k}(t) + max\{0, \alpha[V_{i,k}(t) - V_{j,k}(t)]\}, \text{ for all } k = 1, 2, ..., K \quad (6)$$

The α captures an aspect of knowledge diffusion and transfer. It is important since in some cases, knowledge is only partly available. Similarly to previous models, this model of collective can only be used for a specific class of problems. It has slightly different approach to model collective than DeGroot [4] and Wagner [16]. Here we could observe the conditions that have to be fulfilled to transfer knowledge. Also, the knowledge transfer does not depend on a single number that describes the relation between two members but the similarity measure. Authors of this model definition seem to focus more on aspects omitted in DeGroot [4] and Wagner [16], e.g., this model allows to calculate diversity. In the same time, they are focusing more on collective members, and authors do not pay attention to interactions in collective. The aspects of independence in collective seem to be forgotten in this model. Therefore, despite the wide collective member description, this model cannot be considered as a complex model of the collective, due to simplification of interaction aspect. This model has some properties that could be useful in DeGroot [4] and Wagner [16] models, while at the same time it would be beneficial for this model to use some aspects exploited in DeGroot [4] and Wagner [16]. This transition of aspects of both models could be hard due to the fact that both models start from different aspects of modeling. This situation again shows a great need for meta-model of collective that would allow to easily exchange some aspects between models.

Last but not least approach discussed here was presented in [13]. Authors describe collective by distinguishing three networks:

- a social network - the goal of this network is to describe social connections between collective members
- a semantic network - the goal of this network is to describe links between concepts
- a socio-semantic network - the goal of this network is to links collective members to concepts

This approach is entirely different than the previous one. This model focuses on crowd structure, but also the structure of the concepts, what is an entirely new approach. However, the model does not allow to model any aspects of the collective. Due to the fact, that whole representation of the collective is based only on the graph structure, many restrictions are present, such as a more complex representation of collective member. Lack of such representation omits much of information about a collective. As a result, some properties could not be described, e.g., diversity or independence. This model presents a different approach to model collective than others, but at the same time, it seems to be the

---

[1] Without any consequent loss of knowledge to agent i.

less mature idea. This model requires further development, and it would be very beneficial to use some concepts from other models presented above. This task would be much easier with meta-model of collective (as it was described above).

As was showed above, many models of collective were created. Most of them focus on one aspect of a wise crowd and omit or simplify the others. These restrictions sometimes make it impossible to measure or model some factors of the collective. Very narrow specialization of the models' forces to use many models to fully describe collective. Some models cover the same semantic features of crowd description, but lack of meta-model for collective does not allow to see it on the first sight. At the same time, many models would benefit a lot from concepts defined in other models. Therefore some model would be beneficial in that matter. In this article, we would like to address both problems.

3   Proposed Solution

The extensive study, that was partly presented in previous section, led authors to the conclusion that there is no single and complete approach that would allow transparent definition of agents and crowds. While some sources focus on introducing features that describe collective, they omit its members. Others in turn take deep consideration on the connections between crowd members, their type or properties, but neglect any other aspects, such as assessing possible structure of the crowd as such. There are also approaches that mainly deal with members and their features, but do not pay deep attention to the crowd structure. In their approach authors decided to combine most of aforementioned ideas and on base of them introduce formal approach to the crowd modeling based on graph theory. It is assumed that collective forms a graph, where nodes denote members of the collective, while edges represent possible connections between them.

Lets define the **collective** as a tuple:

$$C = (M, E, t) \tag{7}$$

where

M is a set of collective members,
E is a set of edges,
t is collective *target*.

t is **collective target**

$$target : M \to t \tag{8}$$

that means each collective member m has the same target t

$$\forall i \in \{1, 2, \ldots, mn\} \ (target(m_i) = t) \tag{9}$$

Set of collective **members** is defined as

$$M = \{m_1, m_2, \ldots, m_{mn}\} \tag{10}$$

where $mn = |M|$ is a number of members. Collective members do not have to share a common characteristic. Because of that, in the worst scenario, every member of the crowd would have specific features and properties describing it. Thus, each element of the set M can have its type defined, where $\sigma(M)$ is a tuple representing member attributes.

$$\sigma(M) = (a_1, a_2, \ldots, a_{man}) \tag{11}$$

where man is number of attributes. Member **attribute** $a \in MA$ is defined as a tuple build from $name$ and $type$.

$$a = (name, type) \tag{12}$$

MA is a set of member attributes

$$MA = \{a_1, a_2, \ldots, a_{man}\} \tag{13}$$

Collective member can be thus understood as $m \in M$ being a tuple of values

$$m = (v_1, v_2, \ldots, v_{man}) \tag{14}$$

Each value $v \in V$ of collective member $m \in M$ corresponds to appropriate attribute $a \in MA$ of type $\sigma(M)$

$$MemberValue : M \times MA \rightarrow V \tag{15}$$

E is a set of edges, denoting connection among collective members

$$E = \{e_1, e_2, \ldots, e_{en}\} \tag{16}$$

where $en = |E|$ is number of edges.
$e \in E$ is **edge** connecting members $m_x, m_y \in M$

$$e = (m_x, m_y, rel, infl, ep) \tag{17}$$

where:

– $rel \in REL$ is **relation kind** and REL is a set of kinds of relations,
– $infl \in [0, 1]$ is a **level of influence** member m_x on member m_y,
– ep is a **edge property**, that $ep \in EP$.

Edge property is defined as a tuple of values describing edge e

$$ep = (v_1, v_2, \ldots, v_{epn}) \tag{18}$$

with

$$v \in EPV \tag{19}$$

Each element of the set EP has a type $\sigma(EP)$ defined as a tuple of attributes

$$\sigma(EP) = (a_1, a_2, \ldots, a_{epn}) \tag{20}$$

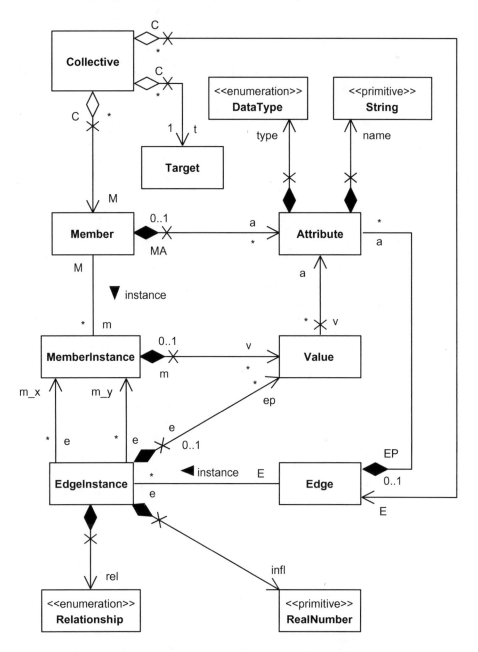

Fig. 1. Model of collective expressed in UML

Number of edge properties is understood as

$$|EPA| = epn \tag{21}$$

and

$$a \in EPA \tag{22}$$

Attribute a was defined in Eq. 12. Each value $v \in EPV$ of edge property $ep \in EP$ corresponds with appropriate attribute a of type $\sigma(EP)$

$$EdgePropertyValue : EP \times EPA \rightarrow EPV \tag{23}$$

Collective members $m_x, m_y \in M$ are connected by edge e representing relationship of kind rel. Influence $infl$ of collective member m_x on member m_y through edge e_z will be denoted as follows

$$m_x \xrightarrow{e_z(infl)} m_y \tag{24}$$

The definitions provided above create a theoretical background for crowd definition. These definitions were processed by the authors to introduce the object-oriented model presented as a UML class diagram (Fig. 1). The model consists of 8 classes, namely `Collective`, `Target`, `Member`, `Attribute`, `MemberInstance`, `Value`, `EdgeInstance`, `Edge`, and several associations depicting the relationships among them. This model should be treated as a base for further study and possible implementation.

4   Defining Crowd Measures

The definition of the collective provided in the previous section allows introducing generic metrics that let us assess the quality of the crowd. In this paper, we will focus on the taxonomy of proposed types of metrics and model's elements that are used to define them Fig. 1. The authors do not intend to provide one and ultimate solution for each metrics since there always will be a possibility to introduce new, better one. However, we would like to set the common ground for each of them to be defined.

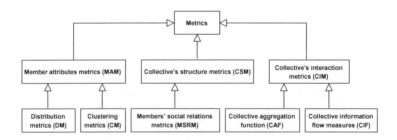

Fig. 2. Taxonomy of collective's metrics expressed in UML

There are different types of metrics that might be important to assess the intelligence of the crowd. We can divide them into the following groups (Fig. 2):

- members' attributes based,
- collective's structure based,
- collective's interaction based.

In the following subsections of the article, we will discuss each group separately.

4.1   Members' Attributes Based Metrics

The collective is build up from its members. At first we will discuss group of measures that use the members' attributes. Equation 13 defines the set of member attributes, however in order to introduce the measure for the collective itself we need to define SMA – super set of all member attributes as:

$$SMA = \bigcup_{i=1}^{mn} MA_i \tag{25}$$

One of the Surowiecki conditions for the crowd to be wise is *diversity* [15], that refers to private knowledge of the member in regard to some fact. Authors believe that the **diversity** refer to the homogeneity of values held by collective members for a given attribute. On that basis lets consider two metrics' types that can be defined for that.

- **Distribution metrics (DM)** – used to asses the one-dimensional distribution of attribute values among collective members. They can be defined on the base of a statistic function, e.g. variance, median, quadrilles etc. The parameters might be calculated and further analyzed for more attributes. However, **DM** is not intended to conduct with it any extended analysis regarding, e.g. dependency among attributes.
- **Clustering metrics (CM)** – used to analyze multi-dimensional aspects of attribute values distribution in members society. Clustering can be used to divide the members set into subsets, and the clustering metrics will allow calculating the distribution of members into those subsets. In other words, this metric is defined on top of clustering results to assess distribution of collective members to clusters. **CM** can be defined as e.g., variance, median, quadrilles, etc. calculated for the clustering results represented by the list of pairs: *cluster name, the number of members.*

4.2   Collective's Structure Based Metrics

Another aspect of the collective is the connections between its members. According to the definition 7, these connections are edges, whose meaning was provided in Eq. 16. These measures aim at assessing members independence, as well as collective centralization. We can distinguish the following types of measures:

- **Collective's structure metrics (CSM)** – used to analyze the structure of collective connections. They are measures used for assessing information regarding graph structure. Among many others, we can thus distinguish measures such as *the longest path, the average number of incoming and outgoing edges* from the node, *reachability* of the nodes, etc. Those metrics are mainly based on the set of members M and the set of edges E defined for the collective C. The analysis of the **CSM** can be conducted to define e.g.

- how *dense is communication* in the collective,
- are there any edge clusters (*centralization of communication*),
- are there any hermit nodes (low communicated nodes) etc.

Authors do not propose any desirable values for the aforementioned measures as there was no extensive research in this area conducted at this moment.

- **Members' social relations metrics (MSRM)** – used to analyze social connections among members of the crowd. They are derivatives (subclasses) of CSM in the sense that they take under consideration properties of the edge that connects nodes. The rel is used here to define social relation type between members, while $infl$ is providing the information regarding its strength. All the specific measures available for computation for CSM are also valid for MSRMs. Since there can be many relation types, the MSRMs should be calculated for each of them separately. However, the analysis of their values can and even should take all of them under consideration parallelly. For very complex systems describing collectives, we can calculate the MSRMs for any subset of edges. For denoting of the subgroup, we can use any ep.

4.3   Collective's Interaction Based Metrics

The groups above quantify a structural aspect of the collective and its members. Last but not least group of measures defined to assess the quality of the crowd has more behavioral nature. Authors assumed that it is possible to determine the properties of the members as well as their connections with quite high confidence. However, it is harder to model each member's behavior (answer) understood as the reaction to the given task (question). Despite known properties and connections with other members, authors have assumed that actions of the members have *black box* nature. The measures defined in this section allow to bring it closer, however, are not meant to unravel it.

- **Collective information flow metrics (CIF)** – used to determine the information flow (propagation) among members of the collective. These are temporal metrics, i.e., they are used to describe the way collective reacts to a problem. Since these metrics define the reaction of the crowd, there are multiple iterations of the system, and after each of them, we can assess the state of the member. The state of the member identifies the m (tuple of values defined in Eq. 14) and the answer to the query. The CIF evaluates the change by comparison of these values after each iteration. Exemplary CIFs are e.g.:
  - the number (percentage) of nodes that changed their state or opinion,
  - the number of edges that appeared/disappeared,
  - the number (percentage) of edges that changed their state, etc.

The list of possible measures is not closed and can change according to the needs of the model. The more thorough analysis might reveal which of the relations' types are most likely to participate in information propagation and under what circumstances. This issue, however, exceeds this paper scope and won't be elaborated.

Essential issue of crowd evaluation is the way that it delivers the answer (recommendation or opinion). Precisely speaking it isn't the measure to assess the properties of the crowd. However, the aggregation method is crucial to be defined. Authors assumed that there should be no restriction on the number of approaches in this regard.

– **Collective aggregation function (CAF)** – used to transform answers (opinions or recommendations) given by members of the collective into one unified response. For most of the models, it should be sufficient to use functions such as average, median, etc. But, there are no contraindications to propose a more sophisticated method.

Appropriate choice of the aggregation method is most crucial for the collective model definition and thus should be well justified. In the authors' opinion, oversimplifying of this model aspect might be a reason why some models do not meet expectations. This exciting aspect of collective modeling will be pursued in the future by the authors, but due to limitations of this paper won't be further discussed here.

5   Conclusion and Future Work

The paper provides the definition of a graph-based framework for collective description. Moreover, a UML class diagram was provided for the possible implementation of the system. The authors not only defined the boundaries to represent the crowd with graph theory but also discussed various metrics' types to assess its properties. It is not easy to identify the features of collective that would provide valuable output. According to the authors, the use of the proposed framework will make it easier, as it gives common ground to relate different collectives to each other. In this paper, only the taxonomy of metrics was defined with no reference to actual functions or their values. That topic will be a subject of future works, along with the guideline how to understand values calculated for each of the metrics.

References

1. Bates, T.C., Gupta, S.: Smart groups of smart people: evidence for IQ as the origin of collective intelligence in the performance of human groups. Intelligence **60**, 46–56 (2017)
2. Chatterjee, S., Seneta, E.: Towards consensus: some convergence theorems on repeated averaging. J. Appl. Probab. **14**(1), 89–97 (1977)

3. Cowan, R., Jonard, N.: The dynamics of collective invention. J. Econ. Behav. Organ. **52**(4), 513–532 (2003)
4. DeGroot, M.H.: Reaching a consensus. J. Am. Stat. Assoc. **69**(345), 118–121 (1974)
5. DeMarzo, P.M., Vayanos, D., Zwiebel, J.: Persuasion bias, social influence, and unidimensional opinions. Q. J. Econ. **118**(3), 909–968 (2003)
6. Golub, B., Jackson, M.O.: Naive learning in social networks and the wisdom of crowds. Am. Econ. J. Microecon. **2**(1), 112–149 (2010)
7. Lévy, P.: From social computing to reflexive collective intelligence: The IEML research program. Inf. Sci. **180**(1), 71–94 (2010)
8. Lorenz, J.: A stabilization theorem for dynamics of continuous opinions. Physica A Stat. Mech. Appl. **355**(1), 217–223 (2005)
9. Malone, T.W., Bernstein, M.S.: Handbook of Collective Intelligence. MIT Press, Cambridge (2015)
10. Nurmi, H.: Some properties of the Lehrer-Wagner method for reaching rational consensus. Synthese **62**(1), 13–24 (1985)
11. Palak, R., Nguyen, N.T.: Prediction markets as a vital part of collective intelligence. In: 2017 IEEE International Conference on INnovations in Intelligent SysTems and Applications (INISTA), pp. 137–142. IEEE (2017)
12. Palak, R., Nguyen, N.T.: An independence measure for expert collections based on social media profiles. In: Nguyen, N.T., Gaol, F.L., Hong, T.-P., Trawiński, B. (eds.) ACIIDS 2019. LNCS (LNAI), vol. 11432, pp. 15–25. Springer, Cham (2019). https://doi.org/10.1007/978-3-030-14802-7_2
13. Pereira, C., Sousa, C., Lucas Soares, A.: A socio-semantic approach to collaborative domain conceptualization. In: Meersman, R., Herrero, P., Dillon, T. (eds.) OTM 2009. LNCS, vol. 5872, pp. 524–533. Springer, Heidelberg (2009). https://doi.org/10.1007/978-3-642-05290-3_66
14. Schmitt, F.F.: Consensus, respect, and weighted averaging. Synthese **62**(1), 25–46 (1985)
15. Surowiecki, J.: The Wisdom of Crowds. Anchor (2005)
16. Wagner, C.: Consensus through respect: a model of rational group decision-making. Philos. Stud. **34**(4), 335–349 (1978)
17. Woolley, A.W., Chabris, C.F., Pentland, A., Hashmi, N., Malone, T.W.: Evidence for a collective intelligence factor in the performance of human groups. Science **330**(6004), 686–688 (2010)

Towards the Pattern-Based Transformation of SBVR Models to Association-Oriented Models

Marcin Jodłowiec[✉] and Marcin Pietranik

Faculty of Computer Science and Management,
Wrocław University of Science and Technology, Wrocław, Poland
{marcin.jodlowiec,marcin.pietranik}@pwr.edu.pl

Abstract. The following research paper deals with the issue of automatic modeling of information systems models based on requirements. The requirements of information systems can be defined in different manner, e.g. in natural language or some formal, or semi-formal language. We have shown the assumptions for the approach, which employs patterns defined in SBVR metamodel and results with AOM models.

1 Introduction

The following paper signalizes the possible approach to a the problem of automatic modeling of IT systems models based on requirements. The requirements of information systems can be defined in different manner, e.g. in natural language or more formally in the form of Semantics of Business Vocabulary and Rules (SBVR), which is the standard proposed by Object Management Group (OMG) [14]. These requirements may apply to the business logic layer and other layers of the IT system, including the data storage layer, or the user interface.

The improvement of effectiveness of this process should focus on its automation, which will improve both the effectiveness and the quality of developed information system. The most important motivation for undertaking this topic is the desire for improving of the effectiveness of the implementation of the requirements while modeling information systems. *Effectiveness* is here understood as productivity of transition from the system requirements to the model stage and also the level of compatibility of requirements with modeled system. Productivity is the crucial element of engineering practice and decides about real costliness of produced software. In particular, it can be applied to the number of resources involved in given time range. The complexity of built information systems successively increases. This is due to more developed requirements, but also due to increasing possibilities in terms of modeling, design and implementation. Thus, effectiveness of the requirement realization becomes more and more practically important both from the quality point of view and the software development economics.

The undertaken research problem can be defined as the development of the automatic translation method, which converts the requirements into model.

© Springer Nature Switzerland AG 2019
N. T. Nguyen et al. (Eds.): ICCCI 2019, LNAI 11683, pp. 79–90, 2019.
https://doi.org/10.1007/978-3-030-28377-3_7

An important assumption is that the target model should be implementable, i.e. would not be only conceptual description of reality, but also a model, which can be directly implemented in given environment. Therefore, the Association-Oriented Metamodel (AOM) has been chosen as the model layer. Each and every modeling level is realized within the AOM without the necessity of transformation between different kinds of metamodel.

This assumption arises from the will to avoid the problem connected with the loss of change of semantic information while transition between the metamodels, e.g. Entity-Relationship Model (ER) [2] ↦ Relational Database Model (RDB) [3], Unified Modeling Language (UML) ↦ RDB, ER ↦ UML, etc. Preservation of the original semantics enclosed within the requirement and constraint specification is crucial for the following research. It will be the basis for the evaluation of the quality of developed translation methods. The other important issue is the automation of this process, which has a huge impact on the efficiency of modeling as well as its precision. We understand precise modeling as modeling without errors or mistakes based on poor understanding or avoidance of some requirements or constrains. Another advantage is formalization of requirements and constraints, which is provided by SBVR.

The choice of SBVR as the language of requirement and constraint definition guarantees the freedom of their specification. The formal character of this standard also simplifies the automation of translation process to the system model. SBVR is a standard defined by the recognized organization OMG. Despite the formalization, SBVR gives the huge freedom of expression construction.

AOM has been chosen as the language for domain modeling, because it meets the following four assumed basic properties: *Implementability*, *Unambiguity*, *Semantic capacity* and *Expressiveness*. This notions are understood as follows: *Implementability* – this means the possibility to create native, physical data sets without translation to other metamodels without any simplifications and with preservation of all the properties and mechanisms occurring at the conceptual and logical level. This is important feature from the point of view of further transformations of a model and hence change or loss of semantics included in the requirements and constraints. *Unambiguity* means the cardinality of the ways of interpretation of metamodel categories and particular elements of grammatical constructions. If a metamodel contains this feature, it can be easily used as a source model for building an algorithm that transforms unambiguous set of templates to unambiguous set of design patterns. *Semantic capacity* means the cardinality of the set of the thought concepts, which can be presented in the form of categories and grammatical constructions of a metamodel. This allows for representation of the widest possible range of simple and complex conceptual constructions expressed using e.g. natural language or SBVR. The term *Expressiveness* is understood as the level of complexity of thought constructions being modeled relative to the level of complexity of metamodel's grammatical constructions. It provides brevity of developed design patterns. The project referred here as AOM is the generalization of database-related project created under the name Associaton-Oriented Database Metamodel (AODB) [7].

AOM is the area of application of AODB in terms of information system domain modeling. The discussed issue concerns the requirements defined according to the OMG SBVR standard regarding the information model. The research objective is to develop and implement a method for automatic conversion of requirements given in SBVR language into elements of association-oriented modeling. It is assumed that the input information will be SBVR expressions, while the result will be data structures, data and query language expressions in the AOM [5,7], as well as the general purpose programming language code.

2 Related Work

The concept of SBVR-based transformation has been used in numerous approaches for various phases of model-based software development processes. The SBVR standard was developed from 2003 until 2008, when OMG proposed its 1.0 version. The issue of business dictionaries mapping formalized in SBVR is an active one and eagerly undertaken by researchers, mainly in the field of transformation between the various Model-Driven Architecture (MDA) components developed by OMG. The literature on the subject provides achievements in the field of the use and mapping from and to the SBVR language of various models in the following areas: generating UML diagrams [15], including the following: class diagrams [12,16], activity diagrams [12,16], sequence diagrams [16], generating UML diagrams annotated with Object Constraint Language (OCL) expressions [12]. generating database models [13] and supporting the creation of business process models in Business Process Model and Notation (BPMN) [18].

Another interesting field of research is the acquisition of formalized rules in the form of SBVR from natural language [11]. SBVR is also used in contemporary model-driven methods in regard to automatic mapping of requirements between Use Case UML diagrams and semi-natural language [17].

The subject of the transformation of the Business Model to Platform Independent Model (PIM), and consequently to Platform Specific Model (PSM) was described by Linehan in [10] while working on the SBVR standard itself. Linehan describes the framework for the Model-Driven Business Transformation (MDBT) methodology developed at BM TJ Watson Research Center, which aims to create executable implementations from business models. The methodology assumes using a tool that supports the definition of rules to avoid ambiguity in the grammatical analysis of natural language. The transformation uses, among others, rules written in RuleML [1], while Linehan only specifies UML artifacts that should be created, i.e. class diagrams, state machine diagrams and use case diagrams, along with pre-conditions expressed in OCL. In 2008, Linehan defined a method to map SBVR expressions to use cases based on the analysis of specific types of SBVR rules.

An interesting scientific achievement in the field of transformation of SBVR business design to UML models is the methodology proposed by Raj in [16]. Raj used a vocabulary and rules written in SBVR to automate the creation of structural and behavioral models expressed in the UML metamodel: activity diagrams, sequence diagrams and class diagrams. The basis of his approach is the distinction, which rules are imperative and express the layer of algorithms formalized as activity diagrams. The methodology distinguishes two types of support for mapping behavioral (operational) rules: automated – no rules are processed entirely by the IT system, without user intervention, supported – the system provides only support for rule processing. The creation of activity diagrams is based on the detection of activity based on the appropriate, logical formulation of rules in the form of if-then rule or the Event-Condition-Action scheme, what leads to appropriate processing by the Rule Sequencing Engine. The creation of sequence diagrams is based on checking generated activity diagrams, extracting sent messages from the rules and determining who is the sender and the recipient of this message. The approach does not involve the detection of actors, but a lexical analysis of the activity from which objects sending messages are extracted. The creation of class diagrams is based on the use of the SBVR $\mapsto$ UML-CD transformation methods specified in the SBVR specification for extracting class and instance names, attributes, generalization-specialization relationships. In addition, Raj's methodology defines mapping rules for class functions and binary associations, including their multiplicities.

An important contribution for transformation of SBVR expressions into UML and OCL is VeTIS tool [12]. This tool allows for direct mapping of SBVR structural rules into UML class diagrams and operational rules into UML operations. Moreover, modal rules (both aletic and deontic) are transformed into OCL constraints. However, the VeTIS methodology recommends independent definition of business process logic in form of e.g. UML activity diagrams or BPMN diagrams. Usage of SBVR should be only the support for this process.

3   Association-Oriented Modeling

The research on AOM and hence effective association-oriented modeling come from years of work in the field of knowledge representation system named Semantic Knowledge Base (SKB) [9]. While creation of SKB's model many modeling approaches have been utilized, including relational modeling, object-oriented modeling, entity-relationship modeling, but each of them have been problematic in terms of precise expression of model's semantics. As a result, it was decided to create new data metamodel, which would contain a number of needed properties as follows: full separation of categories representing data and categories representing relationships, independent inheritance within data containers and relationship containers taking into consideration rights to fulfill roles, full unambiguity of metamodel categories, i.e. to one modeling function corresponds only one category and vice versa, virtuality within inherited components, full support (implementational) for relationships of any arity.

AOM [5,7] is a novel solution which benefits for modeling database layer for complex systems, which require rich semantics in the database model, including knowledge representation systems. It enables modeling in the conceptual and physical level in the same metamodel, using the same set of concepts.

AOM helps to define semantics-rich database models, i.a. by complex definition of relationship roles, which contain many mechanisms offloading the system logic.

Precise metamodel description in terms of abstract and concrete syntax, semantics and comparison with such database metamodel solutions as *relational model, (extended) enity relationship model* and *object model* has been carried out in [5,6].

3.1 Aspects of Association-Oriented Database Metamodel

Below is a brief description of AOM concepts that should help the reader to understand foundations of the AODB metastructure.

The database (*Db*) consists of list of collections (*Coll*) and list of associations (*Assoc*). Intensionally, association contains a set of roles (*Role*). Moreover, it has the reference to a describing collection (*Coll*). Furthermore, both association (*Assoc*) and collection (*Coll*) are generalized to abstract basenodes (*BaseNode*) and have name, information about abstractness, navigability and inheritance. Role (*Role*) has name, information about virtuality, navigability, directionality, multiplicities, compositionality (lifetime dependency between relationship and relationship participant), uniqueness, describing collection (*Coll*) and type of participants, i.e. elements that can be role's (*Role*) destination. Role (*Role*) is anchored in association (*Assoc*), which is its owner. Collection (*Coll*) comprise a set of attributes (*Attr*). Attribute (*Attr*) has name, information about virtuality, inheritability, type and cardinality of elements and default value. Object (*Obj*) is built of values. Furthermore, it contains unique invariant identifier. Association object (*AssocObj*) contains a set of role objects (*RoleObj*), reference to describing object (*Obj*) and unique invariant identifier. Role object (*RoleObj*) contains set of references to database elements ((*Obj*) or (*AssocObj*)) and reference to describing object (*Obj*).

4   Basic Reality Description Patterns

Basic patterns are elementary meta-structures expressing fundamental methods of conceptualizing the reality. They are reflected in various metamodels of databases, including AOM, at the same time being defined in a high level of abstraction. Some already identified basic patterns are explained in the Table 1. The third column contains the AOM formal expressions. The description of its syntax as well the syntax of modelling language can be found in the publications [5].

Dedicated patterns are characteristic constructions for association-oriented modeling. Unlike basic patterns, their pragmatics cannot be considered beyond the AOM. The example of AOM dedicated design pattern is Bicompositive Association-Collection Tandem (BACT) [4] (Fig. 6), witch can be used to express the structure for complex entities, that is such entities, which both define and store data as well as store relationships within other entities. The other example

Table 1. Basic data modeling patterns and their association-oriented representations

Pattern name	Description	AOM generic pattern
List	Connection of two element types, where one of them is grouping and the other is grouped element (Fig. 1)	$\diamond List \overset{+E}{\bullet\!-\!} \left(\diamond E \overset{+E}{\bullet\!-\!\blacklozenge} \square E \right)$
Dictionary	Models a reference of one entity to the entity of different kind in order to minimize the redundancy in reality description (Fig. 2)	$\diamond Dict \left\{ \begin{array}{l} \overset{+Dict}{\bullet\!-\!\longrightarrow} \square Dict \\ \overset{+E}{\bullet\!-\!} \square E \end{array} \right.$
Gen-spec	Models a situation, when elements of one type are also elements of other type (Fig. 3)	$\square Spec \overset{a^+ f^v}{\longrightarrow} \square Gen$
Autoreference	Models a relationship in which entities are connected with other entities of the same type (Fig. 4, described in [8])	$\diamond E \overset{+E}{\bullet\!-\!} \diamond E$
n-ary relationship	Models a connection of many element types, avoids the necessity of creating artificial binary relationships (Fig. 5, technique described in [5])	$\diamond R \left\{ \begin{array}{l} \overset{+E_1}{\bullet\!-\!} \diamond E_1 \\ \overset{+E_2}{\bullet\!-\!} \diamond E_2 \\ \overset{+E_3}{\bullet\!-\!} \diamond E_3 \end{array} \right.$

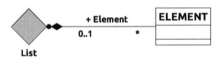

Fig. 1. The *List* pattern in AOM

Fig. 2. The *Dictionary* pattern in AOM

of AOM dedicated pattern is Association Complex (AC) [4], which allows to create structures forming complex relationships in terms of their composition and polymorphic character. These patterns have been used in various association-oriented models, including Extended Semantic Networks Module of SKB [9].

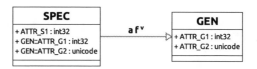

Fig. 3. The *Gen-spec* pattern in AOM

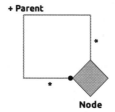

Fig. 4. The *Autoreference* pattern in AOM

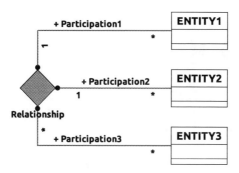

Fig. 5. The *n-ary relationship* pattern in AOM

5   Transformation Framework

In the conducted studies on association-oriented modeling, patterns (both basic and dedicated) are understood as the basic semantic unit of models. This means that, in the applicant's perspective, models are conceptualized to form assemblies of patterns, and other grammatical elements of a metamodel should be considered only as a last resort, or in a situation where two pattern instances

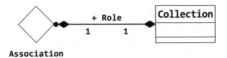

Fig. 6. BACT association-oriented design pattern

are required to glue together. Such an assumption during the methodology development allows to automate the activities related to the design and to provide a higher level of modeling abstraction. Modeling person should only focus on conceptions that should be modeled, and the way it will be implemented should only in the background. This approach was assumed both for issues related to modeling and transformation between different data metamodels. Therefore, some formalization regarding to translation process has been made. This involved the necessity to define formalisms for such terms as the mapping pattern, the mapping convention and the data model translation itself. The P mapping pattern is a mapping that allows you to map the structural elements of a source metamodel to the structural elements in the target metamodel, such that:

$$P : E_{M_{src}} \mapsto E_{M_{trg}}, E_M = K_M \cup S_M, \tag{1}$$

where: K_M – set of all syntactical categories of M metamodel, S_M – set of all grammatical constructions possible to create over M metamodel, E_M – set of all structural elements of M metamodel, M_{scr} – source data metamodel, M_{trg} – target data metamodel.

Based on the mapping pattern, one can determine the mapping convention C, that means set of mapping patterns that is sufficient enough to project any model expressed in source metamodel to the model expressed within target metamodel.

$$C_{M_{src} \mapsto M_{trg}} = \{P_1, P_2, \ldots, P_n\} \tag{2}$$

The translation T is an operation that transforms source model into target model according to defined convention.

$$m_{src} \overset{C_{M_{src} \mapsto M_{trg}}}{\longmapsto} m_{trg}, \tag{3}$$

where: $m_{src} \in S_{M_{src}}$ – data model in source metamodel, $m_{trg} \in S_{M_{trg}}$ – data model in target metamodel.

These results constitute an important foundation for further work, as they form the basic structures and theory that stands behind association-oriented modeling. The structures such as presented above will be the target structures for the definition of mapping convention $C_{SBVR \mapsto AOM}$.

6   Methodology

The first step is to provide the conceptualization of modeling reality. The purpose of this analysis is to identify techniques and ways to describe the complexity of the world. In particular, a few modeling languages such as ORM, EER and UML have been analyzed at all levels of abstraction in order to specify and unify elementary and complex thought concepts for modeling (Fig. 7). Examples of thought concepts may be the concept of a relationship, and in the further consequence multiplicity of relationship, navigability, lifetime dependency, etc. The diagram is an effect of the analysis and represents the a coherent and possibly the most complementary ontology describing possible ways of data modeling ontology with the mutual relations between the extracted modeling concepts have been developed.

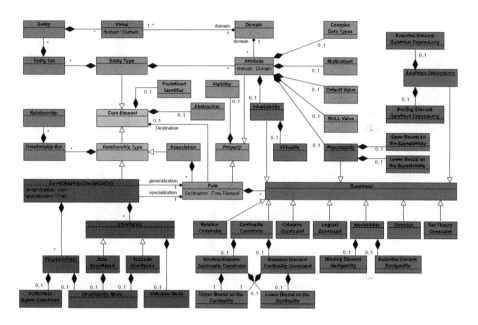

Fig. 7. UML class diagram depicting modeling concepts

Next step will consist of transforming the modeling concepts specified in previous step into the form of templated expressions in SBVR language. The methodology of building templates will be based on elementary constructions E comprising at least two concepts playing specific roles in a given relationships. The following E tuples will be considered:

$$E = (R, \{(\rho_1, C_1), \ldots, (\rho_n, C_n)\}), \tag{4}$$

where $n \geq 2$ and R represents a relationship, ρ_i – a role within relationship, C_i – a concept, and $i = 1..n$, n is the relationship arity. Due to formalism applied to the description of ontology (UML), the concepts will be represented as classes, roles as association ends and relationships as associations. For instance, taking into consideration thought conception of generalization, one can distinguish the concepts of two entities ($entity$) playing roles of (gen) and ($spec$) respectively, which are linked by the relationship ($genspec$) making a tuple:

$$E_{genspec} = (genspec, \{(gen, entity), (spec, entity)\}).\qquad(5)$$

Each of the tuples of the form (4) will be transformed into one template T. The template T will be parameterizable with n concrete terms $t_1, t_2, \ldots, t_n$, $n > 0$ comprising a tuple of placeholders in terms of template definition. Taking the above into consideration, the creation of SBVR template will be the mapping $TemplateCreation$ defined as follows:

$$TemplateCreation : E \mapsto T(t_1, t_2, \ldots, t_n).\qquad(6)$$

In the next step the two types of patterns will be prepared: association-oriented design patterns $PaternAOM_i$, $i = 1..m$ and mapping patterns P_i, $i = 1..m$. Despite the common $pattern$ member in its name, these two are different types of patterns. The first are the generic reusable parametrizable structures of AOM, which solve specific well-defined problem, while the latter will describe how to map sets of SBVR templates $\{T_1, T_2, \ldots, T_n\}$, $n > 0$ into the form of association-oriented design patterns.

$$P_i : \{T_1, T_2, \ldots, T_n\} \mapsto PatternAOM_i.\qquad(7)$$

According to the expression (2), the set comprising each developed mapping pattern $\{P_1, P_2, \ldots, P_n\}$ will be the mapping convention $C_{SBVR \mapsto AOM}$ defined as follows:

$$C_{SBVR \mapsto AOM} = \{P_1, P_2, \ldots, P_n\}.\qquad(8)$$

Determination of each of the SBVR expression template set $\{T_1, T_2, \ldots, T_n\}$ will begin with the choice of some pivotal T_k. The choice will follow the analysis of the UML class diagram from the Fig. 7 and applicant's own experience in the field of modeling information systems. In the next step the grammatical construction of AOM metamodel will be found and selected to correspond to the chosen template. In general, one has to assume that the construction will require more AOM elements. By the method of iteration and mutual adjustation of the set of templates and newly created or existing association-oriented design pattern. This template set $\longleftrightarrow$ association-oriented pattern adjustment will be based on the completing both the set of templates as well as constructing or reconstructing the association-oriented pattern so that they would be compatible from the semantics point of view and at the same time would solve one and only one elementary modeling issue.

The verification of the methodology and tools will be carried out i.a. while the seminars with the participation of experts from the area of data and knowledge modeling in a broad sense. For each of the developed patterns the discussion will be carried out which aims to determine, whether given pattern realizes each of the assumptions of thought constructions, which are the base of its creation.

Within the next step the mapping convention $C_{SBVR \mapsto AOM}$ according to the Eq. (8) will be determined. Whereas within the previous step, the algorithms that allow to utilize these mappings the will be developed. For each of the sets comprising templates of requirements and constraints and corresponding AOM pattern the consecutive steps of the procedure realizing the mapping will be settled.

The first step of the process is to define the meaning of semantics and the semantics loss in context of the expression templates and patterns within considered metamodels. The next step is the development of evaluation method by the specification of the metrics by which the quality of requirement and constraints realization will be measured. This metrics will be elaborated by the definition of the feature space, which describe the quality of transformations and the distance measure of specific transformations. Evaluation studies will be based on the classification of the methods of translation according to their quality understood in the sense of minimization of the semantics loss.

7   Conclusions

In this paper we have presented the issue of transformation of SBVR models to AOM models. To achieve the described main research objective, the specific research will be needed:

1. formulation of generalized modeling methods in the form of grammatical structures SBVR describing requirements and constraints by developing templates of expressions,
2. elaboration of semantically equivalent grammatical constructions of Association-Oriented Metamodel for constructed SBVR expression templates by development of association-oriented design patterns, which are semantically compatible with SBVR expression templates,
3. ensuring the possibility of automatic translation of SBVR expression templates to the form of association-oriented design patterns realized by the development of algorithms transforming specific expressions into the elements of information system model,
4. evaluation of transformation quality realized by definition of metrics allowing the determination the extent to which the set of expressions has been transformed into association-oriented design patterns.

References

1. Boley, H., Tabet, S., Wagner, G.: Design rationale of RuleML: a markup language for semantic web rules. In: Proceedings of the First International Conference on Semantic Web Working, SWWS 2001, pp. 381–401. CEUR-WS.org, Aachen, Germany (2001). http://dl.acm.org/citation.cfm?id=2956602.2956628
2. Chen, P.P.S.: The entity-relationship model - toward a unified view of data. ACM Trans. Database Syst. **1**(1), 9–36 (1976). https://doi.org/10.1145/320434.320440. http://doi.acm.org/10.1145/320434.320440
3. Codd, E.F.: A relational model of data for large shared data banks. Commun. ACM **13**(6), 377–387 (1970)

4. Jodłowiec, M.: Complex relationships modeling in association-oriented database metamodel. In: Nguyen, N.T., Hoang, D.H., Hong, T.-P., Pham, H., Trawiński, B. (eds.) ACIIDS 2018. LNCS (LNAI), vol. 10752, pp. 46–56. Springer, Cham (2018). https://doi.org/10.1007/978-3-319-75420-8_5

5. Krótkiewicz, M.: Association-oriented database model - n-ary associations. Int. J. Softw. Eng. Knowl. Eng. **27**(2), 281–320 (2017). https://doi.org/10.1142/S0218194017500103

6. Krotkiewicz, M.: Formal definition and modelling language of association-oriented database metamodel (AssoBase). Vietnam J. Comput. Sci. (2018). https://doi.org/10.1142/s2196888819500052

7. Krótkiewicz, M.: A novel inheritance mechanism for modeling knowledge representation systems. Comput. Sci. Inf. Syst. **15**(1), 51–78 (2018). http://doiserbia.nb.rs/Article.aspx?id=1820-02141700046K

8. Krótkiewicz, M., Jodłowiec, M.: Modeling autoreferential relationships in association-oriented database metamodel. In: Świątek, J., Borzemski, L., Wilimowska, Z. (eds.) ISAT 2017. AISC, vol. 656, pp. 49–62. Springer, Cham (2018). https://doi.org/10.1007/978-3-319-67229-8_5

9. Krótkiewicz, M., Jodłowiec, M., Wojtkiewicz, K.: Semantic networks modeling with operand-operator structures in association-oriented metamodel. In: Nguyen, N.T., Papadopoulos, G.A., Jędrzejowicz, P., Trawiński, B., Vossen, G. (eds.) ICCCI 2017. LNCS (LNAI), vol. 10448, pp. 24–33. Springer, Cham (2017). https://doi.org/10.1007/978-3-319-67074-4_3

10. Linehan, M.H.: SBVR use cases. In: Bassiliades, N., Governatori, G., Paschke, A. (eds.) RuleML 2008. LNCS, vol. 5321, pp. 182–196. Springer, Heidelberg (2008). https://doi.org/10.1007/978-3-540-88808-6_20

11. Mickeviciute, E., Butleris, R., Gudas, S., Karciauskas, E.: Transforming BPMN 2.0 Business Process Model into SBVR Business Vocabulary and Rules, pp. 360–371 (2017)

12. Nemuraite, L., Skersys, T.: VETIS tool for editing and transforming SBVR business vocabularies and business rules into UML&OCL models. In: 16th International Conference on Information and Software Technologies, pp. 377–384. Kaunas University of Technology, Kaunas (2010)

13. Njonko, P.B.F., El Abed, W.: From natural language business requirements to executable models via SBVR. In: 2012 International Conference on Systems and Informatics, ICSAI 2012 (ICSAI), pp. 2453–2457 (2012). https://doi.org/10.1109/ICSAI.2012.6223550

14. OMG: Object Management Group, Semantics Of Business Vocabulary And Rules 1.4 (2014). http://www.omg.org/spec/SBVR/1.4/

15. OMG: Object Management Group, Unified Modeling Language (UML) superstructure version 2.5 (2015). http://www.omg.org/spec/UML/2.5/

16. Raj, A., Prabhakar, T.V., Hendryx, S.: Transformation of SBVR business design to UML models. In: Business, pp. 29–38 (2008). https://doi.org/10.1145/1342211.1342221, http://portal.acm.org/citation.cfm?doid=1342211.1342221

17. Skersys, T., Danenas, P., Butleris, R.: Extracting SBVR business vocabularies and business rules from UML use case diagrams. J. Syst. Softw. **141**, 111–130 (2018). https://doi.org/10.1016/j.jss.2018.03.061

18. Skersys, T., Tutkute, L., Butleris, R.: The enrichment of BPMN business process model with SBVR business vocabulary and rules. J. Comput. Inf. Technol. **20**(3), 143–150 (2012). https://doi.org/10.2498/cit.1002090

Social Networks and Recommender Systems

Twitter User Modeling Based on Indirect Explicit Relationships for Personalized Recommendations

Abdullah Alshammari$^{(\boxtimes)}$, Stelios Kapetanakis$^{(\boxtimes)}$,
Nikolaos Polatidis$^{(\boxtimes)}$, Roger Evans$^{(\boxtimes)}$, and Gharbi Alshammari$^{(\boxtimes)}$

School of Computing, Engineering and Mathematics,
University of Brighton, Brighton, UK
{A.Alshammaril, S.Kapetanakis, N.Polatidis,
R.P.Evans, g.alshammari}@brighton.ac.uk

Abstract. Information overload has increased due to social network website use in recent times. Social media has increased the popularity of websites such as Twitter. It is believed that a rich environment is provided through Twitter whereby information sharing will be able to aid in recommender system research. This paper will focus upon Twitter user modeling through the utilization of indirect explicit relationships that exist amongst users. The further aim of this paper is to ensure that personal profiles are built via the use of information that will be sourced from Twitter so as to provide recommendations that are more accurate. The proposed method adopts Twitter user's indirect explicit relationships in order to get information which is vital in the process of building personal user profiles. The proposed method has been validated through the implementation of an offline evaluation using real data. Proposed user profiles' performances have been compared with each other and against the baseline profile. The performance of this has been validated using real data and is both practical and effective.

Keywords: Recommender systems · User modeling · User profiling · Explicit relationships · Twitter

1 Introduction

Real-time web is rising as a technology or platform that enables users to share information and communicate in different contexts like Twitter, which is one of the most popular micro-blogging platforms today [16]. It is used by millions of people around the world. Through this platform, users are able to share short messages, up to 280 characters in length, referred to as tweets [16]. It is a very popular means of sharing information as well as effectively reaching a wide audience. It can also be considered as a distinctive shaper of social network platforms because it presents relationships between users based on a review strategy. This platform makes it very different in comparison to other reciprocal social networking platforms such as Facebook. Relationships between Twitter users can either be informational (i.e., reading news) or social (i.e., interacting with friends). Also, users can follow other users in order to

© Springer Nature Switzerland AG 2019
N. T. Nguyen et al. (Eds.): ICCCI 2019, LNAI 11683, pp. 93–105, 2019.
https://doi.org/10.1007/978-3-030-28377-3_8

receive informational posts [1]. The features of Twitter make it useful as a major source for the modeling of users involved in networks characterized by interactions and relationships [1, 17].

Researchers in [1] have demonstrated that Twitter is an important resource in regard to recommender systems, which are a powerful and integral part of the web as well as mobile applications. Such systems do have a primary objective, which is to ensure that context-aware, personalized, and real-time information is provided in order to raise sales as well as user satisfaction. Numerous researchers have exploited Twitter for modeling users, building user profiles, and recommending items in an accurate way such as building a profile based upon user tweets to recommend useful news. The usual way of building such a profile lacks up-to-date information about users' interests. The authors in [4] have solved this problem by using friends' recent tweets to enhance the user's profile with up-to-date information.

This paper is focused on modeling Twitter users through the exploitation of relationships with the aim of enhancing recommendations in the recommender systems. It is an extension of the previous work of the researchers of this paper [4] which was focused on direct explicit relationships (friends' accounts only), whereas this paper focuses on indirect explicit relationships. Indirect explicit relationships contain accounts that the user receives in their tweets from outside the friends list, such as friends of friends. Proposed profiles will contain tweets from these accounts for a period of 2 weeks (short-term profiles) to make sure that profiles contain recent activity that reflects users' interests. The methodology will contain a user profile designed or built from accounts that are outside the user's friends list. The proposed model makes use of the influence rule put forth in the authors' previous work [4], which will be explained generally in the following section. The influence rule will be used for the identification of influential friends. Therefore, their tweets will be used in the building of the user profile via an examination of each tweet received within the last two weeks (short-term). In light of the presented methodology, the following suppositions are made:

- We propose a method that builds user profiles from the tweets of accounts that have indirect explicit relationships with the user.
- The proposed method has been experimentally evaluated using a real dataset, well-known metrics, and against a baseline; thus, the recommendations delivered are more accurate compared to the baseline.

The rest of the paper is constructed as follows: Sect. 2 delivers the related work, Sect. 3 presents the proposed method, Sect. 4 explains the experimental evaluation and Sect. 5 contains the conclusions.

2   Related Work

A method proposed by the authors in [11] was utilized so that a recommender system is designed based on tweets from Twitter to ensure that the accuracy of recommended news articles is improved. In order to build the user profile, the nouns were extracted from the user's tweets as well as retweets. The results indicated that the recommendations (Twitter activity-based) seem to be more accurate when compared to random recommendations. The authors in [8] also proposed TRUPI system that combined the user's tweets history with social features. Also, the system tried to identify the dynamic interest of the user on various topics and to measure how the interest of the user will change over a given period of time.

Temporal dynamics (in profiles of Twitter) were analysed by the researchers in [1] to understand personalized recommendations. The profiles that they built were based on entities (celebrities and places) and hashtags. Variables that were taken into consideration are enrichments (use of external resources like Wikipedia) and user's activity. Results revealed that entity-based profiles, which were built through the use of short-term time (recent activities) as well as enrichment, perform much better compared to other profile types. However, there is a problem in that a number of users lack sufficient data to enable the creation of reliable user profiles. In the research of [12], the authors identified that applying a decay function on long-term profiles, which gives more weight value to recent or newer topics than older topics of interests, showed much better performance in delivering recommendations when compared to long-term profiles not using this function. Also, the researchers in [2] have previously shown that short-term profiles are superior to complete profiles.

A major solution can be enacted through the enrichment of a user profile with other data. Twitter user profiles were modeled by the authors in the study of [2] using various dimensions. Each of their qualities was compared, including the enrichment dimension. The outcomes indicated that utilizing external resources, news articles for instance, seem to be much better than compared to reliance only on Twitter data.

User profile enrichment has been carried out in various ways. These can be done using textual external resources or by exploiting tweets' URLs. Through the exploitation URLs from tweets, a Cat stream system was proposed by [9] which used traditional classification techniques in profiling users of Twitter. It concentrated only on URLs attached in tweets. However, this system is not appropriate for users who do not provide a sufficient number of tweets that contain URLs. A group of tweets was categorised by the authors in [3] as interesting or uninteresting. This categorisation was done through the use of crowd sourcing. This method showed that a URL link's existence is a feature which is successful when it comes to the selection of high accuracy interesting tweets. This factor has its own shortcoming, in that it may classify a tweet incorrectly when linked with un-useful content. Also, users normally do not post enough URLs in their tweets [10].

In regard to the external resources technique, it has been shown by [1, 9] that profiles that included external resources outperformed those profiles which were built using just Twitter activity. As a result, there is an adequate supply of user profiles with more information, which can lead to an improvement in the recommender system accuracy. However, there is data gathered from external resources that will not be relevant to the interest of the user. This can negatively affect the recommender system's performance.

The relationship which exists amongst Twitter users is a field that is yet to be studied. Such research can help to ensure that a user is characterized, thereby improving the recommender system's performance based on profiles enriched by the tweets of others who participate in these relationships. It is very clear that any single user who tends to produce short-text data (retweets and tweets) can be modelled based on his behaviour and history through a collection of historical data (also known as timeline) that has been generated by the user himself. However, in order to provide enough information for building profiles, such a method needs a design system that reaches deeper into the past for data collection. Moreover, the collected information might be too out of date to be used in profiling as users' interests change. Also, the recent activities of most users do not have sufficient data or URL data to enrich their profiles from them. To address the problem of data shortage, the authors in [4] showed that direct explicit links between users should be used for the purpose of enriching the user profile. This finding will help expand the recent activities that are relevant. This method has an advantage, which is that profiles are built from activities that are more recent. Through this method, the recommender system's performance, which is based on these tweets, will be improved. This paper continues the exploration of these links between users within a network to improve the profile through exploiting indirect explicit relationships.

In order for the following links to be exploited, influential users will be gleaned from the user's friends of friends. The majority of research focuses on the influence of a particular user, which is based on that users popularity. This rate is indicated by the number of friends and followers of the user. How a user's interaction with others serves as an influence was also clarified in previous researches [5–7, 18]. Additionally, various Twitter influence measures were collected as well as classified from the literature in [13]. These studies explained that trying to deem someone as influential in a social network is a conceptual problem. They further stated that there is no agreement regarding who or what is an influential user. Subsequently, the authors in [4] argued that there is a need for creating a method which will be able to generate or produce an influence score based on the perspective of the normal user in relation to his or her interaction and behaviour. Their proposed influence score was higher when it identified influential friends of the user and then utilized those friends as a valuable source for building the user profile. As a result, more accurate recommendations were delivered.

3   Proposed Methodology

Generally, the recommender system consists of two phases: (1) user profiling and (2) item ranking. User profiles here are constructed as an extended version of our previous work [4]. Moreover, more resources will be identified through the indirect explicit relationships. The user's tweets will then be extracted and added to the profile. After that, and based on the user profile, recommendation items are ranked.

The general framework of our proposed approach is shown in Fig. 1. By using the Twitter API, the user's data is collected and then processed in order to identify influential friends and build the primary profile (STBLCinf) based on important keywords written by the user and his friends. This step is the basic idea in the previous work [4], and the proposed profiles in this approach will be an extended version of the STBLCinf profile. The steps of each phase will be explained in detail in the following subsections.

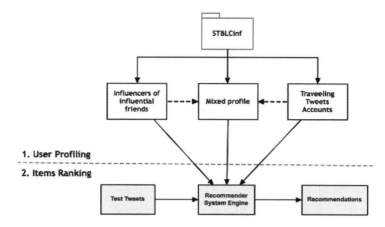

Fig. 1. The main stages of the proposed approach.

3.1 User Profiling

In this phase and in general, tweets that are posted by other users, those who have explicit relationships with the user (i.e., friends), are used in building the profiles. All profiles are built and represented by keywords (bag of words), while pre-processing is applied in order to filter tweets by extracting only important content. Tweets posted and re-tweeted by the user shows the user's interests. On the other hand, tweets received and collected via explicit relationships through the following of links require examination and classification in order to include them in the profiles.

In our previous work [4], the proposed influence score algorithm was able to identify the influential friends of the user and their tweets within a brief time, which are used in building the profile (STBLCinf profile). By exploiting the indirect explicit relationships, two different sources were used in this paper to build the user profile from namely influential friends of influential friends and accounts of travelling tweets. These profiles will be an extended version of the STBLCinf profile.

In inf of inf source and for each user in dataset, the timeline tweets, favourited tweets, and friends list are collected for each influential user in the friends list. Additionally, this information is collected for each influential friend. Then, the influence score is computed between the user and his friends in order to rank his friends based on their influence score and to identify those that are influential. Next, friends are clustered into three categories based on the K-means algorithm: influential, less influential, and non-influential friends. The tweets of influential friends will be added to the profile. While the tweets of non-influential friends will be excluded. Tweets of less influential friends will be classified into representative (re-tweetable) or not representative (not re-tweetable). As in our previous work in [4], the trained classifier that has the highest accuracy in the training set, and was used to classify tweets before, is used here to classify the tweets of less influential friends. Furthermore, various classifiers were used in training the labelled dataset that is built from the user's tweets. Thus, the tweets classified as representative (re-tweetable) are added to the tweets in the profile.

Algorithm 1. The steps of building the inf of inf profile

```
1:     Start with user
2:        Get influential friends of user
3:        For each influential friend
4:               Collect timeline tweets, favourite tweets and friends list
5:               Calculate influence score between him and his friends
6:               Cluster friends list based on influences score with K-means
7:               Collect short-term tweets of influential and less influential
8:               IF tweet is from "influential"
9:                      Store to the user profile
10:           ELSE
11:                  Classify tweet
12:                  IF tweet is classified as re-tweetable
13:                         Store tweet in user profile
14:                  ELSE
15:                         Exclude tweet
```

In the second source, travelling tweets accounts (TTA) are identified. This is done by extracting the accounts that appeared in the user timeline but are not in the user's friends list. Moreover, the user showed some interests by re-tweeting their tweets. After that, tweets from these accounts are collected within brief timespan. The same classifier is used here for classifying tweets into representative (re-tweetable) or not representative (not re-tweetable). The former tweets will be included in the user profile. By the end of this stage, three profiles are built in order to measure their efficiency in the recommender system, which are: inf of Inf, TTA, and the mixed profile (inf of inf + TTA).

Algorithm 2. The steps of building the TTA profile

```
1:     Start with user
2:        Extract accounts from the timeline
3:        For account in accounts:
4:               IF account is not in Friends list:
5:                  Collect short-term tweets
6:                  Classify tweets
7:                  IF tweet is classified as re-tweetable:
8:                         Store tweet in user profile
9:                  ELSE
10:                        Exclude tweet
```

3.2 Items Ranking

Recommendation items in this stage will be represented by those tweets which the user has shown interest in by retweeting. The model which will be used is Vector space representation since it will take recommendation items and the user profile as vectors. The angle which exists between them will then be computed.

In order to rank the various groups of tweets, user profiles that have been developed as explained in the former subsection will be used. All tweets inside the recommendation items will need to be evaluated based on how similar they are to user's profiles. Tweets will be excluded whenever the text contains less than 3 words. Lastly, the similarity score is computed through cosine similarity equation. Therefore, every recommendation item is ranked, and then the recommendation tweets are delivered to user.

4   Experimental Evaluation

For our proposed method's advantages to be validated, there is the implementation of the tweets recommender system. There was also the performing of the offline evaluation using some users. By using Twitter API, which can be found on the website's development section, the timelines of 40 users chosen at random were collected and examined. The dataset, which contains the 40 users, is balanced in terms of activity (active and less active users) and engagement (tweeters and re-tweeters). In the recommendation items, test tweets are collected from the user's timelines based on actions of interests that the user showed via re-tweeting. The following section explains the mechanism of collecting test tweets.

4.1   Experiment Setup

When the information is collected from the examined user's timeline, the dataset is split into three-time frames as it was done in previous work [4].

The tweets that are in the first timeframe (the last 2 weeks) will be used as test items (test tweets). The tweets that are from the second timeframe (between 2 and 4 weeks prior) will be used in building profiles from the mentioned resources. The third timeframe (more than 4 weeks prior) will be used alongside the second timeframe for computing the influence score generated from the influential friends' timelines. Additionally, information gathered from the timeline of the user during the set timeframe will be used in the machine learning classifiers.

Profiles: In this experiment, three profiles will be built, compared against each other, and compared against the profile created in the previous research [4] of the authors. All profiles were built within short-time frame. The profiles are:

- The influential tweets of friends (STBLCinf): This profile includes the timeline tweets, influential tweets, and less influential tweets that are classified as representative (re-tweetable). This profile is considered as the basis of our proposed method because the other profiles are extended versions of this one.
- Influential of influential (inf of inf): This profile includes all tweets from STBLCinf, tweets of influential friends of influential friends, and those classified as less influential friends of influential friends' tweets, which are considered as representative.

- Travelling Tweets Accounts (TTA): This profile contains all tweets from STBLCinf and the tweets from accounts of travelling tweets that are classified as representative.
- Mixed profile (inf of inf + TTA): this profile contains tweets of STBLCinf, inf of inf, and TTA.

Test tweets will be used for evaluating how accurate the recommender system is based on each proposed profile. They are collected from the first timeframe (the last 2 weeks) as clarified previously, and they will be utilized as recommendation items. Each tweet in the test tweets can be relevant or non-relevant. Relevant tweets are tweets that the user re-tweeted whereas the non-relevant tweets are tweets that the user did not show interest in by retweeting.

Evaluation Metrics: Offline evaluation has been used in measuring the accuracy of the recommender system using various profiles [15]. The built user profiles will be plugged into the same recommender system with the same test tweets in order to compare their performance. The metrics used in this study for measuring the system's performance accuracy are average of precision @k (P@k), average precision (AP), and mean average precision (MAP) [14]. Average of precision is used in measuring how good the system is in retrieving relevant items @k, and MAP is used in measuring how useful the system is for retrieving all items that are relevant in a good order. P@k is the amount of correct recommendations in the top-n list of recommendations and is defined in Eq. 1. AP is defined in Eq. 2 where p(k) is the precision @k and rel(k) is an indicator counting as 1 when the item is relevant or zero. Moreover, items not retrieved, but considered relevant, receive a score of zero. Lastly, MAP, which is defined in Eq. 3, has Q being a query and the equation returning the mean of the average precision scores for a set of queries.

$$P@k = \frac{relevant\ recommended\ items}{total\ recommended\ items} \tag{1}$$

$$AP = \frac{\sum_{k=1}^{n}(p(k) * rel(k))}{number\ of\ relevant\ recommendations} \tag{2}$$

$$MAP = \frac{\sum_{q=1}^{Q} AP(q)}{Q} \tag{3}$$

4.2 Results

In this subsection, the profiles that were built from tweets, and derive from different resources of the indirect explicit relationships of the examined user, will be compared against each other and the profile mentioned from the previous research in [4], which is the STBLCinf. The purpose of this step is to be able to determine which profile performs better and to ascertain the required scope for collecting relative tweets. Results from this stage have already been presented in the previously mentioned research. The tested values of k are from 1 to 10. In the metrics of the P@top-k recommendations, when the TTA and Inf of Inf were compared, the results show that the Inf of Inf profile outperformed the TTA profile in all P@top-10 recommendations. When both were compared to the mixed profile, which is TTA + Inf of Inf, results showed that the Inf of Inf profile outperformed the others 9 times in the top 10 recommendations. In contrast, the performance of the mixed profile was better than the TTA profile because it achieved a higher AP value 5 times at k = 1, 3, 8, 9 and 10. Moreover, the TTA profile achieved a higher AP value in only 3 instances. When all the profiles were compared against the baseline, which is STBLCinf, the results showed that the Inf of Inf profile performed better than other profiles, especially STBLCinf. In contrast, its performance was better in 5 of the top 10 recommendations whereas the STBLCinf was better 3 times. (See Fig. 2a).

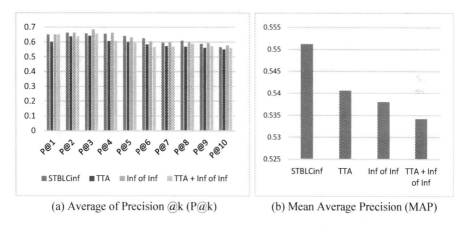

(a) Average of Precision @k (P@k)   (b) Mean Average Precision (MAP)

Fig. 2. Average of precision @k from 1 to 10 and the Mean average precision (MAP) of the profiles.

In the metric of MAP, the profiles were compared in order to see their overall performance in recommending all relative items. The results showed that the TTA profile achieved a higher MAP value than the Inf of Inf profile by 0.2%. The mixed profile achieved less MAP value than the TTA by 0.6% and less than the Inf of Inf by 0.4%. On the other side, the STBLCinf performance was compared to the profiles, and the results showed that it performed better than the TTA, Inf of Inf, and the mixed profile by 1%, 1.2%, and 1.6% respectively. (See Fig. 2b).

4.2.1   Dividing Dataset Based on Activity

The dataset is divided based on activity in order to see deeper analysis and to understand the results in an advanced way. The activity (engagement) of each user was computed using the equation below proposed by [16], which calculates how active a user has been on Twitter since joining.

$$Engagement(Activity) = \frac{Tweets + Retweets + Replies + Favourite}{Account\_Age} \qquad (4)$$

After calculating the activity, users in the dataset are ranked in ascending order based upon their activity scores. Then, they are divided into active and less active, each division having 20 users. In the less active user group, and using the metric of P@top-10 recommendations, Fig. 3a shows that the Inf of Inf profile outperformed the TTA and the TTA + Inf of Inf profiles 9 out of 10 recommendations. In comparison to the STBLCinf profile, the Inf of Inf profile achieved a higher AP value in 3 instance whereas the former achieved a better performance score in 4 instances. In comparison, the mixed profile was slightly better than the TTA profile in delivering related items in the top 10 recommendations. Also, both profiles achieved the lowest performance. In the MAP metric, the result was similar to the general evaluation before the dataset was divided. It showed that the profiles TTA, Inf of Inf, and TTA + Inf of Inf achieved a lower MAP value than the STBLCinf by 1.6%, 2.6%, and 3.1% respectively. (See Fig. 3b).

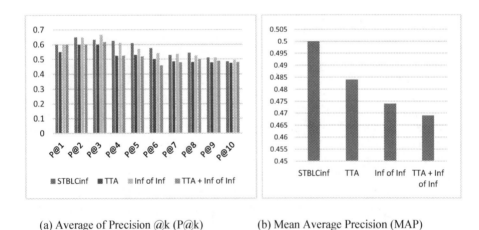

(a) Average of Precision @k (P@k)   (b) Mean Average Precision (MAP)

Fig. 3. Average of precision @k = 1–10 and the Mean average precision of the profiles of less active users in the dataset.

In the Active user group, the results clarified that the Inf of Inf profile outperformed all other profiles in 4 instances (See: Fig. 4a). Surprisingly, the STBLCinf profile did not outperform all the profiles in any of the k values. The TTA profile achieved the lowest AP in 4 instances. When the top 10 recommendations were delivered, results proved that the Inf of Inf profile was able to deliver related recommendations to the active users more accurately than the other profiles. In the MAP metric, surprisingly, the Inf of Inf profile achieved the highest value. Moreover, it was better than the STBLCinf. However, the TTA and TTA + Inf of Inf profiles achieved lower MAP values. This may prove that the Inf of Inf profile is more suitable for the active users than the less active users. (See Fig. 4b).

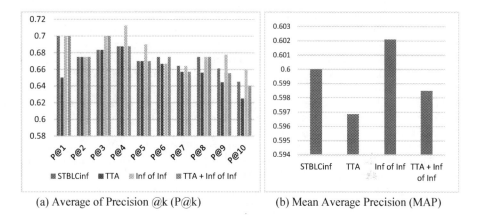

(a) Average of Precision @k (P@k)   (b) Mean Average Precision (MAP)

Fig. 4. P@k = 1–10 and MAP of the profiles of active users in the dataset.

5   Conclusion

In conclusion, this research proposed a new technique for building a user's profile based on exploiting the Twitter explicit links structure with the aim of improving the performance of recommender systems that are based on tweets. This innovative profile takes advantage of the links between a user and his or her friends in order to gather a tweets set within a brief timeframe and to utilize them in profile building. Moreover, the redefined influence rule in our previous work helped us to cluster friends of influential friends into three categories: influential, less influential, and non-influential. Consequently, tweets of influential users were added directly to the profile while tweets of non-influential users were excluded. Tweets of less influential users were classified, and the re-tweetable tweets were included in the created profile. An offline evaluation experiment was done by using a tweets-recommender system, which was used to validate the effectiveness of this proposed technique. Its effectiveness has been shown by comparing and testing it against the baseline profile built from the direct explicit relationships (STBLCinf). Therefore, the profile developed through proposed method was able to outperform the other profiles in recommending the top 10 recommendations. Also, it was the best performing profile with active users. In future work, more exploration can be done to discover through the use of explicit relationships more relationship types that exist among a user and his or her friends. Additionally, we would like to further investigate the similarity that is exists between a user and his or her followers in order to extend the tweets set that forms the interests of the user.

References

1. Abel, F., Gao, Q., Houben, G.J., Tao, K.: Analyzing temporal dynamics in twitter profiles for personalized recommendations in the social web. In: Proceedings of the 3rd International Web Science Conference, p. 2. ACM, June 2011
2. Abel, F., Gao, Q., Houben, G.J., Tao, K.: Twitter-based user modeling for news recommendations. In: IJCAI, vol. 13, pp. 2962–2966, August 2013
3. Alonso, O., Carson, C., Gerster, D., Ji, X., Nabar, S.U.: Detecting uninteresting content in text streams. In: SIGIR Crowdsourcing for Search Evaluation Workshop, July 2010
4. Alshammari, A., Kapetanakis, S., Evans, R., Polatidis, N., Alshammari, G.: User modeling on twitter with exploiting explicit relationships for personalized recommendations. In: Paper presented to the 18th International Conference on Hybrid Intelligent Systems, Porto, 13–15 December 2018
5. Anger, I., Kittl, C.: Measuring influence on Twitter. In: Proceedings of the 11th International Conference on Knowledge Management and Knowledge Technologies, p. 31. ACM, September 2011
6. Bakshy, E., Hofman, J.M., Mason, W.A., Watts, D.J.: Everyone's an influencer: quantifying influence on twitter. In: Proceedings of the Fourth ACM International Conference on Web Search and Data Mining, pp. 65–74. ACM, February 2011
7. Chen, C., Gao, D., Li, W., Hou, Y.: Inferring topic-dependent influence roles of Twitter users. In: Proceedings of the 37th International ACM SIGIR Conference on Research and Development in Information Retrieval, pp. 1203–1206. ACM, July 2014
8. Elmongui, H.G., Mansour, R., Morsy, H., Khater, S., El-Sharkasy, A., Ibrahim, R.: TRUPI: twitter recommendation based on users' personal interests. In: Gelbukh, A. (ed.) CICLing 2015. LNCS, vol. 9042, pp. 272–284. Springer, Cham (2015). https://doi.org/10.1007/978-3-319-18117-2_20
9. Garcia Esparza, S., O'Mahony, M.P., Smyth, B.: CatStream: Categorising tweets for user profiling and stream filtering. In: Proceedings of the 2013 International Conference on Intelligent User Interfaces, pp. 25–36. ACM, March 2013
10. Karidi, D.P., Stavrakas, Y., Vassiliou, Y.: A personalized tweet recommendation approach based on concept graphs. In: 2016 International IEEE Conferences on Ubiquitous Intelligence and Computing, Advanced and Trusted Computing, Scalable Computing and Communications, Cloud and Big Data Computing, Internet of People, and Smart World Congress (UIC/ATC/ScalCom/CBDCom/IoP/SmartWorld), pp. 253–260. IEEE, July 2016
11. Lee, W.J., Oh, K.J., Lim, C.G., Choi, H.J.: User profile extraction from twitter for personalized news recommendation. In: Proceedings of the 16th Advanced Communication Technology, pp. 779–783 (2014)
12. Piao, G., Breslin, J.G.: Exploring dynamics and semantics of user interests for user modeling on twitter for link recommendations. In: Proceedings of the 12th International Conference on Semantic Systems, pp. 81–88. ACM, September 2016
13. Riquelme, F., González-Cantergiani, P.: Measuring user influence on Twitter: a survey. Inf. Process. Manag. **52**(5), 949–975 (2016)
14. Shani, G., Gunawardana, A.: Evaluating recommendation systems. In: Ricci, F., Rokach, L., Shapira, B., Kantor, Paul B. (eds.) Recommender Systems Handbook, pp. 257–297. Springer, Boston (2011). https://doi.org/10.1007/978-0-387-85820-3_8

15. Uysal, I., Croft, W.B.: User oriented tweet ranking: a filtering approach to microblogs. In: Proceedings of the 20th ACM International Conference on Information and Knowledge Management, pp. 2261–2264. ACM, October 2011
16. Vosoughi, S.: Automatic detection and verification of rumors on Twitter. Doctoral dissertation, Massachusetts Institute of Technology (2015)
17. Weng, J., Lim, E.P., Jiang, J., He, Q.: TwitterRank: finding topic-sensitive influential twitterers. In: Proceedings of the Third ACM International Conference on Web Search and Data Mining, pp. 261–270. ACM, February 2010

A Temporal-Causal Network Model for Age and Gender Difference in Choice of Emotion Regulation Strategies

Zhenyu Gao, Rui Liu, and Nimat Ullah[(✉)]

Vrije Universiteit Amsterdam, Amsterdam, The Netherlands
vu.gaozhy@gmail.com, nimatullah09@gmail.com,
liurui_better@163.com

Abstract. Emotion regulation is an essential part of human's life as it enables people to manage their emotions and to avoid negative consequences of them and/or situations triggering them. The choice of an emotion regulation strategy in a specific situation has a profound impact on someone's psychological well-being. Several psychological studies also have highlighted age and gender differences in choice of emotion regulation strategies specifically in relation to cognitive reappraisal and expressive suppression. This paper, for the first time, presents a computational model for the role of age and gender differences in the choice of emotion regulation strategies. Simulation results are reported for various combinations of age and gender and the respective choices of regulation strategies as found in empirical literature.

Keywords: Emotion regulation · Cognitive reappraisal ·
Expressive suppression · Gender differences ·
Temporal causal network modeling

1 Introduction

Emotion regulation (ER) refers to the set of processes whereby people seek to redirect the spontaneous flow of their emotions [1]. ER plays an important role in the social life of individuals, as emotional problems may unpredictably occur several times a day, and without regulation it may badly influence our daily life. Not only efficient emotion regulation has a positive psychological outcome [1], failure in effectively regulating emotion also results in vital psychological consequences [2, 3]. There are various ER strategies [4], the efficacy of which is solely dependent on the situation [5].

Several studies, from social sciences, have also shown age and gender difference in the choice & the effectiveness of ER strategies. Considering gender, previous experiments indicate that men are more likely to use suppression when faced with negative stimuli, while women prefer reappraisal rather than suppression [6, 7]. Similarly, regarding age, studies show that as men grow older, they tend to move to reappraisal, while in case of women, the shift takes place towards increase in suppression with age [8]. Based on these findings from social sciences, a computational model has been developed to give in-depth overview of the choices of ER strategies overtime by

© Springer Nature Switzerland AG 2019
N. T. Nguyen et al. (Eds.): ICCCI 2019, LNAI 11683, pp. 106–117, 2019.
https://doi.org/10.1007/978-3-030-28377-3_9

employing Network-Oriented Modeling approach based on temporal-casual networks [9]. This approach has been used because emotion and its regulation involve a cyclic and temporal process that network oriented temporal casual modeling particularly focuses on. Although, quite some work has already been done on emotion regulation using this modeling approach; for instance, [10, 11] present models for the role of ER strategies on mood and its consequences. [12] considers the sensitivity level in the choice of ER strategies. Similarly, [13] presents a model for contextual emotion regulation. This paper is specifically unique in the sense that it for the first time considers age and gender differences in the choice of ER strategies. The rest of the paper is organized as follows. Section 2 provides the background knowledge for the model. Section 3 presents the conceptual and numerical representation. The scenarios and simulation results are explained in Sect. 4, and the validation is presented in Sect. 5. Finally, the paper is concluded in Sect. 6.

2   Background

Studies from psychology and social sciences reveal that both gender and age differences play an important role in expression [14, 15] and regulation of emotions. For instance, in case of sadness and anger, contrary to men, women are known to express their sadness while suppressing their anger [16]. Similarly, these differences are also obvious in ER strategies. [6] put forward the view that men turn to suppression more often than women do, in general. [17] further narrow down this choice to young men who turn to suppression in comparison to young women. Similarly, [7] report more frequent use of reappraisal by women contrary to men. [6] considers parental role responsible for these differences in choice of ER strategies, as parents motivate sons to have more emotional control than daughters [18] and boys are expected to inhibit emotional expressions to a greater extent than girls. It is also discussed that women tend to appraise stressors more severely than men do, so they report more use of positive reappraisal [19].

However, contrary to men, [20] concludes excessive use of suppression with age for women while classifying ages 20 to 35, 45 to 55 and 65 to 75 as young, middle and adult, respectively. For men, as they become more aware of the positive aspects with age, so they tend to use reappraisal [8].

Cognitive reappraisal and expression suppression are the most studied strategies for such differences. Reappraisal refers to changing the interpretation of the situation thus changing the influence of the stimuli [21]. It is an antecedent-focused strategy that addresses states in the causal paths toward generation of the emotion response. As a result, reappraisal is efficient to down-regulate the negative emotion, and reduces all experiential and behavioral components of negative emotion [6]. Suppression refers to the inhibition of one's own emotional expressive behavior while emotionally aroused [22]. As a response-focused strategy, suppression addresses state in the causal paths after an emotion; although it should be effective in cutting the behavioral expression of the negative emotion, the expression of positive emotion may also be decreased [6].

3 Conceptual Representation of the Model

The proposed computational model is explained in this section. This model is based on the Network-Oriented Modeling approach based on temporal-casual networks [9], briefly explained below; see also [23].

Table 1. Conceptual and numerical representations of a temporal-causal network model.

Concept	Conceptual representation	Explanation
States and connections	$X, Y, X{\rightarrow}Y$	Describes the nodes and links of a network structure (e.g., in graphical or matrix form)
Connection weight	$\omega_{X,Y}$	The *connection weight* $\omega_{X,Y} \in [-1, 1]$ represents the strength of the causal impact of state X on state Y through connection $X{\rightarrow}Y$
Aggregating multiple impacts on a state	$c_Y(..)$	For each state Y a *combination function* $c_Y(..)$ is chosen to combine the causal impacts of other states on state Y
Timing of the effect of causal impact	η_Y	For each state Y a *speed factor* $\eta_Y \geq 0$ is used to represent how fast a state is changing upon causal impact
Concept	Numerical representation	Explanation
State values over time t	$Y(t)$	At each time point t each state Y in the model has a real number value in $[0, 1]$
Single causal impact	$\text{impact}_{X,Y}(t) = w_{X,Y}X(t)$	At t state X with a connection to state Y has impact on Y, using connection weight $\omega_{X,Y}$
Aggregating multiple causal impacts	$\text{aggimpact}_Y(t) = c_Y(\text{impact}_{X_1,Y}(t),\ldots,$ $\text{impact}_{X_k,Y}(t)) = c_Y(w_{X_1,Y}X_1(t),\ldots,w_{X_k,Y}X_k(t))$	The aggregated causal impact of multiple states X_i on Y at t, is determined using combination function $c_Y(..)$
Timing of the causal effect	$Y(t+\Delta t) = Y(t) + \eta_Y[\text{aggimpact}_Y(t) - Y(t)]\Delta t =$ $Y(t) + \eta_Y[c_Y(w_{X_1,Y}X_1(t),\ldots,\omega_{X_k,Y}X_k(t)) - Y(t)]\Delta t$	The causal impact on Y is exerted over time gradually, using speed factor η_Y; here the X_i are all states with outgoing connections to state Y

The Network-Oriented Modeling approach provides different ways to specify how casual impacts are aggregated on a specific state by using certain combination functions. For this purpose not only a library of standard combination functions is available, own-defined functions can also be added.

A conceptual representation of a temporal-causal model can be transformed into a numerical representation as follows:

1. For each time point t every X has an activation level between 0 and 1, indicated by $X(t)$.
2. The impact of state X on state Y at time point t is computed as $\text{impact}_{X,Y}(t) = \omega_{X,Y}\mathbf{X}(t)$ where $\omega_{X,Y}$ is the weight of the connection from X to Y.
3. The aggregated impact on Y is determined by the (multiple) states X_1 to X_k with outgoing connections to Y based on the combination function of Y by

$$\mathbf{aggimpact}_Y(t) = c_Y(\mathbf{impact}_{X1,Y}(t),\ldots,\mathbf{impact}_{Xk,Y}(t))$$
$$= c_Y(\omega_{X1,Y}X_1(t),\ldots,\omega_{Xk,Y}X_k(t))$$

where X_i are the states with outgoing connections to state Y

4. The effect of **aggimpact**$_Y(t)$ on Y is exerted over time gradually, depending on the speed factor η_Y:

$$Y(t + \Delta t) = Y(t) + \eta_Y[\textbf{aggimpact}_Y(t) - Y(t)]\Delta t$$
$$or\, \textbf{d}Y(t)/\textbf{d}t = \eta_Y[\textbf{aggimpact}_Y(t) - Y(t)]$$

5. Thus, the following difference and differential equations are obtained:

$$y(t + \Delta t) = Y(t) + \eta_Y[\textbf{c}_Y(\omega_{X1,Y}X_1(t),\ \ldots, \omega_{Xk,Y}X(t)) - Y(t)]\Delta t$$
$$or\, \textbf{d}Y(t)/\textbf{d}t = \eta_Y[\textbf{c}_Y(\omega_{X1,Y}X_1(t),\ \ldots, \omega_{Xk,Y}X(t)) - Y(t)]$$

The computational model in Fig. 1 shows how the choice of ER strategies changes with age and gender. All except the connection in orange carries positive weights.

The world state (ws$_s$) refers to stimuli s in the world which triggers some emotions resulting in a series of process (ss$_s$, srs$_s$, ps$_a$, es$_a$) to be performed. The bs$_-$ refers to negative belief about the stimuli which activates the body state b (ss$_b$, srs$_b$, fs$_b$, ps$_b$, & es$_b$). The preparation state (ps$_b$) and execution state (es$_b$) gives feedback and enhances response to the s through an as-if-body loop [24].

The choice of using specific strategy is determined by two external conditions/factors i.e. ws$_{ppl}$ and ws$_{prnt}$. ws$_{ppl}$ refers to the people factor in choice of ER strategies (specifically keeping gender in view). ws$_{prnt}$ refers to the parents' influence [6, 18] in choice of ER strategies (especially in young age). This phenomenon is best explained in Sect. 4, Table 4.

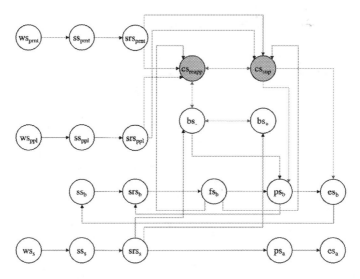

Fig. 1. Conceptual representation of the model.

Table 2. Nomenclature of the model

Notation	Description	Notation	Description
ws_s	World state for stimulus s	bs_+	Positive belief state about the stimulus s
ss_s	Sensor state for stimulus s	bs_-	Negative belief state about the stimulus s
srs_s	Sensory rep: state for stimulus s	ws_{prnt}	World state for parent
ps_a	Preparation state for action a	ss_{prnt}	Sensor state for parent
es_a	Execution state for action a	srs_{prnt}	Sensory rep: state for parent
ss_b	Sensor state for body state b	ws_{ppl}	World state for people
srs_b	Sensory rep: state for body state b	ss_{ppl}	Sensor state for people
fs_b	Feeling state for body state b	srs_{ppl}	Sensory rep: state for people
ps_b	Preparation state for body state b	cs_{reapp}	Control state for reappraisal
es_b	Execution state for body states b	cs_{sup}	Control state for suppression

The control state of reappraisal cs_{reapp} suppresses bs_-, i.e. changing interpretation of the stimuli while control state for suppression (cs_{sup}), suppresses the expression of emotion while the negative belief still remains high. As a result, the person may feel even higher intensity of the negative stimuli but he keeps suppressing his body state.

4 Scenarios and Simulation Results

This section shows simulations results and the parameters used to obtain these results so that it exhibits the same pattern as found by various studies from social sciences (Table 3). Based on the computational model and literature above, here's an example scenario of the model:

> "*When a person finds it difficult to make it to an important appointment. Negative emotion arises. For regulation of such negative emotions, young men are expected to turn to suppression as they are taught to do so (Gross & John, 2003, Underwood et al., 1992), while older men tend to reappraise, because they look more at the positive side as they grow older (Masumoto et al., 2016). Young women prefer reappraisal, while older women may use suppression more often which may reflect the uncontrollable nature of the stresses they face [25].*"

Table 3. Connection weights used in the model

Connection	Weight	Connection	Weight	Connection	Weight
$\omega_{wss,\ sss}$	1	$\omega_{fsb,\ cssup}$	0.1	$\omega_{psb,\ srsb}$	0.3
$\omega_{sss,\ srss}$	1	$\omega_{bs-,\ psb}$	0.4	$\omega_{psb,\ esb}$	0.6
$\omega_{srss,\ psa}$	0.2	$\omega_{bs-,\ csreapp}$	0.1	$\omega_{esb,\ ssb}$	1
$\omega_{srss,\ bs+}$	0.45	$\omega_{wsprnt,\ ssprnt}$	1	$\omega_{bs+,\ bs-}$	−0.4
$\omega_{srss,\ bs-}$	0.8	$\omega_{ssprnt,\ srsprnt}$	1	$\omega_{bs-,\ bs+}$	−0.4
$\omega_{psa,\ esa}$	0.1	$\omega_{srsprnt,\ csreapp}$	0.35	$\omega_{csreapp,\ cssup}$	−1
$\omega_{ssb,\ srsb}$	0.5	$\omega_{srsprnt,\ cssup}$	0.35	$\omega_{cssup,\ psb}$	−0.3
$\omega_{srsb,\ fsb}$	1	$\omega_{wsppl,\ ssppl}$	1	$\omega_{cssup,\ esb}$	−0.4
$\omega_{fsb,\ psb}$	0.4	$\omega_{ssppl,\ srsppl}$	1	$\omega_{cssup,\ csreapp}$	−1
$\omega_{fsb,\ csreapp}$	0.4	$\omega_{csreapp,\ bs-}$	−0.5		

The aspects relevant for the effect of age and gender are modeled by the world state ws_{prnt} representing the role of parents, and by different values of connection weights see Table 4. Activation of ws_{prnt} represents simulation for young boys/girls where the parents has influence on the choice of ER strategies. In contrast, the absence of parents (non-activation of ws_{prnt}) represent older age men and women, the ER choice of which is further differentiated by the connection weight given in Table 4.

Table 4. Key parameters for different scenarios

Initial value of ws_{prnt}	$\omega_{srsppl,\ csreapp}$	$\omega_{srsppl,\ cssup}$	Situation	Strategy
1	0.2	0.8	Young men	Suppression
1	0.8	0.2	Young women	Reappraisal
0	0.2	0.8	Older women	Suppression
0	0.8	0.2	Older men	Reappraisal

The identity function has been used for states with only one incoming connection and advanced logistic function has been used for states with more than one incoming connections, given below:

$$\mathbf{id}(V) = V$$
$$\mathbf{alogistic}_{\sigma,\tau}(V_1,\ldots,V_k) = [(1/(1+e^{-\sigma(V_1+\ldots+V_{k-\tau})})) - (1/(1+e^{\sigma\tau}))](1+e^{-\sigma\tau})$$

σ represent steepness and τ is threshold value of the particular state.

The speed factor (η) for each state represents the speed with which this state will change due to causal impact exerted upon it by other states.

Table 5. Combination functions and speed factors used in the network model

State	σ	τ	η	State	σ	τ	η
ws_s	0	0	0	bs_+	5	0.2	0.2
ss_s	0	0	0.2	bs_-	8	0.2	0.2
srs_s	0	0	0.2	ws_{prnt}	0	0	0
ps_a	0	0	0.2	ss_{prnt}	0	0	0.2
es_a	0	0	0.2	srs_{prnt}	0	0	0.2
ss_b	0	0	0.2	ws_{ppl}	0	0	0
srs_b	5	0.2	0.2	ss_{ppl}	0	0	0.2
fs_b	0	0	0.2	srs_{ppl}	0	0	0.2
ps_b	5	0.2	0.1	cs_{reapp}	8	0.5	0.015
es_b	5	0.2	0.1	cs_{sup}	8	0.4	0.015

These parameters are model specific to achieve what findings from psychological literature suggests.

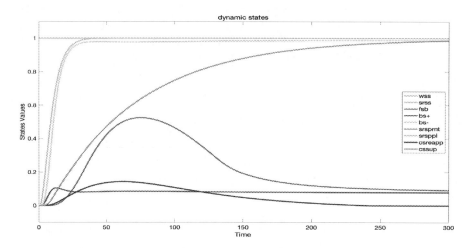

Fig. 2. Simulation of young men suppressing their emotion

Figure 2 shows stimulation result of young men dealing with his emotion. As young men suppress their emotions (because of the parental role), it can be seen that the srs_s and bs_- remain high all the time but as cs_{sup} gets activated, ps_b and es_b gets suppressed and comes down. This means that in expressive suppression, the expression of the body state is suppressed rather than any cognitive change.

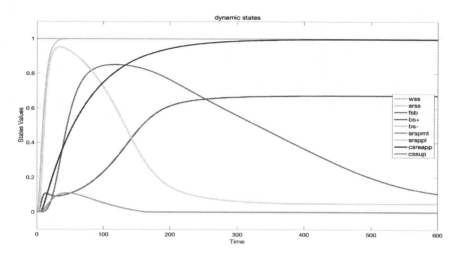

Fig. 3. Simulation of young women reappraising her belief

Figure 3 presents stimulation results for a young woman dealing with her emotion. In the figure it can be seen that initially all the states, become higher until cs_{reapp} gets activated. cs_{reapp} reappraises her belief about the stimulus, so, the negative belief gets suppressed and positive belief grows. This change in the belief also makes her fs_b decrease.

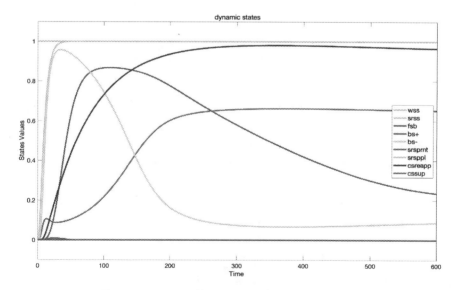

Fig. 4. Simulation of older men reappraising his belief

In both Figs. 4 and 3 the emotion is effectively regulated but the main difference is that they represent different genders and different ages employing different ER strategies. The most notable difference between these two figures is the activation of the ER strategies by the control states cs_{reapp} and cs_{sup}. In young age as the parental role has influence on the choice of ER strategies, therefore, in Fig. 3 it can be seen that initially suppression also gets activated a little bit but as young girls are guided to reappraise so reappraisal finally gets dominant. In Fig. 4, however, the choice of strategies is independent of parent influence from the very beginning, so suppression gets dominated from the very beginning.

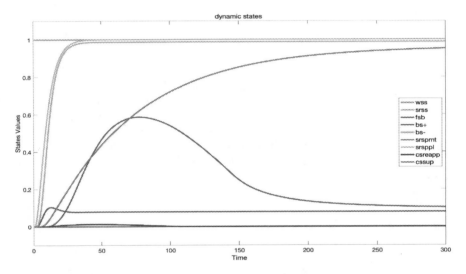

Fig. 5. Simulation of older women suppressing her emotion

Figures 5 and 2 have the same relation as discussed earlier for Figs. 4 and 3. In young age, the uncertainty activates both the strategies but finally the one motivated by parents gets dominated. In contrast, in adulthood/older age the choice is very clear from the beginning and therefore only one strategy gets activated from the beginning.

The simulation results clearly demonstrate as findings from psychological literature suggest.

5   Verification and Validation

5.1   Parameter Tuning

For validation of the model, we have considered a third scenario: older men using reappraisal for downregulating their emotion. The empirical data is based on the findings of [8]. It was learned that the activation of various states by a stimulus and later on the cognitive process taking place by employing reappraisal is slower as compared to that of our model. Based on this assumption, the graph in Fig. 6 gives the comparative overview of the empirical vs simulated results. The doted lines represent the empirical curves in Fig. 6. Therefore, parameter tuning was applied on the speed factors to decrease the gap between the results. Contrary to Table 5, after parameter tuning we got the speed factor given in Table 6. The Root Square Mean (RSM) value before tuning was 0.3917; after tuning the RSM value is 0.2315.

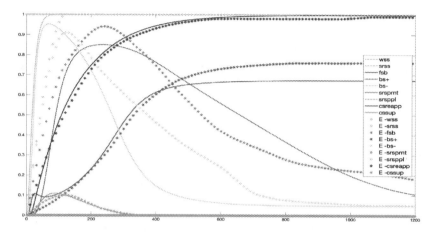

Fig. 6. Empirical data and the simulated data

Table 6. Speed factor after parameter tuning

State X_i	ws_s	ss_s	srs_s	ps_a	es_a	ss_b	srs_b	fs_b	ps_b	es_b
Speed factor	0.002	0.084	0.894	0.823	1	0.101	0.923	0.183	0.909	0.817
State X_i	bs_+	bs_-	ws_{prnt}	ss_{prnt}	srs_{prnt}	ws_{ppl}	ss_{ppl}	srs_{ppl}	cs_{reap}	cs_{sup}
speed factor	0.92	0.177	0.1	0.084	0.986	0.001	0.082	0.922	0.003	0.818

5.2 Verification by Analysis of Stationary Points

In this part, we discuss how we have considered the first scenario (choice of young men using suppression) as an example to verify the model. For t < 100, we choose 7 stationary points for 7 different states and checked with what accuracy the stationary point equations hold for them as shown in Table 6. The stationary point equation derived from the difference equation in a temporal causal network model is aggimpact$_{Xi}(t) = X_i(t)$.

Table 7. Stationary points and the values

State X_i	ss_b	srs_b	fs_b	ps_b	es_b	bs_+	cs_{reapp}
Time point t	62	70	75	70	56.5	13	62
$X_i(t)$	0.2697	0.5278	0.5248	0.6545	0.2725	0.1045	0.1426
aggimpact$_{X_i}(t)$	0.2694	0.5276	0.5250	0.6547	0.2722	0.1019	0.1437
aggimpact$_{X_i}(t) - X_i(t)$	−0.0003	−0.0002	0.0002	0.00020	−0.0003	−0.0026	0.0011

From Table 6 we can see that except for $bs_+(13)$, all other values of aggimpact$_{X_i}(t)$ $- X_i(t)$ are within the range of $[-0.002, 0.002]$. The deviation in $bs_+(13)$ is a bit higher because the inflection in the curve of bs_+ is sharp (and $\Delta t = 0.5$). As there is little difference between the value from our model and the verified value, we can say that the model generated the correct values.

6 Conclusion

The choice of ER strategies has various dynamics. Age and gender are two such important dynamics which completely changes the choice of ER strategies. In young age, as learning takes place under guidance, mostly under parents, so the choice of ER strategies is also under their influence. In contrast, the choice of strategies starts changing with increase in age. One reason for this change can be the possible independence of decision in choice of such strategies. Another reason for this change may be the learning overtime. As age increases, experience increase, more knowledge about different things is gained which completely change such choices overtime. Apart from the above-mentioned facts, adaptivity is another factor which plays a key role in choice of ER strategies. It is learned over time which strategy is more effective and which is not much effective. This also changes the priority of ER strategies. Future work on this topic may address the above-mentioned learning factors over time which changes the choice of ER strategies on the basis of past experiences where a specific strategy proved effective or not effective.

References

1. Koole, S.L.: The psychology of emotion regulation: an integrative review. Cogn. Emot. **23** (1), 4–41 (2009)
2. Aldao, A., Nolen-Hoeksema, S.: Specificity of cognitive emotion regulation strategies: a transdiagnostic examination. Behav. Res. Ther. **48**, 974–983 (2010). https://doi.org/10.1016/j.brat.2010.06.002
3. Gross, J.J. (ed.): Handbook of Emotion Regulation, 2nd edn. Guilford, New York (2012)
4. Gross, J.J.: The emerging field of emotion regulation: an integrative review. Rev. Gen. Psychol. **2**, 271–299 (1998). https://doi.org/10.1037/1089-2680.2.3.271
5. Aldao, A., Sheppes, G., Gross, J.J.: Emotion regulation flexibility. Cogn. Ther. Res. **39**(3), 263–278 (2015). https://doi.org/10.1007/s10608-014-9662-4
6. Gross, J.J., John, O.P.: Individual differences in two emotion regulation processes: implications for affect, relationships, and well-being. J. Pers. Soc. Psychol. **85**, 348–362 (2003)

7. Spaapen, D.L., Waters, F., Brummer, L., Stopa, L., Bucks, R.S.: The emotion regulation questionnaire: validation of the ERQ-9 in two community samples. Psychol. Assess. **26**(1), 46–54 (2014)
8. Masumoto, K., Taishi, N., Shiozaki, M.: Age and gender differences in relationships among emotion regulation, mood, and mental health. Gerontol. Geriatr. Med. **2**, 1–8 (2016)
9. Treur, J.: Network-Oriented Modeling: Addressing Complexity of Cognitive, Affective and Social Interactions. Springer, New York (2016). https://doi.org/10.1007/978-3-319-45213-5
10. Abro, A.H., Klein, M.C.A., Manzoor Rajper, A., Tabatabaei, S.A., Treur, J.: Modeling the effect of regulation of negative emotions on mood. Biologically Inspired Cogn. Architectures **13**, 35–47 (2015). https://doi.org/10.1016/j.bica.2015.06.003
11. Abro, A.H., Manzoor Rajper, A., Tabatabaei, S., Treur, J.: A computational cognitive model integrating different emotion regulation strategies. In: Georgeon, O.L. (ed.), Proceedings of the 6th Annual International Conference on Biologically Inspired Cognitive Architectures, BICA 2015, pp. 157–168 (2015). Procedia Computer Science. Elsevier. https://doi.org/10.1016/j.procs.2015.12.187
12. Manzoor, A., Abro, A.H., Treur, J.: Monitoring the impact of negative events and deciding about emotion regulation strategies. In: Criado Pacheco, N., Carrascosa, C., Osman, N., Julián Inglada, V. (eds.) EUMAS/AT -2016. LNCS (LNAI), vol. 10207, pp. 350–363. Springer, Cham (2017). https://doi.org/10.1007/978-3-319-59294-7_30
13. Ullah, N., Treur, J., Koole, S.L.: A computational model for flexibility in emotion regulation. Procedia Comput. Sci. **145**, 572–580 (2018)
14. Brody, L.R., Hall, J.A.: Gender, emotion, and expression. In: Lewis, M., Haviland, J.M. (eds.) Handbook of Emotions, 2nd edn, pp. 338–349. Guilford Press, New York (2000)
15. Shields, S.A.: Speaking from the Heart: Gender and the Social Meaning of Emotion. Cambridge University Press, Cambridge (2002)
16. Timmers, M., Fischer, A., Manstead, A.: Gender differences in motives for regulating emotions. Pers. Soc. Psychol. Bull. **24**, 974–985 (1998). https://doi.org/10.1177/0146167298249005
17. John, O.P., Gross, J.J.: Healthy and unhealthy emotion regulation: personality processes, individual differences, and life span development. J. Pers. **72**, 1301–1333 (2004)
18. Underwood, M.K., Coie, J.D., Herbsman, C.R.: Display rules for anger and aggression in school-age children. Child Dev. **63**, 366–380 (1992)
19. Tamres, L.K., Janicki, D., Helgeson, V.S.: Sex differences in coping behavior: a meta-analytic review and an examination of relative coping. Pers. Soc. Psychol. Rev. **6**(1), 2–30 (2002)
20. Nolen-Hoeksema, S., Aldao, A.: Gender and age differences in emotion regulation strategies and their relationship to depressive symptoms. Pers. Individ. Differ. **51**, 704–708 (2011)
21. Buhle, J.T., et al.: Cognitive reappraisal of emotion: a meta-analysis of human neuroimaging studies. Cereb. Cortex **24**(11), 2981–2990 (2014)
22. Gross, J.J., Levenson, R.W.: Emotional suppression: physiology, self-report, and expressive behavior. J. Pers. Soc. Psychol. **64**(6), 970–986 (1993)
23. Treur, J.: The Ins and Outs of network-oriented modeling: from biological networks and mental networks to social networks and beyond. In: Nguyen, N.T., Kowalczyk, R., Hernes, M. (eds.) Transactions on Computational Collective Intelligence XXXII. LNCS, vol. 11370, pp. 120–139. Springer, Heidelberg (2019). https://doi.org/10.1007/978-3-662-58611-2_2
24. Damasio, A.R.: Self Comes to Mind: Constructing the Conscious Brain. Pantheon Books, New York (2010)
25. Blanchard-Fields, F.: Everyday problem solving and emotion: an adult developmental perspective. Curr. Dir. Psychol. Sci. **16**(1), 26–31 (2007)

Modelling Stereotyping in Cooperation Systems

Wafi Bedewi[1(✉)], Roger M. Whitaker[1], Gualtiero B. Colombo[1],
Stuart M. Allen[1], and Yarrow Dunham[2]

[1] School of Computer Science and Informatics, Cardiff University, Cardiff, UK
{BedewiWA,WhitakerRM,ColomboG,AllenSM}@cardiff.ac.uk
[2] Department of Psychology, Yale University, New Haven, CT 06511, USA
yarrow.dunham@yale.edu

Abstract. Cooperation is a sophisticated example of collective intelligence. This is particularly the case for indirect reciprocity, where benefit is provided to others without a guarantee of a future return. This is becoming increasingly relevant to future technology, where autonomous machines face cooperative dilemmas. This paper addresses the problem of stereotyping, where traits belonging to an individual are used as proxy when assessing their reputation. This is a cognitive heuristic that humans frequently use to avoid deliberation, but can lead to negative societal implications such as discrimination. It is feasible that machines could be equally susceptible. Our contribution concerns a new and general framework to examine how stereotyping affects the reputation of agents engaging in indirect reciprocity. The framework is flexible and focuses on how reputations are shared. This offers the opportunity to assess the interplay between the sharing of traits and the cost, in terms of reduced cooperation, through opportunities for shirkers to benefit. This is demonstrated using a number of key scenarios. In particular, the results show that cooperation is sensitive to the structure of reputation sharing between individuals.

Keywords: Stereotyping · Cooperation · Indirect reciprocity ·
Reputation

1 Introduction

Cooperation is a sophisticated form of collective intelligence where individuals become incentivised to help one another and benefit from a coalition. One particularly interesting but challenging form of cooperation is *indirect reciprocity*, which is complex because it involves donating to a third party without any guarantee of future reciprocation. Cooperation in this form involves a small cost to the donor, and a much larger benefit to the recipient. This is a hallmark of human behaviour that leads to a societal benefit, by providing a resource through which unrelated individuals support each other [1,3].

© Springer Nature Switzerland AG 2019
N. T. Nguyen et al. (Eds.): ICCCI 2019, LNAI 11683, pp. 118–129, 2019.
https://doi.org/10.1007/978-3-030-28377-3_10

Extensive research has been successful in establishing conditions and mechanisms that promote indirect reciprocity. However, as machines are developed that feature cognition and autonomy, interest in cooperation is reaching beyond humans [20]. Transportation is just one emerging example where technology, through autonomous vehicles, will encounter cooperative decision making [14]. This scenario features latent indirect reciprocity, such as when one driver allows another to manoeuvre in traffic. Journeys in congestion often depend on this, such as when exiting a T-junction, without which safe progress would be impossible in many cities.

Beyond technological scenarios, persistent human scenarios such as intergroup conflict [37] continue to motivate the exploration of cooperation, and the basis for it being sustained. The decision on whether or not to cooperate, when called upon, is the fundamental issue. *Reputation* is an important component that provides a currency through which cooperation can be recognised and signalled [24], allowing individuals to leverage future help when needed [22]. In recent times reputation systems have also emerged to support decision making in diverse areas of e-commerce [19, 31, 40] for example. There are also many areas of work in multi-agent systems where the focus is to engineer protocols or rules that seek to ensure cooperation is followed [46].

The origins of reputation systems come from behaviour in groups with humans being adept at using reputation to assess the integrity of others [34], as a means to promote their survival. This allows groups to function and humans are adept at creating heuristics, or cognitive short cuts, that allow them to find potential cooperators without extensive deliberation. However these cognitive short cuts can also have negative implications. In the context of driving dynamics for example, the type of vehicle, its manufacturer, the age, gender or other characteristics of the driver may well influence whether one driver helps another. While this may appear insignificant, in the wider human context this behaviour can have a major impact, being responsible for bias that fuels stereotyping [12], resulting in potentially unwarranted discrimination and the spread of prejudice [26]. Divisive social consequences may result [15], leading to categorisation, where the reputation that an individual incurs has no alignment to their actual behaviour. This is a key component in theories concerning intergroup conflict. These issues are also transferred to technological scenarios, depending on the capacity of machines to align with human bias or foster it themselves [43].

1.1   Contribution

Our contribution in this work is a new and flexible framework that allows us to explore how the sharing of reputation, by means of shared traits, affects cooperation. The approach used involves agent-based simulation, where agents have some freedom in how they adapt their behaviour based on probabilistically copying the strategy of others, based on their success. This approach allows us to explore conditions that either promote or impede cooperation. It should not be confused with agent based approaches in knowledge engineering, where protocols are sought that allow cooperation to be enforced based on individual behaviour (e.g., [46]). It can be noted that the vast majority of psychological treatments of stereotyping focus on the single trait case, despite increasing demands to capture the ground truth of social organisation [4].

Given very limited treatment of stereotyping from a complex systems perspective, the authors model it with abstraction, seeking to quantify the effects of stereotyping initially in general terms. Indirect reciprocity is the basis for our model, but other forms of cooperation could also be applied. The approach is novel because models of indirect reciprocity conventionally assume that each individual is represented by a unique reputation: in other words an individual's behaviour is entirely judged by their own actions. Stereotyping disrupts this one-to-one mapping, resulting in reputations being implicitly shared by different actors. In the context of cooperation, this means that individuals become dependent on the donation behaviour of others for an element of their reputation.

Furthermore, our framework does not assume that "groups" to which individuals belong are mutually exclusive. Reputations are calculated on traits, any number of which can be held by an individual. This better represents the fluidity that is seen in the real world, where individuals are rarely totally defined by a single group affiliation, but may be represented as a combination of characteristics and affiliations. The paper examines how both repeated sharing of the same trait, and sharing across multiple traits, affects the emergence of cooperation. This provides a mechanism to assess the cost associated with stereotyping, in terms of the effect on cooperation. To the best of our knowledge, no such previous insight has been made in this direction.

2   Key Related Literature

This research focuses on indirect reciprocity, groups and the role of reputation. Indirect reciprocity is frequently considered in the context of the donation game, where an agent has to make a decision on whether or not to provide a donation. This results in a cost c to the donor, and a benefit b to the recipient, and necessarily $c < b$ [5,24]. Reputation systems act to signal an agent's overall donation behaviour to the wider population. Because other agents may use an agent's reputation in deciding when or not to donate, there is an incentive for all potential recipients to maintain reputation at a sufficient level to yield future donations [9,21,41].

Critical within reputation systems are assessment rules. These are the criteria by which a donor's reputation is adjusted in light of their actions, and therefore govern the extent of reward over penalty. In this sense they have been considered as a model for morality [1]. Three main alternatives for assessment of cooperative action are *image scoring*, *standing* and *judging*. The first development was standing [33], which was originally conceived for binary reputations. This assessment rule effectively classifies each individual in the population as either good or bad, penalising the good if they donate to the bad.

Image scoring [23,41] presented the first significant alternative, where reputation is simply incremented or decremented in response to donation or defection respectively. A limitation of image scoring is that those who choose not to cooperate with defectors may be unfairly labelled as less cooperative [17,28]. Consequently, with their roots in the work of Sugden [33], *standing* [28] and *judging* [6] have emerged as the alternatives that capture "legitimate shirking" [10,24,30]. These discrimination rules have mainly been studied assuming that reputation has a binary representation [5,27], although this was generalised for standing in [42].

The overwhelming convention is that individuals hold their own individual reputation with similarity of reputation only introduced to address uncertainty (e.g., [17,23]). The point of deviation from this has occurred in the biological literature, specifically concerning the plausibility of group selection [32,44]. These models assume that individuals belong to precisely one group, and it is the group entity that determines whether or not individuals propagate to future generations. This was largely dismissed by the biological literature but was revisited when the idea of multi-level selection was proposed [45], where individual and group identity coexist and may promote cooperation [25]. Reputation systems can feature in this context, allowing individuals to potentially switch between individual and group reputations [18,34]. However this still remains controversial [29] as an explanation for biological evolution.

Psychological processes of categorisation are well seen in human behaviour, and work relating to groups and cooperation has featured consideration of both in-group bias [11,13] and out-group prejudice [7,43], while not necessarily invoking the use of a group reputation. These contributions reflect the disposition of individuals to differentiate, either implicitly or explicitly, based on their strong identification with self-similar individuals [16]. Stereotyping is a related extension of this, where third party individuals are categorised together through a perception of common characteristics [12]. This is well known to be a divisive phenomenon in the human world [8,36,39].

In the case of reputation systems, only a few contributions consider categorisation. In [2] the impact of group reputation is considered through multi-agents. Here, the concept of group reputation is shared by all individuals within a group when they interact with out-group members. This is calculated as the average of all individual reputations in a group, and assumes that group reputation is an aggregation of the behaviour of individuals. Similarly in [18], a group structure is proposed where individuals interact within their groups using a personal reputation. When they play out-group, individuals adopt a group-level reputation. This model also assumes that reputation is binary. These models do not allow for individuals to share subsets of traits, or aspects of their identity, and depend on individuals belonging to a single group. Our approach is to allow individuals to have a more complex composition of their identity, based on assessment of multiple traits against which reputations are maintained.

3   Model

The simulation model that is introduced pays attention to the structure of reputation that agents hold when engaged in a cooperative dilemma (indirect reciprocity). Rather than individuals necessarily holding their own unique reputation, or being identified by a single group membership, the concept of *traits* is introduced to represent how individuals may be perceived as belonging to groups and judged through stereotypes. Traits are immutable features that are held by agents, and represent identifiable characteristics. All agents have at least one trait, and each trait may belong to one or more agents.

Rather than reputation being associated with individual agents or mutually exclusive groups, it is assumed that each trait t has associated with it a reputation r_t, and an agent i derives its personal reputation r^i from the reputations of the traits associated with i. Specifically, for an agent i, let T_i denote its associated set of traits, and then $r^i = \sum_{t \in T_i} r_t / |T_i|$. In other words, an agent's reputation is the average of the reputation of its associated traits.

This arrangement allows stereotyping to be considered: traits belonging to an agent and shared by others are used as a proxy for their individual reputation. Furthermore, traits do not necessarily partition agents into mutually exclusive sets or groups, providing a useful generalisation. This approach is applied using cooperation in the form of indirect reciprocity.

Indirect Reciprocity. The donation game is adopted, which is a subclass of the mutual aid game [33] where the donor incurs a cost with no guarantee of reciprocation from the beneficiary, or any other individual. This is modelled through prosocial donations which result in a cost c to the donor agent and a benefit b to the recipient, where $b > c > 0$. There are wide ranging models for indirect reciprocity (e.g., [17,23,27,38]), however this work uses the recent and remarkably simple approach of *social comparison* of reputation [42]. This follows the human disposition to make relative judgements about the standing of others.

Each agent i carries a binary vector of variables (s_i, u_i, d_i) which represents i's current *action rule* with respect to i's donation behaviour when it is called upon to consider making a donation to another agent j. The action rule indicates whether or not i donates when similarity (s_i), upward (u_i), or downward self-comparison (d_i) is observed by i in respect of j's reputation (r^j), as compared to i's own reputation value (r^i). Similarity in self-comparison is identified when $r^j = r^i$, upward self-comparison occurs when $r^j > r^i$, and downward self-comparison occurs when $r^j < r^i$.

Periodically each agent updates its action rule through social learning, as a consequence of observing others in the population. It is known [42] that evolution promotes the action rule $(1, 1, 0)$, allowing agents to discriminate against those having a lower reputation than themselves, thereby representing a relative threat.

Updating Reputation. Every time an agent i is called to play the donation game with a potential recipient j, i's donation decision depends on the agent's action rule and reputation is updated as a consequence. The concept of standing is used. Specifically, it is assumed that agent i has a set of traits T_i. If i donates, then r_t is incremented, for all $t \in T_i$. If $r^j \geq r^i$ and i defects then the reputation of trait t, r_t is decremented, for all $t \in T_i$. This means that an individual's actions equally affect the traits by which it is represented. Note that the updating approach ensures that a reduction in reputations does not occur when i fails to donate and j is of a lesser reputation, providing a defence against shirkers. Each trait's reputation is allowed to vary in the integer range $[-5, 5]$.

Performing the Game. The donation game is performed on a set of agents A representing a population of individuals, in this case $|A| = 100$. Each agent i has four key fundamental attributes: its set of traits T_i, its action rule (s_i, u_i, d_i), its reputation r^i and its fitness f_i. Note that $r^i = \sum_{t \in T_i} r_t / |T_i|$, and r^i allows agents to play the donation game and fitness represents the accumulation of costs and benefits that are paid and received by i over a generation. A generation involves making 5,000 random selections of a potential recipient j, from the population, to play the donation game. For an agent j, the potential donor agent i is selected from the sub-population having at least one trait from T_j, with probability s. Here s is a global parameter (not to be confused with s_i) that governs the extent to which an agent is disposed to playing in-group (i.e., with similar others).

At the end of a generation, reproduction occurs. This can be thought of as social learning where agents probabilistically copy the action rules of others, taking into account the success of other agents based on their fitness. Specifically, each agent i in the population copies the action rule of another agent j with probability $f_j / \sum_{k=1}^{n} f_k$, upon which i adopts j's action rule for the next generation.

At this point mutation is applied to each element of an action rule with probability $1/100$. Prior to commencing a new generation, fitness f_i is set to zero ($f_i = 0, \forall i$) and for all traits t, $r_t = 0$ is set. Throughout a c/b ratio of 0.7 is applied. 100,000 generations are performed and the simulation is principally evaluated by comparing the total number of instances of cooperation (i.e., i donating to j in a donation game) across all generations. Average figures of cooperation over 5 randomly seeded runs are used.

4   Experiments

The model provides the option for agents to experience different types of reputation sharing with other agents. An agent is *dependent* if it shares at least one trait with another agent. Otherwise the agent is *independent*. If an agent i is such that $|T_i| > 1$ then i is a *multi-trait* agent. Otherwise i is a *single-trait* agent. Dependent agents provide the means for stereotyping to take hold. This is investigated in two ways: firstly the effect of dependent single-trait agents on the evolution of cooperation (Sect. 4.1); secondly the effect of a dependent multi-trait agent on the evolution of cooperation (Sect. 4.2).

4.1   Dependent Single-Trait Agents

This section considers the effects of a single common trait t being shared by a set of single-trait agents. Let G_t be the set of all agents i having $T_i = \{t\}$.

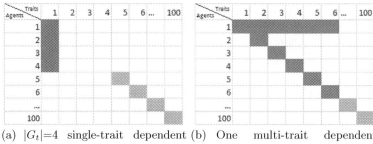

(a) $|G_t|=4$ single-trait dependent agents who share trait $t = 1$.

(b) One multi-trait dependent agent, and five single trait dependent agents.

Fig. 1. Alternative agent-trait relationships for single-trait and multi-trait agents.

Specifically, the maximum size of G_t is determined through which cooperation can be sustained. Note that if all agents are single-trait and independent, their reputation is based entirely on their own past interactions and the results in [42] are replicated. At the other extreme, if all agents are dependent and share a single trait, then agents are (almost) entirely judged on the actions of others, and a greater incentive to defect is expected. The format of this experiment is visualised in Fig. 1(a) and the results are shown in Fig. 2(a). Two patterns emerge: firstly cooperation declines rapidly after 15 dependent single-trait agents share a common trait. Secondly, the average cooperation declines as s increases.

The lack of a distinguishable personal reputation for dependent single-trait agents means that the reputational benefit of donation is shared with others, but the cost is borne by the individual. This provides an opportunity for defective strategies to take hold, where free riders can benefit from enjoying a shared reputation without donating. However this cannot be sustained at scale, leading to the global collapse of cooperation. In fact, as the number of dependent agents increases, the reputation of the shared trait can also increase in value. This leads to greater exploitation by free riders.

Figure 3, shows the action rules of agents across different values of s, comparing instances of the defector strategy $(0, 0, 0)$ with instances of the discriminator strategy $(1, 1, 0)$; which has been known to be dominant when all agents carry their own unique reputation [42]. Prioritising interaction with those who share the same trait (i.e., high s) accelerates the collapse of cooperation further as the discriminative strategy directs donations towards agents with similar reputation. When s is low, dependent single-trait agents interact mainly with those who don't share their reputation as they are still incentivised to adopt cooperative strategies to maximise their fitness with a reduced risk of exploitation.

4.2   Dependent Multi-trait Agents

This section considers the effect of introducing a single dependent multi-trait agent in a population of single-trait agents, as shown in Fig. 1(b). The results

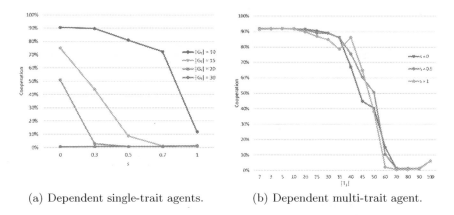

(a) Dependent single-trait agents.   (b) Dependent multi-trait agent.

Fig. 2. Figure (a) shows the relationship between cooperation, parameter s, and the size of the set G_t of agents sharing a common trait (see Fig. 1(a)). Figure (b) shows the effect of increasing the size of the set of traits T_1 of a single multi-trait agent on cooperation, in a scenario where all other agents are single trait (see Fig. 1(b)).

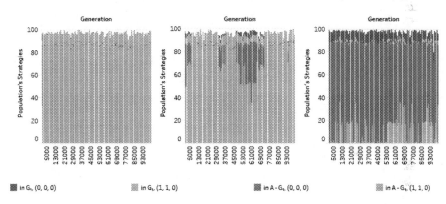

Fig. 3. Distribution of action rules $(0, 0, 0)$ and $(1, 1, 0)$ by generation for the sets of single-trait dependent agents G_t and independent agents $A - G_t$. $|G_t| = 10$ and $s = 0$ (left), 0.5 (middle), and 1 (right).

(Fig. 2(b)) show that as the size of the set T_1 of the multi-trait agent increases, cooperation diminishes. The sharing of the multi-trait agent's reputation is dispersed across single-trait agents who between themselves have no trait in common. This helps to suppress the rise of defective action rules, as compared to the previous scenario (Sect. 4.1). In fact, $|T_1|$ can reach a considerable size (e.g., 30–35 traits) before which cooperation starts to significantly diminish.

In this scenario, single-trait dependent agents rely entirely on themselves and the multi-trait agent for their reputation. Each single-trait dependent agent can also free ride on the single multi-trait agent, and this opens the opportunity for defection to establish itself, although to a lesser extent than the case presented in Sect. 4.1. When the number of traits of the multi-trait agent is relatively

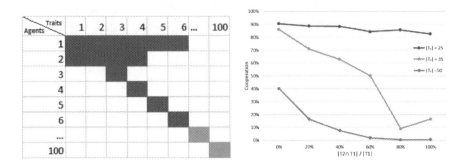

Fig. 4. The figures show the relationship between agents and traits for two dependent multi-trait agents (left) and the average cooperation produced as a function of the size of the intersection between the sets belonging to agents one and two for different values of $|T_1|$ where $s = 0$ (right).

small, the presence of free riding dependent single-trait agents can be sustained without too much disruption to the reputation of the multi-trait agent. As $|T_1|$ increases, and the number of dependent single-trait agents increases, there is a greater opportunity for free-riding action rules to take hold. At the same time, there are fewer independent single trait agents available in the population. This promotes the collapse of cooperation. As soon as a defective strategy takes hold across the population, it then opens the opportunity for this to spread to other agents. Interestingly, s has relatively little impact on whether dependent agents prioritise playing with those that have a common trait. However, they are less likely to have equal reputation in this instance.

Finally a second multi-trait agent is added, by replacing a single-trait agent (agent number 2) in Fig. 1(b), where $T_2 \subseteq T_1$. Figure 4 shows the effect of varying $|T_2 \cap T_1|$, that is the extent to which T_2 has the same traits as T_1. These results show that high proportions of shared identity through multi-trait agents undermine the reputation system. Because the second multi-trait agent can hold a large subset of the first agent's traits, it can heavily disrupt the first agent's reputation, by using defection as its action rule. This effect is more pronounced than that of a dependent single trait agent sharing reputation with the multi-trait dependent agent, and increases as $|T_2 \cap T_1|$ increases.

5   Discussion and Conclusion

Through a general framework for considering reputation, the authors have found that reputation systems for cooperation are heavily disrupted by the sharing of reputation through common traits. Stereotyping takes place, where traits are used as proxy for indirectly assessing an individual's reputation. This introduces the opportunity for agents to disconnect their actions from their reputation. Agents can deploy defective strategies: that is an agent can avoid paying the full costs of donation but receives donations based on the reputation aligning with its associated traits. How the reputation is shared, through inheritance of traits, is highly influential. Holding multiple traits presents an opportunity for agents to share a limited proportion of their identity with others. In doing so they have the potential to better control their exposure to defectors.

Single-trait and multi-trait agents are differentiated in how other agents can share their traits. Under uniform conditions, single-trait agents have a reduced chance of others having a trait in common. However, when another agent shares their trait, their reputation becomes susceptible to the actions of a third party. In contrast, for multi-trait agents, increasing the number of traits can give them a chance to retain an element of unique personal identity, through traits that aren't shared with others. Moreover, for multi-trait agents, sharing can occur with a number of agents that have no dependency between them, in terms of common traits.

Given the enormous number of possible ways in which traits can be shared, in this work our focus has concerned assessing basic aspects of sharing, surrounding the number of traits held by an agent. The results show that reasonable levels of cooperation can be sustained while there is a modest level of sharing of identity in the population, after which cooperation collapses.

This highlights the importance of individual versus group identity in reputation systems. It also warrants further investigation, being an important issue relevant to identity fusion [35], where effectively an individual's personal identity becomes identical to that of the group - in other words, distinguishable personal traits diminish. Understanding the extent to which personal identity, group identity and cooperation trade-off against each other, is an important future goal. The exploratory work in this paper validates the framework presented as a means to accomplish this.

Acknowledgements. W. Bedewi is funded by King Abdulaziz University, Saudi Arabia. Additionally the research was sponsored by the U.S. Army Research Laboratory and the U.K. Ministry of Defence under Agreement Number W911NF-16-3-0001. The views and conclusions contained in this document are those of the authors and should not be interpreted as representing the official policies, either expressed or implied, of the U.S. Army Research Laboratory, the U.S. Government, the U.K. Ministry of Defence or the U.K. Government. The U.S. and U.K. Governments are authorized to reproduce and distribute reprints for Government purposes not with standing any copyright notation hereon. This research was also supported by the Supercomputing Wales project, which is part-funded by the European Regional Development Fund (ERDF) via Welsh Government.

References

1. Alexander, R.D.: The Biology of Moral Systems. Transaction Publishers, Piscataway (1987)
2. Baranski, B., et al.: The impact of group reputation in multiagent environments. In: Proceedings of CEC 2006, pp. 1224–1231 (2006)
3. Bear, A., Rand, D.G.: Intuition, deliberation, and the evolution of cooperation. Proc. Nat. Acad. Sci. **113**(4), 936–941 (2016)

4. Bowleg, L.: Intersectionality: an underutilized but essential theoretical framework for social psychology. In: Gough, B. (ed.) The Palgrave Handbook of Critical Social Psychology, pp. 507–529. Palgrave Macmillan, London (2017). https://doi.org/10. 1057/978-1-137-51018-1_25

5. Brandt, H., Ohtsuki, H., Iwasa, Y., Sigmund, K.: A survey of indirect reciprocity. In: Takeuchi, Y., Iwasa, Y., Sato, K. (eds.) Mathematics for Ecology and Environmental Sciences. Biological and Medical Physics, pp. 21–49. Springer, Heidelberg (2007). https://doi.org/10.1007/978-3-540-34428-5_3

6. Brandt, H., Sigmund, K.: The logic of reprobation: assessment and action rules for indirect reciprocation. J. Theor. Biol. **231**(4), 475–486 (2004)

7. Brewer, M.B.: The psychology of prejudice: ingroup love and outgroup hate? J. Soc. Issues **55**(3), 429–444 (1999)

8. Dovidio, J.F., Gaertner, S.L., Validzic, A.: Intergroup bias: status, differentiation, and a common in-group identity. J. Pers. Soc. Psychol. **75**(1), 109 (1998)

9. Fehr, E.: Human behaviour: don't lose your reputation. Nature **432**(7016), 449–450 (2004)

10. Fishman, M.A.: Indirect reciprocity among imperfect individuals. J. Theor. Biol. **225**(3), 285–292 (2003)

11. Fu, F., Tarnita, C.E., Christakis, N.A., Wang, L., Rand, D.G., Nowak, M.A.: Evolution of in-group favoritism. Sci. Rep. **2**, 460 (2012)

12. Galinsky, A.D., Moskowitz, G.B.: Perspective-taking: decreasing stereotype expression, stereotype accessibility, and in-group favoritism. J. Pers. Soc. Psychol. **78**(4), 708 (2000)

13. Hammond, R.A., Axelrod, R.: The evolution of ethnocentrism. J. Conflict Resolut. **50**(6), 926–936 (2006)

14. Imbsweiler, J., Ruesch, M., Weinreuter, H., León, F.P., Deml, B.: Cooperation behaviour of road users in t-intersections during deadlock situations. Transp. Res. Part F: Traffic Psychol. Behav. **58**, 665–677 (2018)

15. Kawakami, K., Amodio, D.M., Hugenberg, K.: Intergroup perception and cognition: an integrative framework for understanding the causes and consequences of social categorization. Adv. Exp. Soc. Psychol. **55**, 1–80 (2017)

16. Launay, J., Dunbar, R.I.M.: Playing with strangers: which shared traits attract us most to new people? PLoS ONE **10**, 1–17 (2015)

17. Leimar, O., Hammerstein, P.: Evolution of cooperation through indirect reciprocity. Proc. Roy. Soc. B: Biol. Sci. **268**(1468), 745–753 (2001)

18. Masuda, N.: Ingroup favoritism and intergroup cooperation under indirect reciprocity based on group reputation. J. Theor. Biol. **311**, 8–18 (2012)

19. Melnik, M.I., Alm, J.: Does a seller's ecommerce reputation matter? evidence from eBay auctions. J. Ind. Econ. **50**(3), 337–349 (2002)

20. de Melo, C.M., Marsella, S., Gratch, J.: Human cooperation when acting through autonomous machines. Proc. Nat. Acad. Sci. **116**(9), 3482–3487 (2019)

21. Milinski, M., Semmann, D., Krambeck, H.J.: Reputation helps solve the 'tragedy of the commons'. Nature **415**(6870), 424–426 (2002)

22. Molleman, L., van den Broek, E., Egas, M.: Personal experience and reputation interact in human decisions to help reciprocally. Proc. R. Soc. B **280**(1757), 20123044 (2013)

23. Nowak, M.A., Sigmund, K.: Evolution of indirect reciprocity by image scoring. Nature **393**(6685), 573–577 (1998)

24. Nowak, M.A., Sigmund, K.: Evolution of indirect reciprocity. Nature **437**(7063), 1291–1298 (2005)

25. Nowak, M.A., Tarnita, C.E., Wilson, E.O.: The evolution of eusociality. Nature **466**(7310), 1057 (2010)

26. Oakes, P.J., Turner, J.C.: Social categorization and intergroup behaviour: does minimal intergroup discrimination make social identity more positive? Eur. J. Soc. Psychol. **10**(3), 295–301 (1980)

27. Ohtsuki, H., Iwasa, Y.: The leading eight: social norms that can maintain cooperation by indirect reciprocity. J. Theor. Biol. **239**(4), 435–444 (2006)

28. Panchanathan, K., Boyd, R.: A tale of two defectors: the importance of standing for evolution of indirect reciprocity. J. Theor. Biol. **224**(1), 115–126 (2003)

29. Pinker, S.: The false allure of group selection (2012)

30. Rand, D.G., Nowak, M.A.: Human cooperation. Trends Cogn. Sci. **17**(8), 413–425 (2013)

31. Resnick, P., Kuwabara, K., Zeckhauser, R., Friedman, E.: Reputation systems. Commun. ACM **43**(12), 45–48 (2000)

32. Smith, J.M.: Group selection and kin selection. Nature **201**(4924), 1145 (1964)

33. Sugden, R.: The Economics of Rights, Co-operation and Welfare. Blackwell, Oxford (1986)

34. Suzuki, S., Akiyama, E.: Reputation and the evolution of cooperation in sizable groups. Proc. Roy. Soc. B: Biol. Sci. **272**(1570), 1373–1377 (2005)

35. Swann Jr., W.B., Gómez, Á., Seyle, D.C., Morales, J., Huici, C.: Identity fusion: the interplay of personal and social identities in extreme group behavior. J. Pers. Soc. Psychol. **96**(5), 995 (2009)

36. Tajfel, H., Billig, M.G., Bundy, R.P., Flament, C.: Social categorization and intergroup behaviour. Eur. J. Soc. Psychol. **1**(2), 149–178 (1971)

37. Tajfel, H., Turner, J.C.: An integrative theory of intergroup conflict. Soc. Psychol. Intergroup Relat. **33**(47), 74 (1979)

38. Takahashi, N., Mashima, R.: The importance of subjectivity in perceptual errors on the emergence of indirect reciprocity. J. Theor. Biol. **243**(3), 418–436 (2006)

39. Turner, J.C., Hogg, M.A., Oakes, P.J., Reicher, S.D., Wetherell, M.S.: Rediscovering the Social Group: A Self-Categorization Theory. Basil Blackwell, Oxford (1987)

40. Wasko, M.M., Faraj, S.: "it is what one does": why people participate and help others in electronic communities of practice. J. Strateg. Inf. Syst. **9**(2–3), 155–173 (2000)

41. Wedekind, C., Milinski, M.: Cooperation through image scoring in humans. Science **288**(5467), 850–852 (2000)

42. Whitaker, R.M., Colombo, G.B., Allen, S.M., Dunbar, R.I.: A dominant social comparison heuristic unites alternative mechanisms for the evolution of indirect reciprocity. Sci. Rep. **6**, 31459 (2016)

43. Whitaker, R.M., Colombo, G.B., Rand, D.G.: Indirect reciprocity and the evolution of prejudicial groups. Sci. Rep. **8**(1), 13247 (2018)

44. Wilson, D.S.: A theory of group selection. Proc. Nat. Acad. Sci. **72**(1), 143–146 (1975)

45. Wilson, D.S., Sober, E.: Reintroducing group selection to the human behavioral sciences. Behav. Brain Sci. **17**(4), 585–608 (1994)

46. Wu, J., Balliet, D., Van Lange, P.A.: Reputation, gossip, and human cooperation. Soc. Pers. Psychol. Compass **10**(6), 350–364 (2016)

Homophily, Mobility and Opinion Formation

Enas E. Alraddadi$^{(\boxtimes)}$, Stuart M. Allen, and Roger M. Whitaker

School of Computer Science and Informatics, Cardiff University, Cardiff, UK
{AlraddadiE,AllenSM,WhitakerRM}@cardiff.ac.uk

Abstract. Understanding the evolution and spread of opinions within social groups gives important insight into areas such as public elections and marketing. We are specifically interested in how psychological theories of interpersonal influence may affect how individuals change their opinion through interactions with their peers, and apply Agent Based Modelling to explore the factors that may affect the emergence of consensus.

We investigate the coevolution of opinion and location by extending the Deffuant-Weisbuch bounded confidence opinion model to include mobility inspired by the psychological theories of homophily and dissonance, where agents are attracted or repelled by their neighbours based on the agreement of their opinions. Based on wide experimentation, we characterise the time it takes to converge to a steady state and the local diversity of opinions that results, finding that homophily leads to drastic differences in the nature of consensus.

1 Introduction

Human behaviour, and particularly the interactions we have with our peers, has a profound effect on the nature of consensus that emerges within social groups. Due to the rise of online social networks, it is increasingly easy to widely share opinion on a given subject, and thereby influence peers. Understanding how individual interactions in between agents lead to the formation of shared opinions is vitally important, particularly in light of the potential for malicious influence around political decisions. In this paper, we investigate the role of mobility in guiding the dynamics of opinion formation in such systems.

A wide range of models for opinion dynamics have been considered, which can be broadly categorised into *discrete* and *continuous* representations. Notable discrete approaches include voter models [11] or those inspired by physics such as the Ising model [29], however in this work we focus on the widely studied *bounded confidence* model proposed by Deffuant et al. [7]. In this model, opinions are represented by real values in [0, 1] and agents interact with their peers and adjust their opinion whenever the difference between their respective opinions is within a specified threshold. A thorough review of the breadth of approaches can be found across several surveys [1,5,21,30,31].

© Springer Nature Switzerland AG 2019
N. T. Nguyen et al. (Eds.): ICCCI 2019, LNAI 11683, pp. 130–141, 2019.
https://doi.org/10.1007/978-3-030-28377-3_11

Despite the wide range of different approaches in the literature, very few take into account the fundamental principle of human mobility, which forms the basis of investigation in this paper. Mobility is commonly implemented through models in which the agents move constantly at random, such as [12,28,32]. In contrast, [26] presents a model of discrete opinions based on Brownian motion, while [24] considers a lattice model in which movement is triggered by disagreement. Disagreement is also used to trigger changes in structure in [13], however this is based on social group membership without including location.

As highlighted in [5], it is important that the mathematical rules used to model social mechanisms and simulate opinion dynamics are referenced to psychological and/or sociological studies. In this paper, we address this by drawing on the well-studied psychological theories of homophily [23] and dissonance [9] to motivate our rules.

The aim of this paper is to investigate the effect of homophily and dissonance on the speed and structure of opinion convergence among agents that are free to move within a two dimensional region. Comparisons are made with a random mobility model, evaluated over a range of parameters, highlighting clear differences in behaviour.

The paper introduces the general known framework of opinion modelling and extends it to add mobility inspired by psychological and sociological studies. After discussing related work in the next section, we describe our model in Sect. 3. We synthesize and discuss results for two proposed mobility models in Sect. 4 and conclude with a brief summary in Sect. 5.

2 Related Work

The Deffuant-Weisbuch bounded confidence model (denoted DW) of opinion dynamics [7] builds upon previous work of Axelrod [2] (which was framed in terms of the evolution of culture rather than opinion). Axelrod described the culture (opinion) space as a vector of discrete multiple features, and studied the interactions that were most effected between similar people. The DW model was inspired by this notion of homophilic attraction, however represented opinions as a value in the continuous interval $[0, 1]$. DW is one of the most well-studied models, since it represents a number of common scenarios, such as where the political spectrum of an individual is not restricted to an extreme right or left wing but also positions in between [5,7,21] with one and zero representing the two extremes [22]. The Hegselmann-Krause model [18] was developed based on the DW model, by extending influence to groups rather than pairwise interactions, and has also led to a wide body of related research.

We now briefly highlight the key features of opinion models within a general framework (see Fig. 1a). More detail can be found in a number of comprehensive survey papers [1,5,21,30,31].

Many opinion models do take locality into consideration (for example [2, 6,14,29]). However, in reality people's location and opinions are dynamic, but rarely do you find a model that adds mobility [5,15,26,27,30], social interactions

(a) Static

(b) With mobility

Fig. 1. General framework

are not static. Given all the social psychological research on the relationship between impact and distance (proximity-influence relationship), to date, there hasn't been much research on opinion evolution in naturalistic dynamic settings. Most research in this area is conducted on static settings.

One of the main determinants of social influence is similarity [2,23]. We believe influence can be modelled and mapped on location just as opinions. Mobile agents were implemented in different social context. One, is the study of pedestrian crowd [19], this area started off with models on cellular automata and shifted to models where agents can move in continuous space successfully [5]. Furthermore, mobility has been also studied for residential housing patterns [15,25] and emerging communities [24]. Others propose a two-dimensional factorization of perceived personality in crowd simulations with mobile agents [17].

2.1   Interaction Scheme

One of the important features in opinion formation models is the interaction scheme, which defines how the agents are selected to interact. Approaches in the literature include random selection on a global basis [7], various measures of local selection [2,7,12,14,18,24,26,28,29,32], or some combination of both local and global [13,16]. Empirical evidence from social psychology highlights geographical proximity as an indicator of increased interactions between peers [20] or increased probability of friendship [10]. Global interactions as in the original DW model mean that an agent has the same probability to interact with anybody within the entire space, lattice or network, counter to these sociology theories.

2.2   Influence Scheme

Many theories of social interaction are based on interpersonal communication and characterised by mutual attraction and proximity among local individuals of similar characteristic such as age, gender or social class. The psychological theory of *homophily* [23] describes the tendency of an individual to interact with others depending their similarity. This is often expressed by the proverb 'Birds of a feather flock together'. The original DW model is based on this concept, whereby agents that are close in opinion will interact, and adjust their opinion to be closer. In our model, we will also apply the concept to mobility, with agents moving closer to peers following a successful interaction.

A further profound concept is social impact theory [20], which explains that the amount of influence a person experiences in group settings depends on (a) strength (power or social status) of the group, (b) immediacy (physical or psychological distance) of the group, and (c) the number of people in the group exerting the social influence (i.e., number of sources). Latane found that the impact exerted by a source decreases with increasing distance, however, this work has also been criticised for neglecting a number of realistic features of social interaction, such as the possibility to actually move in physical space [5, 26].

The final psychological theory we note is that of *cognitive dissonance* [9], which describes our subconscious desire for internal consistency. More specifically, it is the cognitive discomfort experience by a person who has two contradicting beliefs. Due to this psychological discomfort, a person tends to act to reduce the cognitive dissonance, either adding new parts to the cognition or by actively avoiding social situations or contradicting information.

2.3   Mobility Scheme

Several approaches to mobility have been taken in the literature on opinion dynamics. The most structured of these consider agents that are located on a lattice (e.g. [15, 24, 28, 32]), which move to an empty space (when available). Although this allows computationally efficient simulations, the limited space available greatly constrains movement, which impacts on the formation of groups with any similarity. Network based models, such as [13, 16], share similar issues to lattices, however, allow more realistic social structures.

2.4   Contribution

Inspired by the theory of cognitive dissonance, we propose a new model (Fig. 1b) for the co-evolution of opinion and location. Our model introduces a fixed interaction radii r_s to describe the neighbourhood of an agent, which is modified as agents move freely within the space. The use of free Euclidean space contrasts with forced interactions with the same neighbours for the entire simulation as in the static opinion formation models implemented in [7, 18, 29] or network/lattice models of social structures. Agents in our model do not form or break explicit links, but interact with their local peers at any point in time.

3   Methodology

Our investigation is based on *Agent Based Modelling (ABM)*, an approach that works as electronic laboratory especially for cases where high quality data of opinion spread is not available [3, 4, 20].

3.1   Model

In this section we propose a model for the co-evolution of opinion and location. We consider a population of n agents, $A = \{a_1, \ldots, a_n\}$, where each agent a_i is defined by a location $xy_i = (x_i, y_i)$ and opinion $op_i \in [0, 1]$. Following the DW model [7], a pair of agents a_i, a_j will interact if and only if their respective opinions (op_i, op_j) are within an opinion threshold ϵ. If this is the case, they each update their opinion as shown in Algorithm 1, where μ is a global parameter controlling the effect of a peer's opinion (termed convergence rate in the original model [7]).

Algorithm 1. Simulation framework

Initialise: Create population A of n agents
for each iteration in range($limit$) **do**
        Select agent a_i and neighbour $a_j \in N(i, r_s)$ at random
        if $|op_i - op_j| \leq \epsilon$ **then**
                $op_i = op_i + \mu(op_j - op_i)$
                $op_j = op_j + \mu(op_i - op_j)$
                # Update location based on mobility model
        else
                # Update location based on mobility model
        end if
end for

We modify the DW model by only allowing interactions between agents that are close in both opinion and location, and similarly updating both opinions and location following an interaction. Let $d(i, j)$ denote the Euclidean distance between agents a_i and a_j, and let $N(i, d) = \{a_j \in A - \{a_i\} : d(i, j) \leq d\}$ be the set of agents that are at most distance d from agent a_i. For each interaction we select an agent a_i at random from the population A, and select an a peer at random from $N(i, d)$. The opinions of i and j are the updated following the DW model, before updating the location of i as the instigator of the interaction. We compare the effect of two mobility models:

Random Mobility. Under this model, agent a_i relocates to a random location within a local neighbourhood with probability p if an interaction with a peer is unsuccessful. However if they agree, both agents remain in their current locations. More formally, let λ be a constant input parameter, and let $U(0, 1)$ denote a random number uniformly selected from $[0, 1]$. If agent a_i selects another agent a_j to interact with, then a_i updates it's location according to the Algorithm 2.

Homophilous Mobility. Our second model (shown in Algorithm 3) is inspired by the psychological theory of homophily [23], where agents are more attracted towards similar peers. Following an interaction, agent a_i moves closer to their peer a_j if they are close in opinion, and further away if they differ. A parameter λ is applied to control the scale of movement, with $\lambda = 0$ leading to no movement, and $\lambda = 1$ denoting that a_i moves to the same position as a_j.

Algorithm 2. Random movement

---

if $p > U(0,1)$ **and** $|op_i - op_j| > \epsilon$ **then**
    $r = r_s\lambda\sqrt{U(0,1)}$
    $\theta = 2\pi U(0,1)$
    $xy_i = (x_i + r\cos\theta, y_i + r\sin\theta)$
else
    # Don't move
end if

Algorithm 3. Homophilous movement

---

if $p > U(0,1)$ **then**
    if $|op_i - op_j| \leq \epsilon$ **then**
        $xy_i' = xy_i + \lambda(xy_j - xy_i)$ # Move closer
    else
        $xy_i' = xy_i - \lambda(xy_j - xy_i)$ # Move away
    end if
else
    # Don't move
end if

3.2   Evaluation Metrics

We consider four metrics to assess emergent behaviours. **Convergence time** measures the number of iterations required before a steady state of opinions is reached. The convergence time of a simulation run is defined to be the lowest value of t such that no agent changes their opinion by more than δ between iteration t and $t + N_F$ (with N_F and δ set as input parameters).

The DBSCAN algorithm [8] is used to identify **clusters** of agents that are close in opinion and/or location once the system has converged. Note that the algorithm detects clusters a minimum of five agents, otherwise these are considered as noise. Clusters based on opinion only were identified by considering the distance between two agents a_i and a_j to be $|op_i - op_j|$, and setting the DBSCAN threshold to be δ. To identify clusters that are close in both opinion and location, the distance between a_i and a_j is set to the Euclidean distance between xy_i and xy_j if $|op_i - op_j| < \delta$, and an arbitrary large value otherwise. A threshold of $\frac{2}{3}\lambda r_s$ is then used within the DBSCAN algorithm to identify adjacent agents.

Finally, we define two metrics to measure the distribution of opinion in the immediate locality of each agent, looking at both the number of agents that disagree and the size of this disagreement. **Local disagreement** is calculated as the mean percentage of local agents that hold a different opinion once convergence has occurred.

$$N'(i, r_s) = \{j \in N(i, r_s) : |op_j - op_i| > \delta\}$$
$$dis = \frac{1}{n} \sum_{i \in \{j : |N(j, r_s)| > 0\}} \frac{|N'(i, r_s)|}{|N(i, r_s)|}$$

Local diversity measures the average difference of opinion among the neighbours of each agent:

$$div = \frac{1}{n} \sum_{i=1}^{n} \left[\frac{1}{|N(i, r_s)|} \sum_{j \in N(i, r_s)} |op_i - op_j| \right]$$

4   Results

Experiments were conducted with a population of n agents located in a 10×10 bounded 2D space. The initial position of each agent $i \in n$ was chosen uniformly randomly within the region, with $xy_i = (U(0, 10), U(0, 10))$, and an opinion $op_i = U(0, 1)$. When an agent's mobility would take it beyond the confines of the region, it bounces back to remain within boundaries.

A general property [7] of the DW model is that when $\epsilon \geq 0.3$ then the system reaches complete opinion consensus (only one opinion exists), and that $\epsilon \leq 0.2$ leads to polarization, where two opinions survive. Further study of the model [13] shows that an opinion threshold above 0.267 leads to complete consensus. We therefore restrict our attention to the cases $\epsilon = 0.1, 0.2$ and 0.3, and for each case vary the probability (p) and scale (λ) of movement.

Simulations were run for a maximum of 40,000 iterations and the results presented are averaged over 20 independent simulation runs with different random seeds. Other simulation parameters are listed in Table 1. We obtain qualitatively

Table 1. Simulation parameters

Parameter	Description	Value
n	Number of agents	100
$limit$	Iterations per run	40000
r_s	Interactive radius	2
ϵ	Opinion threshold	$[0.1, 0.2, 0.3]$
μ	Convergence rate	0.5
p	Probability of movement	$[0.1, 0.2, 0.4, 0.6, 1]$
λ	Movement scale factor	$[0.1, 0.2, \ldots, 1.0]$
δ	Opinion change threshold	0.01
N_F	Number of iterations without opinion change	10000

similar results for both a 20×20 space with the same population density, and an average over 40 random seeds. As a baseline for comparison, all figures show results for the corresponding DW model as a constant line (as this does not depend on λ). Results are shown for both random (ran) and homophilous (hom) movement and a range of values for p. For $p = 0$, both mobility models are identical, hence only the random case is shown.

4.1 Convergence Time

Figure 2 shows the convergence times for both models over a range of opinion thresholds, probability of movement (p), and distance moved (λ). For both models, convergence is quicker when agents are more mobile (i.e. as the probability of movement p increases), with the highest mobility approaching the convergence time of the standard DW model with global interactions (denoted *Deff* in the figures). As may be expected, convergence is quickest with no movement ($p = 0$), where there are limited opportunities for agents to interact and change their opinion.

The impact of λ as a control on the distance moved is more pronounced for lower opinion thresholds ($\epsilon = 0.1, 0.2$), but interestingly, shows an increasing correlation for random movement, but a decreasing relationship for homophilous movement. As with the original DW model, there appears to be a step change in behaviour when moving from an opinion threshold of 0.1 to 0.2 or 0.3, with the effect of mobility drastically reducing.

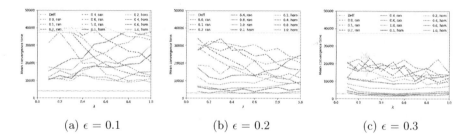

(a) $\epsilon = 0.1$ (b) $\epsilon = 0.2$ (c) $\epsilon = 0.3$

Fig. 2. Mean convergence time for values of p

4.2 Opinion Diversity

Figure 3 highlights that the faster convergence for homophilous movement is also associated with lower local disagreement. In particular, for $\epsilon \geq 0.2$, homophilous movement results in each agent being surrounded by local groups that entirely agree with their opinion (i.e. with opinion differences below δ), while random mobility allows limited diversity to persist. In contrast, the behaviour of random movement is extremely consistent across all values of p and λ, which is similar to the case when agents are stationary ($p = 0$). Similar differences between random and homophilous are also seen in the mean local diversity shown in Fig. 4.

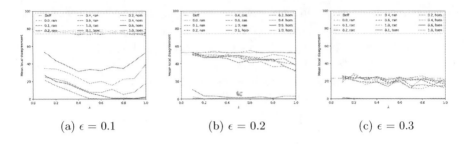

(a) $\epsilon = 0.1$ (b) $\epsilon = 0.2$ (c) $\epsilon = 0.3$

Fig. 3. Mean local disagreement for values of p

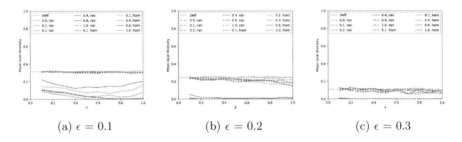

(a) $\epsilon = 0.1$ (b) $\epsilon = 0.2$ (c) $\epsilon = 0.3$

Fig. 4. Mean local diversity for values of p

4.3 Clusters

Finally, we investigate how agents are clustered following convergence, considering only opinion (Fig. 5) and opinion combined with location (Fig. 6). In contrast to the original DW model, restricting interactions to a local area allows consensus to form around a larger number of opinions, confined to geographic groupings. For low values of λ with random movement, DBSCAN typically classes all agents as noise, and is unable to identify any clusters. Note that limiting the scale of mobility, either through lower values of p or λ, allows larger numbers of discrete opinions to survive under homophilous movement. As with previous evaluation, there is a marked difference between the mobility models, with random movement behaving similarly to no movement. In particular, homophilous movement allows the formation of geographically separate clusters with similar opinions.

4.4 Discussion

The results consistently show that random movement produces very similar effects to the original static DW model with global selection of interactions, with very little variation due to the probability p or scale λ of movement. Differences are only evident for the speed of convergence, and the interesting formation of geographically distinct clusters which nevertheless share similar opinions. Our new model based on homophily in movement results in radically different results

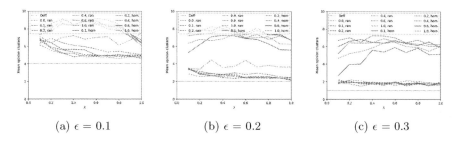

(a) $\epsilon = 0.1$ (b) $\epsilon = 0.2$ (c) $\epsilon = 0.3$

Fig. 5. Mean opinion clusters for values of p

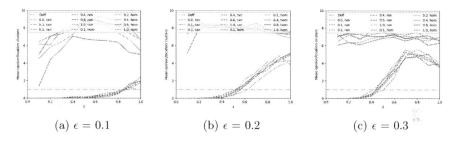

(a) $\epsilon = 0.1$ (b) $\epsilon = 0.2$ (c) $\epsilon = 0.3$

Fig. 6. Mean opinion/location clusters for values of p

for all evaluation measures, demonstrating a greater propensity for clusters of distinct opinions to survive, which each show greater levels of consensus.

5   Conclusions

We have demonstrated that the nature of mobility plays an important role in how groups of shared opinions evolve. Inline with other studies that consider opinion formation with models of random mobility (e.g. [28,32]), we find that increased mobility (either manifested through higher probability of relocating or larger range of movement) leads to faster convergence. However, we have also shown that the opinion groups formed under random movement are similar to the static case, with relatively high local diversity and low numbers of distinct opinions surviving.

As an alternative to random movement, we have proposed a model for the co-evolution of opinion and location based on the psychological principles of *homophily* and *dissonance*, whereby agents move towards peers with a similar opinion, and away from those they disagree with. Results show this model allows a greater number of opinions to survive, with groups separating geographically to avoid conflict. Increased mobility in this case leads to less local diversity and more opinion clusters. This highlights the importance of considering mobility and our psychological behaviour in modelling opinion, with implications for scenarios where individuals have control over their social structures.

Acknowledgement. This research was supported by the Supercomputing Wales project, which is part-funded by the European Regional Development Fund (ERDF) via Welsh Government.

References

1. Abid, O., Jamoussi, S., Ayed, Y.B.: Deterministic models for opinion formation through communication: a survey. Online Soc. Netw. Media **6**, 1–17 (2018)
2. Axelrod, R.: The dissemination of culture: a model with local convergence and global polarization. J. Conflict Resolut. **41**(2), 203–226 (1997)
3. Banisch, S., Araújo, T., Louçã, J.: Opinion dynamics and communication networks. Adv. Complex Syst. **13**(01), 95–111 (2010)
4. Bruch, E., Atwell, J.: Agent-based models in empirical social research. Sociol. Methods Res. **44**(2), 186–221 (2015)
5. Castellano, C., Fortunato, S., Loreto, V.: Statistical physics of social dynamics. Rev. Modern Phys. **81**(2), 591 (2009)
6. Chen, G., et al.: Deffuant model on a ring with repelling mechanism and circular opinions. Phys. Rev. E **95**(4), 042118 (2017)
7. Deffuant, G., Neau, D., Amblard, F., Weisbuch, G.: Mixing beliefs among interacting agents. Adv. Complex Syst. **3**(01n04), 87–98 (2000)
8. Ester, M., Kriegel, H.P., Sander, J., Xu, X., et al.: A density-based algorithm for discovering clusters in large spatial databases with noise. In: KDD, vol. 96, pp. 226–231 (1996)
9. Festinger, L.: A Theory of Cognitive Dissonance, vol. 2. Stanford University Press, Stanford (1957)
10. Festinger, L., Schachter, S., Back, K.: Social Pressures in Informal Groups; A Study of Human Factors in Housing. Harper & Brothers, New York (1950)
11. Galam, S.: Real space renormalization group and totalitarian paradox of majority rule voting. Physica A: Stat. Mech. Appl. **285**(1–2), 66–76 (2000)
12. Galam, S., Chopard, B., Masselot, A., Droz, M.: Competing species dynamics: qualitative advantage versus geography. Eur. Phys. J. B-Condens. Matter Complex Syst. **4**(4), 529–531 (1998)
13. Gargiulo, F., Huet, S.: Opinion dynamics in a group-based society. EPL (Europhys. Lett.) **91**(5), 58004 (2010)
14. Grabowski, A.: Opinion formation in a social network: the role of human activity. Physica A: Stat. Mech. Appl. **388**(6), 961–966 (2009)
15. Gracia-Lázaro, C., Lafuerza, L.F., Floría, L.M., Moreno, Y.: Residential segregation and cultural emination: an axelrod-schelling model. Phys. Rev. E **80**(4), 046123 (2009)
16. Guo, L., Cheng, Y., Luo, Z.: Opinion dynamics with the contrarian deterministic effect and human mobility on lattice. Complexity **20**(5), 43–49 (2015)
17. Guy, S.J., Kim, S., Lin, M.C., Manocha, D.: Simulating heterogeneous crowd behaviors using personality trait theory. In: Proceedings of the 2011 ACM SIGGRAPH/Eurographics Symposium on Computer Animation, pp. 43–52. ACM (2011)
18. Hegselmann, R., Krause, U., et al.: Opinion dynamics and bounded confidence models, analysis, and simulation. J. Artif. Soc. Social Simul. **5**(3) (2002)
19. Helbing, D., Farkas, I.J., Molnar, P., Vicsek, T.: Simulation of pedestrian crowds in normal and evacuation situations. Pedestr. Evacuation Dyn. **21**(2), 21–58 (2002)

20. Latané, B.: The psychology of social impact. Am. Psychol. **36**(4), 343 (1981)
21. Lorenz, J.: Continuous opinion dynamics under bounded confidence: a survey. Int. J. Modern Phys. C **18**(12), 1819–1838 (2007)
22. Martins, A.C.: Continuous opinions and discrete actions in opinion dynamics problems. Int. J. Modern Phys. C **19**(04), 617–624 (2008)
23. McPherson, M., Smith-Lovin, L., Cook, J.M.: Birds of a feather: homophily in social networks. Ann. Rev. Sociol. **27**(1), 415–444 (2001)
24. Pfau, J., Kirley, M., Kashima, Y.: The co-evolution of cultures, social network communities, and agent locations in an extension of axelrod's model of cultural dissemination. Physica A: Stat. Mech. Appl. **392**(2), 381–391 (2013)
25. Schelling, T.C.: Dynamic models of segregation. J. Math. Sociol. **1**(2), 143–186 (1971)
26. Schweitzer, F., Hołyst, J.: Modelling collective opinion formation by means of active brownian particles. Eur. Phys. J. B-Condens. Matter Complex Syst. **15**(4), 723–732 (2000)
27. Sobkowicz, P.: Modelling opinion formation with physics tools: call for closer link with reality. J. Artif. Soc. Soc. Simul. **12**(1), 11 (2009)
28. Sousa, A., Yu-Song, T., Ausloos, M.: Effects of agents' mobility on opinion spreading in Sznajd model. Eur. Phys. J. B-Condens. Matter Complex Syst. **66**(1), 115–124 (2008)
29. Sznajd-Weron, K., Sznajd, J.: Opinion evolution in closed community. Int. J. Modern Phys. C **11**(06), 1157–1165 (2000)
30. Xia, H., Wang, H., Xuan, Z.: Opinion dynamics: a multidisciplinary review and perspective on future research. Int. J. Knowl. Syst. Sci. (IJKSS) **2**(4), 72–91 (2011)
31. Xie, Z., Song, X., Li, Q.: A review of opinion dynamics. In: Zhang, L., Song, X., Wu, Y. (eds.) AsiaSim/SCS AutumnSim - 2016. CCIS, vol. 646, pp. 349–357. Springer, Singapore (2016). https://doi.org/10.1007/978-981-10-2672-0_36
32. Zhang, Y., Liu, Q., Wang, Z., Zhang, S.: On the opinion formation of mobile agents with memory. Physica A: Stat. Mech. Appl. **492**, 438–445 (2018)

Predicting S&P 500 Based on Its Constituents and Their Social Media Derived Sentiment

Rapheal Olaniyan[1,2], Daniel Stamate[1,2(✉)], Ida Pu[1,2], Alexander Zamyatin[1,3], Anna Vashkel[1], and Frederic Marechal[1]

[1] Data Science & Soft Computing Lab, London, UK
[2] Computing Department, Goldsmiths, University of London, London, UK
d.stamate@gold.ac.uk
[3] Institute of Applied Mathematics and Computer Science, Tomsk State University, Tomsk, Russia

Abstract. Collective intelligence, represented as sentiment extracted from social media mining, is encountered in various applications. Numerous studies involving machine learning modelling have demonstrated that such sentiment information may or may not have predictive power on the stock market trend, depending on the application and the data used. This work proposes, for the first time, an approach to predicting S&P 500 based on the closing stock prices and sentiment data of the S&P 500 constituents. One of the significant complexities of our framework is due to the high dimensionality of the dataset to analyse, which is based on a large number of constituents and their sentiments, and their lagging. Another significant complexity is due to the fact that the relationship between the response and the explanatory variables is time-varying in the highly volatile stock market data, and it is difficult to capture. We propose a predictive modelling approach based on a methodology specifically designed to effectively address the above challenges and to devise efficient predictive models based on Jordan and Elman recurrent neural networks. We further propose a hybrid trading model that incorporates a technical analysis, and the application of machine learning and evolutionary optimisation techniques. We prove that our unprecedented and innovative constituent and sentiment based approach is efficient in predicting S&P 500, and thus may be used to maximise investment portfolios regardless of whether the market is bullish or bearish.

Keywords: Collective intelligence · Sentiment analysis ·
Stock market prediction · Feature selection · Feature clustering ·
PCA · Jordan and Elman Neural Networks · Evolutionary computing ·
Statistical tests · Granger causality

1 Introduction

Stock market is considered to be highly volatile. With this inherent problem, developing an efficient predictive model using purely traditional stock data to

© Springer Nature Switzerland AG 2019
N. T. Nguyen et al. (Eds.): ICCCI 2019, LNAI 11683, pp. 142–153, 2019.
https://doi.org/10.1007/978-3-030-28377-3_12

capture its trends, is considered to be hard to achieve. On the other hand, behavioural finance relaxes the assumption that investors act rationally. It underlines the importance of sentiment contagion in investment. Since then, researchers have been focusing on the relationship between sentiment and the stock market. For example, Shiller [19] and Sprenger et al. [20] observed that factors related to the field of behavioural finance influence the stock market as a result of psychological contagion which makes investors to overreact or under-react. They imply that investors have the tendency to react differently to new information which could be in the form of business news, online social networking blogs, and other forms of online expressions.

Observations from related research works sprang up interest in advancing the standard finance models to include collective intelligence information represented by sentiment extracted from social media mining, in the predictive model development, with the aim of enhancing the model reliability and efficiency. Yet in order to statistically validate this inclusion, one needs to consider the source of the sentiment, examine its statistical significance and the Granger causality [7] between the sentiment and the stock market variables by using appropriate approaches.

Gilbert and Karahalios [6] investigated the causal relationship between the stock market returns for S&P 500 and the sentiment based on a collection of Live-Journal blogs. The sentiment was considered as a proxy for public mood. Using a linear framework they showed that sentiment possesses predictive information on the stock market returns. An obviously arising question in such a context is: is the linear framework robust enough to examine the Granger causality between stock market returns and sentiment? Olaniyan et al. [16] presented their finding from the re-assessment of the work conducted by Gilbert and Karahalios [6]. They showed that the models in [6] presented flaws from a statistical point of view. [16] further investigated the causality direction between sentiment and the stock market returns using a non-parametric approach and showed that there is no line of Granger causality between the stock market returns and sentiment in the framework considered in [6].

The influence of sentiments on the stock market has been extensively studied and so are the asymmetric impacts of positive and negative news on the market. But little has been done in devising efficient predictive models that can help to maximise investment portfolios while taking into consideration the statistical relevance of sentiment, and the proposed work addresses this concern. The main aim of this research is to predict reliably the directions of the S&P 500 closing prices, by proposing a predictive modelling approach based on integrating and analysing data on S&P 500 index, its constituents, and sentiments on these constituents. Indeed, this study is the first work to use constituent sentiments and its closing stock prices containing over 800 variables (combined closing stock prices of the S&P 500 constituents and their respective sentiment data without taking into account lagging - which further increases data dimensionality in a n-fold fashion) to predict the stock market.

First we tackle the data high dimensionality challenge by devising and proposing a method of selecting variables by combining three steps based on variable clustering, PCA (Principal Component Analysis) [12], and finally on a modified version of the Best *GLM* variable selection method developed by McLeod and Xu [15].

Then we propose an efficient predictive modelling approach based on Jordan and Elman recurrent neural network algorithms. To avoid the pitfall of time invariant relationship between the response and the explanatory variables in the highly volatile stock market data, our approach captures the dynamic of the explanatory variables set for every rolling window. This helps to incorporate the time-variant and dynamic relationship between the response and explanatory variables at every point of the rolling window using our variable selection technique mentioned above. Finally, we propose an efficient hybrid trading model that incorporates a technical analysis, and machine learning and evolutionary optimisation algorithms.

We prove that our constituent and sentiment based approach is efficient in predicting S&P 500, and thus may be used to maximise investment portfolios regardless of whether the market is bullish or bearish[1]. This study extends our previous recent work on XLE index constituents' social media based sentiment informing the index trend and volatility prediction [14].

The remainder of this paper is organized as follows. Section 2 presents our data pre-processing methodology, which is our proposed method for handling the data high-dimensionality challenge outlined above, for selecting the variables with predictive value. Section 3 elaborates on the results of the causality relationship between sentiment and the stock market returns using special techniques of Granger causality. Section 4 presents the predictive modelling approach that we propose based on machine learning techniques including Jordan and Elman recurrent Neural Network algorithms. Section 5 entails our proposed trading model that combines a technical analysis strategy and the estimated results from the machine learning framework to optimise investment portfolios with evolutionary optimisation techniques. Finally Sect. 6 discusses our findings and concludes the paper.

2   Stock Data and Sentiment Information

In order to develop our approach to predicting the S&P 500 close prices, we rely on three main datasets which we integrate. The first dataset involves the collection of all the closing stock prices for the S&P 500 constituents, and is obtained directly from Yahoo Finance website. The second dataset is sentiment

---

[1] Bullish and bearish are terms used to characterize trends in the stock markets: if prices tend to move up, it is a bull market; if prices move down, it is a bear market.

data for the constituents of the S&P 500 index, obtained from Quandle[2] [9]. And the third dataset contains the S&P 500 historical close prices and trading volume, obtained also from Yahoo Finance website.

All the data collected covered the period from 8th of February 2013 to 21st of January 2016. For S&P 500 and its constituents, the stock market return at time t is defined as $R_t = log(SP_{t+1}) - log(SP_t)$, where SP is the closing stock price. The stock market acceleration metric is obtained from the stock market return as $M_t = R_{t+1} - R_t$. Moreover, V_t is expressed as the first difference of the logged trading volume. Finally, the sentiment acceleration metric is defined as $A_t = S_t - S_{t-1}$, where S_t represents sentiment for each constituent of the S&P 500 at moment t.

By combining the three datasets, in all we have more than 800 initial variables to explore (not including lagged variables), which will lead to one of the challenges encountered in our framework in terms of high data dimensionality.

Figure 1 shows the data pre-processing process flow. It highlights all the processes undertaken to refine the data.

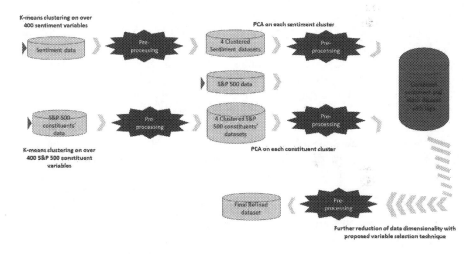

Fig. 1. Data pre-processing process flow that details the processes followed to tackle the complexity of high dimensionality dataset

To handle the high data dimensionality challenge, we propose an approach to reducing the number of dimensions, adapted to our framework, based on 3 steps, consisting consecutively of performing variable clustering, PCA, and by applying a variable selection method that we introduce here based on Best *GLM* variable selection method developed by McLeod and Xu [15]. These steps are described in the following subsection.

---

[2] Quandl collect content of over 20 million news and blog sources real–time. They retain the relevant articles and extrapolate the sentiment. The sentiment score is generated via their proprietary algorithm that uses deep learning, coupled with a bag-of-words and n-grams approach. According to Quandl, negative sentiments are rated between -1 and -5, while positive sentiments are rated between 1 and 5.

2.1 Reducing Data Dimensionality

As mentioned, the prices and sentiments of the S&P 500 constituents are the variables of two of the datasets we dispose of initially. For analysis, it is important to classify each constituent into groups. Of course, classifying the constituents based on their respective industries would have been the easy way to group them since predefined information are readily available. Instead, we follow a more analytically rigorous approach in grouping the constituents based on pattern recognition and similarities in time series by using clustering.

In our case we use K-means clustering on each of the two sets of S&P 500 constituents for closing prices and sentiments respectively in order to group the variables in clusters. On the other hand, as we intend to use a rolling window of 100 days for testing and 10 days for forecasting, we note here that clustering is therefore applied on each rolling window, by forming 4 clusters. We note that by exploring different numbers of clusters between 3 and 10 on a sample sets of 100 days rolling windows, 4 appeared to be the optimal number of clusters in all cases. Due to the generic property of within cluster similarity, it is expected that variables in a cluster are more or less similar.

When it comes to reducing dimensionality of a numeric dataset, one of the most used methods is the well known Principal Component Analysis (PCA) [12]. Instead of applying PCA on all variables at once, we apply it on the groups of variables corresponding to each of the 4 clusters. Results from PCA show that dimensionality for the closing prices of S&P 500 constituents was reduced by 25% on average, and by 20% for sentiments. When we combine the principal components from both sentiments and closing prices we are still faced with a high number of dimensions of the combined dataset. By lagging the combined dataset up to 3 lags, its dimensionality increases to over 1200 variables, which keeps the intended predictive modelling at a challenging level computationally and from a predictive modelling point of view. This led us to propose a variable selection method to handle this complexity in our approach.

As random forest is a popular technique used in variable selection, it was our first choice method to consider in order to further reduce data dimensionality in this 3rd step of our approach. Interestingly, this solution performed very poorly on our dataset, judging by the poor goodness of fit with Adjusted R-Squared being below 0.3. We therefore proposed an alternative solution which is based on the modified best GLM method below developed by McLeod and Xu [15]. The latter selects the best subset of inputs for the GLM family. Given output Y on n predictors $X_1, ..., X_n$, it is assumed that Y can be predicted using just a subset $m < n$ predictors, $X_{i,1}, ..., X_{i,m}$. The aim is therefore to find the best subset of all the 2^n subsets based on some goodness-of-fit criterion. Consider a linear regression model with a number of t observations, $(x_{i,1}, ..., x_{i,n}, y_i)$ where $i = 1, 2, ..., t$. This may be expressed as

$$M_i = \beta_0 + \beta_1 x_{i,1} + ... + \beta_n x_{i,n} + \epsilon_i \tag{1}$$

It is clear that when n is large, building 2^n regressions becomes computationally too expensive, and even untractable in our case with $n > 1200$ predictors, as mentioned above. As such, we modify McLeod and Xu's method of [15] as follows and we call the resulting method MBestGLM. First, the lagged dataset is divided into subsets whereby each subset contains 35 predictors and then the variable selection technique of [15] is applied on each subset with the intention of obtaining statistically significant predictors from each subset. The statistically significant predictors are then combined and the process of dividing the result into other subsets and applying the variable selection technique continues until the set of predictors can no longer be reduced. The regression result from this selected predictors produces a high adjusted R-Squared of over 0.65. The final dataset we obtain has an average number of predictors of 35. Indeed, from experiments we have seen that its number of predictors varies between 30 and 40 according to the instance of the rolling window on which the dataset is generated.

Overall, the dimensionality reduction process including the 3 steps of variable clustering, PCA, and the MBestGLM method we introduced above, are repeatedly applied on the rolling window as we work under the more general and thus more complex assumption of time-variant relationship between independent variables and return.

3   Sentiment's Predictive Information on S&P 500

As mentioned in the Introduction, it has been shown in a series of studies that sentiment variables help improve stock market prediction models ([2,3,6,17]). In light of this it becomes imperative for us to investigate if the sentiment variables of S&P500 constituents included in our framework have some significant predictive power on this stock index.

In examining the relevance of sentiment variables we use two methods, the first based on linear models, and the second one, more general, based on non-linear non-parametric models, respectively. These are Granger causality statistical tests and are used to see if sentiment has predictive information on S&P 500 in our framework.

3.1   Granger Causality Test: The Linear Model

Using the linear model framework represented by the Granger causality statistical test [7], we examine the causal relationship between sentiment and stock market returns. According to [7] we write the general linear VAR models as:

$$Model1 : M_t = \alpha_1 + \Sigma_{i=1}^3 \omega_{1i} M_{t-i} + \Sigma_{i=1}^3 \beta_{1i} Stock_{t-i} + \epsilon_{1t} \qquad (2)$$

$$Model2 : M_t = \alpha_2 + \Sigma_{i=1}^3 \omega_{2i} M_{t-i} + \Sigma_{i=1}^3 \beta_{2i} Stock_{t-i} + \Sigma_{i=1}^3 \gamma_{2i} Sent_{t-i} + \epsilon_{2t} \qquad (3)$$

where M_t is the response variable which is the S&P 500 stock market return at time t, M_{t-i} is the lagged S&P 500 market return with lag period of i, and $Stock$ and $Sent$ are variables generated by our 3-step dimensionality reduction process issued from stock components and sentiment variables respectively. These VAR models *Model*1 and *Model*2 are used to examine if sentiment influences the stock market in our setting. As observed in the two equations, *Model*1 uses the lagged stock market return and the lagged stock market return principal components generated from the close prices of the S&P 500 constituents. In *Model*2 the lagged principal components, generated from sentiment variables related to the S&P 500 constituents, are added to the variables used in *Model*1. That is, *Model*1 does not contain sentiment variables while *Model*2 does. Sentiment variables would be considered to be influential if *Model*2 outperforms *Model*1 in prediction performance based on the adjusted R-squared metric. This is checked by using the standard Granger causality statistical test [7]. In particular we consider the hypothesis H0 that *Model*2 does not outperform *Model*1, and we reject it by obtaining a significant p-value.

Our results show that *Model*2, with the sentiment included in the analysis, outperforms *Model*1, based on the Granger causality F statistics $F_{16,165} = 9.1438$, and the corresponding p-value $p_{Granger} < 0.0001$. Robust tests performed on the estimated residuals show that the residuals do not possess autocorrelation, are normally distributed and homoscedastic in variance (having p-values Ljung-Box > 0.05, and Shapiro-Wilk > 0.05), so the Granger causality test was applied correctly and its conclusion is valid. Thus sentiment has predictive information on S&P 500. In the next subsection we verify this conclusion with a more general non-parametric non-linear Granger causality test.

3.2   Granger Causality Test: The Nonlinear Model

Causality test from the linear model has already shown that sentiment variables have predictive power on the stock market. And the robust tests confirm that the results are not biased by the presence of autocorrelation or heteroscedasticity. Still, we examine the influence of sentimental information on the stock market using a non-linear non-parametric test which was originally proposed by Baek and Brock [1] and was later modified by Hiemstra and Jones [8].

Interestingly, the significant p-values from the nonlinear non-parametric technique (see [5] and [10] for detailed explanation and software used respectively) displayed in Table 1 prove that sentiment has predictive power on the stock market.

Table 1. Nonlinear non-parametric Granger tests. A and M are the sentiment and stock market returns respectively within the period 12/07/2013 and 16/05/2014. $A =>$ M, for example, denotes the Granger causality test with direction from A to M, i.e. sentiment predicts stock market returns. Similarly, $M => A$ is a Granger causality test if stock market predicts sentiment.

$Lx = Ly = 1$	$p\text{-}value$
$A => M$	0.0077
$M => A$	0.0103

As a conclusion of this section, we can confidently state that the inclusion of sentiment variables does improve significantly stock market predictive models in terms of prediction performance, in our framework. Another interesting finding based on the significant p-value of $M => A$ in the nonlinear non-parametric Granger causality test, reveals that the stock market Granger-causes sentiment in this framework of S&P500 with its constituents and their sentiment.

4   Jordan and Elman Neural Network Based Approach to Predicting S&P500 with Sentiment

Linear and non linear models have been employed to assess the influence of sentiments on the stock market and results have shown the statistical significance of sentiments' influence on the stock market in our setting. A linear model has also been developed in the previous section (see $Model2$) to investigate if the future S&P 500 close prices can be predicted with sentiment.

This section evaluates the relative improvements to the linear model when we enhance our approach by using Recurrent Neural Networks algorithms, more specifically for Jordan and Elman networks. The backpropagation algorithm is one of the most popular techniques for training Neural Networks. It has been used in research works such as Collins et al. [4] which applied it to underwriting problems. Malliaris and Salchenberger [13] also applied backpropagation in estimating option prices. To determine the values for the parameters in the algorithms, the gradient descent technique is mostly employed Rumelhart and McClelland [18]. Multilayer, feed-forward, and recurrent Neural Networks such as Jordan and Elman Neural Networks which are used in this study, have become very popular.

As the datasets explored in our framework are highly dimensional, we rely on our variable selection methodology that we proposed in Subsect. 2.1, to assist in selecting a reduced subset of variables based on S&P 500 index, its constituents and their sentiment, to implement a predictive modelling approach with Elman and Jordan Neural Network algorithms. That is, the same variable selection process used to obtain results from the estimated linear model in Sect. 3, is also used with our Neural Network models. It is important to note that in our approach we use a rolling window of 100 days for model development and fitting, and a rolling prediction period of 10 days. This choice was made based on several experiments we ran with our approach, whose details we don't include here due to lack of space. Knowing that the output of Neural Network models is sensitive to the values assigned to the parameters in the models (including the number of hidden layers, the number of their nodes, and the weights), with some computational efforts, fairly optimised Neural Network models have been generated. Since at each rolling window we may have different selection of the set of predictors, the values assigned to Neural Network parameters would therefore be expected to be different for each fairly optimal result.

As observed in Fig. 2, the Elman Neural Network algorithm captures the stock market close price more accurately than the Jordan Neural Network algorithm for both the fitted and predicted values. We conclude this section by mentioning that

Jordan NN   Elman NN

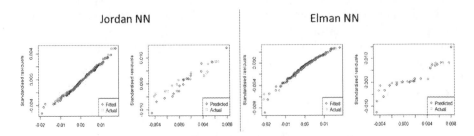

Fig. 2. Jordan Neural Network (Jordan NN) and Elman Neural Network (Elman NN): For each Neural Network, the left figure shows the fitted versus actual values, and the right figure shows the predicted versus actual values, all of which based on the dataset with rolling windows between 20/03/2014 and 12/08/2014

both Neural Network models outperformed the linear model developed in the previous section $Model2$ (details are not included due to lack of space).

5   Evolutionary Optimised Trading Model

In the previous sections we have demonstrated that sentiments influence the stock market prices based on the results from linear and Neural Network frameworks. But with all the information we have so far, are we able to maximise investment portfolio by leveraging on the insightful information from our estimated models? We note that the information available still looks raw and therefore needs refining before we could make good use of it. In the process of refining the information, we resolve to introducing some stock market technical analysis and an evolutionary optimisation algorithm to our developed model. In doing so we propose the following strategies:

1. Active investment in *put* option with the expectation that price will fall in the future. The investor therefore profits from the fall in price. This helps to exploit bearish market.
2. Active investment in *call* option with the expectation that price will rise in the future. The investor therefore profits from the rise in price.
3. Hold position which implies that no investment should be made.
4. Passive investment refers to investment in stock market for a period of time without any optimal investment strategy.

Points 1–3 will be used to maximise investment portfolio under active investment and point 4 will be used to compare active and passive investment strategies.

The active investment strategies use the input from the estimated Neural Network models and also technical analysis data variable K, called the Chaikin Oscillator, which determines the position of the forces of demand and supply - see details on the calculation of the variable in [11]. To maximise the investment

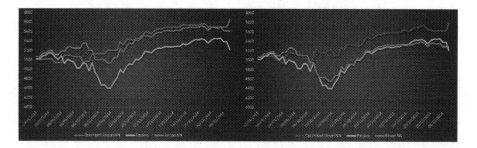

Fig. 3. The three investment portfolios are presented on two separate charts each related to Jordan Neural Networks (Jordan NN) on the left and Elman Neural Networks (Elman NN) on the right. The trends in Blue and Yellow present the optimised models and ordinary Neural Networks active investment portfolios respectively. The trend in Grey represents the passive investment portfolio. (Color figure online)

portfolio we employ an evolutionary optimisation algorithm. Given the objective investment function below:

$$f(call, put) = \begin{cases} Invest_{n-1} + (Price_n - Price_{n-1}) & call \\ Invest_{n-1} + (Price_{n-1} - Price_n) & put \\ Invest_{n-1} & else \end{cases}$$

where
$call : Pred_n > a, \triangle K_{n-1} > b, \triangle K_{n-2} > c, \triangle K_{n-3} > d,$
$put : Pred_n < e, \triangle K_{n-1} < f, \triangle K_{n-2} < g, \triangle K_{n-3} < h,$ $Pred_n$ is the predicted value at day n, $\triangle K_n$ is the change in Chaikin Oscillator at day n, and a, b, c, d, e, f, g, h are variables whose values must be determined. In order to maximise the objective investment function, we consider the following maximization problem:

$$\begin{aligned} &\underset{a,b,c,d,e,f,g,h}{\text{maximise}} \quad \text{f}(call, put) \\ &\text{subject to} \quad -0.4 <= b, c, d, f, g, h <= 0.4 \end{aligned} \tag{4}$$

The evolutionary optimisation algorithm is then applied to Eq. (4) in order to generate the values for $a, b, c, d, e, f, g,$ and h. The objective function is fairly optimised using just the first 35 days and the estimates obtained are kept constant to estimate portfolio values and trends for the next 100 days. Expectations regarding the relevance of this optimisation algorithms and technical analysis method are that trends obtained from the optimised models would be more stable than the ones that are not optimised. Also, we expect rising trends as these trends interpret to portfolio values. Decreasing trends would imply loss in investment. Looking at the results from Fig. 3 it is clear that the optimised active models outperform the ordinary estimated machine learning models and the passive portfolio. This conclusion is based on the fact that the trends in blue appear to be the most stable and fairly rising trends when compared with the trends from the ordinary estimated machine learning models. Even when persistent loss is reported in the passive portfolio in the period 07/10/2014–21/10/2014, trends from the optimised models appear fairly stable and rising. This is due to the fact that the optimised models take account of both bearish and bullish stock market using *put* and *call* options respectively.

6   Discussion and Conclusion

This research work delivers its first novelty by the nature of the data explored, which at our best knowledge, was not considered by previous studies. For analysis purposes, our framework combined the closing prices of S&P 500 constituents and also their related sentiments which in total provides about 800 variables. This dimensionality challenge is n-fold increased due to lagging operation common with time series. To tackle the challenge of high dimensionality of the dataset in a computationally expensive prediction modelling approach that we proposed, a specially designed data pre-processing methodology was introduced. To the best of our knowledge, this is the first work to have used constituent sentiments and its closing stock prices (containing over 800 variables combining closing stock prices of the S&P 500 constituents and their respective sentiment data without lagging) in stock market predictive modelling.

With the rolling window of a 10-day predictions period and time-variant relationship between response variable and predictors - approach which involves obtaining a new set of predictors for every rolling window - the analysis' challenge became compounded. Random forest method failed to do a good predictor selection, as a first method of choice that we considered. As such we proposed a 3-step feature selection methodology involving the consecutive phases of variable clustering, PCA, and our own method of further feature selection that we call MBestGLM.

Having established the most significant variables in our proposed predictive modelling approach, and also justified the inclusion of sentiment in the approach as we proved its predictive value using Granger based methods, we develop models based on Recurrent Neural Network algorithms to predict the S&P 500 closing prices. However, this information per se is not sufficient enough to reliably predict the stock market trends and also maximise investment portfolios. As such, we enhanced our approach by proposing investment strategy models which make use of the generated estimates from the predictive models as input variables to bridge these gaps. Results show that our proposed model appears to be stable even when the stock market is bearish and other approaches are failing. The rationale is that the proposed model is engineered to perform using *put* and *call* options during bearish and bullish moments, respectively. This represents another novelty of our work.

We currently develop further work on exploring the extension of this approach and of the approach proposed in our recent work [14], for several stock market indices.

References

1. Baek, E., Brock, W.: A general test for nonlinear Granger causality: bivariate model, Working paper. Iowa State University (1992)
2. Baker, M., Wurgler, J.: Investor sentiment in the stock market. J. Econ. Perspect. **21**(2), 129–151 (2007)
3. Bollen, J., Mao, H., Zeng, X.: Twitter mood predicts the stock market. J. Comput. Sci. **2**(1), 1–8 (2011)
4. Collins, E., Ghosh, S., Scofield, C.: An application of a multiple neural-network learning system to emulation of mortgage underwriting judgments. In: Proceedings of IEEE International Conference on Neural Networks, pp. 459–466 (1988)
5. Diks, C., Panchenko, V.: A new statistic and practical guidelines for nonparametric Granger causality testing. J. Econ. Dyn. Control **30**(9–10), 1647–1669 (2006)
6. Gilbert, E., Karahalios, K.: Widespread worry and the stock market. In: Proceedings of the 4th International Conference on Weblogs and Social Media, pp. 58–65 (2010)
7. Granger, C.W.J.: Investigating causal relations by econometric models and cross-spectral methods. Econometrica **37**(3), 424–438 (1969)
8. Hiemstra, C., Jones, J.D.: Testing for linear and nonlinear Granger causality in the stock price-volume relation. J. Finan. **49**, 1639–1664 (1994)
9. https://www.quandl.com/databases/NS1/documentation
10. http://research.economics.unsw.edu.au/vpanchenko#software
11. http://stockcharts.com/school/doku.php?id=chart_school:technical_indicators: chaikin_money_flow_cmf
12. Kuhn, M., Johnson, K.: Applied Predictive Modeling. Springer, New York (2013). https://doi.org/10.1007/978-1-4614-6849-3
13. Malliaris, M.E., Salchenberger, L.: A neural network model for estimating option prices. J. Appl. Intell. **3**, 193–206 (1993)
14. Maréchal, F., Stamate, D., Olaniyan, R., Marek, J.: On XLE index constituents' social media based sentiment informing the index trend and volatility prediction. In: Nguyen, N.T., Pimenidis, E., Khan, Z., Trawiński, B. (eds.) ICCCI 2018. LNCS (LNAI), vol. 11056, pp. 366–376. Springer, Cham (2018). https://doi.org/10.1007/978-3-319-98446-9_34
15. McLeod, A., Xu, C.: bestglm: Best Subset GLM (2010). https://CRAN.R-project.org/package=bestglm
16. Olaniyan, R., Stamate, D., Logofatu, D.: Social web-based anxiety index's predictive information on S&P 500 Revisited. In: Gammerman, A., Vovk, V., Papadopoulos, H. (eds.) SLDS 2015. LNCS, vol. 9047. Springer, Cham (2015). https://doi.org/10.1007/978-3-319-17091-6_15
17. Olaniyan, R., Stamate, D., Logofatu, D., Ouarbya, L.: Sentiment and stock market volatility predictive modelling - a hybrid approach. In: Proceedings of the 2nd IEEE/ACM International Conference on Data Science and Advanced Analytics (2015)
18. Rumelhart, D.E., McClelland, J.L.: Parallel Distributed Processing. MIT Press, Cambridge (1986)
19. Shiller, R.J.: Irrational Exuberance. Princeton University Press, Princeton (2000)
20. Sprenger, T.O., Tumasjan, A., Sandner, P.G., Welpe, I.M.: Tweets and trades: the information content of stock microblogs. Eur. Financ. Manag. **20**(5), 926–957 (2014)

Fight or Flight: A Temporal-Causal Analysis of the Behavior of a Bully-Victim

Nizar A. Hirzalla, Thomas M. Maaiveld, and Fakhra Jabeen[(✉)]

Vrije Universiteit, 1081 HV Amsterdam, The Netherlands
{n.a.hirzalla, t.maaiveld}@student.vu.nl,
fakhraikram@yahoo.com

Abstract. This paper presents a temporal-causal network model of a (cyber) bullying victim. Temporal-causal modeling is a tool for examining complex processes by modeling internal states of an agent to examine internal processes. Bullying is a social-cognitive process, that involves mental processes which may put victims at risk for short or long-term physical and psychosocial problems. The temporal causal model for bully-victim is simulated in accordance to react the bully by fight or fly strategy. Subsequently, parameter tuning and mathematical analysis techniques were applied to the simulations to verify and optimize them with respect to patterns derived from empirical literature.

Keywords: Temporal-causal modeling · Bullying · Cyberbullying · Peer victimization

1 Introduction

Bullying is recognized by an unwanted behavior among school adolescents or as a form of peer victimization that involves the targeted intimidation and humiliation of peers [1]. Bullying usually occurs in situations with an observed or perceived power imbalance and may occur repeatedly and in different settings [2]. Incidences of peer victimization can take the form of verbal attacks, or indirect or relational harassment [3]. Cyberbullying shares main characteristics of traditional bullying, but perceived anonymity of online interactions make it more hazardous for mental health, as the obvious consequences are unseen. This gives a feeling of increased tendency for power imbalance, and helplessness on the part of the victim.

Bullying may affect victims across a variety of domains. Bullying has been associated with poor physical and mental health [4]. Negative outcomes may last short-term or swipe in an adulthood, displaying a multitude of adjustment problems. These may include depressed mood and anxiety [5], psychosomatic problems [6]. This is also termed as social pain, which is more painful than physical one, emphasizing the long-term harm. Reported reactions to bullying include depression, fear, sadness, anxiety, suicidal ideation, remorse, worry, stress, embarrassment, and loneliness [7]. Experiences of peer victimization become embedded in the physiology of the developing person, placing him or her at risk for life-long mental and physical health problems [6].

© Springer Nature Switzerland AG 2019
N. T. Nguyen et al. (Eds.): ICCCI 2019, LNAI 11683, pp. 154–166, 2019.
https://doi.org/10.1007/978-3-030-28377-3_13

Research has emphasized the prevalence and consequences of bullying [1]. Research concerning bullying has primarily been conducted through questionnaires in medium- to large-sized cohorts, although the usefulness of computer science applications has been explored previously [8]. However, the impact of a bully over a person is not studied with the perspective of network oriented modeling. In this paper we aim to address two things: It explains (a) how brain of bully victim works if bullied. Moreover, it entails (b) possible reactions of a victim with the help of various factors and internal processes, which drive decision-making and responses to bullying behavior.

The following paper is divided into the following sections. Section 2, describes the related work with respect to neuroscience and computational modeling. Section 3 shows a temporal-causal model developed for a victims perspective. Section 4 presents the simulation scenarios, while Sect. 5 shows mathematical analysis, and paper is concluded by Sect. 6.

2   Related Work

Various estimates have been made of the prevalence of bullying. A meta-analysis of 80 studies carried out in 2014 estimated that around 36% are involved in traditional bullying, while around 15% report being victimized in cyberbullying [9]. Much of neuroscience (fMRI) research focused on the victims of bullying and social exclusion [10].

Research concerning victims of peer aggression is often carried out through endocrinology tests with salivary hormone samples [11]. The hypothalamic-pituitary-adrenal axis (HPA axis) describes a set of interactions among the hypothalamus, pituitary gland and adrenal glands. Among many other functions, the HPA axis controls cortisol levels, a hormone which plays an important role in stress regulation within organisms. Cortisol levels follow a circadian rhythm, with elevated levels in the morning and declining over the course of the day [12]. These levels are elevated in stressful situations, and abnormally high cortisol levels may alter cortisol receptor sensitivity. Such alterations may cause a state of hyperarousal, or, alternatively, result in hypo secretion [4]. Abnormal cortisol patterns are consistent with those found in post-traumatic stress disorder (PTSD) patients [13]. Bullying victims tend to produce below-average cortisol levels. Notably, this effect has been recorded with respect to stress response elevation [11], as well as across the daily cortisol cycle [4], which could be linked to the aforementioned mixed bag of short- and long-term repercussions bully victims endure.

In situations of increased stress, coping responses serve as a type of self-regulation. Such self-regulation strategies may involve the steering of cognition, behaviour, physiology or the environment. These strategies are explored in the model presented in this paper. A framework that is often applied to stress coping is the Approach-Avoidance response framework [5]. In an approach coping response, the victim targets the stressor, while an avoidance coping response attempts to regulate feeling. In peer victimization settings, avoidance responses were associated with wanting to prevent an escalation of the event and approach responses were associated with wanting to defend oneself.

A wide variety of feelings were associated with peer victimization across various studies. Notably, four categories of feeling were derived from various entries in the literature [5]: fear, anger, sadness and rejection. These feelings were found to be associated with approach and avoidance responses [14]. Adolescents associated feelings of sadness and fear with avoidance responses in open questionnaires. Different individuals coped differently with rejection experiences - both aggressive and repressive responses were recorded [14]. Children with poor emotion regulation skills characteristically display reactive aggression, which resulted with increase in anger and correlated negatively with a feeling of sadness [5]. Children who respond to social exclusion by externalizing blame and seeking revenge report a greater frequency of depressive and anxious symptoms, while those who respond with avoidance responses (cognitive restructuring, minimization, ignoring) achieve more positive outcomes [14].

Looking into the temporal causal networks, quite research can be found on PTSD [15], this research indicate that how an event can cause this kind of disorder. There is a research which identifies how bully behaves in a temporal causal domain [16]. However, no research has focused on the factors which can help in order to react over bullying behavior [14].

3   The Temporal-Causal Network Model

This section describes conceptual and numerical representations of the temporal-causal network model designed to study the behavior of a bully-victim. The conceptual representation displays the states of the model along with its connections, which define a causal relationships between the states (Fig. 1). An arrow between two states represents a causal relationship between them [17]. For a given state, the change in its value at time-point t will be propagated through the connections due to its causal effect, affecting another state at time-point t + Δt. Arrowheads are labeled by + or - indicate positive progression or suppression for the following state. Bidirectional arrows indicate the causal impact of state on each other. Equation (1) shows the relationship between a future state $Y(t + \Delta t)$, which is computed by taking a previous state value Y (t) and adding to it the influence of the states affecting it [17]:

$$Y(t + \Delta t) = Y(t) + \eta_Y[c_Y(\omega_{X_1,Y}X_1(t), \ldots, \omega_{Xk,Y}X_k(t)) - Y(t)]\Delta t \tag{1}$$

where $X_1, \ldots X_k$ are the states with outgoing connections to Y.

η_Y = speed factor that modulates the rate of change of state Y's value.
c_Y = combination function used to aggregate impact of states X_i to Y.
$\omega_{Xi,Y}$ = connection weights affecting the impact of states X_i to Y.
Δ_t = step size of time for each interaction from states X_i to Y.

The model basically take input from the bully from es_a state, which indicates a bullying event, and a sensor state to sense an approach response of the victim (this could be the 'rise' the bully is looking for) [16]. The state ws_s here indicates the bully-victim getting stimulus by using the social media. Together with world state ws_s, the bully's execution state activates the sensory apparatus ($ss_{s,b}$ and $srs_{s,b}$) of the victim.

$srs_{s,b}$ activates all feeling states. The victim may experience feeling of fear (fs_f), sadness (fs_{sd}), rejection from society (fs_r), and feeling of anger (fs_a). A victim can choose between two possibilities, either he can avoid or he can confront for the bullying behavior. If the person feels rejected, sad and fear from bully, the respective states will ps_{avd} and es_{avd} will be activated, he can modify the situation. An example of situation modification can be starting reading a book. Similarly, if a person feels angry, rejected, and sad, ps_{app} and es_{app} will be triggered. An executive action unit has been linked to the approach response network in order to model the ownership of the decision to undertake an approach action [17], indicated by pos, ros and srs_{pe}. The control state cs_n regulates feelings which arise in the person.

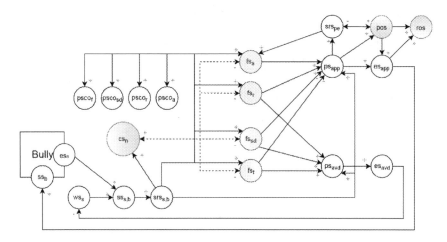

Fig. 1. Conceptual representation of Bully-Victim.

The connections between feelings and the execution states were modeled after the research presented in Sect. 2; fear (fs_f) and sadness (fs_{sd}) increase the likelihood of avoidance (ps_{avd}), while fs_a increases the approach response (ps_{app}) and rejection (fs_r) boosts both. An executive action unit is linked to the approach response network to model the ownership of the decision to undertake an approach action [17]. Lastly, the approach execution state (es_{app}) activates the sensor state of the bully (ss_b), while the avoidance execution state (es_{avd}) modifies situation to resolve the bullying event (ws_s).

Table 1. Nomenclature of the model.

State	Definition
ws_s	World state for stimulus s
ss_x	Sensor state of X; X = bully b and X = s, b presence of stimuli s and b
es_a	Execution state of the bully b
srs_X	Representation state; X = s, b presence s and b or pe = predicted effect
cs_n	Control state for negative feelings

(*continued*)

Table 1. (*continued*)

State	Definition
fs_i	Feeling state for i; i $= f$ (fear), a (anger), r (rejection), sd (sadness)
$psco_i$	Preparation state for communication of feeling i $= f$, a, r, sd
ps_k	Preparation state for the k. k = approach or avoidance response
es_k	Execution state for the k. k = approach or avoidance response
pos	Prior ownership state of action
ros	Retrospective ownership state of action

For simulation connection weights, speed factors were assumed to be in range [0, 1]. The value of ws_s is 1. Different combination functions were used to determine the aggregated causal impact of the states. For the states ss_b, es_b, ws_s, $srs_{s,b}$, cs_n, es_{avd}, srs_{pe} and es_{app}, the identity function **id(V)** = V was used. The advanced logistic sum function was used for the preparation states for action (ps_{app} and ps_{avd}):

$$\mathbf{alogistic}_{\sigma,\tau}(V_1, \ldots, V_k) = \left[\left(\frac{1}{1 + e^{-\sigma(V_1 + \cdots + V_k - \tau)}}\right) - 1/(1 + e^{\sigma\tau})\right](1 + e^{-\sigma\tau})$$

where

$\sigma = 18$ (steepness of the curve), and
$\tau = 0.8$ (threshold)

$V_1, \ldots, V_k$ are variables for single impacts $\omega_{X,Y}X(t)$ and $\omega_{Xk,Y}X_k(t)$, preceding states that affect the state value currently being computed.

For rest of the states ($ss_{s,b}$, $psco_f$, fs_f, $psco_{sd}$, fs_{sd}, $psco_r$, fs_r, $psco_a$, fs_a, pos, ros), the scaled sum function $\mathbf{ssum}_\lambda(V_1, \ldots, V_k) = (V_1 + \ldots + V_k)/\lambda$ was used. Here, λ represents the scaling factor, which is equal to the sum of incoming positive weights for a state. A conceptual representation of a temporal-causal model can be transformed into a numerical representation as follows [17]:

1. Impact of state X on state Y is computed at t as $\mathbf{impact}_{X,Y}(t) = \omega_{X,Y}X(t)$ where $\omega_{X,Y}$ is weight of the connection from X to Y, and $X(t)$ is activation value of the previous state (between 0 and 1)
2. Aggregated impact on Y is computed by combination function of Y from the (multiple) states X_1 to X_k with inward connections to Y.

$$\mathbf{aggimpact}_Y(t) = \mathbf{c}_Y\left(\mathbf{impact}_{X1,Y}(t), \ldots, \mathbf{impact}_{X_k,Y}(t)\right)$$
$$= \mathbf{c}_Y\left(\omega_{X_1,Y}X_1(t), \ldots, \omega_{X_k,Y}X_k(t)\right)$$

where $X_1, \ldots, X_k$ represents the states which have inward connections to Y. $\omega_{x,y}$ represents connection weight between X and Y, and $\mathbf{c}_Y$ represent combination function that is used for state Y.

3. The magnitude of the aggregated impact on Y is controlled by speed factor η_Y to observe the causal effect:

$$Y(t + \Delta t) = Y(t) + \eta_Y[\textbf{aggimpact}_Y(t) - Y(t)]\Delta t \text{ and}$$

$$\frac{\textbf{d}Y(t)}{\textbf{d}t} = \eta_Y[\textbf{aggimpact}_Y(t) - Y(t)]$$

Substituting $\textbf{aggimpact}_Y(t)$ yields the following difference and differential equations:

$$Y(t + \Delta t) = Y(t) + \eta_Y[\textbf{c}_Y(\omega_{X_1,Y}X_1(t), \ldots, \omega_{X_k,Y}X_k(t)) - Y(t)]\Delta t \text{ and}$$

$$\frac{\textbf{d}Y(t)}{\textbf{d}t} = \eta_Y[\textbf{c}_Y(\omega_{X_1,Y}X_1(t), \ldots, \omega_{X_k,Y}X_k(t)) - Y(t)]$$

Using Excel and Matlab software environments, the above steps were automated in order to be able to efficiently test simulations [17]. The numerical representation of the model was also used for mathematical verification of equilibrium state values, which is described in Sect. 6.

4 Simulation Experiments

Simulation experiments based on this model may offer insight into how its states change over time. To evaluate if the model and simulations are valid, the simulation experiments should be optimized by empirical data. Despite that there is extensive literature to be found about bullying and its implications for the victim, direct numerical empirical data related to victim behavior in the context of this paper is not available, therefore we deduced patterns from cited literature to deduce patterns. Table 2 enlist the patterns derived from literature.

Table 2. Patterns derived from empirical literature

Empirical literature	Deduced simulation pattern
Stimulus triggers emotion [18]	Stimulus is present from the start: $ws_s \geq 0, 1$. This activates $ss_{s,b}$ and $srs_{s,b}$
Varying intensity of bullying leads to less emotional reaction [19]	ws_s ranges from 0, 1 to 1, and influences feeling states accordingly
Emotions and feelings that occur consistently and frequently in (cyber)bully victims, correlations from multiple studies to get a more representative list of feelings [5]	From strongest correlation to weakest: (1) Fear (fs_f) (2) Angry (fs_a) (3) Sad (fs_{sd}) (4) Rejected (fs_r). The simulations with the feelings with the strongest correlations and prevalence will have higher values for these feelings in comparison with the other feelings[a]

(continued)

Table 2. (*continued*)

Empirical literature	Deduced simulation pattern
Emotions expression through different means [20]	The feeling states gradually become active and lead to different outcomes, based on the scenario
Feelings fear, sad, angry, rejected are perceived as negative feelings that are suppressed [5]	Control state cs_n increases as a result of higher feeling values. This suppresses the feeling states and prevents them from rising further
Different emotions lead to different responses [14]	Preparation states for avoid and approach ps_{avd} and ps_{app} are activated after the feeling state values begin to increase
Behaviour of a cyberbullying victim: suppressing negative feelings (emotion regulation) [20]	Feeling states either stagnate or decline after action. This depends on the action. Avoid leads to feeling states declining eventually while confronting the bully will let them stagnate due to suppression from the control state even though the bully stimulus remains active
Predictive and inferential processes [17]	The prior-ownership state is involved in prediction of execution of 'approach' concerning aggressive behavior (feeling of angry in this case). The retrospective ownership state and sensory representation for predicted effect srs_{pe} will increase along with pos

[a]Note that different studies use different terminologies to describe feelings. For this study, generic categories were used based on Gimènez et al. [16]; empirical data were interpreted to fit in these categories.

Studies that relied on self-reported data from victims and as such were mostly an indicative of subjective perceptions was taken to deduce qualitative expected patterns. These patterns were used as requirements for the model, in accordance with the fundamentals of requirements engineering in order to emulate different real world scenarios [21]. Following are two scenarios addressed along with the parameter tuning. (a) First scenario simulates an event where a bullying victim avoids bully, while in the second scenario (b) a victim chooses an approach response to the bullying behavior.

4.1   Scenario 1: Choosing the Avoidance Response

As ws_s and bullying event is there, the sensory state and sensory representation state values ($ss_{s,b}$ and $srs_{s,b}$) increase. Subsequently, feeling states increase, thus fs_f has the highest value, followed by fs_{sd} and then fs_r. The corresponding preparation states for communication of these feelings $psco_f$, $psco_{sd}$ and $psco_r$ increase accordingly.

The value of control state cs_n rises alongside the feeling state values, gradually suppressing them. $fs_a = 0$, because it has no association with the avoid action, meaning it is not triggered. As a result, the approach response-related states of pos, ros, srs_{pe} remain at 0. Figure 2 shows the results of the simulation of the avoidance response scenario.

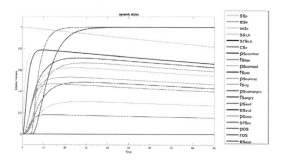

Fig. 2. Victim chooses to avoid the bully, based on Table 1, time point = 0–90

Initially, the state values describing the bullying behaviour (ss_b, es_b), visibly decline again when the victim begins to execute the avoid response. This pattern is expected, since avoiding the bully ceases the interaction and stops exposure to the bullying for the moment by decreasing the value of world state ws_s. This can be observed that all states eventually go towards 0 as a result of the avoid action directly decreasing the stimulus, as described in the model. This can be observed in Fig. 3.

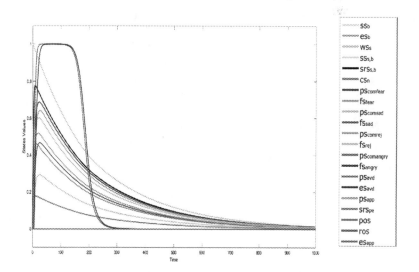

Fig. 3. Victim avoiding bully time point 0–1000

4.2   Parameter Tuning

Parameter tuning is a technique used to optimize various model parameters as to make the simulated model correspond as closely as possible with an empirical pattern-driven model. This optimization is performed by minimizing the error function (usually RMSE) by modulating different parameters. In this case, parameter tuning was applied to the speed factor (η) values used in simulations before. To do this, first we provided patterns presented in Table 2 to a subject matter expert as requirements [22], who helped to extract expected patterns for the model. So, the pattern for states in the approaching scenario were used with the states: $ss_{s,b}$, $srs_{s,b}$, fs_r, fs_a, ps_{app} and es_{app}. For each of these states, 10 discrete data points were taken and interpolated through cubic interpolation technique (Fig. 4).

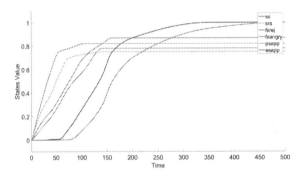

Fig. 4. Patterns for $ss_{s,b}$, $srs_{s,b}$, fs_r, fs_a, ps_{app} and es_{app} after applying cubic interpolation

Secondly, we used Simulated Annealing (SA) optimization for tuning method. Simulated annealing is a technique that attempts to minimize the error function by navigating the model space and finding a minimum on the loss surface (i.e., a set of parameters that minimizes the error between the model and the empirical data). There are many algorithms which are used for optimization of the model [23]. However, Simulated Annealing is considered to be a good choice. A major advantage of SA is that it has increased likelihood of finding a global minima. Figure 5, shows the difference between the initial results of approaching scenario, and the empirical curves.

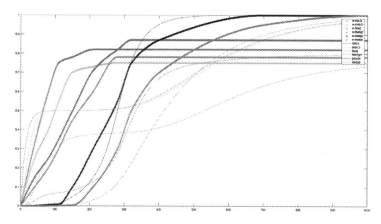

Fig. 5. Plot showing the deviation between empirical values (*) and initial results (−)

Optimization was completed at 2143 iterations, with a linear error root mean square error (RMSE) of 0,162, indicating well-tuned parameter values for the speed factors. This produced the results in Table 3.

Table 3. Speed factor values obtained after parameter tuning.

State	ss_b	$srs_{s,b}$	fs_r	fs_a	ps_{app}	es_{app}
Speed factor (η)	0,708	0,936	0,981	0,925	0,517	0,056

4.3 Scenario 2: Choosing the Approach Response

In this scenario the approach action is selected, an example can be replying him in a text message. Therefore, when ws_s and es_a is high, the preparation state ps_{app} and execution state es_{app} are as expected to get high values (Fig. 6). Consequently, the preparation and execution states for the avoidance response are expected to be 0. The feeling states assume values that describe their correlation with the selected action, regulated by cs_n. In this scenario, all feelings including anger fs_a has high values, leading corresponding psco states to get high. The control state cs_n suppresses the negative feelings. fs_f and fs_{sd} are more suppressed, as these feelings may suppress the approach action. We used tuned speed factors (Table 3) to generate this simulation.

Unlike in the avoidance response scenario, the states regarding the bully behavior (ss_b, es_b) continue to increase towards their maximum value in this scenario. Since approach leads to more interaction with the bully. This means more exposure to bullying, these values do not decline afterwards, despite the fact that the feeling states are heavily suppressed by cs_n and do not increase.

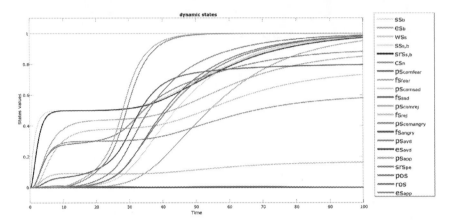

Fig. 6. Victim chooses to approach the bully, based on Table 1.

5 Mathematical Analysis

The model presented can also be verified by mathematical analysis. This can be done by studying the equilibrium property of model. A model is in equilibrium if at a given time-point t all states are stationary points $(\mathbf{dY(t)/dt = 0})$, expressed as [17]:

$$\mathbf{aggimpact}_Y(t) - Y(t) = 0 \iff Y(t) = \mathbf{c}_Y(\boldsymbol{\omega}_{X_1,Y}X_1(t),,\ldots,\boldsymbol{\omega}_{Xk,Y}X_k(t))$$

Mathematical analysis was performed for the scenario when victim chooses to approach bully. For most states, it can be observed that the model starts to converge towards around time point $t = 60$. For instance, most values are converged between the time point of 200 and 250. The differences between simulation values and linear equation solutions were computed by WIMS[1] solver showed that deviations did not exceed 0.02. The results are presented in Table 4 and equations mentioned below.

Table 4. State equilibrium values and linear solver values.

State	ss_b	$srs_{s,b}$	cs_n	$psco_f$	fs_f	$psco_{sd}$	fs_{sd}	$psco_r$	fs_r
Time t	208	140	206	203	112	203	112	150	214
Y(t)	0.9999	0.997	0.6	0.1667	0	0.1667	0	0.8786	0.7600
aggimpact$_Y$(t)	1	1	0.6	0.1651	0.0021	0.1651	0.0015	0.8800	0.7600
Deviation	0.0001	0.0033	0	0.0016	0.0021	0.0016	0.0015	0.0014	0

State	$psco_a$	fs_a	ps_{avd}	es_{avd}	ps_{app}	srs_{pc}	pos	ros	es_{app}
Time t	204	121	126	138	74	76	103	136	206
Y(t)	0.8999	0.7987	0	0	1	1	0.9928	0.9976	1
aggimpact$_Y$(t)	0.9	0.8	0.00001	0.00001	1	1	1	1	1
Deviation	0.0001	0.0013	0.00001	0.00001	0	0	0.0072	0.0024	0

---

[1] http://wims.unice.fr/wims/wims.cgi.

Eq1. $1{,}87ss_b = 0{,}87ss_b + es_{app}$

Eq2. $ws_s = 1$

Eq3. $es_b = ss_b$

Eq4. $2ss_{s,b} = ws_s + es_b$

Eq5. $srs_{s,b} = ss_{s,b}$

Eq6. $cs_n = 0{,}6srs_{s,b}$

Eq7. $1{,}2psco_f = 0{,}2srs_{s,b} + fs_f$

Eq8. $fs_f = -0{,}3cs_n + psco_f$

Eq9. $1{,}2psco_{sd} = 0{,}2srs_{s,b} + fs_{sd}$

Eq10. $fs_{sd} = -0{,}3cs_n + psco_{sd}$

Eq11. $2psco_r = srs_{s,b} + fs_r$

Eq12. $fs_r = -0{,}2cs_n + psco_r$

Eq13. $2psco_a = srs_{s,b} + fs_a$

Eq14. $2fs_a = -0{,}5cs_n + psco_a + srs_{pe}$

Eq15. $ps_{avd} = 0{,}00001$

Eq16. $es_{avd} = 0{,}3ps_{avd}$

Eq17. $ps_{app} = 1$

Eq18. $srs_{pe} = ps_{app}$

Eq19. $2pos = ps_{app} + es_{app}$

Eq20. $2ros = pos + es_{app}$

Eq21. $es_{app} = ps_{app}$

6 Conclusion and Future Work

In this paper a temporal-causal model for a bully victim was presented. Feelings of fear, anger, sadness and rejection along with their relationship to approach and avoidance of bully were explored.

Neurological literature was studied in order to get the expected patterns of the model. Two scenarios were simulated. The regulation involved the control state, which modulated the negative feelings and the corresponding actions were selected. At the end of simulation, parameter tuning was used to optimize the model, and mathematical verification was done, which showed that model behavior was as expected.

Future research could focus more on the role of the prior ownership state. Despite being implemented in the model and functioning as an inhibitor for the anger feeling state (fs_a) through effect prediction, its function was outside the focus of this research. Additionally, the use of empirical data collected in the real world would improve the validity of the methods used in this paper (simulation and parameter tuning), rather than processing expected patterns to subjectively determine parameter settings. Another direction could be to use this model to identify the victims and to provide support of victims.

References

1. Olweus, D.: School Bullying: Development and Some Important Challenges (2013)
2. Gladden, R., Viviolo-Kantor, A., Hamburger, M., Lumpkin, C.: Bullying Surveillance Among Youths (2014)
3. Grotpeter, J.K., Crick, N.R.: Relational Aggression, Overt Aggression, and Friendship (1996)
4. Vaillancourt, T., Duku, E., Decatanzaro, D., Macmillan, H., Muir, C., Schmidt, L.A.: Variation in hypothalamic-pituitary-adrenal axis activity among bullied and non-bullied children. Aggress. Behav. **34**, 294–305 (2008)
5. Ortega, R., et al.: The emotional impact of bullying and cyberbullying on victims: a european cross-national study. Aggress. Behav. **38**(5), 342–356 (2012)

6. Gini, G., Pozzoli, T.: Association between bullying and psychosomatic problems: a meta-analysis. Pediatrics **123**(3), 1059–1065 (2009)
7. Copeland, W.E., Wolke, D., Angold, A., Costello, E.J.: Adult psychiatric outcomes of bullying and being bullied by peers in childhood and adolescence. JAMA Psychiatry **70**, 419–426 (2013)
8. Bellmore, A., Calvin, A.J., Xu, J.M., Zhu, X.: The five W's of 'bullying' on Twitter: who, what, why, where, and when. Comput. Human Behav. **44**, 305–314 (2015)
9. Modecki, K.L., Minchin, J., Harbaugh, A.G., Guerra, N.G., Runions, K.C.: Bullying prevalence across contexts: a meta-analysis measuring cyber and traditional bullying. J. Adolesc. Heal. **55**, 602–611 (2014)
10. https://osf.io/6sqew/
11. Knack, J.M., Jensen-Campbell, L.A., Baum, A.: Worse than sticks and stones? bullying is associated with altered HPA axis functioning and poorer health. Brain Cogn. **77**, 183–190 (2011)
12. Kirschbaum, C., Strasburger, C.J., Jammers, W., Hellhammer, D.H.: Cortisol and behavior: 1. Adaptation of a radioimmunoassay kit for reliable and inexpensive salivary cortisol determination. Pharmacol. Biochem. Behav. **34**, 747–751 (1989)
13. Morris, M.C., Compas, B.E., Garber, J.: Relations among posttraumatic stress disorder, comorbid major depression, and HPA function: A systematic review and meta-analysis. Clin. Psychol. Rev. **32**, 301–315 (2012)
14. Sandstrom, M.J.: Pitfalls of the peer world: how children cope with common rejection experiences. J. Abnorm. Child Psychol. **32**(1), 67–81 (2004)
15. Naze, S., Treur, J.: A computational model for development of post-traumatic stress disorders by Hebbian learning. In: Huang, T., Zeng, Z., Li, C., Leung, C.S. (eds.) ICONIP 2012. LNCS, vol. 7664, pp. 141–151. Springer, Heidelberg (2012). https://doi.org/10.1007/978-3-642-34481-7_18
16. Jabeen, F., Treur, J.: Computational analysis of bullying behavior in the social media era. In: Nguyen, N.T., Pimenidis, E., Khan, Z., Trawiński, B. (eds.) ICCCI 2018. LNCS (LNAI), vol. 11055, pp. 192–205. Springer, Cham (2018). https://doi.org/10.1007/978-3-319-98443-8_18
17. Treur, J.: Network-Oriented Modeling. UCS. Springer, Cham (2016). https://doi.org/10.1007/978-3-319-45213-5
18. Damasio, A.R.: Self Comes to Mind: Constructing the Conscious Brain. Pantheon Books, New York (2010)
19. Archer, J., Coyne, S.M.: An integrated review of indirect, relational, and social aggression. Pers. Soc. Psychol. Rev. **9**, 212–230 (2005)
20. Gross, J.J.: Part I: Foundations. Emotion regulation: conceptual and empirical foundations. vol. 2014 (2013)
21. Pohl, K.: The three dimensions of requirements engineering. In: Bubenko, J., Krogstie, J., Pastor, O., Pernici, B., Rolland, C., Sølvberg, A. (eds.) Seminal Contributions to Information Systems Engineering. Springer, Heidelberg (2013)
22. Ferber, J., Gutknecht, O., Jonker, C.M., Muller, J.-P., Treur, J.: Organization models and behavioural requirements specification for multi-agent systems. In: 2000 Proceedings of Fourth International Conference in Multiagent Systems, pp. 387–388 (2000)
23. Binitha, S., Siva Sathya, S.: A survey of bio inspired optimization algorithms. Int. J. Soft Comput. Eng. **2**(2), 13751 (2012)

A Framework for Research Publication Recommendation System

Bernadetta Maleszka[(✉)] [iD]

Faculty of Computer Science and Management, Wroclaw University of Science
and Technology, Wybrzeze Wyspianskiego 27, 50-370 Wroclaw, Poland
Bernadetta.Maleszka@pwr.edu.pl

Abstract. Information overload is one of the main problem of nowadays
information retrieval systems. To obtain relevant information or items,
many users use recommendation systems which are commonly available:
for products in Internet stores, musics, books, etc. Also in the field of
research papers it is hard to find relevant items. There exists many scientific search engines that retrieve huge databases to find best papers but
it would be comfortable to have an ability to find the best journal or conference where to publish current paper. Every researcher receive many
"calls for papers" but many times the propositions are rather random
and a little correlated with our research. In this paper we explore possibilities of collaborative filtering and content-based approaches to Publication Recommender System. We have presented a simple case study for
a selected group of users.

Keywords: Journal recommendation system ·
Conference recommendation system · Content-based methods ·
Collaborative filtering

1 Introduction

Recommendation systems are present in many areas of our life: books, movies,
music, news recommendation, etc. Many Internet stores implements some recommendation techniques to propose the user relevant goods and to earn more
money. Such systems allow user to find quickly interesting items that the user
could even not know about them before.

Usually, recommendation systems concentrate on the problem of selecting
best items (product) to a final user. The most popular kind of such a system
is documents recommendation system [7] – it is the most frequently situation
when a user retrieve documents connected with particular keywords or topics.
Popular methods are collaborative and content-based filtering and hybrid one.
They collect information about the user and items (features or profiles) and
analyze historical user activities (e.g. likes and dislikes) [5] to manage out a
problem of information overload.

© Springer Nature Switzerland AG 2019
N. T. Nguyen et al. (Eds.): ICCCI 2019, LNAI 11683, pp. 167–178, 2019.
https://doi.org/10.1007/978-3-030-28377-3_14

While many areas are covered by recommendation systems at different stage of development, there are still some fields that can be more explored. According to Wang et al. [9] one of the field that is still not developed is recommendation of scientific venues: conferences or journals. Each researcher receives a lot of "Call for paper" e-mails, which allow to get know about some conferences or journals. On the one hand it is a possibility to choose the best place to publish results but on the other hand huge part of these propositions are out of user research interests.

In the paper we propose a framework to find relevant journals or conferences where a user can submit his or her work and where it is worth to publish. Proposed method takes into account many aspects of retrieval problems: we check where authors of papers about similar research area have published, what are similar conferences or journals (compares scopes of journals and/or conferences) and what is a history of previous authors' publications. The main idea of our approach is based on combination of content-based and collaborative filtering methods that are often used to retrieve similar papers. The main difference in our approach is that we recommend a conference or journal where to publish, while in classic approaches system recommends papers (music, movies, etc.).

The rest of the paper is organized in the following way. Section 2 presents related works correlated with recommendation systems. In Sect. 3 we describe model of user, publication, journal and conference. Algorithms for publication recommendation are described in Sect. 4. Section 5 contains details about experimental evaluation and a case study. Conclusions and ideas for future works are mentioned in the last Sect. 6.

2   Related Works

2.1   Recommendation Systems

Among many recommendation techniques one can find content-based filtering, collaborative filtering (memory- and model-based approaches), hybrid filtering [4] and knowledge-based recommender systems [2].

According to Isinkaye et al. [4] one can differentiate the following stages of recommendation process:

1. Information collection – in this phase necessary relevant information is gathered to build user profile or model in the following ways:
   - Explicit feedback – information is given by the user;
   - Implicit feedback – user behaviour is observed by the system;
   - Hybrid feedback – combination of both explicit and implicit feedback;
2. Learning phase – the aim of this stage is to select significant features about the user from collected data;
3. Prediction/recommendation phase – the system presents possibly relevant items for the user.

Aguilar et al. [1] claim that recommender system should consist of: knowledge representation, learning capabilities, and reasoning mechanisms. They allow to build intelligent recommender system that proceeds knowledge and learns new information.

The most popular kinds of recommendation techniques are collaborative filtering (CF) and content-based methods (CBM) [4].

The first category (CF) can be divided into model-based filtering and memory-based filtering. Some example of model-based algorithms are: clustering, decision tree, association rules, regressions, Bayesian networks or artificial neural networks. Memory-based techniques are clustered into user-based or item-based methods. Among well-known problems of CF, it is worth to mention about cold-start problem (new user or new item without data about ratings); data sparsity problem, scalability and synonymy.

The second approach (CBM) generates recommendation based on information about item's features and user preferences. The most popular techniques are: vector space model or probabilistic models, e.g. Naive Bayes classifier or neural network. This approach does not need information about other users but concentrate of the model and dynamic of the single user or item. It allows also to avoid some of CF problems, like data sparsity and ensure privacy but is very sensitive to completeness of item and user description.

To combine advantages of both approaches and eliminate disadvantages of them, hybrid methods are proposed, e.g. weighted, cascade or mixed combination.

Following the survey presented in [4], we can distinguish different evaluation methods for recommender system:

- Statistical accuracy metrics, e.g. Mean Absolute Error (MAE), Root Mean Square Error (RMSE), Correlation;
- Decision support accuracy metrics, e.g. Reversal rate, Weighted errors, Receiver Operating Characteristics (ROC) and Precision Recall Curve (PRC), Precision, Recall and F-measure, MAP@K (mean average precision at K first result), Recall@K – last two measures are suitable for implicit feedback [10];
- Coverage, which shows the fraction of items and users that a recommender system can provide predictions.

2.2   Publication Recommender System

Publication Recommender System is dedicated for scientific researcher: an item to recommend is a journal, book or conference where it is worth to publish a paper or result of current research. Wang et al. [9] propose a content-based filtering recommendation model using Chi-square and softmax regression, which are combined to construct a real-time online system. They assume that the system should predict journals and conferences at the same time, and automatically update its database (when a new research or paper occurs).

Park et al. [6] explore recommender system trends over few years. They analyze distributions of articles by year of publication, journal in which the article was published and by recommendation fields. Such an approach (exploring collected data and checking some statistical distributions) can be treated as a first step to get know data set. Based on these characteristics, better parameters of recommendation methods can be determined.

During a process of building publication recommendation system, the following aspects should be taken into consideration [8]:

– Data set – which papers should be collected: it can be a set of journal repositories or proceedings of conferences. More features that describe a paper allow better recommendation but it also increases computational complexity. Some exemplary features are:
  • for paper: title, author, journal/conference, abstract, whole text of the paper;
  • for journal/conference: name, categories, IF (for journals) or class of a conference, subscription charges, access options [3];
  • for user: user experience, areas of research interests, previously published papers, etc.
– Infrastructure to store the data set – computational complexity of recommender systems can be reduced by appropriate processing mechanism, e.g. big data infrastructure [10].
– Effective methods and algorithms to process the data. Here can be used all methods that are known in recommendation systems but often they are based on content similarity and user feedback.
– Dynamics of a repository – new papers can be added to the repository every day [3].

Literature in recommender system area is very rich and a lot of recommendation methods and techniques were proposed for different aspects of our life. However, there are still some fields that are not exhaustively explored. One of such a field is journal or conference recommendation. To the best our knowledge, developed methods consider mainly content-based approach and only a few authors analyze content of the paper. It can be worth to develop a system based on collaborative filtering and content-based techniques that can propose a journal or conference where to publish our current researches.

3   A Model of Publication Recommendation System

In this section we present a formal definition of Publication Recommender System and all its components.

Let us assume that Publication Recommender System consists of set of journals, authors and papers:

$$PRS = (J, A, P)$$

where J is a set of journals or conferences where one can publish his or her research; A is a set of publications' authors and P is a set of papers that were published. It should be highlighted that cardinalities of A and P sets increase with every new published papers or new researchers. Some new journals can also occur but such a situation is less frequent.

Below we present sets of attributes of each element component: journal or conference, author and publication.

Let us define a journal or a conference $j \in J$ using the following attributes:

- journal or conference name,
- set of categories,
- IF (for journals) or class of a conference,
- items per year,
- set of published papers,
- subscription charges,
- access options.

A paper $p \in P$ has the following attributes:

- title,
- author,
- type of publication (journal or conference),
- year of publication,
- abstract,
- keywords,
- references.

Attributes of an author $a \in A$:

- author name,
- affiliations,
- experience,
- areas of research interests,
- previously published papers.

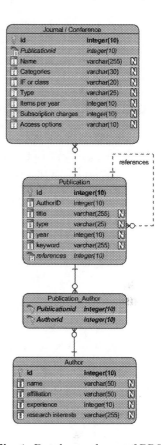

Fig. 1. Database schema of PRS.

Keywords of the paper can be taken directly from the paper (when they are given by the author) or can be determined using some statistical methods, e.g. frequency analysis, TF-IDF. It would be worth to use a thesaurus of concepts that are connected with particular domain. Such a thesaurus allows us also to categorize journals and papers and make it simpler to compare e.g. keywords of the paper with a scope of the conference or the journal. An exemplary poly-hierarchical ontology that can be utilized in semantic web applications were developed by ACM [11].

An overall schema for the PRS is presented in Fig. 1.

4   A Method for Publication Recommendation

In this section we present an idea of recommendation method. The main objective of the method is to analyze author research (scientific paper) and recommend him or her the best place to publish it (e.g. journal or conference).

The system consists of three modules: feature extraction module, collaborative filtering module and content-based module.

First, based on the set of publications, we extract information about authors, journals or conference proceedings and topics. Collaborative filtering and content-based approaches can be performed concurrently or sequentially – the aim is to obtain recommendation of journals or conferences, where to publish. The last step is to combine the results from both algorithms. An overall idea of the system is presented in Fig. 2.

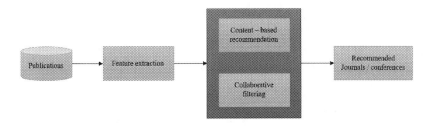

Fig. 2. An overall idea of the journals or conferences recommendation system.

4.1   Feature Extraction Module

The aim of the first module is to collect data about authors, papers, journals and conferences and load them to prepared database schema. There are three possibilities of data source that are easy to access:

- repositories of the journals/conferences – we can download content of them to have a list of papers for each journal item and volume;
- collections of published papers by an author;
- papers correlated with particular topic or keywords – here we can parse results of online search engines.

In all three cases it is assumed that we have access to all necessary elements, especially to full text of publications which allows us to perform text analysis methods. To extract necessary attributes we can use TF-IDF method for indexing papers and Chi-square feature selection method to categorize papers and journals [9].

When data is collected, the next step is to check distributions of some features. It is worth to get know distributions of papers according to categories, years, journals or conferences, author affiliations, etc. It allows us to tune some parameters of the method.

4.2 Collaborative Filtering Module

Recommendation methods are divided into collaborative filtering and content-based approaches. Combining these two approaches are called hybrid methods. Collaborative filtering is used to recommend a user an item that was not yet judged by the user but this item was judged by similar users (neighborhood group). A user is determined as similar to other user if they have judged the same set of items in the similar way.

One can find two ways of presenting the result of collaborative filtering: predicting – when the result is predicted note (judgment) of an item; or recommendation – when items with the highest scores of predictions are presented for the user. In our research we prefer recommendation case: a result list of journals or conferences.

In the case of journal or conference recommendation problem, it is possible to determine a set of journals and conferences where the user has published earlier. The module of CF will find users (authors) that have published in the same or similar issues and determine a set of issues that he or she has not published yet (but other similar users published there).

The list of steps of the module is as follow:

Input: user U, set of all publications P.

Output: list of journals or conferences.

1. For each user U determine a set of user's publications P_U.
2. Extract names of journals and conferences of each P_U.
3. Find users that have published in similar issues.
4. Recommend journals or conferences where the user has not published yet but similar users do.

In classical recommendation systems, the result should not contain the items that user has judged previously. In the case of journal or conferences recommendation, it is possible to publish many times in the same journal or the same conference. An important aspect is a quality of the journal or conference.

To determine a set of similar users and to find a new issue from among many techniques of collaborative filtering, we can explore a few of them, e.g. association rules and artificial neural networks.

Such an approach allows us to find new places where to publish. To explore the possibilities of publishing many times in the same place, we developed content-based approach.

4.3 Content-Based Module

The aim of the content-based module is to find the best place to publish research paper using mainly information about the author. Such an approach requires metadata information about the author, his or her previous publications, journals or conferences. Recommended items (journals or conferences) should be similar to the previous ones, e.g. in terms of scopes.

The main difference with classical recommendation system is the fact that items can be proposed many times (journal's volumes are published a few times in year, conferences are also cyclic events – usually every year or every two years). Also the frequency of submission depends on the type: it is more often situation that authors take part in the same conference every year than situation when they submit papers to the subsequent volumes of the same journal.

The main flow of the content-based approach can be presented in the following steps.

Input: user U, set of all publications P.
Output: list of journals or conferences.

1. Determine a set of user's publications P_U.
2. Develop a profile of user research interests $U_{profile}$ that contains the most important keywords (using e.g. TF-IDF algorithm).
3. Determine a set of keywords for each publication from P.
4. Find the most similar publications to the user profile.
5. Recommend a list of journals or conferences where the most similar publications were published.

The most popular content-based techniques are data mining methods and artificial neural networks, especially, convolutional and recurrent neural networks.

Content-based recommendation methods allow us to build profile of each author. It enables to personalize recommendation results which is not able to perform in the collaborative filtering methods. This is the reason why many recommender systems combine these two techniques.

In our approach we also try to combine collaborative filtering with content-based recommender system. A hybrid approach is explored in a few cases: cascade, weighted hybridization and feature combination [4].

The result can be judged using classic measures like precision, recall or F-measure. The main problem can occur when an author submits a paper to the recommended journal or conference but his or her paper is not accepted for publication.

5   Experimental Evaluation for a Case Study

The main objective of the evaluation process is to check the effectiveness of the recommendation system which is presented in the paper. As the evaluation of the whole system requires time and some volunteers (authors that judge the relevance of the obtained result), we have decided to show only a case study for the authors of the last ICCCI conference (ICCCI 2018 that had taken place in Bristol).

In the following subsection we show the source of data, present ETL process to extract interesting features and some early results that we have obtained.

5.1 Data Set

In order to evaluate proposed Publication Recommender System, we have downloaded XML data from DBLP [12]. We have limited a set of users to authors of papers published in Proceedings of ICCCI 2018. Gathered data were transformed to the schema presented in Fig. 1. DBLP source allows us to collect only a part of attributes that were mentioned in general PRS schema. An ERD diagram for collected data is presented in Fig. 3.

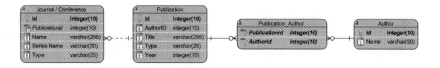

Fig. 3. ERD diagram of experimental data.

It was necessary to extract attributes from XML files and transform them to database. A few features were calculated from downloaded ones, e.g. series name of conference/journal or type of the paper.

5.2 Experimental Results

In the first step of experiments we have checked some statistic properties of collected data. The results are presented in Tables 1, 2, 3 and 4.

The most popular journals are listed in Table 1 and the most popular conferences are listed in Table 2 with numbers of published papers and authors (if author has published many times, he or she is counted multiple times). Average number of authors per paper in journals varies from 1, 1 to almost 4 – it is

Table 1. Top journals based on number of papers.

Journal Name	Number of authors	Number of papers
Computing Research Repository	98	89
Journal of Intelligent and Fuzzy Systems	44	34
Cybernetics and Systems	43	25
T. Computational Collective Intelligence	36	20
Journal of Universal Computer Science	30	21
Computer Science (AGH)	23	13
Journal of Information Telecommunication	17	8
Applied Intelligence	17	13
Expert System Applications	16	10
Knowledge-Based Systems	15	5
Journal of Computer Science	15	4

Table 2. Top conference proceedings based on number of papers.

Conference Name	Number of authors	Number of papers
ICCCI	324	165
ACIIDS	201	101
ICCS	77	50
KES	48	27
IEA/AIE	39	33
KES-AMSTA	33	17

slightly correlated with impact factor and points of the journal (papers in better journal have more average number of authors). In the case of top conferences this ratio is between 1,5 and 2. A range is smaller what can show that the level of these conferences are similar.

In the collaborative approach, when we take into consideration also year of publications in these journals and conferences (appropriately, Tables 3 and 4), we can see that many papers are published almost every year. We can say that activity in top journal publication of ICCCI 2018 conference authors is increasing over years (with a peak in 2017). Conference activity is greater than journal ones. The trend of authors in top conferences is also increasing over years. It is worth to notice that in case of top conferences, there exists a set of "loyal" authors that publish on both ICCCI and ACIIDS conferences. Number for the next conferences are visibly smaller.

Deeper analysis has shown that there exists a set of authors that have published papers every year. Also for top journals and conferences one can observe a pattern that authors "get back" – they have published more papers than one. It shows that it is profitable for authors to publish in these journals and conferences.

Table 3. Top journals based on number of authors over years 2007–2019.

YEAR	2007	2008	2009	2010	2011	2012	2013	2014	2015	2016	2017	2018	2019	SUM
CoRR			1	8	1	6	12	13	14	9	10	19	2	95
JIFS	1	3	4	1	4	2	4	3		3	6	8	4	43
CS			2	2				7	3	2	26			42
TCCI				1	3	4	8	2	1	9	2	2	4	36
JUSC	3	5	4	2		2	3		1	5	2			27
CS (AGH)	2	3		2	1		5			3	1	6		23
JIT											13	3	1	17
App. Int.					1		3		5	3	4			16
ESA							1	1	2	3	8			15
KBS	4	1		1	2	1			1			2		12
JCS			1			2	2	1	1		3			10
SUM	10	12	12	17	12	17	38	27	28	37	75	40	11	336

Table 4. Top conferences based on number of authors over years 2009–2019.

YEAR	2009	2010	2011	2012	2013	2014	2015	2016	2017	2018	2019	SUM
ICCCI	12	6	13	14	15	23	26	24	40	151		324
ACIIDS	5	10	17	13	13	11	10	16	33	39	34	201
ICCS	7		2	3	3	5	8	7	13	2		61
KES	2	7	6	8		3						35
KES-AMSTA	5	4	5	3	4	4						31
ICAART	2				7	6	2	7	4	2		30
IEA/AIE	3	2	5	3								17
SUM	36	29	48	44	42	52	46	54	90	194	34	699

Analysis based on content-based have taken into account scope of top conferences and journals, theirs points, classes of these conferences and impact factor of journals. Also the following features were considered: subscription charges, conference venue and publisher.

Performed evaluations have confirm that authors that have published theirs papers on ICCCI 2018 conference, are interested in a selected areas of computer science – a great part of conferences or journals scope are common. Authors can pay more (subscription charge or conference venue) if the venue is more attractive and choose publishers that are well known in the scientific environment.

6   Conclusions and Future Works

In the paper we have explored CF and CB approaches to determine the best place to submit current research papers. The aim of the system is to recommend an author a journal or conference that fit to his or her researches. We have used some statistical methods to check the publication trends in a group of authors.

In the future works it is worth to perform a complex evaluations of proposed Publication Recommender System for a set of authors and papers published in selected research area, e.g. computer science.

Acknowledgments. This research was partially supported by the Polish Ministry of Science and Higher Education.

References

1. Aguilar, J., Valdiviezo-Diaz, P., Riofrio, G.: A general framework for intelligent recommender systems. Appl. Comput. Inf. **13**, 147–160 (2017)
2. Burke, R.: Knowledge-based recommender systems. In: Encyclopedia of Library and Information Science (2000)
3. Dhanda, M., Verma, V.: Recommender system for academic literature with incremental dataset. Procedia Comput. Sci. **89**, 483–491 (2016)
4. Isinkaye, F.O., Folajimi, Y.O., Ojokoh, B.A.: Recommendation systems: principles, methods and evaluation. Egypt. Inform. J. **16**, 261–273 (2015)

5. Osadchiy, T., Poliakov, I., Olivier, P., Rowland, M., Foster, E.: Recommender system based on pairwise association rules. Expert Syst. Appl. **115**, 535–542 (2019)
6. Park, D.H., Kim, H.K., Choi, I.Y., Kim, J.K.: A review and classification of recommender systems research. In: Proceedings of 2011 International Conference on Social Science and Humanity, IPEDR, vol. 5 pp. VI-290–VI-294 (2011)
7. Ricci, F., Rokach, L., Shapira, B., Kantor, P.B. (eds.): Recommender Systems Handbook. Springer, Boston (2011). https://doi.org/10.1007/978-0-387-85820-3
8. Sardar, A., Ferzund, J., Suryani, M.A., Shoaib, M.: Recommender system for journal articles using opinion mining and semantics. Int. J. Adv. Comput. Sci. Appl. **8**(12), 213–220 (2017)
9. Wang, D., Liang, Y., Xu, D., Feng, X., Guan, R.: A content-based recommender system for computer science publications. Knowl. Based Syst. **157**, 1–9 (2018)
10. Zhang, S., Yao, L., Sun, A., Tay, Y.: Deep learning based recommender system: a survey and new perspectives. ACM Comput. Surv. (2018). https://arxiv.org/abs/1707.07435. Accessed 4 Sept 2019
11. The 2012 ACM Computing Classification System (2012). https://www.acm.org/publications/class-2012. Accessed 1 Apr 2019
12. DBLP computer science bibliography. https://dblp.uni-trier.de/. Accessed 1 Apr 2019

Text Processing and Information Retrieval

Application of Deep Learning Techniques on Document Classification

Mainak Manna[1], Priyanka Das[2(✉)], and Asit Kumar Das[2]

[1] Hyland Software Research & Development, Kolkata, India
moinak.manna@gmail.com
[2] Indian Institute of Engineering Science and Technology, Shibpur,
Howrah 711103, India
priyankadas700@gmail.com, akdas@cs.iiests.ac.in

Abstract. Automatic assignment of documents into some of the categories is highly required for analysing the content of the documents. Thus, document classification plays a significant role in the field of machine learning, artificial intelligence, information extraction, natural language processing and many more. This problem of assigning a document to a particular category or class has been approached in several ways till date, and with numerous new technological advancements, this class of problem has interesting solutions. Apart from the processes related to text analysis and parsing methodologies, deep learning has offered a way to solve this classification scenario. In the present work, we represent a comparative study on some of the basic building blocks used in deep learning, each of which can be applied to get simpler models trying to assign a class of the available documents. The present comparative study shows how these components can vary the impact on the task. The evaluation of the models has been performed on a standard available dataset. The non-linearity provided by these deep learning models are useful in getting state-of-the-art results for text classification problem.

Keywords: Deep learning models · Convolutional neural network ·
Long Short Term Memory · Support Vector Machine · Naïve Bayes

1 Introduction

Classification has been widely studied in the fields of database management, data mining, information retrieval and many more. It is a supervised technique performed when the class label of the data is known to us. The classification task considers two partitions of dataset, i.e., it takes a set of training data $D = \{d_1, d_2, \cdots, d_n\}$, so that each data is assigned with a class value derived from a set of k different discreet values $\{1, \cdots, k\}$. A classification model is prepared that relates the features in the underlying trained data to one of the class values. Then a test data is being considered where the class value is not given and the training model predicts the class of this test data. Nowadays, with the rapid growth of data, categorization of documents has become an important task

© Springer Nature Switzerland AG 2019
N. T. Nguyen et al. (Eds.): ICCCI 2019, LNAI 11683, pp. 181–192, 2019.
https://doi.org/10.1007/978-3-030-28377-3_15

and therefore, researchers are continuously trying to develop new methods for text classification by analysing the content of the documents. Earlier this problem was approached using various methods starting from word-by-word analysis techniques [1] to lexicographical features of the textual data. Harish et al. [2] proposed a feature clustering technique for classifying text documents. Initially, they reduced the dimension of feature vectors and applied the clustering on standard text datasets. Often the word orders are considered to be one of the disadvantages involved in unsupervised approaches. These problems have been later on surpassed by machine learning algorithms. The advent of deep learning algorithms gave this problem a new viewpoint altogether. A research work discussed in [3] developed a model based on both the recurrent neural network and convolutional neural network for dealing with short texts. Their proposed model claimed to achieve state-of-the-art results on three different datasets for dialogue act prediction. Character level convolutional neural networks have also been explored for text classification in [4]. This research constructed their own large scale dataset and also compared their task with the traditional bag of words, n-grams and their TFIDF variants, and deep learning models such as word-based ConvNets and recurrent neural networks and claimed to provide state-of-the-art or competitive results. Also, max-pooling layer has been used to identify the keywords from the text. It is observed that due to enormous increase in the number of text documents, the classification performance of several supervised classifiers has degraded mostly in case of multi-class classification. Therefore, recently, hierarchical deep learning technique [5] has been introduced for text classification. This architecture involves stacks of deep learning architectures to provide specialized understanding at each level of the document hierarchy. Apart from documents and text classification, deep learning techniques are also used in the areas of spam classification, medical data analysis, sentiment analysis and many more.

In the proposed work, different basic deep learning strategies are evaluated against some text datasets to have a comparative study of the various techniques. The basic building blocks of this architectural evolution call for evaluation and comparison. The ensemble of procedures associated with this field and interesting models are considered in this paper. This paper tries to look at some of the primary methods that are being used and mentioned as a significant deep learning breakthrough in recent years. The split of the dataset into train and test part is done using scikit learn split dataset method. We are training with 90% of the dataset with each of this model, and 10% is used to get the performance of the learned model. The vocabulary dataset is formed from the downloaded data along with the frequency of each word in the textual datasets vocabulary. We employ Keras (version 2.2.4) deep learning library with Tensorflow backend to create the models and evaluate them over this dataset. Keras provides many useful API's which are used in some cases custom layers are implemented in Python 3.2.2 for developing the models. The basic steps related to document classification is shown in Fig. 1.

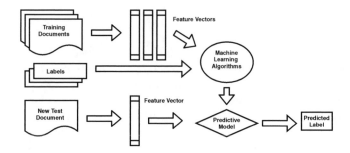

Fig. 1. Supervised learning model for document classification

The remaining part of the paper is organised as follows: Sect. 2 elaborates the existing deep learning models for text document classification. Section 3 exhibits the application of all the existing classification techniques on the existing text datasets and the results of the comparative study are shown in Sect. 3.2. Finally, Sect. 4 concludes the paper.

2   Existing Models for Document Classification

This section mainly provides an elaborate discussion on some of the existing classification models mostly used for classification tasks.

2.1   Bag of Words Model

In this model, the frequency of each word will be a feature in the case of text classification. In these type of problems the machine can not work upon textual data. The conversion from numeric to text data is done using the Keras "Tokenizer" class. The network models will accept the output labels in the same numerical vector format. One hot encoding is used in this case i.e., the labels are converted to the vector where each position denotes the class it represents. This conversion is done using "labelBinarizer" class of scikit learn. This model used the multilayer neural network architecture. The sequential model (using Keras Sequential method) comprises of a dense layer. Then we pass it through the ReLU (Rectified Linear Units) activation. We have added dropout layer with keep probability of 0.5. Again, ReLU activation is used and then similar dropout layer as before is used which then has a layer which will give us the prediction (the final layer). The metrics used in this is 'accuracy' and cross-entropy loss function is calculated with the Adam optimizer.

2.2   Hierarchical Attention Networks

Words making sentences and sentences generating documents is the basic concept behind hierarchical attention networks. But all the words in a document are not equally significant and some of them characterize a sentence more than others. Therefore, it is necessary to develop an attention model that can emphasize more on the sentences having the significant words. The words (the original ASCII text words won't be of any use to the model unless it is being converted to numeric vectors) are transformed into something meaningful to the machine, i.e., vectors. If two words have the same meaning, we expect that their vector would be somewhat pointing to the same direction of sense. Pre-trained word embeddings by Glove [6] are used for achieving this behaviour and then a Bidirectional RNN (Recurrent Neural Networks) with LSTM (Long Short Term Memory) [7] cell is used. This gave similar results when used with GRU (Gated Recurrent Unit) which reads the sequence of words of the documents and encodes each of them to a vector. This representation holds the contextual information of each of the words in the sentence. These token features are later used in attention layer. The attention vector (also known as context vector) dictates which information to drop and the model will learn which data to discard to get the correct behaviour. The vectors that are resulted from the previous step are again passed through a Bi-directional layer with LSTM cell. The concatenated output of forward and backward pass is yet passed through the attention layer to get the document vector representation. This second layer is attending which sentences are of importance for the model to act correctly. The output then is passed through a dense layer with ReLU and softmax activation of 50 and 20 nodes respectively. The final output is then taken into account to calculate the performance.

Attention Model 1. The attention model used here is mentioned by Raffel et al. [8]. The attention is defined as $e_t = ah_t$, where a is the $tanh$ function. α_t = softmax e_t and $c = \sum \alpha_t * h_t$, where h_t is a linear function $(Wh + b)$. The final output c is the summation of attention vector multiplied with feed forward or previous layer output. This reduces the dimension of the valid input over which next levels will work upon.

Attention Model 2. The variation of the above attention mechanism is evaluated in the same computation set-up as mentioned before used in this attention model. Lin et al. [9] suggested an attention that can be denoted by this equation $\alpha = $ softmax $(W_{s_2} * tanh(W_{s_1} * H_t + b))$. Here, W_{s_1} and W_{s_2} are learn-able weight parameters and H_t is the input or previous layer output. Here b is bias (basically denoting the linear function). Though the original proposed model used a penalization term, in our case only categorical cross entropy is used with Adam optimizer. This added parameter W_{s_2} which is basically a matrix that creates a matrix of attention rather than single attention vector.

2.3   Convolutional Neural Networks

Here, we discuss about two convolutional neural network models termed as CNN Model 1 and CNN Model 2.

CNN Model 1. This model is based on the working principle of convolutional neural network. In this case, the embedding matrix is formed using the Glove word vectors. Then we embed this layer into the pipeline. The output from the embedding layer is passed to the 1D convolution layer with 128 being the number of output filters in the convolution (the output dimensionality). The kernel size is taken as 5 and the activation function RELU is used in this case. The next step being the max pooling layer, the pool size is given as 5. It provides the maximum over 5 units of previous output. These two layers are used twice before it is passed to the 1D convolution layer with the global max pooling with pool size of 2 at the end. After that, the output of this layer is passed to the dense layer with RELU activation function with 128 units. The final layer with 20 units and with softmax activation function gives the prediction for a given set of inputs. The loss function used is of categorical cross entropy with RMSProp optimizer.

CNN Model 2. Following Yoon's [10] Convolutional Neural Network, a model has been built to test over the dataset. In this model, we have used pre-trained word vectors generated by the Word2Vec approach [11]. The first layer embeds words into low-dimensional vectors. Convolution is performed in the next layer over the embedded word vectors using multiple filter sizes. This denotes that at a time say, t, $f1, f2, f3$ words are taken into account by the model. Here, $f1, f2, f3$ indicates different filter sizes. In the next step, max-pooling is applied to the result of the convolutional layer. Combining the results of these convolutions a feature vector is formed. Dropout regularization is added after that, and then the classification is done using the softmax layer. Among the 90% train data, 80% of the sample data is used in training the model in this case; rest is used in validation. Upon completion of a few batches, the learning rate is reduced. The minimum learning rate is 0.005, the maximum learning rate is 0.0002 and the decaying term has a value of 2.4.

2.4 Support Vector Machine and Naïve Bayes

Support Vector Machines are based on the concept of decision planes that define decision boundaries. A decision plane is the one that separates between a set of objects having different class memberships. There are various kernels that are used in SVM models. These include linear, polynomial, radial basis function (RBF) and sigmoid. The kernels are defined as follows:

$$K(X_i, X_j) = \begin{cases} X_i.X_j & \text{Linear} \\ (\gamma X_i.X_j + C)^d & \text{Polynomial} \\ exp(-\gamma|X_i - X_j|^2) & \text{RBF} \\ tanh(\gamma X_i.X_j + C) & \text{Sigmoid} \end{cases}$$

Here, $K(X_i, X_j) = \phi(X_i).\phi(X_j)$ that is, the kernel function, represents a dot product of input data points mapped into the higher dimensional feature space by transformation ϕ. γ is an adjustable parameter of certain kernel functions.

On the other hand, Naïve Bayes belongs to the family of probabilistic classifiers based on Bayes' theorem. Naïve Bayes classifiers can handle an arbitrary number of independent variables whether continuous or categorical. Let a set of variables is represented by $X = \{x_1, x_2, \cdots, x_d\}$. The posterior probability for a event say, C_j among a set of possible outcomes can be represented as $C = \{c_1, c_2, \cdots, c_d\}$. Using Bayes' rule it can be said that,

$$p(C_j|x_1, x_2, \cdots, x_d) \propto p(x_1, x_2, \cdots, x_d|C_j)p(C_j)$$

where $p(C_j|x_1, x_2, \cdots, x_d)$ is the posterior probability of class membership, i.e., the probability that X belongs to C_j. Since, Naïve Bayes assumes that the conditional probabilities of the independent variables are statistically independent, we can decompose the likelihood to a product of terms:

$$= p(X|C_j) \propto \Pi_{k=1}^{d}p(x_k|C_j)$$

$$= p(C_j|X) \propto p(C_j)\Pi_{k=1}^{d}p(x_k|C_j)$$

Using Bayes' rule above, we label a new case X with a class level C_j that achieves the highest posterior probability.

Here, in this present work, to compare with the standard benchmarking text classification procedures – the datasets have been tested against Naïve Bayes and Support Vector Machine classifier. After converting the collection of documents into the TF-iDF (Term Frequency-inverse Document Frequency) features we use the Multinomial Naïve Bayes classifier on the data. Similarly, this is done for Support Vector Machine. The data used in both cases are similar, i.e., TF-iDF feature vectors.

2.5   BERT

BERT or Bidirectional Encoder Representations from Transformers is a very new approach to language modelling that applies bi-directional training of transformers. This model reads the whole input sequence all at once and thus it helps in achieving a deeper sense of language context and flow than single-direction language modelling. Using BERT we can use the context specific representation of the words to predict meaningful information. For describing the transformer encoder, it can be said that the input is a sequence of tokens that are vectorised and fed to the neural network. The output is a sequence of vectors in which each vector corresponds to an input token with the same index. While training language models, it is always a challenging task to define a prediction goal and hence BERT uses two training strategies: (i) Masked LM and (ii) Next Sentence Prediction. Unlike other classification models, Gluon NLP library is used in this case. Here we have used the pre - trained model of BERT. The model used is gluonnlp.model.bert_12_768_12. The number of layers (L) is 12, number of units (H) is 768, and the number of self-attention heads (A) is 12. The dataset loaded into this model function is book_corpus_wiki_en_uncased. We have used Adam's optimizer. The learning rate is 6e-6 and epsilon = 1e-9. Gradient clipping is used in this case and the training process is same as before. The result is at last found from the SoftMax layers in this model.

2.6 Bi-directional LSTM

LSTM is being widely used as it overcomes all the disadvantages related to the vanishing gradients of Recurrent Neural Networks. Let an input sequence is given as $x = (x_1, x_2, \cdots, x_T)$, then any RNN computes the hidden vector sequence as $h = (h_1, h_2, \cdots, h_T)$ and output vector sequence $y = (y_1, y_2, \cdots, y_T)$ by iterating the following equations from $t = 1$ to T:

$$h_t = H(W_{xh}x_t + W_{hh}h_{t-1} + b_h)y_t = (W_{hy}h_t + b_o)$$

$$y_t = (W_{hy}h_t + b_o)$$

Here, all the terms related to W are weight matrices, the b terms denote bias vectors and H is the hidden layer function. But in case of LSTM, the same hidden layer function can be calculated as follows:

$$i_t = \sigma(W_{xi}x_t + W_{hi}h_{t-1} + W_{ci}c_{t-1} + b_i)$$

$$f_t = \sigma(W_{xf}x_t + W_{hf}h_{t-1} + W_{cf}c_{t-1} + b_f)$$

$$c_t = f_t c_{t-1} + i_t tanh(W_{xc}x_t + W_{hc}h_{t-1} + b_c)$$

$$o_t = \sigma(W_{xo}x_t + W_{ho}h_{t-1} + W_{co}c_t + b_o)$$

$$h_t = o_t tanh(c_t)$$

Here, the logistic sigmoid function is denoted by σ, the input gate, forget gate, output gate and cell activation vectors are denoted by i, f, o and c respectively and all of these are of same size as h.

In this model, we have used the Glove word embeddings of 300 dimension. Here, in the present work we have followed the same document hierarchy as mentioned by Yang et al. [12]. A sentence consists of words, and those words which are mainly the integer sequences are converted to word vectors by using the Glove embeddings mentioned above and this sequence of vectors are passed to a Bi-directional LSTM. This would generate a vector for each of these sentences. The hierarchy comes into the picture from the fact that now these sentence vectors are now passed to a similar procedure just like the words in a sentence in the previous step. The sentence vectors are given as input into a bi-directional LSTM encoder that outputs a vector which can be considered as a vector denoting the entire document. This vector is then passed to a dense layer. The final layer which is a dense layer with softmax activation does the prediction of the classes of the text datasets.

3   Application on Various Text Datasets

This section describes the application of the existing classification schemes on several existing text datasets.

3.1   Data Preparation

The data for this application comprises several existing datasets like the standard 20 Newsgroups dataset collected from UCI Machine Learning Repository, IMDB Movie Review dataset, Reuters-21578, Crime dataset as mentioned in [13] and Twitter Sentiment Analysis dataset from Kaggle. Once all the datasets are downloaded, they are being tokenized and then the most frequent words like 'a', 'an', 'the' have been removed. The preprocessing steps have been incorporated using the Stanford NLP. By removal of those stopwords, we assigned a lower weight in these models. In some cases the pre-processing of data varied from others, i.e., truncation of sentence or document are needed as described in the corresponding models.

3.2   Experimental Results

The present work has applied all the existing classification schemes against the text datasets mentioned above. The details of the datasets considered for training, validation and testing is given in Table 1.

Table 1. Details of the data

Dataset	Data size	Training sample	Validation sample	Testing sample
20 Newsgroup	20,000	16000	2000	2000
IMDB Movie Review	50,000	40,000	5,000	5,000
Reuters-21578	21,578	17,262	2,158	2,158
Crime dataset	192,424	153,940	19,242	19,242
Twitter Sentiment Analysis	1,578,627	1,262,902	157,863	157,862

As mentioned in Table 1, we have run the models on the training samples of the data. Results have been obtained by running these models in Keras with the Tensorflow GPU backend. For evaluating the classification performance of the classifiers considered in this comparative study, we have measured standard evaluation metrics like, precision (P), recall (R) and F-measure (F) and classification accuracy (A) [14] using (1–4). Here, the evaluation metrics are computed based on the confusion matrix as shown in Table 2. The parameters u, v, w and x are termed as true positive, false negative, false positive and true negative respectively.

$$\text{Precision (P)} = \frac{u}{u + w} \tag{1}$$

$$\text{Recall (R)} = \frac{u}{u + v} \tag{2}$$

$$\text{F-measure (F)} = \frac{2PR}{P + R} \tag{3}$$

Table 2. Confusion matrix

Actual	Predicted	
	Positive	Negative
Positive	u	v
Negative	w	x

$$\text{Accuracy (A)} = \frac{u + x}{u + v + w + x} \tag{4}$$

Tables 3 and 4 show the evaluation result on text datasets in terms of precision, recall, F-measure and accuracy. The accuracy denotes how much of the predicted data are matching with the original label. For each dataset, the highest scores of precision, recall and F-measure and accuracy obtained for the corresponding classifiers are marked in bold faces.

Till date, many research works have been reported the performance of classification models on text datasets. Therefore, we have also made an effort to incorporate a comparative study based on the performance of two very recent classification schemes described in [15] and [16]. The work represented in [15] preserves the sequence of term occurrences in documents. It discarded the conventional vector space models and further proposed to index the terms in B-tree to avoid the issues related to sequential matching. Again, another recent work in [16] introduced a fast and efficient text classification approach using K-Nearest Neighbour classifier using different feature selection schemes. Classification performance has been evaluated based on minimum number of features needed to classify a text document. Here, 80% data has been trained and rest has been tested and the comparison has made based on terms like F-measure and accuracy and the results are shown in Table 5. For comparing the proposed work with these two recent works, we have considered the best F-score and accuracy for each dataset as mentioned in Tables 3 and 4. The best scores for each metric corresponding to each dataset are shown in bold faces. It is observed that most of the results obtained by the proposed experiments are higher compared to the recent existing works.

From the results shown in Tables 3 and 4, it is observed that the CNN Model 2 seems to be performing better than both the SVM and Naïve Bayes and all the other models. In case of MLP BOW model, we considered the document vector to be averaged over the sum of the word vectors. The context information is lost in this case. The value of the document will not give any particular word as an important feature. For the attention-based models the feature extraction is better than the bag of words. Before discussing the improvement, it is better to consider the effect of encoding for Bi-directional LSTM. The encoding extracts better conversion of the sequence of original word vectors to a different sequence which is better at yielding a better result. Context-specific information plays a vital role in this case. The use of LSTM solves the problem of not capturing the full information in the sequence of words that occur when merely averaging

Table 3. Classification performance in (%) MLP with BOW, Attention Model 1, Attention Model 2, CNN 1 and CNN 2

Dataset	ML				A1				A2				C1				C2			
	P	R	F	A	P	R	F	A	P	R	F	A	P	R	F	A	P	R	F	A
20 Newsgroup	74	77	75	71	82	84	83	80	83	86	84	82	82	87	84	89	**86**	**89**	**87**	**92**
IMDB Movie Review	**75**	**77**	**76**	**76**	71	72	71	73	69	73	71	72	68	71	69	74	72	75	73	72
Reuters-21578	71	75	**73**	74	69	**76**	72	73	71	73	72	74	64	71	67	72	**72**	74	**73**	**75**
Crime dataset	75	78	76	80	81	84	82	85	**84**	**87**	**85**	85	84	85	84	83	81	83	82	84
Twitter Sentiment Analysis	81	84	82	86	80	82	81	85	**83**	**85**	**84**	**87**	82	84	83	82	80	82	81	82

Table 4. Classification performance in (%) for Naïve Bayes, SVM, BERT and LSTM

Dataset	NB				SVM				BERT				LS			
	P	R	F	A	P	R	F	A	P	R	F	A	P	R	F	A
20 Newsgroup	80	85	82	85	84	87	85	**91**	**87**	**89**	**88**	**91**	79	84	81	76
IMDB Movie Review	74	79	76	78	71	75	73	77	72	78	74	75	**76**	**81**	**78**	**83**
Reuters-21578	**81**	**81**	**81**	**83**	79	77	78	81	72	78	74	76	75	77	76	75
Crime dataset	72	74	73	77	73	75	74	78	75	77	76	78	**82**	**86**	**84**	**83**
Twitter Sentiment Analysis	**75**	**77**	**76**	76	71	73	72	75	70	73	71	75	71	74	72	**77**

out the word vectors of a sentence which is useful in extended text classification such as document classification just as in this case.

The reason behind the significant increase in performance from BOW and Bi-LSTM would be the introduction of attention layer. Here, the usage of hierarchical attention gives a better result than Bi-LSTM because the presence of different words and then corresponding different sentences are given different weight importance to arrive at a correct classification result. This attention mechanism reduces the dimensionality and only considers those parts which contribute well in making the accurate model prediction. The improvement in performance is because the mechanism correctly captures the context-specific importance. This context is essential since the same word can be of different importance based on the background on which it appears in the text.

The second CNN model uses multiple filters before passing it to the max pooling layer. The operation performed by convolution on a series of text can be observed as going through a set of words. Sometimes it might be two words or three words at once. This repetitive reading is processing the local context. The max pooled output gets the most critical part or contextual information. This is found to be useful in predicting the classes of the newsgroups. Also, the pre-trained word vectors are essential in this case. The model without the word embeddings is not favourable. Multiple feature maps get the correct information from these word vectors rather than from an embedding which is learned on the

Table 5. Comparative results based on F-score and Accuracy in (%) for two existing works

Dataset	Proposed		Work in [15]		Work in [16]	
	F	A	F	A	F	A
20 Newsgroup	**87**	**92**	84	86	81	78
IMDB Movie Review	78	**83**	**79**	80	75	79
Reuters-21578	**81**	**83**	80	**83**	79	82
Crime dataset	**85**	**85**	79	82	76	71
Twitter Sentiment Analysis	**84**	**87**	76	80	79	74

go in this model system. The accuracy found in case of BERT is almost 91% which is close to that obtained by the CNN model trained before. Convolutions being a complicated step is resource intensive as well as time consuming - the time taken was higher than this one. The almost similar result of the can be attributed to the basic building nature of the BERT's context in transformer architecture itself. Each block of the transformer present in BERT transforms the input using linear layers and applies attention to the sequence.

Again, the results shown in Table 5 obtained by comparing with two recent research works, it is observed that results are improved by incorporating deep learning techniques into the classification schemes.

4   Conclusion

It can be concluded that though the application of the convolutional neural network might not be intuitive, it is successful in classifying the document classes with better accuracy. This can be helpful in the field of natural language processing in a different application. The feature extraction and classification is applied over a broad range. With this result, it can be mentioned that CNN can be used for document classification with NLP pipeline as a significant part. The CNN based models could further be observed to get a better model or can be combined with any of the methods previously mentioned to analyse how they perform and this remains as a future work.

References

1. Soumya George, K., Joseph, S.: Text classification by augmenting bag of words (BOW) representation with co-occurrence feature. IOSR J. Comput. Eng. **16**(1), 34–38 (2014)
2. Harish, B.S., Udayasri, B.: Document classification: an approach using feature clustering. In: Thampi, S., Abraham, A., Pal, S., Rodriguez, J. (eds.) Recent Advances in Intelligent Informatics. AISC, vol. 235, pp. 163–173. Springer, Cham (2014). https://doi.org/10.1007/978-3-319-01778-5_17

3. Lee, J.Y., Dernoncourt, F.: Sequential short-text classification with recurrent and convolutional neural networks. CoRR abs/1603.03827 (2016)
4. Zhang, X., Zhao, J.J., LeCun, Y.: Character-level convolutional networks for text classification. CoRR abs/1509.01626 (2015)
5. Kowsari, K., Brown, D.E., Heidarysafa, M., Meimandi, K.J., Gerber, M.S., Barnes, L.E.: HDLTex: hierarchical deep learning for text classification. In: 2017 16th IEEE International Conference on Machine Learning and Applications (ICMLA), pp. 364–371 (2017)
6. Pennington, J., Socher, R., Manning, C.: Glove: global vectors for word representation. In: Proceedings of the 2014 Conference on Empirical Methods in Natural Language Processing (EMNLP), pp. 1532–1543 (2014)
7. Hochreiter, S., Schmidhuber, J.: Long short-term memory. Neural Comput. **9**(8), 1735–1780 (1997)
8. Raffel, C., Ellis, D.P.W.: Feed-forward networks with attention can solve some long-term memory problems. CoRR abs/1512.08756 (2015)
9. Lin, Z., et al.: A structured self-attentive sentence embedding. CoRR abs/1703.03130 (2017)
10. Kim, Y.: Convolutional neural networks for sentence classification. In: Proceedings of the 2014 Conference on Empirical Methods in Natural Language Processing (EMNLP), pp. 1746–1751 (2014)
11. Mikolov, T., Chen, K., Corrado, G., Dean, J.: Efficient estimation of word representations in vector space. CoRR abs/1301.3781, pp. 1–12 (2013)
12. Yang, Z., Yang, D., Dyer, C., He, X., Smola, A., Hovy, E.: Hierarchical attention networks for document classification. In: 2016 Annual Conference of the North American Chapter of the Association for Computational Linguistics, pp. 1480–1489 (2016)
13. Das, P., Das, A.K.: Graph-based clustering of extracted paraphrases for labelling crime reports. Knowl.-Based Syst. (2019)
14. Das, P., Das, A.K., Nayak, J.: Feature selection generating directed rough-spanning tree for crime pattern analysis. Neural Comput. Appl. 1–17 (2018)
15. Harish, B.S., Manjunath, S., Guru, D.S.: Text document classification: an approach based on indexing (2019)
16. Jodha, R., Gaur Sanjay, B.C., Chowdhary, K.R.: Text classification using KNN with different feature selection methods. Int. J. Res. Publ. **8**(1), 1–8 (2018)

Similar Meaning Analysis for Original Documents Identification in Arabic Language

Adnen Mahmoud[1,2(⊠)] and Mounir Zrigui[1]

[1] Algebra, Number Theory and Nonlinear Analyzes Laboratory,
University of Monastir, Monastir, Tunisia
mahmoud.adnen@gmail.com, mounir.zrigui@fsm.rnu.tn
[2] Higher Institute of Computer Science and Communication Techniques,
Hammam Sousse, University of Sousse, Sousse, Tunisia

Abstract. The progressive advancement in technology has become easy to present the language expression of someone else as one's own with similar words semantically. This phenomenon increased the potential source of plagiarism. Its detection is a challenge especially in the case of Arabic paraphrase because of the semantic ambiguity of this language. In recent decades, researches have been hindered by the very limited availability of well-structured datasets. In this context, our main objectives are focused on constructing a corpus for Arabic and presenting thereafter its impact for identifying paraphrase. Indeed, we generated the suspect documents from the Open Source Arabic Corpora (OSAC). Distributed word representation (word2vec) and part-of-speech methods were useful for replacing each original word by its most similar one that had the same grammatical class. Moreover, we captured the structure of Arabic sentences with different window sizes and vector dimensions. Then, we studied how this corpus could be used efficiently in the evaluation of Natural Language Processing (NLP) methods (i.e. Term Frequency-Inverse Document Frequency (TF-IDF), Latent Semantic Analysis (LSA), Latent Dirichlet Allocation (LDA), word2vec, Global Vector Representation (GloVe), and Convolutional Neural Network (CNN)) for paraphrase detection. Experiments revealed which one could outperformed significantly for preserving semantic properties of Arabic words with various linear regularities, alleviating data sparseness and increasing the degree of semantic similarity, in terms of precision and recall.

Keywords: Arabic language · Paraphrase · Semantic similarity ·
Corpus development · Word embeddings · Convolutional Neural Network

1 Introduction

The progressive advancement in technology makes everything freely accessible over the internet, which increases the potential source of paraphrase. It became easy to rewrite ideas of someone else and involve representing their work as one's own without mention the source. Its detection needs a semantic similarity analysis that is a crucial task in Natural Language Processing (NLP). Often, an important problem to solve in the development and evaluation of methods is the lack of benchmark corpora in Arabic language publicly available. It is a fundamental issue understanding more attention to

© Springer Nature Switzerland AG 2019
N. T. Nguyen et al. (Eds.): ICCCI 2019, LNAI 11683, pp. 193–206, 2019.
https://doi.org/10.1007/978-3-030-28377-3_16

researchers to deal with it. Faced with these issues, we develop an Arabic paraphrased corpus preserving semantic and syntactic properties of sentences. Then, we study its impact for identifying original documents. This paper is organized as follows: First, we present previous works of paraphrase detection, in Sect. 2. Then, we describe our methodology in Sect. 3, in which we will detail the phases that it makes up. Subsequently, we present the experimental setup and discussion in Sect. 4. Finally, we end by a conclusion and future work to realize, in Sect. 5.

2   State of the Art

Corpora are the fundamental elements in the development and/or testing of studies in the fields of NLP, Information Retrieval and Computational Linguistics [1]. The collection of documents incorporating real paraphrase usually based on two datasets: Source documents from which passages of text extracted; and suspect documents, in which the aforementioned passages inserted after undergoing obfuscation processing. Therefore, NLP researchers focus on developing freely large-scale resources to investigate paraphrase detection problem according to two ways [2]: The first one is to reuse manually an original document (e.g. copy of words, reconstruction, synonym substitution, and words representation with and without diacritics, etc.). The second one is by applying automatically different strategies of obfuscation (e.g. reference description, shuffling words/sentences, word order changes, synonym substitution, and addition/deletion of words). In this context, many researches have been developed paraphrased corpora in different languages to conduct their experiments:

Microsoft Research Paraphrase Corpus (MRPC) is well used for evaluating English paraphrase detection systems. It contains 5800 pairs of sentences extracted from news sources on the web, along with human annotations indicating whether each pair capture a semantic equivalence relationship. In [3] and [4], this corpus has been used to experiment their systems. They have been studied how word-embedding models could captured different aspects of linguistic properties. These have been inspired them thereafter to learn various pre-trained word embedding's (word2vec, Fast text, GloVe, Baroni, and SL999) and achieved a Pearson's score of 82.45%. In contrast, 160 pdf Thesis in English language extracted from (digilib.uns.ac.id) have been manually reused in [5]. This dataset has been used to evaluate the effectiveness of cosine similarity and conditional probability combination for detecting plagiarism. The best results have been shown from thresholds 0.3 and 0.2 for conditional probability and cosine similarity. For uncovering obfuscated plagiarism for English and Marathi languages, fuzzy semantic based similarity and Naïve Bayes model have been presented in [6]. For experiments, English documents with reuse and large collections of potential source documents have been used, including: PAN-PC-11 and PAN-PC-10 containing 7645 manual paraphrases and 34310 automatic paraphrases; and PAN-PC-09 involving 17127 artificial cases but no simulated plagiarism cases. For Marathi language, manual and artificial paraphrases have been collected for testing. Contrariwise, paraphrased corpus in Japanese language has been built in [7]. Thus, sentential paraphrases have been collected and organized using automatic candidate generation and manual judgment. The first Russian paraphrase detection shared task ParaPhraser held in 2016 has been described in [8]. Thus, Russian corpus has been developed from automatic collection of candidate pairs and manual annotation using crowd sourcing. Experiments have been shown the best scores of 79.92% by using traditional classifiers combined with fine-grained linguistic features, complex neural networks, shallow methods and purely technical methods. Furthermore, benchmark corpus for Urdu News Text Reuse (COUNTER) has been created in [9]. It has been contained 1200 documents with three levels of real text reuse (wholly derived, partially derived and non-derived). Then, a set of similarity estimation methods have been employed such as: content (word n-gram overlap, cosine, Longest Common Subsequence (LCS) and Greedy String Tiling (GST)), structure (stop-words based n-grams overlap) and style (sentence token ratio).

Different from Western languages like English, little attention has been considered for Arabic paraphrase detection. This has been because of the following reasons: Arabic script is written from right to left and rich of morphological features accentuating its complexity by the existence of dots, diacritics, and stacked letters above and below the baseline [10, 11]. It is characterized by inflectional, derivational and no concatenated features that make it clumpy and ambiguous [12, 13]. For example, Corpus of Contemporary Arabic (CCA) has been built from Latifa Al-Sulaiti's webpage [14]. It included 842684 words and 415 texts containing different categories (religion, art, history, biography, science and technology). Then, 200 Arabic documents of about 500 words have been generated from the original documents. In [15], obfuscated documents have been adapted from various resources such as www.alwaraq.com and http://ar.wikisource.org. Subsequently, they have been conducted tests on three software's (plagiarism.net, plagiarism detector, and QARNET). Likewise, news of tweets have been collected from Arabic well-known news agencies of twitter accounts (e.g. Al-Jazeera and Al-Arabiya breaking news), in [16]. The best-achieved results have been when using lexical overlap features with word alignment and topic modeling for features extraction; and Maximum Entropy (MaxEnt) and Support Vector Regression (SVR) classifiers for similarity estimation. In contrast, this method has been weak in identifying the relationship between words with similar meanings, whether they could have a root or synonym form. Furthermore, a fingerprinting and word embedding based approach has been presented in [17] for detecting verbatim and complicated reproduction. Experiments have been carried out on External Arabic Plagiarism Corpus (ExAra-2015). Suspicious documents have been contained artificial (e.g. phrase and word shuffling) and simulated (e.g. synonym substitution, diacritics insertion and paraphrasing) plagiarism cases. Results have been shown recall and precision of 88% and 85%.

Throughout the state of the art, we found a lack of works developing corpora in Arabic language that represent different forms of paraphrase despite its richness of word's construction and diversity meanings. Therefore, developing an efficient intelligent paraphrase detection system depends on the quality of resources used.

3 Proposed Methodology

3.1 Arabic Paraphrased Corpus Construction

An important problem in paraphrase detection system and its evaluation is the lack of well-structured and publicly available corpora representing different forms of reuse. This necessitates text-mining tools to analyze semantic relatedness between documents. As a solution, we intend to develop a corpus and use it to inform the design of an Arabic paraphrase detection system. Figure 1 depicts the construction process containing the following components:

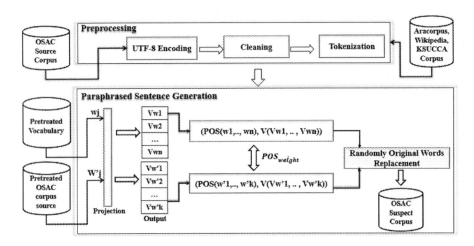

Fig. 1. Proposed model for paraphrased corpus generation.

Data Collection. Paraphrased corpus development needs the following datasets: Open Source Arabic Corpora (OSAC) as a source corpus from which passages of texts extracted and replaced semantically from a vocabulary [16]. It contains 18.183.511 Arabic documents including 10 categories (economics, history, education & family, religious & fatwas, sport, health, Astronomy, low, stories, cooking recipes). Then, a vocabulary model from which original words replaced. It composed by more than 2.3 billion words from different resources including Arabic Corpora Resource (AraCorpus), King Saud University Corpus of Classical Arabic (KSUCCA) and a set of Arabic papers extracted from Wikipedia.

Data Preprocessing. A set of operations should be applied in order to remove worthless data and reduce thereafter the time required for further processing as follows: First, encode all datasets into text files (.txt) by using Unicode Transformation Format (UTF-8). Then, remove unnecessary data (diacritics, extra white spaces, titles numeration, duplicated letters, non-Arabic words, and normalize some writing forms (Hamza "ٱ" and Taa Marboutah "ة" to "ا" and "ه".)). After that, reduce lexical parsimony by splitting and separating words from texts applying tokenization operation.

Degree of Paraphrase Setting. We propose an artificial based approach for developing paraphrased corpus. It is established randomly as follows: we fix the degree of paraphrase D by applying random uniform function according to a random variable x restricted between a finite interval [a, b], defined in Eq. (1):

$$f(x) = \begin{cases} \frac{1}{b-a}, a \leq x \leq b \text{ and } (b-a) \in [1.33,\ldots,2.22] \\ 0, \quad \text{otherwise} \end{cases} \tag{1}$$

According to D fixed between 47% and 75%, we count the number of words to replace P from the OSAC source corpus of N words as follows in Eq. (2):

$$P = N \times D \tag{2}$$

Finally, we apply random Shuffle function to replace source words according to an index chosen randomly.

Similar Words Extraction. Word embedding proposed by Mikolov et al. [17] is one of the most trends in NLP offering more expressive and efficient representation of words with low dimensional vectors. Since paraphrase allows giving the meaning of original words in another form semantically, we use an analogy reasoning to extract its synonyms from the vocabulary model by employing Skip gram model. It predicts the context of middle word according to the unique representation of words w_t in a surrounding window c as input, as shown in Eq. (3):

$$\frac{1}{T} \sum_{t=1}^{T} \sum_{-c \leq j \leq c, j \neq 0} \log p(w_{t+j}|w_t) \tag{3}$$

Part-Of-Speech Annotation. We assign for each original word its grammatical class (noun, verb, adjective, adverbs, quantifiers, personal pronouns, etc.) by using Part-Of-Speech-Tagger (POS) technique proposed by the Stanford NLP group. To preserve both semantic and syntactic changes of the original word w_i, we retrieve its most similar word $Max(Syn_i)$ that has the same POS and add a weight (equal to 0.1) to its score of similarity defined as follows in Eq. (4):

$$POS_{weight}(w_i) = Max\ (Syn_i) + 0.1 \tag{4}$$

Paraphrased Corpus Generation. This phase consists of replacing the original word by its most similar one that has the same grammatical class. In this way, original and paraphrased sentences will have the same syntactic changes with similar words semantically.

3.2   Arabic Original Documents Identification

Since the performance of any paraphrase detection system depends on the quality of data analyzed and the methodology adopted, this section describes our proposed methods for Arabic original documents identification based on semantic analysis.

Traditional Based Methods. We study how semantic vector space models can extract efficiently many hidden relationships between Arabic words. Indeed, we study traditional based methods that rely heavily on the matrix of frequency and the co-occurrence of words. This done by assuming that words in the same contexts share similar or related semantic meanings. Therefore, we study some good models in this category such as: Term Frequency-Inverse Document Frequency (TF-IDF) method determines words that are more descriptive. This is according to their frequency in the document and their importance in document collection. Latent Semantic Analysis (LSA) based on term-term co-occurrence matrix representation and Singular Value Decomposition (SVD). Furthermore, Latent Dirichlet Allocation (LDA) capturing polysemy (each word has multiple meanings) by associating a context with a document. After that, we calculate the overlap of geometric average of the datasets to generate thereafter a vector of similarity scores. This is according to the suspect sentence S_j size until reaching the source sentence S_i size, as follows in Eq. (5):

$$\text{Cos}(S_1, S_2) = \frac{\sum_{i=1}^{k} S_{1i} \times S_{2i}}{\sqrt{\sum_{i=1}^{k} S_{1i}^2} \times \sqrt{\sum_{i=1}^{k} S_{2i}^2}} \tag{5}$$

In contrast, traditional NLP methods cannot accurately capture similarity between words, and do not take efficiently the structure of language into consideration. This is because sentences may not contain any common words or the co-occurrence of words is rarely present.

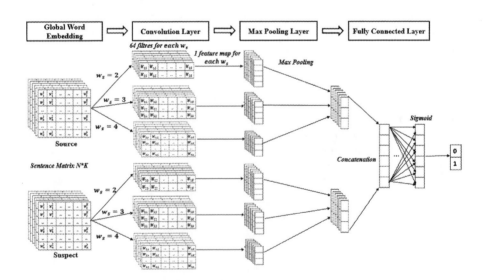

Fig. 2. GloVe-CNN model for Arabic paraphrase detection

Neural Network Based Method. We propose a semantic based approach predicting a given word compared to its neighbors. It consists of the following components (Fig. 2):

Global Embedding. We use Global Vector Representation (GloVe) combining the advantages of count based matrix factorization and contextual Skip Gram model. It examines word-word-co-occurrences, uses statistics efficiently to produce linear direction of meaning, and thereafter, creates a meaningful word vector space by using an objective function J. This function evaluates the sum of squared errors weighted with a function f defined as follows in Eq. (6):

$$J=\sum_{i,j=1}^{V} f(X_{ij}) (w_i^T \widetilde{w}_j + b_i + \breve{b}_j - \log(X_{ij}))^2$$

$$(6)$$

Where: w_i and $\widetilde{w}_j$ are the vectors of words i and j; b_i and $\breve{b}_j$ are the scalar biases of the main word i and the context of word j; V is the vocabulary size and $f(x)$ is the weighting function rare and frequent co-occurrence.

Convolutional Neural Network (CNN). To extract high level of abstract features from different n-gram regularities, we use the outputs of GloVe model as entries in CNN for sentence modeling with different local connections, shared weights and local pooling with fewer adjustable parameters. We encode all semantic interactions between suspect and source documents as follows: First, a convolution layer to learn new features $C[i]$ by using 64 convolution filters with different window sizes $w_s = \{2, 3, 4\}$ in each sentence of $n - w_s + 1$ words, defined in Eq. (7):

$$C[i] = ReLU(w_f . x_{i:i+j-1} + b)$$

$$(7)$$

Where: $b \in R$ is a bias term for polarization; $w_f \in R_{j*k}$ is the weight vector of the filter; and Rectified Linear Units (RELU) is the activation function of words $\{x_{1:j}, x_{2:j+1}, \ldots, x_{n-j+1:n}\}$ inducing sparsity problem in the hidden units.

After that, a max-pooling layer found the most important latent semantic factors on the document defined as follows in Eq. (8):

$$P_s = Max\{C[i]\}$$

$$(8)$$

Then, we consider a join layer concatenating all the intermediate representations into a single feature vector for the penultimate layer. Finally, a fully connected hidden layer generates the output of our proposed GloVe-CNN model. It learns the complex nonlinear interactions and represents the global semantic information. This is by using sigmoid function taking a real-valued number and squashes it to a value in the range between [0, 1], as follows in Eq. (9):

$$\text{Output} = \text{Sigmoid}(x) = \sigma(x) = \frac{e^x}{(1 + e^x)} \tag{9}$$

We propose a binary classification based on the following criteria: if the degree of semantic similarity is higher than a threshold α, sentence pair is considered as paraphrased (class 1). Otherwise, it is considered as not paraphrased (class 0).

4   Experiments and Discussion

4.1   Paraphrased Corpus Development

Word2vec Configuration. To test the effectiveness of our proposed method for artificial developing of paraphrased corpus in Arabic language, we calculate an average of all cosine similarities of word embeddings $\{w_1, \ldots, w_n\}$ extracted from each suspect sentences S_i, as follows in Eq. (10):

$$\text{Sen2vec} = \sum\nolimits_{i=1}^{n} \frac{w_i}{n} \tag{10}$$

Various configurations of word2vec model are studied employing different window sizes and vector dimensions to preserve both syntactic and semantic structures of the source sentence without ambiguities. Then, we add for each original word a weight of 0.1 to its most similar word that has the same grammatical class. More precisely, Table 1 illustrates the best parameters for training word2vec model to develop a well-structured paraphrased sentence that are 300 as a vector dimension, 3 as a window size, and 0.1 as a POS weight. It shows the performance evolution of the average of all words embedding's:

Table 1. Configurations of word2vec with and without POS weighting

Original sentence	لا تتسرع في القيادة 'Do not rush to drive'						
Vector dimension	Window Size						
	1	2	3	4	5	6	7
Model 1	Word2vec						
250	0.678	0.702	0.749	0.786	0.779	0.722	0.547
300	0.682	0.823	0.857	0.842	0.689	0.659	0.639
350	0.603	0.701	0.703	0.772	0.647	0.632	0.582
400	0.628	0.641	0.760	0.711	0.612	0.651	0.636
Model 2	Word2vec-POS						
250	0.778	0.702	0.839	0.736	0.685	0.698	0.650
300	0.801	0.850	0.887	0.821	0.783	0.766	0.688
350	0.767	0.801	0.840	0.762	0.752	0.707	0.612
400	0.741	0.783	0.783	0.806	0.682	0.601	0.606

Consequently, the best parameters of the paraphrased sentence development helping to identify the semantically closest words of the target word are the following in Table 2:

Table 2. Parameters of word2vec model

Parameters	Values
Number of words in the vocabulary	More than 2.3 billion words
Vector dimension	300
Window size	3
Matrix size	2.3 * 300
Minimum count	≤ 5
Workers	8
Iterations number	7

Paraphrased Corpus Analysis. The combination of word2vec and POS is reported to be good in capturing syntactic and semantic properties of words as shown in Table 3:

Table 3. Example of paraphrased sentence generation

Source	لا تتسرع في القيادة 'Do not rush to drive'		
w_i	Similar words extraction	Word2vec	Word2vec-POS
تتسرع 'rush' 'verb'	Sim ('rush' تتسرع, سرعة'speed'' noun') = 0.68 Sim ('rush تتسرع, تستعجل 'hurry up' 'verb') = 0.67 Sim ('rush'تتسرع, عجلة 'hurry''noun') = 0.73	عجلة 'hurry' 'noun' (0.73)	تستعجل 'harry up' 'verb' (0.67+0.1)
قيادة 'drive' 'complement'	Sim (قيادة 'drive', قائد 'leader' noun') = 0.70 Sim (قيادة 'drive', سياقة 'driving''complement') = 0.68 Sim (قيادة 'drive', قاد 'drove'' verb') =0.62	قائد 'leader' 'noun' (0.70)	سياقة 'driving' 'complement' (0.68+0.1)
	Sen2vec	0.857	0.887
Result	لا تستعجل في السياقة 'Do not hurry up driving '		

After many experiments, Table 4 details the topologies characterizing the resulted paraphrased corpus in Arabic language:

Table 4. Topologies of Arabic paraphrased sentences

Topology	Example
Same polarity substitution	لا تستعجل في السياقة
	'Do not hurry up driving '
Add/Deletion of words	لا تستعجل في القيادة
	'Do not hurry up to drive '
Change of order	في القيادة لا تستعجل
	'In the leadership do not rush'
Total copy of words	لا تتسرع في القيادة
	'Do not rush to drive'

4.2   Original Documents Identification

GloVe Configuration. Various datasets are used to train the GloVe model as represented in Table 5:

Table 5. Training datasets

Datasets	Numbers of words
Arabic words Corpora	1.500.000
Akhbar Al Khaleej	3.000.000
AlWatan	10.000.000
KACST Arabic newspaper corpus	2.000.000
King Saud University Corpus of Classical Arabic	50.000.000
Wikipedia	2.158.904.163

Table 6 summarizes the best parameters of GloVe model:

Table 6. Parameters of GloVe model

Parameters	Values
Size of co-occurrence matrix	1.119.436 *1.119.436 words
Embedding size	300
Context size	3
Minimum occurrence	25
Learning rate	0.05
Batch size	512
Numbers of epochs	20

CNN Configuration. For sentence modeling, we fix the following parameters that increased the performance of our proposed CNN model as summarized in Table 7:

Table 7. Parameters of CNN model

CNN layers	Parameters	
Convolution layer	Filters number	64
	Kernel size	2, 3, 4
	Activation function	ReLU
Pooling layer	Type	Max-pooling
	Pooling size	4
Fully connected layer	Activation function	Sigmoid
	Threshold	0.3

Discussion. Based on the complex nature and structure of Arabic language, the quality of a paraphrase detection system depends on the used corpus, its language and the adopted methodology. In fact, the performance of GloVe and word2vec are comparable to detect semantic meaning of words, which also depends on word vector representation. Yet, LDA outperforms better than other traditional methods like TF-IDF and LSA for synonym detection and analogy reasoning in terms of precision of 77% and recall of 75%. Thereafter, we argue that GloVe performs much better on word semantics and similarity rather than state-of-the-art methods on Arabic. It obtained the highest precision of 78% and recall of 76%. According to this observation, we prove that word2vec based on Skip-Gram model with POS weighting technique are efficient to develop an Arabic paraphrased corpus preserving contextual information of words. Thereafter, the use of GloVe embedding improved the representation of words that are highly descriptive in each sentence. It allows scalable fast learning for huge data with better performance even with small corpora. In addition, it performs a dynamic logistic regression examining word-word co-occurrences and capturing statistics efficiently to produce linear direction of meaning. Furthermore, the quality of our proposed system increased using the CNN especially at the level of sentence modeling and semantic similarity estimation. Table 8 summarizes the overall results in terms of precision and recall:

Table 8. Comparison of results

Proposed models		Precision	Recall
Paraphrased corpus	Original documents identification		
Word2vec	TF-IDF	0.63	0.67
	LDA	0.74	0.72
	LSA	0.71	0.70
	Word2vec	0.76	0.74
	GloVe-CNN	0.78	0.76

(continued)

Table 8. (*continued*)

Proposed models		Precision	Recall
Paraphrased corpus	Original documents identification		
Word2vec-POS	TF-IDF	0.69	0.72
	LDA	0.77	0.75
	LSA	0.75	0.77
	Word2vec	0.80	0.78
	GloVe-CNN	0.82	0.80

The overall best performing method is the GloVe-CNN achieving the highest precision of 82% and recall of 80%. The low performances of other methods due to their inability to detect some obfuscation plagiarism cases and the quality of the corpus used. Moreover, our proposed model has proven its ability to capture more semantic features of Arabic texts with different regularities using the combination of word2vec model and POS weighting technique for better-paraphrased sentence generation. Figure 3 represents the overall results of our prosed system regarding the F1 score:

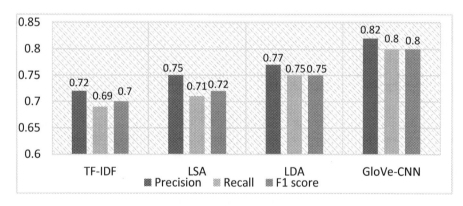

Fig. 3. Overall results

5   Conclusion and Future Work

In this paper, we introduced an Arabic paraphrased corpus automatically preserving semantic and syntactic properties of the original sentences. We replaced source words by their most similar ones and that had the same POS from a vocabulary. Different topologies of paraphrase are obtained presenting different forms of obfuscation (e.g. same polarity, add/deletion of words, order change, and total copy). Then, we studied how this corpus could be useful efficiently in the evaluation of Arabic original documents identification system. Although lexical based method could determine the most descriptive words in the corpus, TF-IDF cannot capture the semantic structure of language into consideration. In contrast, GloVe-CNN model outperformed significantly traditional methods (e.g. word2ec, LSA and LDA) for alleviating data sparseness and Arabic word semantics. This method achieved promising results in terms of precision of 0.82, recall of 0.80 and F1 score of 0.80. For future work, we would like to enhance our corpus using other NLP techniques like collocation, named entity recognition, etc. Furthermore, we will investigate the properties of other models for word embedding's and similar meaning analysis.

References

1. Karaoglan, B., Kışla, T., Kumova Metin, S.: Description of Turkish paraphrase corpus structure and generation method. In: Gelbukh, A. (ed.) CICLing 2016. LNCS, vol. 9623, pp. 208–217. Springer, Cham (2018). https://doi.org/10.1007/978-3-319-75477-2_13
2. Mahmoud, A., Zrigui, M.: Artificial method for building monolingual plagiarized Arabic corpus. Comput. Syst. **22**(3), 767–776 (2018)
3. Tien, N.H., Le, N.M.: An ensemble method with sentiment features and clustering support. In: Eighth International Joint Conference on Natural Language Processing, Taiwan, vol. 1, pp. 644–653 (2017). http://www.aclweb.org/anthology/I17-1065
4. Tien, N.H., Le, M.N., Tomohiro, Y., Tatsuya, I.: Sentence modeling via multiple word embeddings and multi-level comparison for semantic textual similarity, pp. 1–10 (2018). arXiv preprint: arXiv:1805.07882
5. Saptono, R., Prasetyo, H., Irawan, A.: Combination of Cosine similarity method and conditional probability for plagiarism detection in the thesis documents vector space model. J. Telecommun. Electron. Comput. Eng. **10**(2–4), 139–143 (2018)
6. Shenoy, N., Potey, M.A.: Semantic similarity search model for obfuscated plagiarism detection in Marathi language using Fuzzy and Naïve Bayes approaches. IOSR J. Comput. Eng. **18**(3), 83–88 (2016)
7. Fujita, A., Inui, K.: A class-oriented approach to building a paraphrase corpus, pp. 25–32 (2014). http://aclweb.org/anthology/I05-5004
8. Pivovarova, L., Pronoza, E., Yagunova, E., Pronoza, A.: ParaPhraser: Russian paraphrase Corpus and shared task. In: Filchenkov, A., Pivovarova, L., Žižka, J. (eds.) AINL 2017. CCIS, vol. 789, pp. 211–225. Springer, Cham (2018). https://doi.org/10.1007/978-3-319-71746-3_18
9. Sharjeel, M., Rao Muhammad Adeel Nawab, A.M.R., Rayson, P.: COUNTER: corpus of Urdu news text reuse. Lang Resour. Eval. **51**, 777–803 (2017)
10. Mansouri, S., Charhad, M., Zrigui, M.: A heuristic approach to detect and localize text in Arabic news video. Comput. Sist. **23**(1), 75–82 (2018)
11. Mahmoud, A., Zrigui, M.: Semantic similarity analysis for paraphrase identification in Arabic texts. In: 31st Pacific Asia Conference on Language, Information and Computation, PACLIC 31, Philippine, pp. 274–281 (2017)
12. Batita, M.A., Zrigui, M.: Derivational relations in Arabic Wordnet. In: 9th Global WordNet Conference, GWC, Singapore, pp. 137–144 (2018)
13. Mahmoud, A., Zrigui, A., Zrigui, M.: A text semantic similarity approach for Arabic paraphrase detection. In: Gelbukh, A. (ed.) CICLing 2017, Part II. LNCS, vol. 10762, pp. 338–349. Springer, Cham (2018). https://doi.org/10.1007/978-3-319-77116-8_25
14. Ameer, A.A.Y., Juzaiddin, A.A.M.: Enhanced Tf-Idf weighting scheme for plagiarism detection model for Arabic language. Aust. J. Basic Appl. Sci. **9**, 90–96 (2015)

15. Abakush, I.: Methods and tools for plagiarism detection in Arabic documents. In: International Scientific Conference on ICT and E-Business Related Research SINTEZA, Serbia, pp. 173–178 (2016). https://doi.org/10.15308/sinteza-2016-173-178
16. AL-Smadi, M., Jaradat, Z., AL-Ayyoub, M., Jararweh, Y.: Paraphrase identification and semantic text similarity analysis in Arabic news tweets using lexical, syntactic, and semantic features. ACM Digit. Libr. **53**(3), 640–652 (2016)
17. Nagoudi, E.B., Khorsi, A., Cherroun, H., Schwab, D.: A two-level plagiarism detection system for Arabic documents. Cybern. Inf. Technol. **18**(1), 1–18 (2018). https://doi.org/10.2478/cait-2018-0011
18. Saad, M.K., Ashour, W.: OSAC: Open Source Arabic Corpora. In: 6th International Conference on Electrical and Computer Systems, EECS 2010, Lefke, North Cyprus, pp. 1–6 (2010)
19. Mikolov, T., Sutskever, I., Chen, K., Corrado, G.S., Dean, J.: Distributed representations of words and phrases and their compositionality. In: Advances in Neural Information Processing Systems, vol. 26, pp. 3111–3119 (2013)

TimeML Annotation of Events
and Temporal Expressions
in Arabic Texts

Nafaa Haffar$^{(\boxtimes)}$, Emna Hkiri$^{(\boxtimes)}$, and Mounir Zrigui$^{(\boxtimes)}$

Research Laboratory of Algebra, Number Theory and Non-linear Analysis,
University of Monastir, Monastir, Tunisia
`nafaa.haffar.5@gmail.com`, `emna.hkiri@gmail.com`, `mounir.zrigui@fsm.rnu.tn`

Abstract. Events and temporal expressions are crucial elements in the
construction of the text. In this article, we present the first free Arabic
corpus for events and temporal expressions by adapting the TimeML
standard. For this, we first present the concept of events and temporal
expressions as well as their main ontological and grammatical characteristics for the Arabic language and according to the TimeML standard.
Second, we describe our annotation scheme and annotated corpus.

Keywords: Arabic TimeML · Event annotation ·
Temporal expression · GATE platform · Arabic NLP

1 Introduction

The identification of temporal entities such as events and temporal expressions,
as well as the extraction of relation between them, is an important aspect of
understanding Natural Language Processing (NLP). More specifically, the automatic recognition and extraction of these entities and their relations is clearly
susceptible to bring many benefits in various NLP tasks like question answering, information retrieval and temporal information extraction. However, this
task requires annotated corpora that can be used as learning and evaluation for
these systems. The Arabic language is one of the languages where resources are
scarce for temporal information extraction. For that, the community of Arabic
NLP still suffers from the lack of available free annotated corpora, electronic
lexicons and NLP tools. We find in the literature two models geared to extract
event and temporal expressions: Automatic Content Extraction (ACE[1]) [14] and
Time Markup Language (TimeML[2]) [18]. The ACE model defines an event as an
action at which the participants are connected. In this model, only events that
fall into one of 34 predefined categories are annotated. Moreover, the structures
of arguments and temporal information in this model are complex and they are
annotated only when they are explicitly presented [11]. Unlike the ACE model,

---

[1] https://www.ldc.upenn.edu/collaborations/past-projects/ace/annotation-tasks-
and-specifications.

[2] http://www.timeml.org/.

© Springer Nature Switzerland AG 2019
N. T. Nguyen et al. (Eds.): ICCCI 2019, LNAI 11683, pp. 207–218, 2019.
https://doi.org/10.1007/978-3-030-28377-3_17

the TimeML model annotates every event in the text and separates the representation of event and temporal expressions from the anchoring dependencies that may exist in a given text. It defines an event like a word that points to a node in a network of temporal relations. The most important attribute of TimeML which differs from ACE is that it introduces temporal link annotations to establish dependencies (temporal relations) between events and temporal expressions [16]. This difference fundamentally serves to anchor an event to a temporal expression and determine the temporal order between events. This particularity of TimeML becomes our primary consideration in choosing the event and temporal information model for our research.

We propose in this work a new Arabic annotated corpus for event and temporal expressions according to the TimeML model. We use the Gate tool and other NLP tools. The rest of the paper is organized as follows: Sect. 2 presents the specificities of the TimeML standard, their adaptation to the Arabic language and our annotation scheme used. Section 3 provides an overview of existing resources in the literature. In Sect. 4, the methodology implemented is then described: This is based on an automatic pre-annotation phase, followed by a manual correction phase. Section 5 is devoted to the representation of the statistics of our corpus, a comparison with the literature as well as a series of experience for the pre-annotation. Finally, we conclude our work with a few perspectives.

2   Annotation of Event Information

2.1   TimeML Specification Language

TimeML is a temporal information markup language for natural language text. It allows to tag, with a surface viewpoint, the events and temporal expressions, as well as the different relations between them [5]. The first type of tags used in TimeML is <EVENT>. The concept of an event corresponds here to cover all types of situations (actions, states, and processes, etc.). This tag contains a set of attributes for the morpho-syntactic and semantic traits (semantic class, tense, aspect, modality, stem, polarity) of the annotated event. The choice made in TimeML specification is to place the tag on the head of the event group (excluding auxiliaries, adverbs, clitics, etc.) and the annotated events can correspond to various syntactic categories (i.e. noun, verb, adjective, etc.). The second type of tags is <TIMEX3>. It corresponds to the temporal expressions in the text. This tag is used to markup explicit temporal expressions, such as TIME (منتصف النهار, midday), DATE (العام الفارط, Last year), DURATION(سنتين, Two years) and SET (كل سبت, Every Saturday). For annotated relations in TimeML, we find <SLINK>, <ALINK> and <TLINK>. SLINKS links are used to mark subordinate (modal) relations between two events. The ALINKS indicate an aspectual relation between two events. Finally, TLINKS marks the (strictly) temporal relation between the tags. The idea of this standard is not to annotate the meaning itself, but to provide a standardization of the linguistic forms that express the temporality in text by limiting as much as possible the theoretical commitment. For Arabic, this idea is not always true, and some annotations are sometimes based on information that does not only concern surface forms. For example: "The warrior believes that his friend has died in the war": "يعتقد المحارب ان صديقه قد مات في الحرب". The annotation of modal subordination in this example requires knowledge of the syntactic structure of the sentence.

2.2 Adaptations for Arabic Language

ISO-TimeML is a recent standard, first developed for English, and then adapted to other languages, such as French, Italian, Chinese, etc. It is therefore still subject to adaptations and possible changes for another language. And since it has not been adapted to the Arabic language, we try to make our own correspondence.

This correspondence is made, in particular, to take into account times, such as the future, and aspect, as the perfect and progressive in English. In Arabic, an action began in the past and continues in the present is usually rendered by the present in Arabic. The preposition "منذ" (Mundhu) is used to specify how much in the past the action started. As regards the progressive aspect, the present is used in Arabic for continuous and usual actions and states. We will therefore adopt the definition of Arabic grammarians of the verb that is sufficient to assume that any verb refers to an event. Moreover, the Arabic language is not limited to the adoption of verbs as events, but it adds the category of the deverbal nouns and adjectives. The modality in the Arabic language behaves differently from other languages such as English and French. Standard Arabic does not have exact equivalents of these verbs, but it has words that are used in the same way including phrases beginning with (من الـ) like "أنّ من الواجب": "it is necessary to" or with (verb+"أ"). All of these are followed by imperfect verbs ("من الضروري أن نحصل على المال"): "It is necessary that we get the money"). However, if we remove the (أن) we can follow them with a "NOUN: مصدر" ("من الضروري الحصول على المال"): "It is necessary to get money"). This sentences can fall under the reach of polarity operators as "ليس" (laysa) and (لا) (la'a) before the sentence for negation, and tense operators like كان (kana) to indicate the past, and سوف (sawfa) for the future. We propose in our work that modal verbs, nouns and adjectives are marked with the <EVENT> tag under the MODAL class and we provide a set of normalized values for the modality attribute, within a manual annotation context, which reflects the classic classes of event modality [17]: necessity, probability and possibility for epistemic modality, and obligation and permission for deontic modality.

2.3 Annotation Scheme of Our Corpora

Our proposed annotation method is therefore as follows:

```
EVENT
  <
    eid        ::= EventID
    Class      ::= OCCURRENCE | PERCEPTION | REPORTING | ASPECTUAL|
                   STATE | I_STATE| I_ACTION | MODAL
    Tense      ::= PAST | PRESENT | FUTURE | NONE (default)
    Aspect     ::= PERFECTIVE | IMPERFECTIVE | NONE (default)
    Moods      ::= INDICATIVE | SUBJUNCTIVE | JUSSIVE | IMPERATIVE |
                   NONE (default)
    Pos        ::= VERB | NOUN | ADJECTIVE | NONE (default)
    Modality ::= NECESSITY | OBLIGATION | PERMISSION |
                   POSSIBILITY | PROBABILITY | NONE (default)
    Polarity ::= POS | NEG |NONE (default,if absent,is POS)
    Stem       ::=  lemma of words
  >
TIMEX3
  <
    tid    ::= ID
    Type   ::= DATE | TIME | DURATION | SET
    Value ::= Duration | Date | Time | WeekDate | WeekTime |
              Season | PartOfYear
  >
```

3 State of the Art

Several attempts have been made to annotate and create an event corpora. Many corpora have been developed for Latin languages but with a low frequency for the Asian languages. Up to our knowledge, there has been a problem in that no tagged Arabic TimeML corpora are freely available. Most of the Arabic event and temporal corpora that have been created to help researchers in their personal research do not meet the specifications of TimeML or they are not accessible to the public like the corpora created by Aliane et al. [1]. This evolutionary work began with building the TimeBank1.1 [6] which was created at the beginning of TimeML and followed the TimeML 1.1 specifications. This attempt has resulted in several corpora that have played an important role in the creation of many other corpora and the compilation of the event extraction task.

TimeBank1.2[3] is an improvement of TimeBank1.1 and they follow the TimeML 1.2.1 specifications. TimeBank1.2 contains 183 news articles in English that have been annotated with temporal information, adding three tags. events, temporal expressions and temporal links between both of them. It contains 7,935

---

[3] https://catalog.ldc.upenn.edu/docs/LDC2006T08/timebank.html.

annotated events, 1,414 annotations of TIMEX3 and 6,418 for temporal relations. This corpus is the building block of the TempEval training corpora. The latter were created for the Tempeval-1 task as part of the SemEval-2007 competition. The TempEval-2 Corpora [21] were created for the Tempeval-2 task as part of the Semeval-2010 competition. They were a manually annotated corpora based on TimeML specification, they were not parallel and they were multilingual (English, French, Italian, Spanish, Chinese and Korean).

The IT-TimeBank was created by Irena et al. [13]. It was built for Italian language based on TimeML specification and it was fully manually annotated and contained 8,138 events. Similar to the IT-TimeBank, The FR-TimeBank created by Bittar et al. [4] was a French TimeML corpus. It was developed with an automatic pre-annotation phase to speed up the annotation process, followed by a manual correction. For this automatic pre-annotation phase, two tools were used. On the one hand, The TempEx Tagger marked temporal expressions and set the tags attributes. On the other hand, the Event Tagger marked up events. This corpora was, according to the authors, composed of a set of 109 articles from the East-Republican journal (1999–2003) and contained 2,100 event tags and 608 Timex tags.

In addition to the previously mentioned resources in the Tempeval-2 task, we note the existence of the Portuguese TimeBank [7] with 7,926 event tags, the Spanish TimeBank [22] presented with 1,677 event tags and the Romanian TimeBank [9] with 7,887 event tags, which were derived from a translation of English TimeBank1.2 text.

Finally, the AQUAINT TimeBank [21] was another TimeML corpora which contained 4,432 event tags derived from a set of 73 English news report documents. Its content was very similar to TimeBank 1.2 and used the same specifications.

As we can see from the literature, the creation of a TimeML corpus has been the subject of enormous effort. This prompted us to provide an Arabic tagged event corpus specifically designed to serve as training and test data for automatic systems to extract events and temporal expressions from Arabic text. This corpus[4] is available for free and it can also be used in other natural language processing applications.

4   Methodology

4.1   Data Collection

To build our Arabic event corpora, we downloaded the United Nations (UN) Parallel Corpora v1.0 [23] for the years 2015. The United Nations is responsible for publishing documents in six official languages (Arabic, Chinese, English, French, Russian, Spanish) and for creating a considerable archive of parallel documents from its own translation operations in which the primary documents are the English documents. This parallel corpus is composed of official records and other parliamentary documents of the United Nations that are in the public

---

[4] https://github.com/nafaa5/Temporal-ArEvent-Corpora-.

domain. We have chosen for our work both Arabic and English files. The two sets include 4,000 sentences for each document, which correspond to an alignment of 1 to 1 for both languages. We have chosen to use a parallel corpus (English-Arabic) because of the existence of a plugin "Gate-Time" (Integrated in the Gate tool) [8]. This tool uses HeidelTime [19] for temporal labeling. Gate-time also includes a fast English event recognition and classifier that can be combined with different pre-processing annotations. It is based on TimeML and it can help us to correct several errors in the construction of our Arabic corpus during the extraction of nominal events, (as "انتخابات": "election", "حرب": "war") and their associated classes.

4.2 Text Preprocessing

This first step aims to represent data in a form that can be efficiently analyzed and to improve the data quality by reducing the quantity of trivial noise [15]. A large number of NLP tasks requires the text to be free of punctuation or diacritics, if not both [10,24]. Therefore, we have implemented a simple JAVA code to remove punctuation and diacritics. It removes all three forms of diacritics, such as vowel diacritics, "nunation" diacritics and the "shadda". Also, empty lines, double spaces, punctuation and symbols such as $(@\#=+\$*:/])(\_\&\}\{!\S-)$ are removed. We have also replaced incompatible variations like Taa−Marbutah/"ة" with Haa/"ه", the Alf−Maksowrah YAA/"ي" with DOTLESS−YAA/"ى" and the Alf/ "آ، إ، أ" with the abstract version of the letter ALEF/"ا".

4.3 Automatic Pre-annotation

To speed up the annotation process, we have carried out an automatic pre-annotation of tags (events, temporal expressions), followed by a manual correction. For this pre-annotation, we describe in the following our developed modules.

Event Extraction. Our event extraction system identifies the event triggers (verbs, nouns and adjectives) based on detailed lexical resources and various contextual criteria. For this module, we have used General Architecture for Text Engineering (GATE). It is a JAVA open source platform dedicated to textual engineering, and it appears to us well suited for the development of our system. It provides to users a variety of modules dedicated to textual analysis. The most commonly used are tokenizers (segmenters), Part Of Speech (POS) taggers (morpho-syntactic taggers), gazetteers (lexicons) and transducers (JAPE Grammar) [12]. For the Arabic language, GATE does not have a predefined gazetteer for events and does not annotate it for the Arabic text, that is why we have created three new gazetteers for the triggers of verbs, nouns and adjectives. These lists are collected from the mapped DBpedia[5] with SPARQL query, Arabic WordNet [2,3] and Arabic dictionary. We have divided these gazetteers into subclasses to associate every event to their class it represents. At this stage

---

[5] https://wiki.dbpedia.org/datasets/events.

of our work, we do not deal with polysemous events, we just develop gazetteers[6] for monosemic events (see Table 1).

Table 1. Enrichment of Gate gazetteers.

Gazetteers	Predefined entries	Enriched entries
Event-ADJ	0	32
Event-NOUN	0	5200
Event-VERB	0	6079
Total	0	11531

The implementation of the GATE platform requires the use of other nomenclatures and tools, so installing new plugins is necessary. To extract verb events, we use the Stanford POS tagger to mark each word in text that corresponds to a particular POS, such as nouns, verbs, and adjectives. Thus, we have implemented Jape rules that check each POS tag and mark each verb with the <EVENT>tag. For the other types of events, we implement Jape rules that allow us to compare the tokens of the Arabic text to words in both created gazetteers. To classify each tagged event into its associated class, we integrated the morphological analyzer (GATE Morphological Analyzer). This analyzer allow us to obtain, for each tagged event in the Arabic text, the associated lemma. These latter enable us to compare the token to lemmas in the created gazetteers. If the searched word exists in one of the gazetteers, it will be automatically assigned in the associated class. Else, if it does not exist in the gazetteers, it will be assigned to a class by a manual correction. The result of these steps is a set of XML files containing text annotated by events and their attributes (class and stem). In order to complete the other attributes such as tense and aspect, we implement a JAVA code that integrates the MADAMIRA[7] and the "ALP[8]" tools.

TIMEX3 Extraction. For this step, Heideltime[9] tool is used. It is promoted as the best tool in the tempEval-3 [20] which follows the standard TimeML. It is a multilingual, domain-sensitive temporal tagger that currently contains hand-crafted resources for 13 languages. In addition, the most recent version contains automatically created resources for more than 200 languages, which includes Arabic and English. It marks temporal expressions <TIMEX3> and sets the tags attributes with an F-score de 77.61%. One of the important and interesting aspects of this tool is standardization. In other words, the operation consists of turning a temporal expression into a formatted, fully specified representation (this includes finding the absolute value of relative dates). HeidelTime uses the tense of verbs and

---

[6] https://github.com/nafaa5/arabic-event-gazetteers-.
[7] https://camel.abudhabi.nyu.edu/madamira/?locale=en.
[8] http://arabicnlp.pro/alp/.
[9] https://heideltime.ifi.uni-heidelberg.de.

sentences to determine whether the temporal expression refers to the past or the future. The results obtained in this step are satisfactory, but some errors persist. This is often due to the misidentification of the tense in the sentence.

4.4   Manual Annotation and Validation

In this step, The texts previously annotated were corrected by six human experts annotators using GATE and Farassa tools. The gate-time plugin is used in this step to correct some of nominal events and their associated classes By using the alignment of the United nations corpora.

5   Statistics and Evaluation

5.1   Statistics and Comparison of Our Corpora

Our aim in this work is to provide a corpus of a comparable size to the existing resources for the other languages. We recall that our corpus is available online for public use.

Table 2 shows a simple comparison between the size of our corpus and existing TimeML corpora.

Table 2. Comparison of our corpus VERSUS other TimeML corpora.

Corpora	Language	Tokens	Events	Timex	Availability
1. TimeBank1.2	English	61,418	7 935	1,414	NO
2. AQUAINT TB	English	34154	4432	605	Free
3. FR-TB	French	61000	2100	608	Free
4. Korean TB	Korean	—	11522	2552	NO
5. Spanish TB	Spanish	68,000	12,385	2,776	Free
6. IT-TimeBank	Italian	150000	8138	2,314	Free
7. TimeBank-PT	Portuguese	70,000	1677	1244	NO
8. Ro-TimeBank	Romanian	65375	7926	1414	NO
9. Our Corpora	ARABIC	95782	15730	2297	Free

Table 3 presents the distribution of temporal expressions and events annotated in our Arabic corpus. It is shown that the DATE type constitutes almost 88% of the temporal expressions in our corpus, while the other types have relatively low proportions that vary between 2% (49 timex Tags) and 6% (159 timex Tags). For events, we can see that the "occurrence" class represents 51% of all annotated events, almost 5 times more than the second most frequent class, "STATE", with a rate of 11.2%. The modal class is ranked third with 8.1%, suggesting that the modality is a general characteristic of the language used in the description of events. The rest are in relatively very low proportions with a score ranging from 7% to 4%.

Table 3. Statistics of our corpus.

TIMEX	Total
DURATION	159
SET	49
DATE	2015
TIME	69

Class Event	Total
OCCURRENCE	8030
STATE	1770
MODAL	1290
PERCEPTION	1003
I-STATE	646
I-ACTION	751
ASPECTUAL	1180
REPORTING	1090

Figure 1 represents a simple example from our annotated corpus.

```
<?xml version="1.0"?>
<!DOCTYPE TimeML SYSTEM "TimeML.dtd">
<TimeML>
...
</TimeML>
```

Fig. 1. Example of annotated text in our corpus.

5.2 Impact of Automatic Pre-annotation

In this section, we present an evaluation of the effects of pre-annotation on the extraction task of events and temporal expressions in our methodology. We have examined two methods for evaluating the pre-annotation task in TimeML, first, the impact of the quality of the automatic pre-annotation on the annotation task, and second, the impact of a bias introduced by the pre-annotation on the choices of the annotators. To measure the impact of the pre-annotation, we have annotated a 100 lines that contains 2.596 tokens, 390 EVENT and 76 TIMEX and which had already been previously annotated according to our pre-annotation method. The manual annotation of this 100 lines has required an average time of approximately 420 min, while this time has increased to approximately 230 min of manual correction for pre-annotation. This experience shown that this difference in the annotation time is certainly due to the fact that tags contain complex attributes and values for the manual annotation.

The second part of this experiment, called bias, consists at measuring the influence of pre-annotation on the choice of annotator. For this experiment, the 100 lines are annotated manually by three experts in the first time and verified by a fourth one in the second time which had a deep knowledge on temporal annotation. So, The agreement between the three annotators and the expert (SA) was calculated in pairs and gives: 312 events and 68 timex for (A1, SA), 299 events and 70 timex for (A2, SA), 318 events and 74 timex for (A3, SA). This annotation will be considered as a reference that will then be used to compare the manual annotations with those of the pre-annotation to measure the divergence between both of them and the reference. It is therefore assumed that: (C_p) is the pre-annotated corpus, (C_m) is the manual corpus and (C_r) is the reference corpus, annotated by three experts. To obtain a positive bias, it is necessary for a tag or an attribute that (1) C_p and C_r have the same annotation, (2) D_m is different from C_p and C_r, and (3) C_m is false. If C_m is true, then the bias is negative. The equations to calculate the rate of positive and negative bias are as follows:

$$\textbf{Positive bias (\%)} = \frac{\sum error\ rate}{\sum manual\ tags} * 100 \qquad (1)$$

$$\textbf{Negative bias (\%)} = \frac{\sum error\ rate}{\sum C_r\ tags} * 100 \qquad (2)$$

Table 4 shows the rate of manual annotation errors calculated with equation (1) (positive bias) and the errors introduced by the pre-annotation but avoided in the manual annotation calculated with equation (2) (Negative bias). This shows that pre-annotation introduces few errors for the temporal expression task, but most pre-annotation errors are made during the event task.

Table 4. Positive and negative bias of pre-annotation.

Tags		Positive bias (%)	Negative bias (%)
<Timex>	False tag	12	3.2
	Value error	17.9	0.6
	Type error	14.7	1.3
<Event>	False tag	5.8	3
	Attribute error	4.8	1.5

We conclude from these experiences that the use of a pre-annotation phase accelerates the annotation task and reduces the error rate of the human annotator. However, the expert's intervention remains a crucial and important task for evaluation, correction and validation.

6 Conclusion and Future Work

In this paper, we have presented the first free annotated Arabic corpus of events and temporal expressions based on the Timeml specifications. This work has been the result of a well studied methodology, based on an annotation pipeline combining an automatic pre-annotation task, as well as human corrections. This resource is freely available and based on the TimeML specifications. Moreover, the TimeML standard seems relatively stable and could be applied to Arabic through a series of adaptations.

The work on our corpus is still going forward. we will move towards improving to be at the same level of the other TimeBank corpora. We will complete our corpus by adding the temporal relations indicated in the TimeML standard to satisfy all the specifications of this latter.

References

1. Aliane, H., Guendouzi, W., Mokrani, A.: Annotating events, time and place expressions in Arabic texts. In: Proceedings of the International Conference Recent Advances in Natural Language Processing, RANLP 2013, pp. 25–31. INCOMA Ltd., Shoumen, Bulgaria, Hissar, Bulgaria (2013)
2. Batita, M.A., Zrigui, M.: The enrichment of Arabic WordNet antonym relations. In: Gelbukh, A. (ed.) CICLing 2017. LNCS, vol. 10761, pp. 342–353. Springer, Cham (2018). https://doi.org/10.1007/978-3-319-77113-7_27
3. Batita, M.A., Zrigui, M.: Derivational relations in Arabic WordNet. In: The 9th Global WordNet Conference GWC, pp. 137–144. European Language Resources Association (ELRA) (2018)
4. Bittar, A.: ISO-TimeML Annotation Guidelines for French-Version 1.0. ALPAGE and University Paris 7 Didero (2010)
5. Bittar, A., Pascal, A., Pascal, D., Laurence, D.: French TimeBank: an ISO-TimeML annotated reference corpora. In: The 49th Annual Meeting of the Association for Computational Linguistics, Portland, Oregon, United States, pp. 130–134 (2011)
6. Boguraev, B., Pustejovsky, J., Ando, R.K., Verhagen, M.: TimeBank evolution as a community resource for TimeML parsing. Lang. Resour. Eval. 41(1), 91–115 (2007)
7. Costa, F., Branco, A.: TimeBankPT: a TimeML annotated corpus of Portuguese. In: LREC, pp. 3727–3734. European Language Resources Association (ELRA) (2012)
8. Derczynski, L., Strötgen, J., Maynard, D., Greenwood, M.A., Jung, M.: GATE-time: extraction of temporal expressions and event. In: Tenth International Conference on Language Resources and Evaluation (LREC 2016), pp. 3702–3708. European Language Resources Association (ELRA) (2016)

9. Forascu, C., Tufis, D.: Romanian TimeBank: an annotated parallel corpus for temporal information. In: Proceedings of the Eighth International Conference on Language Resources and Evaluation (LREC-2012), pp. 3762–3766 (2012)
10. Haffar, N., Maraoui, M., Aljawarneh, S., Bouhorma, M., Alnuaimi, A.A., Hawashin, B.: Pedagogical indexed Arabic text in cloud e-learning system. IJCAC **7**(1), 32–46 (2017). https://doi.org/10.4018/IJCAC.2017010102
11. Hkiri, E., Mallat, S., Zrigui, M.: Events automatic extraction from Arabic texts. IJIRR **6**(1), 36–51 (2016)
12. Hkiri, E., Mallat, S., Zrigui, M., Mars, M.: Constructing a lexicon of Arabic-English named entity using SMT and semantic linked data. Int. Arab J. Inf. Technol. **14**(6), 820–825 (2017)
13. Irene, R., Tommaso, C., Francesco, R.: Recognizing deverbal events in context. In: Proceedings of 12th International Conference on Intelligent Text Processing and Computational Linguistics (CICLing 2011), Poster Session, Tokyo, Japan. Springer, February 2011
14. LDC: ACE (Automatic Content Extraction) Arabic Annotation Guidelines for Events Version 5.4.4 (2005)
15. Mahmoud, A., Zrigui, A., Zrigui, M.: A text semantic similarity approach for Arabic paraphrase detection. In: Gelbukh, A. (ed.) CICLing 2017. LNCS, vol. 10762, pp. 338–349. Springer, Cham (2018). https://doi.org/10.1007/978-3-319-77116-8_25
16. Mirza, P.: Extracting temporal and causal relations between events. In: Proceedings of the ACL 2014 Student Research Workshop, Baltimore, Maryland, USA, pp. 10–17. Association for Computational Linguistics (2014)
17. Palmer, F.R.: Mood and Modality. Cambridge University Press, Cambridge (1986)
18. Pustejovsky, J., et al.: TimeML: robust specification of event and temporal expressions in text. In: Maybury, M.T. (ed.) New Directions in Question Answering, pp. 28–34. AAAI Press, Menlo Park (2003)
19. Strötgen, J., Armiti, A., Van Canh, T., Zell, J., Gertz, M.: Time for more languages: temporal tagging of Arabic, Italian, Spanish, and Vietnamese. ACM Trans. Asian Lang. Inf. Process. **13**(1), 1:1–1:21 (2014)
20. UzZaman, N., Llorens, H., Derczynski, L., Allen, J., Verhagen, M., Pustejovsky, J.: SemEval-2013 task 1: TempEval-3: evaluating time expressions, events, and temporal relations. In: Second Joint Conference on Lexical and Computational Semantics (*SEM). Volume 2: Proceedings of the Seventh International Workshop on Semantic Evaluation (SemEval 2013), Atlanta, Georgia, USA, pp. 1–9. Association for Computational Linguistics (2013)
21. Verhagen, M., Sauri, R., Caselli, T., Pustejovsky, J.: SemEval-2010 task 13: TempEval-2. In: Proceedings of the 5th International Workshop on Semantic Evaluation, pp. 57–62. Association for Computational Linguistics (2010)
22. Wonsever, D., Rosá, A., Malcuori, M., Moncecchi, G., Descoins, A.: Event annotation schemes and event recognition in Spanish texts. In: Gelbukh, A. (ed.) CICLing 2012. LNCS, vol. 7182, pp. 206–218. Springer, Heidelberg (2012). https://doi.org/10.1007/978-3-642-28601-8_18
23. Ziemski, M., Junczys-Dowmunt, M., Pouliquen, B.: The United Nations parallel Corpus v1.0. In: Proceedings of the Tenth International Conference on Language Resources and Evaluation (LREC 2016). European Language Resources Association (ELRA) (2016)
24. Zrigui, M., Ayadi, R., Mars, M., Maraoui, M.: Arabic text classification framework based on latent Dirichlet allocation. CIT **20**(2), 125–140 (2012)

Ensemble Method for Multi-view Text Clustering

Maha Fraj[(✉)], Mohamed Aymen Ben Hajkacem, and Nadia Essoussi

Institut Supérieur de Gestion, LARODEC, Université de Tunis,
2000 Le Bardo, Tunisia
maha.fraj.m@gmail.com, medaymen.hajkacem@gmail.com,
nadia.essoussi@isg.rnu.tn

Abstract. Textual data frequently occurs as an unlabeled document collection, therefore it is useful to sort this collection into clusters of related documents. On the other hand, text has different aspects, which a single representation cannot capture. To this end, multi-view clustering present an efficient solution to integrate different representations called "views" by exploiting the complementary characteristics of these views. However, the existing methods consider only one representation mode for all views that is based on terms frequencies. Such representation leads to losing valuable information and fails to capture the semantic aspect of text. To overcome these issues, we propose a new method for multi-view text clustering that exploits different representations of text in order to improve the quality of clustering. The experimental results show that the proposed method outperforms other methods and enhances the clustering quality.

Keywords: Text clustering · Multi-view clustering · Ensemble method

1 Introduction

Textual data clustering aims to partition a collection of documents into several clusters, such that documents in the same cluster are as similar as possible, whereas those in different clusters are as dissimilar as possible [1]. To this end, different methods for text clustering have been investigated in the last years. Most of these methods are based on partitional clustering, such as the K-means algorithm or hierarchical clustering, given their simplicity and availability in several machine learning tools [3, 12, 14, 15, 27].

Inevitably, applying clustering algorithms on text data requires a preliminary and fundamental step in which the data is converted into a structured form. The Vector Space Model (VSM) [24] is the most commonly used vector representation of text. On the other hand, text data depicts different aspects, consequently other representation models exist in the literature, such as topic models [5], and word embeddings [20]. To this end, considering different aspects of the data can

© Springer Nature Switzerland AG 2019
N. T. Nguyen et al. (Eds.): ICCCI 2019, LNAI 11683, pp. 219–231, 2019.
https://doi.org/10.1007/978-3-030-28377-3_18

induce improvement in the quality of clustering [33]. Combining multiple representations of data is known as multi-view clustering, the distinct representations are referred to as "views", where each view captures partial information that is not depicted by other views [8,26]. The study in [4] shows that the multi-view versions of K-means and EM achieved better experimental results compared to their single-view equivalents. Furthermore, outliers and data noise which exist in one view may be compensated by other views. Many research works have exploited the aspect of multi-view data by integrating the specific properties of each view in the learning process to improve the performance of existing machine learning algorithms [6,16,17,19].

We are particularly interested in multi-view text clustering. Textual data was examined early on in the context of multi-view, particularly in cross-lingual text categorization where, having each view corresponding to a different language, the data is labeled in one view and not in another, the aim is to use the information in both views to label all data [2,29,30]. In the literature, the existing multi-view clustering methods can be sorted into three categories. The first category, generally known as co-training, integrates the views directly in the objective function of the clustering algorithm [6,16]. The second category is the subspace, where all views are mapped into a low-dimensional space on which the algorithm is applied [11,38]. The third category is the late integration which consists in running one or more algorithms on each view individually and then combining the obtained partitions [13,31,32]. Admittedly, the existing methods have improved the clustering results. However, these methods rely only on the syntactic aspect of text i.e. terms occurrences. In addition, views are represented with a single model, most commonly the Term Frequency weighting [23]. Although such representation is able to give an idea of a word's relative importance in a document, it does not however provide any insight into words semantic links.

In this paper, we aim to tackle the stated limits by developing a new method for multi-view text clustering. We propose to exploit different text representation models to capture and integrate information from each view and maintain the semantic facet of text. Moreover, as opposed to existing methods that rely on the natural split of data, we propose to generate manufactured views to extract various information. In the aim of improving the quality of clusters, the proposed approach considers different partitions that are derived from the different views, and is based on three main steps: first different views are generated based on different text representation models, then a clustering algorithm is applied on each view in order to obtain different partitions, and lastly these partitions are then combined to provide a final clustering.

The remainder of this paper is organized as follows: Sect. 2 reviews related work. The proposed multi-view approach for text clustering is presented in Sect. 3. The experimental results are discussed in Sect. 4, followed by a conclusion.

2   Related Work

Existing multi-view clustering approaches can be presented under three main categories [19]. Algorithms in the first category incorporate multi-view integration into the clustering process directly through jointly optimizing the objective function. The idea was first introduced in [6] in a semi-supervised approach. Since unlabeled data exists plentifully, it is used to enrich the training set of the labeled data, such that given two views the learning algorithm is trained on the labeled data of both views. Eventually, based on the consensus principle, the views should agree on all labeled data. Under the same assumption (i.e. data points that are clustered together in one view should be clustered together in all other views), a co-training approach for multi-view spectral clustering of text data is proposed in [16]. The approach bootstraps the clustering results of two views in order to adjust the graph structure of each one until the clustering is consistent across all views. The second category first seeks a common lower dimensional subspace that represents the intrinsic structure of the multi-view data then run and then applies a clustering algorithm to obtain the partitions. In [11] the subspace learning is formulated as a convex joint optimization problem. A low-rank linear projection is performed in [9] to uncover shared information and minimize the semantic gap across views. The proposed algorithm CoKmLDA in [38] first applies K-means on each view to obtain cluster assignments, the Linear Discriminant Analysis (LDA) is then used to project each view into a lower dimensional subspace. In [34], sparse subspace matrices are constructed from each view then a spectral clustering algorithm is performed. Other approaches were based on Non-negative Matrix Factorization (NMF). The idea is to find a common latent factor among multi-view data through low rank factor matrices. Liu et al. [19] proposed multiNMF which regularizes the coefficient matrices towards a common consensus. Recently, Nie et al. [22] introduced MLAN, a graph-based model that learns a local manifold structure and performs clustering simultaneously. The approach in [36] adopted semi-NMF, a variant of NMF and followed a deep learning strategy. Newly approaches were proposed to tackle incomplete multi-view data [35,37]. The third category is called late integration, it combines clustering results obtained individually from each view on the basis of a consensus. Multi-view kernel k-means clustering ensembles (MvKKMCE) and multi-view spectral clustering ensembles (MvSpecCE) were proposed in [31]. The work in [32] extended a well-known boosting algorithm Adaboost to multi-view learning. Multiple ensemble techniques were exploited in [13] for multi-view document clustering. The approach is based on three different similarity matrices: Cluster Based Similarity Matrix, Affinity Matrix and Pair-wise Dissimilarity Matrix. These matrices are then aggregated in one similarity matrix which is used for the final clustering. Multi-view ensemble learning is also used to deal with high dimensionality [17]. The work presented in [28] applies low-rank and sparse decomposition to obtain the consensus affinity matrix and eventually the final clustering.

In all of the presented methods, the views for textual data is represented using only syntactic features i.e. the bag of words as views, which cannot preserve the semantic aspect of text, and consequently valuable information is lost. In addition, the views either correspond to different sources of the same document or different parts of the documents i.e. for scientific papers a view can refer to the actual text while another view refers to the citations. However, deriving multiple views from the same text document has not been tackled in the literature. Therefore, for the same document, considering different representations of text as views can improve the clustering performance. The proposed approach falls into the third category, in which we combine multiple clusterings and obtain a single consensus clustering.

3   Proposed Approach

In order to cluster text documents, we propose a new multi-view approach which takes as input a collection of document derives views using different representations of text, and finally outputs clusters of documents. The proposed approach consists of three main steps. In the first step, views are generated such that documents are represented with three different representation models. In the second step, clustering algorithm is then applied on each view to get different partitions. The third step consists in using an ensemble technique to combine the different partitionings in order to obtain a final consensus clustering of documents. The overall process in given in Fig. 1.

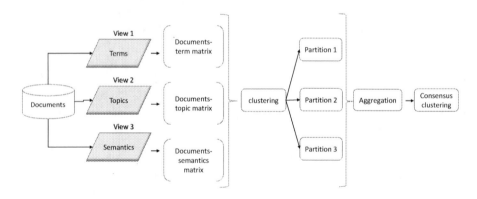

Fig. 1. Graphical representation of the proposed method

3.1   Generation of Views

The first step of the proposed method consists in generating different views based on three text representation models: The VSM, the LDA, and the Skip-gram model that respectively capture the syntactic, the topical and the semantic aspects of text. Moreover, this step aims to demonstrate that manufactured views is able to improve the clustering results.

The Vector Space Model (VSM) [24] is the most commonly used method for text representation. The VSM is an algebraic model in which documents and terms are represented as vectors in a multidimensional space and can be represented as a term-document matrix in which the values correspond to the Term Frequency-Inverse Document Frequency (tf-idf) weights [23]. *TF-IDF* is a weighting method that is used to score the importance of a word in a document based on the number of times it occurs in the document itself and in the entire collection of documents. The intuition behind the TF-IDF weighting measure is that the importance of a word should increase proportionally to the number of times that word appears in a document. Words such as "is", "the", "a" are very common in the English language and tend to appear more often than other words but they carry no meaning in them, therefore their values are offset by their idf weights.

Latent Dirichlet Allocation model (LDA) is a probabilistic topic model that represents each document as a probability distribution over a number of topics while each topic itself is a probability distribution over a number of words [5]. Unlike other models, LDA do not represent words by weights such as their frequencies in documents, instead each word is represented as a probability distribution. The LDA model is used along with Gibbs sampling [7] to discover topics represented by a documents-topic matrix.

The Skip-gram model [20] is a neural network capable of learning word embeddings that capture both semantic and syntactic information of words, and can be used to measure word similarities. To take full advantage of this model, the technique of negative sampling [21] is used in our method. Following [10], the vector representations of words in the corpus are provided by the neural model. The K-means algorithm is then used in order to identify different K groups of words which fit together semantically. The entries of this matrix are tf-idf weights of the semantic cliques, such that:

$$w_{ij} = \frac{tf_{ij} \times idf_i}{\sum\limits_{t \in d_j} tf_{ij} \times idf_i} \qquad (1)$$

where w_{ij} is the weight of the word cluster C_i in the document d_j, tf_{ij} is the frequency of C_i in d_j that is the sum of the tf weights of terms t belonging to cluster C_i and document d_j as expressed by (2), idf_i is the idf weighting of C_i which is the sum of the idf weights of words w in C_i (3). The denominator is for normalization.

$$tf_{ij} = \sum_{l=1} tf(t_l \in C_i, d_j), \ i \in \{1, .., K\}; \ j \in \{1, .., N\} \qquad (2)$$

$$idf_i = \sum_{l=1} idf(t_l \in C_i) \quad i \in \{1, \cdots, K\} \qquad (3)$$

The output of this step is three views corresponding to the different representation models. The VSM yields the first view represented by the documents-term matrix, the LDA based representation provides the second view where data is represented by documents-topic matrix, and from the Skip-gram model, we obtain the third view which is represented by a documents-semantics matrix.

3.2 Views Clustering

Once the views are obtained through the three representation models, a clustering algorithm is applied on each of the matrices given by each view i.e. the documents-term matrix, the documents-topic matrix and the documents-semantics matrix. Consequently, different partitions are generated by running the K-means algorithm using the cosine distance

$$min\ Dis = \sum_{j=1}^{N}\sum_{i=1}^{K} D_{js}(d_j^v, c_i^v), \quad v = \{1, 2, 3\} \tag{4}$$

where, given the *v-th* view, d_j is the vector representation of the *j-th* document given, c_i is the centroid of the *i-th* cluster.

3.3 Aggregation of Views Clustering

The last step of the proposed method consists in combining the different partitions provided by each view in order to obtain a final consensus clustering. As stated beforehand, the method is based on late integration, where multiple partitions are combined without accessing the features or the algorithms used to obtain those partitions. Two techniques i.e. the Cluster Based Similarity Partitioning (CBSP) [25] and the Pairwise Dissimilarity Matrix (PDM) [39], are used to integrate the partitions yielded by each view. The motivation behind the choice of CBSP and PDM is given in the following.

Cluster Based Similarity Partitioning first represents the clustering assignments obtained from each view using a hyper-graph based adjacency matrix. The rows of the hyper-graph adjacency matrix correspond to the N objects, while the columns are a concatenation of all hyper-edges mapping the clusters of each partition. The adjacency matrix is a binary matrix, where 1 indicates that the object is a part of the hyper-edge of its corresponding partition and 0 indicates that it is not. An illustrative example is given in Fig. 2 for 5 documents and K = 3.

P	P1	P2	p3
d_1	1	2	1
d_2	1	2	2
d_3	2	1	3
d_4	3	1	1
d_5	2	3	3

H	P1			P2			P3		
	h_1	h_2	h_3	h_1	h_2	h_3	h_1	h_2	h_3
d_1	1	0	0	0	1	0	1	0	0
d_2	1	0	0	0	1	0	0	1	0
d_3	0	1	0	1	0	0	0	0	1
d_4	0	0	1	1	0	0	1	0	0
d_5	0	1	0	0	0	1	0	0	1

Fig. 2. Hyper-graph based adjacency matrix H

The next step of CBSP is to build a n × n similarity matrix S_H based on the adjacency matrix H, such that:

$$S_H = \frac{1}{m}(H * H^T) \tag{5}$$

where m is the total number of partitions which correspond to the number of views, and H^T is the transpose of H. The motivation behind the choice of CBSP is its capability to depict the relationship between objects in the same cluster which is represented in the matrix S_H. The obtained similarity matrix is used to re-cluster the objects. This method maintains a good performance even in the presence of noise [25].

The Pairwise Dissimilarity Matrix takes into account the disagreement between the partitions with respect to an object. Hence, the pairwise dissimilarity correspond to the number of times two specific objects have been assigned to different clusters in each partition.

To combine the PDM and the similarity matrix of CBSP, the former is transformed into a similarity matrix using the cosine similarity

$$S_{PDM}(i,j) = \cos(d_i, d_j) = \frac{d_i d_j}{\sqrt{(d_i d_j)(d_i d_j)}} \tag{6}$$

where d_i and d_j are the vector representations of documents i and j in the dissimilarity matrix. The PDM based similarity matrix is selected as it considers both the disagreement in the different partitions as well as the relationship between the clustered objects.

Once both the similarity matrices are deduced from the different partitions, the next step consists in combining them in one similarity matrix such that:

$$S = \frac{1}{2}(S_H + S_{PDM}) \tag{7}$$

however, in order to preserve the triangular inequality, $dis(i,j) < dis(i,k) + dis(k,j)$, where $dis(i,j) = 1 - S_{ij}$, we use the ultra-metric as in [39] to enforce this property where:

$$dis(i,j) = min(dis(i,j), max(dis(i,k), dis(k,j))) \tag{8}$$

The new similarity matrix S servers to re-cluster the documents using the hierarchical clustering to obtain the final consensus clustering.

4 Experiments and Results

In order to evaluate the performance of the proposed method, we conduct several experiments on different data sets with regards to three evaluation measures. First, we carry out a comparison with the equivalent single view methods. Precisely, this corresponds to the first two steps of the proposed method without the aggregation step. Second, our method is evaluated against two existing methods for multi-view clustering.

Algorithm 1. Ensemble method for multi-view text clustering

1: **input**: a collection of text documents
2: **output**: final consensus clustering
3: Generate the views based on the VSM, LDA and Skip-gram models and obtain the three representation matrices.
4: Apply the K-means clustering on each matrix.
5: Calculate the cluster based similarity partitioning matrix S_H.
6: Calculate the pairwise similarity matrix S_{PDM}.
7: Aggregate the similarity matrices into one matrix S.
8: Apply the hierarchical clustering on S
9: return the final clustering

4.1   Data Sets Description

The experiments are carried on 4 well known data sets for text mining. The number of data sets classes ranges from 5 to 20, the sample number reaches up to over 4000. *Reuters R8* data sets is a subset of Reuters data set, consists of 2189 documents belonging to 8 classes. *20 Newsgroups* is a collection of 2828 news articles distributed on 20 classes. *WebKB* data set consists of 4168 web pages collected from computer science departments, belonging to 4 classes (student, faculty, project, course). *BBC Sport* consists of 737 documents from the BBC Sport website corresponding to sports news articles belonging to 5 areas: football, rugby, tennis, athletics and cricket. Before applying the clustering algorithms, a preprocessing step is performed on the data sets including stop words removal. Stop words removal consists in eliminating common words that appear frequently, for example words like "the", "and", "to", "it" in the English language, such words offer no additional value in deciphering what a text is about.

4.2   Evaluation Measures

To measure the quality of the clustering and compare it with existing methods, three evaluation measures are utilized: the F-measure [18], the Normalized Mutual Information (NMI) [40], and Purity [22]. Given a set of clusters $C = \{c_1, c_2, \ldots, c_k\}$ and the gold standard classes $G = \{g_1, g_2, \ldots, g_j\}$:

F-measure is a trade-off between *Precision* and *Recall* such that:

$$F - measure(c_k, g_j) = 2 * \frac{Precision(c_k, g_j) \times Recall(c_k, g_j)}{Precision(c_k, g_j) + Recall(c_k, g_j)} \qquad (9)$$

Normalized Mutual Information (NMI) measures the quality of clustering with regards to the number of clusters and their sizes. NMI is defined as:

$$NMI(C, G) = \frac{I(C, G)}{[E(C) + E(G)]/2} \qquad (10)$$

where I is the mutual information and $E(C)$ is entropy.

$$I(C,G) = \sum_k \sum_j \frac{|c_k \cap g_j|}{N} \log \frac{N|c_k \cap g_j|}{|c_k||g_j|} \qquad (11)$$

$$E(C) = -\sum_k \frac{|s_k|}{N} \log \frac{|s_k|}{N} \qquad (12)$$

Purity: measures the number of correctly assigned documents, where each cluster is assigned to the dominant class in that cluster. The larger the number of clusters is, the higher is the Purity. Unlike NMI, Purity cannot trade off the quality of the clustering against the number of clusters

$$Purity(C,G) = \frac{1}{N} \sum_k \max_j |c_k \cap g_j| \qquad (13)$$

For all measures, the values range from 0 to 1, such that values closer to 0 represent poor quality clustering and those closer to 1 indicate high quality clustering.

4.3   Experimental Results and Discussion

For the first comparison, the proposed method is evaluated against the single view based clustering. Each view correspond to a single text representation model which are the VSM, the LDA model, and the Skip-gram model. We use the K-means algorithm for all single view methods.

Table 1. Comparison of clustering results with single view methods

		F-measure	NMI	Purity
Reuters	VSM	0.758	0.553	0.682
	LDA	0.716	0.501	0.645
	Skip-gram	0.765	0.566	0.687
	Proposed method	**0.814**	**0.604**	**0.743**
20 Newsgroup	VSM	0.450	0.446	0.384
	LDA	0.418	0.356	0.322
	Skip-gram	0.497	0.452	0.440
	Proposed method	**0.511**	**0.534**	**0.458**
webKB	VSM	0.650	0.354	0.652
	LDA	0.635	0.301	0.642
	Skip-gram	0.684	0.361	0.653
	Proposed method	**0.694**	**0.387**	**0.660**
BBC Sport	VSM	0.953	0.854	0.953
	LDA	0.947	0.849	0.947
	Skip-gram	0.976	0.919	0.976
	Proposed method	**0.978**	**0.926**	**0.978**

Given the results in Table 1, the proposed approach outperforms the single view based clustering by yielding better results on all four data sets for F-measure, NMI and Purity. This confirms that combining information extracted from the different views of the data improves the learning and the clusters quality. Furthermore, we notice that although the single view clustering based on the Skip-gram model always gives better results than LDA and VSM, the combination of the three did not cause any deterioration in the clustering quality. This only validates the fact that each representation model corresponding to a view is capable of capturing an aspect of the text that is missing in other views. Despite not giving the best results in the single view context, the LDA and VSM based views contributed to achieving better clustering in multi-view context.

To further evaluate the proposed method, we compare it against two other multi-view clustering methods: the Multi-view K-means (MVKM) proposed in [4] and the Multi-view via ensemble method (MVEM) in [13]. The results in Table 2 are averaged on 50 iterations for each method. The proposed approach outperformed the other two methods. We notice that the best results were scored for the BBC Sport data set with an F-measure and Purity of 0.978 and 0.926 for NMI, while the 20 Newsgroup gave the lowest F-measure and Purity. The lowest NMI results were scored for the webKB data set, this could be due to the fact that NMI takes into account the number and the sizes of clusters and the webKB data set is the largest with 4 classes which can be challenging for clustering algorithms. Nonetheless, our method achieved better results on all data sets by a significant margin. This shows that the views representation method for text data affects considerably the quality of the obtained clusters.

Table 2. Comparison of clustering results with multi-view methods

		F-measure	NMI	Purity
Reuters	MVEM	0.490	0.337	0.493
	MVKM	0.648	0.428	0.541
	Proposed method	**0.814**	**0.604**	**0.743**
20 Newsgroup	MVEM	0.380	0.305	0.300
	MVKM	0.431	0.380	0.373
	Proposed method	**0.511**	**0.534**	**0.458**
webKB	MVEM	0.542	0.268	0.448
	MVKM	0.564	0.321	0.460
	Proposed method	**0.694**	**0.387**	**0.660**
BBC Sport	MVEM	0.819	0.717	0.753
	MVKM	0.693	0.546	0.633
	Proposed method	**0.978**	**0.926**	**0.978**

5   Conclusion

In this paper, we proposed a new method for multi-view text clustering based on ensemble method. While the existing methods use only one representation of text based on terms occurrence, the proposed method generates three views based on different text representation models. The syntactic and topical and semantic aspects of text are captured by the VSM, the LDA and the Skip-gram model respectively. The second step of the method consists in applying the K-means algorithm to obtain different partitions from each view. Lastly the partitions are combined using the Cluster Based Similarity Partitioning and the Pairwise Dissimilarity ensemble methods. These latter are combined in one similarity matrix that servers for the re-clustering which results to a final consensus partitioning.

The conducted experimentation shows that, in comparison to single view based clustering, using multiple views improves the clustering quality. The experiments also show that the proposed method yields better results compared to other multi-view clustering methods.

References

1. Aggarwal, C.C., Zhai, C.: Mining Text Data. Springer, New York (2012). https://doi.org/10.1007/978-1-4614-3223-4
2. Amini, M., Usunier, N., Goutte, C.: Learning from multiple partially observed views-an application to multilingual text categorization. In: Advances in Neural Information Processing Systems, pp. 28–36 (2009)
3. Ben N'Cir, C.E., Essoussi, N.: Using sequences of words for non-disjoint grouping of documents. Int. J. Pattern Recognit Artif Intell. **29**(03), 1550013 (2015)
4. Bickel, S., Scheffer, T.: Multi-view clustering. In: ICDM, vol. 4, pp. 19–26 (2004)
5. Blei, D.M., Ng, A.Y., Jordan, M.I.: Latent Dirichlet allocation. J. Mach. Learn. Res. **3**, 993–1022 (2003)
6. Blum, A., Mitchell, T.: Combining labeled and unlabeled data with co-training. In: Proceedings of the Eleventh Annual Conference on Computational Learning Theory, pp. 92–100. ACM (1998)
7. Bolstad, W.M.: Understanding Computational Bayesian Statistics, vol. 644. Wiley, New York (2010)
8. Chao, G., Sun, S., Bi, J.: A survey on multi-view clustering. arXiv preprint arXiv:1712.06246 (2017)
9. Ding, Z., Fu, Y.: Low-rank common subspace for multi-view learning. In: 2014 IEEE International Conference on Data Mining, pp. 110–119. IEEE (2014)
10. Fraj, M., Hajkacem, M.A.B., Essoussi, N.: A novel tweets clustering method using word embeddings. In: 2018 IEEE/ACS 15th International Conference on Computer Systems and Applications (AICCSA), pp. 1–7. IEEE (2018)
11. Guo, Y.: Convex subspace representation learning from multi-view data. In: AAAI, vol. 1, p. 2 (2013)
12. Hassan, M.T., Karim, A., Kim, J.B., Jeon, M.: CDIM: document clustering by discrimination information maximization. Inf. Sci. **316**, 87–106 (2015)
13. Hussain, S.F., Mushtaq, M., Halim, Z.: Multi-view document clustering via ensemble method. J. Intell. Inf. Syst. **43**(1), 81–99 (2014)

14. Jun, S., Park, S.S., Jang, D.S.: Document clustering method using dimension reduction and support vector clustering to overcome sparseness. Expert Syst. Appl. **41**(7), 3204–3212 (2014)
15. Kalogeratos, A., Likas, A.: Document clustering using synthetic cluster prototypes. Data Knowl. Eng. **70**(3), 284–306 (2011)
16. Kumar, A., Daumé, H.: A co-training approach for multi-view spectral clustering. In: Proceedings of the 28th International Conference on Machine Learning (ICML 2011), pp. 393–400 (2011)
17. Kumar, V., Minz, S.: Multi-view ensemble learning: an optimal feature set partitioning for high-dimensional data classification. Knowl. Inf. Syst. **49**(1), 1–59 (2016)
18. Larsen, B., Aone, C.: Fast and effective text mining using linear-time document clustering. In: Proceedings of the Fifth ACM SIGKDD International Conference on Knowledge Discovery and Data Mining, pp. 16–22. Citeseer (1999)
19. Liu, J., Wang, C., Gao, J., Han, J.: Multi-view clustering via joint nonnegative matrix factorization. In: Proceedings of the 2013 SIAM International Conference on Data Mining, pp. 252–260. SIAM (2013)
20. Mikolov, T., Chen, K., Corrado, G., Dean, J.: Efficient estimation of word representations in vector space. arXiv preprint arXiv:1301.3781 (2013)
21. Mikolov, T., Sutskever, I., Chen, K., Corrado, G.S., Dean, J.: Distributed representations of words and phrases and their compositionality. In: Advances in Neural Information Processing Systems, pp. 3111–3119 (2013)
22. Nie, F., Cai, G., Li, X.: Multi-view clustering and semi-supervised classification with adaptive neighbours. In: AAAI, pp. 2408–2414 (2017)
23. Salton, G., Buckley, C.: Term-weighting approaches in automatic text retrieval. Inf. Process. Manage. **24**(5), 513–523 (1988)
24. Salton, G., Wong, A., Yang, C.S.: A vector space model for automatic indexing. Commun. ACM **18**(11), 613–620 (1975)
25. Strehl, A., Ghosh, J.: Cluster ensembles-a knowledge reuse framework for combining multiple partitions. J. Mach. Learn. Res. **3**, 583–617 (2002)
26. Sun, S.: A survey of multi-view machine learning. Neural Comput. Appl. **23**(7–8), 2031–2038 (2013)
27. Tagarelli, A., Karypis, G.: A segment-based approach to clustering multi-topic documents. Knowl. Inf. Syst. **34**(3), 563–595 (2013)
28. Tao, Z., Liu, H., Li, S., Ding, Z., Fu, Y.: From ensemble clustering to multi-view clustering. In: IJCAI (2017)
29. Wan, X.: Co-training for cross-lingual sentiment classification. In: Proceedings of the Joint Conference of the 47th Annual Meeting of the ACL and the 4th International Joint Conference on Natural Language Processing of the AFNLP: Volume 1-Volume 1, pp. 235–243. Association for Computational Linguistics (2009)
30. Wei, B., Pal, C.: Cross lingual adaptation: an experiment on sentiment classifications. In: Proceedings of the ACL 2010 Conference Short Papers, pp. 258–262. Association for Computational Linguistics (2010)
31. Xie, X., Sun, S.: Multi-view clustering ensembles. In: 2013 International Conference on Machine Learning and Cybernetics (ICMLC), vol. 1, pp. 51–56. IEEE (2013)
32. Xu, Z., Sun, S.: An algorithm on multi-view adaboost. In: Wong, K.W., Mendis, B.S.U., Bouzerdoum, A. (eds.) ICONIP 2010. LNCS, vol. 6443, pp. 355–362. Springer, Heidelberg (2010). https://doi.org/10.1007/978-3-642-17537-4_44
33. Yang, Y., Wang, H.: Multi-view clustering: a survey. Big Data Min. Anal. **1**(2), 83–107 (2018)

34. Yin, Q., Wu, S., He, R., Wang, L.: Multi-view clustering via pairwise sparse subspace representation. Neurocomputing **156**, 12–21 (2015)
35. Yin, Q., Wu, S., Wang, L.: Unified subspace learning for incomplete and unlabeled multi-view data. Pattern Recogn. **67**, 313–327 (2017)
36. Zhao, H., Ding, Z., Fu, Y.: Multi-view clustering via deep matrix factorization. In: AAAI, pp. 2921–2927 (2017)
37. Zhao, L., Chen, Z., Yang, Y., Wang, Z.J., Leung, V.C.: Incomplete multi-view clustering via deep semantic mapping. Neurocomputing **275**, 1053–1062 (2018)
38. Zhao, X., Evans, N., Dugelay, J.L.: A subspace co-training framework for multi-view clustering. Pattern Recogn. Lett. **41**, 73–82 (2014)
39. Zheng, L., Li, T., Ding, C.: Hierarchical ensemble clustering. In: 2010 IEEE International Conference on Data Mining, pp. 1199–1204. IEEE (2010)
40. Zhuang, F., Karypis, G., Ning, X., He, Q., Shi, Z.: Multi-view learning via probabilistic latent semantic analysis. Inf. Sci. **199**, 20–30 (2012)

Towards Humanlike Chatbots Helping Users Cope with Stressful Situations

Lenin Medeiros[1,2]([⊠])(iD), Charlotte Gerritsen[1](iD), and Tibor Bosse[2](iD)

[1] Behavioural Informatics Group, Vrije Universiteit Amsterdam,
Amsterdam, The Netherlands
{l.medeiros,c2.gerritsen}@vu.nl
[2] Behavioural Science Institute, Radboud Universiteit, Nijmegen, The Netherlands
t.bosse@ru.nl

Abstract. Many researchers are studying the application of computer-generated emotional support to increase well-being in humans. In this chapter, we investigate some challenges related to the development of effective stress support bots. We developed a chatbot for Facebook Messenger that, using IBM Watson's text mining and machine learning capabilities, can carry out small dialogues with its users and recognise when they are talking about stressful daily-life events. Based on previous studies, our presented bot provides emotionally supportive text messages tailored to the stressors users share with it. Two groups of specialists have interacted with our software and provided useful insights via focus groups. Based on the results of the focus groups, a number of recommendations have been formulated to further improve stress support bots. In future work, we plan to address all the feedback obtained during this study, as well as to conduct an experiment to investigate to what extent our chatbot is able to make people cope with their daily-life stressful situations.

Keywords: Chatbots · Conversational agents ·
Computer-generated emotional support · Text mining ·
Human-computer interaction · Emotion regulation · Stress

1 Introduction

Computer-Generated Emotional Support (CGES) has been proposed in recent years as a promising approach to help people cope with difficult circumstances [5, 10,11,17]. In this project, we aim to explore how chatbots can be used to help people cope online with *everyday stress*: stressful circumstances all of us face from time to time, making us feel a bit tense or even sad, without necessarily related to mental disorders. Relationship problems, work and financial problems, health issues, and family circumstances, are examples of such situations, which we will call stressors in this paper.

At early stages of this project, as reported in [13], we conducted an investigation to collect the most common stressors Twitter users talked about in a time

© Springer Nature Switzerland AG 2019
N. T. Nguyen et al. (Eds.): ICCCI 2019, LNAI 11683, pp. 232–243, 2019.
https://doi.org/10.1007/978-3-030-28377-3_19

window of seven days. Around 10.000 tweets were collected, each one containing at maximum 280 characters. Next to that, we used crowdsourcing to identify supportive strategies people are likely to use, related to the respective stressors, when providing emotional support to peers. These strategies have been categorized according to the emotion regulation strategies proposed by Gross [6]. They are also in line with the results discussed in a previous article [12], where we tried to distinguish a number of requirements for the development of an emotional supportive chatbot. We collected Twitter data because research has demonstrated that Twitter users often talk about their stressful situations (e.g., users sharing tweets about post traumatic stress disorder [3]). In addition, Twitter provides a public API, which makes it easy to use for scientific purposes.

In the final phase of this project, we intend to develop and test an emotionally supportive chatbot that: (1) is able to identify stressors in the text messages shared by users, (2) match them with appropriate supportive strategies, and (3) provides tailored stress support messages to users. The current paper describes some important steps of this development process, as well as some preliminary evaluation.

Hence, the goal of this paper is to report on our progress as well as to discuss the challenges involved in developing such a human-like chatbot aiming to help users cope with daily-life stressful situations. We present a focus group study in which two groups of experts (with a background in Computer Science and Communication Science, respectively) have interacted with our bot and provided us useful insights on these challenges. The precise structure of this document is as follows. In Sect. 2, we present important related work. In Sects. 3 and 4, respectively, we explain both the algorithm and the architecture of our proposed chatbot in detail. In Sect. 5, we discuss use case scenarios of our chatbot and provide the results of our focus group evaluations. Finally, Sect. 6 concludes this paper with a discussion.

2   Background

We use the concept of *emotion regulation*, as proposed by Gross [6], as the theoretical basis to classify and construct the supportive messages that our chatbot will use. As discussed by Gross, human beings use a variety of strategies to regulate their own emotions, which can be classified into distinct categories such as *cognitive change* and *attentional deployment*. However, as we discussed in [12], these strategies can also be used in an 'interpersonal' way (e.g., instead of focusing your own attention on some other entity than the stressor, you can also tell your friend to think of something else). Indeed, as we demonstrated in [13], most of the strategies people use online to provide emotional support to their peers can be mapped onto these categories.

Many researchers have investigated the use of computers to provide emotional support to humans: the so-called Computer-Generated Emotional Support (CGES). Assuming that CGES can be as effective as support provided by a human peer, this approach seems to be very promising from the perspective of a user, since computers can be fully available whenever a given user seeks for support. Moreover, their performance is not hindered by their own negative emotions. Furthermore, *peer-to-peer support*, defined by Kim et al. [9] as 'the process of users with strong social ties helping each other in getting emotional, practical and even social support', has been shown to be effective in promoting health and well-being [1, 2, 7]. As a consequence, as discussed by Hoermann et al. [8] and Mensio et al. [14], there are already commercial applications available that provide artificially generated emotional support to users, such as *Woebot* and *Replika*. The first app, for instance, was evaluated in [4] leading to the conclusion that users might experience "significant reduction in symptoms of depression".

Two papers deserve special notice for the fact they are quite similar to ours. Kindness et al. [10] also investigated appropriate supportive strategies tailored to stressors, as we did in previous works [12, 13]. However, the stressors they address are related to community first responders dealing with medical emergencies, whereas we focus on 'everyday stress'. Another difference it that their strategies are not explicitly related to Gross' emotion regulation theory, even though their strategies can be roughly matched to ours. Secondly, Morris et al. [16] investigated to what extent users can perceive a conversational agent, similar to the one we present in this paper, as expressing empathy. They found out that users tend to prefer supportive messages sent by real peers, even though they might see the computer-generated supportive messages as acceptable enough. In the end, they conclude that developing such a bot, which expresses empathy in order to make its users feel attached to it, is still a big challenge.

As concluded in [10], after discussing a number of relevant papers, humans can indeed have their mood affected positively by support that is provided by software. This discussion leads us to point out two interesting aspects. Firstly, it is worthwhile to explore the potential of computer-generated support for people dealing with everyday stressful circumstances. Secondly, there are some challenges in this field in the sense that it is still quite difficult to develop artificial agents that express empathy to humans in a way that they perceive it is natural. With the current paper, we aim to contribute to the state-of-the-art in this area by developing a prototype of a stress-support chatbot, and evaluating it by means of focus groups.

3   Algorithm

As mentioned in Sect. 1, the algorithm to decide what supportive strategy our chatbot should follow when supporting its users is based on a Twitter investigation conducted earlier [13]. The algorithm is described in detail in the current section. However, before showing it in detail, it is necessary to define a few concepts, in particular regarding the scope of the stressors our chatbot deals with, as well as the supportive strategies it uses.

There are six possible categories of stressors that our chatbot is able to recognise. They concern stressful situations involving: interpersonal relationships (REL); work (WOR); finances (FIN); education environments such as school, universities, etc. (EDU); health issues (HEA); and grief (GRI) (see [12]). Regarding the supportive strategies, our chatbot can follow four different ones, which are defined as follows (see [6]):

- Attentional deployment (AD): to suggest the user to focus their mind on something else, different from the stressful situation. Example: *"Oh, try not to think about this situation. Think about something else that makes you feel better!"*;
- Cognitive change (CC): to try to reinterpret the problem from the user's point of view. Example: *"Oh, but look at the bright side: there are things you have learned from this situation!"*;
- General emotional support (GES): to provide general kind words showing empathy. Example: *"I am truly sorry to hear about this situation from you. I hope you feel better soon!"*;
- Situation modification (SM): to attempt to convince the user they can do something in order to change a given situation. Example: *"Oh, but try to think about how you could change this situation. I am sure there is something you can do about it!"*.

Inspired by our empirical investigation of which support strategies Twitter users use in which situation [13], we have developed a mapping between the stressors and the support strategies. Algorithm 1 depicts, via pseudo code, how our presented application selects the most appropriate text message to send to its users when they are talking about stressful situations. Note that, the algorithm assumes that the message sent by the user is a request for emotional support tailored to a given stressor. More details about how our chatbot deals with any type of text message sent by the user are explained in Sect. 4.

Algorithm 1. Selecting a supportive text message based on a stressor.

---

function HANDLEMESSAGE(message)

    stressor ← GETSTRESSOR(message)
    strategy ← "GES"

    if stressor = "GRI" **then** strategy ← "GES_GRIEF"
    else if stressor = "WOR" ∨ stressor = "EDU" **then** strategy ← "CC"
    else if stressor = "REL" ∧ ISP(message) = TRUE **then** strategy ← "AD"
    ▷ The function *isP* decides whether a relationship situation is permanent or not.
    else if stressor = "FIN" **then** strategy ← RSEL(input ← ["CC", "GES", "SM"])
    ▷ The function *rSel* randomly selects one item of the array passed as parameter.

    supportiveMessage ← GETSUPPORTIVETEXTRESPONSE(strategy)

    return supportiveMessage

According to Algorithm 1 the agent first decides what is the stressor involved in the message shared by the user, and then selects the most appropriate supportive strategy based on the proposed mapping rule. The `getStressor()` function extracts the most likely stressor from the incoming text message. To this end, the system has been trained on examples of texts representing users sharing stressful situations, using IBM Watson. Additionally, specific keywords related to each one of the stress categories were provided as well. Examples of such keywords are: *hospital, ill*, etc. for health; *died, passed away*, etc. for grief; *boyfriend, wife*, etc. for relationships; *work, paperload*, etc. for work; *debts, bills*, etc. for finances; and *midterms, grade*, etc. for education. More than 45 keywords per stressor have been used. The final decision on the stressor, is performed via IBM Watson's natural language processing, sentiment analysis and machine learning techniques. If the sentiment analysis module identifies a negative sentiment present in the text and the machine learning algorithm classifies the sentence as an example of a stressful situation, then the text will be further analysed so that the specific stressor can be identified. When the stressor cannot be identified, the support strategy will be GES, which is the most general one.

When the stressor can be identified, a corresponding support strategy is chosen based on the knowledge identified in [13]. First of all, stressors related to health issues are mapped into GES. However, for the subset of health issues that are related to serious grief (e.g., a loved one passed away), the algorithm must set a flag to identify these messages as grief. In this case, the special support strategy GES_GRIEF is used, because the chatbot should show that it understood that someone the user cares about passed away. Next, stressors of the categories WOR and EDU are related to the support strategy CC. Stressors about relationships problems have one subcategory called permanent, to represent cases where a given interpersonal relationship is over. This is determined by the function isP(), which uses IBM Watson's machine learning and text mining techniques, to compare the user's input to training samples representing users that are talking about cases where their relationship has ended. If a relationship is indeed over, then the selected strategy must be AD (e.g., "Just think about something else!"). If the relationship is not over (which means the situation is still 'repairable'), the strategy will be GES. Furthermore, for financial matters, there will be a random selection between three strategies: the strategy might be CC, GES or SM (see the function rSel()). The reason for using multiple strategies in the case of relationship problems and financial problems is that the results obtained in [13] were inconclusive in the sense that there was not one single strategy that was used significantly more often than other strategies. Therefore, in these cases one of the most frequently used strategies in selected.

The last part of the algorithm addresses the translation from an abstract support strategy to a specific supporting message tailored to the situation. For this, the proposed algorithm uses lists of pre-established sentences (again, inspired by our empirical studies) related to each of the supportive strategies. When giving a response to a user, the algorithm selects one sentence from the appropriate lists and fills in certain slots to make it fit the specific situation.

4   Architecture

The application has been developed such that can easily be managed and extended. We also used well established services as much as possible, enabling us to focus on the algorithm cited in Sect. 3. The presented chatbot[1] was built in *Node.js*, as the authors already had worked with this *JavaScript* run-time environment before and it provides support to the services used in this project: *IBM Watson* (to analyse text messages sent by users and deal with dialogue flow), *Facebook* (user interface) and *mLab* (database).

On a high level, our chatbot works as follows. As soon as our application is up and running, it keeps listening to a server port. It can run locally or on a server. However, in order to make the application available to all Facebook users, it must be hosted on a server that provides a HTTPS connection. Whenever a user sends a message to our bot via Facebook Messenger, the application will make a call to IBM Watson to receive the text message it must send back to the user as a response. In case the response is an emotional support message, Watson will send a code representing the supportive strategy that should be followed to the application. Then, the application will send a query to the database to retrieve the last message of that particular support strategy that has been sent to this user. The application will select the next message from the list (or the first one, if the pointer already achieved the end of the list). This is done to avoid the user receiving the same supportive message multiple times, if they keep talking to the chatbot about the same type of problem (or if, by coincidence, they keep talking about different stressors in a row that match with the same supportive strategy).

The application consists of a front end and a back end module, which are explained below. The front end module contains the code to deal with GET and POST requests, with the application listening to a given port. This module also establishes the connection to the Facebook API, or any other user interface that we would like to use.

The back end module contains the connections with the database and the IBM service. Whenever a user sends a message to our bot, the application stores this message as a JSON document with a field representing the classification performed by Watson, without saving any personal information from the user. We can use this information in the future to perform some analysis, for instance, to understand what are the most common stressors our chatbot users are likely to talk about. Figure 1 shows a visualisation of the architecture.

From the perspective of IBM Watson, our chatbot uses sets of entities, intents and a dialogue tree. Entities are keywords and respective synonyms that represent a given concept. For instance, the keyword `wife` can represent the concept `relationship`, while `office` can be related to `work`. Intents can be seen as the desire of a given user when they send a certain message to the bot. For each intent, Watson must be provided a definition of the intent together with a few

---

[1] Available at: https://github.com/leninmedeiros/dailystressassist. Accessed on January 24, 2019.

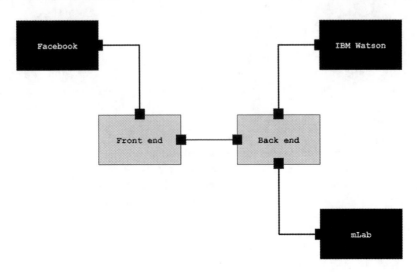

Fig. 1. A scheme representing the architecture of the presented chatbot.

examples of text that represent it. The most important intent in our case is called #sharing-problem. Whenever a user sends a message similar to the ones belonging to this classification, predefined by us, the system can recognise the user is seeking for emotional support tailored to a given stressor. As mentioned before, this comparison is performed by Watson's dedicated Artificial Intelligence techniques. Entities and intents are used in a dialogue tree to evaluate text messages and decide how the bot should respond to an incoming message. A visualization of this dialogue tree is shown in Fig. 2. Here, the most important element in the tree is the node Talking about a stressful event, which is an implementation of the algorithm presented in Sect. 3.

5   Preliminary Evaluation

Due to the explorative nature of our project (i.e., we aim to understand the potential of chatbots as 'artificial friends' that help people cope with stress by engaging in a dialogue with them), we performed a preliminary evaluation of our prototype. To this end, two focus group studies have been performed [15]. Hence, the purpose of these studies is not to test hypotheses regarding the effect the chatbot can have on its users' stress levels. Instead, we were interested in presenting our prototype to experts in order to get useful insights that might be helpful to further develop and improve the system. In this section, we first present some example 'use cases' (i.e., descriptions of the behaviour shown by the chatbot from a user perspective), which is followed by a description of the two focus group studies.

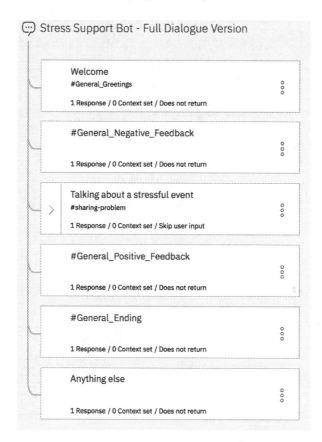

Fig. 2. Visualization of the chatbot's dialogue tree, implemented in IBM Watson.

5.1   Use Cases

The idea is that a user can interact with our chatbot via a given online social network (as explained in Sect. 4) as if it were one of their personal contacts. To illustrate how this works, we depict a number of fragments of conversations the chatbot can have with its users. Due to lack of space, we will only present a brief selection.

At the beginning, the chatbot acts in a reactive way, as the human user should be the one responsible for starting a conversation (see Fig. 3).

The chatbot is able to carry out simple conversations about common topics, such as responding to greetings and negative feedback (see Figs. 4 and 5).

As soon as the chatbot concludes a given user is facing some stressful situation, it will select the most appropriate supportive message to send back based on the stressor identified (see Fig. 6). Note that Figs. 3, 4, 5 and 6 are screenshots from Facebook Messenger. Therefore, in terms of semiotics, the emoticons users might use as well as the default colour scheme to differentiate bot messages from users messages are defined by this platform.

Hello!
Hello. How can I help you? Tell me about something that is bothering you...

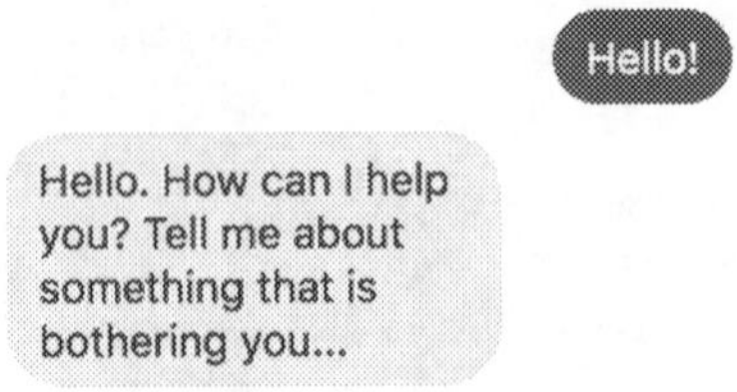

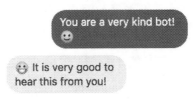

Fig. 3. A user starting a conversation with the chatbot.

You are a very kind bot!
It is very good to hear this from you!

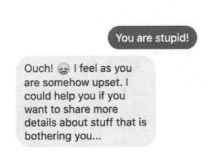

Fig. 4. A user greeting the chatbot.

You are stupid!
Ouch! I feel as you are somehow upset. I could help you if you want to share more details about stuff that is bothering you...

Fig. 5. A user sharing negative sentiment towards the bot.

5.2 Focus Groups

Since this is an inter-disciplinary project which is situated on the boundary of Computer Science and the Social Sciences, we decided to conduct two focus group studies with experts from these two disciplines. Both focus groups involved three participants. The first group was formed by Computer Science specialists from Vrije Universiteit Amsterdam: two PhD candidates and one Master's student. The second focus group was composed by three PhD students in Communication Science from Radboud University Nijmegen. Both focus groups took place in February 2019.

At the start of each focus group, the participants were asked to interact with two versions of our chatbot, in two rounds of five minutes each. One version was only able to have simple interactions with its users: every message sent to the bot was assumed to be a description of a stressful situation, therefore our

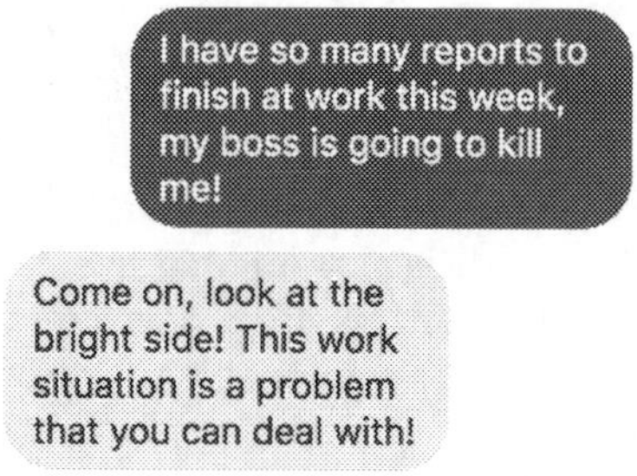

Fig. 6. A user sharing a work related stressful situation with the bot.

algorithm would automatically provide a supportive message to each incoming message. The second version was the one described previously in Sect. 5.1. After each interaction, the participants had the opportunity to discuss about positive and negative aspects of the chatbots via a round table discussion. A summary of the insights extracted from these discussions is provided below.

First of all, all participants liked interacting with the chatbot, and indicated that most of the time it correctly identified the stressors they shared. However, they also tended to agree on the fact the bot must start talking about stress related matters (including offering help and asking for more details) only by request. They thought it is more realistic to carry the conversation going smoothly until the moment the user is confident enough to share a given stressful situation. The participants reported it can be annoying to have the chatbot ask how it could help already at the start of the dialogue. According to them, the decision to start talking about stressful situations should be completely delegated to its users, hence the chatbot should only talk about topics not related to stress and initiated by the users, until the point they start requesting for help by themselves.

Another limitation observed by the participants concerns the 'deepness' of the conversation the chatbot could have about specific stressful situations. As soon as the bot identified a description of a stressful situation, it tried to infer the stressor in order to select the most appropriate response (supportive message). Consequently, the bot sent such a response back to the user without asking for more details about the stressful situation itself, which was perceived as rather unnatural. If the goal is to achieve a humanlike dialogue, the interaction could be more personal: even though the bot recognized the types of the problems described by its users, it did not provide much practical support tailored to the specific stressor a user was talking about. The supportive messages sent by the bot, therefore, must be tailored more to the specific situation.

Finally, the participants also mentioned that, whenever the chatbot said something inappropriate, this substantially decreased the confidence they had in the system. Therefore, it might be a good idea to make the bot first ask for a confirmation about the stressful situation it assumes to have identified. This way, the system can be prevented from giving support that is inappropriate.

6   Discussion

Computer-generated emotional support is a very dynamic research area. Many applications are being developed, but they often lack the ability to truly 'understand' the specific situation (and the corresponding emotional state) of the user and thus to adequately respond. In this project we aim to address this problem by developing an intelligent chatbot that is able to perform short dialogues with users about daily stressful circumstances. The chatbot is able to recognize the stressful situation the user is facing and helps them to cope with it by applying different emotion regulation strategies. The bot is able to distinguish six different types of stressful events, namely interpersonal relationships, work, finances, education, health and grief.

We have tested the bot by organizing two focus groups. The most important feedback we received was that the participants would like to have a more extensive dialogue with the chatbot. In the current test situations, the participants are asked directly to tell something about their stressful experience. The participants agreed that it would be more natural if the bot would start the conversation on a more general level and slowly move towards the topic of stress. Furthermore, they would appreciate it if the conversations would go into more depth. After the bot identifies the stressor, it will determine the correct response and answer without asking more questions related to the stressful event. If the bot would go into more depth it will probably be perceived as being more interested and human-like. Besides this feedback, the participants liked interacting with the bot and agreed that the bot provided correct responses to their stressor.

In future work, we will cover the feedback provided by the focus groups. We will implement some small talk in the beginning of the dialogue and extend the part about the stressor, making the dialogue more natural. Additionally, we will test the effectiveness of the chatbot, in order to assess to what extent it is helpful to let users cope with their everyday stress. There will be room for investigation of the ethical implications as well. For instance, more research is needed to understand to what extent users will possibly build up 'long-term relationships' our chatbot. Also, the question to what extent our chatbot should store the user's personal data in order to make the supportive messages more personal, is another delicate topic that we should investigate in the future.

Acknowledgements. The authors would like to thank the Brazilian government and state that Lenin Medeiros' stay at VU Amsterdam was funded by Science without Borders/CNPq (reference number: 235134/2014-7).

References

1. Cobb, S.: Social support as a moderator of life stress. Psychosom. Med. **38**, 300–314 (1976)
2. Cohen, S., Wills, T.A.: Stress, social support, and the buffering hypothesis. Psychol. Bull. **98**(2), 310 (1985)

3. Coppersmith, G., Harman, C., Dredze, M.: Measuring post traumatic stress disorder in Twitter. In: Eighth International AAAI Conference on Weblogs and Social Media (2014)
4. Fitzpatrick, K.K., Darcy, A., Vierhile, M.: Delivering cognitive behavior therapy to young adults with symptoms of depression and anxiety using a fully automated conversational agent (Woebot): a randomized controlled trial. JMIR Ment. Health **4**(2), e19 (2017)
5. Gockley, R., et al.: Designing robots for long-term social interaction. In: 2005 IEEE/RSJ International Conference on Intelligent Robots and Systems (IROS 2005), pp. 1338–1343. IEEE (2005)
6. Gross, J.J.: Emotion regulation: affective, cognitive, and social consequences. Psychophysiology **39**(3), 281–291 (2002)
7. Heaney, C.A., Israel, B.A.: Social networks and social support. In: Health Behavior and Health Education: Theory, Research, and Practice, vol. 4, pp. 189–210 (2008)
8. Hoermann, S., McCabe, K.L., Milne, D.N., Calvo, R.A.: Application of synchronous text-based dialogue systems in mental health interventions: systematic review. J. Med. Internet Res. **19**(8), e267 (2017)
9. Kim, H.S., Sherman, D.K., Taylor, S.E.: Culture and social support. Am. Psychol. **63**(6), 518 (2008)
10. Kindness, P., Masthoff, J., Mellish, C.: Designing emotional support messages tailored to stressors. Int. J. Hum. Comput. Stud. **97**, 1–22 (2017)
11. Leite, I., Pereira, A., Mascarenhas, S., Martinho, C., Prada, R., Paiva, A.: The influence of empathy in human-robot relations. Int. J. Hum. Comput. Stud. **71**(3), 250–260 (2013)
12. Medeiros, L., Bosse, T.: Empirical analysis of social support provided via social media. In: Spiro, E., Ahn, Y.-Y. (eds.) SocInfo 2016. LNCS, vol. 10047, pp. 439–453. Springer, Cham (2016). https://doi.org/10.1007/978-3-319-47874-6_30
13. Medeiros, L., Bosse, T.: Using crowdsourcing for the development of online emotional support agents. In: Bajo, J., et al. (eds.) PAAMS 2018. CCIS, vol. 887, pp. 196–209. Springer, Cham (2018). https://doi.org/10.1007/978-3-319-94779-2_18
14. Mensio, M., Rizzo, G., Morisio, M.: The rise of emotion-aware conversational agents: threats in digital emotions. In: Companion of the The Web Conference 2018 on The Web Conference 2018, pp. 1541–1544. International World Wide Web Conferences Steering Committee (2018)
15. Morgan, D.L.: The Focus Group Guidebook, vol. 1. SAGE Publications, Thousand Oaks (1997)
16. Morris, R.R., Kouddous, K., Kshirsagar, R., Schueller, S.M.: Towards an artificially empathic conversational agent for mental health applications: system design and user perceptions. J. Med. Internet Res. **20**(6), e10148 (2018)
17. van der Zwaan, J.M., Dignum, V., Jonker, C.M.: A conversation model enabling intelligent agents to give emotional support. In: Ding, W., Jiang, H., Ali, M., Li, M. (eds.) Modern Advances in Intelligent Systems and Tools. SCI, vol. 431, pp. 47–52. Springer, Heidelberg (2012). https://doi.org/10.1007/978-3-642-30732-4_6

Event Detection Based on Open Information Extraction and Ontology

Sihem Sahnoun[1](✉), Samir Elloumi[1](✉), and Sadok Ben Yahia[1,2](✉)

[1] University of Tunis El Manar, Faculty of Sciences of Tunis,
LIPAH-LR11ES14, Tunis, Tunisia
sahnounsihem@yahoo.com, samir.elloumi@fst.utm.tn
[2] Department of Software Science, Tallinn University of Technology, Tallinn, Estonia
sadok.ben@taltech.ee

Abstract. Most of the information is available in the form of unstructured textual documents due to the growth of information sources (the Web for example). In this respect, to extract a set of events from texts written in natural language in the management change event, we have been introduced an open information extraction (OIE) system. For instance, in the management change event, a PERSON might be either the new coming person to the company or the leaving one. As a result, the Adaptive CRF approach (A-CRF) [15] has shown good performance results. However, it requires a lot of expert intervention during the construction of classifiers, which is time consuming. To palpate such a downside, we introduce an approach that reduces the expert intervention during the relation extraction. The named entity recognition and the reasoning which are automatic and based on techniques of adaptation and correspondence. Carried out experiments show the encouraging results of the main approaches of the literature.

Keywords: Information extraction · Event · Named entity · Relationship · OIE · Ontology

1 Introduction

Information Extraction (IE) is one of the hottest areas of the active research in artificial intelligence. It was developed in the late 1980's and 1990's with the Message Understanding Conferences (MUC) [1], in the latter, a set of evaluation campaigns have been suggested and have defined the different tasks of the IE systems. The core task of IE is named entity recognition (NER), which is based on the extraction of categorizable textual objects in classes such as names of people, names of organizations, etc. The relation identification is also a worthy of mention task in the field of IE, which aims to find the mention of a binary relation between two entities in a text [3]. Another specific type of knowledge that can be extracted from the text is the event and can be considered as an object that admits an existence in the time space and depends on other objects [3]. In 2007, the open information extraction (OIE) has appeared and has allowed the task of

© Springer Nature Switzerland AG 2019
N. T. Nguyen et al. (Eds.): ICCCI 2019, LNAI 11683, pp. 244–255, 2019.
https://doi.org/10.1007/978-3-030-28377-3_20

extracting knowledge from texts without much supervision. OIE systems aim to obtain relation tuples with a highly scalable extraction by identifying a variety of relation phrases and their arguments in arbitrary sentences [8]. In this paper, we propose an event extraction approach which reduces the expert intervention by using an OIE system for a relation extraction without supervision, an automatic NER, and an ontology applied for any management change event. We show some case application scenarios for a management change event domain followed by experimental result in terms of recognition rates.

The remainder of this paper is organized as follows. In Sect. 2, we present the related works of the IE domain and its different levels. Section 3 thoroughly describes our new approach for IE. In Sect. 4, we present the experimental results we obtained for the management change event. In Sect. 5, we conclude and sketch issues of future work.

2 Related Work

According to the type of information extracted, different levels are defined in the domain of IE. In the following section we provide a general overview of these levels and elaborate further in subsequent sections.

1. Named Entity Recognition
   NER consists of identifying objects such as the name of people, the name of organizations, the name of places, etc., or numeric entities such as date, money and percentages. There are several NER systems that exist and are classified into three broad families: Systems based on **symbolic approaches**, systems based on **learning approaches** and **hybrid systems** [2]. **The symbolic approach** is based on the use of formal grammars built by hand and exploit syntactic labeling associated with words, such as the grammatical category of the word. It is also based on dictionaries of proper names, which usually include a list of the most common names, first names, place names, and names of organizations. Shaalan and Raza [9] developed their NERA system to extract ten types of NEs. This system relies on the use of a set of NE dictionaries and a grammar in the form of regular expressions. To learn patterns that will recognize entities, **learning-based methods** use annotated data. The annotated data corresponds to documents in which the entities, with their types, are indicated. Subsequently, a learning algorithm will automatically develop a knowledge base using several numerical models such as Conditional Random Fields (CRF), Support Vector Machines (SVM), hidden markov model (HMM), etc., which is not the case for symbolic approaches that only apply the previously injected rules. Benajiba et al. [10] developed an SVM learning technique for their NER system using a set of features of the Arabic language. The combination of the two antecedent approaches represent the emergence of an **hybrid approach**.
2. Relation extraction: Relation extraction (RE) is an important task for many applications and many studies. The RE task involves identifying relationships

between named entities in each sentence of a given document. A relation usually indicates a well-defined relation (having a specific meaning) between two or more NEs. We can distinguish two cases of RE [3]:

– The first concerns the identification of a relationship when both entities are pre-identified in the text. The work by Hearst [11] used hand written rules to automatically generate more rules that were manually evaluated to extract hypernym-hyponym pairs from text. Berland and Charniak [12] used patterns to find all sentences in a corpus containing basement and building.

– The second concerns the identification of all existing relationships between all entities that can be found in an open corpus. There are two generations in OIE that was introduced for the first time by WOE [7] and TextRunner [6] and later in the 2nd generation, by Reverb [4], OLLIE [4] and clauseIE [5]. The goal of these systems is to extract and to present some of the data in the form of (Arg1, Rel, Arg2). "Arg1" and "Arg2" are two nouns, and "Rel" is the relationship between these two arguments. OIE systems of the first generation can suffer from problems such as the extraction of incoherent and non-informative relations. For instance, instead of extracting the relation "is an album by", it only extracts "is" as the relation. The second generation systems deal with inconsistent and non-informative extractions that occur in the first generation by identifying a more meaningful relationship expression.

3. Event recognition: Event extraction is intended to extract from the text a characterization of an event, defined by a set of entities associated with a specific role in the event. Some techniques use **data-driven approaches**, others use **Knowledge-driven approaches** and others use **hybrid approaches**. **Data-driven approaches** require a large text corpora in order to develop models that approximate linguistic phenomena. Data-driven methods require a lot of data and a little domain knowledge and expertise, while having a low interpretability. They don't deal with a meaning explicitly, i.e., they discover relations in corpora without considering semantics.

For example CRF based systems [14] apply the classifier to a set of texts to produce a set of annotated texts. **Knowledge-driven approaches** is often based on models that express rules representing expert knowledge. This alleviates the problems with the statistical methods concerning the meaning of the text. For example, the GLAEE approach [3] is based on a list of keywords and cue words to identify events. **Hybrid approaches** seem to be a compromise between data and knowledge-based approaches, requiring an average amount of data and knowledge and having medium interpretability. For example, the interest of A-CRF [13] is to adapt the recognition of named entities level to the CRF tool based on learning techniques and a correspondence between level 1 learning (PERSON, ORG, DATE, NUMEX, PROFIL) as well as learning level 2 (NEW PERSON, COMING PERSON) which brings us back to a double generation of the classifier.

The diversity of approaches for IE witness the steady interest and usefulness of this domain. Several systems have been proposed in the context of event extraction we have studied their functionality and according to their limits we have introduced our new approach. GLAEE [3] is an approach based on the generation of annotation patterns which involves a list of keywords and cue words. It purposes to identify events by an alignment between the pattern and the new text. Here as stated before, the entities, the keywords and the cue words require human intervention. The template filling through information extraction [16] is an approach that aims to classify sentences according to a predefined event type. The event classification is then generally assimilated to the detection of triggers within the sentence. The trigger type indicates the type of the template form. Here the rules are written manually and require a lot of data. The A-CRF system uses CRFs [14] which are based on a learning phase to manually prepare a set of corpora to train the model and an annotation phase to annotate a new text based on the learned texts and the probability distribution. Hence, the learning phase was applied to generate the level 1 classifier. The corpus is also prepared for deriving the level 2 classifier after an adaptive phase. It means replacing all annotated texts by their corresponding NE. In general, the event extraction task is a dependent domain. It requires human intervention in order to construct manually the annotation rules or to prepare an annotated corpus as an input for the learning phase. In order to reduce the expert intervention, we suggest using ontologies as a knowledge source for describing any event. We suppose that an event-ontology describes the relations between named entities and their possible roles in an event. For instance, in the management change event, a person role might be the new-person i.e. the hired one or the leaving person. To check if a new text informs about a given event in particular the roles of some named entities, a matching process is required between the new text and the ontology. To do that, we suggested the following steps: First we Applied the OIE in order to extract the most relevant relations within a text, then we applied the NER on these relations and finally we made a matching between results of the previous step and the ontology for deriving a possible event.

3   Our Approach: Event Detection Based on Open Information Extraction and Ontology

Our approach admits 2 phases that depend on each other as shown in Fig. 1. The first phase is the modeling of an event by an ontology and constructing a set of rules acquired manually. The second is the recognition phase which includes the RE, the NER and an automatic reasoning between learning rules and an input ontology adaptation. Our aim through two these phases is an event extraction.

3.1   Learning Phase

An event is an object that admits an existence in the space of time and depends on other objects in relation. To cope with such constructs, we construct an ontology manually to model these events in any domain. An ontology is a set

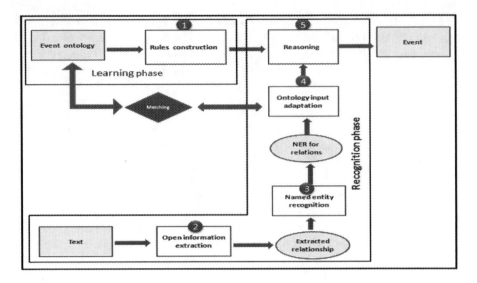

Fig. 1. System architecture

of concepts, as well as relationships between these concepts[1]. The **Algorithm 1** describes the mechanism of the learning phase on a list of named entities, relationships and roles to produce as an output, an ontology and a set of rules. In our case, the concepts stand for the named entities of the event (Person, Organization, etc.) and their roles (Coming_person, Leaving_person, IN_ORG) being in certain relationships.

Figures 2 and 3 illustrate respectively the learning phase which composed of event ontology (classes, subclasses and relations) and rule construction.

The class Person has two subclasses: Coming_person and Leaving_person.

The class Organization has two subclasses: IN_ORG and OUT_ORG.

The class Position has four subclasses: CP_new_position, CP_previous_position, LP_previous_position, LP_new_position.

The class Date has two subclasses: Date_of_coming, Date of leaving.

Our ontology contains a set of predefined relationships to connect two eventual instances such as appoint, resign, promote...

The rules construction is an important step in our approach which drives us, through the ontology and the result of the recognition phase to a possible event extraction. A set of rules are predefined to assign to every instance its role.

For instance the following rule, **Person(?x) ∧ appoint(?o,?x) ∧ Organization(?o)→ IN_ORG(?o) ∧ Coming_Person(?x)** means that any instance "x" of type Person is connected by an 'appoint' relation with any instance of type Organization "o" gives us the result that the instance "x" is a Coming_person and the instance "o" is an IN_ORG.

---

[1] https://www.ontotext.com/knowledgehub/fundamentals/what-are-ontologies/.

Algorithm 1 Learning phase

Input
    L1 : List of entities
    L2 : List of roles
    R : List of relations
Output
    O : Ontology
    RC : Rules Construction
foreach *Entity i in L1* **do**
    Class ← Class ∪ add(i) //*Add named entities as classes in the ontology*
    foreach *Role j in L2* **do**
        Subclass ← Subclass ∪ add(i, Class) // *Add roles as subclasses for named entities that represent classes in ontology*
    end
end
foreach *RelationrinR* **do**
    Relation ← Relation ∪ add(r) //*Add a set of relationships to the ontology*
end
    O ← Event_Ontology(Class, Subclass, Relation) //*The event is modeled by these classes, subclasses and relationships*
    RC ← Rules_Construction(Class, Subclass, Relation) //*The rules are made by these classes, subclasses and by relationships*

For the learning phase we chose protégé as an ontology modeling tool[2]. For the rules construction, we used Semantic Web Rule Language (SWRL) tab. The SWRL tab is a Protégé plugin that provides a development environment for working with SWRL rules. Informally, a rule may be read as meaning that if the antecedent holds (is "true"), then the consequent must also hold.

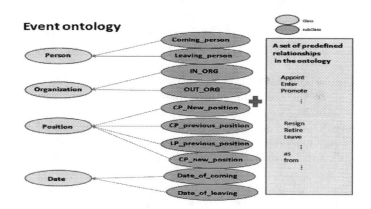

Fig. 2. Example of an Event ontology

Person(?x) ∧ appoint(?o, ?x) ∧ Organization(?o) -> IN_ORG(?o) ∧ Coming_person(?x)
Position(?p) ∧ as(?x, ?p) ∧ Coming_person(?x) -> CP_new_position(?p)
Position(?p) ∧ as(?x, ?p) ∧ Leaving_person(?x) -> LP_previous_position(?p)
Position(?p) ∧leave(?x, ?p) ∧ Leaving_person(?x) -> LP_previous_position(?p)
Person(?x) ∧ resign(?o, ?x) ∧ Organization(?o) -> OUT_ORG(?o) ∧ Leaving_person(?x)

Fig. 3. Example of rules built

---

2 https://protege.stanford.edu/.

3.2   Recognition Phase

The recognition phase operates through four steps which are explained in the following **Algorithm 2**.

Algorithm 2 Recognition phase

   Input
      T : Text
      RC :Rules Construction
      RT :Relation Triplet
   Output
      E : Events
   Begin
      $RT \leftarrow OIE(T)$ *//Relation extraction by an open information extraction tool*
      $R \leftarrow RT.substring(pos(";", RT) + 1, -pos(";", RT) - 1)$ *//Extract the verbal part of the*
   relationships
  foreach *Relation_triplet rt in RT* **do**
      $Token \leftarrow Tokenization(rt)$ *//Cut the relationship triplet into tokens*
     foreach *Token t inrt* **do**
        $NE \leftarrow NER(t)$ *//Named entity recognition automatically*
        $A \leftarrow Adaptation(NE, R, O)$
        $RS \leftarrow Reasoning(A, RC)$
        $E \leftarrow Event\_Extraction(RS)$ *// Event extraction By a reasoner*
     end
  end

Step1: Open information extraction

The input of the system is a text in natural language, the first step of recognition is generated by an OIE system which allows to extract textual relationship triplets existing in each sentence. The relationship triplets contain three textual components (Arg1, Rel, Arg2) where the first and the third stand for the pair of arguments and the second indicates the relationship between them as depicted by Fig. 4. The aim of this step is to restrict the content of the text into relationships that are well defined and have a specific meaning for each sentence in the text. The OLLIE tool produces a strong performance by extracting relationships not only mediated by verbs, but also mediated by nouns and adjectives.[3] It can capture N-ary extractions where the relation phrase only differs by the preposition. OLLIE also captures enabling conditions and attributions if they are present.

Example 1. OLLIE extraction examples
Enabling conditions
Sentence: If I slept past noon, I'd be late for work.
Extraction: (I; 'd be late for; work)[enabler=If I slept past noon]
Attribution
Sentence: Some people say Barack Obama was not born in the United States.
Extraction: (Barack Obama; was not born in; the United States)[attrib=Some people say].
N-ary Extraction
Sentence: I learned that the 2012 Sasquatch music festival is scheduled for May 25th until May 28th.
Extraction: (the 2012 Sasquatch music festival; is scheduled for; May 25th)
Extraction: (the 2012 Sasquatch music festival; is scheduled until; May 28th)
N-ary: (the 2012 Sasquatch music festival; is scheduled; [for May 25th; to May 28th])

---

[3] The OLLIE tool is available at this address: https://github.com/knowitall/ollie.

Step2: Named entity recognition

The input of the NER tool is a triplet found in the previous step. The triplet (Arg1, Rel, Arg2) will have an automatic recognition of named entities after a tokenization step as shown in Fig. 4. In this step, the system can detect person, organization, location, etc., in any part of the triplet. We used Python as one of the languages commonly used for Automatic Language Processing. Its particularity is to be open source and to solve common problems and especially its "libraries" which contain different algorithms directly usable by data scientists. Among these libraries we can mention spaCy and nltk[4]. We chose spaCy for NER and NLTK for lemmatisation and tokenization.

Recognition phase

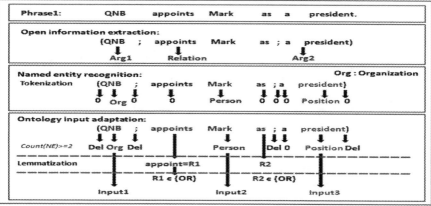

Fig. 4. Example of recognition phase for the phrase "QNB appoints Mark as a president"

Step3: Ontology input adaptation

Algorithm 3 illustrates the adaptation step. After recognizing the NEs, the verbs will be passed through a lemmatization layer that will convert conjugated verbs to their infinitive form. Every token recognized by a NE will be added as an instance in the ontology. During the learning phase, we said that the concepts represent the NEs of the event and their roles. In this step we operate as follows: Tokens are added as instances to the ontology and will be linked by relations whenever the following conditions are fulfilled:

---

[4] https://www.ekino.com/articles/handson-de-quelques-taches-courantes-en-nlp.

Algorithm 3 Adaptation

Input
    NE : Named entity
    R : Relation
    O : Event_Ontology
Output
    tk : tokens_input_ontology
    RL :Relation_lemmatized
Begin

    if $(triplet.Count(NE) >= 2)$ **then**
        $tk \leftarrow NE.token$ // *tk takes tokens that are recognized by named entities*
        if $(R\ in\ O.Relations)$ **then**
        $RL \leftarrow R.Lemmatization$ // *Verbs are transformed into infinitive*
        $Matching(tk, RL, O)$
        end
    end
end

- The number of named entities is greater than or equal to 2 to have a possible relationship among them. The NE can be found in the triplet or in the attribution/condition part (if it exists)
- The lemmatized verb and the other relations between delimiters ";" should be included in the relation list of the ontology and NEs can be linked with these relations.

To automatically add the instances (individuals) to the ontology and to link them by their relationship, We used OWLAPI in a Java code for manipulating the elements that compose an ontology (i.e. classes, individuals, properties, annotations, restrictions, etc.) to the ontology and Owlready2 for the reasoning step as a module for ontology-oriented programming in Python. It can load OWL 2.0 ontologies as objects, modify them, save them, and perform reasoning via the Hermit reasoner (included).

Step4: Reasoning
The reasoning is a stage after entering the instances and linking them by their specific relations. The reasoner is a software which infers logical consequences from a set of rules to affect for each instance its role (event) as shown in Fig. 5. Web Ontology Language (OWL) is based on description logics, and it supports automated reasoning. Protégé OWL provides direct access to reasoners such as Hermit. Hermit can determine whether or not the ontology is consistent, identify subsumption relationships between classes, and much more. The tokens that are recognized by named entities (QNB, Mark and president) will be entered as instances under the classes of the ontology and will be connected by their corresponding relationships (appoint, as). After reasoning, the entries (input1, input2, input3) are automatically linked by their roles (event) in this example

QNB has the role of IN_ORG, Mark has the role of Coming person, president has the role of CP_new_position as shown in Fig. 5.

Algorithm 4 Matching

Input
    O : Ontology
    tk : Tokens_input_ontology
    R : Relation
Output
    O2 : Ontology with instances linked by relations
Begin
if $(O.Class == tk.NE)$ **then** // *if the named entity of the token matches a class of the ontology*
        $tk.addAsInstanceOf(O.Class)$ // *the token will be added as instance under the class*
        $tk.LinkInstancesBy(R)$// *the tokens will be linked by a relation R*
    end
        $O2 \leftarrow New\_OntologyWith(tk, R)$// *a new ontology with instances tk linked by relation R*
    end

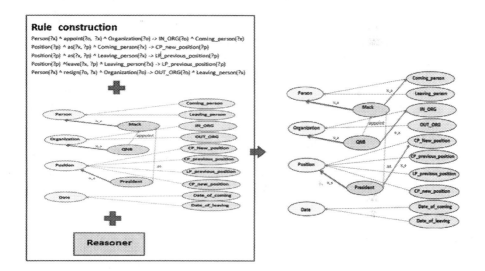

Fig. 5. Example of reasoning step and event extraction for the phrase "QNB appoints Mark as a president"

4   Experimental Results

The main objective of this work is to build a system for an automatic extraction of management change event from texts. We compared our work to a previous applications A-CRF and GLAEE [13]. A-CRF is based on a correspondence between NEs and events. This correspondence is based on a double generation of the classifier: A classifier for the first level's learning (PERSON, POSITION, ORG) and another classifier for the second level's learning (COMING PERSON, NEW POSITION, IN_ORG). GLAEE is based on a list of keywords and cue

Table 1. Comparative study

Role	Our approach	A-CRF	GLAEE
Coming_Person	81%	81%	66.66%
Leaving_Person	92%	49%	33.33%
Date_of_coming	22%	69%	88.88%
Date_of_leaving	50%	61%	60.00%
CP_new_position	60%	81%	84.90%
LP_leaving_position	75%	60%	82.35%

words to identify events. In addition a second application has been applied based on our approach. For the current setting, 40 files for the learning phase are collected and 25 others for the testing phase. To establish a comparative study with an other work in the field of event extraction, so we chose to compare our results against A-CRF and GLAEE by role.

Precision is considered to be a comparative metric between these two approaches. Table 1 presents the results obtained from these two approaches for each role obtained. Even though quite encouraging, we can deduce that we arrived with an acceptable rate to extract from the texts a set of events. The A-CRF approach based on CRF analysis that requires human and manual intervention at the classifiers generation and which take a long time. The GLAEE approach involves a list of keywords and cue words that are manually acquired to identify events by an alignment between the pattern and the new text. Our approach everything was automatic except the part of the rule construction and the ontology which are useful for any event in the management change domain.

5 Conclusion

In this paper, we introduced an event extraction system from textual documents that was able to extract events with an accuracy rate comparable to A-CRF and GLAEE approaches. Our approach is generalized to any type of text in the management change event in particular for the modal of the ontology and the OIE context. We consider as future work, by merging between OIE and open domain event extraction approach [13]. Based on the idea of the open domain, it can give us more effective results. In addition, we plan to use conjugated verbs instead of the lemmatized ones and to assign higher importance to the attribution/condition part to resolve the problem of two different roles in the same sentence and to identify the temporal order of statements.

Acknowledgment. This work was made possible thanks to the Astra funding program Grant 2014-2020.4.01.16-032.

References

1. Grishman, R., Sundheim, B.: Message understanding conference-6: a brief history. In: Proceedings of the 16th Conference on Computational linguistics, pp. 466–471 (1996)
2. Talha, M., Boulaknadel, S., Aboutajdine, D.: Système de Reconnaissance des Entités Nommées Amazighes, In: actes de TALN, pp. 517–524 (2014)
3. Elloumi, S., Jaoua, A., et al.: General learning approach for event extraction: case of management change event. J. Inf. Sci. **39**(2), 211–224 (2013)
4. Fader, A., Soderland, S., Etzioni, O.: Identifying relations for open information extraction. In: Proceedings of the Conference on Empirical Methods in Natural Language Processing, pp. 1535–1545 (2011)
5. Corro, L.D., Gemulla, R.: ClausIE: clause-based open information extraction. In: Proceedings of the 22nd Intlligence Conference on World Wide Web, pp. 355–366 (2013)
6. Banko, M., Cafarella, M.J., Soderland, S., Broadhead, M., Etzioni, O.: Open information extraction from the web. In: Proceedings of the 20th IJCAI 2007, pp. 2670–2676 (2007)
7. Wu, F., Weld, D.S.: Open information extraction using wikipedia. In: Proceedings of the 48th Annual Meeting of ACL 2010, pp. 118–127 (2010)
8. Vo, D.-T., Bagheri, E.: Open Information Extraction, pp. 1–6 (2016)
9. Shaalan, K., Raza, H.: NERA: named entity recognition for arabic. J. Am. Soc. Inform. Sci. Technol. **60**(8), 1652–1663 (2009)
10. Benajiba, Y., Diab, M., Rosso, P.: Using language independent and language specific features to enhance arabic named entity recognition. Int. Arab J. Inf. Technol. **6**(5), 464–473 (2009)
11. Hearst, M.A.: Automatic acquisition of hyponyms from large text corpora. In: Proceedings of the 14th Conference on Computational Linguistics COLING 1992, pp. 539–545 (1992)
12. Berland, M., Charniak, E.: Finding parts in very large corpora. In: Proceedings of the 37th Annual Meeting of the Association for Computational Linguistics on Computational Linguistics, pp. 57–64 (1999)
13. Elloumi, S.: An adaptive model for sequential labeling systems. Multimedia Tools and Applications (2019). https://doi.org/10.1007/s11042-019-7558-8. ISSN: 1573-7721
14. Sarawagi, S., Cohen, W.: Semi-Markov Conditional Random Fields for Information Extraction. pp. 1–8 (2004)
15. Serrano, L., et al.: Vers un système de capitalisation des connaissances: extraction d'événements par combinaison de plusieurs approches, pp. 1–14 (2012)
16. Kodelja, D., Besancon, R., Ferret, O.: Représentations et modèles en extraction d'événements supervisée, CEA, LIST, France, pp. 1–7 (2017)

Data Mining Methods and Applications

Local Models of Interaction
on Collinear Patterns

Leon Bobrowski[1,2](✉) (iD)

[1] Faculty of Computer Science,
Białystok University of Technology, Białystok, Poland
l.bobrowski@pb.edu.pl
[2] Institute of Biocybernetics and Biomedical Engineering, PAS, Warsaw, Poland

Abstract. Data mining algorithms can be used for discovering collinear patterns in data sets composed of a large number of multidimensional feature vectors. Collinear (flat) pattern is observed in data sets when many feature vectors are located on a plane in a feature space. Models of linear interactions between multiple features (genes) can be designed based on collinear patterns. Minimization of the convex and piecewise linear (*CPL*) criterion functions allows for efficient discovering of flat patterns even in cases of large data sets.

Keywords: Data mining · Collinear patterns · Linear interactions models ·
CPL criterion functions

1 Introduction

Data mining methods are being developed extensively for discovering new and useful knowledge in large, multi-dimensional data sets [1, 2]. New knowledge is discovered on the basis of patterns extracted from data sets. Data mining procedures are specified for pattern extraction from data sets. An extracted pattern is expected to be a subset (*cluster*) of such feature vectors that are characterized by some type of regularity (*homogeneity*) [3]. Biclustering procedures are aimed at extracting not only homogeneous groups of feature vectors (patients) in a given feature space, but also at selection of such subsets of feature (genes) specific for particular patterns [4]. Exploration of genomic data sets can be done with clustering or biclustering techniques [5].

A recently developed method of collinear biclustering can be used in extracting local models of multiple interactions from multidimensional data sets [7]. Collinear (*flat*) biclusters can be characterisd as numerous subsets of such feature vectors which are located on vertexical planes of different dimensionality in a given feature space [8]. Flat patterns can be linked to degenerated vertices in the parameter space.

The proposed method of flat patterns extraction from a given data set is based on minimization of the collinearity criterion functions defined on the elements of certain data subsets [9]. The collinearity function belongs to the large family of the *convex and piecewise linear* (*CPL*) criterion functions. This *CPL* family contains, among others, the *perceptron criterion function* [2].

© Springer Nature Switzerland AG 2019
N. T. Nguyen et al. (Eds.): ICCCI 2019, LNAI 11683, pp. 259–270, 2019.
https://doi.org/10.1007/978-3-030-28377-3_21

The optimal parameters (*weights*) which constitute the minimal value of the *CPL* criterion function can be found by using one of the basis exchange algorithms [8]. Basis exchange algorithms are based on the Gauss-Jordan transformation and, mainly for this reason, are similar to the *Simplex* algorithm used in the linear programming [9]. The basis exchange algorithm allows to find efficiently and precisely the weights constituting the minimal value of the *CPL* criterion functions defined on a given data set, even when this set is large and multidimensional.

The presented article is a continuation of the work [11]. The article analyzes the possibility of finding multiple interaction models through searching for collinear patterns. The local model of multiple interactions in a form of a linear equation between selected features (genes) can be formulated on the basis of the extracted local pattern.

The extraction of flat patterns by minimizing the regularized collinear criterion function is considered [8].

2 Vertices in the Parameter Space

We assume that the data set C is composed of m feature vectors $\mathbf{x}_j = [x_{j,1},\ldots, x_{j,n}]^T$ belonging to a given n-dimensional feature space $\mathbf{F}[n]$ $((\forall j \in \{1, \ldots, m\})\ \mathbf{x}_j \in \mathbf{F}[n])$:

$$C = \{\mathbf{x}_j\}, \ where\ j = 1,\ldots, m \tag{1}$$

Components $x_{j,i}$ of the feature vector $\mathbf{x}_j$ can be treated as the numerical results of n standardized measurements (features) X_i of the j-th object (patient) O_j, where $x_{ji} \in \{0,1\}$ or $x_{ji} \in R$.

Each of m feature vector $\mathbf{x}_j$ from the set C (1) defines the following (*dual*) hyperplane h_j in the parameter space R^n:

$$(\forall \mathbf{x}_j \in C)\ h_j = \left\{\mathbf{w} : \mathbf{x}_j^T\mathbf{w} = 1\right\} \tag{2}$$

where $\mathbf{w} = [w_1, \ldots, w_n]^T$ is the parameter (*weight*) vector ($\mathbf{w} \in R^n$).

Each of n unit vectors $\mathbf{e}_i = [0, \ldots, 1, \ldots, 0]^T$ defines the hyperplane h_i^0 in the parameter space R^n:

$$(\forall i \in \{1,\ldots,n\})h_i^0 = \left\{\mathbf{w} : \mathbf{x}_j^T\mathbf{w} = 0\right\} = \{\mathbf{w} : \mathbf{w}_i = 0\} \tag{3}$$

Let us consider the k-th set S_k of n linearly independent vectors $\mathbf{x}_j$ and $\mathbf{e}_i$:

$$S_k = \{\mathbf{x}_j : j \in J_k\} \cup \{\mathbf{e}_i : i \in I_k\} \tag{4}$$

where the index k has a finite number K of values ($k = 1,\ldots, K$).

The set S_k is composed of r_k feature vectors $\mathbf{x}_j$ ($j \in J_k$) and $n - r_k$ unit vectors $\mathbf{e}_i$ ($i \in I_k$), where J_k is the k-th subset of the indices j, and I_k is the k-th subset of the indices i.

The k-th *vertex* $\mathbf{w}_k$ in the parameter space R^n is the intersection point of r_k hyperplanes h_j (2) determined by the feature vectors $\mathbf{x}_j$ ($j \in J_k$) and $n - r_k$ hyperplanes or h_i^0 (3) determined by the unit vectors $\mathbf{e}_i$ ($i \in I_k$) from the set S_k (4). The intersection point (*vertex*) $\mathbf{w}_k = [\mathbf{w}_{k, 1},..., \mathbf{w}_{k,n}]^T$ is defined by the below linear equations:

$$(\forall j \in J_k)\mathbf{w}_k^T\mathbf{x}_j = 1 \tag{5}$$

$$(\forall i \in I_k)\mathbf{w}_k^T\mathbf{e}_i = 0, or\ \mathbf{w}_{k,i} = 0 \tag{6}$$

The Eqs. (5) and (6) can be represented in the matrix form:

$$\mathbf{B}_K = [\mathbf{X}_{j(1)},\ldots,\mathbf{X}_{j(1)},\ \mathbf{e}_{i(rk+1)},\ldots,\mathbf{e}_{i(n)}]^T \tag{7}$$

The square, nonsingular matrix $\mathbf{B}_k$ is the k-th *basis* linked to the vertex $\mathbf{w}_k$:

$$\mathbf{B}_K = [\mathbf{X}_{j(1)},\ldots,\mathbf{X}_{j(rk)},\mathbf{e}_{i(rk+1)},...,\mathbf{e}_{i(n)}]^T \tag{8}$$

$$and\ \mathbf{w}_k = \mathbf{B}_K^{-1}\mathbf{1}' = [\mathbf{r}_1,\ldots,\mathbf{r}_n]\mathbf{1}' = \mathbf{r}_1 + \ldots + \mathbf{r}_{rk} \tag{9}$$

where the symbol $\mathbf{r}_i$ means the i-th column of the inverse matrix $\mathbf{B}_k^{-1} = [\mathbf{r}_1,...., \mathbf{r}_n]$.

Definition 1: The *rank* r_k ($1 \le r_k \le n$) of the k-th vertex $\mathbf{w}_k$ (9) is defined as the number of the non-zero components $\mathbf{w}_{k,i}$ ($\mathbf{w}_{k,i} \ne 0$) of the vector $\mathbf{w}_k = [\mathbf{w}_{k, 1}, ...,\mathbf{w}_{k,n}]^T$ (9).

Definition 2: The basis $\mathbf{B}_k$ (8) linked to the vertex $\mathbf{w}_k$ of the rank r_k is *standard*, when it is composed of r_k feature vectors $\mathbf{x}_{j(i)}$ from the set C (1) and $n - r_k$ unit vectors $\mathbf{e}_i$.

Definition 3: The *degree of degeneration* d_k of the vertex $\mathbf{w}_k$ (9) of the rank r_k is defined as the number $d_k = m_k - r_k$, where m_k is the number of such feature vectors $\mathbf{x}_j$ from the set C (1), which define the hyperplanes h_j (2) passing through this vertex ($\mathbf{w}_k^T\mathbf{x}_j = 1$). The vertex $\mathbf{w}_k$ (9) is *degenerated* if the degree of degeneration d_k is greater than zero ($d_k > 0$).

In accordance with the Eq. (6), the i-th component $\mathbf{w}_{k,i}$ of the vector $\mathbf{w}_k = [\mathbf{w}_{k, 1}, ..., \mathbf{w}_{k,n}]^T$ (9) is equal to zero ($\mathbf{w}_{k,i} = 0$), if the i-th unit vector $\mathbf{e}_i$ belongs to the basis $\mathbf{B}_k$ (8):

$$(i \in I_k) \Rightarrow (w_{k,i} = 0) \tag{10}$$

The reverse sentence is not always true. It can be given examples of such nonsingular matrices $\mathbf{B}_k$ (8) that the vector $\mathbf{x}_{j(i)}$ from the set C (1) constituting the i-th row of the matrix $\mathbf{B}_k$ results in the i-th component $\mathbf{w}_{k,i}$ (9) equal to zero ($\mathbf{w}_{k,i} = 0$).

3   Vertexical Planes in Feature Space

The hyperplane $H(\mathbf{w}, \theta)$ in the feature space $F[n]$ is defined in the below manner [2]:

$$H(\mathbf{w}, \theta) = \{\mathbf{x} : \mathbf{w}^T\mathbf{x} = \theta\} \tag{11}$$

where $\mathbf{w}$ is the *weight vector* ($\mathbf{w} \in R^n$) and θ is the *threshold* ($\theta \in R^1$).

Remark 1: If the threshold θ is different from zero ($\theta \neq 0$), then the hyperplane $H(\mathbf{w}, \theta)$ (11) can be represented as the hyperplane $H(\mathbf{w}', 1) = \{\mathbf{x}: (\mathbf{w}/ \theta)^T\mathbf{x} = 1\}$ with the weight vector $\mathbf{w}' = \mathbf{w}/\theta$ and the threshold θ equal to one ($\theta = 1$).

The $(r_k - 1)$ – dimensional *vertexical plane* $P_k(\mathbf{x}_{j(1)},..., \mathbf{x}_{j(rk)})$ based on the k-th *supporting vertex* $\mathbf{w}_k$ (9) of the *rank* r_k is defined as the standardized linear combination of the r_k ($r_k > 1$) *supporting vectors* $\mathbf{x}_{j(i)}$ ($j(i) \in J_k$) (4) from the basis $\mathbf{B}_k$ (8) [7]:

$$P_k\left(\mathbf{x}_{j(1)}, \ldots, \mathbf{x}_{j(rk)}\right) = \{\mathbf{x} \in \mathbf{F}[n] : \mathbf{x} = \alpha_1(\mathbf{x})\mathbf{x}_{j(1)} + \ldots + \alpha_{rk}(\mathbf{x})\mathbf{x}_{j(rk)}\} \tag{12}$$

where $j(i) \in J_k$ (5) and the r_k parameters $\alpha_i(\mathbf{x})$ ($\alpha_i(\mathbf{x}) \in R^1$) fulfill the below *standardization condition* [7]:

$$(\forall \mathbf{x} \in \mathbf{F}[n]) \, \alpha_1(\mathbf{x}) + \ldots + \alpha_{rk}(\mathbf{x}) = 1 \tag{13}$$

Lemma 1: The vertexical plane $P_k(\mathbf{x}_{j(1)},...,\mathbf{x}_{j(rk)})$ (12) supported by the vertex $\mathbf{w}_k$ (9) with the rank r_k ($r_k > 1$) is equal to the hyperplane $H(\mathbf{w}_k, 1) = \{\mathbf{x}: \mathbf{w}_k^T\mathbf{x} = 1\}$ (11) defined by the vertex $\mathbf{w}_k$ (9) in the n - dimensional feature space $\mathbf{F}[n]$.

Theorem 1: The j-th feature vector $\mathbf{x}_j$ ($\mathbf{x}_j \in C$ (1)) is located on the vertexical plane $P_k(\mathbf{x}_{j(1)}, ..., \mathbf{x}_{j(rk)})$ (12) if and only if the j-th dual hyperplane h_j (2) passes (5) through the supporting vertex $\mathbf{w}_k$ (9) of the rank r_k ($\mathbf{w}_k^T\mathbf{x}_j = 1$).

The proofs of the above *Lemma 1* and the *Theorem 1* can be found in the paper [7].

4   Collinearity Criterion Function

The *collinearity penalty functions* $\varphi_j(\mathbf{w})$ are defined by each feature vectors $\mathbf{x}_j$ from the data set C (1) in the below manner [8]:

$$(\forall \mathbf{x}_j \in C) \, \varphi_j(\mathbf{w}) = \left|1 - \mathbf{x}_j^T\mathbf{w}\right| = \begin{array}{l} 1 - \mathbf{x}_j^T\mathbf{w} \;\; if \;\; \mathbf{x}_j^T\mathbf{w} \leq 1 \\ \mathbf{x}_j^T\mathbf{w} - 1 \;\; if \;\; \mathbf{x}_j^T\mathbf{w} > 1 \end{array} \tag{14}$$

Each of n unit vectors $\mathbf{e}_i$ defines the *regularizing function* $\varphi_i^0(\mathbf{w})$ in the n-dimensional parameter space R^n ($\mathbf{w} = [w_1,..., w_n] \in R^n$):

$$(\forall i \in \{1, \ldots, n\}) \, \varphi_i^0(\mathbf{w}) = \left|\mathbf{e}_i^T\mathbf{w}\right| = |w_i| = \begin{array}{l} -w_i \;\; if \;\; w_i \leq 0 \\ w_i \;\; if \;\; w_i > 0 \end{array} \tag{15}$$

The collinearity penalty functions $\varphi_j^1(\mathbf{w})$ (14) are linked to the hyperplanes h_j (2). Similarly, the regularizing functions $\varphi_i^0(\mathbf{w})$ (15) are linked to the hyperplanes h_i^0 (3). Both the collinearity penalty functions $\varphi_i^1(\mathbf{w})$ (14) and the regularizing functions $\varphi_i^0(\mathbf{w})$ (15) are convex and piecewise linear (*CPL*).

The regularized criterion function $\Psi_{k,\lambda}(\mathbf{w})$ is defined on elements $\mathbf{x}_j$ of the k-th data subset C_k ($C_k \subset C$ (1)) as the sum of the penalty functions $\varphi_j(\mathbf{w})$ (14) and the regularizing functions $\varphi_i^0(\mathbf{w})$ (15):

$$\Psi_{k,\lambda}(\mathbf{w}) = \sum_{j \in Jk} \varphi_j(\mathbf{w}) + \lambda \sum_{i=1,\ldots,n} \gamma_i |w_i| \qquad (16)$$

where $J_k = \{j : \mathbf{x}_j \in C_k \subset C \,(1)\}$, λ is the *regularizing parameter* ($\lambda \geq 0$), and γ_i is the cost parameter of the i-th feature X_i ($\gamma_i \geq 0$). The standard values of the cost parameters γ_i are equal to one ($\gamma_i = 1$).

It can be proved that the minimal value $\Psi_{k,\lambda}(\mathbf{w}_{k,\lambda}^*)$ of the convex and piecewise linear criterion function $\Psi_{k,\lambda}(\mathbf{w})$ (18) can be found in one of the vertices $\mathbf{w}_k$ (9):

$$(\forall \lambda \geq 0)\,(\exists \mathbf{w}_{k,\lambda}^*)\,(\forall \mathbf{w})\,\Psi_{k,\lambda}(\mathbf{w}) \geq \Psi_{k,\lambda}(\mathbf{w}_{k,\lambda}^*) \geq 0 \qquad (17)$$

This propertycan be proved by using the *fundamental theorem of linear programming* [9].

The *optimal vertex* $\mathbf{w}_{k,\lambda}^*$ constitutes the minimal value $\Psi_{k,\lambda}(\mathbf{w}_{k,\lambda}^*)$ (17) of the *CPL* criterion function $\Psi_{k,\lambda}(\mathbf{w})$ (16). The basis exchange algorithm allows to find efficiently and precisely the minimal value $\Psi_{k,\lambda}(\mathbf{w}_{k,\lambda}^*)$ (19) of the regularized criterion functions $\Psi_{k,\lambda}(\mathbf{w})$ (19) and the optimal vertex $\mathbf{w}_{k,\lambda}^*$ (9) even in the case of large, multidimensional data subsets C_k [10].

Theorem 2: The minimal value $\Psi_{k,0}(\mathbf{w}_{k,0}^*)$ (17) of the regularized criterion function $\Psi_{k,\lambda}(\mathbf{w})$ (16) with $\lambda = 0$ is equal to zero ($\Psi_{k,0}(\mathbf{w}_{k,0}^*) = 0$) if and only if all the feature vectors $\mathbf{x}_j$ from the subset C_k can be located on some hyperplane $H(\mathbf{w}, \theta)$ (10) with $\theta \neq 0$.

The proof of a similar theorem is given in the paper [8].

5   Collinear Biclusters

The optimal vertex $\mathbf{w}_{k,\lambda}^*$ (17) constitutes the minimal value $\Psi_{k,\lambda}(\mathbf{w}_{k,\lambda}^*)$ of the regularized criterion function $\Psi_{k,\lambda}(\mathbf{w})$ (17) which is defined on the elements $\mathbf{x}_j$ of the k-th data subset C_k ($C_k \subset C$ (1)) and can influenced by the regularizing parameter λ.

In accordance with the *Definition* 1, the rank r_k of the optimal vertex $\mathbf{w}_{k,\lambda}^*$ (17) is equal to the number of the non-zero components ($w_{k,i}^* \neq 0$) of the vector $\mathbf{w}_{k,\lambda}^*$ (9). The standard basis $\mathbf{B}_k^*$ (8) linked to the optimal vertex $\mathbf{w}_k^*$ (17) of the rank r_k is composed of r_k feature vectors $\mathbf{x}_{j(i)}$ ($j(i) \in J_k$) from the k-th data subset C_k (1) and $n - r_k$ unit vectors $\mathbf{e}_i$ ($i \in I_k$).

Remark 2: The rank r_k $(r_k > 0)$ of the optimal vertex $\mathbf{w}^*_{k,\lambda}$ (17) can be decreased through increasing the regularizing parameter λ $(\lambda \geq 0)$ in the criterion function $\Psi_{k,\lambda}(\mathbf{w})$ (17).

Increasing the regularizing parameter λ $(\lambda \geq 0)$ in the function $\Psi_{k,\lambda}(\mathbf{w})$ (16) may cause the increasing of the number $n - r_k$ of the unit vectors $\mathbf{e}_i$ $(i \in I_k)$ in the standard basis $\mathbf{B}^*_{k,\lambda}$ (8) linked to the optimal vertex $\mathbf{w}^*_{k,\lambda}$ (20). The presence of the unit vector $\mathbf{e}_i$ $(i \in I_k)$ in the optimal basis $\mathbf{B}^*_{k,\lambda}$ (8) means that the i-th component $\mathbf{w}^*_{k,i}$ of the optimal weight vector $\mathbf{w}^*_{k,\lambda} = [\mathbf{w}^*_{k,1}, \ldots, \mathbf{w}^*_{k,n}]^T$ (17) is equal to zero $(\mathbf{w}^*_{k,i} = 0)$.

Remark 3: Features X_i linked to the weights $\mathbf{w}^*_{k,i}$ equal to zero $(\mathbf{w}^*_{k,i} = 0)$ in the optimal vertex $\mathbf{w}^*_{k,\lambda}$ (17) are removed from the feature set $F[n] = \{X_1, \ldots, X_n\}$ [13].

The *relaxed linear separability* (RLS) method of feature subset selection has been based on the above feature reduction rule [14]. Vertexical subset of features $F_{k,\lambda}[r_k]$ $(F_{k,\lambda}[r_k] \subset F[n] = \{X_1, \ldots, X_n\})$ and the feature subspace $\mathbf{F}_{k,\lambda}[r_k]$ $(\mathbf{F}_{k,\lambda}[r_k] \subset \mathbf{F}[n])$ are defined on the basis of the k-th optimal vertex $\mathbf{w}^*_{k,\lambda}$ (20) of the rank r_k [12].

The k-th *vertexical subset of features* $F_k[r_k]$ $(F_k[r_k] \subset F[n])$ is obtained from the initial set of features $F[n] = \{X_1, \ldots, X_n\}$ by reducing such $n - r_k$ features X_i which are linked to the weights $\mathbf{w}^*_{k,i}$ equal to zero $(\mathbf{w}^*_{k,i} = 0)$, where $\mathbf{w}^*_{k,i}$ is the i-th component of the k-th optimal vertex $\mathbf{w}^*_{k,\lambda} = [\mathbf{w}^*_{k,1}, \ldots, \mathbf{w}^*_{k,n}]^T$ (17):

$$(\forall i \in \{1, \ldots, n\}) \text{ } \textit{if } w_{k,i} = 0, \text{ } \textbf{then} \text{ the } i \text{ - th feature } X_i \text{ is } \textit{removed}$$
$$\text{from the feature set } F[n] \tag{18}$$

Definition 4: The k-th *vertexical feature subset* $F_k[r_k]$ $(F_k[r_k] \subset F[n])$ is composed of such r_k features X_i which are linked to the non-zero weights $\mathbf{w}^*_{k,i}\left(\mathbf{w}^*_{k,i} \neq 0\right)$ in the optimal vertex $\mathbf{w}^*_{k,\lambda}$ (17).

We can remark again that the unit vector $\mathbf{e}_i$ in the basis $\mathbf{B}^*_k$ (8) linked to the optimal vector $\mathbf{w}^*_{k,\lambda} = [\mathbf{w}^*_{k,1}, \ldots, \mathbf{w}^*_{k,n}]^T$ (20) causes the i-th weight $\mathbf{w}^*_{k,i}$ equal to zero $\left(\mathbf{w}^*_{k,i} = 0\right)$ and the reduction of the i-th feature X_i from the initial feature set $F[n]$ in accordance with the rule (18).

Definition 5: The *reduced vectors* $\mathbf{y}_j = [y_{j,1}, \ldots, y_{j,rk}]^T$ $(\mathbf{y}_j \in \mathbf{F}_k[r_k])$ are obtained from the feature vectors $\mathbf{x}_j = [x_{j,1}, \ldots, x_{j,n}]^T$ $(\mathbf{x}_j \in C_k \subset C$ (1)$)$ through reducing (21) such $n - r_k$ components $x_{j,i}$ which are linked to the unit vectors $\mathbf{e}_i$ in the basis $\mathbf{B}_k$ (8) and by a new indexing i of the remaining r_k components $y_{j,i}$ $(i = 1, \ldots, r_k)$. Similarly, the *reduced weight vector* $\mathbf{v}^*_{k,\lambda} = [v^*_{k,1}, \ldots, v^*_{k,rk}]^T$ is obtained from the k-th optimal vertex $\mathbf{w}^*_{k,\lambda} = [\mathbf{w}^*_{k,1}, \ldots, \mathbf{w}^*_{k,n}]^T$ (17) of the rank r_k by reducing such $n - r_k$ components $\mathbf{w}^*_{k,i}$, which are equal to zero $\left(\mathbf{w}^*_{k,i} = 0\right)$.

Definition 6: The k-th *collinear bicluster* $\mathbf{B}_k(m_k, r_k)$ based on the degenerated optimal vertex $\mathbf{w}_{k,\lambda}^*$ (20) of the rank r_k is defined as the set of such m_k ($m_k > r_k$) reduced feature vectors $\mathbf{y}_j$ ($\mathbf{y}_j \in \mathbf{F}_k[r_k]$), which fulfill the equation $(\mathbf{v}_{k,\lambda}^*)^T \mathbf{y}_j = 1$:

$$B_k(m_k, r_k) = \{\mathbf{y}_j : (\mathbf{v}_{k,\lambda}^*)^T \mathbf{y}_j = 1\} \tag{19}$$

The k-th collinear (*flat*) bicluster $B_k(m_k, r_k)$ (19) based on the degenerated vertex $\mathbf{w}_{k,\lambda}^*$ (17) is characterized by the two numbers r_k and m_k, where r_k is the number of features X_i in the vertexical feature subspace $\mathbf{F}_k[r_k]$ ($\mathbf{F}_k[r_k] \subset \mathbf{F}[n]$) (19), and m_k is the number of such feature vectors $\mathbf{x}_j$ ($\mathbf{x}_j \in \mathbf{F}[n]$) which define the dual hyperplanes h_j (2) passing through this vertex ($(\mathbf{w}_{k,\lambda}^*)^T \mathbf{x}_j = 1$) .

Remark 4: The collinear bicluster $\mathbf{B}_k(m_k, r_k)$ (19) based on the k-th vertex $\mathbf{v}_k$ is a set of such m_k reduced vectors $\mathbf{y}_j$ ($\mathbf{y}_j \in \mathbf{F}_k[r_k]$) which are located on the hyperplane $H(\mathbf{v}_k,$ 1) $= \{\mathbf{y}: \mathbf{v}_k^T \mathbf{y} = 1\}$ in the k-th vertexical feature subspace $\mathbf{F}_k[r_k]$ (*Definition 5*). If the basis $\mathbf{B}_k$ (8) linked to the supporting vertex $\mathbf{v}_k$ of the rank r_k is standard (*Definition 2*), then the all r_k components $v_{k,i}$ of the reduced weight vector $\mathbf{v}_k = [v_{k,1},...,v_{k,rk}]^T$ are different from zero ($\forall i \in \{1,...., r_k\}$ $v_{k,i} \neq 0$).

One can also notice that each of the m_k feature vectors $\mathbf{x}_j = [x_{j,1},...,x_{j,n}]^T$ located on the vertexical plane $P_k(\mathbf{x}_{j(1)},..., \mathbf{x}_{j(rk)})$ (14) is also represented in the collinear bicluster $\mathbf{B}_k(m_k, r_k)$ (22) as the reduced vector $\mathbf{y}_j = [y_{j,1},...,v_{j,rk}]^T$ and vice versa [7]:

$$(\forall j \in \{1,...,m\})\,(\mathbf{x}_j \in P_k(\mathbf{x}_{j(1)},..., \mathbf{x}_{j(rk)})\,(12)) \Leftrightarrow (\mathbf{y}_j \in B_k(m_k, r_k)\,(19)) \tag{20}$$

6   Linear Models of Multiple Interactions

Feature vectors $\mathbf{x}_j = [x_{j,1},...,x_{j,n}]^T$ ($\mathbf{x}_j \in C_k \subset C$ (1)) located on the vertexical plane $P_k(\mathbf{x}_{j(1)},..., \mathbf{x}_{j(rk)})$ (14) can be represented as the linear combination of the r_k ($r_k > 1$) supporting vectors $\mathbf{x}_{j(i)}$ from the basis $\mathbf{B}_k$ ($j(i) \in J_k$) (4) [8]:

$$(\forall j \in \{1,...,m\})\,(\mathbf{x}_j \in P_k(\mathbf{x}_{j(1)},..., \mathbf{x}_{j(rk)})\,(12)) \Leftrightarrow (\mathbf{x}_j = \alpha_{j,1}\mathbf{x}_{j(1)} + ... + \alpha_{j,rk}\mathbf{x}_{j(rk)})$$
$$\tag{21}$$

where

$$(\forall j \in \{1,...,m\})\,(\forall i \in \{1,...,r_k\})\alpha_{j,i} \in R^1, \text{ and } \alpha_{j,1} + ... + \alpha_{j,rk} = 1 \tag{22}$$

Definition 7: The data subset C_k ($C_k \subset C$ (1)) of a large number m_k of the feature vectors $\mathbf{x}_j$ ($\mathbf{x}_j \in C_k$) is the *flat pattern* if and only if and only if each element of this subset is located on the vertexical plane $P_k(\mathbf{x}_{j(1)},..., \mathbf{x}_{j(rk)})$ (12) defined by the k-th supporting vertex $\mathbf{w}_k$ (9) of the rank r_k ($m_k \geq \geq r_k$).

Remark 5: Each of the m_k feature vectors $\mathbf{x}_j$ belonging to the flat pattern C_k is represented in the collinear bicluster $B_k(m_k, r_k)$ (22) as the reduced vector $\mathbf{y}_j$ (*Definition 5*), and vice versa.

Let us assume that a large number m_k ($m_k \geq \geq r_k$) of the feature vectors $\mathbf{x}_j$ ($j \in J_k(m_k, r_k)$) is located on the vertexical plane $P_k(\mathbf{x}_{j(1)},..., \mathbf{x}_{j(rk)})$ (14) supported by the optimal vertex $\mathbf{w}_k$ (19) of the rank r_k. In accordance with the *Theorem 1*, such feature vectors $\mathbf{x}_j$ which are located on the plane $P_k(\mathbf{x}_{j(1)},..., \mathbf{x}_{j(rk)})$ (14) fulfil the equations:

$$(\forall j \in J_k(m_k, r_k))\mathbf{w}_k^T\mathbf{x}_j = \mathbf{v}_k^T\mathbf{y}_j = 1 \tag{23}$$

where $J_k(m_k, r_k)$ is the set of indices j of such m_k hyperplanes h_j (2) which pass through the vertex $\mathbf{w}_k$, $\mathbf{y}_j = [y_{j,1},...,y_{j,rk}]^T$ ($\mathbf{y}_j \in F_k[r_k]$) are the reduced feature vectors (*Definition 5*), and $\mathbf{v}_k = [v_{k,1},...,v_{k,rk}]^T$ is the reduced weight vector with the all r_k components $v_{k,i}$ different from zero ($v_{k,i} \neq 0$).

Remark 6: The Eq. (27) describes the linear dependence between such r_k components $x_{j,i}$ of m_k feature vectors $\mathbf{x}_j = [x_{j,1},...,x_{j,n}]^T$ ($j \in J_k(m_k, r_k)$) which are linked to the r_k weights $w_{k,i}$ different from zero in the k-th vertex $\mathbf{w}_k = [w_{k,1},...,w_{k,n}]^T$ (9).

The linear dependence (27) between r_k components $x_{j,i}$ of the feature vectors $\mathbf{x}_j$ ($j \in J_k(m_k, r_k)$) reflects such linear dependence between corresponding r_k features X_i ($i \in I_k(m_k, r_k)$), where

$$I_k(m_k, r_k)) = \{i\colon w_{k,i} \neq 0\} \tag{24}$$

The dependence (28) between r_k features $X_{i(l)}$ ($i(l) \in I_k(m_k, r_k)$) can be represented in the form of the below linear model with the r_k different from zero coefficients α_i:

$$\alpha_1 X_{i(1)} + \ldots + \alpha_{rk} X_{i(rk)} = 1 \tag{25}$$

where ($\forall i \in \{1,....,r_k\}$) $\alpha_i = v_{k,i} \neq 0$, and $v_{k,i}$ is is the i-th component ($v_{k,i} \neq 0$) of the the reduced weight vector $\mathbf{v}_k = [v_{k,1},...,v_{k,rk}]^T$ in the optimal vertex $\mathbf{w}_{k,\lambda}^*$ ($\mathbf{v}_k = \mathbf{w}_{k,\lambda}^*$ (20)).

The Eq. (25) can be treated as the *local model* of *multiple linear interactions* between the r_k selected features $X_{i(l)}$ ($i(l) \in I_k(m_k, r_k)$ (23)). The model (29) is *local* because the linear dependence between the r_k components $x_{j,i}$ is fulfilled exactly only for the m_k selected feature vectors $\mathbf{x}_j$ ($j \in J_k(m_k, r_k)$ (23)). The m_k selected feature vectors $\mathbf{x}_j$ ($j \in J_k(m_k, r_k)$ (23)) and the r_k selected features $X_{i(l)}$ ($i(l) \in I_k(m_k, r_k)$ (24)) define the collinear bicluster $B_k(m_k, r_k)$ (19).

7 Designing Models of Interaction

It follows from *Theorem* 2 that the minimal value $\Psi_{k,0}\left(\mathbf{w}^*_{k,0}\right)$ (17) of the *CPL* criterion function $\Psi_{k,0}(\mathbf{w}_{k,0})$ (16) is equal to zero if and only if all m_k feature vectors $\mathbf{x}_j$ from the k-th data subset C_k ($C_k \subset C$ (1)) are located on the hyperplane $H(\mathbf{w}^*_{k,0}, 1)$ (11) which is defined by the optimal vertex $\mathbf{w}^*_{k,0}$ of the rank r_k. The optimal vertex $\mathbf{w}^*_{k,0}$ (17) is *highly degenerate* if the number m_k of feature vectors $\mathbf{x}_j$ (hyperplanes h_j (2)) in this vertex is much greater than his rank r_k ($m_k \geq \geq r_k$). An extraction of a highly degenerate vertex $\mathbf{w}^*_{k,0}$ (20) allows to define local model of interaction (25). In result, the extracting linear models of interaction (25) can be carried out through the minimization of the regularized criterion functions $\Psi_{k,\lambda}(\mathbf{w})$ (16).

The k-th *CPL* criterion function $\Psi_{k,0}(\mathbf{w}_{k,0})$ (16) is defined on elements $\mathbf{x}_j$ of the k-th data subset C_k ($C_k \subset C$ (1)). Feature vectors $\mathbf{x}_j$ constituting the given data subset C_k may be located on not only one vertexical plane $P_k(\mathbf{x}_{j(1)},\dots, \mathbf{x}_{j(rk)})$ (14). This case is described in the below example (Fig. 1).

Example 1: The k-th *collinear pattern* appears when the number m_k of the dual hyperplanes h_j (2) passing through the vertex $\mathbf{w}_k$ is greater than his rank r_k ($m_k \geq \geq r_k$). Three collinear (*flat*) patterns in the two-dimensional feature space R^2 ($\mathbf{x}_j \in R^2$) are shown in the Fig. 1 (*left*). The flat paterns are composed here from $m_1 = 4$, $m_2 = 6$, and $m_3 = 5$ elements $\mathbf{x}_j = [x_{j,1}, x_{j,2}]^T$, adequately. These collinear patterns are represented in the parameter space by the three degenerated vertices of the rank r_k equal to 2 (*right*).

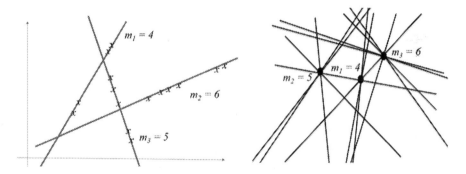

Fig. 1. An example of the three collinear patterns in the two-dimensional feature space (*left*) and in the parameter space (*right*). The degree of degeneration $d_k = m_k - r_k$ ($k = 1, 2, 3$) of the vertices $\mathbf{w}_1$, $\mathbf{w}_2$ and $\mathbf{w}_3$ (9) are equal to $d_1 = 2$, $d_2 = 2$, and $d_3 = 4$ (*Definition 4*).

The Eq. (25) represents deterministic model of interactions between the r_k selected features $X_{i(l)}$ ($i(l) \in I_k(m_k, r_k)$ (24)). This model has a *local character* because it was based not on all the feature vectors $\mathbf{x}_j$ from the global data set C (1) but only on elements $\mathbf{x}_j$ of the k - th subset C_k. Each of the data subset C_k and each of the three collinear patterns on the Fig. 1 has its own interaction model (25). In this case, particular linear models (25) differ only by the coefficients $v_{k,i}$. In a more general case of the multidimensional data sets, particular linear models (25) may differ also by subsets of selected features $X_{i(l)}$ ($i(l) \in I_k(m_k, r_k)$ (24)).

Minimizing the criterion functions $\Psi_{k,\lambda}(\mathbf{w})$ (16) gives possibility to extract many collinear patterns of different ranks r_k from the data set C (1). The regularized criterion function $\Psi_{k,\lambda}(\mathbf{w})$ (16) is defined on elements $\mathbf{x}_j$ of the k-th data subset C_k ($C_k \subset C$). The following *property of monotonicity* holds for the function $\Psi_{k,\lambda}(\mathbf{w})$ (16) [8].

$$(C_k \subset C_{k'}) \Rightarrow \Psi_{k,\lambda}(\mathbf{w}_{k,\lambda}^*) \leq \Psi_{k',\lambda}(\mathbf{w}_{k',\lambda}^*) \tag{26}$$

where $\Psi_{k,\lambda}\left(\mathbf{w}_{k',\lambda}^*\right)$ is the minimal value $\Psi_{k',\lambda}\left(\mathbf{w}_{k',\lambda}^*\right)$ (17) of the *CPL* criterion function $\Psi_{k',\lambda}(\mathbf{w})$ (16) which is defined on elements $\mathbf{x}_j$ of the k-th data subset $C_{k'}$.

In accordance with the implication (26) reducing the supporting data subset $C_{k'}$ $C_{k'} \subset C$ (1)) may lead to decreasing of the the minimal value $\Psi_{k,\lambda}\left(\mathbf{w}_{k',\lambda}^*\right)$ (17).

The minimal value $\Psi_{k,\lambda}\left(\mathbf{w}_{k',\lambda}^*\right)$ (17) of the convex and piecewise linear (*CPL*) criterion function $\Psi_{k,\lambda}(\mathbf{w})$ (16) can be found in one of the vertices $\mathbf{w}_k$ (9) ($\mathbf{w}_{k,\lambda}^* = \mathbf{w}_k$). The basis exchange algorithm allows to find efficiently and precisely the minimal value $\Psi_{k,\lambda}\left(\mathbf{w}_{k',\lambda}^*\right)$ (17) of the regularized criterion functions $\Psi_{k,\lambda}(\mathbf{w})$ (16) and the optimal vertex $\mathbf{w}_{k',\lambda}^*$ (9) [8].

Remark 7: The minimal value $\Psi_{k,0}\left(\mathbf{w}_{k,0}^*\right)$ (17) of the criterion function $\Psi_{k,\lambda}(\mathbf{w})$ (16) with $\lambda = 0$ is equal to zero ($\Psi_{k,0}\left(\mathbf{w}_{k,0}^*\right) = 0$) if the supporting data subset C_k ($C_k \subset C$ (1)) is the flat pattern (*Definition* 7).

The statement is based on the *Theorem* 2. It can be proved also that the minimal value $\Psi_{k,0}\left(\mathbf{w}_{k,0}^*\right)$ (17) of the criterion function $\Psi_{k,\lambda}(\mathbf{w})$ (16) defined on elements $\mathbf{x}_j$ of the flat pattern C_k is equal zero if the regularizing parameter λ is small enough ($0 \leq \lambda < \lambda_k$), where λ_k is a certain border value.

Remark 8: If a noisy data subset C_k contains the flat pattern (*Definition* 7) with some noise, then the minimization of the regularized criterion functions $\Psi_{k,\lambda}(\mathbf{w})$ (16) gives possibility to extract this pattern from this data subset (1).

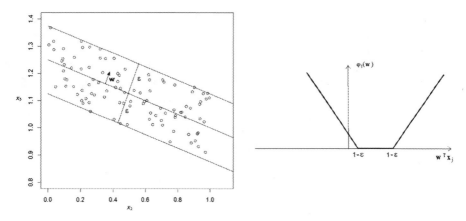

Fig. 2. The penalty function $\varphi_j^\varepsilon(\mathbf{w})$ (27) (*right*) and the ε - layer $\boldsymbol{L}^\varepsilon(\mathbf{w})$ (27) (*left*) [11].

Modifications of the collinearity penalty functions $\varphi_j(\mathbf{w})$ (14) may allow for further increase of the possibility of flat patterns extraction from data sets C with some disruptions. The following penalty functions $\varphi_j^\varepsilon(\mathbf{w})$ with the margin ε ($\varepsilon \geq 0$) were introduced for this purpose [11] (Fig. 2):

$$(\forall \mathbf{x}_j \in C) \; \varphi_j^\varepsilon(\mathbf{w}) = \begin{array}{ll} 1 - \varepsilon - \mathbf{w}^T\mathbf{x}_j & \textit{if } \mathbf{w}^T\mathbf{x}_j < 1 - \varepsilon \\ 0 & \textit{if } 1 - \varepsilon \leq \mathbf{w}^T\mathbf{x}_j \leq 1 + \varepsilon \\ \mathbf{w}^T\mathbf{x}_j - 1 + \varepsilon & \textit{if } \mathbf{w}^T\mathbf{x}_j > 1 + \varepsilon \end{array} \qquad (27)$$

The penalty functions $\varphi_j^\varepsilon(\mathbf{w})$ with the margin ε ($\varepsilon \geq 0$) allow to locate feature vectors $\mathbf{x}_j$ ($\mathbf{x}_j \in C$ (1)) in the below ε - *layers* $\boldsymbol{L}^\varepsilon(\mathbf{w}_k)$ in the feature space $\mathbf{F}[n]$ ($\mathbf{x} \in \mathbf{F}[n]$):

$$L^\varepsilon(\mathbf{w}_k) = \{\mathbf{x} : 1 - \varepsilon \leq \mathbf{w}_k^T\mathbf{x} \leq 1 + \varepsilon\} \qquad (28)$$

The ε - layers $\boldsymbol{L}^\varepsilon(\mathbf{w}_k)$ (31) allow to generalize the local model (25) of multiple linear interactions. The Eq. (25) is approximately met for all feature vectors $\mathbf{x}_j$ ($\mathbf{x}_j \in C$ (1)) belonging to the ε - layers $\boldsymbol{L}^\varepsilon(\mathbf{w}_k)$ (28) Data sets C (1) used in practice may contain many collinear patterns. A simple case of this type is shown in Fig. 1. The problem of extraction of more than one collinear patterns from a given data set C (1) could be a more complicated. This problem can be solved through extractions and removal of single flat patterns in successive stages.

8   Concluding Remarks

The local model (25) of multiple linear interactions has been formulated and analyzed in the presented paper. The interaction model (25) has the form of a linear combination of the selected features X_i.

A set of selected features X_i as well as the coefficients $v_{k,i}$ to the linear combination (25) are estimated on the basis of the data subset C_k ($C_k \subset C$ (1)) which is composed from multidimensional feature vectors $\mathbf{x}_j$.

The proposed approach to the problem of extraction of multiple interactions has been based on finding higly degenerated vertices $\mathbf{w}_k$ (9) in the parameter space. The basic role in the search for interaction models (25) is played by the collinear biclusters $B_k(m_k, r_k)$ (19). The k-th collinear bicluster $B_k(m_k, r_k)$ (19) is supported by a highly degenerated k-th vertex $\mathbf{w}_k$ (17). The search for highly degenerated verticex $\mathbf{w}_k$ (17) can based on the minimization of the regularized criterion functions $\Psi_{k,\lambda}(\mathbf{w})$ (16). The basis exchange algorithm which is based on the Gauss-Jordan transformation allows to find efficiently and precisely the optimal vertex $\left(\mathbf{w}^*_{k/,\lambda}\right)$ (9) constituting the minimal value $\Psi_{k,\lambda}\left(\mathbf{w}^*_{k/,\lambda}\right)$ (17) of the regularized criterion functions $\Psi_{k,\lambda}(\mathbf{w})$ (16).

Acknowledgments. The presented study was supported by the grant S/WI/2/2019 from Bialystok University of Technology and funded from the resources for research by Polish Ministry of Science and Higher Education.

References

1. Hand, D., Smyth, P., Mannila, H.: Principles of data mining. MIT Press, Cambridge (2001)
2. Duda, O.R., Hart, P.E., Stork, D.G.: Pattern classification. J. Wiley, New York (2001)
3. Bishop, C.M.: Pattern Recognition and Machine Learning. Springer, New York (2006)
4. Madeira, S.C., Oliveira, S.L.: Biclustering algorithms for biological data analysis: a survey. IEEE Trans. Comput. Biol. Bioinform. **1**(1), 24–45 (2004)
5. Pontes, B., Giraldez, R., Aguilar-Ruiz, J.S.: Biclustering on expression data: A review. J. Biomed. Inform. **57**, 163–180 (2015)
6. Bobrowski, L.: Biclustering based on collinear patterns. In: Rojas, I., Ortuño, F. (eds.) IWBBIO 2017. LNCS, vol. 10208, pp. 134–144. Springer, Cham (2017). https://doi.org/10. 1007/978-3-319-56148-6_11
7. Bobrowski, L.: Discovering main vertexical planes in a multivariate data space by using CPL functions. In: Perner, P. (ed.) ICDM 2014. LNCS (LNAI), vol. 8557, pp. 200–213. Springer, Cham (2014). https://doi.org/10.1007/978-3-319-08976-8_15
8. Bobrowski, L.: Data Exploration and Linear Separability, pp. 1–172. Lambert Academic Publishing (2019)
9. Simonnard, M.: Linear Programming. Prentice – Hall, Englewood Cliffs, New York (1966)
10. Bobrowski, L., Zabielski, P.: Models of multiple interactions from collinear patterns. In: Rojas, I., Ortuño, F. (eds.) IWBBIO 2018. LNCS, vol. 10813, pp. 153–165. Springer, Cham (2018). https://doi.org/10.1007/978-3-319-78723-7_13
11. Bobrowski, L., Zabielski P.: Flat patterns extraction with collinearity models. In: 9th *EUROSIM* Congress on Modelling and Simulation, *EUROSIM* 2016, IEEE Conference Publishing Services (CPS), pp. 518–524. Linköping University Electronic Press, Linköping (2018)
12. Bobrowski, L., Łukaszuk, T.: Relaxed Linear Separability (*RLS*) approach to feature (Gene) subset selection. In: Xia, X (ed.) Selected Works in Bioinformatics, *INTECH*, pp. 103–118 (2011)

Two Phase Failure Detection
Using Fuzzy Logic

David Sec$^{(\boxtimes)}$ and Peter Mikulecky

Faculty of Informatics and Management,
University of Hradec Kralove, Hradec Kralove, Czech Republic
david.sec@uhk.cz

Abstract. Control systems certainly deserve increased attention, as they can be found in many industrial environments, they are exploitable for military purposes, in transportation, and in many other areas. In this paper we propose the implementation of a control system for sensor failures detection using fuzzy logic approach for data analysis. We divide the system into two separate subsystems to ensure better suitability and adaptation to specific sensor data. One of these subsystems will be implemented exactly in the nodes which collect data from sensors. The second one will be implemented on the (cloud) server where all the signals are collected. The system implemented on the nodes will ensure that all the data are in the correct range of the monitored sensor and it could initiate the measurement repeatedly when the first measurement failed or its value is corrupted. This phase is able to check all the values in real time, therefore it can be considered as the main method for identification of major problems in the system. In the server part, all the collected values will be analyzed in order to identify other failures like gradual variation of sensor data due to polluted sensor parts, an others. The outcomes identified by this method could be removed or marked as the value that is not corresponding to the real world situation. These data can be ignored by the control system or can be used in some less critical application later on. The proposed system could be of importance in any control or manufacturing process were any redundant sensors and collected data directly affect parameters of the process.

Keywords: Failure detection · Sensor failure · Fourier transform · Control systems · Residuals

1 Introduction

In accord with a popular definition, a control system is a device, or set of devices, that manages, commands, directs or regulates the behavior of other devices or systems. Various types of control systems are used in industrial production, in military, transportation, and in many other branches of real life. Control systems monitor measured environment or manufacturing processes and provide a desired system response using connected actuators which could change the process or environment variables.

© Springer Nature Switzerland AG 2019
N. T. Nguyen et al. (Eds.): ICCCI 2019, LNAI 11683, pp. 271–282, 2019.
https://doi.org/10.1007/978-3-030-28377-3_22

Sensors are the most important part of each control system. Every control system is dependent on the data which are produced by the sensors.

However, sometimes sensors could not reflect correctly the data corresponding with the measured environment. This can be caused for example by sensor aging or pollution, zero shift, electromagnetic interference's in wiring, network disturbance, and so on. According to [5], control systems become more sophisticated from year to year, and any sensor failure can degrade the system's performance and it can possibly lead to total system failure. Such a system failure can be the source of instabilities and cause of financial loss, injures or human casualties, and moreover, they could lead to potentially dangerous situations. In this paper we introduce new methods for detecting these situations and for preventing their appearance.

Failure detection is the main task for identifying these defected data and for excluding them from any further processing. A traditional solution here relies on using many sensors measuring the same value and comparing these values using voting or neighborhoods like method [8] or [2]. In the case of a failure, there is always at least one backup sensor which could be used for sensing actual conditions. In the case of a number of different outcomes, the right value could be obtained by voting. Although this method looks like a best solution, it is the most expensive from any others mentioned in this article. Another very popular method is using of a reference model or Neural Networks (NN) in the process of data learning in order to simulate manufacturing process and comparing the actual data with these obtainable from the model [2,7]. The main weakness of this solution is in model classification process, which usually needs a thousands of process cycles needed for the process understanding and providing its faithful simulation. The main principle of fault detection system is based on the development of a reference model which represents standard operating process signature. To identify system failure there are typically measured deviations from this model and the alert is executed when any variable exceeds the selected threshold. According to [9], every failure detection system can be designed as consisting of two steps: building a process model and choosing metrics for testing its faults.

This article provides design and implementation of a failure detection system divided into two separate parts (or phases). Each phase has different function and is located in the different part of the proposed system.

In the first part of the proposed control system we implement the layer for identification of those values that are definitely corrupted. These can be values, which are out of measured sensor range due to sensor shortcut, wires cut-off or a number of other reasons. The system disposes these corrupted values and tries to initialize new measurements. If this failed too, the system will notice user about the sensor failure and avoids sending of another data. The values which meet condition in this phase will be sent to the server and processed using another methods.

In the second part of the control system, particular statistical methods for checking collected data and comparing them with historical data in same context, will be implemented. The result will be represented with probability of possible sensor failure from zero to one. In the experimental section we shall present some examples of data from a home autonomous system with several failures detected.

Recently, various papers to this topic have been published, for instance [5, 6, 9–11]. These will be briefly introduced below.

2 Related Works

A network based failure detection filter, which reduces network delays and packet dropouts in sampler-to-control systems, has been introduced in [11]. This filter has been used for ensuring sensitivity of residual signals to external disturbances faults in Unmanned Surface Vehicles (USV).

An alternative approach to data filtering can be found in [10]. This paper focuses on the design of a reliable filter ensuring the mixed passivity and *H-infinity* performance level of the resulting filtering error system in the presence of sensor failures.

The article [9] focuses on industrial environment and deals with process monitoring industrial systems and perspectives in design of process monitoring systems. Authors briefly described all trends in process monitoring and identification techniques in past twenty years, and offers opportunities and new challenges for future research.

A solution in the form of a two-dimensional detection algorithm for sensor-based fault detection and isolation schemes in industrial environment was proposed in [6]. In this article a control system is monitored in its common state, and machine learning together with data mining techniques were used for failures and variations in environmental process detection, as well as for comparison with reference model in order to assess the degree of correlation. In the last part of this article this interesting solution was demonstrated on a control system of burners in industrial gas turbines. Here multiple correlated data sets have been used for identification of deviations between sensors. This solution also enable detection of some behavior characteristic which could not be detected by single sensor unit. A disadvantage of this solution can be seen in quite a lot of redundancy. Main advantage of it is, that gas combustion is a process which can be easily described by physical models and it is relatively easy to create and classify this model for a control system.

As the last article the paper [5] should be mentioned, focused on sensor failures detection, identification, and accommodation (SFDIA). Here a description of these methods in the safety critical systems can be found. A solution of SFDIA scheme on Aircraft systems is presented, using fully connected cascade neural network, based on [4] aircraft pitch, roll, and yaw rate sensor. For fault detection, identification and accommodation multiple redundant sensors were used. On the basis of this hardware redundancy the voting processes can be initialized in order to detect faulty sensor. In the role of a reference model a neural network based model is used, which determinate expected value and residual difference could be estimated on this basis. Some experiments based on plane simulator model have been executed as well.

Another topics related to our research focused on failure detection or sensor multiplication in automation systems can be found in [1–3,5–7,10,11].

The novelty of our approach, presented in this article, is in dividing control system into two separate parts. Each part has different effects, so our solution can ensure faster detection of main failures and repeated measurement execution. This solution may identify the most of corrupted values with minimal effect to the rest of the system and its performance. The first part of the system is implemented directly on the sensors data collection gateway, i.e. the nodes. This gateway contains only very reduced algorithms to filter main errors and faster measure initialization of a new measurement. These methods are described in further sections. Complex data analysis and dependencies detection are situated on the main server, where also data from all sensors and computing resources are stored in order to enable executing of the algorithms.

3   Methodology

Each sensor value could be affected by many different errors and may be described as follows:

$$Y(t) = V(t) + n(t) + f(t) \tag{1}$$

where Y_t is the real output from a sensor in specified time t, $V(t)$ is measured sensor data, $n(t)$ means noise which could be caused by electromagnetic interferes and $f(t)$ is the sensor failure. Each failure could be caused by many different factors and according to [1] each one could have very different properties. In the next section these failures will be described briefly.

Bias offset failure is caused by incorrect sensor calibration and it is characterized by a constant signal offset β in each measurement in the time t. The bias failure can be formalized as:

$$f(t) = X(t) + \beta(t) \tag{2}$$

Second very common type of failures is the *Drift failure*. This failure can be caused by a partial sensor degradation, temperature changes or the sensor pollution. This failure type is typical for many kinds of analog sensors.

$$f_t = X(t) + \delta(t) \tag{3}$$

where $\delta(t)$ is time varying offset.

In the *Scaling failure* some values may be scaled by a factor $\alpha(t) > 0$. This failure is mostly caused by several small diversions in the manufacturing process. For this failure it is typical that the same sensors from different manufacturing series measure different values. This values are highly correlated but the measured values are slightly different. This difference should appear within the tolerance defined by the manufacturer.

$$f_t = \alpha(t) * X(t) \tag{4}$$

Another failure type is the *hard failure*. This type of a failure is mainly caused by a wire-break, electric shortcuts or sensor stuck in a constant state (as an example water level sensors could serve). In this case the sensor output is 0 or a constant value from the sensor's range depending on the kind of sensors or used analog to digital converter.

The *hard failure analyzer* is the first part of the signal processing model figured on the Fig. 1. The main objective of this layer is to identify situations when no value from sensors could be read or the collected value is out of the sensor's range and obviously incorrect. At this time the system tries to initialize repeated measurement and will inform the user about a hard failure if this new measurement fails too.

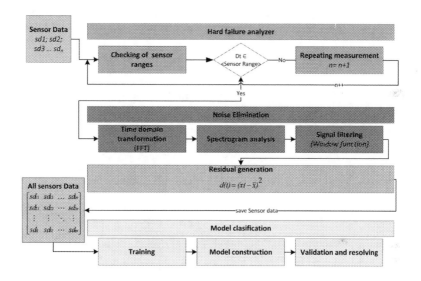

Fig. 1. Flowchart of the failure detection system topology

In this case the counter c is defined, which identifies the number of repeated measurements. When a hard failure is detected, the counter is increased by one $c = c + 1$ in every measurement cycle. When the value obtained is satisfying all the conditions, the counter is reset back to zero $c = 0$. However, when the counter reaches the threshold defined by the user, the system will notify the user about hard sensor failures and no more values could be received from this sensor until the sensor's manual inspection or replacement.

3.1 Noise Reduction Methods

The data received from sensors may contain noises of many forms, introduced in the previous section. In this section, some methods will be introduced for eliminating these errors and extracting the undesirable signal components from real signals.

The real environment variables are represented in the form of a continuous signal. By sensing, samples of this continuous signal are created. When a continuous signal is sampled by the selected frequency, the discrete signal is obtained, and each value $\forall x, y \in R$ in the sequence is then called a sample. When the discrete signal is quantizating, a digital signal is obtained where $\forall x, y \in R$ are turned into a binary digital signal. It is needed to know, that a part of the signal information will be lost after quantization. In order to maintain the signal shape it is necessary to select sampling frequency S higher than twice the desired maximum transmitted frequency f_{max} to prevent an aliasing.

$$S > 2 * f_{max} \tag{5}$$

On the other hand, there are many methods how to change discrete and digital signals back into the continuous signal by interpolation methods. This interpolated signal is similar, but not the same to the original continuous signal. The Figs. 2, 3, 4 and 5 show differences between them.

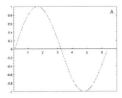

Fig. 2. Continuous signal

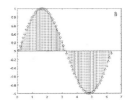

Fig. 3. Discrete signal

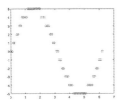

Fig. 4. Digital signal

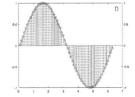

Fig. 5. Interpolated signal

Fourier transforms are methods to identify all frequency components of the signal in a time domain.

The *Fast Fourier transform (FFT)* is a form of the discrete Fourier transform algorithm of $x(t)$ which enable to convert discrete piece-wise continuous signal to a frequency domain $X(f)$ using the following definition (6). We are using FFT for the description of a frequency spectrum of the signal and for the identification of the main frequencies using their magnitudes.

$$\sum_{n=0}^{N-1} a_n e^{-2\pi i nk/N} = \sum_{n=0}^{N/2-1} a_{2n} e^{-2\pi i(2n)k/N} + \sum_{n=0}^{N/2-1} a_{2n+1} e^{-2\pi i(2n+1)k/N}$$

$$= \sum_{n=0}^{N/2-1} a_{2n}^{even} e^{-2\pi i nk/(N/2)} + e^{-2\pi i k/N} \sum_{n=0}^{N/2-1} a_n^{odd} e^{-2\pi i nk/(N/2)}$$

$$(6)$$

The first form of incorrectness in sensing is guaranteed within its absolute or relative accuracy by the manufacturer. Under the ideal conditions, if measured signal is constant, the sensors are measuring the constant signals as well. But in the case of real sensors the measured value will oscillate around this constant value due to the sensing accuracy. In the case of analog sensors these errors are often extended by the resistance of wires and electromagnetic interference. This type of noise is typical by generally higher frequencies than nominal signal, so we could successfully identify main frequencies by its magnitudes and use the filtering methods for separating of noise frequencies and the real signal.

We used the concrete Gaussian pulse filter as the signal filtering method, which enable allowing only a selected portion of the frequency spectrum and decreases other elements of the functions. The graph of the Gaussian pulse is a symmetric real function of x with parameters a, b, c.

$$f(x) = a * e^{-\frac{(x-b)^2}{2c^2}} \tag{7}$$

where a is the height of the curve's peak, b is the position of the center of the pulse and c indicates the weight of the pulse. These parameters could be selected on the base of the magnitudes of major frequencies of a signal converted into a frequency domain using the Fourier transform. As a result of this process a signal without high harmonics frequencies is obtained which could be used as the reference model for failures identification.

3.2   Residual Generation

As described earlier, in this system the real incoming data were cleaned up of undesirable signal components and these values have been used for residuals d determination for sensor failures identification. The residuals are generated by squaring the difference between the original sensor measurement and the value calculated from the reference model (8).

$$d(t) = (x_t - \bar{x})^2 \tag{8}$$

In (8), $d(t)$ is the residual at specified time t, where x is the real sensor measurement, and $\bar{x}$ is the estimated value specified by the model at time t.

Sensor failure is detected when residual $d(t)$ calculated by Eq. (8) exceeds the user defined threshold τ. This threshold should be defined with respect to the selected sensor and measured values. Ideally, the measured values should be equal to the estimated ones, therefore the generated residual will be $d(t) = 0$ or $d(t) \neq 0$ in the case of a failure. In a practical system, some kind of the threshold τ must be defined. When the residual $d(t)$ crosses the threshold of the sensor τ_s failure, an alarm will be triggered. In an ideal detection system τ_r should be kept close to 0 for faster failure detection ($\tau_r \approx 0$).

However, in a practical system, the sensor measurements are not equal to the calculated value due to the sensor's noise and inaccuracies in the reference model. This means that the residual $d(t)$ is not equal to zero in the case if no failure has been occurred. Due to this reason, an improper recognition of a failure could occur frequently when the threshold is close to zero $\tau_r \approx 0$. This can be resolved by raising the value of τ_r, however, this threshold rising may cause potential risks in the sense, that some failures could remain undetected. Therefore, it is important to determine a balance between false alarms and reliable fault detection.

3.3   Dependencies Detection

The last part of our research was focused on the fuzzy verification model implementation for detecting inconsistencies in the system. Most of the control system needs to verify if the selected action has an adequate reaction. Many systems use several different sensors to sensing more variables in an environment process. The measured variables are often interdependent, so a change of the value in one variable may cause a difference in others. The detection system is checking these dependencies and helps to decide the rate of the failure.

In our proposed system we supposed a positive correlation between variables A and B, which means, that both variables increases (Inc) or decreases (Dec) jointly. A positive correlation exists when one variable decreases as the other variable decreases, or one variable increases while the other increases too. There are four possible states for two variables in the binary logic shown in the Table 1. Output Y shows if variables are correlated ($Y = 0$) or not ($Y = 1$).

Table 1. Logical XOR in binary logic.

Signal (A)	Signal (B)	Output (Y)
Inc.	Inc.	0
Inc.	Dec.	1
Dec.	Inc.	1
Dec.	Dec.	0

Our aim is to convert this binary logic into the fuzzy logic and try to express a degree of correlation in it. For this purpose we will measure the level of increases or decreases.

A function is increasing when $x_N - x_{N-1} > 0$, and decreasing when $x_N - x_{N-1} < 0$.

Because each sensor model should have different sensing range, it is necessary to normalize incoming data into interval $(0;1)$ which ensures, that all data will be in a same range and suitable for a next processing by fuzzy logic.

To convert a digitized signal to the fuzzy logic the following equation was used which correspond to the outputs shown in the Table 1.

$$Y_n = \frac{A_N - max_A}{max_A - min_A} + \frac{B_N - max_B}{max_B - min_B} - (2 * \frac{A_N - max_A}{max_A - min_A} * \frac{B_N - max_B}{max_B - min_B}) \quad (9)$$

4 Experiments

For the purpose of an experiment, one month data from a smart home system [3] has been selected. More than 25.000 samples of measured data from 8 different sensors have been used. The data were focused on temperature, humidity, and motion sensors. The sampling frequencies have varied, from one second to several minutes. These data have been stored in the database, organized to subsets and sorted by their time marks. However, it was no need to analyze and exhibit all of them.

Although the hard failure detection is not a main purpose of this research, four hard failures in the measurement process were identified. All of them have been detected by the system and new measurements were initialized. However, in one case the sensor wires have been corrupted and no value retrieved.

Briefly, we implemented the FFT to a set of parameters for the data filtration. On the basis of these parameters the Gaussian pulse filter has been constructed. In this experiment the sampling frequencies equaled to one sample from a sensor each ten minutes, which was suitable for slowly changing temperatures. The process of noise elimination is introduced on the Figs. 6, 8 and 9. The Fig. 6 shows the part of an originally sampled signal in the period between third and twelfth day of the measurement. The horizontal axis represent the day of the month and the vertical axis shows actual temperature in degrees of Celsius.

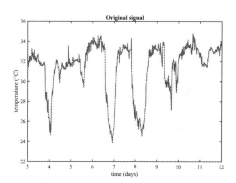
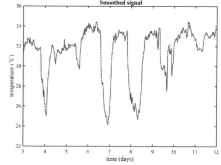

Fig. 6. Original signal   **Fig. 7.** Smoothed signal after filtration

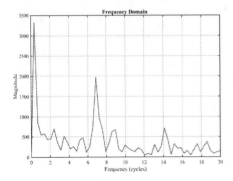

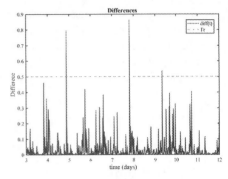

Fig. 8. Frequency domain overview of the sampled signal

Fig. 9. Differences between signals computed using an Eq. 8

The Fig. 8 shows the frequency domain of the whole signal. Two major magnitudes are characteristic there in areas from 0.5 to 1 cycles and the second one around 7 cycles. These two frequencies has been used to a Gaussian pulse construction and after the filtration they has been summarized together. The Fig. 7 shows the result. This smoothed signal was used to residuals computation which are shown on the Fig. 9. The threshold $\tau_r = 0.5$ was used in this experiment, so two corrupted values were identified in the days five and eight. In the scope of the whole data set of 4800 samples, 17 sensor failures were identified with the threshold $\tau_r = 0.5$.

To the fuzzy dependency detection purpose the data from two temperature sensors were used. The Fig. 10 shows two correlated temperature sensors. The Fig. 11 shows the output of the dependencies detection system. The blue line shows results of the binary logic and the red line represents results of the fuzzy logic.

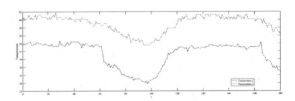

Fig. 10. Example of a two correlated variables

5   Results Evaluation

In our research we proposed a failure detection system which can be used in various industrial systems, in the IoT or IIoT solutions in combination with cloud or external storage systems. There was no aim to detect all the possible

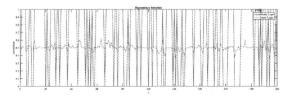

Fig. 11. Result of a Fuzzy dependency detection

sensor failures but to chart the major reasons of the system failure and to provide some mechanisms to prevent it. We introduced new methods, e.g., noise elimination methods, for identification of failures of sensors in a control system. In the verification phase we analyzed sampled digital signal from eight different sensors of a smart home control system. The system identified all the hard sensor failures, and provided new methods for reducing the signal noise, as well as for identification of those values which are not consistent with the predicated model.

6   Conclusion and Discussion

Sensors are important parts of all control systems and the collected data provided base for any control mechanisms. It is necessary to be sure, that every single sensor is capable of producing data and that all these incoming data are correct and corresponding to the measured variable.

We proposed the failure detection system with practical implementation of this system in the form of a real enterprise environment control system. The first part of the control was realized using simple mathematical methods for the hard failures detection, using a feedback of the subsystem with the sensing module for repeating the failed measurement. Sensors stuck are analyzed by counting the time between the value change and alert setting when the defined threshold has been reached. In the second part of the system the FFT was used for analyzing all the compounds of incoming signal data from the sensors. These data should be used for setting noise filtering parameters methods to help reducing a noise interfered to the measured values and to provide correct data to the later parts. Main advantage of this solution is in fast detection of the hard failure and in an easy initialization of new measurement instead of including these values into a next processing and eliminating them in later parts helping to reduce error propagation.

The main purpose of this solution are filtration methods and model composition for a failure detection. The FFT in combination with a Gaussian pulse has been used because the FFT provides acceptable outcomes with respect to the computational complexity and the Gaussian pulse has a minimum possible group delay in compression with low pass filters or median filters which have non linear characteristics.

In the second part we introduced a fuzzy method to identify correlations between values in the same context or a manufacturing process. These correlations can be used to identify main areas where a failure could be detected and will help to reduce whole data set into a couple of areas which could be deeply analyzed by any robust algorithms. This system will be implemented as a part of the HAUSY system described in the [3]. In the future research the statistical part could be replaced by any form of neural network processes or a computer learning process which may result in a kind of the model improvement, providing thus better results. Some effort in the direction of optimizing this solution to be run in runtime on a small IoT devices instead of cloud is expected as well.

Acknowledgment. The research has been partially supported by the Faculty of Informatics and Management UHK specific research project 2107 *Computer Networks for Cloud, Distributed Computing, and Internet of Things II*. The financial support is gratefully acknowledged.

References

1. Balaban, E., Saxena, A., Bansal, P., Goebel, K.F., Curran, S.: Modeling, detection, and disambiguation of sensor faults for aerospace applications. IEEE Sens. J. **9**(12), 1907–1917 (2009)
2. Goupil, P.: Airbus state of the art and practices on FDI and FTC in flight control system. Control Eng. Pract. **19**(6), 524–539 (2011)
3. Horálek, J., Matyska, J., Stepan, J., Vancl, M., Cimler, R., Soběslav, V.: Lower layers of a cloud driven smart home system. In: Barbucha, D., Nguyen, N.T., Batubara, J. (eds.) New Trends in Intelligent Information and Database Systems. SCI, vol. 598, pp. 219–228. Springer, Cham (2015). https://doi.org/10.1007/978-3-319-16211-9_23
4. Hussain, S., Mokhtar, M., Howe, J.M.: Aircraft sensor estimation for fault tolerant flight control system using fully connected cascade neural network. In: The 2013 International Joint Conference on Neural Networks (IJCNN), pp. 1–8. IEEE (2013)
5. Hussain, S., Mokhtar, M., Howe, J.M.: Sensor failure detection, identification, and accommodation using fully connected cascade neural network. IEEE Trans. Industr. Electron. **62**(3), 1683–1692 (2015)
6. Maleki, S., Bingham, C., Zhang, Y.: Development and realization of changepoint analysis for the detection of emerging faults on industrial systems. IEEE Trans. Industr. Inf. **12**(3), 1180–1187 (2016)
7. Naidu, S.R., Zafiriou, E., McAvoy, T.J.: Use of neural networks for sensor failure detection in a control system. IEEE Control Syst. Mag. **10**(3), 49–55 (1990)
8. Napolitano, M.R., An, Y., Seanor, B.A.: A fault tolerant flight control system for sensor and actuator failures using neural networks. Aircr. Des. **3**(2), 103–128 (2000)
9. Severson, K., Chaiwatanodom, P., Braatz, R.D.: Perspectives on process monitoring of industrial systems. IFAC-PapersOnLine **48**(21), 931–939 (2015)
10. Shen, H., Wu, Z.G., Park, J.H.: Reliable mixed passivae and $\mathscr{H}\infty$ filtering for semi-Markov jump systems with randomly occurring uncertainties and sensor failures. Int. J. Robust Nonlinear Control **25**(17), 3231–3251 (2015)
11. Wang, Y.L., Han, Q.L.: Network-based fault detection filter and controller coordinated design for unmanned surface vehicles in network environments (2016)

Hand Gesture Recognition System Based on LBP and SVM for Mobile Devices

Houssem Lahiani[1,2,3(✉)] and Mahmoud Neji[1,2,3]

[1] National School of Electronics and Telecommunications,
University of Sfax, Sfax, Tunisia
lahianihoussem@gmail.com, mahmoud.neji@gmail.com
[2] Faculty of Economics and Management, University of Sfax, Sfax, Tunisia
[3] Multimedia Information Systems and Advanced Computing Laboratory,
Sfax, Tunisia

Abstract. With the advent of smart devices and the massive use of smartphones, hand gesture recognition by mobile devices is being a major difficulty due to their technical specificities. To find a balance between speed and accuracy, we propose a new approach to recognize hand gestures by a smart device. This topic has some current interest and future applicability. In this paper, we present a new gesture detection framework for mobile devices based on LBP and SVM. LBP provides good texture representation properties. First, the proposed LBP on each non-overlapping blocks of a hand pose image is computed and a histogram of these LBPs is obtained. Those histograms are used as feature vectors for gesture classification as they demonstrate their robustness against compression and uniform intensity variations. The classification has been done by using Support Vector Machine (SVM). Since SVM is commonly used for pattern recognition, it is good for the explicit classification of form-dependent data, such as hand gestures. A recognition rate of approximately 93% is obtained based the enhanced NUS database I. In addition, the impact of using such a hand pose estimation task in an embedded device is studied. We conduct experiments on the speed of detection on different mobile devices. The impact of using SVM as a classifier for a gesture recognition task in an embedded device like smartphone is studied.

Keywords: Android · LBP · Hand gesture · SVM · Human-mobile interaction

1 Introduction

These days, small mobile devices such as cell phones, smartwatches and Google glasses have emerged and have become used by the majority of human beings. However, reducing the size of these devices has limited the operating space. Subsequently, a new way of interacting with these devices is required. In this context, the recognition of hand gestures by a mobile device is proposed as a better alternative to existing interaction systems. Indeed, hand gesture classification for mobile devices is one of the most challenging problems for researchers. Similar to any pattern recognition problems, hand gesture classification has two key points, which are feature extraction and pattern classification. Hand gesture recognition for mobile devices has attracted researcher's

N. T. Nguyen et al. (Eds.): ICCCI 2019, LNAI 11683, pp. 283–295, 2019.
https://doi.org/10.1007/978-3-030-28377-3_23

attention over the past decade because it is challenging to recognize hand poses with variations, occlusion, ethnicity changes and blur by a limited devices in term of computational capacities. In the last decade, mobile devices become at the heart of the way we live today due to their great influence. After the good performance of accelerometers, gyroscopes and touch screens, researchers ought to improve the user experience more and more. A modernization that will undoubtedly draw attention is an integrated hand pose estimation system in smartphones based only on vision. As hand poses are an intuitive means of communication, vision based hand pose estimation has been commonly applied in the field Human Machine Interaction, which makes its integration necessary in today's mobile devices. Thus, due to the computational limits of smartphones and the visual discomfort of gestures, integrated hand gesture recognition on mobile devices become a challenging task. In fact, when the smartphone's camera captures a hand gesture, it interprets it in order to recognize sign language or to place order without any need to touch the screen. Concerning our work, the smartphone's camera is used to capture frames before the real-time processing of the captured gesture. Regarding this paper, the system is designed for Android ecosystem. Several reasons led to choose this ecosystem. For now, Android and iOS are the most used operating systems in the world. Other dedicated systems for mobile devices on the market have a very low usage rate. Android is the most commonly used operating systems in the world [2] and the majority of today's mobile devices are running on Android ecosystem [1]. As well as, Android devices may have better hardware specifications than Apple devices, as well as Android is better than iOS in terms of cost and can be obtained by most of people [20]. In the other hand, the use of Computer Vision in mobile applications has grown tremendously over the years, thanks in part to powerful sensors and processors that continue to make their way into mobile devices. In addition, Android platform allows integrating image-processing libraries like OpenCV library [3]. According to openCV web site, the library has more than 47,000 users and about 14 million downloads. As well as, according to a comparative between iOS and android in term of image processing tasks, Android platform achieved better performance [4]. The mainly challenge of vision based tasks in our case is the computational limits of smartphones [23] and in the other hand, the computational cost of vision based tasks is expensive. Among approaches applied for hand gesture recognition in mobile devices, we find glove-based approaches [5, 6]. Unfortunately, these approaches are cumbersome for users. Thus, Vision-based methods [7–10] constitute a better alternative. Despite the simplicity of use for vision-based approaches, they are still vulnerable against changes in lighting. The proposed work is based on a LBP (Local Binary Pattern) features and SVM (Support Vector Machine). The problem to be solved here is to find a new way of interacting with mobile devices more intuitively than existing methods. The recognition of gestures in space is one of the best alternatives, especially with the advent of smart devices such as Google glasses and smartwatches. Another problem to be solved here is to find algorithms and methods capable of giving better detection rate with the fact of being suitable for limited computing devices furthermore.

2 Literature Review

Several works in hand pose estimation field using mobile devices and many works that use LBP and SVM for gesture recognition have been studied. The simplicity in use of the smartphones has prompted researchers to integrate gesture recognition tasks into them. Several approaches and methods have been developed for that issue. The vision-based approach constitute one of them and it uses only the camera of the device to recognize gestures. However, it meets challenges like lightening variations and difference of skin colors. Thus, that risks to produce lower recognition rate compared to other approaches. Therefore, we adopt an approach non-vulnerable to illumination changes on the one hand, and which uses non-greedy techniques in term of consuming computational resources of the mobile device. LBP features and SVM have been widely used in gesture recognition due to their robustness against illumination changes. The challenges imposed by vision-based systems have led researchers to experiment with non-vision based recognition system around mobile devices. At this level, many researchers have tried to find new ways to interact with the device. For example, using infrared sensors (IR) or an accelerometer and the integrated micro gyroscope of the mobile device. Others have tried to solve this problem by using sensors and gloves. In [6] Xie et al. developed a system based on smartphone sensors. The system is made to recognize 8 gestures that include capital letters of English alphabet and 4 Arabic numerals. The system used the built-in micro gyroscope of the phone and accelerometers since they can generate input data based on measures provided by the accelerations and angular velocities along x-, y- and z-axis. Authors have computed the energy of input data to reduce the effect of the posture variations of the device. For the classification, they used SVM that had an accuracy rate of 93.84%, KNN that had an accuracy rate of 90.54% and HMM that had an accuracy rate of 91.79%. In [26] Mr. Seymour et al. have created a system that recognizes South African Sign Language (SASL). This system requires an instrumented glove connected via Bluetooth to the smartphone. The system is designed for Android platform. Three classifiers were deployed to make a comparison: Logsigmoid with 93.8% accuracy and 6.21 µs as a classification time, Symmetric Elliott with 95.7% accuracy and 4.26 µs as the detection time and SVM with 99.2% accuracy and 81.99 µs as classification time. Despite the accuracy rate was high for the three classifiers, the classification time was considerably high because the sensors attached to the glove were connected to an Arduino board connected to the smartphone via Bluetooth. Thus, this system requires user instrumentation, which constitute a major obstacle to adoption and limit seamless unencumbered user interaction. Systems cited above require user instrumentation or specific configuration, and often external processing. These problems pose serious barriers to adoption by users. All this constitutes a discomfort for users, which makes vision-based systems a better alternative.

In [11] Lahiani et al. presented a system based on a combination of HOG and LBP features to recognize hand gestures by a smartphone. The training was done based on an enhanced 'NUS hand gesture dataset I'. A detection rate of 92% was obtained. The issue here is the combination of two features, which affects the execution time. In [12] Lahiani et al. developed a system based on LBP features and gentle AdaBoost to recognize hand gestures in real time by a smartphone. Recognition rate was about 88%. In [14] Lahiani et al. designed a system for based on Haar-like features and adaptive boosting to detect the "Nus dataset" gestures by smartphones. Recognition rate was about 89%. The weakness of these two systems in [12] and [14] lies in the recognition rate, which is a little low compared to other systems. In [13] a translator of American Sign Language by smartphone was made by C. Jin et al. Canny edge detector and SURF algorithm were used to extract features and SVM for classification. The application was made to interpret 16 ASL postures with a detection rate of 97.13%. The use of Canny edge detector represents a vulnerability in this system, because it requires a greedy consumption of resources, which is not good for mobile devices. Although it is known by its good detection and good locating (objects) performance, the Canny edge detection algorithm contains many preprocessing and post processing steps and is more computationally complex than other detection algorithms. This imposes heavy memory requirements and results in significant latency that makes real-time implementation of Canny's edge detection algorithm very delicate and critical [25]. This makes its use in a mobile device application very critical. In [15] an Android application was made by Setiawardhana et al. to recognize hand gestures. Recognition process starts by detecting the hand using boosted Haar cascade and ends by recognizing hand gestures using K-NN classifier. The recognition rate is equal to 100% if the distance is less than or equal to 50 cm. On the other hand, it becomes equal to 25% if the distance is equal to 75 cm. The limits of this system boils down to have good detection rate only when the hand and camera are close enough. In [16] an ASL translator was made by Prasuhn et al. for android devices. In this system HOG features were deployed due to their invariance against rotation. The problem of this system is summarized in its client-server architecture, which depends on the network that could affect the response time. In this work, we will not only try to enhance the detection rate compared to other works but we will also try to find computationally inexpensive techniques that do not affect the performances of the mobile device.

3   Overview

With the advent of small mobile devices, the style of interaction with them must evolve to provide a better user experience. As we said in the previous section, several researchers have tried to recognize gestures in the air using materials such as glove and sensors. These systems require a specific configuration for each device, as well as external processing. These problems are serious obstacles to user adoption. On the other hand, vision-based systems are comfortable for the user. Unfortunately, these systems face a lot of challenges and difficulties due to the complexity of the recognition task and the technical limitations of the mobile device

In our paper, we describe a Human-Mobile Interaction system based on hand gestures, which must allow the user to interact in a natural and intuitive way with smartphones. In this work, the application is made for Android smartphones. The captured image of hand gesture by the camera of the smartphone constitute the input of our application. We tried to use approaches that need less computational power to be suitable for smartphones. The main steps of our system are presented in Fig. 1.

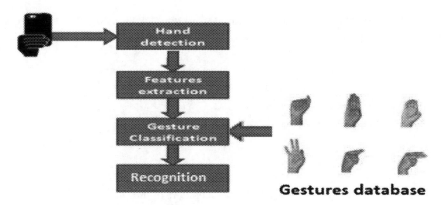

Fig. 1. Overview of our system

3.1 Pose Capturing

Hand Pose Estimation systems aim to recognize the signs made by people based on mathematical algorithms. They represent an HCI and a manner for smartphones to understand behavior. In our case, the smartphone camera that constitutes the input device, detects frames. Those frames are then interpreted using AI (Artificial Intelligence) algorithms.

For any system based on vision, the first step consists on extracting the region of interest (hand) from the frame, which could be tricky if this frame has cluttered background that contains many objects, which could disturb the right detection of the posture.

3.2 Feature Extraction: Local Binary Patterns (LBP)

Local Binary Pattern is a highly descriptive and simple technique to classify objects as part of a computer vision application. It is a standard approach that solves several problems basing on its discriminatory capacity. LBP features are characterized by their robustness against luminance changes.

The most important characteristic of the LBP operator in real-world applications is its tolerance against lighting changes. In addition, its simplicity of computation makes it possible to analyze images under challenging real time conditions. Indeed, this makes using LBP operator for hand pose estimation task by mobile device suitable.

Local binary patterns characterize textures as long as the image is a gray-scale image. Their role consists of attributing a value to every pixel (P) in the image. These values are calculated following a comparison of the gray levels between the central pixel (P) and its neighbors. LBP concept is simple; it assigns a binary code to a pixel according to its neighborhood. The local texture of a region is computed by thresholding a neighborhood with the central pixel gray level. A comparison between the gray scale levels of the central pixel 'i_c' of coordinates '(x_c, y_c)' and its neighbors 'i_n' is made following these formulae:

$$LBP(x_c, y_c) = \sum_{m=0}^{p-1} s(i_n - i_c)2^n \qquad (1)$$

$$s(i_n - i_c) = 1 \text{ if } i_n - i_c \geq 0$$

$$s(i_n - i_c) = 0 \text{ if } i_n - i_c < 0$$

p represents the neighboring pixels number

The binary pattern is generated when the neighbors of the current pixel take the "1" value if their values are equal to or greater than the value of the current one or "0" otherwise. The LBP code of the current pixel is generated by multiplying the pixels of this binary pattern by weights and then summed. Therefore, for the entire image, we obtain pixels whose intensity is between 0 and 255, as in an ordinary 8-bit image.

3.3   Gesture Classification: SVM

The Support Vector Machine (SVM) is a supervised learning tool invented by Vapnik and Chervonenkis in 1964 in the context of statistical learning theory (Vapnik and Chervonenkis 1964). We had to wait the mid-1990s to see an SVM implementation with the introduction of kernel trick and non-separable generalization [17]. Since then, the SVM have experienced many developments and gained popularity in various areas such as machine learning, optimization and functional analysis. This is one of the most successful learning algorithms. Its ability to compute complex models for the computational cost of a very simple model has made it a key component of the machine-learning domain where it has been particularly successful in image or character recognition. The SVM algorithm aims to find the separation between two or many classes of objects with the idea that the larger the separation is, the more robust the classification is. In its simplest form.

Among the different machine learning methods, SVM has attracted a lot of attention from researchers and practitioners [18].

Our trained model was obtained using LIBSVM wrapper for android [27]. We specified a training dataset file and a model file. Information of trained model are put into that file. The training dataset file, where our extracted features were stored into a "sparse matrix form", demonstrates the standard format for training file. In our study, we will try to see the effect of using SVM in a hand gesture application designed for embedded devices like smartphone and which run on real-time.

4   Training and Evaluation

4.1   Training Data

For our system, the first version of "NUS hand gesture database" was used [19]. "NUS database I" contains 240 captures containing different hand postures. It has 10 classes of gestures. Each class contains 24 captures that were taken by varying the position and size of the hand in the frame.

The Training process requires a great number of captures containing gestures to obtain an accurate classifier. For that reason, we tried to enhance the database by adding to each class 51 captures that contain the hand pose. Captures were taken in different backgrounds, with different persons and lightening conditions. Therefore, an enhanced NUS dataset is obtained and that has 75 captures per class (Fig. 2).

For the training process, the 75 captures of each class were chosen as positive samples. We cropped the captures to get only the region of interest that contains only the posture. The ratios of the cropped captures must not be too different. The good results come from positive examples that look exactly like the ones we want to recognize. We assigned to each hand posture a letter or a word for testing purposes (Fig. 3).

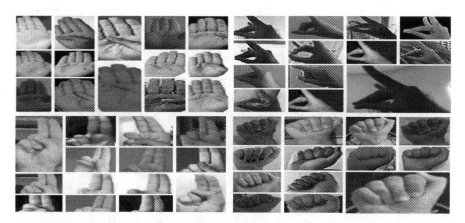

Fig. 2. Postures of the enhanced NUS database I

Training process requires also negative examples that do not contain the region of interest. More than 4000 negative samples that do not contain postures were used.

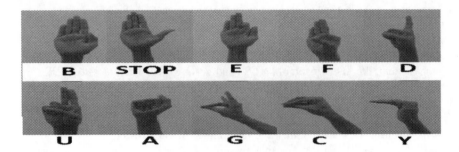

Fig. 3. Assigned letters to gestures

4.2 Evaluation

As long as our system is designed for handheld devices, which have computational limits, and because our application is made to run in real-time, we chose to perform the tests using real-time evaluation to identify the detection rate and to know the execution time required per task. To identify the real time recognition rate, we invite many persons to test the system in different lightning condition and backgrounds. For every gesture, fifty frames were taken with cluttered backgrounds and in different lightning condition. Figure 4 shows gestures made by different persons recognized correctly by our system in real time and in different background and lightening conditions. The name of each gesture is shown on the top of the green box.

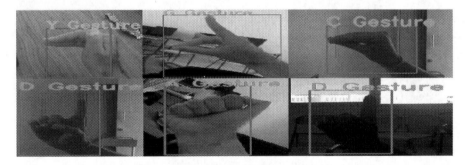

Fig. 4. Gestures detection

In order to make a comparison, we subjected our system to the same training conditions (the same database) and evaluation as the systems we developed previously. Table 1 gives the results obtained by the different systems. For each hand posture, fifty captures were detected in different lightening condition and with cluttered background. In this work, Tegra Android Development Pack (TADP) was used to made the Android application.

The Table 1 summarizes the results obtained by different methods. It provides a comparison between the results obtained by different systems and their detection rates. In order to make a comparison, we subjected our system to the same training conditions and to the same evaluation process as systems developed before. For comparison purpose, the same experimental methodology as [11, 12, 14 and 23] is adopted.

Table 1. Recognition rate of different hand poses estimation systems.

Distance <= 75 cm								
Feature		HOG		LBP		HOG-LBP		LBP
Classifier		AdaBoost [23]		AdaBoost [12]		Adaboost [11]		SVM
Sign	Number of capture	Recognized	Recognition rate	Recognized	Recognition rate	Recognized	Recognition rate	Recognized	Recognition rate
B	50	48	96%	45	90%	48	96%	47	94%
STOP	50	45	90%	45	90%	48	96%	46	92%
E	50	43	86%	43	86%	45	90%	48	96%
F	50	46	92%	44	88%	47	94%	48	96%
D	50	45	90%	44	88%	45	90%	47	94%
U	50	40	80%	45	90%	44	88%	46	92%
A	50	47	94%	45	90%	47	94%	46	92%
G	50	45	90%	42	84%	45	90%	47	94%
C	50	45	90%	44	88%	44	88%	45	90%
Y	50	43	86%	43	86%	45	90%	46	92%
Average			89,4%		88%		91.6%		93.2%

According to the experimental results in Table 1, the distance between the hand and the camera affects the recognition rate. The results could be optimal if the distance is less than or equal to 75 cm. To develop this system, we used a laptop equipped with in Intel Core i7 Central Processor Unit and 8 GB RAM. To test the system we used two mobile devices: the first one has a 13 Mega Pixel camera, Android5.1 (Lollipop version) and equipped with a 1.5 GHz octa-core processor and 1.5 GB "Read Only Memory: RAM". The second one uses a 4 Mega Pixel camera, Android 4.4 (KitKat version) and equipped with 1.3 Ghz Dual Core Cortex Processor and 512 MB RAM.

4.3 Execution Time

As we said before, mobile devices have limitations in terms of computational capacities and power. We have studied the execution time required for the recognition task of each gesture using TimingLogger [21] (Fig. 5). TimingLogger allows displaying the result of the execution time through the logcat [22] in the IDE (Integrated Development Environment) when the recognition task is executed in a mobile device connected to the IDE via a USB cable. Generally, the logcat is designed to display the logs of the application. The application based on LBP and AdaBoost and the other one based on HOG and AdaBoost have the fastest execution time, an average time of 1 ms was found almost for each posture detection using the first smartphone cited above. Therefore, the system based on HOG-LBP and AdaBoost and the system based on LBP and SVM have the greatest execution time (2 ms for each gesture). Execution time made by the second smartphone was greater than the results obtained by the first one.

It is because the Octa-core processor of the first smartphone is made up of eight processor cores. It enables smartphones to carry out more advanced tasks such as handling high-resolution videos and graphic-heavy games without draining the battery, making the devices capable and efficient. Octa-core processor also gives devices faster load times.

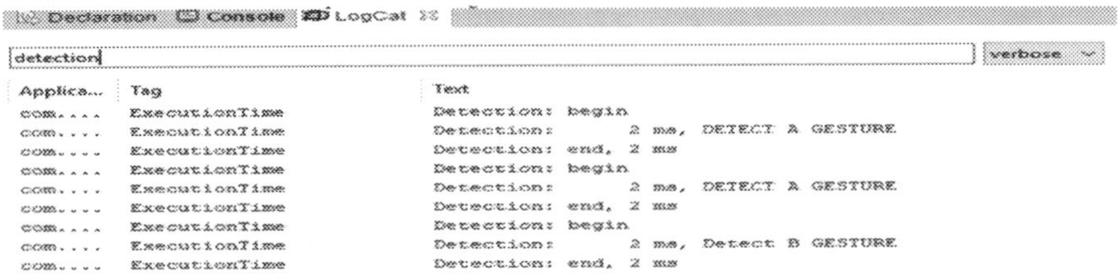

Fig. 5. Execution time for some gesture recognition tasks

To better assess the performance of the system, we applied the precision and recall concept (pr). Pr curves are better than ROC Curve (Receiver Operating characteristic Curves) to evaluate models [24].

$$Precision = TP/(TP + FP) \quad Recall = TP/(TP + FN)$$

F1 Score = 2*(Recall * Precision) / (Recall + Precision) With: TP: true positive which represents a good detection, FP: false positive, which is a detection for which no gesture exists, FN: false negative is a gesture for which no detection exists and F1 score: weighted average of Precision and Recall. Precision, recall and F1 score were evaluated basing on a test set formed by 35 images for each class of postures. These images have been chosen from version II of the NUS dataset, which contains hand

Table 2. Precision, Recall and F1 score for LBP-SVM system with compred results

Sign	PRECISION		RECALL		F1 SCORE	
	LBP and SVM	HOG-LBP and AdaBoost [11]	LBP and SVM	HOG-LBP and AdaBoost [11]	LBP and SVM	HOG-LBP and AdaBoost [11]
A	0.65369	0.45679	0.81564	1	0.725739	0.627119
B	0.954789	0.935484	0.81425	0.828571	0.878937	0.878788
C	0.513658	0.421053	0.84985	0.914286	0.640307	0.576577
D	0.787654	0.617762	0.914758	0.925267	0.846461	0.740874
E	0.784526	0.625471	0.841256	0.954796	0.811901	0.755818
F	0.845362	0.754892	0.84369	0.916582	0.844525	0.827916
G	0.645825	0.584253	0.745832	0.910203	0.6922351	0.711682
U	0.694761	0.619892	0.84391	0.996974	0.7621067	0.764462
Y	0.683945	0.611458	0.949123	0.997035	0.7950041	0.758033
STOP	0.756492	0.618532	0.846952	0.989752	0.7991703	0.761300

postures with human noise and noisy backgrounds. Table 2 gives an overview of the obtained results for the LBP-SVM system. The same testing process like [11] was deployed.

Table 2 gives obtained results for our system. The same evaluation process as [11] was used for comparison purposes. Precision answers the following question: What proportion of positive identifications was actually correct? The recall answers the following question: What proportion of actual positive results has been identified correctly? To evaluate the performance of a model, both the precision and the recall should be evaluated.

5   Conclusion

In this work, we proposed a human-mobile interaction system based on hand gestures. We developed a system that detected static poses of the hands. The results of the experiment have proved the robustness of the system despite certain limitations. LBP features were used because they are very fast to calculate and they are invariant with respect to monotonic grayscale transformations and scaling. The SVM classifier has demonstrate the best recognition rate. Unfortunately, he showed the worst execution time. The first version of the "NUS dataset" was used to train our model, and some images of the second version of the NUS dataset were used for evaluation purposes. In a future work, to improve the trained model, we will try to use the NUS hand gestures dataset II that contains more gestures and images. We will also try to use deep learning algorithms for hand pose estimation tasks using smartphones to see their impact and effect on mobile devices. In addition, a comparison between different systems in term of battery power consumption could be assessed to see the impact of different systems on energy consumption.

References

1. Manjoo, F: A Murky Road Ahead for Android, Despite Market Dominance. The New York Times. ISSN 0362-4331. Retrieved May 27 2015
2. Statcounter company web site. http://gs.statcounter.com/press/android-overtakes-windows-for-first-time. 3 April 2017
3. OpenCV. http://opencv.org/platforms/android.html
4. Cobârzan, C., Hudelist, M.A., Schoeffmann, K., Primus, M.J.: Mobile image analysis: Android vs. iOS. In: 21st International Conference on MultiMedia Modelling (MMM), pp. 99–110 (2015)
5. Seymour, M., Tšoeu, M.: A Mobile Application for South African Sign Language (SASL) recognition. In: IEEE Africon, pp 281–285 (2015)
6. Xie, C., Luan, S., Wang, H., Zhang, B.: Gesture recognition benchmark based on mobile phone. In: You, Z., Zhou, J., Wang, Y., Sun, Z., Shan, S., Zheng, W., Feng, J., Zhao, Q. (eds.) CCBR 2016. LNCS, vol. 9967, pp. 432–440. Springer, Cham (2016). https://doi.org/10.1007/978-3-319-46654-5_48

7. Lahiani, H., Elleuch, M., Kherallah, M.: Real time hand gesture recognition system for android devices. In: 15th International Conference on Intelligent Systems Design and Applications (ISDA), pp. 592–597 (2015)

8. Lahiani, H., Elleuch, M., Kherallah, M.: Real time static hand gesture recognition system for mobile devices. J. Inf. Ass. Secur. **11**, 067–076 (2016). ISSN: 1554-1010

9. Lahiani, H., Kherallah, M., Neji, M.: Hand pose estimation system based on Viola-Jones algorithm for android devices. In: 13th ACS/IEEE International Conference on Computer Systems and Applications, (AICCSA) (2016)

10. Lahiani, H., Kherallah, M., Neji, M.: Vision based hand gesture recognition for mobile devices: a review. In: Abraham, A., Haqiq, A., Alimi, Adel M., Mezzour, G., Rokbani, N., Muda, A.K. (eds.) HIS 2016. AISC, vol. 552, pp. 308–318. Springer, Cham (2017). https://doi.org/10.1007/978-3-319-52941-7_31

11. Lahiani, H., Neji, M.: Hand gesture recognition method based on HOG-LBP features for mobile devices. In: 22nd International Conference on Knowledge-Based and Intelligent Information & Engineering Systems (KES), pp. 254–263 (2018)

12. Lahiani, H., Kherallah, M., Neji, M.: Hand gesture recognition system based on local binary pattern approach for mobile devices. In: 17th International Conference on Intelligent Systems Design and Applications (ISDA) 2017

13. Jin, C., Omar, Z., Jaward, M.H.: A mobile application of american sign language translation via image processing algorithms. In: 2016 IEEE Region 10 Symposium (TENSYMP), pp. 104–109 (2016)

14. Lahiani, H., Kherallah, M., Neji, M.: Hand pose estimation system based on a cascade approach for mobile devices. In: Abraham, A., Muhuri, Pranab Kr., Muda, A.K., Gandhi, N. (eds.) ISDA 2017. AISC, vol. 736, pp. 619–629. Springer, Cham (2018). https://doi.org/10.1007/978-3-319-76348-4_60

15. Setiawardhana, R.Y. Hakkun, Baharuddin, A.: Sign language learning based on android for deaf and speech impaired people. In: 2015 International Electronics Symposium (IES) 2015, pp. 114–117 (2015)

16. Prasuhn, L., Oyamada, Y., Mochizuki, Y., Ishikawa, H.: A HOG-Based hand gesture recognition system on a mobile device. In: IEEE International Conference on Image Processing (ICIP), pp. 3973–3977 (2014)

17. Cortes, C., Vapnik, V.: Support-vector networks. Mach. Learn. **20**(3), 273–297 (1995)

18. Burges, J.C.: A tutorial on support vector machines for pattern recognition. Data Min. Knowl. Disc. **2**, 121–167 (1998)

19. The NUS hand posture datasets I. https://www.ece.nus.edu.sg/stfpage/elepv/NUS-HandSet

20. Jamdaade, K., Khairmode, A., Kamble, S.: A comparative study between Android & iOS. Int. J. Curr. Trends Eng. Res. (IJCTER) **2**(6), 495–501 (2016). e-ISSN 2455–1392

21. TimingLogger| Android Developers. https://developer.android.com/reference/android/util/TimingLogger.html

22. Logcat Command-line Tool. https://developer.android.com/studio/command-line/logcat.html

23. Lahiani, H., Neji, M.: Comparative study between hand pose estimation systems for mobile devices. J. Inf. Ass. Secur. **12**, 218–226 (2017). ISSN: 1554-1010

24. Howse, J., Puttemans, S., Hua, Q., Sinha, U.: Object detection performance testing in "OpenCV 3 Blueprints"

25. Chandrashekar N.S., Nataraj, K.R.: NMS and Thresholding Architecture used for FPGA based Canny Edge Detector for Area Optimization. In: Proceedings of International Conference on Control, Communication and Power Engineering, pp 80-84 (2013)
26. Qifan, Y., Hao, T., Xuebing, Z, Yin, L., Sanfeng, Z.: Dolphin: ultrasonic-based gesture recognition on smartphone platform. In: IEEE 17th International Conference on Computational Science and Engineering, pp. 1461–1468 (2014)
27. Libsvm ported to Android jni environment. https://github.com/cnbuff410/Libsvm-androidjni

Parkinson's Disease Development Prediction by C-Granule Computing

Andrzej W. Przybyszewski[1,2]([⊠]) [iD]

[1] Polish-Japanese Academy of Information Technology,
02-008 Warsaw, Poland
przy@pjwstk.edu.pl
[2] Department of Neurology UMass Medical School,
Worcester, MA 01655, USA

Abstract. Both Rough Set Theory (RST) and Fuzzy Rough Set Theory (FRST) are related to intelligent granular computing (GrC) but primary with help of static granules. Our granules are sets of attributes measured from Parkinson's disease (PD) patient in a certain moment of his/her disease. In order to look into PD development in time during our longitudinal study, we have introduced the complex granule (c-granule) approach with properties of granules that are evolving with disease progression.

We have used a RST/FRST approach in order to find similarities between attributes of different patients in different disease stages to another group of more advanced PD patients. We have compared group (G1) of 23 PD with attributes measured three times (visits V1 to V3) every half of the year (G1V1, G1V2, G1V3) to other group of 24 more advanced PD (G2V1). By means of RST/FRST we have found rules describing symptoms of G2V1 and applied them to G1V1, G1V2, and G1V3. With RST (FRST) we've got the following accuracies: G1V1 – 59 (38)%; G1V2 – 68(54)%; G1V3 – 86(61)% but global coverage for FRST was better. This means that c-granule attributes became more similar to the model.

Keywords: Granular computing · Similarity · Aggregation ·
Disease progression · Disease model

1 Introduction

Our goal was to simulate Parkinson's disease (PD) development in time with help of granular computing (GrC) methods [1, 2]. As PD related neurodegeneration (ND) starts about 20 years before first symptoms and during this period of time ND process is effectively compensated by brain plasticity, each patient's PD progressions are different.

In this work, we have used intelligent granular computing based on the principle of complex object classifications from the visual brain [3, 4]. As states in the schematic (Fig. 1) properties of the unknown object p are represented as α and compared with the model α_M (in the brain – possible objects [3], here symptoms of more advanced PDs). It results rules β that determine new object's properties or PD time development.

© Springer Nature Switzerland AG 2019
N. T. Nguyen et al. (Eds.): ICCCI 2019, LNAI 11683, pp. 296–306, 2019.
https://doi.org/10.1007/978-3-030-28377-3_24

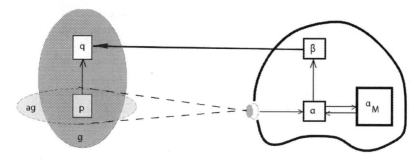

Fig. 1. It is a principal schematic of the intelligent granular computing base on the brain intelligence. We observe a limited part of c-granule g that is generally subpart ag of environment env in a time interval [t − Δ, t]. Interaction between env and ag in time t during Δ Int g,t,Δ (env, ag) represents α and results that rule $(\alpha \cap \alpha_M, \gamma)->\beta$ is learned by ag, where γ represents properties of the structure g, and α property of the interaction process, and β describes unknown, expected properties other part of g that might be reason for future changes into the disease; α_M it is the model of the world that interacts with α in order to extracts its significant features (modified after [5]).

2 Methods

Our data mining analysis is based on granular computing implemented in RST (rough set theory proposed by Pawlak [1] and FRTS (fuzzy rough set theory) by extending RST indiscernibility with concepts of the tolerance Zadeh [2].

   Our data is converted to the decision table where rows were related to different measurements and columns represent different attributes. An information system [1] a pair $S = (U, A)$, where U, A are nonempty finite sets called the universe of objects U and the set of attributes A. If $a \in A$ and $u \in U$, the value a(u) is a unique element of V (where V is a value set).

   We define as in [1] for RST the indiscernibility relation of any subset B of A or IND (B) as: $(x, y) \in IND(B)$ or $xI(B)y$ iff $a(x) = a(y)$ for every $a \in B$ where the value of $a(x) \in V$. It is an equivalence crisp relation $[u]_B$ that we understand as a B-elementary granule. The family of $[u]_B$ gives the partition U/B containing u will be denoted by B (u). The set $B \subset A$ of information system S is a reduct $IND(B) = IND(A)$ and no proper subset of B has this property [1]. In most cases, we are only interested in such reducts that are leading to expected rules (classifications). On the basis of the reduct we have generated rules using four different ML methods (RSES 2.2): exhaustive algorithm, genetic algorithm, covering algorithm, or LEM2 algorithm.

   A *lower approximation* of set $X \subseteq U$ in relation to an attribute B is defined as all elements have B attribute: $\underline{B}X = \{u \in U : [u]_B \subseteq X\}$. The upper approximation of X is defined as some elements have B attribute: $\overline{B}X = \{u \in U : [u]_B \cap X \neq \phi\}$. The difference of $\overline{B}X$ and $\underline{B}X$ is the boundary region of X that we denote as $BN_B(X)$. If $BN_B(X)$ is empty then set than X is exact with respect to B; otherwise if $BN_B(X)$ is not empty and X is not rough with respect to B.

A decision table (training sample in ML) for S is the triplet: $S = (U, C, D)$ where: C, D are condition and decision attributes [1]. Each row of the decision table gives a particular rule that connects condition and decision attributes for a single measurements, RST generalizes these particular rules into universal hypotheses (object or disease classification.

Dubois and Prade [6] have generalized RST to FRTS (fuzzy rough set theory) by extending RST indiscernibility with concepts of tolerance after Zadeh's membership degrees in fuzzy sets [2].

As the consequence, 'crisp' dependences were replaced by a fuzzy tolerance or similarity relations $R_a(x, y)$ as a value between two observations x and y. As $R_a(x, y)$ is a similarity relation, it must be reflexive, symmetric and transitive. As summarized in [7] there are several tolerance relationships such as the normalized difference (so-called 'Eq. 1') or Gaussian or exponential differences [7]. There are also formulas related to normalized differences between pairs of attributes. The most common are **Łukasiewicz (t.norm)** and **t.cos** $- \tau$ [7]. As decision attributes are nominative we used crisp relations between them.

We define B-lower and B-upper approximations for each observation x in FRST as following: *B-lower* approximation as: $(R_B)(x) = \inf_{y \in U} I(R_B(x, y), X(y))$ where I is an *implicator* [7]. The B-lower approximation for the observation x is then the set of observations, which are the most similar to observation x and it can predict the decision attribute with the highest confidence, based on conditional attributes B.

The B-upper approximation is defined by $(R_B)(x) = \sup_{y \in U} \tau(R_B(x, y), X(y))$, where τ is the t-norm. The B-upper approximation is a set of observations for which the prediction of decision attribute has the smallest confidence [7].

Notice that rules in FRST have dissimilar formation than in RST. They are based on the tolerance classes and appropriate decision concepts. The fuzzy rule is a triple (B, C, D), where B is a set of conditional attributes that appear in the rule, C stands for fuzzy tolerance class of object and D stands for decision class of object.

We have used RST algorithms implemented as the RSES 2.2 (logic.mimuw.edu.pl/ ~ rses/get.html) Exploration Program Rough System and FRST implemented as Rough Set package in R [7].

2.1   Measured Attributes

We have tested two groups of PD patients: the first group (G1) of 23 patients was measured three times every half of the year (visits were numbered as V1, V2, V3), and the second group (G2) had more advanced 24 patients and were a reference model of disease progression in the first group. Both groups of patients were only on medication. The major medication in this group was L-Dopa that increases concentration of the transmitter dopamine in the brain as it that is lacking in Parkinson's patients. In the most cases PD starts with neurodegeneration in substantia nigra that is responsible for the release of the dopamine.

All patients were measured in two sessions: MedOFF (session S#=1 without - medication) and MedON (session S#=2 patients on medications). In addition all patients have the following procedures: neuropsychological tests: PDQ39 (quality of life), Epworth (sleepiness test); neurological tests: eye movements and standard PD test: UPDRS (Unified Parkinson's Disease Rating Scale). All tests were performed in Brodno Hospital, department of Neurology, Faculty of Health Science, Medical University Warsaw, Poland. In the present work, we have tested and measured fast eye movements: reflexive saccades (RS) as described in our previous publications [8, 9]. In summary, every subject was sitting in a stable position without head movements and watching a computer screen before him/her. At the beginning he/she has to fixate in the center of the screen, and to keep on moving light spot. This spot was jumping randomly, ten degrees to the right or ten degrees to the left. Patient has to follow movements of the light spot and following parameters were measured: latency (RSLat) – time difference between beginning of spot and eyes movements, saccade duration (RSDur); saccade amplitude (RSAmp) and saccade velocity (RSVel).

3 Results

For the first group of PD patients we have performed three tests, every half-year, whereas the second group of more advanced PD we have measured only one time. The mean age of the first group (G1) was 57.8+/−13 (SD) years with disease duration 7.1+/−3.5 years; UPDRS MedOff/On was 48.3+/−17.9 and 23.6+/−10.3 for the first visit (V1); 57.3+/−16.8 and 27.8+/−10.8 for the second visit (V2), 62.2+/−18.2 and 25+/−11.6 for the third visit (V3). The second group (G2) of patients was more advanced with mean age 53.7+/−9.3 years, and disease duration 10.25+/−3.9 years; UPDRS MedOff/On was 62.1+/−16.1 and 29.9+/−13.3 measured one time only. Data were placed in four information tables: G1V1, G1V2, G1V3, and G2V1.

Table 1. Part of the decision table for three G1V1 patients

P#	Ses	tdur	PDQ39	Epworth	RSLat	RSDur	RSAmp	RSVel	UPDRS
10	1	5.3	90	17	205	51	9.8	343	58
10	2	5.3	90	17	182	56	10	333	35
11	1	15	122	8	245	55	12	503	57
11	2	15	122	8	266	55	12	431	40
12	1	5.5	20	3	178	54	10	421	25
12	2	5.5	20	3	161	58	13	505	15
13	1	4.8	68	9	299	59	13	472	46
13	2	4.8	68	9	234	57	11	367	26

Table 1 has 46 rows: 23 patients measured in two sessions each. Condition attributes patient number P#, S# session number, tdur – disease duration, PDQ39, Epworth (as above), RS parameters (above). The decision attribute is UPDRS that is proportional to the disease progression, it increases from G1V1 to G1V3 and it will be referred to G2V1.

3.1 Rough Set Approach

In the next step, Table 1 is discretized by RST and part of the table for G1V1 patients in Table 2 below. Notice that some less significant attributes were by algorithm of RSES 2.2 discarded: RSDur, RSAmp, and RSVel – duration, amplitude and velocity of reflexive saccades.

Table 2. Discretized-table Table 1 for three G1V1 patients

P#	Ses	tdur	PDQ39	Epworth	RSLat	RSDur	RSAmp	RSVel	UPDRS
10	1	"(-Inf,5.65)"	"(50.5,Inf)"	"(14,Inf)"	"(-Inf,264)"	*	*	*	"(43,63)"
10	2	"(-Inf,5.65)"	"(50.5,Inf)"	"(14,Inf)"	"(-Inf,264)"	*	*	*	"(33.5,43)"
11	1	"(5.65,Inf)"	"(50.5,Inf)"	"(-Inf,14)"	"(-Inf,264)"	*	*	*	"(43,63)"
11	2	"(5.65,Inf)"	"(50.5,Inf)"	"(-Inf,14.)"	"(264,Inf)"	*	*	*	"(33.5,43)"
12	1	"(-Inf,5.65)"	"(-Inf,50.5)"	"(-Inf,14)"	"(-Inf,264)"	*	*	*	"(-Inf,33.5)"
12	2	"(-Inf,5.65)"	"(-Inf,50.5)"	"(-Inf,14)"	"(-Inf,264)"	*	*	*	"(-Inf,33.5)"
13	1	"(-Inf,5.65)"	"(50.5,Inf)"	"(-Inf,14.0)"	"(264,Inf)"	*	*	*	"(43,63)"
13	2	"(-Inf,5.65)"	"(50.5,Inf)"	"(-Inf,14.)"	"(-Inf,264)"	*	*	*	"(-Inf,33.5)"

By means of the discretization RSES software RSES 2.2 (see Methods) UPDRS was divided into 4 ranges: "(-Inf, 33.5)", "(33.5, 43.0)", "(43.0, 63.0)", and "(63.0, Inf)". All other attributes, except symbolic attributes P# (number given to each patient) and S# (session number) were also discretized (Table 2).

Cross validation (6-fold) based on the decomposition tree of the first visit G1V1 data gave the global accuracy 0.896 and global coverage 0.35. Prediction, based on rules from G1V1, of UPDRS in G1V2 and G1V3 gave global accuracy 0.7 with coverage 1, and these results do not indicate time related disease progression.

For G2V1 group rules from G1V1 gave global accuracy 0.64 and coverage 0.5. However, it was more interesting to estimate G1V1 to G1V3 from other more advanced model group of patients G2V1.

This way we can follows our c-granular approach (Fig. 1) where the model are granules of attributes of G2V1 that might predict PD time: G1V1, G1V3, G1V3 development. With help of RSES we have found rules describing relationships between condition and decision attributes in G2V1 and we are using these rules to predict disease symptoms in G1 group for each visit V1, V2, and V3. If the disease progression has direction going to the model (G2V1) group then are predictions should increase with the time of the disease. We demonstrate our predictions in three following Tables 3, 4 and 5.

Table 3. Confusion matrix for UPDRS of G1V1 patients by rules obtained from G2V1 patients with RST

Actual	Predicted				
	"(63.0, Inf)"	"(33.5, 43.0)"	"(43.0, 63.0)"	"(-Inf, 33.5)"	ACC
"(63.0, Inf)"	2.0	0.0	0.0	0.0	1.0
"(33.5, 43.0)"	1.0	0.0	1.0	1.0	0.0
"(43.0, 63.0)"	6.0	0.0	1.0	0.0	0.14
"(-Inf, 33.5)"	3.0	0.0	2.0	17.0	0.77
TPR	0.17	0.0	0.25	0.94	

TPR: True positive rates for decision classes; ACC: Accuracy for decision classes: the global accuracy was 0.59 and global coverage was 0.74

Table 4. Confusion matrix for UPDRS of G1V2 patients by rules obtained from G2V1 patients with RST

Actual	Predicted				
	"(63.0, Inf)"	"(33.5, 43.0)"	"(43.0, 63.0)"	"(-Inf, 33.5)"	ACC
"(63.0, Inf)"	3.0	0.0	1.0	0.0	0.75
"(33.5, 43.0)"	0.0	0.0	2.0	1.0	0.0
"(43.0, 63.0)"	4.0	0.0	0.0	0.0	0.0
"(-Inf, 33.5)"	0.0	0.0	1.0	16.0	0.94
TPR	0.43	0.0	0.0	0.94	

TPR: True positive rates for decision classes; ACC: Accuracy for decision classes: the global accuracy was 0.68 and global coverage was 0.61.

Table 5. Confusion matrix for UPDRS of G1V3 patients by rules obtained from G2V1 patients with RST

Actual	"(63.0, Inf)"	"(33.5, 43.0)"	"(43.0, 63.0)"	"(-Inf, 33.5)"	ACC
"(63.0, Inf)"	3.0	0.0	0.0	0.0	1.0
"(33.5, 43.0)"	0.0	0.0	1.0	2.0	0.0
"(43.0, 63.0)"	0.0	0.0	0.0	0.0	0.0
"(-Inf, 33.5)"	0.0	0.0	2.0	16.0	1.0
TPR	1.0	0.0	0.0	1.0	

TPR: True positive rates for decision classes; ACC: Accuracy for decision classes: the global accuracy was 0.86 and global coverage was 0.48.

In Table 3 are prediction of the UPDRS for the first visit group of patients (G1V1). Notice that in this and two other tables (Tables 4 and 5) we could not predict UPDRS between 33.5 and 43. The accuracy in Table 3 was below 60%, but it increases for each following visit: G1V2 has global accuracy 68% and G1V3 – 86%. Therefore patients' symptoms become with time more similar to G2V1 group.

An important part in these estimations is to find rules that are enough general to be patient independent (there are different patients in G1 and G2 groups) and not too general in order to find differences between different visits.

There were all together 71 rules, e.g.

$$(Ses=2)\&(PDQ39="(-Inf,50.5)")=>(UPDRS="(-Inf,33.5)"\ [10]) \tag{1}$$

$$\begin{aligned}(Ses=2)\&(Epworth="(-Inf,14.0)")\&(RSLat="(264.0,Inf)")\\ =>(UPDRS="(63.0,Inf)"[4])\end{aligned} \tag{2}$$

$$\begin{aligned}(dur="(5.65,Inf)")\&(Ses=2)\&(RSLat="(-Inf,264.0)")\\ =>(UPDRS="(-Inf,33.5)"[14])\end{aligned} \tag{3}$$

$$\begin{aligned}(Ses=1)\&(PDQ39="(-Inf,\ 50.5)")\&(RSLat="(264.0,Inf)")\\ =>(UPDRS="(63.0,Inf)"[1])\end{aligned} \tag{4}$$

Equations (1–3) were for *Ses* = 2 (patient on medication) and they were fullfield by 10 (1), 4 (2) and 14 (3) cases, whereas Eq. 4 was for 1 case only.

We can read (1) as for patients on medication *(Ses = 2)* and with *PDQ39* (quality of life test result) smaller than *50.5* then his/her *UPDRS will be smaller than 33.5*.

3.2 Fuzzy Rough Set Approach

We have obtained our predictions using the generalized fuzzy rough set rules (GFRS) with aggregation by the t.norm **Łukasiewicz**, similarity expressed as tolerance Eq. 3 (modified Gaussian from [7]), and implicator – Łukasiewicz; alpha precision was 0.05. As the decision attribute must be nominal, so we have chosen classes that are similar to already used in our previous section: "(-Inf, 33.5)' = "1"; "(33.5, 43.0" = "2"; "(43.0, 63.0)" = "3",: "(63, Inf)" = "4". The examples of FRST rules are below:

$$(Ses=1)\&(Epworth="16")\&(RSLat="192")=>(UPDRS="3") \tag{5}$$

$$(Ses=2)=>(UPDRS="1") \tag{6}$$

$$(Ses=1)\&(Epworth="1")\&(RSLat="289")=>(UPDRS="4") \tag{7}$$

We can read Eq. (5) as for patients without medication (s#=1) and with Epworth (quality of sleep test result) about 16 and saccade latency about 192 then his/her UPDRS will be about 3 (between 34 and 63).

FRST rules have some similarities to RST rules but there are not 'crisp' there are fuzzy and more difficult to interpret as their fuzziness are not given directly as they are dependent on aggregation, tolerance and implicator equations. Their advantage to RST rules is that they cover all cases with the global coverage = 1. As above we have found FRST rules for our model group of patients G2V1 and applied these rules to other groups G1V1, G1V2, and G1V3 (Tables 6, 7 and 8).

Accuracies of out FRST predictions were inferior in comparison to FRS predictions, but as before accuracy is increasing with each visit: G1V1 – accuracy was below 40%, for G1V2 – 54% and for G1V3 visit was over 60%. Also notice that we did not get right predictions for UPDRS nominal values 2 and 3 that were between (33.5 and 43) and between (43 and 63), but we have got relatively good predictions for classes 1 and 4 were accuracy for decision classes ACC was almost for all estimations near 1.

Table 6. Confusion matrix for UPDRS of G1V1 patients by rules obtained from G2V1 patients with FRST

Actual	Predicted				
	"1"	"2"	"3"	"4"	ACC
"1"	19	0	0	5	0.79
"2"	2	0	0	4	0.0
"3"	2	0	0	11	0.0
"4"	0	0	0	3	1
TPR	0.826	0.0	0.0	0.13	

TPR: True positive rates for decision classes; ACC: Accuracy for decision classes: the global accuracy was 0.38 and global coverage was 1.

Table 7. Confusion matrix for UPDRS of G1V1 patients by rules obtained from G2V1 patients with FRST

Actual	Predicted				
	"1"	"2"	"3"	"4"	ACC
"1"	18	0	0	0	1.0
"2"	4	0	0	2	0.0
"3"	2	0	0	13	0.0
"4"	0	0	0	7	1.0
TPR	0.75	0.0	0.0	0.32	

TPR: True positive rates for decision classes; ACC: Accuracy for decision classes: the global accuracy was 0.54 and global coverage was 1.

Table 8. Confusion matrix for UPDRS of G1V3 patients by rules obtained from G2V1 patients with FRST

Actual	Predicted				
	"1"	"2"	"3"	"4"	ACC
"1"	17	0	0	0	1.0
"2"	5	0	0	3	0.0
"3"	2	0	0	8	0.0
"4"	0	0	0	11	1.0
TPR	0.74	0.0	0.0	0.5	

TPR: True positive rates for decision classes; ACC: Accuracy for decision classes: the global accuracy was 0.61 and global coverage was 1.

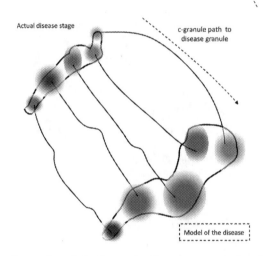

Fig. 2. C-granule path in disease development compared to the model

4 Discussion

In this work we have used c-granular computing to estimate disease progression in time (longitudinal study) of patients with Parkinson's disease (PD). As in each individual PD symptoms and their developments are different (**"No two people face Parkinson's in quite the same way"**) we would like to know if we could predict a particular patient progression by looking to more advanced group of patients.

We have used granular computing (GrC) with RST (rough set theory) and FRST (fuzzy rough set theory). RST looks into 'crisp' granules and estimates objects by upper and lower approximations that determine precision of the description as dependent from properties of granules. Therefore RST can give very precise estimation but not for all objects (patients). This we can see in our results where we can precisely predict symptoms (measured as UPDRS) of patients, but not all of them (global coverage less than 1). If we make our granules fuzzy (not crisp) they can describe properties of all objects (patients) with global coverage = 1, but less precisely. Our present results might be a good example of these differences.

Another important aspects of our approach are similarities between findings all-important aspects (symptoms) of the disease and recognition of the complex object (Fig. 1). In the visual brain we are trying to infer not clear visible object's properties from attributes we have classified from a to b and back to a new part (q) of the object. However, it is a very important principle of our vision – the Model. It consists world, particular environment and known objects. We are able to precisely classify a complex, unknown object as we are tuning and comparing it particular attributes in many different levels (and even with different logics [1]). The model is important part of our approach. Our model is determined by attributes of the more advanced group of PD – G2V1. As it is illustrated in Fig. 2 granules describing different disease stages might develop or stay constant. In each disease stage we are comparing actual symptoms with the model and look for the similarities. We have demonstrated on group of over 20 patients that even if each one has different symptoms their path (c-granule) is going in the direction of our model.

Changing treatment it might push patient symptoms to the different path. In order to test such options we need several models and to measure how to change the treatment to direct patients to different model. By testing several different patient's groups, we have demonstrated that the certain long lasting treatments can change disease develop to new directions that are not similar to classical medication treatments [10].

In such cases one possible solution is to increase number of granules (dimension of attributes) but adding new attributes that might 'sense' new direction of the disease development. We are actually testing influence of the depression on the direction of the symptoms changes, as depression is characteristic not only for Parkinson's disease but also for more common Alzheimer's (AD) where late (after 65 years of age) onset AD (LOAD) is in 50% related to depression. Others have proposed similar AI predictive methods: to voice changes [11], by using supporting vector machine [12] or modular approach [13] based on interactions between motor and psychological tests [14, 15].

In summary, we have demonstrated that by using approach similar to the visual brain intelligence might give us a new way of look into similarities between different groups of patients. In addition, we might see longitudinal studies as c-granules and measure symptoms by distance to the Model (advance stage of the disease).

References

1. Pawlak, Z.: Rough Sets - Theoretical Aspects of Reasoning About Data. Kluwer Academic Publisher, Dordrecht (1991)
2. Zadeh, L.A.: From computing with numbers to computing with words - from manipulation of measurements to manipulation of perceptions. Int. J. Appl. Math. Comput. Sci. **12**, 307–324 (2002)

3. Przybyszewski, A.W.: The neurophysiological bases of cognitive computation using rough set theory. In: Peters, J.F., Skowron, A., Rybiński, H. (eds.) Transactions on Rough Sets IX. LNCS, vol. 5390, pp. 287–317. Springer, Heidelberg (2008). https://doi.org/10.1007/978-3-540-89876-4_16

4. Przybyszewski, A.W.: SI: SCA measures - fuzzy rough set features of cognitive computations in the visual system. J. Intell. Fuzzy Syst. (2018, pre-press). https://doi.org/10.3233/JIFS-18401

5. Skowron, A., Dutta, S.: Rough sets: past, present, and future. Nat. Comput. **17**, 855–876 (2018)

6. Dubois, D., Prade, H.: Rough fuzzy sets and fuzzy rough sets. Int. J. Gen. Syst. **17**, 91–209 (1990)

7. Riza, L.S., et al.: Implementing algorithms of rough set theory and fuzzy rough set theory in the R package RoughSets. Inf. Sci. **287**, 68–69 (2014)

8. Przybyszewski, A.W., et al.: Multimodal learning and intelligent prediction of symptom development in individual Parkinson's Patients. Sensors **16**(9), 1498 (2016). https://doi.org/10.3390/s16091498

9. Przybyszewski, A.W.: Fuzzy RST and RST rules can predict effects of different therapies in parkinson's disease patients. In: Ceci, M., Japkowicz, N., Liu, J., Papadopoulos, G.A., Raś, Z.W. (eds.) ISMIS 2018. LNCS (LNAI), vol. 11177, pp. 409–416. Springer, Cham (2018). https://doi.org/10.1007/978-3-030-01851-1_39

10. Przybyszewski, A.W., Szlufik, S., Habela, P., Koziorowski, D.M.: Multimodal learning determines rules of disease development in longitudinal course with parkinson's patients. In: Bembenik, R., Skonieczny, Ł., Protaziuk, G., Kryszkiewicz, M., Rybinski, H. (eds.) Intelligent Methods and Big Data in Industrial Applications. SBD, vol. 40, pp. 235–246. Springer, Cham (2019). https://doi.org/10.1007/978-3-319-77604-0_17

11. Tiwari, A.K.: Machine learning based approaches for prediction of Parkinson's disease. Mach. Learn. Appl. Int. J. (MLAIJ) **3**(2), 33–39 (2016)

12. Lerche, S., Heinzel, S., et al.: Aiming for study comparability in Parkinson's disease: proposal for a modular set of biomarker assessments to be used in longitudinal studies. Front. Aging Neurosci. (2016). https://doi.org/10.3389/fnagi.2016.00121

13. Singh, G., Vadera, M., Samavedham, L., Lim, E.C.: Machine learning based framework for multi-class diagnosis of neurodegenerative diseases: a study on Parkinson's disease. IFAC PaperOnLine **49**(7), 990–995 (2016)

14. Goldman, J.G., Holden, S., Ouyang, B., Bernard, B., Goetz, C.G., Stebbins, G.T.: Diagnosing PD-MCI by MDST ask force criteria: how many and which neuropsychological tests? Mov. Disord. **30**, 402–406 (2015)

15. Lawton, M., Kasten, M., May, M.T., et al.: Validation of conversion between mini-mental state examination and Montreal cognitive assessment. Mov. Disord. **31**, 593–596 (2016)

Component-Based Gender Identification Using Local Binary Patterns

Salma M. Osman[1], Nahla Noor[1], and Serestina Viriri[2($\boxtimes$)]

[1] College of Computer Science and Information Technology,
Sudan University of Science and Technology, Khartoum, Sudan
[2] School of Mathematics, Statistics and Computer Science,
University of KwaZulu-Natal, Durban, South Africa
viriris@ukzn.ac.za

Abstract. In this paper a component-based gender identification model from facial images has been proposed. The paper enhances the gender identification by using individual facial components (forehead, eyes, nose, cheeks, mouth and chin). Group of frontal facial images are used to validate the proposed model, feature extraction technique Local Binary Patterns (LBP) is implemented, then KNN and SVM classification techniques are applied to accomplish the gender identification model. The results achieved in this research work show an improved accuracy rate when face components (eyes, nose, mouth) are used for gender identification instead of the whole facial image. These results indicate that there are some facial parts which are not necessary for facial image recognition related application like gender identification.

Keywords: Face detection · Facial component · Feature extraction · LBP

1 Introduction

The face is an important biometric feature trait for human beings recognition [1]. Faces are accessible *windows* into the mechanisms that govern our emotional and social lives. Face identification is an interesting sub-area in the field of object recognition and can be defined as identifying or verifying human subjects in various scenes from a digital image or a video source [2]. A successful gender classification method has many potential applications such as human identification, smart human computer interface, computer vision approaches for monitoring people, demographic data collection. However, the gender classification tasks can be carried out easily by a human being but not by machines without any intelligence [3].

This work focuses on facial component-based gender identification from facial images. The facial components investigated include; the forehead, eyes, nose, cheeks, mouth and chin. The main steps of a gender classification system are *face detection*: extracts the region of interest which is the human faces in digital images, *feature extraction*: extraction of distinctive facial features, *classification*: categorizing the extracted data (patterns) through a learning process.

© Springer Nature Switzerland AG 2019
N. T. Nguyen et al. (Eds.): ICCCI 2019, LNAI 11683, pp. 307–315, 2019.
https://doi.org/10.1007/978-3-030-28377-3_25

There are several different techniques are used for facial recognition in the literature. The most common techniques are: Eigenfaces, Local Feature Analysis, Elastic Graph Matching, Active Appearance Model and 3D Morphable Model [4–8]. The Eigenfaces represent pictures of faces using Principal Component Analysis (PCA). The different forms of Eigenfaces are used as a base for other face recognition techniques. In general, the Eigenfaces find the similarities between faces with minimal controlled environments.

Heisele et al. [9–11] proposed a method to automatically detect and recognize facial components in term of Component Analysis for Facial Recognition. 14 points of reference are selected in the object window based on their 3D correspondences from a morphable model. The detection of facial components is computed by finding the maximum output of the smaller rectangular area with each component being classified using linear Support Vector Machine (SVM). The coordinates of the position of the maximum output of each component classifier is recorded with the position. The Haar transform is applied on the frontal faces to obtain the feature vectors.

Atharifard and Ghofrani [12–14] presented a robust component face detection algorithm based on the colour features. The algorithm is efficient in time complexity. In order to apply the component detectors, extra pixels, including non-skin regions, were removed. Mainly, the detected facial components are eyes and mouth. Ravi and Wilsonin [15] presented a novel face detection and gender classification strategy in color images under non uniform background.

Component-based gender identification related studies are not that many in the literature. Even methods which compute similarity measures at specific facial landmarks, such as Elastic-Bunch Graph Matching (EBGM) [16] do not operate in a per-component manner. This work focuses on gender identification based on facial component. The strategy seeks to utilize successfully detected facial components to recognize and verify the gender from images.

The rest of the paper is organized as follows: Sect. 2 describes the overall methodology of the study, and describe the overall face recognition system. Section 3 outlines the experiments, results and discusses the outcome of the study, and Sect. 4 concludes the paper and discusses possible extensions and the future work.

2   Methods and Techniques

The proposed facial component-based gender identification model is depicted in Fig. 1. Figure 1 shows all the steps of the proposed model starting from the image acquisition up to the classification stage.

2.1   Face Detection and Prepossessing

The first stage of face recognition is face detection, which is the detection of the facial region of interest. The region of interest is detected using Viola and Jones face detection technique that searches the face portion, this detector extract faces

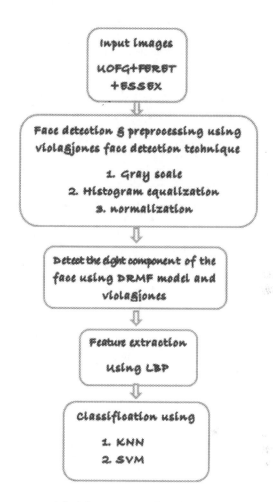

Fig. 1. The proposed facial component-based gender identification model

Fig. 2. (a) Original image (b) Face detection (c) Gray scale (d) Histogram equalization (e) Detected the components

from the image by starting from top left corner, it goes down to the bottom right corner [4]. It has three main steps: *(i)* The images are represented in the form of *Integral Image*; (ii) Features selection module is using the Ad boost learning algorithm; *(iii)* The cascade of Ad boost classifier is used eliminate background regions of the image.

The image is converted into grey level, and the grey level value indicates the brightness of a pixel. The Eq. (1) illustrates how the grey level is computed.

$$RGBTOGray : Y \leftarrow 0.299 \ast R + 0.587 \ast G + 0.114 \ast B \qquad (1)$$

where Y is the new grey scale pixel value, R is the red pixel value, B is the blue pixel value and G is the green pixel value.

The facial images are normalized, which is composed of two stages: geometric normalization component which rotates and scales the face to the same position among all images, and photometric normalization component which performs illumination adjustments [5]. The Eq. (2) defines the normalization process:

$$NF(x) = \frac{F(x)}{max(F(x))} \qquad (2)$$

Where $F(x)$ represents the extracted features and $max(F(x))$ represent the maximum values corresponding to the extracted features $F(x)$.

The Histogram equalization, is a technique for adjusting image intensities to enhance contrast as shown in Fig. 2. The Eq. (3) defines the Histogram equalization.

$$H^{'}(i) = \sum_{0 \leq j \leq i} H(j) \qquad (3)$$

Where $H^{'}(i)$ is the re-mapped intensity value, $H(j)$ is the original intensity value.

2.2   Detection of Facial Components

In component based gender identification, the most challenging task is to locate the components from the face. The Viola and Jones [17] algorithm is one of the powerful algorithms to perform this, although it does not cover all the components. The Discriminative Response Map Fitting (DRMF) model automatically detects the 66 landmark points on the face and estimates the rough 3D head pose. The Fig. 3 shows the resultant 66 landmark points of the DRMF model, and Fig. 4 shows the detected eight facial components.

2.3   Feature Extraction

Features extraction is one of the main steps in the gender identification process. In this step, we extract unique features from an image, these features called descriptor which used to describe the image.

DRMF Algorithm

- **Input: Data X.**
- **Output: Low-rank L; Outliers S.**

- **Iterate (block coordinate descent):**
  − Let **C = X − S**. Do rank-K SVD: **L = SVD(C, K)**.
  − Let **E = X − L**. Do thresholding: $S_{ij} = \begin{cases} E_{ij} & |E_{ij}| > t \\ 0 & \text{otherwise} \end{cases}$
    • t: the e-th largest elements in $\{|E_{ij}|\}$.

Fig. 3. Detected component using DRMF model

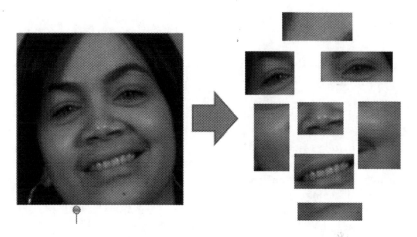

Fig. 4. Eight facial components detected

Local Binary Patterns (LBP). The Local Binary Patterns (LBP) [18] is a non-parametric descriptor that efficiently summarizes the structure of the image. Local Binary Pattern is considered to be tolerant of monotonic illumination changes and simple to compute. It is a texture analysis method but can also define local structures. Local Binary Pattern is computed by obtaining a decimal number for each pixel. Each pixel is then compared with the eight neighbouring pixels to the central pixel. The comparison is done by subtracting the central pixel from the neighbouring pixel, shown in equation (below). If the obtained value is negative then the pixel is assigned a 0; if a positive value is obtained, then that pixel is given a 1. The binary value is then read in a clockwise direction starting in the top left hand corner. The binary value that is obtained from each of these pixels is then converted to a decimal value. This decimal value that is obtained is then the pixel value, this value is between 0 and 255 pixel intensity.

Computation of the LBP descriptor can be summarized in a four-step process and is explained below:

1. For every pixel (x, y) in an image I, choose P neighboring pixels at a radius R.
2. Calculate the intensity difference of the current pixel i_c, with the P neighboring pixels i_p.
3. Threshold the intensity difference, such that all the negative differences are assigned 0 and all the positive differences are assigned 1, forming a bit vector.
4. Convert the P-bit vector to its corresponding decimal value and replace the intensity value at i_c with this decimal value.

Thus, the LBP descriptor for every pixel is given as

$$LBP(P, R) = \sum_{p=0}^{p-1} s(i_p - i_c)2^p \tag{4}$$

where i_c and i_p denote the intensity of the current and neighboring pixel, respectively. P is the number of neighboring pixels chosen at a radius R.

2.4   Classification

Classification involves taking the feature vectors extracted from the image and using them to automatically classify an images gender. This is done by using different machine learning algorithms. In this research work, a number of supervised machine learning algorithms were used to obtain the images gender. The supervised machine learning algorithm involves training the feature vector in order to compare an unknown feature vector with the trained data. The supervised machine learning algorithms used KNN and SVM.

K-Nearest Neighbor (KNN). The KNN [19] is an algorithm that stores all the cases and classifies the new case based on the similarity measure. The K-Nearest Neighbour method is used both in statistical estimation and pattern recognition. The whole dataset is classified into either the training or the testing sample data. From the training sample point, the distance is calculated using the Euclidean Distance. This equation is shown below. If the result is less than the neighbours around that data, then it is considered the neighbour.

$$d = \sqrt{\sum_{i=1}^{n}(x_i - q_i)^2} \tag{5}$$

Where n is the size of the data, xi is an element in the dataset and qi is a central point.

Support Vector Machine (SVM). The SVM [20] is a trained algorithm for learning classification and regression rules from data. SVM is based on structural risk minimization and is related to regularization theory. The parameters are found by solving a quadratic programming problem with linear equality and inequality constraints. Using the kernel function allows for flexibility and can search for a wide variety in the dataset. The defined algorithm searches for an optimal separating surface, known as the hyper plane. All the data is then separated using the hyper plane. If there are too many outliers using the calculated hyper plane, a new hyper plane is calculated until the simplest hyper plane is formulated.

Cross Validation. Cross-Validation is a statistical process of evaluating and comparing learning algorithms by dividing data into two parts: one used to learn or train a model and the other used to validate the model. Here we used 10 fold cross-validation which the data is randomly split into 10 equally (or nearly equally) sized segments or folds. Then 10 iterations of training and validation are performed such that within each iteration a different fold of the data is held-out for validation while the remaining 9 folds are used for learning [1]. The accuracy rate is computed using the equation:

$$Accuracy = \frac{true(positive) + true(negative)}{true(positive) + true(negative) + false(positive) + false(negative)} * 100$$

3 Experimental Results and Discussion

In this study the facial datasets used are the ESSEX, FERET and UOFG frontal face databases. The ESSEX database consists of facial images with 153 different objects (every object have 20 images) with green background. The FERET database consists of 485 images for training and 416 images for testing. The image has the size of 256×384 pixels with grey scale and color images. The UOFG dataset contains 10000 frontal images in age about 18 to 23 years old. The performance of detecting the whole face and some regions of the face compared, using Viola and Jones face detection technique and (DRMF) model, LBP feature extraction technique and two classifiers K-nearest neighbour algorithm (k-NN)and support vector machine (SVM). The gender classification rates are shown in Table 1 and Fig. 5.

The experiment results show that the best recognition appear when we using UOFG dataset with SVM classifier on 4 facial components (forehead, eyes, nose, and mouth). In general, better results are achieved without making use of the whole face. This could indicate that there are some facial components which are more distinctive for human gender identification. The time complexity is not much of an issue due to multi-processing capability currently available.

Table 1. The accuracy rate when we used UOFG, FERET and ESSEX with KNN and SVM classifier

Dataset	UofG		FERET		ESSEX	
Classifier	KNN	SVM	KNN	SVM	KNN	SVM
Whole face	77.09%	91.35%	75.08%	83.44%	78.22%	90.53%
8 facial components	89.25%	96.16%	80.90%	86.85%	88.21%	90.85%
4 facial components	93.12%	98.55%	89.12%	91.00%	92.3%	93.93%

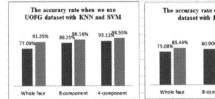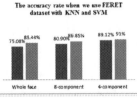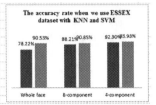

Fig. 5. The accuracy rates on three dataset, using the whole face, 4 facial components 8 facial components

4   Conclusion

In this paper, we presented a gender classification method based on the facial components. The results achieved show that the whole face is not necessarily required for gender identification from facial images. The Discriminative Response Map Fitting model is used to detect the facial components (forehead, eyes, nose, cheeks, mouth and chin). An accuracy rate of 98.55% was achieved, and the most distinctive facial components are the forehead, eyes, nose and mouth. For further work, it is envisioned that this model be extended to facial recognition in general and other facial characterization such age detection to determine the most distinctive and time-invariant facial components. Moreover, this research work can be extended to deep learning.

References

1. Raniwala, A., Chiueh, T.: Architecture and algorithms for an IEEE 802.11 based multi-channel wireless mesh network. In: IEEE Conference on Computer Communications (2005)
2. Abdullah, B., Abd-Alghafar, I., Salama, G.I., Abd-Alhafez, A.: Performance evaluation of a genetic algorithm based approach to network intrusion detection system. In: 13th International Conference on Aerospace Sciences and Aviation Technology, Military Technical College, Kobry Elkobbah, Cairo, Egypt (2009)
3. Alam, M.M.: Gender detection from frontal face images. Dissertation, BRAC University (2016)

4. Du, H., Salah, S.H., Ahmed, H.O.: A color and texture based multi-level fusion scheme for ethnicity identification. In: SPIE Sensing Technology + Applications, p. 91200B (2014)
5. Fu, Y., Cao, L., Guo, G., Huang, T.S.: Multiple feature fusion by subspace learning. In: Proceedings of the 2008 International Conference on Content-based Image and Video Retrieval, pp. 127–134 (2008)
6. Geertz, C.: The integrative revolution: primordial sentiments and civil politics in the new states. In: Old Societies and New States, p. 150 (1967)
7. Green, E.D.: Redefining ethnicity. In: 47th Annual International Studies Association Convention (2011)
8. Bradski, G., Kaehler, A.: Learning OpenCV: Computer Vision with the OpenCV Library. O'Reilly Media Inc., Sebastopol (2008)
9. Bonnen, K., Klare, B.F., Jain, A.K.: Component-based representation in automated face recognition. Inf. Forensics Secur. **8**(1), 239–253 (2013)
10. Heisele, B., Serre, T., Pontil, M., Poggio, T.: Component-based face detection. Comput. Vis. Pattern Recogn. **1**, 657 (2001)
11. Horowitz, D.L.: Ethnic Groups in Conflict. University of California Press, Oakland (1985)
12. Huang, J., Blanz, V., Heisele, B.: Face recognition using component-based SVM classification and morphable models. In: Pattern Recognition with Support Vector Machines, pp. 334–341 (2002)
13. Isaacs, H.R.: Idols of the Tribe: Group Identity and Political Change. Harvard University Press, Cambridge (1975)
14. Jafri, R., Arabnia, H.R.: A survey of face recognition techniques. J. Inf. Process. Syst. **5**(2), 41–68 (2009)
15. Belhumeur, P.N., Hespanha, J.P., Kriegman, D.J.: Eigenfaces vs. fisherfaces: recognition using class specific linear projection. Pattern Anal. Mach. Intell. **19**(7), 711–720 (1997)
16. Nazir, M., Ishtiaq, M., Batool, A., Jaffar, A., Mirza, M.: Feature selection for efficient gender classification. In: 11th WSEAS International Conference, pp. 70–75 (2010)
17. Hma Salah, S., Du, H., Al-Jawad, N.: Fusing local binary patterns with wavelet features for ethnicity identification. In: Proceedings of the IEEE International Conference Signal Image Process, vol. 21, pp. 416–422 (2013)
18. Domingos, P.: A few useful things to know about machine learning. Commun. ACM **55**(10), 78–87 (2012)
19. Kanungo, T., Mount, D.M., Netanyahu, N.S., Piatko, C.D., Silverman, R., Wu, A.Y.: An efficient k-means clustering algorithm: analysis and implementation. IEEE Trans. Pattern Anal. Mach. Intell. **24**(7), 881–892 (2002)
20. Refaeilzadeh, P., Tang, L., Liu, H.: Cross-validation. In: Ling Liu, M., Tamer, Ö. (eds.) Encyclopedia of Database System, pp. 532–538. Springer, New York (2009). https://doi.org/10.1007/978-0-387-39940-9_565

Age Estimation of Real-Time Faces Using Convolutional Neural Network

Olatunbosun Agbo-Ajala and Serestina Viriri[(✉)]

School of Mathematics, Statistics and Computer Sciences,
University of Kwazulu-Natal, Durban, South Africa
ajalabosun@gmail.com, viriris@ukzn.ac.za

Abstract. Age classification of an individual from an unconstrained real-time face image is rapidly gaining more popularity and this is because of its many possible applications from security control, surveillance monitoring to forensic art. Several solutions have been proposed in the past few years in solving this problem. Many of the existing traditional methods addressed age classification from face images taken from a controlled environment, only a few studied an unconstrained imaging conditions problem from real-time faces. However, deep learning methods have proven to be effective in solving this problem especially with the availability of both a large amount of data for training and high-end machines. In view of this, we propose a deep learning solution to age estimation from real-life faces. A novel six-layer deep convolutional neural network (CNN) architecture, learns the facial representations needed to estimate ages of individuals from face images taken from uncontrolled ideal environments. In order to further enhance the performance and reduce overfitting problem, we pre-trained our model on a large IMDB-WIKI dataset to conform to face image contents and then tuned the network on the training portions of MORPH-II and OIU-Adience datasets to pick-up the peculiarities and the distribution of the dataset. Our experiments demonstrate the effectiveness of our method for age estimation in-the-wild when evaluated on OIU-Adience benchmark that is known to contain images of faces acquired in ideal and unconstrained conditions, where it achieves better performance than other CNN methods. The proposed age classification method achieves new state-of-the-art results with an improvement of 8.6% (Exact) and 3.4% (One-off) acccuracy over the best-reported result on OIU-Adience dataset.

Keywords: Age estimation · Face images · Convolutional neural network · Deep learning

1 Introduction

Age estimation using face images is an interesting and a very challenging task [1,2]. The features from the face images are used to determine age, gender, ethnic background, and emotional state of people [3]. Among this set of features,

© Springer Nature Switzerland AG 2019
N. T. Nguyen et al. (Eds.): ICCCI 2019, LNAI 11683, pp. 316–327, 2019.
https://doi.org/10.1007/978-3-030-28377-3_26

age estimation can be particularly useful in many possible real-time applications [4] which include biometrics [3], security and surveillance [5], electronic customer relationship management [6], human-computer interaction [5], electronic vending machines [6], forensic art [7], entertainment [8], cosmetology [1] among others.

The conventional hand-crafted methods relied on the differences in dimensions of facial features [4], and face descriptors like local binary patterns and Gabor features [9, 10]. Most of these techniques only designed classification methods for age estimation task that utilize face images captured under controlled conditions [11]; few of those methods are designed to handle the many challenges of unconstrained imaging conditions. The images in these categories have some variations which may affect the ability of the computer vision system to accurately estimate the age. More recently, convolutional neural network (CNN) based methods have proven to be effective for age estimation task due to its superior performance over existing methods. Availability of both large data for training and high-end machines, also help in the adoption of the deep CNN methods for age classification problems.

In this paper, we present an age estimation system (in Fig. 1) that uses a deep CNN method to estimate the age of face images of an individual taken from unconstrained real-time scenarios. The design is a six-layer network architecture of four convolutional layers and two fully connected layers pre-trained on a large IMDB-WIKI dataset and tuned on the training portions of MORPH-II and OIU-Adience datasets for further learning the traits of face images in each datasets. The proposed system includes three stages of image preprocessing phase that prepare the face images before being fed into the designed network for age classification process (details of image preprocessing method is presented in Sect. 3.1). The newly designed network was evaluated on OIU-Adience benchmark for age classification of unfiltered face images. The method outperforms the other methods in the literature, showing an improvement on the current state-of-the-art methods.

The remainder of this paper is structured as follows: Sect. 2 presents a review of the related works, Sect. 3 describes the proposed method, Sect. 4 presents the experiments while conclusion and future works are drawn in Sect. 5.

2   Related Works

The study of age estimation from face images has been in existence for decades. Various methods have been employed in the time past to address this problem, with varying levels of achievement. A comprehensive study of some of the past but recent approaches to age estimation from facial images are presented by Angulu et al. in [12].

Some of the very early past methods approached an age estimation problem by manually extracting the facial features using differences in facial features dimension. Although those methods have proven to be effective when classifying images from a constrained environment, only a few have attempted to address the problems that arise from real-time images with the variations in

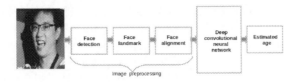

Fig. 1. A schematic diagram of the proposed age estimation system.

Fig. 2. Image preprocessing phase

pose, illumination, expression, and occlusion [4]. Kwon and Lobo [13] presented an age estimation solution that extracted and used wrinkles features. They used distance ratios between frontal face landmarks to separate babies from adults and separated the young adults from senior adults by using the wrinkle indices. However, their method lacks the ability to classify face images from in-the-wild scenarios due to the presence of varying degrees of variations in those images. Ramanathan and Chellappa in [14] proposed a model that predicted an age progression and face recognition of young faces from 0 to 18 years. They used images from FG-NET aging dataset and a private dataset for evaluation and testing. In [15] Horng et al. used both geometric and wrinkles features. They used geometric features to distinguish a baby face from an adult face and wrinkles for classifying adult faces into three different adult groups. They employed Sobel edge operator and region labeling to locate the positions of features to extract. The approach achieved a better result than the state-of-the-art methods on constrained face images. Jana et al. in [16] also investigated a method that used spatial local binary patterns (LBP) histograms to classify face images into six different age (groups). They employed minimum distance, nearest neighbor and k-nearest neighbour classifiers at the classification stage. The result showed a reasonable improvement on the existing age estimation methods on face images from controlled environments.

Although, all of these methods on age classifications have proven to be effective on constrained images, they are not suitable to tackle large variations experienced in an ideal real-world images. In order to effectively solve the task of age classification of real-time face images, increasing attention is drawn to the use of machine learning and deep CNN. Eidinger et al. in [4] developed a solution that estimates humans age from facial images acquired in a challenging in-the-wild condition. They collected face images labeled for age that are acquired from an ideal world environment and employed a robust face alignment with a dropout-support vector machine approach to estimate the ages of individuals from face images taken from a real-time environment. Their approach significantly outperformed the state-of-the-art methods when evaluated. Levi and Hassner [11] investigated a deep CNN approach for age estimation from an unconstrained image. They developed a simple CNN architecture that can estimate ages of individuals using face images from real-time scenarios that reflect different levels of variations in appearance. Their method achieved 50.7% (Exact) and 84.7% (One-off) accuracy when it was evaluated on OIU-Adience dataset for age. Ekmekji [17] proposed a study that classified humans age by extending the already existing approaches. Qawaqneh *et al.* in [18] studied a solution that used an already trained deep CNN to estimate the age of unconstrained face images. The study used a network that was initially trained on face recognition dataset to carry out the age estimation task. Their approach outperformed the previous works when evaluated on the challenging OIU-Adience database. Liu *et al.* [19] also developed an approach that focused on the distribution of data rather than modifying the already existing network architectures. They proposed a CNN model that used a multi-class focal loss function instead of the conventional softmax function. Fortunately, their experimental approach showed better performance over the state-of-the-art techniques.

In summary, it has been proven in the literatures that CNN can achieve great success on age estimation task, significantly achieving better performance. Although most of the recent works improved classification accuracy by modifying the existing network architecture, age classification can still obtain a higher accuracy with a better CNN architecture. In this study, we propose a novel CNN method, a six-layer CNN architecture of four convolutional layers and two fully connected layers. The proposed method is fortified with a robust image processing technique that impact the performance of our approach. Furthermore, our optimization algorithm that adaptively tunes the learning rate as the network trains and a regularization method, contributed to the effectiveness of our approach. Our method resulting in a better performing network, showing an improvement on the state-of-the-art methods.

3   Proposed Method

The proposed method follows the pipeline in Fig. 1, in this section, we describe each step of the pipeline in detail.

Fig. 3. Face images from IMDB-WIKI, Adience and MORPH-II datasets

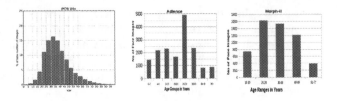

Fig. 4. Age distribution in IMDB-WIKI, Adience and MORPH-II datasets

3.1   Image Preprocessing

Some of the datasets employed in this work do not show centered frontal-faces but rather faces in-the-wild, we need to detect and align the faces for both training and testing. As such there is need to prepare and preprocess the face images for classification task before feeding them into the designed network. The image preprocessing phases are explained in more detailed below:

Face Detection: In order to detect the facial landmark of the input images, there is need to localize the face in the image and detect the key facial structures on the face. In this work, a face detector *Haar Feature-based Cascade Classifier* proposed by Viola and Jones [20] for face detection was employed. The classifier returns an output that is a bounding rectangle that contains the face image.

Landmark Detection: To represent salient facial regions like mouth, right eyebrow, left eyebrow, right eye, left eye, nose and jaw, a pre-trained Dlib model *shape_predictor_68_face_landmarks* that was an implementation of Kazemi and Sullivan [21] for face landmark detection was used. It estimates the location of $68(x, y)$-coordinates that map to facial structures on the face images. With this method, the key structures in our face images were localized.

Face Alignment: There is need to align the face images for both training and testing to further boost our work for higher accuracy. To this effect, there is need to compute the angle between the *(x, y)-coordinates* of the eyes, generated the midpoint between the eyes then applied affine transformation to warp the images into a new output coordinate space. With this, the face is centered in the image, rotated with the eyes lying along the same *y-coordinates* and then scaled with the size of all faces approximately equal. As expected, cropping the detected face for the age estimating processing rather than using the entire image, obtained a massive improvement in performance. Image preprocessing stage are shown in Fig. 2.

3.2   Network Architecture

We proposed an architecture (see Table 1) that contain six layers; four convolutional layers and fewer nodes with two fully-connected layers, The proposed network is a sequential CNN model that is capable of extracting the facial features needed to distinctively estimate the age of an individual via face image.

The method introduced a regularization technique (a dropout and data augmentation) to reduce the risk of overfitting and improve performance of our work. A batch normalization is used in place of the conventional local response normalization used by Levi *et al.* to further improve the performance of the network. We further prepare the face images by scaling them into 256×256 and then cropped into 227×227 pixel to boost the accuracy of our method. The six-layer CNN based architecture is structured as follow:

The first convolutional layer learned 96, 7×7 kernels with a stride of 4×4 to reduce the spatial dimensions of the input 227×227 images. Each convolutional layer is followed by an activation layer then a batch normalization with a max-pool of kernel size of 3×3 and a stride of 2×2 operating at the end of the convolutional block. After series of empirical experiments, a small dropout of 0.25 was utilized to reduce overfitting. The second series of convolutional layer applied the same structure, but with an adjustment to learn 256, 5×5 filters. The third is near identical to the other convolutional layers but with an increase in the number of filters to 384 and a reduction of the filter size to 3×3. The final convolutional layer set has a filter of 256 and a filter size of 3×3. All the convolutional layers are sandwiched with a dropout of 0.25 at the end of each layer set. The first fully-connected layer received the output of the fourth convolutional layer and learn 512 nodes with an activation layer followed by a batch normalization and with a dropout of 0.50 while the second and last fully connected layer maps to the final classes for age. In our case, we employed a softmax loss classifier to assign a probability for each class. The softmax classifier as a linear classifier, uses the cross-entropy loss function; the gradient of the cross-entropy function inform a softmax classifier how exactly to update its weights. The Softmax loss is defined in Eq. 1:

$$\sigma(z)_j = \frac{e^{z_j}}{\sum_{k=1}^{k} e_k^z} \tag{1}$$

where z is a vector of the inputs to the output layer and j indexes the output units.

For the cross-entropy loss of a multi-class classification, we calculate a separate loss for each class label per observation and sum the result. This is defined as presented in Eq. 2:

$$-\sum_{c=1}^{M} y_{o,c} \log(p_{o,c}) \tag{2}$$

where M is the number of classes, y is the binary indicator $(0 or 1)$ if class label c is the correct classification for observation o and p is the predicted probability observation o that is of class c.

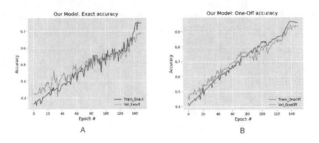

Fig. 5. Graph of Exact and One-off accuracy against Epoch

3.3   Evaluation Metrics

In order to evaluate our approach, we use two different established metrics.

Exact Accuracy: Exact accuracy metric is used to define the effectiveness of an age estimator. It is calculated as the percentage of face images that were classified into correct age-groups. Equation 3 presents its mathematical equation.

$$Exact\ accuracy = \frac{no\ of\ accurate\ prediction}{total\ no\ of\ prediction\ made} \tag{3}$$

One-Off: One-off evaluation metric measures whether the ground-truth class label matches the predicted class label. It allows for a deviation of at most one bucket from the real age range. One-off is calculated as a ratio of the correct predictions to the total number of data points.

3.4   Network Training

The proposed network is trained on IMDB-WIKI dataset, a very challenging dataset, to conform to face image contents and then tuned on the training portion of both MORPH-II and OIU-Adience datasets to pick-up the peculiarities and the distribution of each dataset. All these datasets are with varying degrees of variations, as such, there is need to preprocess the face images to decrease the influence of the background of images and resized the images to 256 × 256 pixel. Data augmentation is also needed to increase the amount of relevant data within a training dataset and reduce the risk of overfitting of the network, and this is done by creating an altered copies of the face images during the training stage. For the estimation, we utilized 70% OIU-Adience for training, and the other 30% for validation and testing. To further boost the accuracy of our approach, 10-crop oversampling method was employed to extract 227 × 227 region of the images and this increased the training data and consequently improved our result. Moreover, rather than computing the loss and the gradient of the entire training set, a sample of small sets of training examples (mini batch) was used to compute the estimate of the full sum and that of the true gradient, a Stochastic Gradient Descendent (SGD) optimizer was adopted with a mini-batch size of 64 for training. The optimizer was chosen ahead of other known ones in order

Table 1. Summary of our Network Architecture

Layer type	Output size	Filter size/Stride
INPUT IMAGE	$227 \times 227 \times 3$	–
CONV1	$56 \times 56 \times 96$	$7 \times 7/4 \times 4$
ACT	$56 \times 56 \times 96$	-
BN	$56 \times 56 \times 96$	-
Maxpool	$28 \times 28 \times 96$	$3 \times 3/2 \times 2$
dropout	$28 \times 28 \times 96$	-
CONV2	$28 \times 28 \times 256$	5×5
ACT	$28 \times 28 \times 256$	-
BN	$28 \times 28 \times 256$	-
Maxpool	$14 \times 14 \times 256$	3×3
dropout	$14 \times 14 \times 256$	-
CONV3	$14 \times 14 \times 384$	3×3
ACT	$14 \times 14 \times 384$	-
BN	$14 \times 14 \times 384$	-
Maxpool	$7 \times 7 \times 384$	3×3
dropout	$7 \times 7 \times 384$	-
CONV4	$7 \times 7 \times 384$	3×3
ACT	$7 \times 7 \times 256$	-
BN	$7 \times 7 \times 256$	-
Maxpool	$1 \times 1 \times 256$	3×3
dropout	$1 \times 1 \times 256$	-
FC1	512	-
ACT	512	-
BN	512	-
dropout	512	-
FC2	8	-

to compute an update for each example $(x^{(i)}, y^{(i)})$ that was uniformly sampled from the training dataset; it calculates the gradient of the parameters by using only a few training samples. This is calculated as shown in Eq. 4 below:

$$\theta = \theta - \alpha \nabla_\theta J(\theta; x^{(i)}, y^{(i)}) \tag{4}$$

where α is the learning rate, $\nabla_\theta J$ is the gradient of the loss term with respect to the weight vector θ.

Data Augmentation: Figure 4 reveals the uneven distribution of the age in the employed datasets. To address this problem, we employed an adaptive augmentation method that increases the number of altered copies of the face images and also makes the age distribution of the training set even. In this work, we applied an augmentation approach that includes random cropping, zooming, random mirror, and rotation.

Table 2. Age classification: Exact and One-off results on OIU-Adience benchmark.

Methods	Exact (%)	One-off (%)
Eidinger *et al.* [4]	45.1	79.5
Ekmekji [17]	54.5	84.1
Levi *et al.* [11]	50.7	84.7
Liu *et al.* [19]	54.0	88.2
Proposed	**63.1**	**91.6**

4   Experiments

In this section, we present the results of our empirical experiments. We introduce the datatsets used and then show the performance of our proposed method on the validation datasets.

4.1   Datasets

The availability of relevant facial aging databases plays an important role in the performance of an age estimator. In this work, we employed the three most relevant facial aging databases to either train, or validate our approach.

IMDB-WIKI: IMDB-WIKI [22] is the largest publicly-available dataset for age estimation of people in-the-wild, containing more than half a million images with accurate age labels between 0 and 100 years. IMDB contains 460,723 images of 20,284 celebrities and Wikipedia with 62,328 images. The images of IMDB-WIKI dataset are obtained directly from the website, as such the dataset contains many low-quality images, such as human comic images, sketch images, severe facial mask, full body images, multi-person images, blank images, and so on.

MORPH-II: MORPH-II database [23] is a publicly-available aging database collected at the University of North Carolina at Wilmington by the face aging group. The database records linked attributes such as age, gender, ethnicity, weight, height, and ancestry. The whole database is divided into two albums; album I and album II. Album II contains 55,134 face images obtained from more than 13,000 subjects.

OIU-Adience: OIU-Adience database [4] is a collection of face images from an ideal real-life and unconstrained environments. It reflects all the features that are expected of an image collected from challenging real-world scenarios. OIU-Adience images, therefore, exhibit a high level of variations in noise, pose, appearance among others. It is used in studying age and gender classification system. The entire collection of OIU-Adience database is about 26,580 face images of 2,284 subjects and with an age-group label of eight comprising: 0–2, 4–6, 8–13, 15–20, 25–32, 38–43, 48–53, 60+. Samples of the face images are presented in Fig. 3.

Fig. 6. Samples of face images with correct estimation

Fig. 7. Samples of face images with wrong estimation

4.2   Experimental Result

In this section, we assess our method for predicting age-groups. The purpose is to predict whether a person's age falls within some age range rather than predicting the precise age. We evaluate the performance of our classifier on OIU-Adience dataset using Exact and One-off accuracy metrics. We achieved an Exact accuracy of 63.1% and One-off accuracy of 91.6%. The graph in Fig. 5 presents the results for Exact accuracy and One-off accuracy. Table 2 presents our result and the results of the current state-of-the-art methods for age-group classification on OIU-Adience benchmark. Our approach achieves the best results, not only improving the Exact accuracy but also the One-off accuracy; it outperforms the current state-of-the-arts methods.

In Figs. 6 and 7, we present the predictions of some of the face images from the OIU-Adience (validation set) by our classifier. In many instances, our solution is able to correctly predict the age-group of faces. Failures (Fig. 7) may be as a result of two major reasons: The first is the failure to either detect or align the face. The second is because of some extreme conditions of variability such as non-frontal, blurring, low resolution, occlusion, heavy makeup.

5   Conclusions and Future Work

The proposed six-layer CNN based method shows the state-of-the-art result on OIU-Adience dataset. With a robust image processing design, our method handles some of the variability noticed in the face images from real life's scenarios. This validates the applicability of our method to age classification in-the-wild. Pre-training on the IMDB-WIKI and fine-tuning on MORPH-II and OIU-Adience datasets, result in a large boost in the performances. In the future, we hope that a larger dataset will be available in age (groups) estimation so as to employ a deeper convolutional neural network architecture for age estimation of real-time faces. Fine-tuning the face detector on the target dataset(s) can also lessen the failure rate of the face detection phase. A more robust landmark detector can also lead to better alignment and performance.

References

1. Drobnyh, K.A., Polovinkin, A.N.: Using supervised deep learning for human age estimation problem. In: ISPRS - International Archives of the Photogrammetry, Remote Sensing and Spatial Information Sciences, vol. XLII-2/W4, pp. 97–100, May 2017
2. Huerta, I., Fernández, C., Segura, C., Hernando, J., Prati, A.: A deep analysis on age estimation. Pattern Recogn. Lett. **68**, 239–249 (2015)
3. Bouchrika, I., Harrati, N., Ladjailia, A., Khedairia, S.: Age estimation from facial images based on hierarchical feature selection. In: 16th International Conference on Sciences and Techniques of Automatic Control and Computer Engineering - STA 2015, Monastir, Tunisia, pp. 393–397 (2015)
4. Eidinger, E., Enbar, R., Hassner, T.: Age and gender estimation of unfiltered faces. IEEE Trans. Inform. Forensics Secur. **9**(12), 2170–2179 (2014)
5. Abbas, A.R., Kareem, A.R.: Intelligent age estimation from facial images using machine learning techniques. Iraqi J. Sci. **59**(2A), 724–732 (2018)
6. Mandal, S., Debnath, C., Kumari, L.: Automated age prediction using wrinkles features of facial images and neural network. Int. J. Emerg. Eng. Res. Technol. **5**(2), 12–20 (2017)
7. Shen, W., Guo, Y., Wang, Y., Zhao, K., Wang, B., Yuille, A.: Deep regression forests for age estimation. In: CVPR, pp. 2304–2313 (2017)
8. Wen, Y., Liu, W., Yang, M., Fu, Y., Xiang, Y., Hu, R.: Structured occlusion coding for robust face recognition. Neurocomputing **178**, 11–24 (2016)
9. Badame, V., Jamadagni, M.: Study of approaches for human facial age. Int. J. Innov. Res. Sci. Eng. Technol. **6**(8), 2347–6710 (2017)
10. Feng, S., Lang, C., Feng, J., Wang, T., Luo, J.: Human facial age estimation by cost-sensitive label ranking and trace norm regularization. IEEE Trans. Multimedia **19**(1), 136–148 (2017)
11. Levi, G., Hassner, T.: Age and gender classification using convolutional neural networks. In: IEEE Conference on Computer Vision and Pattern Recognition Workshops, pp. 34–42 (2015)
12. Angulu, R., Tapamo, J.R., Adewumi, A.O.: Age estimation via face images: a survey. EURASIP J. Image Video Process. **2018**, 42 (2018)
13. Kwon, Y.H.: Age classification from facial images. Zhurnal Eksperimental'noi i Teoreticheskoi Fiziki **74**(1), 1–21 (1997)
14. Ramanathan, N., Chellappa, R.: Modeling age progression in young faces. In: Proceedings of the 2006 IEEE Computer Society Conference on Computer Vision and Pattern Recognition, CVPR 2006, February 2016

15. Horng, W.B., Lee, C.P., Chen, C.W.: Classification of age groups based on facial features. Tamkang J. Sci. Eng. **4**(3), 183–192 (2001)
16. Jana, R., Pal, H., Chowdhury, A.: Age group estimation using face angle. IOSR J. Org. **7**(5), 1–5 (2012)
17. Ekmekji, A.S.U.: Convolutional Neural Networks for Age and Gender Classification Research paper (2016)
18. Qawaqneh, Z., Mallouh, A.A., Barkana, B.D.: Deep Convolutional Neural Network for Age Estimation based on VGG-Face Model. arXiv, September 2017
19. Liu, W., Chen, L., Chen, Y.: Age classification using convolutional neural networks with the multi-class focal loss. In: IOP Conference Series: Materials Science and Engineering, vol. 428, no. 1 (2018)
20. Viola, P., Jones, M.: Rapid object detection using a boosted cascade of simple features. In: Proceedings of the 2001 IEEE Computer Society Conference on Computer Vision and Pattern Recognition, CVPR, vol. 1 (2001)
21. Kazemi, V., Sullivan, J.: One millisecond face alignment with an ensemble of regression trees. In: Proceedings of the IEEE Computer Society Conference on Computer Vision and Pattern Recognition, pp. 1867–1874 (2014)
22. Zhang, K., et al.: Age group and gender estimation in the wild with deep RoR architecture. IEEE Access **5**(X), 22492–22503 (2017)
23. Ricanek, K., Tesafaye, T.: MORPH: a longitudinal image database of normal adult age-progression. In: Proceedings of 7th International Conference on Automatic Face and Gesture Recognition, pp. 341–345 (2006)

Demand Forecasting Using Random Forest and Artificial Neural Network for Supply Chain Management

Navneet Vairagade[1(⊠)], Doina Logofatu[1(⊠)], Florin Leon[2], and Fitore Muharemi[1(⊠)]

[1] Frankfurt University of Applied Sciences, Frankfurt am Main, Germany
logofatu@fb2.fra-uas.de
[2] Technical University of Iaşi, Iaşi, Romania

Abstract. Demand forecasting is affecting the success of Supply Chain Management (SCM), and the organizations which support them and are in the early stage of a digital transformation. In a near future it could represent the most significant change in the integrated SCM era in today's complex, dynamic, and uncertain environment. The ability to adequately predict demand by the customers in an SCM is vital to the survival of any business. In this work, we have tried to solve this problem using various demand forecasting models to predict product demand for grocery items with machine learning techniques. A representative set ML-based forecasting techniques have been applied to the demand data and the accuracy of the methods was compared. As measurement metrics we have used R2 score, Mean Squared Error score and Mean Absolute Error score. Based on ranking, Random Forest classifier gives better performance result on this specific demand forecasting problem compared with the Artificial Neural Network falling behind in the tested category.

Keywords: Supply Chain Management · Demand forecasting ·
Random Forest · Artificial Neural Network

1 Introduction

In the era of greater demand uncertainty, higher supply risk, and increasing competitive intensity, Supply Chain Management (SCM) excellence often depends on the organization's ability to integrate the entire spectrum of end-to-end processes of acquiring components or materials, converting them into finished goods, and delivering them to customers. Since such an ability can be improved by increased visibility across the end-to-end SCM processes and many leading-edge organization's have attempted to enrich their information sources and share real-time information with Supply Chain (SC) partners [1]. SCM is the lifeblood of any business, impacting everything from the quality, delivery, and costs of business products and services to customer service and satisfaction to ultimately profitability and return on assets. The requirements and pressures on

© Springer Nature Switzerland AG 2019
N. T. Nguyen et al. (Eds.): ICCCI 2019, LNAI 11683, pp. 328–339, 2019.
https://doi.org/10.1007/978-3-030-28377-3_27

SC teams-including those for sustainability, cost efficiency, and disruption and risk mitigation-are increasing and growing in complexity. Unfortunately, most of the SC organization's are operating with systems built for another era. They lack the transparency and visibility needed to predict better and mitigate disruptions and imbalance. As a result, SC organization's struggle to collect and make sense of an overwhelming amount of data scattered across different processes, sources and, systems. Under these conditions it is incredibly challenging to manage and monitor the complete SC, resulting in undesirable risk exposure, delays, disruptions, and as well as increased costs [2]. Thus SCM is becoming more information intensive, and its focus has been shifted toward the substitution of assets like inventory, Warehouses, transportation equipment with information. Recognizing the increasing significance of information to SC success, SC professionals have explored various ways to manage information better and leverage it to make better business decisions. Some of those ways include Artificial Intelligence (AI), Machine Learning (ML) has been in existence for decades but has not been fully utilized in the area of SCM.

1.1 Supply Chain Management

The term 'SCM' refers to a network of organization's involved in generating value for the end customer in the form of products and services via upstream or downstream links in different processes and activities as shown in Fig. 1. SCM enables an organization to source the components and raw materials that are needed to create a service or product and deliver that service or product to customers [3].

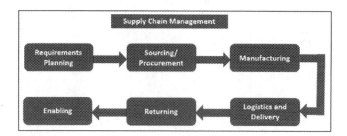

Fig. 1. Supply Chain Management process

The components involved in SCM are:

1. **Requirements Planning:** Enterprises need to plan and manage all resources required to meet customer demands for their product or service. They also need to design their SC and then determine which metrics to use to ensure the SC is efficient, effective, delivers value to customers and meets enterprise goals [4].
2. **Sourcing/Procurement:** Companies must choose suppliers to provide the goods and services needed to create their product. After suppliers are under contract, SC managers use a variety of processes to manage and monitor supplier relationships. Key processes include ordering, managing inventory, receiving and authorizing supplier payments [4].

3. **Manufacturing:** SC managers coordinate the activities required to accept raw materials, manufacture the product, test for quality, the package for shipping and schedule for delivery. Most enterprises measure quality, production output, and worker productivity to ensure the enterprise creates products that meet quality standards [4].

4. **Logistics and Delivery:** This involves coordinating customer orders, dispatching loads, scheduling delivery, invoicing customers and receiving payments. It depends on a fleet of vehicles to ship products to customers. Many organization's outsource large parts of the delivery process to specialist organization's, particularly if the product has to be delivered to a consumer's home or requires special handling [4].

5. **Returning:** The supplier needs a responsive and flexible network to take back excess, unwanted and damaged products. If the product is defective, it must be scrapped or reworked. If the product is merely excess or unwanted, it must be returned to the warehouse for sale [4].

6. **Enabling:** To operate efficiently, the SC requires many support processes to monitor information throughout the SC and assure compliance with all regulations. Enabling processes include portfolio management, finance, HR, IT, facilities, product design, sales and quality assurance [4].

2   Problem Statement

Latest technology can be beneficial and profitable in SCM. However, to get a budget or management support the fastest, the first question should be What needs to be improved in SCM right now? [5]. The following examples are as follows:-

1. Hard to plan for demand (demand forecasting) [5].
2. Excessive safety stocks and bullwhip effect [5].
3. Supplier unreliability [5].
4. Transport network unpredictability [5].
5. Looking at the real bottom line impact of supply chain decisions [5].

The forecasting of demands is one of the most challenging phases in SCM. The current technologies for forecasting the demand are often presented the user with incorrect results, causing them to make severe financial mistakes. They cannot correctly understand the growing market patterns and market fluctuations, and this hampers its power to calculates market trends and provide results accordingly adequately. What makes demand forecasting so challenging and complex? Rather than looking like a logical series of numbers, in today's business environment, we see demand like a pattern of partially constrained chaos. Demand is highly influenced by various internal and external factors that drive it up and down in ways that can not be understood by merely looking at a historical time-series of aggregated demand buckets. Instead, demand should be viewed as a complex series of indicators that can be nearly impossible to manage with traditional forecasting algorithms.

3   Related Work

This section discusses an understanding of different machine learning techniques that were used for demand forecasting in SCM. The sections below represent the summarization of the related work used for demand forecasting in SCM. Kalyan Mupparaju, Anurag Soni, Prasad Gujela, and Matthew A Lanham in the research *A Comparative Study of Machine Learning Frameworks for Demand Forecasting* built various demand forecasting models to predict product demand for millions of items at a store and day level for a South American grocery chain using Python's deep learning library. The purpose of their predictive models is to compare the performance of different open-source modeling techniques to predict a time-dependent demand at a store-SKU level. These demand forecasting models were developed using Keras and scikit-learn packages in Python. The forecasting models used in this study are Gradient Boosting, Factorization Machines, and Deep Neural Networks [11].

Carbonneau Real, Vahidov Rustam, and Laframboise Kevin in the research *Machine Learning-Based Demand Forecasting in Supply Chains* investigated the applicability of ML techniques and compared the performances with more traditional methods to improve demand forecast accuracy in Supply Chains in *Statistics Canada manufacturing survey* data-set. The forecasting models used in this study are Artificial Neural Network, Recurrent Neural Network, and Support Vector Machines [12].

Yue et al. [10], have shown the effectiveness of Support Vector Machine model in demand forecasting which. In this research, the model of SVM is introduced into the retail industry for demand forecasting, and the experiment results show that the performance of SVM is superior to traditional statistical models and the traditional Radius Basis Function Neural Network (RBFNN). The authors conclude that the prediction accuracy of SVM can still be improved by using ensemble-learning techniques.

4   Proposed Approaches

Extensive research on forecasting has provided a large number of forecasting techniques and algorithms in mathematics, statistics, operations management, and supply chain academic outlets. This section explains the approaches in our research and introduction to the data-set that has been used for demand forecasting. We have used Random Forest and Keras Regression - Neural Network regression algorithms for predictions and calculated R2 score, Mean Squared Error (MSE) score and Mean Absolute Error (MAE) score for both of the algorithms.

4.1   Random Forest

Random Forest is a supervised machine learning algorithm which is a combination of many tree predictors such that each individual tree depends on the values of a random vector sampled independently with the same distribution for all trees that are included in the forest [6,9]. We have chosen Random Forest algorithm because it builds multiple decision trees and merges them to get a more accurate and stable prediction. It makes powerful models with the ability to limit overfitting without substantially increasing error due to bias and they are very quick to train the huge samples. Random Forest is a very convenient and easy to use algorithm, because of default hyper-parameters often produce a good prediction result.

4.2   Keras Neural Network

Keras is a powerful Deep Learning library written in Python and has made a significant contribution to the advancement of artificial intelligence. We have chosen the Keras Neural Network because it is a user-friendly Neural Network library that can reliably process large volumes of data, and it was developed with a focus to enable fast experiments with high accuracy. It is simple to use, and it allows you to build powerful Neural Networks in just a few lines of code [7]. The implementation of the neural network classifier is based on the traditional back-propagation algorithm, and on a 5 hidden-layers network.

4.3   Keras Neural Network Life Cycle

Figure 2 below is an overview of the 5 steps in the Keras Neural Network model life cycle:

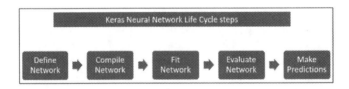

Fig. 2. Keras Neural Network Life Cycle steps [8].

1. **Define Network:** The first step is to define a Neural Network, and they are defined in Keras as a sequence of layers. The package for these layers is the Sequential class. First, the instance of the Sequential class is created, then create multiple layers and add them sequentially in the order that they should be connected [8]. The first layer in the network defines the number of inputs with activation function as *ReLU (Rectified Linear Unit)*.
2. **Compile Network:** After defining the network, the compilation is an important step. It transforms the sequence of layers that we have defined into a highly proficient series of the matrix, transforms in a format proposed to be executed on your GPU or CPU. Compilation requires many parameters to be specified, specifically tailored to training your network. Specifically the optimization algorithm, i.e., *adam* is used to train the network and the loss function i.e., *mse* is used to estimate the network that is minimized by the optimization algorithm.

3. **Fit Network:** After compiling the network, it can be fit, which means adapt the weights on a training data-set. Fitting the network requires the training data-set to be specified, with a matrix of input patterns (X) along with an array of matching output patterns (Y). The network is then trained using the backpropagation algorithm and optimized according to the optimization algorithm and loss function specified while compiling the model.

4. **Evaluate Network:** After the network is trained, it has to be evaluated on the training data, but this will not provide a meaningful indication of the performance of the network as a predictive model, as it has already observed all of this data before so we have to evaluate the network performance on a different data-set, i.e., validation or test which is unseen during testing.

5. **Make Predictions:** This is the final step after network evaluation and satisfying the performance of the fit model, we can use it to make predictions on new data. This is done by just calling the *predict()* function in Python on the model with an array of new input patterns.

4.4   Keras Neural Network Workflow

Figure 3 below shows the complete Workflow of Keras Neural Network. There is training data-set with samples and given these samples as input to Input layer for Keras Neural Network. Followed by the Input layer there is a Hidden layer and at last Output layer to display the output.

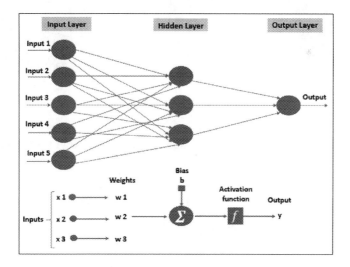

Fig. 3. Keras Neural Network Workflow.

5   Implementation

This section includes discussion regarding detailed implementation for improving accuracy of demand forecasting in Supply Chain Management using Random Forest and Neural Network algorithms, results of the implementation including all the possible aspects. The data used in this research is from the *Kaggle competition* with the purpose to forecast demand for millions of items for a South American grocery chain in the Ecuadorian supermarket chain. The programming language used for demand forecasting is *Python* and IDE used is *Pycharm* with *Anaconda* package.

Figure 4 below shows a data-set model of how each each data-set and features are map to each other.

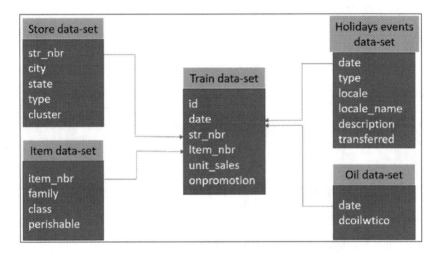

Fig. 4. Data-set model.

The data-set consists of a set of multiple input files used for demand forecasting are as follows:

Table 1. Summarization of store data-set.

Column name	Column data type	Column description
store_nbr	int64	Store identifier
city	object	City in which store is located
state	object	State in which store is located
type	object	Internal store categorization
cluster	int64	Internal store clustering

Table 2. Summarization of items data-set.

Column name	Column data type	Column description
item_nbr	int64	Item identifier
family	object	The family of item
class	int64	Class of items
perishable	int64	Whether the item is perishable

1. **Store data-set:** It consists of 54 "Corporacion Favorita" chain stores including city, state, type, and cluster. Table 1 provides the detailed description of the store data-set.
2. **Items data-set:** It consists of 4,100 items including their belonging families, classes and whether they are perishable or not. Table 2 provides the detailed description of items data-set.
3. **Oil data-set:** It consists of 1,218 items, daily oil price from 2013-01-01 to 2017-08-31. Table 3 provides the detailed description of the oil data-set.
4. **Holidays events data-set:** It consists of 350 information about holidays in Ecuador. Holidays are again sub-categorized in types of holidays i.e. Local, Regional and National. Table 4 provides the detailed description of the holidays events data-set.
5 **Train data-set:** It consists of 125,497,040 sales observations which include the target unit sales by date, store number, and item number and unique id to label rows. Table 5 provides the detailed description of the train data-set.

Table 3. Summarization of oil data-set.

Column name	Column data type	Column description
date	object	Date of daily oil prices
dcoilwtico	float64	Oil prices

Table 4. Summarization of holidays events data-set.

Column name	Column data type	Column description
date	object	Dates of holidays
type	object	Types of Holidays
locale	object	Types of local holidays
locale_name	object	Name of local holidays
description	object	Description of holidays
transferred	bool	Transferred holidays

Table 5. Summarization of train data-set

Column name	Column data type	Column description
id	int64	Identifier
date	object	Date of sales
store_nbr	int64	Store identifier
item_nbr	int64	Item identifier
unit_sales	float64	Sales defined at the date-store-item-promotion level
onpromotion	object	Whether the item is on promotion

5.1   Data Preprocessing

This section explains how the preprocessing stage of data-set work has been done on the original data-set. This includes various steps performed during the predictions which are as follows:-

1. Analyze the data-types, dimensions, and missing values in all data-sets.
2. Overview of the trends of total sales of all stores and items over time.
3. Visualize the data distribution of individual features including stores, items, oil price, and holiday events.
4. Explore the different individual features that affects grocery sale volumes.
5. Modify the original training data-set.
6. Change the data type of the modified train data-set.
7. Build models to forecast daily grocery sales and test on validation data-set.

5.2   Modify Train Data-Set

Train data-set has grocery sales data obtained from Ecuadorian grocery chain store *Corporacion Favorita* which contains information of *125 million* sale events of 4,100 grocery items from 54 different chain stores over 1,218 days from 2013-01-01 to 2017-08-31.

Select Duration for Predictions: In our research, we have predicted demands from 2013-01-01 till 2013-03-05 and they were analyzed with the aim of identifying features influencing daily grocery sales and to build a predictive model to forecast these sales.

Merge Data-Sets: Train data-set has fields id, date, store number, item number, on-promotion. We have merged store, items, oil, holiday events data-sets into train data-set to make a good and accurate model for predictions.

Predictions for 10 Most Purchased Products: We have extracted the 10 most purchased products from Ecuadorian grocery chain store.

Create Dummy Variables: It is an artificial variable which is created to represent an attribute with two or more distinct categories or levels. We have used dummy variables to create binary variables using the pandas library.

Scale Variables: We have scaled the variables so that they are normalized with *0* mean and with a standard deviation equal to *1*.

Split Data-Set: We have split the train data-set into a train and a validation data-set using the function *train_test_split* in Python.

6   Experimental Results and Statistical Analysis

This section is based on the experimental data results for two approaches for our real-world application, we did some evaluation for two approaches considering different key parameters. The two models we used for demand forecasting are regression models.

6.1   Evaluation of the Two Approaches Based on the Experimental Results

Traditional k-fold cross-validation methods of model evaluation have limitations for time series data, as time series data is characterized by the correlation between observations that are near in time. To validate the classifiers, we use time series cross-validator, as it is very important to evaluate our model for time series data on "future" ervations least like those that are used to train the model. Time series cross-validator is a variation of k-fold which returns first k fold as train set and the (k+1)th fold as the test set. Differently from standard cross-validation methods, here the successive training sets are super-sets of those that come before them, it also adds all surplus data to the first training partition which is always used to train the model.

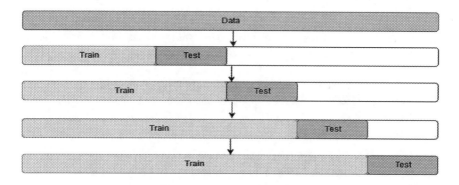

Fig. 5. Time Series Validator

We have split the training data to four partitions as described in Fig. 5.

The Table 6 represents the comparison between observations based on the R2 score, MSE score, and MAE score in demand forecasting using the Random Forest and Neural Network regression algorithms.

Table 6. Experimental parameters and result based on the evaluation.

	Random Forest	Neural Network
Duration for prediction	2013-01-01 to 2013-03-05	2013-01-01 to 2013-03-05
R2 Score	0.8308844919132312/1.0	0.8150293303537545/1.0
MSE Score	0.0011800437881035438/0.0	0.0012906769590013843/0.0
MAE Score	0.022340968892558138/0.0	0.02357178899431181/0.0
Total sample size	28871	28871
Train sample size	23096	23096
Validation sample size	5775	5775

Based on the experimental results and Fitted vs. Observed plots, Random Forest has better R2, MSE, and MAE scores compared to Keras Neural Network.

7 Conclusion and Future Work

In this paper, we have used Random Forest and Keras Neural Network regression algorithms to improve demand forecasting in SCM. Each of the algorithms has been evaluated according to its key parameters. Many factors are considered for demand forecasting in SCM including oil dates, oil prices, holiday events, store types, item types, item descriptions, cities, states in Ecuador. The computational results provide some interesting conclusions. Various sensitivity analysis is done to explore the impact of various parameters on the success of algorithms. Based on the experimental results, the analysis is done to and out which is the better approach to predict the sales in SCM. The key observation we found are listed below:

1. In the Random Forest approach, we have evaluated R2, MSE, MAE scores, and Observed vs. Fitted graph for sales predictions and we considered it as a good result.
2. In Keras Neural Network, we have evaluated R2, MSE, MAE scores, and Observed vs. Fitted graph for sales predictions and the results are similar to Random Forest.
3. For this case study, Random Forest is more efficient than Neural Network.

In the context of demand forecasting problems, many challenges remain open to research to improve SCM efficiency. As the study is specific to the demand forecasting phase, we can apply ML techniques to other phases in the future as a future work as described below:-

1. Chatbots for Operational Procurement.
2. Autonomous Vehicles for Logistics and Delivery.
3. Machine Learning for Warehouse Management.
4. Natural Language Processing (NLP) for Data Cleansing and Building Data Robustness.
5. ML and Predictive Analytics for Supplier Selection and Supplier Relationship Management (SRM).

References

1. Min, H.: Artificial intelligence in supply chain management: theory and applications. Int. J. Logist. Res. Appl. **26**, 13–39 (2019). https://doi.org/10.1080/13675560902736537. ISSN: 0018-9162
2. Stank, T., Scott, S., Hazen, B.: A savy guide to the digital supply chain. Appendix of Safeware: System Safety and Computers (2018). https://haslam.utk.edu/sites/default/files/GSCI.WhitePaper.Savvy_.FINALFORISSUU.pdf. Accessed Jan 2019
3. Keunstler, B.: Guideline supply chain management in electronics manufacturing. ZVEI - German Electrical and Electronic Manufacturers Association (2014). https://www.zvei.org/fileadmin/user_upload/Presse_und_Medien/Publikationen/2014/november/Guideline_Supply_Chain_Management_in_Electronics_Manufacturing/Guideline-Supply-Chain-Management.pdf. Accessed Jan 2019
4. Perkins, B., Wailgum, T.: What is supply chain management (SCM)? Definitions and best practices. CIO from IDG Commun., August 2017. https://www.cio.com/article/2439493/supply-chain-management/supply-chain-management-supply-chain-management-definition-and-solutions.html. Accessed Jan 2019
5. Byrne, R.O.: How AI helps build the supply chain that thinks for itself. Logistics Bur. https://www.logisticsbureau.com/how-ai-helps-build-the-supply-chain-that-thinks-for-itself/. Accessed Jan 2019
6. Breiman, L.: Random forests (2001). https://www.stat.berkeley.edu/~breiman/randomforest2001.pdf. Accessed Feb 2019
7. Keras: The Python deep learning library. https://keras.io/. Accessed Jan 2019
8. Brownlee, J.: 5 step life-cycle for neural network models in Keras (2016). https://machinelearningmastery.com/5-step-life-cycle-neural-network-models-keras/. Accessed Jan 2019
9. Navlani, A.: Understanding random forests classifiers in Python. https://www.datacamp.com/community/tutorials/random-forests-classifier-python. Accessed Jan 2019
10. Yue, L., Yafeng, Y., Junjun, G., Chongli, T.: Demand forecasting by using support vector machine. In: Third International Conference on Natural Computation, ICNC 2007, pp. 272–276 (2007)
11. Mupparaju, K., Soni, A., Gujela, P., Lanham, M.A.: A comparative study of machine learning frameworks for demand forecasting. Academia (2018). http://matthewalanham.com/Students/2018_MWDSI_A%20Comparative%20Study%20of%20Machine%20Learning%20Frameworks%20for%20Demand%20Forecasting.pdf. Accessed Feb 2019
12. Carbonneau, R., Vahidov, R., Laframboise, K.: Machine learning-based demand forecasting in supply chains. IJIIT, **3** (2007). https://doi.org/10.4018/jiit.2007100103. https://www.researchgate.net/publication/220208887_Machine-Learning-Based_Demand_Forecasting_in_Supply_Chains. Accessed Feb 2019

Exploring the Impact of Purity Gap Gain on the Efficiency and Effectiveness of Random Forest Feature Selection

Mandlenkosi Victor Gwetu[✉], Jules-Raymond Tapamo, and Serestina Viriri

University of KwaZulu-Natal, Private Bag X54001, Durban 4000, South Africa
gwetum@ukzn.ac.za

Abstract. The Random Forest (RF) classifier has the capacity to facilitate both wrapper and embedded feature selection through the Mean Decrease Accuracy (MDA) and Mean Decrease Impurity (MDI) methods, respectively. MDI is known to be biased towards predictor variables with multiple values whilst MDA is stable in this regard. As such, MDA is the predominantly preferred option for RF-based feature selection, despite its higher computational overhead in comparison to MDI. This research seeks to simultaneously reduce the computational overhead and improve the effectiveness of RF feature selection. We propose two improvements to the MDI method to overcome its shortcomings. The first is using our proposed Purity Gap Gain (PGG) measure which has an emphasis on computational efficiency, as an alternative to the Gini Importance (GI) metric. The second is incorporating a Relative Mean Decrease Impurity (RMDI) score, which aims to offset the bias towards multi-valued predictor variables through random feature value permutations. Experiments are conducted on UCI datasets to establish the impact of PGG and RMDI on RF performance.

Keywords: Random Forest · Mean Decrease Accuracy ·
Mean Decrease Impurity · Purity Gap Gain ·
Relative Mean Decrease Impurity

1 Introduction

Although feature selection [3] is commonly applied to avoid the curse of dimensionality in contexts such as text and DNA microarray analysis, it is also useful as a machine learning preprocessing step. It ensures that all variables that are included in a predictive model are not redundant, so as to meaningfully contribute towards its discriminative ability. The benefits of feature/variable selection include improved prediction accuracy and efficiency, reduced overfitting, as well as easier understanding, interpretation and control over model training [5].

Algorithms used for establishing a set of useful features can be categorized as either filter, wrapper or embedded methods [7]. Filter methods ensure feature usefulness using statistical metrics such as chi square, fisher score and variance; which evaluate intrinsic properties of features without considering their relationship to the target variable. Wrapper methods use cross-validation techniques

© Springer Nature Switzerland AG 2019
N. T. Nguyen et al. (Eds.): ICCCI 2019, LNAI 11683, pp. 340–352, 2019.
https://doi.org/10.1007/978-3-030-28377-3_28

to select features that optimize classifier performance; examples include genetic algorithms, sequential selection and recursive elimination. Embedded algorithms use the model learning process to gather useful statistics on the utility of each feature; example classifiers that can be used to gather such statistics include decision trees and SVMs [8].

The Random Forest (RF) classifier facilitates both wrapper and embedded feature selection through the Mean Decrease Accuracy (MDA) and Mean Decrease Impurity (MDI) methods, respectively [10]. One disadvantage of MDI is its bias towards predictor variables with multiple values. Since MDA is stable in this regard [4], it is generally the default option for RF-based feature selection, despite its higher computational overhead when compared to MDI. This study proposes to improve MDI by using the Purity Gap Gain (PGG) measure which is designed for computational efficiency, as an alternative to the Gini Importance (GI) metric. Secondly, a Relative Mean Decrease Impurity (RMDI) score is incorporated, in an attempt to offset the bias towards multi-valued predictor variables through random feature value permutations. Experiments are conducted on UCI datasets to compare the effectiveness and efficiency of PGG against that of GI, in the context of RMDI.

In the remainder of this paper, we begin with a detailed overview of RFs and then proceed to introduce our proposed improvements to MDI feature selection. Experimental details are then presented and results discussed.

2 Random Forests

Ensemble classification methods are premised on a training phase which generates several individual base classifiers and a testing phase which aggregates classifier predictions into a consolidated result [9]. The most common examples include boosting [14], bagging [1] and Random Forests (RFs) [2], all of which are based on decision trees. In boosting, trees are trained in succession and emphasis is placed on instances that are misclassified by previous classifiers; the ensemble is therefore a committee of evolving trees that increasingly adapt towards learning how to correctly predict the most difficult training instances. In bagging, trees can be trained concurrently and emphasis is placed on creating bootstrapped samples; the ensemble is therefore a committee of trees which have random similarities and differences. RFs complement bagging by introducing an extra level of stochastic behavior in the selection of features involved in node split point optimization. As a result, RFs are known to (1) have reliable classification performance that is comparable to Support Vector Machines (SVMs), (2) be tolerant of noise and robust to over fitting, and (3) be fast and simple to use since they only rely on 2 main parameters [9].

We proceed to outline the adopted notation for representing the various components of a RF and introduce some of its internal measures. As a supervised machine learning algorithm, RFs receive a training set X, of N instances, each of which can be represented by $X(i, \_) = (\mathbf{x}, y)$, where $1 \leq i \leq N$ and $\mathbf{x} = (x_1, x_2, \ldots, x_A)$, is a vector of A components. Each instance $\mathbf{x}$ has a corresponding label y such that $1 \leq y \leq C$, from the set of C possible class values. X can be presented as a table in which the rows and columns correspond with the dataset's instances and features respectively. Accordingly, the notations $X(i, \_)$ and $X(\_, j)$ represent views of the ith instance and j^{th} feature respectively. A set of samples $\{X_k, 1 \leq k \leq T\}$, each of size N, is drawn with replacement from X^1 and used to create a RF classifier $h(x)$ made up of T corresponding decision tree classifiers $h_1(\mathbf{x}), h_2(\mathbf{x}), \ldots, h_T(\mathbf{x})$. The RF algorithm can therefore be said to accept a training set X as input and output an ensemble classifier $h(x)$. During the classification stage, $h_k(x) = 0$ denotes a correct prediction whereas $h_k(x) = y$ specifies that x has been incorrectly labelled as a member of class y.

The sample X_k is used to create a root node Θ_{k0} of the kth tree (h_k), which is built by recursively splitting nodes until given conditions are satisfied. We denote any node at a valid depth $d \geq 0$ in h_k and its size by Θ_{kd} and $|\Theta_{kd}|$ respectively. It can therefore be said that $\Theta_{kd} \in h_k$. Let $\Phi(\Theta_{kd}, j)$ represent the set of all possible ways of partitioning node Θ_{kd} into B branches based on attribute j and $\phi \in \Phi(\Theta_{kd}, j)$ be one such partition. ϕ^* is the adopted partition as it is the most optimal in terms of decreasing the impurity of child nodes. When a partition is enforced, $\phi(z), 1 \leq z \leq B$ is the resulting child node of Θ_{kd} at depth $d + 1$. For the sake of simplicity we represent $\phi(z)$ as Θ_{kd+1}. The probability of landing on branch z from Θ_{kd} when splitting based on ϕ is represented by $p(z)$. The probability of class y in node Θ_{kd} and the probability of class y in branch z of Θ_{kd} are represented by $p(y)$ and $p(y|z)$ respectively.

2.1   Gini Impurity

Individual decision trees within a RF, use conditional rules to recursively partition a sample Θ_{kd} in an attempt to produce pure child nodes with instances belonging to the same class. Although the Gini Index (GI) [13] was the original measure chosen by Breiman [2] for measuring the level of decrease in impurity along a RF decision tree path, it is still widely used due to its general effectiveness [6,17]. The Gini index of a node Θ_{kd} is defined as follows:

$$GI\left(\Theta_{kd}\right) = 1 - \sum_{y=1}^{C} p\left(y\right)^2. \tag{1}$$

Given that a partition $\phi \in \Phi(\Theta_{kd}, j)$ splits Θ_{kd} into B child nodes $(\phi(z))$, the resulting decrease in impurity is calculated as follows:

$$\delta GI\left(\phi\right) = -\sum_{y=1}^{C} p\left(y\right)^2 + \sum_{z=1}^{B} p\left(z\right) \sum_{y=1}^{C} p\left(y|z\right)^2. \tag{2}$$

Here, the GI is used to measure the impurity of Θ_{kd} and the weighted impurity of its child nodes $(\phi(z))$. $\delta GI\left(\phi\right)$ is therefore a measure of the change in impurity caused by the partition ϕ; it is commonly referred to as the Gini impurity

---

[1] Note that although X_k is drawn from X, the latter is a set while the former is a multiset.

[7] metric for simplicity. The optimal partition ϕ^* for splitting a node Θ_{kd} on attribute j^* is deduced as follows:

$$\phi^* = \operatorname*{argmax}_{\phi \in \Phi(\Theta_{kd},j)} \delta GI(\phi). \tag{3}$$

Note that attribute j^* is the feature that yields the highest value of $\delta GI(\phi)$ after considering all possible split values from all features j. The process of training a RF classifier is essentially an iterative algorithm (commonly referred to as Forest-RI) in which a node Θ_{kd} is split into its child nodes. Each child node Θ_{kd+1} is likewise split and this process continues until specified conditions such a maximum node purity level or depth, are met. During each iteration, a predefined number of features is chosen randomly, without replacement. This extra level of stochastic behaviour distinguishes the RF algorithm from bagging and facilitates greater variation among the trees of a RF.

2.2   Random Forest Strength

In the typical RF algorithm, N instances are drawn from the training set with repetition. On average, a third of the training set is not used by each tree, due to this bootstrapped sampling [13]. This excluded collection of instances is known as the Out Of Bag (OOB) set, which is useful for determining feature importance as well as RF internal estimates for error, strength and correlation; in the context of the training set [2].

Let $P_o(\mathbf{x}, y)$ be the proportion of votes allocated to class y when an OOB instance $(\mathbf{x}, y), \mathbf{x} \notin \Theta_{k0}$ is classified by the RF trees. This proportion is defined by:

$$P_o(\mathbf{x}, y) = \frac{\sum_{k=1}^{T} I\left(h_k(\mathbf{x}) = y; (\mathbf{x}, y) \in O_k\right)}{\sum_{k=1}^{T} I\left((\mathbf{x}, y) \in O_k\right)}, \tag{4}$$

where O_k is the OOB set for classifier $h_k(\mathbf{x})$. It follows that $X \setminus X_k = O_k$. $I(c)$ is an indicator function which returns 1 if the condition c is true and 0 otherwise. The margin on an OOB instance reflects the extent to which votes for the correct class exceed votes for any other class and is represented by:

$$mr(\mathbf{x}, y) = P_o(\mathbf{x}, 0) - \max_{y=1}^{C} P_o(\mathbf{x}, y). \tag{5}$$

The strength of a RF is an internal measure of the average expected margin over the whole training set [13]:

$$s(X) = \frac{1}{N} \sum_{i=1}^{N} mr(X(i, \_)). \tag{6}$$

2.3   Random Forest Variable Selection Methods

Although RFs are predominantly used as classifiers, one of their important byproducts is variable importance measures. There are two such common measures: MDI and MDA.

Mean Decrease Impurity. MDI is also referred to as Gini importance and it measures the average Gini impurity δGI for a given training set X and feature j, as shown below:

$$MDI(X,j) = \frac{1}{T}\sum_{k=1}^{T}\sum_{\Theta_{kd}\in h_k:\Theta_{k0}=X_k}\sum_{\phi\in\Phi(\Theta_{kd},j)}\delta GI\left(\phi\right)I(\phi = \phi^* \wedge j = j^*), \quad (7)$$

where $I(\phi = \phi^* \wedge j = j^*)$ is an indicator function call which returns 1 if j yields the optimal split ϕ^* and 0 otherwise. Equation 7 is essentially computing the average δGI arising from all the cases during the induction of $h(x)$ when feature j yields an optimal split. An attribute j will have a high MDI value if it frequently yields high δGI values during RF induction. MDI is a typical example of an embedded feature selection method since it utilizes information generated in the RF learning process; this makes it a computationally attractive option. Its overhead in terms of space is of the order A since it needs to keep track of total Gini impurity values for each attribute. This method is however not often used because of its bias towards variables with multiple values [4], this means that any real valued variable is likely to generate lower impurity scores than a binary valued one. This drawback makes the feature rankings that are generated by this method less objective [7,15], since typical dataset features do not necessarily have the same value distribution.

Mean Decrease Accuracy. MDA evaluates variable importance based on the relative OOB error rate when an entire feature is replaced with its identically distributed perturbed version. In order to formally describe this process, we introduce some extra notation. Let $\bar{X}$ represent a modified version of a training set X such that $\bar{X}(\_,j)$ is a randomly generated permutation of $X(\_,j)$, where $1 \leq j \leq A$. Let $\tilde{X}^{(v)}$ represent another modified version of X such that $\tilde{X}^{(v)}(\_,v) = \bar{X}(\_,v)$ and $\tilde{X}^{(v)}(\_,j) = X(\_,j)$ for $j \neq v$, where $1 \leq j,v \leq A$. We define a mapping function $\wp(x,v) : X \mapsto \tilde{X}^{(v)}$ that generates elements $\wp(x,v) \in \tilde{X}^{(v)}$ which are adaptations of $x \in X$ such that the vth attribute is perturbed. We use the term perturb to refer to the process of replacing every instance's value for attribute v with the corresponding permuted value in $\bar{X}(\_,v)$.

Given a classifier h_k, we define its OOB error as the rate of incorrect classifications over O_k as follows:

$$OOB\_Error\,(k) = \frac{\sum_{x\in X} I\left(h_k\left(\mathbf{x}\right) \neq y; (\mathbf{x},y) \in O_k\right)}{|O_k|}. \quad (8)$$

A similar error rate can be formulated for $\tilde{X}^{(v)}$ as follows:

$$OOB\_Error^{(v)}\,(k) = \frac{\sum_{x\in X} I\left(h_k\left(\wp(\mathbf{x},v)\right) \neq y; (\mathbf{x},y) \in O_k\right)}{|O_k|}. \quad (9)$$

The MDA of an attribute j with respect to a classifier h_k aggregates the above-mentioned error rates as follows:

$$MDA(j) = \sum_{k=1}^{T} \frac{OOB\_Error^{(j)}(k) - OOB\_Error(k)}{T}. \tag{10}$$

Any attribute j will demonstrate the highest MDA if it has the highest dissimilarity between $X(\_, j)$ and $\tilde{X}^{(j)}(\_, j)$. Conversely, if a random permutation of j yields little difference in MDA when compared against its original version, j is assumed to be of little importance since its specific values do not seem to make any difference with respect to classification accuracy. MDA is generally preferred over MDI because of its better tolerance of the different levels of feature value granularity [4,7,15]. It is however computationally expensive since it requires the training of T trees followed by the testing of each of these trees, A times; since each attribute has to be perturbed.

3   Proposed MDI Improvements

We propose two avenues for improving MDI. The first is the replacement of the Gini impurity with a similar but computationally more efficient alternative, Purity Gap Gain (PGG). The second is the incorporation of the concept of random feature value permutation observed from MDA. We ultimately seek to reduce the susceptibility of MDI to feature value granularity so as to jointly optimize the effectiveness and efficiency RF feature selection.

3.1   Purity Gap Gain

The first difference between PGG and Gini impurity is the use of a product of node proportions instead of the Gini Index (GI). One of these proportions is known as node purity [18] and is defined as follows:

$$\hat{p}(\Theta_{kd}) = \max_{y=1}^{C} p(y). \tag{11}$$

The other proportion is simply the minimum class proportion within a node. The concept of purity gap effectively rewards a smaller difference between the maximum and minimum proportions within a node as shown below:

$$PG(\Theta_{kd}) = 1 - \max_{y=1}^{C} p(y) \min_{y=1}^{C} p(y). \tag{12}$$

PG is maximized when the minimum and maximum proportion in a node are the same. In the case of two classes, this occurs when each class has a proportion of $\frac{1}{2}$. Thus PG models GI in that it is maximized when class proportions are equal in a node and it is minimized when there is a clear bias towards one of the class proportions. A notable difference between Eqs. 1 and 12 is the computational simplicity of the latter over the former. PG simply deduces the maximum and minimum class proportions, while the Gini index requires the calculation of the sum of all class proportions squared within a node. PGG is the weighted average change in PG over a branch from Θ_{kd} to Θ_{kd+1} as defined below:

$$PGG\left(\phi\right) = \sum_{z=1}^{B} p\left(z\right) PG\left(\phi(z)\right) - PG\left(\Theta_{kd}\right). \tag{13}$$

Although we have previously explored the concept of PGG for measuring RF tree confidence [16], its implementation in this study is simpler[2] and geared more towards mimicking GI in an efficient manner.

3.2   Relative Mean Decrease Impurity

Inspired by MDA, we adopt the concept of Relative Mean Decrease Impurity (RMDI) proposed by Nguyen et al. [12], which captures the difference between the MDI values derived from $X(\_, j)$ and $\tilde{X}^{(j)}(\_, j)$ as shown below:

$$RMDI(j) = MDI(X, j) - MDI(\tilde{X}^{(j)}, j). \tag{14}$$

In contrast to MDA, feature permutations are introduced at the start of the learning phase of a RF. Once a permutation of each feature is generated, these are injected into the dataset such that the number of features is now $2A$. If the number of features randomly selected during each iteration of Forest-RI is predetermined as A, the modified learning algorithm would generally take twice as long to train. It is however important to note that if common convention [2,13] is followed, the computational overhead of the modified algorithm is reduced to $\sqrt{2A} - \sqrt{A}$, since $\sqrt{2A}$ features are now selected instead of $\sqrt{A}$.

Although the split values of permuted attributes are actually computed, nodes are never split based on such attributes, in order to retain the integrity of RF training. ϕ^* is therefore restricted to original features only; permuted features are mainly used for offsetting the total split scores of original features. Instead of simply observing the MDI of an attribute as a measure of attribute importance, we now consider how different this MDI is from the MDI of a permuted version of the attribute. We envisage that the incorporation of this relative comparison will offset the MDI's bias towards multi-valued attributes. Although RMDI may result in a slight increase in computational requirements when compared to MDI, the resulting time complexity will still be superior to that of MDA.

While the emphasis of the study by Nguyen et al. [12] was on reducing RF bias in the context of high dimensional data, the concept of RMDI is incorporated into this study mainly for its reported effectiveness in reducing bias towards multivalued features. Our ultimate goal is a suitable means of selecting the most discriminative feature from a set of proposed Gabor features for use in automatic thresholding. It is important that such a selection should be robust to the varying granularity of these features, to avoid a skewed outcome.

---

[2] Information about node depth is not considered in the current implementation.

4   Experimental Protocol

The experiment used in this study is designed to achieve 2 objectives: (1) to assess the reliability of RMDI as a feature selection strategy and (2) to provide a preliminary comparison between Gini impurity and PGG and split metrics during RF induction. All experiments were conducted using our own C++ implementation of dichotomous ($B = 2$) RFs that use the following standard settings [2,13]:

- Each RF is made out of $T = 100$ trees.
- The number of randomly selected attributes at each node of a tree is set to $\sqrt{A}$.
- The size of each bootstrapped sample Φ_{k0} is N, the size of X.
- Node splitting is stopped when either $|\Theta_{kd}| \leq 5$, $\hat{p}(\Phi_{kd}) = 1$, or a depth $d = 30$ is reached.

Experiments were conducted on a Windows PC[3] and took a combined running time of approximately 1 h 30 min over all data sets.

4.1   Experiment Description

To achieve the first objective, we perform repeated random sub-sampling validation 30 times. In each case, the dataset is split using an 80%:20% split ratio into training and validation data respectively. Feature ranking is based on RMDI scores achieved on the training data. We partition the feature set into strong and weak features using the top and bottom half of features in the RMDI rank respectively. The corresponding validation data is then used as a training sample for strong and weak features separately. We then calculate the strengths of the strong and weak feature based RFs, as defined in Eq. (6). We use the paired T-test to determine whether the mean difference between the two RF strengths is zero. We formally define our hypotheses as follows:

- The null hypothesis (H_0) assumes that the true mean difference (μ_d) between the strengths of the strong and weak feature based RFs is zero.
- The alternative hypothesis (H_1) assumes that μ_d is non zero.

If RMDI is a reliable means of feature selection, the experimental results should demonstrate sufficient evidence for us to reject (H_0) in favor of (H_1). Since the two forests utilize features of different combined usefullness, we do not expect their average strengths to be equal.

To achieve the second objective, we compare the strengths and running times of the RFs based on strong features for both Gini impurity and PGG. The same dataset splits are used in each case; the main difference is the split criteria used for RF induction. We are primarily interested in comparing the effectiveness and efficiency of these two metrics.

---

[3] 2 cores running at 2.70 GHz and 2 GB of RAM.

4.2   Data Sets

The effectiveness of the methods proposed in this study is tested using 4 data sets from the UCI repository [11]. These data sets are drawn from Robnik [13] and Breiman's [2] studies on RFs. The characteristics of the chosen data sets are summarized in Table 1, which reveals the diversity of the problems represented, in terms of data set size $(N^*)^4$, number of features (A) and number of classes (C).

Table 1. UCI datasets

Dataset	N^*	A	C	Dataset	N^*	A	C
Ecoli	336	7	8	Segmentation	2310	19	7
Ionosphere	351	34	2	Sonar	208	60	2

5   Results

After features are sorted using RMDI scores derived from RF induction, features in the top half of this sorted list are presumed to be weaker[5] than those in the bottom half. Similarly, subsequent RFs built from the top half of this sorted list should ideally be weaker than those built from the bottom half. Tables 2 and 3 present the strengths of 30 RF pairs, using top and bottom half features. RFs are induced twice, using δGI and PGG as alternative split metrics. The headings δGI_T and PGG_T identify RFs built using the top half features when sorting is based on δGI and PGG based RMDI respectively. Likewise δGI_B and PGG_B are associated with the bottom half features.

We observe that the relative strengths of the majority of RF pairs were in line with our expectations. The ecoli and segmentation datasets each had only one anomaly in a PGG based RF. Out of 60 RF inductions, the isonosphere and sonar datasets had 10 and 6 odd cases respectively. It can be noted that the datasets with one anomaly have an odd number of features (A). A likely reason for this outcome is the fact that the top half of sorted features was smaller than the bottom half. Since the bottom half had stronger and more features than the top half, it is expected that the strengths of RFs corresponding to the former would be higher than those of the latter.

We use the mean (μ) strength over 30 RF inductions to rate the relative effectiveness of the 4 RF categories. This comparison is objective since for each run, the same Θ_{k0} is used to induce 4 different RFs. These mean values also confirm that the top half features were weaker than the bottom half for all datasets. A comparison of δGI_B and PGG_B mean RF strengths shows that

---

[4] This value is larger than N, the size of a training set, X which is drawn from a data set.

[5] Sorting is done in ascending order, hence the list is arranged from weakest to strongest.

the δGI based RFs were stronger than their PGG counterparts in all cases except the sonar dataset. These findings are also confirmed by the paired T-test which yields p-values less that 1% for each of the comparisons: δGI_T vs δGI_B, PGG_T vs PGG_B and δGI_B vs PGG_B. This indicates that there is less than 1% likelihood that the observed trends are a mere coincidence, hence we reject the null hypothesis (H_0) in favor of the alternative hypothesis (H_1).

Table 2. Random Forest strengths for Ecoli and Isonosphere datasets

Run	Ecoli				Isonosphere			
	δGI_T	δGI_B	PGG_T	PGG_B	δGI_T	δGI_B	PGG_T	PGG_B
1	−0.027146	0.389795	0.047715	0.070317	0.556447	0.582385	**0.514891**	**0.511525**
2	0.152976	0.436591	0.043644	0.076737	0.550569	0.590034	0.481161	0.555759
3	0.152096	0.387711	0.050019	0.104831	0.560526	0.570626	0.484594	0.543271
4	0.145038	0.365383	0.087261	0.149182	0.516025	0.556717	**0.525872**	**0.524723**
5	0.061024	0.416723	0.094282	0.161514	0.520416	0.599395	0.490189	0.549813
6	0.181508	0.444353	**0.160363**	**0.07783**	**0.568939**	**0.560921**	0.53242	0.533997
7	−0.023615	0.408102	0.071638	0.117691	0.561062	0.586017	0.510265	0.560203
8	−0.00364	0.391702	0.083588	0.142523	0.519336	0.582497	0.482497	0.556673
9	0.02483	0.415895	0.092955	0.137078	0.530046	0.61077	0.50587	0.551568
10	0.170839	0.441432	0.057166	0.107488	0.508288	0.56497	**0.541541**	**0.540246**
11	0.019756	0.415132	0.079084	0.106102	**0.589797**	**0.568449**	0.524403	0.500343
12	−0.007194	0.431746	0.08335	0.124272	**0.585577**	**0.574657**	**0.540212**	**0.524845**
13	0.150296	0.442049	0.080319	0.114403	0.545405	0.570824	0.524202	0.558661
14	0.076479	0.445552	0.049069	0.132312	0.541053	0.582383	0.485662	0.544718
15	0.058208	0.441629	0.089712	0.102199	0.545074	0.612689	0.50907	0.543123
16	0.157126	0.459481	0.084636	0.13876	0.513623	0.566544	0.488532	0.565566
17	0.003931	0.421854	0.081421	0.092023	0.541315	0.576777	0.493366	0.539206
18	−0.01861	0.420028	0.04713	0.083462	0.556248	0.596467	0.476581	0.568932
19	0.042306	0.430415	0.091708	0.162491	0.546211	0.590314	0.484315	0.564066
20	0.182107	0.45673	0.050223	0.104296	**0.551437**	**0.542613**	0.473955	0.523157
21	0.049584	0.420147	0.078497	0.142797	0.541913	0.569445	0.515962	0.527477
22	0.029947	0.423455	0.032072	0.117826	**0.582216**	**0.557931**	0.500887	0.528861
23	0.021469	0.414482	0.065759	0.105622	0.52593	0.560144	0.55522	0.557496
24	0.004867	0.387004	0.091882	0.130458	0.567995	0.587164	0.47623	0.549819
25	0.013595	0.406981	0.04701	0.134774	0.539891	0.573105	0.507317	0.533809
26	−0.004538	0.371943	0.047229	0.093141	0.528445	0.589206	0.505377	0.535757
27	0.085616	0.428243	0.082603	0.136401	0.553018	0.586033	0.504947	0.572588
28	0.098499	0.449171	0.024366	0.094602	0.538827	0.58456	0.497916	0.552165
29	0.066641	0.415959	0.062593	0.100947	**0.597805**	**0.589895**	0.501625	0.575789
30	−0.035408	0.400474	0.068714	0.125563	0.545177	0.602018	0.525964	0.566263
μ	0.060953	0.419339	0.070867	0.116255	0.547620	0.579505	0.505368	0.545347

In proposing PGG as a split metric, we sought to provide an effective and efficient alternative to δGI. Figure 1 demonstrates that over all datasets, experiments using PGG had lower computational overhead than those using δGI. The difference in running times seems to get more pronounced as the dataset size increases. We observe that the mean strengths for δGI_B and PGG_B were close in value (0.5795 vs 0.5453), with fewer anomalies for the latter than the former over the isonosphere dataset. This could be an indication that the PGG split metric is promising in such contexts.

Table 3. Segmentation dataset Random Forest strengths

Run	Segmentation				Sonar			
	δGI_T	δGI_B	PGG_T	PGG_B	δGI_T	δGI_B	PGG_T	PGG_B
1	0.280749	0.451078	0.026682	0.216214	**0.277886**	**0.267121**	0.196934	0.345602
2	0.382937	0.443338	0.065954	0.210795	0.271027	0.279378	0.189782	0.30134
3	0.150113	0.471911	0.02725	0.190696	0.218538	0.287594	0.221478	0.268406
4	0.307423	0.430391	0.084253	0.147266	**0.293588**	**0.264731**	0.215746	0.320396
5	0.275586	0.436293	0.070093	0.148077	0.250705	0.307684	0.248996	0.302134
6	0.184008	0.46554	0.06357	0.174442	0.252636	0.259464	0.197973	0.296295
7	0.292195	0.442552	0.06355	0.155224	0.302454	0.30526	0.204969	0.320364
8	0.173639	0.446667	0.057788	0.16547	0.2361	0.28515	0.268867	0.317392
9	0.353221	0.455366	0.074285	0.154391	0.207769	0.337482	**0.317218**	**0.310252**
10	0.269949	0.451071	−0.000421	0.217403	0.1418	0.289696	0.226896	0.316504
11	0.385196	0.449063	0.035755	0.202914	0.187644	0.263049	0.23491	0.283686
12	0.387249	0.423394	0.085668	0.176955	0.216668	0.325378	0.224855	0.364993
13	0.373037	0.457085	**0.129758**	**0.125576**	0.217332	0.285277	0.209871	0.317247
14	0.261068	0.445298	0.044706	0.182459	0.262298	0.329419	0.244875	0.313514
15	0.286878	0.473829	0.063416	0.148759	0.247052	0.264555	0.264563	0.334389
16	0.365537	0.443747	0.06488	0.170588	0.271854	0.287196	0.290693	0.290879
17	0.033245	0.471337	0.076697	0.16636	**0.283797**	**0.262356**	0.227599	0.289655
18	0.244264	0.461377	0.063161	0.149092	0.212502	0.272545	0.170465	0.326425
19	0.315729	0.426779	0.072084	0.154189	0.184329	0.274708	0.226859	0.325275
20	0.205651	0.472926	0.079125	0.167418	0.264698	0.271629	**0.305203**	**0.26897**
21	0.140948	0.434108	0.125577	0.130802	0.249948	0.274471	0.282349	0.299947
22	0.215783	0.41543	0.08794	0.169451	0.279594	0.322566	0.169293	0.295569
23	0.149275	0.461224	0.047319	0.149366	0.241776	0.257334	0.205737	0.294691
24	0.276067	0.434075	0.099273	0.10654	0.199526	0.287055	0.284262	0.313362
25	0.301123	0.49464	0.067388	0.167487	0.273647	0.299759	0.266106	0.333127
26	0.242784	0.496258	0.042917	0.181709	0.258242	0.288529	0.263361	0.271273
27	0.021848	0.458347	0.041644	0.169971	0.259743	0.281895	0.309879	0.301405
28	0.196497	0.448907	0.082877	0.128287	0.255122	0.325952	0.200246	0.306815
29	0.289368	0.424298	0.083893	0.142953	0.256761	0.285733	0.192828	0.293787
30	0.317692	0.443497	0.053572	0.17874	0.191721	0.313998	**0.315653**	**0.28764**
μ	0.255969	0.450994	0.066022	0.164987	0.242225	0.288566	0.239282	0.307045

In order to evaluate the potential of using RMDI scores for feature ranking, we observe a sample of actual feature ranks from the ecoli dataset[6] in Table 4. Although the δGI metric seems to produce varying ranks, some intuitive finding can be made. It can be noted that features 2 and 3 are generally weak, since they consistently occur within the top two rank positions. In contrast to this, feature 5 potentially has high discriminative power since it prominently occurs within the bottom half of the ranking order. The PGG metric showed greater stability than δGI, with only one variation in ranking order through out all 30 runs. This variation happens to be the only anomaly for the PGG metric over the ecoli dataset. This observation once again demonstrates the potential of PGG as a split criteria in RFs.

---

[6] This dataset is easier to analyze since it has fewer features.

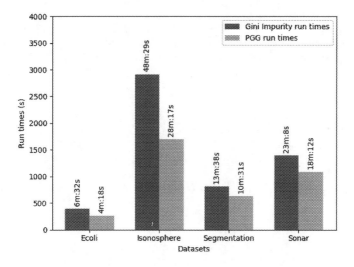

Fig. 1. Running times by dataset and split metric

Table 4. A Sample of Ecoli dataset feature ranks

Run	Feature ranks	
	δGI	PGG
1	2, 3, 4, 0, 1, 6, 5	0, 1, 2, 3, 4, 5, 6
2	2, 3, 6, 0, 5, 1, 4	0, 1, 2, 3, 4, 5, 6
3	3, 2, 0, 4, 6, 1, 5	0, 1, 2, 3, 4, 5, 6
4	3, 2, 0, 1, 4, 5, 6	0, 1, 2, 3, 4, 5, 6
5	2, 3, 1, 6, 0, 4, 5	0, 1, 2, 3, 4, 5, 6
6	3, 2, 6, 4, 1, 0, 5	1, 5, 3, 6, 4, 2, 0

6   Conclusion

This study sought to improve the MDI RF feature selection approach by proposing a new split metric (PGG) and applying the RMDI feature score. PGG has shown potential for use in large datasets as its effectiveness and efficiency seemed more pronounced in this context. Given the fact that RFs comprising features with higher RMDI scores had higher strength and the datasets used included multi-valued predictor variables, we conclude that our approach was reliable in partitioning strong and weak features. The observed rankings were however generally very fluid, making it difficult to establish a clear order of features in terms of discriminative ability.

Although this study may be useful as a first step towards improving MDI RF feature selection, more work needs to be done in order to gain better understanding of the contextualized costs and benefits of the proposed methods. Future work will focus on deeper analyses such as (1) comparison against existing feature selection strategies that focus on large datasets, and (2) detailed characterization of proposed methods in terms of convergence behavior.

References

1. Breiman, L.: Bagging predictors. Mach. Learn. **24**(2), 123–140 (1996)
2. Breiman, L.: Random forests. Mach. Learn. **45**(1), 5–32 (2001)
3. Dash, M., Liu, H.: Feature selection for classification. Intell. Data Anal. **1**(3), 131–156 (1997)
4. Genuer, R., Poggi, J.M., Tuleau-Malot, C.: Variable selection using random forests. Pattern Recogn. Lett. **31**(14), 2225–2236 (2010)
5. Guyon, I., Elisseeff, A.: An introduction to variable and feature selection. J. Mach. Learn. Res. **3**, 1157–1182 (2003)
6. Hu, C., Chen, Y., Hu, L., Peng, X.: A novel random forests based class incremental learning method for activity recognition. Pattern Recogn. **78**, 277–290 (2018)
7. Kawakubo, H., Yoshida, H.: Rapid feature selection based on random forests for high-dimensional data. Expert Syst. Appl. **40**, 6241–6252 (2012)
8. Lal, T.N., Chapelle, O., Weston, J., Elisseeff, A.: Embedded methods. In: Guyon, I., Nikravesh, M., Gunn, S., Zadeh, L.A. (eds.) Feature Extraction, pp. 137–165. Springer, Heidelberg (2006). https://doi.org/10.1007/978-3-540-35488-8_6
9. Liaw, A., Wiener, M., et al.: Classification and regression by randomForest. R News **2**(3), 18–22 (2002)
10. Louppe, G., Wehenkel, L., Sutera, A., Geurts, P.: Understanding variable importances in forests of randomized trees. In: Advances in Neural Information Processing Systems, pp. 431–439 (2013)
11. Newman, C.B.D., Merz, C.: UCI repository of machine learning databases (1998). http://www.ics.uci.edu/~mlearn/MLRepository.html
12. Nguyen, T.T., Huang, J.Z., Nguyen, T.T.: Unbiased feature selection in learning random forests for high-dimensional data. Sci. World J. 2015 - volume number (2015)
13. Robnik-Šikonja, M.: Improving random forests. In: Boulicaut, J.-F., Esposito, F., Giannotti, F., Pedreschi, D. (eds.) ECML 2004. LNCS (LNAI), vol. 3201, pp. 359–370. Springer, Heidelberg (2004). https://doi.org/10.1007/978-3-540-30115-8_34
14. Schapire, R.E., Freund, Y., Bartlett, P., Lee, W.S.: Boosting the margin: a new explanation for the effectiveness of voting methods. Ann. Stat. **26**, 1651–1686 (1998)
15. Strobl, C., Boulesteix, A.L., Zeileis, A., Hothorn, T.: Bias in random forest variable importance measures: illustrations, sources and a solution. BMC Bioinform. **8**(1), 25 (2007)
16. Surname, N.: Publication details withheld for peer review purposes. In: Publication, pp. 1–5000. Organization (2030)
17. Wang, Y., Xia, S.T.: Unifying attribute splitting criteria of decision trees by Tsallis entropy. In: 2017 IEEE International Conference on Acoustics, Speech and Signal Processing (ICASSP), pp. 2507–2511. IEEE (2017)
18. Witten, I.H., Frank, E., Hall, M.A., Pal, C.J.: Data Mining: Practical Machine Learning Tools and Techniques. Morgan Kaufmann, Burlington (2016)

Applying ML Algorithms to Video Game AI

Marek Kopel$^{(\boxtimes)}$ and Adam Pociejowski

Faculty of Computer Science and Management,
Wroclaw University of Science and Technology,
wybrzeze Wyspiańskiego 27, 50-370 Wroclaw, Poland
marek.kopel@pwr.edu.pl

Abstract. In this paper a comparison of selected algorithms used to learn intelligent behavior of characters in video games was presented. The experiment environment was created using Unity3D and TensorFlow. After brief description of the algorithms, the comparison of results is presented for three algorithms: Genetic Algorithm, Deep Q-Learning and Actor-Critic Algorithm.

Keywords: AI · NPC · Video game · Neural network

1 Introduction

With rapid development of video games in the last thirty years, the need for introducing smart behavior for non-playable characters (NPC) has increased. Non-playable character behaviors in the game has a significant impact on the gameplay quality. To create more realistic behaviors of NPC, game developers started using machine learning (ML) algorithms to make their games environments smarter and more realistic.

In recent years deep learning algorithms has become more popular. The reason for that was still growing computing power and the need for the market. Currently, ML is used not only for big data analysis to return optimized predictions. That type of ML is called supervised learning. ML can also learn in real time by adapting to the environment, that type of algorithms in machine learning is called reinforcement learning.

1.1 Reinforcement Learning

Reinforcement learning (RL) is a common choice used to train AI in games. This kind of machine learning approach is inspired by behaviorist psychology. It is follows the way in which people and animals learn to take decisions based on negative and positive rewards received by their environment [8].

In recent years reinforcement learning algorithms have been used with great success. RL algorithms can beat world champion at the game of GO or human experts at playing Atari games [1].

© Springer Nature Switzerland AG 2019
N. T. Nguyen et al. (Eds.): ICCCI 2019, LNAI 11683, pp. 353–362, 2019.
https://doi.org/10.1007/978-3-030-28377-3_29

2   Algorithms

2.1   Genetic Algorithm

Evolutionary algorithms is a class of stochastic search and optimization techniques obtained by natural selection and genetic mutations. This kind of algorithms are based on populations and follow evolution theory of the natural ecosystem. During evolution process algorithm creates various forms of entities that in process of artificial evolution becomes more adapted to the task they are supposed to perform.

Big advantage of genetic algorithms (GA) is that they can be used when problem cannot be defined using numerical expressions and when optimal solution is not required. It is successfully used along with neural networks e.g. for jobs like [4]. These types of machine learning algorithms are also often used in fighting action games. In that type of games chromosomes include information about what action NPC should take depending on previous opponent actions and distance between them [3].

Crossover and mutation are most crucial stages of the algorithm. They way they are implemented may vary in different approaches. Another crucial aspect of the method is the adaptation function, which calculates the assessment of the solution quality. This function, based on values of genes in chromosomes, evaluates the adaptation value of a given individual and returns the result in numerical form. Value returned by adaptation function is called fitness. The better adapted individuals, the greater value they receive. In games, fitness value is often associated with reward received from environment in process of reinforcement learning. The most popular selection strategies are: ranking list, tournament and roulette.

2.2   Deep Q-Learning

Another popular RL algorithm is Deep Q-Learning (DQN), which is used to determine optimal policy for agent in video games. In this algorithm we are using function Q (quality), which takes two parameters: state and action of agent and returns quality of this combination. For example if we have $Q(S, A) = R$, it means that quality of action A in state S has value R. Learned action-value function Q directly approximates the optimal action-value function independent of the policy being followed [6].

The biggest disadvantage of Q-Learning is a table representation of Q function and the problem of its non-scalability. In complex environments with millions of possible states Q, the table can grow to large sizes and calculations would be too expensive. To solve this problem, neural network is used to represent values of Q function. In this approach we can treat states as input vector to our neural network, which can be any set of observations received from the environment. Quality of actions are represented as output vector of neural network. Output layer should have as many nodes as there are possible actions.

Q-Learning was described in more detail in previous report [5].

The following, three improvements have been implemented to Q-learning and tested as another approach:

1. Experience sampling - network is trained by sampling mini-batches of experience set uniformly at random.
2. Fixed Q_{target} - using same weights ω for estimating Q_{target} (maximum value in the next state) and Q_{value} (current prediction of the network) has a consequence of high correlation between them. To solve this problem a second network with weights ω' is introduced.
3. Double DQNs - using the same values to select and evaluate action, by DQN max operator, can lead to overoptimistic value estimates. To solve this problem a second neural network is used to calculate Q_{target} value for taking action at the next state [7].

2.3   Actor-Critic Methods

Actor-Critic (AC) algorithms is a temporal difference (TD) learning approach to RL, which tries to eliminate the drawbacks of previous methods [2]. In this approach the algorithm do not suffer from the bias present in Deep Q-Learning. The algorithm uses two entities, each represented as separate neural network: Actor - neural network that makes decision which action will be taken based on a given state; and Critic - neural network that returns value of an action in a given state. Based on that value Actor network is being optimized.

3   Experiment

To perform a comparison of selected ML algorithms, a simple game was created using Unity 3D engine. The game is a death match of two tank teams. Each tank has the ability to move and shoot. To speed up the learning process no textures were used and players were modeled as cubes. Player receives points for eliminating (shooting) an enemy (the other team's tank) and loses points for eliminating a friend (same team's tank). So the reward values were set accordingly: 1 for defeating an enemy and -1 for eliminating a friend tank. When a player is defeated, he re-appears (respawns) in a random place at the arena and continues the game. Player that scores the most points wins. Agent for each player can perform one of the six predefined actions:

- 0 - do nothing
- 1 - move forward
- 2 - move backward
- 3 - turn left
- 4 - turn right
- 5 - shoot (available once a second)

Observations are collected by agents using ray casting that can detect nearest observable objects. The rays start in the center of the player and extend horizontally over a certain distance, in the way shown in Fig. 1. Vector with observations generated by single ray cast can be defined as follows: $r = [o_1, o_2, .., o_n, d, l]$, where:

- o_i - information whether one of three types of objects - friend, enemy, arena border - is observable using i ray (value: 1), otherwise 0. Only closest objects can be detected by ray cast.
- d - distance between agent and closest detected object.
- l - 1 when no object was detected by raycast, 0 otherwise.

Additionally, to observation vector has been added value of actual agent's speed and time to his next shoot. This gives a total length of observation vector equal 87.

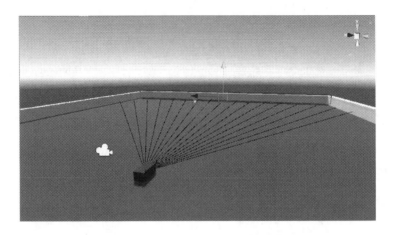

Fig. 1. Visualization of a player agent performing a ray cast.

The experiment was carried out for all tested algorithms using the same neural network architecture as presented in Fig. 2. It has four layers. First layer has 87 neurons, one for each input from observation vector. Both hidden layers are dense connected and have 128 neurons each. Activation function used for them is called ReLU (rectified linear unit) which is one of the most frequently used activation function in the field. It looks as follows:

$$f(x) = max(0, x) \tag{1}$$

Last output layer is dense connected layer with 6 neurons, one for each action.

The network was implemented in Python, using TensorFlow - an open source library created by Google Brain Team. The learning process implementation was done with Machine Learning Agents Toolkit (ML-Agents Toolkit) - an open-source Unity plugin.

4 Results

The experiment was performed with fours algorithms described in Sect. 2. To compare the results the common way to compare reinforcement learning algorithms. i.e. compare their mean reward received during training session. That is

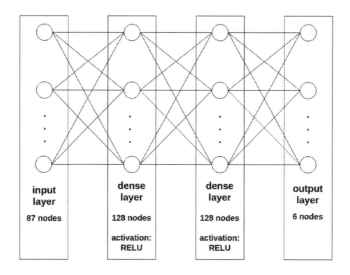

Fig. 2. Architecture of the implemented neural network.

why for every algorithm ten training sessions were held. Each training session lasted for 1,000,000 game iterations with 64 simultaneous agents and all their rewards have been averaged.

4.1 Genetic Algorithm

As shown in Table 1, GA using neural network reached mean reward per 1000 steps at the end of session equal 5.76. Comparing this to results of other tested algorithms genetic algorithm reached worse mean reward at the end of session. Mean training session time for GA was 6.76 h.

As shown in Fig. 3 algorithm in early few episodes taken actions practically randomly, the agents moved towards the walls (arena borders) and get stuck. After about 50,000 session iterations algorithm started to learn that the goal of the game is to eliminate enemies.

The Problem with using GA to learn network weights in more complex problems, is that genetic algorithm generates weights randomly and choose individuals with best fitness to next population, but when neural network is complex there are too many possibilities of neural weights and genetic algorithm has a problem to generate optimal weights.

A solution for this problem may be reducing the number of weights, but then again less complex network will not reach best results in more complex environment. Another possible solution is to increase the size of a population, but again in more complex environment this solution will increase the training time significantly.

Table 1. Rewards for 10 sessions of 1,000,000 iterations each, using Genetic Algorithm.

Session	Max	Mean	At the end	Time [h]
1	6.08	4.81	5.28	6.37
2	6.47	4.37	4.39	6.64
3	7.11	5.46	6.42	6.85
4	7.62	4.87	7.62	7.16
5	5.97	4.73	4.95	7.00
6	8.47	7.06	7.77	7.02
7	5.62	4.42	4.28	6.92
8	7.38	5.65	6.83	7.00
9	7.11	5.75	5.69	7.19
10	5.67	4.26	4.33	5.46
Avg	6.75	5.14	5.76	6.76

4.2   Deep Q-Learning

Table 2 shows results from testing Q-Learning algorithm. Weights of neural network were initialized randomly using uniform distribution. In this case base version of Deep Q-Learning was tested using single neural network and experience sampling.

Table 2. Rewards for 10 sessions of 1,000,000 iterations each, using Deep Q-Learning.

Session	Max	Mean	At the end	Time [h]
1	17.98	13.43	13.50	6.63
2	17.19	13.31	13.47	6.65
3	19.09	14.21	15.75	7.15
4	19.06	14.19	16.38	7.21
5	19.52	14.68	16.52	7.17
6	17.27	13.58	14.25	6.76
7	14.67	11.59	12.41	5.35
8	17.86	11.84	10.78	5.58
9	16.58	12.58	14.61	6.03
10	18.33	12.79	16.42	6.06
Avg	17.75	13.22	14.41	6.46

As shown in Fig. 3, after about 300,000 iterations of training session, Deep Q-Learning algorithm reached mean reward per 1000 iterations equal 14.5. After that point further improvements of algorithm were insignificant and mean reward remained at a similar level until the end of the session.

4.3   Deep Q-Learning /w Improvements

As shown in Table 3, Deep Q-Learning with improvements achieved even better results than base Deep Q-Learning algorithm. Mean reward per 1000 iterations at the end of sessions was 17.18. This is an improvement of around 20%. Mean reward of all 10 training sessions was 16.39.

Table 3. Rewards for 10 sessions of 1,000,000 iterations each, using Deep Q-Learning with improvements: Experience sampling, Fixed Q, Double DQNs.

Session	Max	Mean	At the end	Time [h]
1	20.38	17.15	16.12	31.11
2	20.94	16.61	15.67	25.14
3	20.44	17.02	17.31	31.10
4	20.09	16.84	17.08	30.03
5	19.70	15.66	17.23	25.31
6	19.30	15.75	17.53	22.47
7	21.52	15.84	17.05	24.06
8	22.12	15.92	17.62	25.10
9	21.50	16.21	16.45	28.59
10	21.12	16.90	19.70	26.04
Avg	20.71	16.39	17.18	26.89

One disadvantage of the algorithm was a longer time of learning: about 4 times longer than in case of base Deep Q-Learning. The main reason for this is that base Deep Q-Learning algorithm uses only one neural network to predict moves. In case of improved version with double DQNs algorithm also uses another neural network for better predictions.

As shown in Fig. 3, improved Deep Q-Learning reached its peak faster than base version of Deep Q-Learning. After about 200,000 iterations of training mean reward per 1000 iterations was about 17.5 and remained at a similar level to the very end.

4.4   Actor-Critic Algorithm

Again, Table 4 shows Actor-Critic algorithm achieved best results. Even better than those reached by Deep Q-Learning with improvements. Mean reward per 1000 iterations at the end of sessions was 23.10, this is an improvement of around 30% to Deep Q-Learning with improvements and about 60% better than base Deep Q-Learning. Mean reward of all 10 training sessions was 21.47. Mean training session time was 12.68 h, which is about two times more than in case of GA and base Deep Q-Learning algorithm. This is due to the fact that in the learning process with Actor-Critic algorithm, two neural networks are used.

Table 4. Rewards for 10 sessions of 1,000,000 iterations each, using Actor-Critic algorithm.

Session	Max	Mean	At the end	Time [h]
1	27.61	22.80	23.62	13.04
2	25.66	21.34	22.98	12.15
3	26.78	23.03	22.72	13.79
4	26.52	22.09	23.44	13.37
5	26.88	23.12	23.45	13.44
6	28.08	21.33	22.34	11.73
7	27.88	21.57	24.53	12.13
8	24.59	19.83	21.41	12.65
9	24.91	19.91	24.91	11.74
10	22.86	19.65	21.62	12.73
Avg	26.18	21.47	23.10	12.68

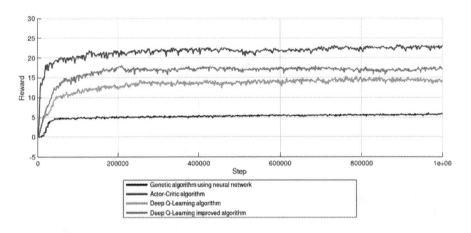

Fig. 3. Mean reward of all training sessions for the four compared algorithms.

4.5 Aggregation

Table 5 shows that Actor-Critic algorithm achieved best results, much better than the remaining algorithms. Actor-Critic algorithm reached at the end of training session mean reward equal 23.10. This is about 35% better than that reached by Deep Q-Learning with improvements algorithm that reached result equal 17.18 and about 60% better result than Deep Q-Learning algorithm that reached result equal 14.41. The worst result was achieved by GA. The mean reward at the end of session was only 5.76, about 4 times worse result than that reached by Actor-Critic algorithm.

Table 5. Results aggregation.

Algorithm	Max	Mean	End of session	Time [h]
GA	6.75	5.14	5.76	6.76
DQL	17.75	13.22	14.41	6.46
iDQL	20.71	16.39	17.18	26.89
Actor-Critic	26.18	21.47	23.10	12.68

In terms of training time DQL and GA reached similar results. Mean training time of 1,000,000 iterations for DQN algorithm was 6.46 h and for GA - 6.76. These algorithms reached best results in terms of time because of less complexity. Both used single neural network to predict actions.

Actor-Critic algorithm training time was about 2 times longer, because this algorithm uses 2 neural networks. The longest training time shows for iDQN.

4.6 Statistical Significance

Statistical significance was tested using Student's t-test. Table 6 presents results received from paired-sample t-test. They confirm observations from previous subsection. P-value less than statistical significance factor $\alpha = 0.05$, means that hypothesis H0, (X = Y) was rejected at the 5

Table 6. One-sided pair-sampled Student's t-test results.

X \Y	GA	DQL	iDQL	Actor-Critic
GA	-	0.9999	1.0	1.0
DQL	1.027e-13	-	0.9999	1.0
iDQL	3.528e-18	4.668e-08	-	0.9999
Actor-Critic	8.709e-18	3.3755e-12	8.546e-10	-

5 Conclusions

All algorithms presented in this work can be successfully used in video games for adding intelligent behaviors to non-player characters. Algorithms such as Deep Q-Learning or Actor-Critic seem to have an advantage over evolutionary algorithms such as genetic algorithm to solve more complex problems. Another advantage of Deep Q-Learning or Actor-Critic algorithms is that they are temporal difference type of machine learning algorithms. They can learn at each step of training sessions in contrast to algorithms such as Genetic Algorithms that must wait until end of episode to make evolutionary operations such as crossover or mutation.

Choosing the right algorithm to learn intelligent behaviors characters in games is very important, but it is also very important to choose correct architecture that, for example neural network or table in case of Genetic Algorithm or Q-Learning. Another very important thing in machine learning is to select correct parameters like number and types of network layers, activation functions and hyper-parameters such as learning rate or decay rate. Selection of correct parameters can improve the results of the model and increase the time of the learning process.

5.1   Future Works

There are many other methods that can be compared with the algorithms presented in this work. Imitation learning is one of them. It can learn from data generated by human or other bots it can, for example learn from replays recorded from game sessions. Another family of algorithms can could be compared to tested algorithms is Proximal Policy Optimization (PPO) algorithm, this is actual state of art algorithm that was used by OpenAI Five to competition with humans in such complex game as Dota 2.

Another thing that can be investigated in the future is the comparison of the results achieved by the examined algorithms with those reached by humans. For this purpose, a representative sample of games played by people should be collected.

References

1. Bellemare, M.G., Naddaf, Y., Veness, J., Bowling, M.: The arcade learning environment: an evaluation platform for general agents. J. Artif. Intell. Res. **47**, 253–279 (2013)
2. Bhatnagar, S., Sutton, R.S., Ghavamzadeh, M., Lee, M.: Natural actor-critic algorithms. Automatica **45**(11), 2471–2482 (2009)
3. Cho, B.H., Park, C.J., Yang, K.H.: Comparison of AI techniques for fighting action games - genetic algorithms/neural networks/evolutionary neural networks. In: Ma, L., Rauterberg, M., Nakatsu, R. (eds.) ICEC 2007. LNCS, vol. 4740, pp. 55–65. Springer, Heidelberg (2007). https://doi.org/10.1007/978-3-540-74873-1_8
4. Kempa, O., Lasota, T., Telec, Z., Trawiński, B.: Investigation of bagging ensembles of genetic neural networks and fuzzy systems for real estate appraisal. In: Nguyen, N.T., Kim, C.-G., Janiak, A. (eds.) ACIIDS 2011. LNCS (LNAI), vol. 6592, pp. 323–332. Springer, Heidelberg (2011). https://doi.org/10.1007/978-3-642-20042-7_33
5. Kopel, M., Hajas, T.: Implementing AI for non-player characters in 3D video games. In: Nguyen, N.T., Hoang, D.H., Hong, T.-P., Pham, H., Trawiński, B. (eds.) ACIIDS 2018. LNCS (LNAI), vol. 10751, pp. 610–619. Springer, Cham (2018). https://doi.org/10.1007/978-3-319-75417-8_57
6. Sutton, R.S., Barto, A.G.: Reinforcement Learning: An Introduction. MIT Press, Cambridge (2018)
7. Wang, Z., Schaul, T., Hessel, M., Van Hasselt, H., Lanctot, M., De Freitas, N.: Dueling network architectures for deep reinforcement learning. arXiv preprint arXiv:1511.06581 (2015)
8. Yannakakis, G.N., Togelius, J.: Artificial Intelligence and Games, vol. 2. Springer, Heidelberg (2018). https://doi.org/10.1007/978-3-319-63519-4

Apartment Valuation Models for a Big City Using Selected Spatial Attributes

Michał Talaga[1], Mateusz Piwowarczyk[1], Marcin Kutrzyński[1],
Tadeusz Lasota[2], Zbigniew Telec[1], and Bogdan Trawiński[1]([✉])

[1] Faculty of Computer Science and Management,
Wrocław University of Science and Technology, Wrocław, Poland
michal.jan.talaga@gmail.com,
{mateusz.piwowarczyk,marcin.kutrzynski,zbigniew.telec,
bogdan.trawinski}@pwr.edu.pl
[2] Wrocław Institute for the Application of Spatial Information and Artificial
Intelligence, Wrocław, Poland
tadeusz.lasota@wp.pl

Abstract. This paper addresses a property valuation problem with machine learning models with pre-selection of attributes. The study aimed to examine to what extent the environmental attributes influenced real estate prices. Real-world data about purchase and sale transactions derived from a cadastral system and registry of real estate transactions in one of Polish big cities were employed in the experiments. Machine learning models were built using basic attributes of apartments and environmental ones taken from cadastral maps. Five market segmentations were made including administrative cadastral regions of a city and quality zones delineated by an expert, and classes of apartments. Feature selection was accomplished and property valuation models were built for each division of a city area. The study allowed also for a comparative analysis of performance of ensemble learning techniques applied to construct predictive models.

Keywords: Property valuation · Sales comparison approach · Feature selection · Expert algorithms · Ensemble learning · Prediction models

1 Introduction

Thanks to the technological progress that have taken place over the last years, huge amounts of computing power and many advances in artificial intelligence allowed for many improvements in different domains and fields of science. Lots of these improvements appear to be connected with methods based on machine learning [19,28,29]. One of the phenomena which had peculiarly attracted attention of many scientist all over the world in different domains is very significant progress in big data analysis [4,6,16] and neural networks [14,22]. This progress allows us to use different data resources and learn new facts about them form

© Springer Nature Switzerland AG 2019
N. T. Nguyen et al. (Eds.): ICCCI 2019, LNAI 11683, pp. 363–376, 2019.
https://doi.org/10.1007/978-3-030-28377-3_30

the statistical perspective. Computational processing power currently available allows to cut the time needed for training specific machine learning algorithms in order to be able to to achieve the best possible results. Such algorithms are used not only in computer science, but also in many other fields like medicine (for example, the analysis of human genotypes [15,18]), banking, (forecasting trends in financial markets [5]) or trade (predicting behaviour of customers of customers based on previous purchases [27]). The issue of this research on the other hand is the real estate appraisal. Many attempts over the last years have been carried out in order to achieve best accuracy of automated valuation models in this domain [9,12,13]. Improvements in this topic is very demanded by professional appraisals, financial institutions, investors and property developers. Due to the multiplicity and diversity of attributes that can be assigned to the particular real estate, this case is very good subject for machine learning and Big Data researchers [8]. Recent years brings many studies examining machine learning models for real estate price prediction. Some of them focuses mainly not on transactional prices [2,10], which in many countries like Poland are not publicly available but on predicting price based on environmental [23], spatial and surroundings features, which can be easily received form open data sources. Multiplicity and diversity of such data is the main problem. They consist of many features, that alone have only little impact on the final price of property but combined together could be very significant predictor. The family of machine learning methods called ensemble learning [3,21] tries to tackle this problem by combining many weak, specialised predictors for building one, general and strong one. As previous research shows this techniques could result in better performance not only compared to machine learning models from other families but also compared to prices predicted using similar methods, that professional appraisers use [24,26]. Some of this methods were used in this research and achieved better results compared to the other ones.

   The aim of the study was to investigate how spatial and environmental attributes influence real estate price prediction machine learning models and do they have greater impact on price than basic attributes of the property such as area, year of construction or number of storeys. Another important problem in real estate appraisal is selecting clusters of neighbourhoods or buildings similar in the context of their price [11,20]. To address this problem special methods of properties cluster division were proposed in this paper. The original dataset was divided into 5 sub-sets, from which training and test sets were separated. The machine learning data driven models were built over the data prepared in such a way and their performance was examined in terms of the MAPE measure. Additionally, due to the growing popularity of the Gradient Boosting [1,7], it was checked whether it achieves better results in comparison to other popular machine learning techniques: decision trees, neural networks, random forest, linear regression and bagging of neural networks and decision trees.

2   Dataset Description

Dataset used in this research consisted of almost 21,000 records of sale and purchase transactions conducted on the real estate market in one of big cities in Poland in the years 2007–2015. This data came from the registry of real estate transactions and referred to apartments. The basic attributes of the properties in our collection were usable *area* of the premises, *year of construction* of the building in which the premises are located and *number of storeys* in the whole building. In addition, the transaction records contained 25 spatial attributes of individual premises. These attributes are listed in the Table 1.

Table 1. Transaction attributes considered in study.

Attribute label	Type	Category	Description
area	A	DOM	Total area of the building plot
city_center	L	GEO	Distance to the Wroclaw city center
highway	L	RAR	Distance to the nearest highway
national_road	L	RAR	Distance to the nearest national road
prov_road	L	RAR	Distance to the nearest provincial road
railway_line	L	RAR	Distance to the nearest railway line
railway_station	L	COM	Distance to the nearest railway station
transport_stop	L	COM	Distance to the nearest public transportation stop
transport_hub	L	COM	Distance to the transportation hub
shopping_mall	L	SHO	Distance to the nearest shopping center (33 largest and multifunctional shopping centers with at least one grocery store)
primary_school	L	EDU	Distance to the primary school building
middle_school	L	EDU	Distance to the middle school building
high_school	L	EDU	Distance to the high school building
university	L	EDU	Distance to the university building
area_ind500	L	IND	Industrial built-up area and storage sites in the 500-m radius
area_ind1500	L	IND	Industrial built-up area and storage sites in the 500–1500-m radius
area_ind > 1500	L	IND	Industrial built-up area and storage sites in the above 1500-m radius
area_for500	E	FOR	Forest area within the 500-m radius
area_for1500	E	FOR	Forest area within the 500–1500-m radius
area_for > 1500	E	FOR	Forest area above the 1500-m radius
river	E	WAT	Distance to the nearest main river
river_trib	E	WAT	Distance to the nearest river tributary
nature_bd	E	NAT	Distance to the Nature 2000 protection area under the Birds Directive
nature_hb	E	NAT	Distance to the Nature 2000 protection area under the Habitats Directive
nature_lp	E	NAT	Distance to the nearest landscape park

The response variable taken into account to train the models was transactional price updated to 1. January 2016. This allowed us to reliably compare performance of machine learning models against constantly changing real estate market.

3   Setup of Evaluation Experiments

To increase the accuracy of machine learning models, dataset has been divided into groups with sub-sets. This was to ensure that the value of attributes would be less variable, which should result in better performance. The first two groups resulted directly from the dataset. These were groups with 69 cadastral regions depicted on Fig. 1 and 23 expert zones proposed by real estate market experts resulting from their experience (Fig. 2). The expert zones have been delineated to embrace areas in which the prices of premises were changing over years in a similar way.

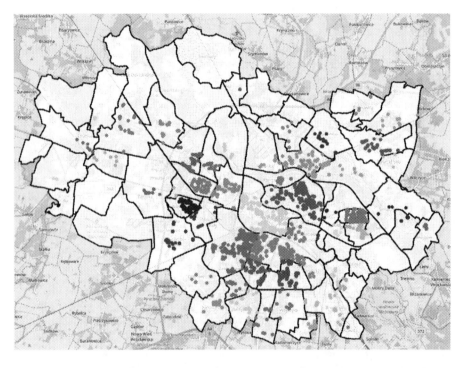

Fig. 1. Visualization of purchase and sale transactions of apartments over 69 cadastral regions.

For selected basic numerical attributes of real estate (number of storeys, area and year of construction) their division into classes and subclasses was

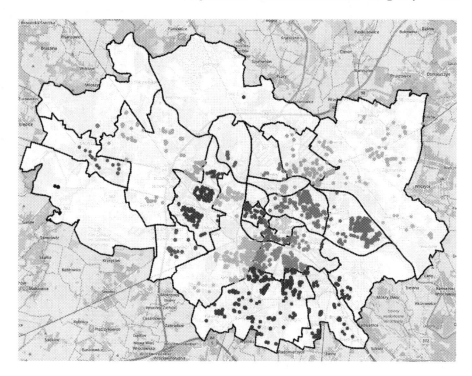

Fig. 2. Visualization of purchase and sale transactions of apartments over 23 expert zones.

determined. Subclass division is presented in Tables 2, 3 and 4. It was carried out taking into account the development conditions in the city. The division according to the years of construction results also from historical conditions.

Table 2. Subclass division S based on number of storeys in the building.

Number of storeys	Subclass value
From 1 to 2	1
From 3 to 5	2
Above 5	3

On the basis of the subclasses, it was possible to divide whole dataset of sale/purchase records into target classes. The target property class was determined as a tuple of record subclass values, The target class set P_{class} consisted of records that belonged to the same subclasses (Eq. 1). Class division was made on the whole dataset and particular subsets of cadastral regions and expert zones.

$$P_{class} = \{p \mid p = \langle s, a, y \rangle \ and \ s \in S, a \in A, y \in Y\} \tag{1}$$

Table 3. Subclass division A based on property area.

Area	Subclass value
Under 40 m2	1
From 40 m2 to 60 m2	2
Above 60 m2	3

Table 4. Subclass division Y based on year of construction.

Year of construction	Subclass value
To 1918	1
From 1919 to 1945	2
From 1946 to 1975	3
From 1976 to 1995	4
From 1996	5

where:

S - Subclass set based on number of storeys in the building
A - Subclass set based on property area
Y - Subclass set based on year of construction

The final result was the selection of 5 main data groups containing smaller sub-sets. A necessary condition for leaving a specific subset was its cardinality of at least 100 records. The list of selected groups with the number of their subsets (165 subsets in total) is as follows:

- Cadastral regions - 33 subsets
- Expert zones - 17 subsets
- Classes in the city of Wrocław - 24 subsets
- Classes in particular cadastral regions - 48 subsets
- Classes in particular expert zones - 43 subsets

Mean Absolute Percentage Error measurement briefly described in Eq. 2 was used to examine the accuracy of individual models.

$$MAPE = \frac{100}{n} \sum_{i=1}^{n} \frac{|y_i - x_i|}{y_i} \tag{2}$$

where:

n – number of records
y_i – actual value (in this case the actual transaction price of the property)
x_i – predicted value (in this case the value of the property resulting from the model)

For comparison the results with each other and check statistically significant differences between them many methods could be used. One of them is the Student's t-test, which compares two samples based on the arithmetic averages of their results but due to the multitude of calculations needed, authors decided to replace the Student's t-test with the Wilcoxon tests to check the statistically significance differences between the results for the individual machine learning algorithms and the Friedman test to rank the algorithms based on the results achieved. The Wilcoxon test is popular alternative to the Student's t-test and does not require the use of multiple test attempts. Since the parametric Student's t-test requires special criteria to be met, the Wilcoxon test is better suited to this paper issue. It is a non-parametric test and compares two sets of data. It's important advantage is that it adapts well to small sets of observations. The Friedman test at the other hand consists in ordering groups of observations on the basis of rank. At least three groups of data are needed to act properly. Just like the Wilcoxon test it is non-parametric test. We cannot check on its basis which group is the best. We can only deduce which group performed best compared to the others following [25].

Before training individual models, feature selection process was conducted for selection best fitting attributes [17]. The filtering class of feature selection algorithms has been used for this purpose. The selected algorithms belonged to the WEKA [30] software:

- CfsSubsetEval
- PrincipalComponents
- CReliefFAttributeEval

Each of the above algorithms was run for each subset (before the division into training and test data). The result of each algorithm was presented as a series of attributes from the most influential to the least influential. Depending on the position in the series, a given attribute was assigned a weight, where the higher the ranking position, the lower the weight was assigned. After weighting, the results of all three algorithms were combined to form a final ranking. The smaller the sum of the values for a particular attribute was, the higher the ranking position it occupied. Test datasets containing 2, 5, 15 and 25 of the best attributes respectively were created from the final, ordered set of attributes. In addition, a set *AYH* containing only 3 basic attributes (*area, year of construction* and *number of storeys*) was created for comparison. All sets prepared in this way were transferred to machine learning algorithms. The exception was the XGBoost algorithm, which received a full set of 28 attributes. The aim of this step was to check if due to this fact XGBoost algorithm will get the best results.

The following symbols have been proposed for models:

- Random forest (FOR)
- Linear regression (LIN)
- Decision tree (TRE)
- Multilayer Perceptron Neural network (NEU)
- 50 MP5 Decision trees bagging (TRE_BAG)

- 50 Multilayer Perceptron Neural networks bagging (NN_BAG)
- XGBoost with linear regression (XGB)
- XGBoost with regression based on tweedie distribution (XGB_T)

and the following symbols have been adopted for sets of attributes:

- Set with 2 best attributes (FS_2_ATTR)
- Set with 5 best attributes (FS_5_ATTR)
- Set with 15 best attributes (FS_15_ATTR)
- Set with 25 best attributes (FS_25_ATTR)
- Set with only basic attributes [area, year of construction, number of storeys] (AYH)

4   Analysis of Experimental Results

Figures 3, 4, 5, 6 and 7 show the medians of MAPE performance obtained for particular groups of division. Due to the fact that the XGBoost algorithm received a full set of attributes, the columns containing its results do not take into account the division into the number of attributes.

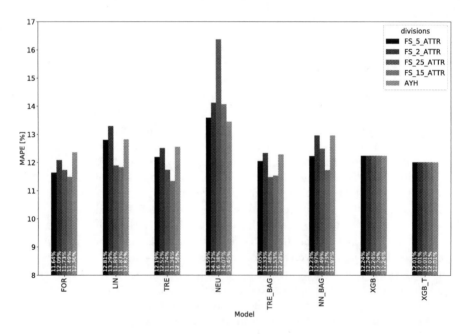

Fig. 3. Medians of MAPE performance for individual models with class division.

Based on the analysis of median MAPE performance values, we can see that the results for individual models do not differ significantly from each other.

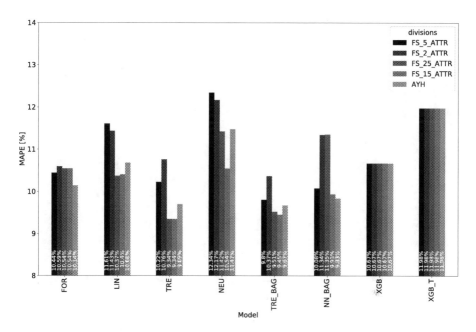

Fig. 4. Medians of MAPE performance for individual models with cadastral region division.

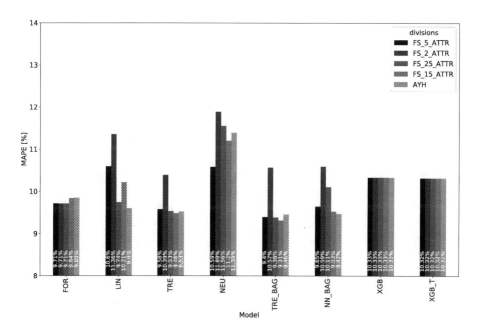

Fig. 5. Medians of MAPE performance for individual models with class within cadastral regions division.

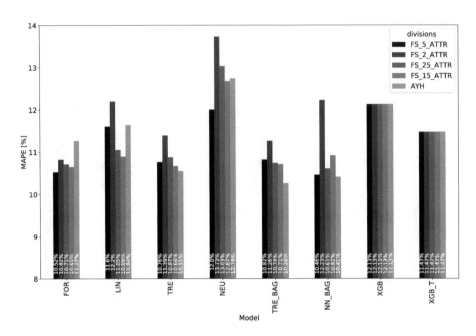

Fig. 6. Medians of MAPE performance for individual models with expert zone division.

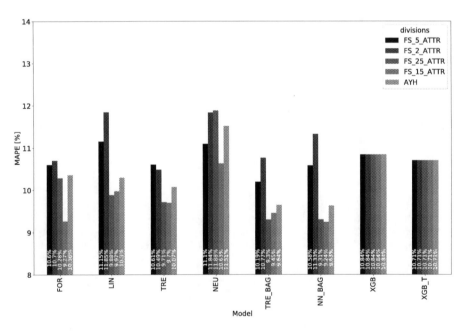

Fig. 7. Medians of MAPE performance for individual models with class within expert zones division.

In most test cases, the lowest values were recorded for decision tree bagging (TRE_BAG) and neural network bagging (NN_BAG). The highest MAPE performance values in most cases were achieved by single multilayer perceptron neural networks (NEU). This may have been due to too small training dataset. Both XGBoost approaches (linear and tweedie), despite the advantage of having more initial attributes, achieved results in most cases in the middle of the ranking. Here, too, a small number of test data may have had an impact.

The number of attributes also influenced the results. In most cases, the lowest error values were recorded for sets with 15 attributes (FS_15_ATTR). This was due to the fact that each of the machine learning algorithms has implemented an attribute selection algorithm, which additionally took into account which attributes from among those provided in the training dataset should have the greatest impact on the result. According to this, the best results should be obtained by the set that has the highest number of attributes. In this case, due to the small test sets, overfitting may have occurred, which negatively impact the results. We can also see that spatial attributes has influence on performance. Sets containing only basic attributes only in a few cases showed better performance than others.

Taking into account the division of sets into groups, the lowest values of errors were recorded for the division into classes within expert zones and cadastral regions. This is due to the fact that the properties in these sets were the most similar to each other, and machine learning models built on them were the best suited to the test data. The highest error values were obtained for models built on the basis of classes. Despite the fact that these sets contained similar values of basic attributes, the spatial attributes selected for each set may have caused the results to be less accurate.

In the case of statistical analysis, when comparing algorithms in pairs, in most cases where there was a significant statistical difference, neural networks were the worst. In all comparisons they turned out to be worse than the algorithm with which they were compared. The situation is similar in the case of both variants of the XGBoost algorithm. Only in few cases did they perform better than neural networks and random forest. When comparing the two variants, when there were significant statistical differences, the variant based on Tweedie's distribution turned out to be better. The best in direct comparisons turned out to be the bagging of decision trees. In most cases, there were significant statistical differences in comparison with other algorithms, and in these comparisons it was better than the second algorithm.

5   Conclusions and Future Work

In this paper an attempt was made to show that not only basic attributes of premises such as area or year of construction, but also spatial and environmental attributes retrieved from open repositories and cadastral maps have an impact on their prices. Due to the characteristics of the place where this premises are located, each group has a set of attributes that affect their price the most.

In some places it may be the distance from a shopping centre, in others it may be the distance from the nearest public transportation stop. The aim of this paper was to investigate are machine learning algorithms are able to adapt to diverse real estate datasets with many property attributes. Selection of these attributes was made combining few methods from WEKA package. For each set of attributes, a corresponding machine learning model was created. These models were trained on the basic property attributes and accordingly 2, 5, 15 and 25 attributes picked by mix of feature selection techniques. The results obtained by algorithms were tested for statistical significance with the Wilcoxon and the Friedman tests to indicate how the individual algorithms performed in comparison to the others.

The results obtained during the research confirmed the aim of the work. They showed lower values of obtained errors in the case of using spatial attributes than in the case of using only basic attributes. Taking into account the machine learning algorithms, the advantage in the number of initial attributes for the Gradient Boosting algorithm, the lowest error values were recorded for the decision tree bagging. The statistical significance tests confirmed these results by comparing the algorithms in pairs. In all pairs where there was a statistically significant difference, the bagging of decision trees outperformed other algorithms. Neural networks were the worst in the tests of statistical significance - in all comparisons where there was a statistically significant difference, they were worse than in the other ones. This work was only a prelude to possible further work on machine learning models for property valuation. First of all, it is worthwhile to obtain more training data. Due to the fact that some of subsets had only 100 properties, the algorithms were not able to train well, which resulted in decreased accuracy. Another possible development path is the comparison of machine learning algorithms investigated in this paper with the results obtained by expert algorithms. This would allow open discussions on modernising actual expert methods of property valuations and adapt machine learning to be legally used in professional appraisal.

References

1. Chen, T., Guestrin, C.: XGBoost: a scalable tree boosting system. In: Proceedings of the 22nd ACM SIGKDD International Conference on Knowledge Discovery and Data Mining, pp. 785–794. ACM (2016)
2. De Nadai, M., Lepri, B.: The economic value of neighborhoods: predicting real estate prices from the urban environment. In: 2018 IEEE 5th International Conference on Data Science and Advanced Analytics (DSAA), pp. 323–330. IEEE (2018)
3. Dieterich, T.G.: Ensemble methods in machine learning. In: Kittler, J., Roli, F. (eds.) MCS 2000. LNCS, vol. 1857, pp. 1–15. Springer, Heidelberg (2000). https://doi.org/10.1007/3-540-45014-9_1
4. Erevelles, S., Fukawa, N., Swayne, L.: Big Data consumer analytics and the transformation of marketing. J. Bus. Res. **69**(2), 897–904 (2016)
5. Fischer, T., Krauss, C.: Deep learning with long short-term memory networks for financial market predictions. Eur. J. Oper. Res. **270**(2), 654–669 (2018)

6. Gandomi, A., Haider, M.: Beyond the hype: big data concepts, methods, and analytics. Int. J. Inf. Manag. **35**(2), 137–144 (2015)
7. Ke, G., et al.: LightGBM: a highly efficient gradient boosting decision tree. In: Advances in Neural Information Processing Systems, pp. 3146–3154 (2017)
8. Kok, N., Koponen, E.L., Martínez-Barbosa, C.A.: Big data in real estate? From manual appraisal to automated valuation. J. Portf. Manag. **43**(6), 202–211 (2017)
9. Lasota, T., Łuczak, T., Trawiński, B.: Investigation of rotation forest method applied to property price prediction. In: Rutkowski, L., Korytkowski, M., Scherer, R., Tadeusiewicz, R., Zadeh, L.A., Zurada, J.M. (eds.) ICAISC 2012. LNCS (LNAI), vol. 7267, pp. 403–411. Springer, Heidelberg (2012). https://doi.org/10.1007/978-3-642-29347-4_47
10. Lasota, T., Mazurkiewicz, J., Trawiński, B., Trawiński, K.: Comparison of data driven models for the valuation of residential premises using keel. Int. J. Hybrid Intell. Syst. **7**(1), 3–16 (2010)
11. Lasota, T., Sawiłow, E., Trawiński, B., Roman, M., Marczuk, P., Popowicz, P.: A method for merging similar zones to improve intelligent models for real estate appraisal. In: Nguyen, N.T., Trawiński, B., Kosala, R. (eds.) ACIIDS 2015. LNCS (LNAI), vol. 9011, pp. 472–483. Springer, Cham (2015). https://doi.org/10.1007/978-3-319-15702-3_46
12. Lasota, T., Telec, Z., Trawinski, B., Trawinski, G.: Evaluation of random subspace and random forest regression models based on genetic fuzzy systems. In: KES, pp. 88–97 (2012)
13. Lasota, T., Telec, Z., Trawinski, B., Trawinski, K.: Investigation of the ets evolving fuzzy systems applied to real estate appraisal. Mult.-Valued Log. Soft Comput. **17**(2–3), 229–253 (2011)
14. LeCun, Y., Bengio, Y., Hinton, G.: Deep learning. Nature **521**(7553), 436 (2015)
15. Leung, M.K., Delong, A., Alipanahi, B., Frey, B.J.: Machine learning in genomic medicine: a review of computational problems and data sets. Proc. IEEE **104**(1), 176–197 (2015)
16. Li, J., Tao, F., Cheng, Y., Zhao, L.: Big Data in product lifecycle management. Int. J. Adv. Manuf. Technol. **81**(1–4), 667–684 (2015)
17. Li, J., et al.: Feature selection: a data perspective. ACM Comput. Surv. (CSUR) **50**(6), 94 (2018)
18. Libbrecht, M.W., Noble, W.S.: Machine learning applications in genetics and genomics. Nat. Rev. Genet. **16**(6), 321 (2015)
19. Lötsch, J., et al.: Machine-learning-derived classifier predicts absence of persistent pain after breast cancer surgery with high accuracy. Breast Cancer Res. Treat. **171**(2), 399–411 (2018)
20. Malinowski, A., Piwowarczyk, M., Telec, Z., Trawiński, B., Kempa, O., Lasota, T.: An approach to property valuation based on market segmentation with crisp and fuzzy clustering. In: Nguyen, N.T., Pimenidis, E., Khan, Z., Trawiński, B. (eds.) ICCCI 2018. LNCS (LNAI), vol. 11055, pp. 534–548. Springer, Cham (2018). https://doi.org/10.1007/978-3-319-98443-8_49
21. Polikar, R.: Ensemble learning. In: Zhang, C., Ma, Y. (eds.) Ensemble Machine Learning, pp. 1–34. Springer, Boston (2012). https://doi.org/10.1007/978-1-4419-9326-7_1
22. Silver, D., et al.: Mastering the game of go with deep neural networks and tree search. Nature **529**(7587), 484 (2016)
23. Sylla, M., Lasota, T., Szewrański, S.: Valuing environmental amenities in peri-urban areas: evidence from poland. Sustainability **11**(3), 570 (2019)

24. Trawiński, B., Lasota, T., Kempa, O., Telec, Z., Kutrzyński, M.: Comparison of ensemble learning models with expert algorithms designed for a property valuation system. In: Nguyen, N.T., Papadopoulos, G.A., Jędrzejowicz, P., Trawiński, B., Vossen, G. (eds.) ICCCI 2017. LNCS (LNAI), vol. 10448, pp. 317–327. Springer, Cham (2017). https://doi.org/10.1007/978-3-319-67074-4_31
25. Trawiński, B., Smetek, M., Telec, Z., Lasota, T.: Nonparametric statistical analysis for multiple comparison of machine learning regression algorithms. Int. J. Appl. Math. Comput. Sci. **22**(4), 867–881 (2012). https://doi.org/10.2478/v10006-012-0064-z
26. Trawiński, B., et al.: Comparison of expert algorithms with machine learning models for real estate appraisal. In: 2017 IEEE International Conference on INnovations in Intelligent SysTems and Applications (INISTA), pp. 51–54. IEEE (2017)
27. Vafeiadis, T., Diamantaras, K.I., Sarigiannidis, G., Chatzisavvas, K.C.: A comparison of machine learning techniques for customer churn prediction. Simul. Model. Pract. Theory **55**, 1–9 (2015)
28. Voyant, C., et al.: Machine learning methods for solar radiation forecasting: a review. Renew. Energy **105**, 569–582 (2017)
29. Webb, S.: Deep learning for biology. Nature **554**(7693), 555–557 (2018)
30. Witten, I.H., Frank, E., Hall, M.A., Pal, C.J.: Data Mining: Practical Machine Learning Tools and Techniques. Morgan Kaufmann (2016)

Valuation of Building Plots in a Rural Area Using Machine Learning Approach

Mateusz Piwowarczyk[1]([⊠]) [iD], Tadeusz Lasota[2] [iD],
Zbigniew Telec[1] [iD], and Bogdan Trawiński[1] [iD]

[1] Faculty of Computer Science and Management,
Wrocław University of Science and Technology, Wrocław, Poland
{mateusz.piwowarczyk, zbigniew.telec,
trawinski}@pwr.edu.pl
[2] Wrocław Institute for the Application of Spatial Information
and Artificial Intelligence, Wrocław, Poland
tadeusz.lasota@wp.pl

Abstract. Among many factors influencing the prices of building plots in rural areas, one can distinguish location factors related to the proximity and availability of many public services and transport hubs, as well as environmental factors, which are mainly related to the proximity of forests, parks or rivers. This paper examines how strongly such attributes of a property influence its price in rural areas. The experiments were carried out using top-notch machine learning methods and real-world data derived from the real estate price register and publicly available geographical data sets. The study showed that environmental features of building plots in a rural area had rather a small impact on their prices whereas location features turned out to be more important.

Keywords: Machine learning · Land valuation · Building plots · Rural area · Mass appraisal

1 Introduction

Traditional methods of property valuation were created at a time when there was no common access to large online databases allowing insights and investigation of many peculiar attributes of individual properties. These traditional methods are based on techniques in which domain experts with advanced knowledge in the field of real estate appraisal attempt to assess the similarity among selected properties as objectively as possible, according to criteria based on developed industry standards. Based on this assessed similarity and past prices of similar properties in the neighbourhood, predicted price of valuated property is calculated. Also extracting these similarity zones constitutes a big challenge [1–3]. Traditional expert methods have proven to be sufficiently effective for professional purposes, especially when there is lack of additional data [4], but they require large amount of work in expertise of evaluated individual properties, and they are relying on subjectively selected key variables. Traditional comparable methods clearly do not derive any value from the new methods and solutions that have emerged since the recent Big Data era [5].

© Springer Nature Switzerland AG 2019
N. T. Nguyen et al. (Eds.): ICCCI 2019, LNAI 11683, pp. 377–389, 2019.
https://doi.org/10.1007/978-3-030-28377-3_31

Access to big data sets and diversity of available data cause that methods which can achieve best accuracy after training them on a large amount of data gain in popularity. Moreover, common and public access to various collected statistics and other public domain data sets made it possible to combine facts from many data sources and find correlations between different dependencies [6].

Regarding property valuation methods, such previously unavailable data sources can be online databases on crime accidents [7] or air pollution in the regions [8]. Access to the large amount of property sale-purchase transaction data itself has also increased, allowing statistical methods to be more effective.

Building plots are the object of interest for potential investors. Accurate prediction of real estate prices based on features commonly available in public data repositories and conclusions derived from analysing price change trends in may have a real impact on investors decisions regarding the purchase of real estate for investment purposes. The issue of searching for real estate for investments has been the subject of many studies. Some of them show that machine learning methods can surpass traditional methods of real estate appraisal [9, 10].

The practical goal of this paper is to check how strong influence on the price of a building plot can have environmental and location features such as distance from a forest, river or shopping mall. At it is known, ecosystem and natural environment surroundings could have great impact on human well-being [11]. There is a gap in research on influence of environmental amenities, especially on rural areas [12]. Information about such amenitiesis available in public geographical databases. We can deliberate what could be more significant for buyers in rural area: proximity to nature or communication and public services points. Is it even possible to accurately predict price of a property having only this range of data? [13]. The conclusions drawn from answer to this question can influence on potential investors decisions. To estimate the prices of potential investment plots in selected areas machine learning mass appraisal methods and publicly available data were used.

Unlike traditional methods of property valuation, where only a few highly price forming attributes play a major role in forecasting the price, the machine learning approach and publicly available data allow for the identification of a large number of attributes with a weak impact on the price individually, but together could be a strong predictor, when appropriately selected and combined. This approach reflects very well the way ensemble machine learning model are formed, where many weak predictors are combined, to produce a single accurate predictor [14, 15]. Ensemble methods were used in this research, resulting in the best accuracy with comparison to other types of machine learning algorithms.

2   Dataset Description

For the purpose of building machine learning models 9114 records concerning sale-purchase transactions completed in the real estate market during the years 2004–2016 were used. These data were taken from the actual real estate price register and included several attributes for environmental and spatial characteristics of building plots intended for development of single-family houses in the agglomeration of the city

Wrocław, excluding the area of the city itself as shown in Fig. 3. Provided data includes only transactions where the price was at least 10 PLN per square meter. There were 28 different attributes used for training. These attributes are briefly described in Table 1.

Table 1. Transaction attributes considered in study

Attribute label	Type	Category	Description
area	A	DOM	Total area of the building plot
avg_price	M	DOM	Average price per square meter within a property cadastral region
city_center	L	GEO	Distance to the Wroclaw city center
highway	L	RAR	Distance to the nearest highway
national_road	L	RAR -	Distance to the nearest national road
prov_road	L	RAR	Distance to the nearest provincial road
railway_line	L	RAR	Distance to the nearest railway line
railway_station	L	COM	Distance to the nearest railway station
transport_stop	L	COM	Distance to the nearest public transportation stop
transport_hub	L	COM	Distance to the transportation hub
shopping_mall	L	SHO	Distance to the nearest shopping center (33 largest and multifunctional shopping centers with at least one grocery store)
primary_school	L	EDU	Distance to the primary school building
middle_school	L	EDU	Distance to the middle school building
high_school	L	EDU	Distance to the high school building
University	L	EDU	Distance to the university building
area_ind500	L	IND	Industrial built-up area and storage sites in the 500-m radius
area_ind1500	L	IND	Industrial built-up area and storage sites in the 500–1500-m radius
area_ind>1500	L	IND	Industrial built-up area and storage sites in the above 1500-m radius
area_for500	E	FOR	Forest area within the 500-m radius
area_for1500	E	FOR	Forest area within the 500–1500-m radius
area_for>1500	E	FOR	Forest area above the 1500-m radius
river	E	WAT	Distance to the nearest main river
river_trib	E	WAT	Distance to the nearest river tributary
nature_bd	E	NAT	Distance to the Nature 2000 protection area under the Birds Directive
nature_hb	E	NAT	Distance to the Nature 2000 protection area under the Habitats Directive
nature_lp	E	NAT	Distance to the nearest landscape park
shape_index	O	SHP	Shape Index expressed in Formula 1
perimeter	O	SHP	Perimeter of the plot

All explanatory variables have been divided into 11 categories, which was: domain (DOM), geographical (GEO), roads and railways (RAR), commute and transportation (COM), shopping (SHO), education (EDU), industrial areas (IND), forests (FOR), water (WAT), nature (NAT), shape (SHP) and 5 types including area (A), location (L), environmental (E), average price per square metre within a property cadastral region (M) and others related to size and shape of the plot (O). Types of variables were used to divide attributes into separate data sets used to train machine learning models.

There were two calculated attributes. First of them was *avg_price*. This variable was calculated from the average price of all transactions concluded on the market during the period considered in a cadastral region. The use of this attribute was dictated by the need to obtain information on pricing attributes for the valued land properties, such as availability of utilities or location of the property. In professional appraisal such data are obtained from geodetic maps, land and mortgage registers, on-site inspection or development plans and, in accordance with the professional standards, they usually have the greatest impact on the price of the property. We were not able to obtain values for these attributes, therefore the attribute of an average price was introduced. The task of this attribute is to average infrastructure and geodetic conditions for a selected cadastral region. This will help to reduce the error in the predicted property price resulting from the lack of key price forming attributes.

The second calculated variable was *shape_index*. It was calculated using Formula 1 introduced in [16]. In this case if shape index is closer to 1, then the shape of building plot is closer to square. This could be very helpful in terms of investigating very narrow or untypically shaped building plots, on which building family houses could be more complicated. Shape index is an efficient way of numerical approximation of the shape [17, 18]. Shape is one of the main price forming attributes of building plots.

$$Shape\_Index = \frac{perimeter}{4\sqrt{area}} \tag{1}$$

Then, in order to reduce the number of attributes and thus reduce the tendency of machine learning models to overfit the most correlated environmental and location attributes was rejected from final set of attributes. Correlation of the attributes was analyzed using the Pearson correlation coefficient. The result of the analysis is presented in Fig. 1. As strongly correlated groups of attributes, those whose correlation coefficient was greater than or equal to 0.6 were selected. After such analysis, 3 main groups of correlated attributes presented in Table 2 were selected. Bolded attributes were chosen to be used in the final experiment, as the most representative form the group. This selection was based on the attribute importance provided by *Random Forest* for the whole set of attributes. The rank of attributes by importance is presented in (Figs. 1 and 2).

Table 2. Groups of correlated attributes

Group 1	**shopping_mall**, city_center, university, transport_hub
Group 2	**railway_station**, railway_line
Group 3	**national_road**, highway

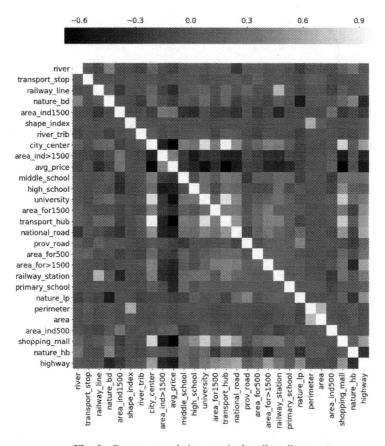

Fig. 1. Pearson correlation matrix for all attributes

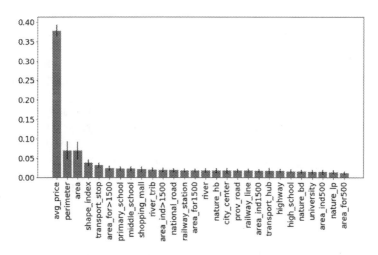

Fig. 2. The rank of attributes provided by Random Forest

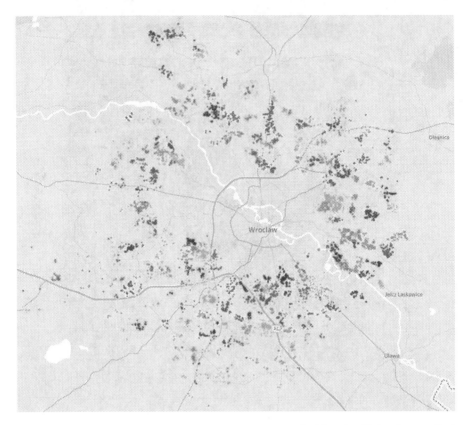

Fig. 3. Valuated building plots by cadastral region annotated with color (Color figure online)

3   Setup of Evaluation Experiments

For such selected attributes 6 different types of machine learning models were trained on the 8 different datasets, that contained selected attributes presented in Table 3. Models were constructed using *scikit-learn* machine learning library for python programming language. The trained machine learning types of models was *Linear Regression (LIN), Decision Tree (TRE), Random Forest (FOR), Bagging* of 150 decision trees *(BAG). Gradient Boosting (GBR)* and *K-Nearest Neighbors (KNN)*. All of selected attributes were normalized in the pre-processing stage with *sklearn.pre-processing.Normalizer* with L2 norm. ALEMO data set was employed for tuning the parameters of machine learning models using the *scikit-learn* class: *sklearn.-model_selection.RandomizedSearchCV*. Several different setups was randomly combined to tune best parameters across different machine learning models. All of them are presented in Table 4. Bolded parameter values were selected for training models during the experiment.

Table 3. Datasets description

Dataset label	Dataset features
AL	Area of property, Location features
AE	Area of property, Environmental features
ALE	Area of property, Location features, Environmental features
ALEO	Area of property, Location features, Environmental features, Other features (perimeter and shape index)
ALM	Area of property, Location features, Average price per square metre within a property cadastral region
AEM	Area of property, Environmental features, Average price per square metre within a property cadastral region
ALEM	Area of property, Location features, Environmental features, Average price per square metre within a property cadastral region
ALEMO	Area of property, Location features, Environmental features, Average price per square metre within a property cadastral region, Other features (perimeter and shape index)

A - Area of property, L - Location features, E - Environmental features, M - Average price per square metre within a property cadastral region, O - Other features

Table 4. Machine learning model parameters used for tuning phase

Parameter name	Model using this parameter	Considered values
max_depth	TRE, FOR, BAG, GBR	1, 3, 5, 7, 10, 15, 20, 30, 40, **None**
min_samples_split	TRE, FOR, BAG, GBR	**2**, 3, 5, 7, 10, 15, 20, 30, 40
min_samples_leaf	TRE, FOR, BAG, GBR	**1**, 3, 5, 7, 10, 15, 20, 30, 40
n_estimators	FOR, BAG, GBR	2, 5, 10, 30, 50, 100, **150**
n_neighbors	KNN	3, 5, **7**, 10, 20, 50, 100
leaf_size	KNN	3, 5, **10**, 20, 30, 50, 100, 150

In order to check the statistical significance of the obtained results, the whole dataset of our transactional records was randomly divided into two separate groups. Training set contained 70% of the whole dataset and test set comprised 30% of records.

The following procedure was implemented to compare the performance of the *LIN, TRE, FOR, BAG, GBR, KNN* algorithms over the *AL, AE, ALE, ALEO, ALM, AEM, ALEM, ALEMO* datasets. The prices of 100 building plots randomly drawn from the test set were computed with individual algorithms and datasets. Then, the performance measure *MAE* (*mean absolute error*) was determined for each run in accordance with Formula 2, where P_i^a and P_i^p denote the actual and predicted prices respectively and n stands for the number of building plots being estimated in each run.

$$MAE = \frac{1}{n} * \sum_{i=1}^{n} \left| P_i^p - P_i^a \right| \tag{2}$$

This schema was repeated 100 times yielding 100 values of *MAE* for each algorithm and dataset which enabled us to conduct the *ANOVA* test in the group of machine learning algorithms, to check if there are any significant differences in this groups and Tukey's multi-comparison method for statistical significance among particular groups.

4   Analysis of Experimental Results

It the first place, statistically significant differences between groups of data sets for a given model (Table 5) and between models within a given data set (Table 6) were examined. This was checked with the usage of the *ANOVA* test. There were statistically significant differences in performance in terms of *MAE* of given models among given dataset (marked with + sign). However, in the case of *FOR*, *BAG* and *KNN* no statistically significant differences in performance over different data sets were observed (− sign). For rejection of H_0 the 0.05 p-value threshold was used in all tests.

Table 5. ANOVA test for MAE performance among all datasets

Model	p-value	F-value	Reject H_0
LIN	>0.0001	76.61026	+
TRE	0.00338	3.07107	+
FOR	0.54646	0.84946	−
BAG	0.47743	0.93631	−
GBR	0.00299	3.11648	+
KNN	0.51132	0.89301	−

Table 6. ANOVA test for MAE performance among all types of models

Dataset	p-value	F-value	Reject H_0
AL	>0.0001	105.86413	+
AE	>0.0001	169.9786	+
ALE	>0.0001	107.23304	+
ALEO	>0.0001	108.52238	+
ALM	>0.0001	71.69764	+
AEM	>0.0001	85.03717	+
ALEM	>0.0001	77.37814	+
ALEMO	>0.0001	76.78763	+

With the usage of Tukey test, differences in performance between the types of machine learning models within each data set were checked. The results of this analysis are presented in Tables 7, 8, 9, 10, 11, 12, 13 and 14. The following denotation was applied:

≈ There were no significant statistical differences
+ Model marked in the row turned out to have better MAE performance
− Model marked in the column revealed better MAE performance

No statistically significant differences between Bagging and Random Forest were observed over all data sets.

Table 7. Tukey test for MAE performance over ALEMO dataset

	FOR	GBR	KNN	LIN	TRE
BAG	≈	+	+	+	+
FOR		+	+	+	+
GBR			−	−	≈
KNN				≈	+
LIN					+

Table 8. Tukey test for MAE performance overALEM dataset

	FOR	GBR	KNN	LIN	TRE
BAG	≈	+	+	+	+
FOR		+	+	+	+
GBR			−	−	≈
KNN				≈	+
LIN					+

Table 9. Tukey test for MAE performance over AEM dataset

	FOR	GBR	KNN	LIN	TRE
BAG	≈	+	+	+	+
FOR		+	+	+	+
GBR			−	≈	≈
KNN				≈	+
LIN					+

Table 10. Tukey test for MAE performance over ALM dataset

	FOR	GBR	KNN	LIN	TRE
BAG	≈	+	+	+	+
FOR		+	+	+	+
GBR			−	−	≈
KNN				≈	+
LIN					+

Table 11. Tukey test for MAE performance over ALEO dataset

	FOR	GBR	KNN	LIN	TRE
BAG	≈	+	+	+	+
FOR		+	+	+	+
GBR			−	≈	≈
KNN				+	+
LIN					≈

Table 12. Tukey test for MAE performance over ALE dataset

	FOR	GBR	KNN	LIN	TRE
BAG	≈	+	+	+	+
FOR		+	+	+	+
GBR			−	≈	≈
KNN				+	+
LIN					≈

Table 13. Tukey test for MAE performance over AE dataset

	FOR	GBR	KNN	LIN	TRE
BAG	≈	+	+	+	+
FOR		+	+	+	+
GBR			−	+	≈
KNN				+	+
LIN					−

Table 14. Tuckey test for MAE performance on AL dataset

	FOR	GBR	KNN	LIN	TRE
BAG	≈	+	+	+	+
FOR		+	+	+	+
GBR			−	≈	≈
KNN				+	+
LIN					≈

When analysing the results of the experiment, we can observe that the data set which achieves the highest accuracy in price prediction of the building plot is ALEMO containing full set of attributes of the plot (both environmental and location features along with shape related ones). Averaged results from all 100 measurements for MAE are presented in Table 15. The most accurate type of machine learning models for land property valuation turned out to be *Random Forest (FOR)* along with *Bagging (BAG)*. These two ensemble based machine learning regressors gave noticeably better results than other machine learning models in all evaluated sets of attributes (Fig. 4).

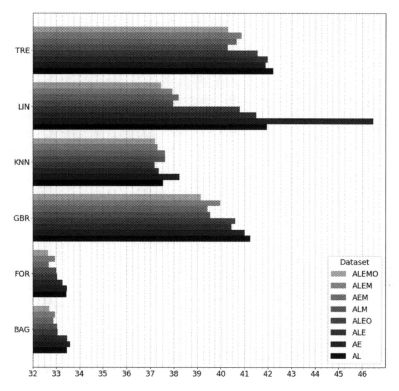

Fig. 4. Performance comparison of individual models over individual datasets

Table 15. Average MAE result from 100 test runs

	AL	AE	ALE	ALEO	ALM	AEM	ALEM	ALEMO
BAG	33.45	33.60	33.47	33.05	33.03	32.88	32.96	32.70
FOR	33.44	33.45	33.27	33.03	33.00	32.68	32.94	32.65
GBR	41.25	41.02	40.44	40.60	39.55	39.45	39.98	39.14
KNN	37.54	38.23	37.36	37.18	37.63	37.63	37.30	37.20
LIN	41.94	46.49	41.49	40.80	37.97	38.20	37.94	37.45
TRE	42.22	41.90	41.98	41.55	40.28	40.65	40.88	40.30

5 Conclusions and Future Work

The issue of property valuation is very complicated and requires a lot of domain knowledge. Modern methods of data exploration and publicly available geographical datasets allow us to bring improvements in this field, especially in the mass appraisal methods. An important role in estimating the value of real estate is played by attributes selected for valuation process, which describe the property. A reasonable selection of similar real estate for comparison is also important in the case of comparative approach.

The prices of individual properties may be affected by various factors. A big challenge is to create valuation standards that would allow us to regulate which attributes in which cases should be considered in the valuation of real estate.

The influence of selected environmental attributes on the accuracy of estimating real estate prices using selected machine learning models was investigated in this paper. This influence was relatively small when comparing to other localization and infrastructural attributes, but it gave significantly better results compared to machine learning models which were built without these features.

It is also worth noting that the accuracy of predicting property prices by the models discussed in this paper could be increased if the important price forming attributes for building plots such as infrastructure, including access roads, electricity, water, and gas, would be available. Therefore, automated extraction of such data from geodetic maps is needed to enhance the considered models in the future research.

References

1. Lasota, T., Sawiłow, E., Trawiński, B., Roman, M., Marczuk, P., Popowicz, P.: A method for merging similar zones to improve intelligent models for real estate appraisal. In: Nguyen, N.T., Trawiński, B., Kosala, R. (eds.) ACIIDS 2015. LNCS (LNAI), vol. 9011, pp. 472–483. Springer, Cham (2015). https://doi.org/10.1007/978-3-319-15702-3_46

2. Lasota, T., et al.: Enhancing intelligent property valuation models by merging similar cadastral regions of a municipality. In: Núñez, M., Nguyen, N.T., Camacho, D., Trawiński, B. (eds.) ICCCI 2015. LNCS (LNAI), vol. 9330, pp. 566–577. Springer, Cham (2015). https://doi.org/10.1007/978-3-319-24306-1_55

3. Malinowski, A., Piwowarczyk, M., Telec, Z., Trawiński, B., Kempa, O., Lasota, T.: An approach to property valuation based on market segmentation with crisp and fuzzy clustering. In: Nguyen, N.T., Pimenidis, E., Khan, Z., Trawiński, B. (eds.) ICCCI 2018. LNCS (LNAI), vol. 11055, pp. 534–548. Springer, Cham (2018). https://doi.org/10.1007/978-3-319-98443-8_49

4. Pagourtzi, E., Assimakopoulos, V., Hatzichristos, T., French, N.: Real estate appraisal: a review of valuation methods. J. Prop. Invest. Finance 21(4), 383–401 (2003)

5. Peterson, S., Flangan, A.B.: Neural network hedonic pricing models in mass real estate appraisal. J. R. Estate Res. 31(2), 147–164 (2009)

6. Zhang, C., Fang, J., Yu, T.: A study of real estate demanding index based on massive website log data. In: Proceedings of the 2018 9th International Conference on E-business, Management and Economics, pp. 55–59. ACM (2018)

7. Tita, G.E., Petras, T.L., Greenbaum, R.T.: Crime and residential choice: a neighborhood level analysis of the impact of crime on housing prices. J. Quant. Criminol. 22(4), 299 (2006)

8. Anderson Jr., R.J., Crocker, T.D.: Air pollution and residential property values. Urban Stud. 8(3), 171–180 (1971)

9. Trawiński, B., Lasota, T., Kempa, O., Telec, Z., Kutrzyński, M.: Comparison of ensemble learning models with expert algorithms designed for a property valuation system. In: Nguyen, N.T., Papadopoulos, George A., Jędrzejowicz, P., Trawiński, B., Vossen, G. (eds.) ICCCI 2017. LNCS (LNAI), vol. 10448, pp. 317–327. Springer, Cham (2017). https://doi.org/10.1007/978-3-319-67074-4_31

10. Trawiński, B., et al.: Comparison of expert algorithms with machine learning models for a real estate appraisal system. In: The 2017 IEEE International Conference on INnovations in Intelligent SysTems and Applications INISTA 2017. IEEE (2017). https://doi.org/10.1109/inista.2017.8001131

11. Haines-Young, R., Potschin, M.: The links between biodiversity, ecosystem services human well-being. In: Raffaelli, D.G., Frid, C.L.J. (eds.) Ecosystem Ecology: A New Synthesis, pp. 110–139. Cambridge University Press, Cambridge (2010)

12. Sylla, M., Lasota, T., Szewrański, S.: Valuing environmental amenities in peri-urban areas: evidence from Poland. Sustainability 11(3), 1–15 (2019)

13. De Nadai, M., Lepri, B.: The economic value of neighborhoods: predicting real estate prices from the urban environment. In: 2018 IEEE 5th International Conference on Data Science and Advanced Analytics (DSAA), pp. 323–330. IEEE (2018)

14. Rokach, L.: Ensemble-based classifiers. Artif. Intell. Rev. 33(1–2), 1–39 (2010)

15. Kazienko, P., Lughofer, E., Trawiński, B.: Hybrid and ensemble methods in machine learning. J. Univers. Comput. Sci. 19(4), 457–461 (2013)

16. Solecka, I., Sylla, M., Świąder, M.: Urban sprawl impact on Farmland conversion in suburban area of Wroclaw, Poland. In: IOP Conference Series: Materials Science and Engineering, vol. 245, no. 7 (2017). https://doi.org/10.1088/1757-899x/245/7/072002

17. McGarigal, K., Marks, B.J.: FRAGSTATS: spatial pattern analysis program for quantifying landscape structure. General technical report PNW-GTR-351, USDA Forest Service, Pacific Northwest Research Station, Portland, OR (1995)

18. Jiao, L., Liu, Y.: Analyzing the shape characteristics of land use classes in remote sensing imagery. ISPRS Ann. Photogramm. Remote Sens. Spat. Inf. Sci., I-7(September), 135–140 (2012)

Computer Vision Techniques

Detection and Modeling of Alcohol Intoxication Dynamic from IR Images Based on Clustering Driven by ABC Algorithm

Jan Kubicek[✉], Alice Krestanova, Marek Penhaker, David Oczka,
Martin Cerny, and Martin Augustynek

VSB-Technical University of Ostrava, FEECS,
K450, 17. Listopadu 15, Ostrava-Poruba, Czech Republic
{jan.kubicek,alice.krestanov,marek.penhaker,
david.oczka,martin.cerny,martin.augustynek}@vsb.cz

Abstract. Alcohol detection is a challenging issue due to many aspects, especially to security reasons. Conventional measuring systems usually utilize a direct contact with the human body to obtain on spot alcohol level estimation. Nevertheless, it is well known that there are several side effects including the facial temperature distribution for alcohol detection. Since the facial temperature map is observable from the infrared (IR) records, we have performed a set of experimental measurements allowing for dynamical tracking of time-dependent effect of the alcohol intoxication. In this paper, we have proposed the clustering multiregional segmentation driven by the genetic optimization, particularly the Artificial Bee Colony (ABC) algorithm for the facial IR segmentation. The genetic optimization determines an optimal distribution of the initial cluster's centroids, which represent the main part of a proper clustering. Based on the segmentation procedure, we have proposed a dynamical model allowing for prediction of time-dependent alcohol intoxication features.

Keywords: Image segmentation · IR image · Alcohol features ·
ABC algorithm · Clustering · K-means

1 Introduction

Worldwide, alcohol, and in this case, ethanol represent one of the most frequently used drugs. Also, alcohol is responsible for many diseases and hospital admissions. From the aforementioned reasons, it is one of the most challenging areas of the new methods development allowing for detection and tracking of the alcohol content [1–3].

From a chemical point of view, the molecule responsible for alcohol intoxication is the ethanol (C_2H_6O). Present in all alcoholic beverages, ethanol reaches the blood vessels system through normal digestion. Recognized as a toxin, ethanol will be destroyed by the body, and mainly in the liver as it filters blood. When the input of ethanol in the body is superior to the liver's absorption capacity, like when we drink, ethanol stacks in the bloodstream, and begins to have all sorts of effects. As a small molecule, ethanol will make its way through most of our organs, including the brain, which induces the most visible part of the intoxication [4–6].

© Springer Nature Switzerland AG 2019
N. T. Nguyen et al. (Eds.): ICCCI 2019, LNAI 11683, pp. 393–402, 2019.
https://doi.org/10.1007/978-3-030-28377-3_32

Shortly after reaching the blood vessel system, as the blood travels through the lungs, ethanol can be found in the expired air. Air concentration is supposed to be proportional to the blood concentration (x2100 at 294 °K), making it a very good estimator, in theory. As accessing the breath of a person is relatively easy, this technique has been the most widely used to estimate BAC(Blood Alcohol Content), through devices now called the breathalyzers [7–9].

Breathalyzers come in three types: electrochemical, based on the oxidation of ethanol into acetic acid and water, producing a measurable anode-cathode current; semiconductor-based, using a material whose resistance varies with the amount of ethanol on its surface; spectrophotometers, operating in the Near InfraRed spectrum (NIR), which are able to detail the exhaled air's composition. The latter is extremely accurate and can be used in the police stations [9, 10, 15].

Most of the conventional methods require a direct contact with a tested person to precisely measure current alcohol content. Such approach may be inconvenient for various reasons. It is important to realize that we measure only on spot alcohol values, and we cannot track dynamical progress of the alcohol intoxication. Furthermore, such methods require a direct contact with a tested person and their agreement [11–14, 16].

In this paper, we take advantage a fact that the alcohol intoxication may be measured and tracked by touchless methods, when observing side effects of the alcohol in the human's body. One of such effects is the facial temperature distribution. Temperature distribution exhibits the dynamical features over the time. It predetermines that alcohol intoxication can be observed whilst person drinking.

2 Problem Definition

Breath analyzers and blood tests ensure mostly reliable results, but those standards represent contact methods which can be carried out only with agreement of the tested subject. Furthermore, some of these tests can only be done in clinical conditions.

It is known that the alcohol intoxication causes vasodilation, but this can be very hard to recognize visually, even on the face, where the blood vessels are located closer to the surface of the skin. Fortunately, it is also known that the blood, travelling through the inner body, is hotter than the outer skin. We consequently expect the global temperature of the face to rise, as the 'hot blood'/'cold skin' ratio increases.

For this reason, the infrared imagery centered approximately on 9.5 μm seems promising to acquire relevant data. Furthermore, it has at least two other advantages. Firstly, it is almost insensitive to luminosity variations, and as the identifications have a very high chance of being conducted at night, (where the lack of luminosity would greatly disturb analysis in the visible spectrum), this is highly interesting. Secondly, infrared radiation of a body is also determined by the emissivity of its surface, but even with variety of human skins, this value barely changes and remains between 0.98 and 0.99 (% of what the human body would radiate if it was a perfect black body) for black and white skins around these wavelengths.

Temperature change caused by the alcohol intoxication is well observable on the face. In this regard it is important to determine which facial areas reliably reflect the ethanol effect. An important question is: what outcomes are expected from the thermographic analysis, and does this analysis have a potential to overcome standardly used methods?

The processing of the thermographic records should bring information to determine if a person is sober or drunk, but we also want to know if this analysis has the potential to develop a predictive model estimating different levels of BAC.

3   Definition of Alcohol-Temperature Features

As we have stated before, the alcohol intoxication is observable from the IR image records. In this task, it is needed to define certain spots representing reliable and significant features for the alcohol effect tracking.

Based on the experimental measurements, two facial areas show significantly various temperature variations whilst alcohol drinking. Firstly, it is the nose area. Judging by the experimental measurement, in a sober state, the nose area shows mostly blue color spectrum indicating cold temperature map. Whilst drinking, such cold temperature is being reduced. Second important dynamical feature is the forehead area. In this area, when person is sober, minor proportion of the hot color is registered. Within the alcohol intoxication, this hot color area is getting increasingly expanded

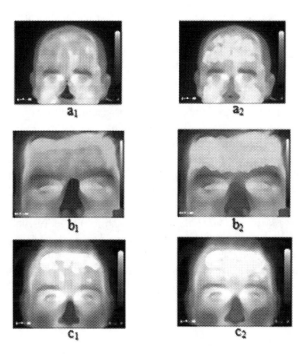

Fig. 1. Comparison of IR images in monochromatic spectrum in a sober state (1) and after 200 ml 40% alcohol (2).

within the forehead. Examples of such alcohol features are reported in the Fig. 1. In this figure, we report a comparative analysis in a sober state and after consuming 200 ml of 40% alcohol. Even on the base of the visual comparing, the hottest spectrum on the forehead, and the coldest spectrum on the nose are being changed, within the alcohol intoxication.

4   IR Image Dataset

In this section, we describe a process of the data acquisition. We analyze a dataset containing 20 tested persons. In order to prevent adjacent effects that might influence the facial IR images, all the tested persons rested 30 min in the room conditions, after arrival. For all the tested persons, six images have been taken. All the images were acquired in a standardized resolution: 480×360 pixels. First one in the sober state, and others after each 40 ml (42%) alcohol drink. A time interval between individual measurements was 30 min. The thermographic camera was focused on the forehead and nose.

5   Proposal of Facial IR Image Segmentation

In this section, we introduce a complex algorithm structure for the facial IR image segmentation. The facial model is composed from three main parts. Firstly, the images are pre-processed. Image pre-processing is intended for the IR image quality enhancement. In this step, we utilize a combination of the median filter and the image interpolation.

We generally suppose that the IR images may be corrupted by the image noise or artefacts. They can be caused by the inhomogeneities, which may influence the facial temperature distribution. Therefore, we have applied the median filter with the mask 6×6 pixels for the high-frequency noise suppression. Consequently, the cubic interpolation of the sixth order is applied. This procedure improves the facial images resolution. Since the original IR images have relatively weak resolution (800×600), this unfavourable fact may be compensated by the interpolation.

In the consequent step, the IR image decomposition is carried out. The input IR images are represented by the color spectrum. Such spectrum is mathematically represented by three matrices making up the RGB model. Since we intend to develop the segmentation model operating with two-dimensional images, the RGB decomposition is done. For this task, we are using the averaged sum of the individual RGB channels, and simultaneous extraction of individual channels. Based on such operation, we should recognize which model the best reflects the alcohol features and should be used for the segmentation. The Fig. 2 shows a comparative analysis of the RGB model decomposition of the three IR facial images.

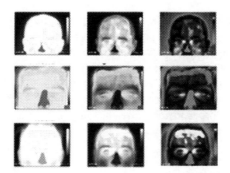

Fig. 2. RGB model decomposition: R channel (left column), G channel (middle column) and B channel.

Based on the RGB model decomposition, we can R channel exclude from the analysis due to a fact that the alcohol features are not observable. Rest two channels (G and B) well reflect the forehead area and the nose temperature spectrum. When comparing contrast of these images, we have decided to use the B channel.

The last part of the model deals with a proposal of the segmentation method for the forehead and nose temperature spectrum extraction. For this task, a standard version of the K-means is adopted. This conventional algorithm is driven by the genetic optimization in order to obtain qualitatively better distribution of the image clusters more reliably approximating the facial temperature areas.

6   IR Facial Image Segmentation Based on Modified K-Means Algorithm

We suppose that the IR facial area is represented by the colour spectrum. Such color spectrum may be grouped to specific areas reflecting individual face parts, as well as colder and hotter spectrum. Since we are going to develop a model differentiating the forehead and nose areas indicating temperature changes with the alcohol drinking, the multiregional segmentation appears as a good compromise. We suppose developing the multiregional segmentation model being able to differentiate temperature into predefined classes, where we can specify particular class or classes detecting the colour spectrum reflecting the alcohol intoxication.

For the multiregional segmentation, the clustering, particularly K-means is adopted. This method utilizes two stages for the clustering. (1) Initial centroids are defined. This is a crucial step of the clustering influencing algorithm's convergence. Number of such centroids corresponds with a number of the clusters. (2) In the assignment stage, all the pixels are being classified to a respective class, where a pixel has the minimal Euclidean distance. By this way, all the pixels are classified into clusters (segmentation classes). Consequently, the centroids are recalculated by means of the average value from the pixels belonging to a respective cluster, and assignment stage is repeated. Such procedure is performed as many times till, in two consequent iterations, any pixels change their clusters. This state represents the algorithm's convergence.

The major limitation of the K-means is the initial phase, where the initial centroids are defined. There is not unified approach, which would correctly classify pixels into clusters to the K-means reaches convergence in a few iterations. When even selecting completely unsuitable centroids (far from the histogram peaks), the K-means is unable reach convergence. Based on the aforementioned reasons, we optimize the initial stage of the clustering by using the genetic optimization. Here, we are searching for optimal clusters distribution in order to minimize the inner statistical variance of the pixels inside all the clusters.

7   ABC Algorithm for Clustering Optimization

The ABC algorithm is composed from three parts comprising the optimization process. Firstly, a set of the initial centroids (X_n, n stands for number of solutions) are defined. In our approach, we are using 250 initial combinations of centroids. For each X_n is set an alternative V_n. Their fitness functions *(fit)* are compared. When $fit_V < fit_X$ then V_n is stored in a memory as possible solution of the optimization problem. Otherwise, different V_n is generated. Such process is maximally repeated ten-times, after that such X_n is perceived as exhausted source. This phase is called employed bees.

In the next stage (onlooker bees), a roulette selection is applied. The roulette selection is applied as many times as many initial solutions we set. We randomly select, for each round, one solution X_n, and its probability is computed by the following definition:

$$p_i = \frac{fit_i}{\sum_{j=1}^{n} fit_n} \tag{1}$$

In the end on this stage, the solution X_n having the largest p_n is selected. Others are rejected as less suitable results.

In the last stage, which is called scout bees, the abandoned solutions from the first stage are figured out. Scouts are capable of finding the abandoned solutions, replace them by alternatives, and the whole algorithm is repeated. These three stages of the ABC are being repeated within predefined number of the iterations, we use 100 iterations. It was set a compromise between the computing time and algorithm effectivity.

8   Modeling of IR Facial Records

As we stated earlier, the forehead and nose are the most significant to the alcohol intoxication. Firstly, we have applied the multiregional clustering driven by the ABC algorithm containing eight segmentation classes. This algorithm is applied separately on the forehead and nose area. In the Fig. 3, we report experimental segmentation results in the nose area, while Fig. 4 reports the forehead area.

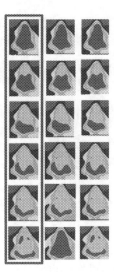

Fig. 3. Modeling of the nose area by using the K-means driven by ABC algorithm: for 250 generations (left column), 70 (middle column) and 120 (right column) while using 100 itterations. (Color figure online)

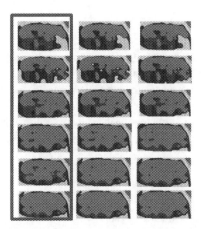

Fig. 4. Modeling of the forehead area by using the K-means driven by ABC algorithm: for 250 generations (left column), 70 (middle column) and 120 (right column) while using 100 itterations. (Color figure online)

The experimental results show two important facts. When segmenting the nose area, from the sober state (Fig. 3 first row) up to the maximum amount of the consumed alcohol (Fig. 3 last row), the segmentation class representing the coldest color, indicated as red is getting disappeared. Contrarily, the hottest color, indicated as violet in the forehead area (Fig. 4) is getting expanded. It predetermines a fact that such dynamical features well reflect the alcohol intoxication, as well as allow for building of the prediction model for intoxication forecasting.

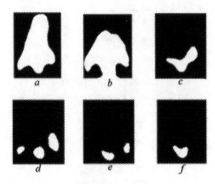

Fig. 5. Nose binary model reflecting area of the coldest temperature spectrum extracted from the segmentation model: (a) sober state, (b) 40 ml of alcohol, (c) 80 ml of alcohol, (d) 120 ml of alcohol, (e) 160 ml of alcohol and (f) 200 ml of alcohol.

In the last part of the model building, the binary classification is carried out. The binary classification procedure detects only a class representing the hottest spectrum in the forehead and the coldest spectrum in the nose, where rest of the segmentation model is suppressed. We report example of such nose binary model in the Fig. 5.

9   Quantitative Testing

In the last part of our analysis, the quantitative testing is carried out. We have divided this performance in two parts. Firstly, we have measured the computing time for the forehead and nose. We are aware that the segmentation procedure is as effective as work fast. The computing time is depended on various factors including number of the segmentation classes, and parameters of the genetic optimization. The Table 1 reports the averaged execution time for twenty tested persons.

Table 1. Time complexity for the segmentation model: 8 classes, 250 generations and 100 iterations

Image resolution	Sober person	40 ml of alcohol	80 ml of alcohol	120 ml of alcohol	160 ml of alcohol	200 ml of alcohol
800 × 600 px	80.5 s	78.6 s	81.3 s	82.3 s	88.3 s	65.9 s

Lastly, we have performed a quantitative comparison of the proposed model against gold standard representing the ground truth data. The gold standard was generated for all the twenty persons by manual segmentation. We have carried out this objective comparison based on the Correlation coefficient (*Corr*) and Mean Squared Error (*MSE*), as we report in the Table 2.

Table 2. Quantitative comparison for twenty IR images

Parameter	Sober person	40 ml of alcohol	80 ml of alcohol	120 ml of alcohol	160 ml of alcohol	200 ml of alcohol
Corr	0.91	0.78	0.88	0.87	0.91	0.93
MSE	33.12	32.15	26.45	35.12	32.84	33.13

10 Conclusion

In this paper, we have proposed model allowing for dynamical tracking and objectification of the alcohol intoxication dynamical effect. The proposed algorithm is composed from the data pre-processing, and the segmentation procedure based on the clustering driven by the genetic optimization. This heuristic clustering algorithm is able to precisely extract model of the temperature variations whilst alcohol drinking. Judging by the quantitative comparison results the algorithm works effectively. Correlation coefficient achieves around 90% agreement with the gold standard. In the future time we are going to focus on building of the prediction model allowing for utilization of this segmentation model for classification of the alcohol intoxication.

Acknowledgment. The work and the contributions were supported by the project SV450994 Bio-medicínské inženýrské systémy XV'. This study was also supported by the research project The Czech Science Foundation (GACR) 2017 No. 17-03037S Investment evaluation of medical device development run at the Faculty of Informatics and Management, University of Hradec Kralove, Czech Republic. This study was supported by the research project The Czech Science Foundation (TACR) ETA No. TL01000302 Medical Devices development as an effective investment for public and private entities.

References

1. Kubicek, J., Augustynek, M., Penhaker, M., Cerny, M., Oczka, D.: Analysis and modeling of alcohol intoxication from IR images based on multiregional image segmentation and correlation with breath analysis. In: 2017 IEEE Conference on Big Data and Analytics, ICBDA 2017, January 2018, pp. 49–54 (2018)
2. Mallard, T.T., Ashenhurst, J.R., Harden, K.P., Fromme, K.: GABRA2, alcohol, and illicit drug use: an event-level model of genetic risk for polysubstance use. J. Abnorm. Psychol. **127**(2), 190–201 (2018)
3. Hallgren, K.A., McCrady, B.S., Caudell, T.P., Witkiewitz, K., Tonigan, J.S.: Simulating drinking in social networks to inform alcohol prevention and treatment efforts. Psychol. Addict. Behav. **31**(7), 763–774 (2017)
4. Luo, X., Li, X., Wang, P., Qi, S., Guan, J., Zhang, Z.: Infrared and visible image fusion based on NSCT and stacked sparse autoencoders. Multimed. Tools Appl. **77**, 1–25 (2018)
5. Zeng, D., Zhu, M.: Multiscale fully convolutional network for foreground object detection in infrared videos. IEEE Geosci. Remote Sens. Lett. **15**(4), 617–621 (2018)
6. Blokhinov, Y.B., Gorbachev, V.A., Rakutin, Y.O., Nikitin, A.D.: A real-time semantic segmentation algorithm for aerial imagery. Comput. Opt. **42**(1), 141–148 (2018)

7. Kubicek, J., Penhaker, M., Augustynek, M., Cerny, M., Oczka, D., Maresova, P.: Detection and dynamical tracking of temperature facial distribution caused by alcohol intoxication with using of modified OTSU regional segmentation. In: Nguyen, N.T., Hoang, D.H., Hong, T.-P., Pham, H., Trawiński, B. (eds.) ACIIDS 2018. LNCS (LNAI), vol. 10752, pp. 357–366. Springer, Cham (2018). https://doi.org/10.1007/978-3-319-75420-8_34

8. Wu, Y., Sun, H., Liu, P.: A novel fast detection method of infrared LSS-Target in complex urban background. Int. J. Wavelets Multiresolution Inf. Process. **16**(1), 1850008 (2018)

9. Piniarski, K., Pawlowski, P.: Efficient pedestrian detection with enhanced object segmentation in far IR night vision. In: Signal Processing - Algorithms, Architectures, Arrangements, and Applications Conference Proceedings, SPA, September 2017, Article no. 8166857, pp. 160–165 (2017)

10. Suchotzki, K., Gamer, M.: Alcohol facilitates detection of concealed identity information. Sci. Rep. **8**(1) (2018). Article no. 7825

11. Cao, M., Li, L.: New models for predicting workability and toughness of hybrid fiber reinforced cement-based composites. Constr. Build. Mater. **176**, 618–628 (2018)

12. Probst, C., Manthey, J., Merey, A., Rylett, M., Rehm, J.: Unrecorded alcohol use: a global modelling study based on nominal group assessments and survey data. Addiction **113**(7), 1231–1241 (2018)

13. Viry, O., Boom, R., Avison, S., Pascu, M., Bodnár, I.: A predictive model for flavor partitioning and protein-flavor interactions in fat-free dairy protein solutions. Food Res. Int. **109**, 52–58 (2018)

14. Hu, X., Du, X., Kerich, M., Lohoff, F.W., Momenan, R.: Random forest based classification of alcohol dependence patients and healthy controls using resting state MRI. Neurosci. Lett. **676**, 27–33 (2018)

15. Fida, B., Bernabucci, I., Bibbo, D., Conforto, S., Schmid, M.: Pre-processing effect on the accuracy of event-based activity segmentation and classification through inertial sensors. Sensors **15**, 23095–23109 (2015)

16. Bibbo, D., Conforto, S., Bernabucci, I., Carli, M., Schmid, M., D'Alessio, T.: Analysis of different image-based biofeedback models for improving cycling performances. In: Egiazarian, K.O., Agaian, S.S., Gotchev, A.P., Recker, J., Wang, G. (eds.) Image Processing: Algorithms and Systems X and Parallel Processing for Imaging Applications Ii, vol. 8295 (2012)

Fusion of LBP and Hu-Moments with Fisher Vectors in Remote Sensing Imagery

Ronald Tombe and Serestina Viriri$^{(\boxtimes)}$

School of Mathematics, Statistics and Computer Science,
University of KwaZulu-Natal,
Westville Campus, Durban 4000, South Africa
ronaldtombe@gmail.com, viriris@ukzn.ac.za

Abstract. There are huge volumes of scene images generated periodically by satellite technology which require effective processing for intelligent decisions. The satellite sensed images contain diverse image contents such as shape, color, texture, spectral, and spatial resolutions. These variables are further affected with varying illumination conditions which result to noisy images. This poses a challenge to image analysis methods thus limiting their capabilities tasks of image understanding and interpretation. Remote sensing imagery classification task hence need advanced methods which can characterize images better so as to achieve higher accuracy results on scene images classification. This research proposes a feature-fusion-strategy of complementary image features, this is, Local Binary Patterns (LBP) and Hu Moments are fused with fisher vectors and the resultant is more discriminative feature representation that yield better image scene classification accuracy of 50.12% as demonstrated in with experimental results. This is an improvement compared to some pixel-based image descriptor methods in literature that are implemented. Although there are other methods in literature with superior classification accuracies than the proposed method, its is evident that fusion of complementary-features result to better classification accuracy.

Keywords: Remote sensing · Local binary patterns · Feature-fusion · Hu-moments

1 Introduction

Satellite technology generates numerous image information everyday that need to be processed for intelligent decisions [1]. Remote sensing aims in utilizing satellite images with the aid of image analysis algorithms for image understanding and interpretation for effective earth observations and periodic monitoring of land activities such as, the structural changes in residential areas over time due to population increase, examining agricultural activities, and managing natural resources. The advances in image-sensor technology yield high resolution images

© Springer Nature Switzerland AG 2019
N. T. Nguyen et al. (Eds.): ICCCI 2019, LNAI 11683, pp. 403–413, 2019.
https://doi.org/10.1007/978-3-030-28377-3_33

with detail information on image properties which include shape, texture, color, different spectral information, etc. [2]. Additionally these variables are affected with varying illumination conditions that result to noisy images. All these factors pose a huge challenge for remote sensing image classification task, hence there is need for robust methods which can characterize images effectively for image understanding, interpretation and other processing tasks that are based on the image content such as recognition and classification.

Efforts are being made to apply computer vision techniques on remote sensing imagery [3]. Some of the popular computer vision methods in literature include the local scale invariant features (SIFT) [4], the local binary patterns [13], bag of visual words [19], the computer vision tasks in remote sensing imagery include: image scene classification [5], natural hazard detection [6], land-use-land cover determination [7]. Every image analysis technique attempts to describe an image richly in adverse situations that could result due to variations in viewpoints, lighting, alterations because of rotations, scale etc. The scale-invariant feature transform (SIFT) is a famous descriptor which generates the descriptors using 3D histogram about gradient location and orientation [3]. The uniqueness of SIFT has attracted revisions and enhancements resulting to a number of proposed methods, among them are: PCA-SIFT [9], Gradient location and orientation histogram GLOH [8] and speed up robust features (SURF) [10]. PCA-SIFT use principal components analysis (PCA) to minimize feature dimensionality, whereas SURF Method creates descriptors with an integral image which compute derivatives of the image. Although SIFT method is popular in view matching, it fail to settle the inexactness which occur from locally similar patches [11]. Additionally, errors in point of interest detection can possibly result to poor performance. A common texture analysis method is the local binary pattern (LBP) which describes the contrast of local image texture [13], however LBP sensitive to non-monotonic illumination variations, thus it's performance is poor in the presence of random noise [11]. Hu [31] proposed Hu-moments, a feature characterization method which measure data spread, the is invariant to translation, scale and rotation. Arandjelovic [14] showed that Hu-Moments is illumination and shape invariant.

Feature fusion of image descriptor algorithms is thought as a viable strategy of integrating complementary image features for better object identification and view matching [15–17]. Various strategies are proposed in literature, Tan [18] fuse Gabor and LBP for robust feature representation on face recognition task in difficulty lighting conditions, Zhu [16] fuse local and global features. This trend shows that complementary feature fusion can achieve higher accuracy for recognition and classification tasks.

The main contributions of this paper are:

1. A Feature-fusion technique using LBP and Hu-moments is introduced for remote sensing imagery. The proposed method is effective in image feature characterization and hence it gives superior accuracy results on performance as compared results of the local binary pattern [13] on UC-Merced dataset [19].

2. This paper demonstrate the application of fisher vectors [20] in achieving feature fusion [2].

This paper is organized as follows: in Sect. 2, an overview of feature characterization methods with their application is given and more detail is given to the methods that are applicable to this research work. Section 3 presents the proposed feature-fusion technique, in Sect. 4, experimentation, evaluation metrics discussed. Section 5 concludes the paper with ideas for the future works.

2 Feature Characterization Methods

Effective image feature representation is key for image understanding and interpretation to enable accurate classification of scene images into correct classes. Numerous approaches are proposed [13,21,22] for image analysis and interpretation for classification task depending on the image content owing to wide applications of remote sensing [24,25]. Image analysis methods in literature are divided into three general classes [3], that is, (1) handcraft-feature-methods, examples in this class are LBP [13] and SIFT [4], (2) unsupervised learning-feature based methods [26,27] and deep neural networks (DNNs) commonly referred to as deep learning methods [23,28–30]. This research centers on hand crafted feature descriptor techniques which are sometimes referred to as pixel-based methods.

2.1 Local Binary Patterns (LBP)

The LBP [13] characterizes local image texture by considering it's center pixel gray value, p_c. The neighbor pixels are equally spaced from the center radius r at location p_c. When the coordinates of p_c are (0,0), $(n-1)$ neighbor pixels $\{p_i\}_{i=0}^{n-1}$ are thresholded with the center pixel. LBP is calculated by thresholding neighbor $\{p_i\}_{i=0}^{n-1}$ pixels with the center p_c to generate n-bit binary number that is converted to a decimal number as specified in Eq. (1)

$$LBP_{n,r}(p_c) = \sum_{i=0}^{n-1} s(p_i - p_c)2^i = \sum_{i=0}^{n-1} s(d_i)2^i, s(x) = \{_{0,x<0}^{1,x>0} \tag{1}$$

Where $d_i = (p_c - p_i)$ denotes the difference of center pixel and its neighboring pixel p_i. The result is characterized spatial local pixel structure on the center pixel location.

Non-monotonic illumination changes affect LBP leading to poor performance in the presence of random noise [18]. Xia [12] applied LBP method on aerial scene image datasets: UC-Merced [19], Aerial Image Dataset (AID) [12] where the accuracy classification performance achieved by the LBP method was less than 40% in the aforementioned datasets.

2.2   Hu Moments

Hu Moments [31] describe an image characteristics with $(p+q)^{th}$ moment (M_{pq}), i.e. an image is defined as a two-dimensional density distribution continuous function which for discrete cases is a summation equation (2) [32].

$$M_{pq} = \sum_{x=1}^{i} \sum_{y=1}^{j} x^p y^q f(x,y) \tag{2}$$

Where i and j denote size of the gray-level image $f(x,y)$.

The moments generated by Eqs. 2 and 3 measure the data spread which are invariant to translation, scale changes and rotation [31].

3   The Proposed Method

This research proposes a model illustrated in Fig. 1 for more efficient scene object classification. The technique employ earlier feature fusion [33] with fisher vectors [20] to combine the features of image descriptor LBP [13] and hu-moments [21] to a concatenated feature vector representation ($z_n = v_{LBP} + v_{HuMoments}$), a more discriminant method, that yield superior performance as demonstrated by the experiment results. In the Subsects. 3.1 and 3.2 the proposed method mechanics are discussed.

3.1   Image Preprocessing

Remote sensed images are considered to have additive random noise [34] due to variations in illumination and atmospheric conditions, imperfect instruments, and transmission errors. Owing to this factors image denoising prior to it's feature extraction enhances the performance of features descriptor algorithms. Motwani et al. [34] describes different approaches in literature for image denoising. This research work adopts the adaptive Gaussian filter [35] explained in Eq. (3), to achieve noise reduction, contrast enhancement, smoothing and sharpening prior to image characterization with the descriptor algorithms LBPs and Hu Moments.

$$G(x,y) = \frac{1}{2\pi\sigma^2} e^{-\frac{x^2+y^2}{2\sigma^2}} \tag{3}$$

3.2   Fisher Vector Feature Representation

Fisher vector encoding strategy is applied to encode the features generated by LBP and Hu-Moments to a discriminative representation. The Fisher vector transforms J-dimensional data into one-dimension [20] representation. Consider $Z = \{z_n, n = 1, 2..., N\}$ where N is a sample of observations $z_n \in Z$. Take μ_λ as a probability density function which models the generative process of the elements in Z. $\lambda = [\lambda_1, \lambda_2, ...\lambda_J]' \in R^J$ shows the vector J parameters for μ_λ. Using statistics the $score function$ is the gradient log-likelihood of the data model.

$$G_\lambda^Z = \nabla_\lambda \log \mu_\lambda(Z). \tag{4}$$

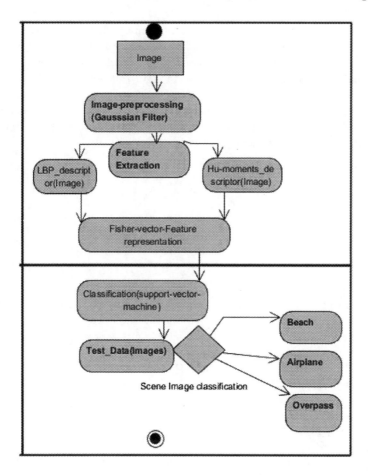

Fig. 1. Remote Sensing Images Scene classification based on LBPs and Hu Moments

A gradient function given in Eq. 4 explain the contribution of each parameter to the generative process. Observe that $G_\lambda^Z \in R^J$, thus dimensionality of G_λ^Z is determined by the number of parameters J in λ and not on the sample size N.

Application to Images. For J-dimensional features extracted from an image with extractor methods LBP [13] and Hu Moments [14], $Z = \{z_n, n = 1, 2, ..., N\}$ is the descriptor Model. Suppose that samples are independent, Eq. (5) is written as:

$$g_\lambda^Z = \sum_{n=1}^{N} L_\lambda \nabla_\lambda \log \mu_\lambda(z_n).$$

(5)

The Fisher Vector is a computed sum of the normalized gradient stats $L_\lambda \nabla_\lambda \log \mu_\lambda(z_n)$ computed for every descriptor method. This operation is as per Eq. (6):

$$x_t \rightarrow \varphi_{FK}(z_n) = L_\lambda \nabla_\lambda \log \mu_\lambda(z_n)$$

(6)

Based on this equation the image descriptor method z_n is embedded into a higher-dimensional space which responsive to linear classification. From computer vision literature [36], the Gaussian Mixture Model (GMM) is a generation process that selects high dimensional features of the image descriptors for the classification task. In this research μ_λ is a GMM with approximate parameters probabilistic distribution. For parameters in a class i, the GMM is denoted as $\lambda = \{w_i, \mu_i, \sum_i, i = 1, ...I\}$ where w_i, μ_i, and $\sum_i$ are the mixture weight, mean vector and covariance matrix of a Gaussian i respectively.

$$\mu_\lambda(z) = \sum_{i=1}^{I} w_i \mu_i(z), \tag{7}$$

where μ_i denote Gaussian i.

It is expected that:

$$\forall_i : w_i \geq 0, \sum_{i=1}^{I} w_i = 1, \tag{8}$$

Which ensures that $\mu_\lambda(z)$ is a valid likelihood distribution. Supposing that diagonal covariance matrices are standard, then variance vector is depicted with σ_i^2, i.e., diagonal of $\sum_i$. The GMM parameters are approximated on the image training dataset with local image descriptor methods with the expectation maximization (EM) algorithm [37] which is the posterior probability of Gaussian i computed as per Eq. 9 [20].

$$\gamma_n(i) = \frac{w_i \mu_i(z_n)}{\sum_{i=1}^{I} w_i \mu_i(z_n)} \tag{9}$$

Local image descriptor methods are represented with gradient formulas: scalars $g_{\alpha i}^Z$, means $g_{\mu i}^Z$, and the standard deviations $g_{\sigma i}^Z$, these are the J-dimensional vectors. Resultant Fisher vector representation is a concatenation of the gradients for $i = 1, ...I$ and thus the dimension $E = (2J + 1)I$. From samples Z the distribution $\gamma_n(k)$ is the value of local image descriptor z_n. This is described using statistics of the zero-order, first-order and second order that are expressed with Eqs. (10–12).

$$S_i^0 = \sum_{n=1}^{N} \gamma_n(i) \tag{10}$$

$$S_i^1 = \sum_{i=1}^{N} \gamma_n(i) z_n \tag{11}$$

$$S_i^2 = \sum_{n=1}^{N} \gamma_n(i) z_n^2 \tag{12}$$

where $S_i^0 \in R$, $S_i^1 \in R^J$ and $S_i^2 \in R^J$, are term-to-term operations.

Algorithm 1. LBP and Hu-moment feature-fusion with Fisher-Vectors

---

    train data image (X)
- Fusion of features $z_n = feature_{LBP} + feature_{HuMoments}$
- $Z = z_n \in R^J, n = 1, .., N,$
- GMM parameters $\lambda = w_i, \mu_i, \sigma_i, i = 1, ..I$

    Output
- Fisher vector discriminant representation $g_\lambda^Z \in R^{I(2J+1)}$

1: **procedure** CALCULATE FEATURE STATISTICS
    1. For $i = 1, ..., I$ accumulator variables initialization:
      – $S_i^0 \leftarrow 0$, $S_i^1 \leftarrow 0$, $S_i^2 \leftarrow 0$
    2. For $n = 1, ...N$:
      – Calculate $\gamma_n(i)$ with equation (9)
      – For $i = 1, ..I$:
        • $S_i^0 \leftarrow S_i^0 + \gamma_n(i)$,
        • $S_i^1 \leftarrow S_i^1 + \gamma_n(i)z_n$,
        • $S_i^2 \leftarrow S_i^2 + \gamma_n(i)n_n^2$,
    3. Calculate Fisher vector's
      – For $i = 1, ..., I$:
        • $g_{\alpha_i}^Z = (S_i^0 -_N wi/)\sqrt{w_i}$
        • $g_{\mu_i}^Z = (S_i^1 - \mu_i S_i^0)/(\sqrt{w_i}\sigma_i)$
        • $g_{\sigma_i}^Z = (S_i^2 - 2\mu_i S_i^1 + (\mu_i^2 - \sigma_i^2)S_i^0)/(\sqrt{2w_i\sigma_i^2})$
      – Combine Fisher vector components into one vector.
      – $g_\lambda^Z = (g_{\alpha_1}^Z, ...g_{\alpha_I}^Z, g_{\mu_1}^{Z'} ..., g_{\mu_K}^{Z'}, g_{\sigma_1}^{Z'}, ..g_{\sigma_I}^{Z'})$
2:     image classification
3:     **END**;

---

4 Experimentation, Evaluation Metrics and Discussion

The Proposed method is evaluated with UC Merced Land Use dataset [19], which has 21 classes with 100 images per class. This experiment employ the Support Vector Machine (SVM) and the hyper-parameter setting were set with K-fold cross-validation is technique, that is, the dataset is randomly partitioned into 5 equal subsets with 20 images from every class of the 21 classes. During training, four subsets are used while the remaining one is used for testing. The classification accuracy is the average of test class data evaluations(see [5]) for more information on various evaluation metrics. The feature sets from the images are extracted as described in Algorithm 1. A sample of 21 images from UC-Merced dataset showing various semantics are shown in Fig. 2.

4.1 Evaluation Metrics and Discussion

This research employ average classification accuracy [5]. The results on accuracy of classification performance attained with proposed feature-fusion method are provided in Table 1. The results are compared with those in literature. Observe that results of the local binary pattern appears twice in Table 1 because it is

Fig. 2. Example image of the UC Merced Land Use dataset classes

obtained from two sources, that is, from the experiment of this paper and from other works in literature.

Image semantics vary greatly in remotely sensed images due to a variety of image contents. This is possibly the reason for lower performance of in image classification accuracy for individual image descriptor operators for LBP and Hu moments as reported in Table 1. Comparing these results with the proposed feature-fusion technique, that is, when LBP fused with Hu Moments, there is a significant accuracy improvement of cross to 11%. This demonstrate that complementary feature-fusion result to a more discriminating feature vector representation which characterize the image better for classification as evidently demonstrated by experiment results. Comparative analysis of the results on classification performance in literature, i.e. those of Gabor Histogram and of SIFT in Table 1 demonstrate superior results with the proposed feature fusion method.

Table 1. The classification Performances of image descriptors UC Merced Land Use Dataset

Descriptor methods	Accuracy (%)
Hu moments	40.40
Local binary patterns	35.12
Local binary patterns [12]	36.29
Gabor histogram [38]	38.9
SIFT [12,38]	29.30
LBP + Hu moments	50.12

5   Conclusion

This research work present a feature characterization method that is based on complementary features-fusion of LBP and Hu moments with fisher vectors. The proposed technique achieve superior accuracy results on scene image classification. Given the high volumes of images generated periodically by satellites technology, it can only be possible to derive intelligent decisions based on image content via machine learning and other computer vision applications. In actual remote sensing application it is essential for image denoising due to variations in image illuminations resulting from weather patterns changes, sensor defects, and transmission which considerably degrade performance of image descriptor algorithms, hence a preprocessing stage in the proposed technique prior to feature extraction with LBP and Hu-moments. Although there are other methods in literature with superior classification accuracies than the proposed method, its is evident that fusion of complementary-features results to better classification accuracy in remote sensing images. In our future work we explore on applying deep learning for feature classification.

References

1. Gómez-Chova, L., Tuia, D., Moser, G., Camps-Valls, G.: Multimodal classification of remote sensing images: a review and future directions. Proc. IEEE **103**(9), 1560–1584 (2015)
2. Ghassemian, H.: A review of remote sensing image fusion methods. Inf. Fusion **32**, 75–89 (2016)
3. Tombe, R., Viriri, S.: Local descriptors parameter characterization with fisher vectors for remote sensing images. In: 2019 Conference on Information Communications Technology and Society (ICTAS), pp. 1–5. IEEE (2019)
4. Lowe, D.G.: Distinctive image features from scale-invariant keypoints. Int. J. Comput. Vis. **60**(2), 91–110 (2004)
5. Cheng, G., Han, J., Lu, X.: Remote sensing image scene classification: benchmark and state of the art. Proc. IEEE **105**(10), 1865–1883 (2017)
6. Li, X., Cheng, X., Chen, W., Chen, G., Liu, S.: Identification of forested landslides using LiDar data, object-based image analysis, and machine learning algorithms. Remote Sens. **7**(8), 9705–9726 (2015)
7. Qi, K., Wu, H., Shen, C., Gong, J.: Land-use scene classification in high-resolution remote sensing images using improved correlatons. IEEE Geosci. Remote Sens. Lett. **12**(12), 2403–2407 (2015)
8. Mikolajczyk, K., Schmid, C.: A performance evaluation of local descriptors. IEEE Trans. Pattern Anal. Mach. Intell. **27**(10), 1615–1630 (2005)
9. Ke, Y., Sukthankar, R.: PCA-SIFT: a more distinctive representation for local image descriptors. In: Proceedings of the 2004 IEEE Computer Society Conference on Computer Vision and Pattern Recognition, CVPR 2004, vol. 2, p. II. IEEE, June 2004
10. Bay, H., Ess, A., Tuytelaars, T., Van Gool, L.: Speeded-up robust features (SURF). Comput. Vis. Image Underst. **110**(3), 346–359 (2008)
11. Jabid, T., Kabir, M.H., Chae, O.: Local directional pattern (LDP) for face recognition. In: 2010 Digest of Technical Papers International Conference on Consumer Electronics (ICCE), pp. 329–330. IEEE, January 2010

12. Xia, G.S., et al.: AID: a benchmark data set for performance evaluation of aerial scene classification. IEEE Trans. Geosci. Remote Sens. **55**(7), 3965–3981 (2017)

13. Ojala, T., Pietikainen, M., Maenpaa, T.: Multiresolution gray-scale and rotation invariant texture classification with local binary patterns. IEEE Trans. Pattern Anal. Mach. Intell. **24**(7), 971–987 (2002)

14. Arandjelović, O.: Computationally efficient application of the generic shape-illumination invariant to face recognition from video. Pattern Recogn. **45**(1), 92–103 (2012)

15. Zhang, L., Zhang, J.: A new fusion method for remote sensing images based on salient region extraction. In: 2017 IEEE International Conference on Image Processing (ICIP), pp. 1960–1964. IEEE, September 2017

16. Zhu, Q., Zhong, Y., Zhao, B., Xia, G.S., Zhang, L.: Bag-of-visual-words scene classifier with local and global features for high spatial resolution remote sensing imagery. IEEE Geosci. Remote Sens. Lett. **13**(6), 747–751 (2016)

17. Ma, T., Oh, S., Perera, A., Latecki, L.: Learning non-linear calibration for score fusion with applications to image and video classification. In: Proceedings of the IEEE International Conference on Computer Vision Workshops, pp. 323–330 (2013)

18. Tan, X., Triggs, W.: Enhanced local texture feature sets for face recognition under difficult lighting conditions. IEEE Trans. Image Process. **19**(6), 1635–1650 (2010)

19. Yang, Y., Newsam, S.: Bag-of-visual-words and spatial extensions for land-use classification. In: Proceedings of the 18th SIGSPATIAL International Conference on Advances in Geographic Information Systems, pp. 270–279. ACM, November 2010

20. Sánchez, J., Perronnin, F., Mensink, T., Verbeek, J.: Image classification with the fisher vector: theory and practice. Int. J. Comput. Vis. **105**(3), 222–245 (2013)

21. Yan, F., Mei, W., Chunqin, Z.: SAR image target recognition based on Hu invariant moments and SVM. In: Fifth International Conference on Information Assurance and Security, IAS 2009, vol. 1, pp. 585–588. IEEE, August 2009

22. Cheng, G., Han, J., Guo, L., Liu, Z., Bu, S., Ren, J.: Effective and efficient midlevel visual elements-oriented land-use classification using VHR remote sensing images. IEEE Trans. Geosci. Remote Sens. **53**(8), 4238–4249 (2015)

23. Zhang, F., Du, B., Zhang, L.: Scene classification via a gradient boosting random convolutional network framework. IEEE Trans. Geosci. Remote Sens. **54**(3), 1793–1802 (2016)

24. Han, J., Zhang, D., Cheng, G., Guo, L., Ren, J.: Object detection in optical remote sensing images based on weakly supervised learning and high-level feature learning. IEEE Trans. Geosci. Remote Sens. **53**(6), 3325–3337 (2015)

25. Han, J., et al.: Efficient, simultaneous detection of multi-class geospatial targets based on visual saliency modeling and discriminative learning of sparse coding. ISPRS J. Photogramm. Remote Sens. **89**, 37–48 (2014)

26. Li, Y., Tao, C., Tan, Y., Shang, K., Tian, J.: Unsupervised multilayer feature learning for satellite image scene classification. IEEE Geosci. Remote Sens. Lett. **13**(2), 157–161 (2016)

27. Yuan, Y., Wan, J., Wang, Q.: Congested scene classification via efficient unsupervised feature learning and density estimation. Pattern Recogn. **56**, 159–169 (2016)

28. Hu, F., Xia, G.S., Hu, J., Zhang, L.: Transferring deep convolutional neural networks for the scene classification of high-resolution remote sensing imagery. Remote Sens. **7**(11), 14680–14707 (2015)

29. Yao, X., Han, J., Cheng, G., Qian, X., Guo, L.: Semantic annotation of high-resolution satellite images via weakly supervised learning. IEEE Trans. Geosci. Remote Sens. **54**(6), 3660–3671 (2016)
30. Zou, Q., Ni, L., Zhang, T., Wang, Q.: Deep learning based feature selection for remote sensing scene classification. IEEE Geosci. Remote Sens. Lett. **12**(11), 2321–2325 (2015)
31. Hu, M.K.: Visual pattern recognition by moment invariants. IRE Trans. Inf. Theory **8**(2), 179–187 (1962)
32. Flusser, J.: Moment invariants in image analysis. Proc. World Acad. Sci. Eng. Technol. **11**(2), 196–201 (2006)
33. Piras, L., Giacinto, G.: Information fusion in content based image retrieval: a comprehensive overview. Inf. Fusion **37**, 50–60 (2017)
34. Motwani, M.C., Gadiya, M.C., Motwani, R.C., Harris, F.C.: Survey of image denoising techniques. In: Proceedings of GSPX, pp. 27–30, September 2004
35. Deng, G., Cahill, L.W.: An adaptive Gaussian filter for noise reduction and edge detection. In: 1993 IEEE Conference Record Nuclear Science Symposium and Medical Imaging Conference, pp. 1615–1619. IEEE, November 1993
36. Lagrange, A., Fauvel, M., Grizonnet, M.: Large-scale feature selection with Gaussian mixture models for the classification of high dimensional remote sensing images. IEEE Trans. Comput. Imaging **3**(2), 230–242 (2017)
37. Levitan, E., Herman, G.T.: A maximum a posteriori probability expectation maximization algorithm for image reconstruction in emission tomography. IEEE Trans. Med. Imaging **6**(3), 185–192 (1987)
38. Deselaers, T., Keysers, D., Ney, H.: Features for image retrieval: an experimental comparison. Inf. Retr. **11**(2), 77–107 (2008)

An Enhanced Deep Learning Framework for Skin Lesions Segmentation

Adekanmi Adegun and Serestina Viriri[✉]

School of Mathematics, Statistics and Computer Science,
University of KwaZulu-Natal,
Durban 4000, South Africa
adegun.adekanmi@lmu.edu.ng, viriris@ukzn.ac.za

Abstract. Reliable and accurate segmentation of skin lesions images is an essential step in analysing skin lesions for the clinical diagnosis and treatment of melanoma skin cancer. Skin cancer analysis and detection has been automated over the years using various computing techniques and algorithms. Machine learning techniques such as deep learning methods have also been recently applied in diagnosing the disease. Segmentation identifies the shape of the features and the region of interest for analysis. Inconsistency in the delicate arrangement of skin lesions, coupled with possible presence of noise and artefacts such as hairs, air or oil bubbles on skin lesions, weak edges, irregular and fuzzy borders, marks, dark corners, skin lines and blood vessels on skin lesions has made automation of skin lesions segmentation challenging. The proposed deep learning framework is composed of a deep convolutional neural network with an encoder-decoder type architecture that fully integrates a dice coefficient loss function and employs elastic transformation techniques for data augmentation. The multi-stage segmentation approach adopted in this work learns contextual information by extracting discriminative features at the encoder stage of the system and also captures the object boundaries of the skin lesions images at the decoder stage. This enable the system to effectively segment the challenging and inconsistent skin lesion images. This system is further improved with the combination of effective data augmentation technique and the dice loss function. The performance evaluation of the proposed model with evaluation metrics such as Dice Coefficient, Jaccard index, Accuracy and Sensitivity gives improved and promising results when compared with some existing state-of-the-arts techniques.

Keywords: Melanoma · Skin lesion segmentation · Deep learning · Deep convolutional neural network · Encoder-decoder · Dice loss function · Data augmentation

1 Introduction

Melanoma skin cancer is one of the most common type of human malignancy [1]. Early detection of skin lesions is vital for timely diagnosis and treatment of the

© Springer Nature Switzerland AG 2019
N. T. Nguyen et al. (Eds.): ICCCI 2019, LNAI 11683, pp. 414–425, 2019.
https://doi.org/10.1007/978-3-030-28377-3_34

disease and also to improve the survival rate of patients [2]. This task is more complex to the dermatologist that rely solely on manual methods such as visual inspection, clinical screening, dermoscopic analysis, biopsy and histopathological examination for the diagnosis of skin lesion [1].

Various computing techniques and algorithms have been used in the past for segmentation and analysis of skin lesions to discover melanoma. Image segmentation which is regarded as a pre-processing step for image analysis and visual comprehension is always used to classify each pixel in the image and break the image into visually meaningful regions [3]. Segmentation of skin lesions images is carried out to extract the lesion areas which are the spots on skin that are infected [4]. Researchers have proposed methods such as thresholding methods, clustering-based segmentation methods and graph-based partitioning segmentation methods for performing image segmentation over the past decades [3].

These methods have been limited due to the challenging appearance of skin lesions. According to [5], automatic segmentation of skin lesion is challenging because of the possible presence of noise and artefacts such as hairs, air or oil bubbles on skin lesions, low contrast and variegated colouring, weak edges, irregular and fuzzy borders, marks, dark corners, skin lines and blood vessels. Vesal et al. [2] also stated that skin lesion segmentation challenges are due to the low contrast of lesions and the high similarity between the appearance of the lesions and the healthy tissue [2]. Figure 1 below shows the examples of the challenging skin lesions images.

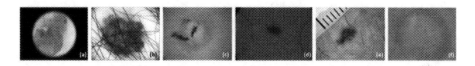

Fig. 1. Examples of skin lesions with various visual characteristic such as fuzzy boundaries (a, b, c, e), presence of hair (b, e), inhomogeneity (a, c) and low-contrast to the background (d, f) which adds complexity to automated image analysis [6].

Computer-aided-diagnostic systems that enable automatic and accurate skin lesion detection and segmentation are thus very essential [4]. Recently, Deep Learning approach has provided state-of-the-art performance for image segmentation and classification [7].

This paper proposes a model that integrates a convolutional encoder-decoder type architecture with dice loss function for the segmentation of skin lesions. The architecture is made up of both the encoding and decoding sections. The encoding section which comprises of convolution neural network and max-pooling function learns features from the lesion images. The features are further down-sample. The output is sent into the decoder stage for up-sampling and mapping of the low-resolution features. Softmax function is then applied to produce the predicted segmented output. The dice loss function minimises the loss by reducing the deviation of predicted image pixels from the ground truth label pixels in the training phase [8]. The performance evaluation of the proposed model carried out with evaluation metrics such as Dice Coefficient, Jaccard index and Accuracy shows higher performance over some existing state-of-the-arts techniques. The result gives an average dice coefficient of 92% when evaluated on skin lesion challenge dataset in ISIC 2018 dermoscopic images archives.

The remaining part of this paper is arranged as follows: the first part is the review of related works. The next section presents overview of methods and results. The is followed by outlines the system evaluation using performance metrics such as accuracy, dice coefficient, jaccard index and sensitivity and finally the conclusion.

1.1   Related Works

Recently, some deep learning based methods have been proposed and applied for automatic skin lesion segmentation. However, there is still room for improving segmentation performance and reducing the overhead cost of these methods. This work aims at less overhead and higher performance. Some of the existing deep learning methods have a tendency to over-segment lesions [6]. Li et al. [9] presented a semi-supervised method for skin lesion segmentation. In their work, weight combination of a common supervised loss for labelled inputs and a regularization loss for both labelled and unlabelled data were used for network optimization.

Convolutional neural network frameworks for skin lesions segmentation and features extracted have been proposed. A convolutional neural network (CNN) called SkinNet which is a modified version of U-Net was proposed by Vesal et al. [2]. The system employed dilated convolutions in the lowest layer of the encoder branch of the U-Net to provide a more global context for the features extracted from the image. Another form of convolutional neural network that combined the strengths of Convolutional Neural Networks (CNNs) and Conditional Random Fields (CRFs)-based probabilistic graphical modelling was recently introduced [11]. The framework still however lacks wide-ranging application and the cost still high. Deep learning framework consisting of two fully convolutional residual networks that can simultaneously segment and classify skin lesions was proposed by [2]. A deep learning approach called fully convolutional residual network (FCRN) with more than 50 layers for segmentation and classification of skin lesions was proposed by [10]. Zhao et al. [3] employed fully convolutional networks (FCN) to obtain pixel-level semantic features that utilized simple linear iterative clustering (SLIC) to generate superpixel-level region information. Colour and the position information of pixels were used to improve the semantic segmentation accuracy using the pixel-level prediction capability of CRFs. However, FRCN comes with a larger size which increases the complexity.

Deep dense deconvolution network based on dermoscopic images was proposed by Xinzi et al. [12]. The deep dense layer and a generic multi-path Deep RefineNet were combined to improve the segmentation performance. In the work, the deep representation of all available layers was aggregated to form the global feature maps using skip connection. The dense deconvolution layer was also leveraged to capture diverse appearance features through the contextual information. The dense deconvolution layer was then finally applied to smooth the segmentation maps and obtain final high-resolution output [12]. Liang-Chieh et al. [13] extended DeepLabv3 by adding a simple and effective decoder module to refine the segmentation results especially along object boundaries to develop DeepLabv3+. Liang-Chieh et al. [13]. They further explored the Xception model and applied the depthwise separable convolution to both Atrous Spatial Pyramid Pooling and decoder modules. Deep dense deconvolution and DeepLabv3+ are complicated and huge in size.

This work proposes a well refined deep learning framework that applied Max Pooling Indices to upsample in multi-stage and multi-scale segmentation process with less overhead cost. Using MaxPooling gives better performance than FCN, DeepLabv1 and DeconvNet [14]. The proposed framework is designed to be efficient both in terms of memory and computational time during inference. It also possesses smaller number of trainable parameters than other competing architectures.

1.2   Main Contribution

In this work an approach of a new deep learning framework for skin lesions segmentation towards melanoma detection has been proposed. Three key ideas of this approach are as follows:

First, a deep convolutional network that employs encoder-decoder type architecture has been proposed for skin lesion segmentation. Max Pooling Indices are applied to upsample feature maps and process the low-resolution input features from the encoder through the decoder units. This is achieved in multi-stage procedure with less overhead cost.

Secondly, the dice loss function is adopted to improve segmentation and accuracy by producing a smoother segmentation prediction.

Thirdly, the data augmentation techniques through elastic transformation of the dataset will increase the amount of training sets in the system. This results in better performance of the proposed system.

The approach stated above will result to a deep learning framework that has the capacity to handle tasks with fine-grained variability through its multi stage segmentation approach for skin lesions segmentation. The overall complexity of the proposed has been reduced, thus making the new model practically applicable to multiscale segmentation that can train any size and resolution of images with less computational resources.

2   Method

2.1   Overview of the Framework

In this research work, an enhanced deep learning framework which employs deep convolutional encoder-decoder type architecture with dice loss function is proposed for segmentation of skin lesions. The framework uses an encoder network to map raw image inputs to feature representations as feature map. The decoder network accepts this feature maps and processes the low-resolution input features through the up-sampling function. This is then sent into the softmax function for pixel wise prediction to produce segmented output. The dice loss function works on minimising the loss and deviation experienced between the predicted output and the ground truth label. This is further illustrated by the general framework shown in the Fig. 2 below.

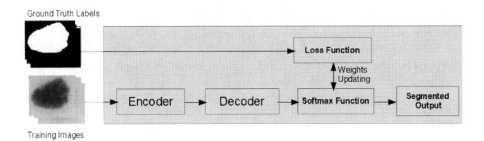

Fig. 2. General overview of the framework

The proposed encoder-decoder network is a multistage approach in which the initial stage, encoder, learns coarse appearance and localization information by capturing and interpreting the semantic and contextual information through learning and training while the later stage, decoder, learns the characteristics of the lesion boundaries to recover spatial information for output prediction [6]. This process trains skin lesion images from end-to-end and pixels to pixels using pixels and disease labels to produce pixel-wise prediction.

The encoder network performs convolution on skin lesion image as input to produce a set of feature maps. It is composed of the convolution layers, ReLU activation function and the max-pooling function. The activation function which is an element-wise rectified linear unit (ReLU) is applied together with the convolution layers on the input image set to extract feature maps. The max-pooling function then downsample the extracted feature maps before being transferred to the decoding section. The Max-pooling function performs downsampling in order to achieve translation invariance over small spatial shifts in the input image for better classification [14].

The decoder network upsamples performs convolution with upsampling of the feature maps from the encoder section. This results in sparse feature maps output. The feature maps are then convolved with a trainable decoder filter bank to produce dense feature maps. The decoders in the network produce feature maps with the same number of size and channels as their encoder inputs. The final decoder output with high dimensional feature representation is fed into a trainable M-class soft-max classifier. The softmax classifier predicts the class for each pixel where M is the number of classes and the output is a M channel image of probabilities.

The Dice loss function tends to minimise acquired in the process of pixel-wise predictions. This function calculates the deviation of the predicted image pixels from the ground truth label pixels using the differentiated gradient. This is then used to update the model weight as shown in Fig. 2. The final predicted segmentation therefore corresponds to the class with maximum probability at each pixel [14].

2.2 Proposed Model Network

The proposed model network can be illustrated with the Eq. 1 stated below. The image inputs are fed into the encoder section which transforms these into the feature maps. The output feature maps are generated by convolving with kernels W, down sampling with max-pooling function s and finally adjusting the bias b appropriately:

$$f(x, w) = w * x + b \qquad (1)$$

where x is the input feature map vector, w denotes weight vector also known as convolutional kernel, b is the bias function that aids model learning.

The system performs the up-sampling at the decoder section. This is represented by the Eq. 2 stated below.

$$Y = U(f(x, w)) \qquad (2)$$

where Y is the output result at the decoder section, $f(x, w)$ is the input feature map produced from the encoder section. U represents the upsampling function that up-samples of the feature map to ensure that the output and input have the same resolution and size.

The final decoder output is fed to a multi-class soft-max classifier to produce class probabilities for each pixel independently. This is connected to the loss function that calculates the per-pixel logistic loss between the ground truth labels and the predicted results. This is used for the weight adjustment and updating of the softmax function and it is done repeatedly. Dice loss function computes the losses for each class separately and then find the average to yield a final score [15]. The equation is stated below.

$$DiceLoss = 1 - \frac{2 \sum_i Y_t Y_p}{\sum_i Y_t^2 + \sum_i Y_p^2} \qquad (3)$$

where i is the pixels, Y_t denotes the ground truth label, Y_p denotes the predicted image output. This is fed back into the system as illustrated in the Fig. 2.

2.3 Model Training

The proposed Deep Convolutional Encoder-Decoder Model Architecture operates by learning from pixels to pixels in an end to end manner. The dataset used was collected from ISIC Skin Lesion Challenge [16]. The dataset includes both the training image dataset and corresponding ground truth image. Due to the limited size of the dataset, a data augmentation techniques by elastic transformation through the deformation of the image dataset is employed to increase the amount of training image sets in the system [17]. The input image dataset is accepted through the receptive layer which is always the first layer of the encoder part as shown in the Fig. 3 stated below.

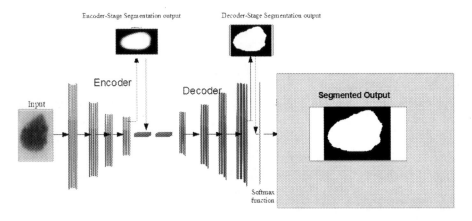

Fig. 3. The Figure illustrates data flow and the general architectural diagram of the proposed multi-stage deep convolutional networks with dice loss function

Each stage is made up of set of layers. In the encoder stage, each of the layer is made up of convolution network, pooling unit and the ReLU activation function. In the decoder each of the layer is made up of the upsampling function and convolution layer. Input images will be transformed into feature map and taken through set of convolutional layers combined with max-pooling function for down sampling. This process reduces the size of the input feature map which are restored by up-sampling process that takes place through the deconvolution layers. This ensures that the input and the output feature map have the same size. The form of training adopted by the model is a supervised form of training whereby the ground truth images which is also the target goal is supplied together with the input images. The output data from the prediction will finally be compared with the target goals for accuracy and the performance metrics evaluated.

3   Experimental Results and Discussion

To achieve the improved results stated below, segmentation was performed on 2000 skin lesion images containing both melanoma and non-melanoma cases. The dataset used is repository in ISIC archive [16].

3.1 Datasets

The method was evaluated on publicly available dermoscopic images from the ISIC Dermoscopic Archive [16]. This dataset was categorized into training and testing image set both comprising of images and ground truth labels respectively. The training images are set of 2000 images for both the training and the ground truth respectively. The input data are dermoscopic lesion images in JPEG format while the ground truth are mask image in PNG format. The ground truth label are provided for training and internally scoring validation and test phases data using the evaluation metrics. Ground truth images are normally generated through Fully-automated algorithm, reviewed and accepted by a human expert.

3.2 Evaluations Metric

The most common skin lesion segmentation evaluation metrics were used for comparison including: dice similarity coefficient (DSC.), jaccard index (Jac.) and accuracy (Acc.). These metrics were used for evaluation of the model. They are illustrated below:

Dice Similarity Coefficient: It measures the similarity or overlap between the ground truth and the automatic segmentation. It is defined as

$$\text{DSC} = \frac{2TP}{FP + 2TP + FN} \tag{4}$$

Jaccard Index: It is defined as the intersection between the two sets divided by their union, that is

$$\text{Jac} = \frac{2TP}{FP + 2TP + FN} \tag{5}$$

It is related with the dice coefficient as shown below

$$\text{Jac} = \frac{DSC}{2 - DSC} \tag{6}$$

Accuracy: It measures the proportion of true results (both true positives and true negatives) among the total number of cases examined.

$$\text{Accuracy} = \frac{TP + TN}{TP + TN + FP + FN} \tag{7}$$

Where FP is the number of false positive pixels, FN is the number of false negative pixels, TP is the number of true positive pixels and TN is the number of true negative pixels. These equations are used to compute the performance of the system. The unit of the values in Table 1 can be taken as a percentage of 1.

3.3 Discussion

The proposed model produces state-of-the-arts performance on skin lesions image datasets. Figure 4 displays the original images that were tested on the

Table 1. Segmentation performance metric.

Method	Jaccard index
Proposed model	0.83
Deep Residual method [18]	0.79
FCN method [19]	0.78
Deep Convolution Network method [20]	0.83

proposed model. Figure 5 shows the segmented output from the model. Figure 6 shows the corresponding ground truth label for our internal evaluation. A close look at Fig. 5 indicates very high similarity with Fig. 6 which are the ground truth labels. The results displayed in Table 1 above shows that the jaccard index of the proposed model which shows similarity and intersection between the predicted result and the ground truth label is at par with the best performing technique when compared with some techniques recently used in the segmentation of skin lesion images on the same database.

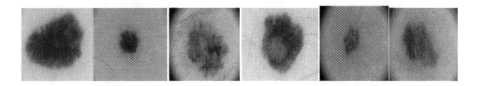

Fig. 4. Original images from Skin lesion images Dataset.

Fig. 5. Images segmentation results using Proposed model.

This shows high similarity between the ground truth and the result of the automatic segmentation using the proposed model. Secondly, the accuracy result of the proposed model as shown in Fig. 7 curve gives promising result of more than 93%. The curve shows that any substantial increase in the number of training epochs will still push the accuracy percentage up further and can still be projected to around 98% with further improvement. Also Fig. 7 shows that the training loss diminishes to less than 10%. There is a direct relation between the loss rate and the overlapping of the ground truth labels and the predicted segmentation under test. Any reasonable reduction in the loss rate also indicates

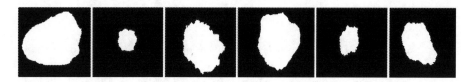

Fig. 6. Ground truth Label for the Original images.

improved performance and will increase the dice coefficient and jaccard index. There is also direct relationship between the dice coefficient and the jaccard index as shown in Eq. 6. Finally, the result indicates that the system has high level of accuracy and reliability.

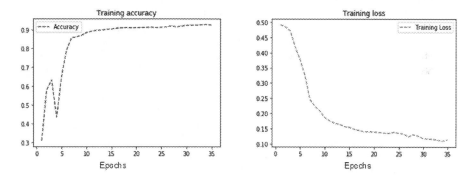

Fig. 7. This displays two figures showing the training accuracy and loss curve respectively for the training of the proposed model on Skin lesion Dataset.

4   Conclusion

In this paper, an encoder-decoder architecture with dice loss function is proposed for segmentation of skin lesions towards melanoma detection. The encoder-decoder architecture adopted in this work is able to train skin lesion images from end-to-end and pixels to pixels using the image pixels and labels to produce pixel-wise prediction. The proposed system adopts multi stage segmentation approach for skin lesions segmentation. This can train multi-scale and multi-resolution images. It has been established that the approach can handle challenging skin lesions images with presence of noise and artefacts such as hairs, air or oil bubbles on skin lesions, low contrast and variegated colouring, weak edges, irregular and fuzzy borders, marks, dark corners, skin lines and blood vessels. Experiments on well-established public datasets demonstrated that the proposed model achieved state-of-the-arts performance and outperformed some of the existing techniques. In the future, the proposed system will be adapted to other datasets and medical images. Further improvement will still be worked on for border and edges improvement.

References

1. Esteva, A., et al.: Dermatologist-level classification of skin cancer with deep neural networks. Nature **542**, 115–118 (2017)
2. Vesal, S., Ravikumar, N., Maier, A.: SkinNet: a deep learning framework for skin lesion segmentation (2018). Preprint: https://arxiv.org/abs/1806
3. Zhao, W., Fu, Y., Wei, X., Wang, H.: An improved image semantic segmentation method based on superpixels and conditional random fields. Appl. Sci. **8**(5), 837 (2018)
4. Sumithra, R., Suhil, M., Guru, D.S.: Segmentation and classification of skin lesions for disease diagnosis. Procedia Comput. Sci. **45**, 76–85 (2015)
5. Olugbara, O.O., Taiwo, T.B., Heukelman, D.: Segmentation of melanoma skin lesion using perceptual color difference saliency with morphological analysis. Math. Probl. Eng. **2018**, 19 (2018)
6. Bi, L., Kim, J., Ahn, E., Kumar, A., Fulham, M., Feng, D.: Dermoscopic image segmentation via multistage fully convolutional networks. IEEE Trans. Biomed. Eng. **64**(9), 2065–2074 (2017)
7. Alom, M.Z., Hasan, M., Yakopcic, C., Taha, T.M., Asari, V.K.: Recurrent residual convolutional neural network based on U-Net (R2U-Net) for medical image segmentation (2018). arXiv preprint: arXiv:1802.06955
8. Livne, M., et al.: A U-Net deep learning framework for high performance vessel segmentation in patients with cerebrovascular disease. Front. Neurosci. **13** (2019)
9. Li, X., Yu, L., Chen, H., Fu, C.-W., Heng, P.-A.: Semi-supervised skin lesion segmentation via transformation consistent self-ensembling model (2018). arXiv preprint: arXiv:1808.03887
10. Li, Y., Shen, L.: Skin lesion analysis towards melanoma detection using deep learning network. Sensors **18**(2), 556 (2018)
11. Zheng, S., et al.: Conditional random fields as recurrent neural networks. In: Proceedings of the IEEE International Conference on Computer Vision, pp. 1529–1537 (2015)
12. He, X., Yu, Z., Wang, T., Lei, B., Shi, Y.: Dense deconvolution net: multi path fusion and dense deconvolution for high resolution skin lesion segmentation. Technology and Health Care Preprint, pp. 1–10 (2018)
13. Chen, L.-C., Zhu, Y., Papandreou, G., Schroff, F., Adam, H.: Encoder-decoder with atrous separable convolution for semantic image segmentation. In: Ferrari, V., Hebert, M., Sminchisescu, C., Weiss, Y. (eds.) ECCV 2018, Part VII. LNCS, vol. 11211, pp. 833–851. Springer, Cham (2018). https://doi.org/10.1007/978-3-030-01234-2_49
14. Badrinarayanan, V., Kendall, A., Cipolla, R.: SegNet: a deep convolutional encoder-decoder architecture for image segmentation. IEEE Trans. Pattern Anal. Mach. Intell. **3912**, 2481–2495 (2017)
15. Fidon, L., et al.: Generalised Wasserstein dice score for imbalanced multi-class segmentation using holistic convolutional networks. In: Crimi, A., Bakas, S., Kuijf, H., Menze, B., Reyes, M. (eds.) BrainLes 2017. LNCS, vol. 10670, pp. 64–76. Springer, Cham (2018). https://doi.org/10.1007/978-3-319-75238-9_6
16. Codella, N.C.F., et al.: Skin lesion analysis toward melanoma detection: a challenge at the 2017 International Symposium on Biomedical Imaging (ISBI), Hosted by the International Skin Imaging Collaboration (ISIC). In: 2018 IEEE 15th International Symposium on Biomedical Imaging (ISBI 2018), pp. 168–172. IEEE (2018)

17. Eduardo, C., Cardoso, J.S., Pereira, J.C.: Elastic deformations for data augmentation in breast cancer mass detection. In: 2018 IEEE EMBS International Conference on Biomedical and Health Informatics (BHI), pp. 230–234. IEEE (2018)
18. Lei, B., Jinman, K., Euijoon, A., Dagan, F.: ISIC 2017- Automatic Skin Lesion Analysis using Large-scale Dermoscopy Images and Deep Residual Networks. https://arxiv.org/ftp/arxiv/papers/1703/1703.04197.pdf. Accessed 27 June 2018
19. Yading, Y.: ISIC 2017: Automatic skin lesion segmentation with fully convolutional-deconvolutional networks. https://arxiv.org/pdf/1703.05165.pdf. Accessed 27 June 2018
20. Matt, B.: ISIC 2017- Skin Lesion Analysis Towards Melanoma Detection. https://arxiv.org/ftp/arxiv/papers/1703/1703.00523.pdf. Accessed 27 June 2018

Fully Convolutional Encoder-Decoder Architecture (FCEDA) for Skin Lesions Segmentation

Adekanmi Adegun and Serestina Viriri[✉]

School of Mathematics, Statistics and Computer Science,
University of KwaZulu-Natal, Durban 4000, South Africa
adegun.adekanmi@lmu.edu.ng, viriris@ukzn.ac.za

Abstract. Segmentation which is identification of regions of interest (ROIs) in medical images is a very important step for image analysis in computer-aided diagnosis systems. Accurate segmentation of skin lesions images plays a vital role in efficient diagnosis of melanoma skin cancer. Diagnosis of melanoma cancer through the segmentation of skin lesions is a challenging task due to possible presence of noise and artefacts such as hairs, air or oil bubbles on the skin lesion images. Skin lesions images are also sometimes characterized with weak edges, irregular and fuzzy borders, marks, dark corners, skin lines and blood vessels on skin lesions. Recently, segmentation methods based on Fully Convolutional Encoder-Decoder Architecture (FCEDA) have achieved great success in medical images. This work presents automatic skin lesion segmentation method that is based on Fully Convolutional Encoder-Decoder Architecture. Two types of FCEDA namely U-Net and SegNet architectures, have been examined and utilized for segmentation of skin lesion images. The performance analysis of the two architectures have been conducted. Evaluation and comparison of these two architectures were also carried out. This work finds out and proposes possible improvements of these methods on the segmentation of skin lesions. It is also a systematic comparison of U-Net and SegNet models on the segmentation of skin lesion images. The paper discovers how deep learning methods can be explored using a supervised approach to get accurate results with less complexity possible. The models were evaluated on skin lesion challenge dataset in ISIC 2018 dermoscopic images archives.

Keywords: Melanoma · U-Net · Deep learning · FCEDA · Encoder-decoder · SegNet · Segmentation

1 Introduction

Deep learning methods have tremendously transformed the field of medical imaging [1]. Fully Convolutional Encoder-Decoder based architecture have been recently applied to the segmentation of medical images for proper analysis.

© Springer Nature Switzerland AG 2019
N. T. Nguyen et al. (Eds.): ICCCI 2019, LNAI 11683, pp. 426–437, 2019.
https://doi.org/10.1007/978-3-030-28377-3_35

A Fully Convolutional Encoder-Decoder network provides state-of-the-art results for image segmentation tasks in computer vision [2]. Two types FCEDA namely U-Net and SEGNET architectures have been investigated and explored in this work for the segmentation of skin lesion images.

Deep learning methods based on Fully Convolutional Encoder-Decoder Networks have achieved great success in image segmentation-related challenges [3]. In recent years Deep Learning has brought about a breakthrough in Medical Image Segmentation [4]. Convolutional neural networks (CNNs) have achieved state-of-the-art performance for automatic medical image segmentation.

The popular architectures of deep neural network in the medical imaging include state-of-the-art deep learning segmentation models which are U-Net [4] and SegNet [5]. These two networks employ Fully Convolutional Encoder-Decoder based architecture. The architecture is a multi-stage approach to image segmentation that trains images through an end-to-end and pixel-to-pixel procedure. It is mainly composed of the encoder and decoder units. The encoder is composed of convolution and pooling layers while the decoder is made up of convolution and up-sampling layers. Application of this approach in skin lesion segmentation for melanoma detection has produced promising results. Figure 1 below shows example of skin lesion images and the corresponding ground truth images for the lesions segmentation.

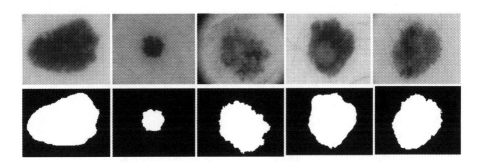

Fig. 1. Examples of skin lesions images for segmentation: the first row identifies the lesion images and the second row identifies the corresponding ground truth labels

Diagnosis of diseases from the analysis and segmentation of medical images require reliable and accurate performance. This has led to the wider acceptability of Fully Convolutional Networks (FCNs) based on Encoder-Decoder architecture in the analysis and detection of diseases. FCNs adopt a skip architecture that combines semantic information with appearance information, by which they acquire the capability to produce accurate segmentation results. Some segmentation tasks based on FCNs, such as skin lesions segmentation, brain tumor segmentation and retinal vessel segmentation has produced good results [6,7].

Accurate segmentation of melanoma is extremely challenging due to artifacts presence such as hair, reflections, air and oil bubbles [8,9] on these images.

Over the years computing techniques have been applied to carry out this task. There is a need for a system that can perform proper and accurate analysis of skin lesions images. In this work, the state-of-the-art architecture of Fully Convolutional Encoder-Decoder Networks has been explored on segmentation of skin lesions images. This paper finds out and proposes possible improvements of these methods on the segmentation of skin lesions. It also performs a systematic comparison of U-NeT and SegNet models on the segmentation of skin lesion images. This paper discovers that the U-NET architecture outperforms the SegNet models. The performance of the models was evaluated using metrics such as accuracy, recall and mean intersection over union (mIoU).

1.1   Related Works

Recently, deep learning methods based fully Convolutional Encoder-Decoder network architecture have been largely applied in medical image segmentation towards disease diagnosis. Variants of Fully Convolutional Encoder-Decoder network methods have achieved state-of-the-art performance for various automatic medical image segmentation. The application of some of these methods on some disease diagnosis has been reviewed in this work.

Alom et al. [10] proposed and tested a recurrent convolutional neural network (RCNN) and a Recurrent Residual Convolutional Neural Network (RRCNN) based on U-Net models named RU-Net and R2U-Net respectively for the segmentation of three image datasets of skin cancer, lung lesion, and retina images. Chen et al. [11] investigated the segmentation results of different U-Net models based on three architectures using different ensemble strategies such as weighted average, unweighted average and hierarchical average was investigated. Venkatesh et al. [12] proposed a methodology for automatic skin lesion region segmentation based on U-Net and residual network.

Identification of cell nuclei in certain images using fully convolutional network (FCN) based on U-Net was carried out by Bartolome et al. [13]. The model is a modified U-Net architecture which retains feature maps from the encoding phase to be used at the decoding phase. Bartan et al. [14] applied deep learning methods to cell nuclei segmentation in tissue images taken over a certain range of modalities and conditions. They used a modified U-Net architecture that retains feature maps produced in the encoding phase for the decoding phase to develop an optimal model.

Kumar et al. [15] proposed a Fully Convolutional Neural network tool from the hybrid of two deep learning architectures of SegNet and U-Net for improved brain tissue segmentation. A skip connection inspired from U-Net was used in the SegNet architecture to incorporate fine multi scale information for better tissue boundary identification. A novel architecture, MultiResUNet, was also developed from U-Net architecture for segmenting multimodal medical images by Nabil et al. [4]. Lastly a Deep Fully Convolutional Neural Network for pixel-wise semantic segmentation called Squeeze-SegNet was introduced [16]. A SqueezeNet-like encoder and a decoder was formed. The upsample layer used pooling indices like in SegNet and a deconvolution layer was added to provide final multi-channel feature map.

1.2   Main Contribution

The contributions of this work can be summarised as follows:

(1) Two models U-Net and SegNet based on fully convolutional encoder-decoder architecture have been investigated for medical image segmentation.
(2) Experiments were conducted on skin lesion images to detect melanoma cancer.
(3) Performance evaluation of the models was conducted for the end-to-end image-based approach for skin lesions segmentation tasks.
(4) Systematic comparison of the state-of-the-art methods that shows superior performance of the U-Net method against the SegNet method.

2   Method

2.1   FCEDA-Based Segmentation Method for Skin Lesion Analysis

The first approach uses the popular U-net architecture which was built on fully convolutional network (FCN) [2] that is based on encode-decoder mechanisms for skin lesion segmentation. The U-net architecture is majorly composed of a contracting path known as encoder and an expanding path known as decoder. The network accepts a set of larger skin lesion images and the corresponding ground truth labels as input. It applies a supervised learning model. The encoder is made up of set of convolutional and max-pooling layers. The network uses a Rectified Linear Units (RELU) activation function at each layer. The rectifier linear unit is used as activation function for non-linearly transformation of image dataset within each layer of the convolutional network. The function is defined as:

$$f(x) = max(0, x) \tag{1}$$

where x represents the image dataset. The convolutional layers perform extraction of feature maps from the input image sets by copying and cropping the maps. The pooling layers gradually decrease the size of the feature maps. The architecture extends the encoder section with shortcut skip connections made up of set of convolutional layers where the encoder and the decoder network meets as shown if Fig. 3. The shortcut connections are used to help decoder recover the object details better and enlarge the receptive field of the convolutions to provide a multi-scale context for the input image. The decoder which is the expanding path decoder gradually recovers and restores the object details and spatial dimension of the reduced feature maps from the encoder section through the up-sampling layers. The decoder layer is made up of convolutional layers and the up-sampling layer. The last layer of the decoder section is a softmax classifier that predicts pixel-wise labels for output which has the same resolution as the input image as shown in Fig. 2. The softmax compute the conditional distribution over the ground truth labels. The output of the softmax layer is used together with a loss function which aims to minimize the error between the ground truth labels and the final segmentation output through training and learning procedure. This can be simply represented as:

$$y = \sum_{1=1}^{n} w_i x_i + \theta \qquad (2)$$

Where y is the segmented image output, xi is the input image pixels, i is pixels number, n is the total number of pixels in image features, θ is proportional to the offset of the input from the origin and w is the weight vector also known as kernel used in training for prediction adjustment. Both θ and w are used in learning and training.

The second approach uses SegNet architecture also built on fully convolutional network (FCN) based on encode-decoder mechanisms. Both architectures are similar in operation but differs in some few aspects. The SegNet architecture also possesses a contracting path known as encoder and an expanding path known as decoder but differs from the U-Net architecture in when connecting the encoder with the decoder. It adopts indices to connect the encoder with the decoder in place of the shortcut connections used in the U-Net architecture. instead of copying the encoder features as in FCN, indices from max-pooling are copied. This makes SegNet more memory efficient than U-Net but the performance is reduced.

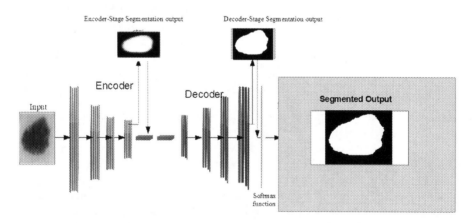

Fig. 2. Fully Convolutional Encoder-Decoder Architecture: The blue lines represent the convolution network layers and the green lines represent the pooling layers in the encoder section. Red lines represent the up-sampling layers and the deep blue lines represent the convolution layers in the decoder section. In between the encoder and the decoder are the two boxes that represent the short circuit connection and transfer the feature maps produced at the encoder section of the UNet model. The last layer represented by a yellow line is the softmax layer that performs the final segmentation and produces the segmented output. (Color figure online)

2.2   General Architectures of SegNet and U-Net

A Fully Convolutional Encoder-Decoder network provides state-of-the-art results for image segmentation tasks in computer vision [2]. Two types of FCEDA have been utilized in this work. These include U-Net and SegNet models. The two methods have been applied in this work on some set of skin lesion images for segmentation. The methods operate by learning a mapping from pixels to pixels in an end-to-end manner. This is illustrated in the Fig. 3 below. The general architecture is divided into the following major parts as shown in the figure:

Data Preparation

The input image sets go through re sampling and resizing. The image sets are made up of training images with their corresponding ground truth and the validation set also with their own ground truth. The images are resized and cropped to the fixed size of the encoder layers. Some level of noise is also removed from the training images before being sent into the model. We used 2000 images set for the training dataset and 800 images set for the validation.

Encoder

The encoder is made up of set of convolution and pooling layers. It also contains the ReLU activation function. The convolution layer part performs features extraction from the input image and the pooling layers reduce the resolution of the image feature maps. This is sent to the decoder section.

Decoder

The decoder is made up of convolution and up-sampling layers. It also works with ReLU activation function. The decoder works on the discriminative features with lower resolution learnt from the encoder. The up-sampling layer increases the resolution of feature map. This is sent to the final layer for prediction.

Prediction

This section contains softmax classifier function. This is used to predict pixel-wise labels by performing pixel-wise mapping that leads to segmentation of the skin lesions image. This produces the final output which has the same resolution as the input image. The general layout is illustrated in Fig. 3.

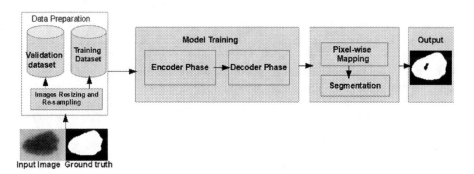

Fig. 3. General Layout diagram for Fully Convolutional Encoder-Decoder network

2.3 SegNet Model

SegNet model uses the encoder-decoder architecture. The unique feature of this model is its ability to transfer encoder features using the pooling indices. Each up-sampling and the convolution layer in the decoder stage corresponds to max-pooling and the convolution layer in the encoder. Input image set are received as feature maps, taken through set of convolutional layers combined with max-pooling function for down sampling in the encoder section and trained from end-to-end. The encoder features are transferred to the decoder through the pooling indices as shown in diagram in Fig. 4 below. The feature maps restored in the decoder to the original resolution and are then fed to the softmax classifier to produce the final segmentation.

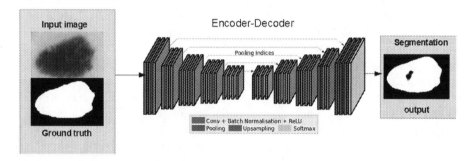

Fig. 4. Architectural Diagram for the SegNet model (Adapted from SegNet architecture Badrinarayanan et al. [5])

2.4 U-Net Model

It is also basically made up of an encoder and decoder. The encoder part is composed of four set of convolution layers composing 32, 64, 128 and 256 channels respectively. Each of the layers applies Rectified Linear Units (RELU) activation function and a pooling (max-pooling function) layer. Features extraction are carried out at each stage of the convolution layer with the pooling layer reducing the resolution of the feature maps. The encoder section is connected with the decoder section through shortcut connections made up of convolution layers. The decoder part is also made up of four (4) convolution layers that matches the four (4) convolution layers in the encoding part directly. It also makes use of the RELU activation function at each layer. The system concatenates and merges the encoder feature maps to up sampled feature maps from the decoder at every stage. This architecture allows the decoder at each stage to learn back relevant features that are lost when pooled in the encoder through concatenation connections [17].

3   Experimental Results and Discussion

3.1   Datasets

Segmentation was preformed on skin lesion images containing both melanoma and non-melanoma cases. The dataset used is repository in ISIC 2018 archive [18]. The dataset contains 2600 samples in total. It consists of 2000 training samples in JPEG format and 600 testing samples. The original size of each sample was 700×900, which was rescaled to 256×256 for this implementation. The training samples include the original images and the corresponding ground truth label in PNG format.

This dataset was categorized into:

Training Image Sets. We have:
1. Training images
2. Ground truth images

Testing Image Sets. We have:
1. Testing images
2. Ground truth images

3.2   Evaluations Metrics

The most common skin lesion segmentation evaluation metrics were used for comparison including: mean intersection over union (mIoU), sensitivity (Sen.) and accuracy (Acc.). These metrics were used for evaluation of the model. They are illustrated below:

• Mean Intersection over Union (mIoU): It is the measure of (intersection and union)similarity or overlap between the ground truth and the automatic segmentation. It is defined as

$$\mathbf{mIoU} = \frac{TP}{FP + TP + FN} \tag{3}$$

• Sensitivity: This proportion of actual positives which are predicted positive in cases examined.

$$\mathbf{Sensitivity} = \frac{TP}{TP + FN} \tag{4}$$

• Accuracy: It measures the proportion of true results (both true positives and true negatives) among the total number of cases examined.

$$\mathbf{Accuracy} = \frac{TP + TN}{TP + TN + FP + FN} \tag{5}$$

Where FP is the number of false positive pixels, FN is the number of false negative pixels, TP is the number of true positive pixels and TN is the number of true negative pixels.

Table 1. Segmentation performance metric.

Method	Accuracy	mIOU	Sensitivity
U-Net model	0.95	0.90	1.00
SegNet	0.91	0.85	0.80

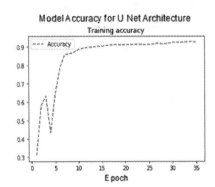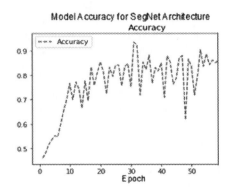

Fig. 5. Examples of train accuracy plots for two different Fully Convolutional Encoder-Decoder networks, UNet and SegNet. As shown by the x-axis, the number of epochs used for training the two architectures differs due to early stopping criteria. The accuracy reaches the highest level of 95% for UNet model and 91% for the SegNet model.

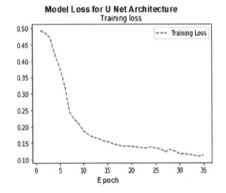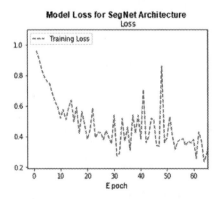

Fig. 6. Examples of train loss plots for two different Fully Convolutional Encoder-Decoder networks, UNet and SegNet using Adam algorithm. As shown by the x-axis, the number of epochs used for training the two architectures differs due to early stopping criteria. In both cases the loss reaches lowest level of 0.10 and 0.20 respectively.

3.3   Segmentation Results

See Fig. 7.

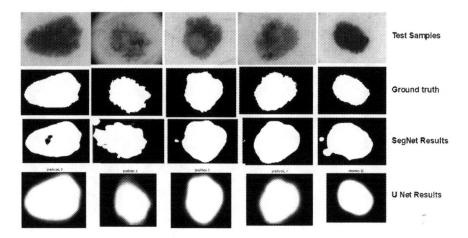

Fig. 7. Comparison of U-Net and SegNet segmentation results: The first row shows the lesion images that was segmented; the second row displays segmentation Experts' manual segmentation, i.e. ground truth mask; the third row shows the mask of the test image.

3.4   Discussions

Table 1 and Figs. 5, 6 and 7 show that the U-Net model outperforms the Seg-Net model in the segmentation of skin lesions. The difference between these two methods demonstrates the advantage of shortcut connection in between the encoder and decoder units of the U-net model, which enables the system to have continuous flow of image features from the encoder to the decoder. This also enables better training and learning during the segmentation process. This also explains the disparity in the segmentation output results of the two models as shown in Fig. 7. The accuracy results shown in Fig. 6 produces training accuracy with highest level of 95% for U-Net model and 91% for the SegNet model. The loss function can also be improved further. As shown in Fig. 6, the lowest training loss reached in the U-Net model was 10% and 20% for the SegNet model. Figure 6 shows that the loss diminishes to less than 10% for the U-Net model which again indicates more reliability.

4   Conclusion

In this paper, we utilized the U-Net and SegNet architectures for the segmentation of skin lesions. These models were evaluated on ISIC 2018 dataset. The experimental results demonstrate that the U-Net model shows better performance than the SegNet model in segmentation tasks with the same number of network parameters. The results also show that U-Net model produces better performance during training and in testing phase than SegNet model. In future, a novel feature fusion strategy from encoding to the decoding section units is being proposed for the U-Net model. The application of dilated network or residual network in-between the encoder and decoder of the U-Net model will be explored for the segmentation of skin lesions. The loss function will also be improved further. Ensemble methods of the improved U-Net model with some other state-of-the arts techniques will be worked on.

References

1. Razzak, M.I., Naz, S., Zaib, A.: Deep learning for medical image processing: overview, challenges and the future. In: Dey, N., Ashour, A.S., Borra, S. (eds.) Classification in BioApps. LNCVB, vol. 26, pp. 323–350. Springer, Cham (2018). https://doi.org/10.1007/978-3-319-65981-7_12
2. Long, J., Shelhamer, E., Darrell, T.: Fully convolutional networks for semantic segmentation. In: Proceedings of the IEEE Conference on Computer Vision and Pattern Recognition, pp. 3431–3440 (2015)
3. Bi, L., Kim, J., Ahn, E., Feng, D., Fulham, M.: Semi-automatic skin lesion segmentation via fully convolutional networks. In: 2017 IEEE 14th International Symposium on Biomedical Imaging (ISBI 2017), pp. 561–564. IEEE (2017)
4. Ibtehaz, N., Sohel Rahman, M.: MultiResUNet: rethinking the U-Net architecture for multimodal biomedical image segmentation (2019). arXiv preprint: arXiv:1902.04049
5. Badrinarayanan, V., Kendall, A., Cipolla, R.: SegNet: a deep convolutional encoder-decoder architecture for image segmentation. IEEE Trans. Pattern Anal. Mach. Intell. **39**(12), 2481–2495 (2017)
6. Jian, J., et al.: Fully convolutional networks (FCNs)-based segmentation method for colorectal tumors on T2-weighted magnetic resonance images. Australas. Phys. Eng. Sci. Med. **41**(2), 393–401 (2018)
7. Bi, L., Kim, J., Ahn, E., Kumar, A., Fulham, M., Feng, D.: Dermoscopic image segmentation via multistage fully convolutional networks. IEEE Trans. Biomed. Eng. **64**(9), 2065–2074 (2017)
8. Adeyinka, A.A., Viriri, S.: Skin lesion images segmentation: a survey of the state-of-the-art. In: Groza, A., Prasath, R. (eds.) MIKE 2018. LNCS (LNAI), vol. 11308, pp. 321–330. Springer, Cham (2018). https://doi.org/10.1007/978-3-030-05918-7_29
9. Pennisi, A., Bloisi, D.D., Nardi, D., Giampetruzzi, A.R., Mondino, C., Facchiano, A.: Skin lesion image segmentation using Delaunay Triangulation for melanoma detection. Comput. Med. Imaging Graph. **52**, 89–103 (2016)
10. Alom, M.Z., Hasan, M., Yakopcic, C., Taha, T.M., Asari, V.K.: Recurrent residual convolutional neural network based on U-Net (R2U-NET) for medical image segmentation (2018). arXiv preprint: arXiv:1802.06955
11. Chen, L.-C., Zhu, Y., Papandreou, G., Schroff, F., Adam, H.: Encoder-decoder with atrous separable convolution for semantic image segmentation. In: Ferrari, V., Hebert, M., Sminchisescu, C., Weiss, Y. (eds.) ECCV 2018, Part VII. LNCS, vol. 11211, pp. 833–851. Springer, Cham (2018). https://doi.org/10.1007/978-3-030-01234-2_49

12. Venkatesh, G.M., Naresh, Y.G., Little, S., O'Connor, N.E.: A deep residual architecture for skin lesion segmentation. In: Stoyanov, D., et al. (eds.) OR 2.0/CARE/CLIP/ISIC 2018. LNCS, vol. 11041, pp. 277–284. Springer, Cham (2018). https://doi.org/10.1007/978-3-030-01201-4_30

13. Zhang, Y., Bartolome, C., Ramaswami, A.: DeepCell: automating cell nuclei detection with neural networks. cs230.stanford.edu

14. Bartan, B., Pao, J., Knapp, B.: Nucleus detection using deep learning. cs230.stanford.edu

15. Kumar, P., Nagar, P., Arora, C., Gupta, A.: U-Segnet: fully convolutional neural network based automated brain tissue segmentation tool. In: 2018 25th IEEE International Conference on Image Processing (ICIP), pp. 3503–3507. IEEE (2018)

16. Nanfack, G., Elhassouny, A., Thami, R.O.H.: Squeeze-SegNet: a new fast deep convolutional neural network for semantic segmentation. In: Tenth International Conference on Machine Vision (ICMV 2017), vol. 10696, p. 106962O. International Society for Optics and Photonics (2018)

17. Ronneberger, O., Fischer, P., Brox, T.: U-Net: convolutional networks for biomedical image segmentation. In: Navab, N., Hornegger, J., Wells, W.M., Frangi, A.F. (eds.) MICCAI 2015, Part III. LNCS, vol. 9351, pp. 234–241. Springer, Cham (2015). https://doi.org/10.1007/978-3-319-24574-4_28

18. Codella, N.C.F., et al.: Skin lesion analysis toward melanoma detection: a challenge at the 2017 International Symposium on Biomedical Imaging (ISBI), hosted by the International Skin Imaging Collaboration (ISIC). In: 2018 IEEE 15th International Symposium on Biomedical Imaging (ISBI 2018), pp. 168–172. IEEE (2018)

Decision Support and Control Systems

Decision Support System for Assignment of Conference Papers to Reviewers

Dinh Tuyen Hoang[1], Ngoc Thanh Nguyen[2], and Dosam Hwang[1(✉)]

[1] Department of Computer Engineering, Yeungnam University,
Gyeongsan, South Korea
hoangdinhtuyen@gmail.com, dosamhwang@gmail.com
[2] Faculty of Computer Science and Management,
Wroclaw University of Science and Technology, Wrocław, Poland
Ngoc-Thanh.Nguyen@pwr.edu.pl

Abstract. Research conferences are held to share research progress and novel findings among scientists and encourage the growth of academic communities. Assigning papers to reviewers is the most critical and arduous task for conference organizers. Usually, conference committees must distribute hundreds of publications to reviewers in a short time. Moreover, other restrictions—such as a limited number of reviewers and avoiding conflict of interest—make the process of wholly distributed more difficult. Manually choosing reviewers can be an unfair and time-consuming process. In this study, we developed a support system for automatically assigning submitted papers to reviewers. For this, we extracted features from reviewer profiles and their networks to compute their quality and relevance with respect to the submitted papers. Experiments on a DBLP dataset showed that our system achieved more accurate results than other methods.

Keywords: Reviewer assignment · Decision support system ·
Conference paper review

1 Introduction

Research conferences are a place for scientists to share their research process and new findings to the scientific community, thereby contributing to the development in their academic discipline. Assigning submitted papers to reviewers is one of the most crucial tasks for conference organizers, and receiving high-quality reviews is of great significance to the quality and reputation of a conference. Moreover, conference organizers often are required to distribute papers to reviewers within a few days of the conference submission deadline—a massive burden for conference chairs. Regular conferences receive hundreds or thousands of papers that must be assigned to hundreds of reviewers. Assigning each submitted paper to an appropriate group of reviewers requires knowledge of both reviewer expertise and paper topics. Therefore, it is extremely difficult for a conference chair to assign all submitted papers to reviewers while avoiding existing

© Springer Nature Switzerland AG 2019
N. T. Nguyen et al. (Eds.): ICCCI 2019, LNAI 11683, pp. 441–450, 2019.
https://doi.org/10.1007/978-3-030-28377-3_36

problems, such as reviews are nonobjective, conflicts of interest, and a fixed number of reviewers for each paper. Additionally, most conference organizers assign reviewers a pool, which they already know. This leads to the omission of many potential reviewers—especially in rapidly developing areas such as artificial intelligence and machine learning. Automating the assignment of reviewers is necessary to reduce the time required to assign the submitted papers and increase the objectiveness of the process.

The quality of the reviewer assignment process is a profound concern of scientists because their academic careers are directly affected by it. As such, several approaches have been proposed to enhance the process that mainly involve a bidding process and the matching of a paper's topic with a reviewer's expertise [2,3,11,13].

However, the bidding process still has limitations: A reviewer may bid on papers for their novelty instead of matching to their research area. Besides, reviewers often do not examine all submitted papers; instead, they use specific keywords to search, which leads to noise into the process. On the other hand Alternatively, the choosing of the reviewers by the program committee is still a significantly time-consuming.

In this study, we built a support system to automatically assign submitted papers to reviewers. The contribution of our proposed method can be described as follows:

(1) The quality of a reviewer is determined according to their quantity and activity.
(2) The relevance between a submitted paper and reviewer is estimated based on the content similarity and referring network.
(3) The matching degree between a submitted paper and reviewer is computed and then considers the assigning rule for paper assignments.

The remainder of this paper is constructed as follows: In Sect. 2, related works on conference review assignment are reviewed briefly. Section 3 presents our proposed method in detail. The experiments are explained in Sect. 4. Lastly, the conclusion and directions for future work are presented in Sect. 5.

2   Related Works

Although existing peer review systems encourage the growth of the academic community, conference paper assignment remains a profound concern of scientists because it affects most of their career [5,7]. In general, there have been three typical approaches: decision support, machine learning, and recommender systems [9].

Decision support systems have often been applied for tasks surrounding scientific works. Tian et al. [15] built an organizational decision support system for R&D project selection. Xu et al. [17] developed a group decision support system for evaluating reviewers' performances in the peer review process. The competitiveness and relevance between reviewers and submitted papers were computed to solve the paper assignment process. Fan et al. [4] proposed an genetic algorithm for proposal grouping, in which knowledge rules were considered for the identification and classification of proposals. Nguyen et al. [11] proposed an ordered weighted averaging aggregation function to compile information from different sources and rank potential reviewers for each paper.

The machine learning approach is often used when dealing with large datasets that cannot be processed manually and has been successfully applied for information retrieval. Mori et al. [10] developed a system to discover new business partners. The correlative relationships among partners could be found with the help of machine learning techniques. Pavlov and Ichise [12] introduced a method for finding experts by considering the co-authorship networks. Structural properties from past collaborations networks were used to predict experts using supervised learning algorithms.

Recommender systems have also been applied to suggest reviewers for papers. Hoang et al. [5] built a group recommender system to recommend a group of experts to solve a specific problem. Protasiewicz [13] introduced a support system for selecting reviewers to evaluate research proposals or articles. Keywords from the publications of researchers were extracted to compute the content similarity between research proposals or articles and researcher profiles.

The recent related works have pointed out that the paper assignment problem needs further research. In this work, we propose a method for automatically solving conference paper assignment without human intervention. We extract features from a reviewer's profile to estimate their quality. Subsequently, we measure the relevance between a submitted paper and the reviewer. Assigning rules such as CoI, and limited assignment number, are then applied for paper assignment.

3   Proposed Methodology

This section describes our proposed method for solving the reviewer assignment problem. The matching degree between a submitted paper and reviewers is computed according to the quality of the reviewer and the relevance between the two.

3.1   Reviewer and Paper Identification

In this subsection, we present a reviewer identification method by considering the researchers' profile and their behavior for matching reviewers to predefine topics T. Previous works assume that the matching degree of a reviewer r on topic $t \in \{1...T\}$ is represented as a probability $P_{(r,t)}$ with $\sum_t P_{(r,t)} = 1$. Likewise, a submitted paper p is represented as T-dimensional topic $P_{(p,t)}$ distribution with $\sum_t P_{(p,t)} = 1$ [11]. However, the imbalance of reviewer candidates among different topics means more prevalent topics will be biased, and vice versa. Therefore, we extract features and use the learning-to-rank approach to identify reviewers for each topic. We consider two crucial factors: reviewer quality and relevance between reviewer and paper for identifying reviewers.

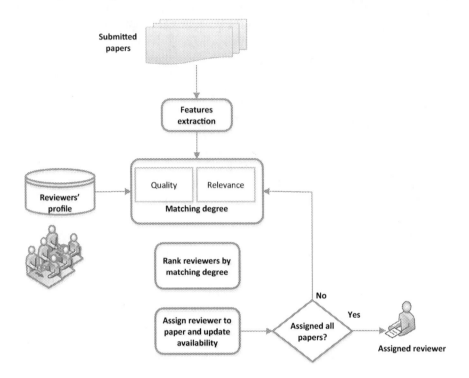

Fig. 1. Framework of the decision support system

Quality describes a reviewer's publishing achievements and productivity in recent years. The relevance between a reviewer and paper is represented by the matching degree between the reviewer fields and submitted paper.

Reviewer Quality. Quality of an reviewer is a important factor affecting the quality of the review process. We measure the quality of a reviewer in two main aspects: *Quantity* and *Activity*.

Quantity: We consider three features to determine the quantity of reviewer r_i, the number of publications (Pu_{r_i}), number of citations (C_{r_i}), and h-index (H_{r_i}). Usually, the number of citations of each author is higher than the number of papers. According to Thomson Reuters, the number of citations for the average paper is four. Thus, we add $\frac{1}{4}$ as a constant to normalize the competence function.

Definition 1. *The Quantity of reviewer r_i is defined as follows:*

$$Quantity_{r_i} = \frac{1}{1 + e^{-\frac{1}{3}(Pu_{r_i} + \frac{1}{4}C_{r_i} + H_{r_i})}} \tag{1}$$

The sigmoid function is used to scale the value to fit in the range $(0, 1)$, which is the same domain as other factors.

Activity: The activity of a reviewer represents the current research situation and work performance in the past N years. According to [8] "recent research or similar activity which assures maintenance of research competence is essential to full credit for past accomplishments." This is explained to mean that the total research career should be evaluated, and then if lack of recency exists, full credit should not be given.

The timeframe is determined to realize that some scientists will have no final publication in any one rating year and should not necessarily be rated low because of this. The activity of a reviewer is measured by according to the number of publications $(Pu_{N_{r_i}})$, number of collaborators $(C_{N_{r_i}})$, and h-index $(H_{N_{r_i}})$ in the past N years.

Definition 2. *The activity of reviewer r_i is defined as follows:*

$$Activity_{r_i} = \frac{1}{1 + e^{-\frac{1}{3}(Pu_{N_{r_i}} + \frac{1}{4}C_{N_{r_i}} + H_{N_{r_i}})}} \qquad (2)$$

where N is the number of years consider. As a general rule, 3 to 5 years is the timeframe commonly used to assess the activity of a scientist.

Definition 3. *The quality of reviewer r_i is defined as follows:*

$$Quality_{r_i} = \alpha \times Quantity_{r_i} + (1 - \alpha) \times Activity_{r_i} \qquad (3)$$

where $0 \leq Quality_{r_i} \leq 1$, and indicates the academic standing and authority of reviewer r_i in the scientific community. Parameter α is a constant $(\alpha \in [0,1])$, which controls the rates of reflecting the importance values of the *quantity* and *activity* of reviewer r_i.

Relevance Between Reviewer and Paper. Research topics can be obtained in several ways. For instance, in the paper-reviewer task, each reviewer can choose his or her topics from predefined categories. Other work can apply statistical topic modeling to automatically extract topics from the data and match them with predefined topics.

We determine the relevance between reviewer and paper based on two main assumptions:

(1) Given that the research topics of a reviewer are often expressed in his/her publications, the similarity between a reviewer's publication and a submitted paper is used to measure the relevance between the reviewer and paper.
(2) Two papers that refer to the same reference will have similar research fields.

First, the similarity of reviewer r_i with submitted paper p is calculated by measuring the similarity value as follows:

$$Similarity(r_i, p) = \frac{|V_p \times V_{r_i}|}{|V_p| \times |V_{r_i}|} \qquad (4)$$

where V_p is a vector of submitted paper p and V_{r_i} represents a vector of the publications of reviewer r_i using the word embedding method [6].

Second, common reference between a reviewer's publication and a submitted paper is computed by considering the co-citation network [8]. There are two types of common references:

- Submitted paper p cites one of reviewer r_i's publications. - Submitted paper p and reviewer r_i refer to the same reference.

$$Referring(r_i, p) = \frac{1}{2}\left(\frac{|Cite_{r_i}|}{|Pu_{r_i}|} + \frac{|Co-cite|}{|Cite_p|}\right) \qquad (5)$$

where $Cite_{r_i}$ is the number of citations that submitted paper p cited from reviewer r_i's publications. $Co - cite$ is the number of like references between p and r_i, and $Cite_p$ is the number of references in p.

Definition 4. *The relevance between reviewer r_i and submitted paper p is defined as follows:*

$$Relevance(r_i, p) = \beta \times Similarity(r_i, p) + (1 - \beta) \times Referring(r_i, p) \qquad (6)$$

where $0 \leq Relevance(r_i, p) \leq 1$, and represents the degree of relevance between the reviewer r_i and submitted paper p. Parameter β is a constant ($\beta \in [0, 1]$), which controls the rates of reflecting the importance values of the similarity and common references between r_i and p.

Matching Degree Between Reviewers and Papers. The matching degree is used to identify the importance of a reviewer's expertise and relevance to a submitted paper.

Definition 5. *The matching degree between reviewer r_i and submitted paper p is defined as follows:*

$$Matching(r_i, p) = \gamma \times Quality(r_i, p) + (1 - \gamma) \times Relevance(r_i, p) \qquad (7)$$

where the range of $Matching(r_i, p)$ is from 0 to 1, which represent the matching degree between reviewer r_i and submitted paper p. Parameter γ is a constant ($\gamma \in [0, 1]$), which determines the rates of reflecting the importance values between $Quality(r_i, p)$ and $Relevance(r_i, p)$.

3.2   Assigning Reviewers to Papers

The assigning process determines a set of reviewers who meet the requirements of a submitted paper. In order to assign a reviewer to a submitted paper, we apply the following rules:

(1) Avoid conflict of interest (CoI): We consider two types of CoI: Co-author and shared affiliation. If one of the authors of submitted paper p has a shared affiliation or co-authorship in at least one publication with reviewer r_i, r_i cannot be assigned to p.

(2) Quality of reviewers: We favor assigning a reviewer with a higher quality value.

(3) Assignment limit: A reviewer cannot be assigned more than a maximal number, P_{max} of papers, while each submitted paper should be reviewed by R_m reviewers.

The assigning process consists of the following four steps:

Step 1. For each submitted paper $p, (p \in P)$, CoI is checked to avoid any conflicts of interest.

Step 2. For each reviewer $(r_i \in R)$, the matching degree with submitted paper p is computed.

Step 3. The matching degrees are ranked in descending order.

Step 4. Assign submitted paper p to the R_m reviewers who have the largest matching degree and update the availability.

4 Experiments

4.1 Datasets

We collected approximately 400 papers and 200 reviewers to evaluate our proposed method. As such, each reviewer was assigned two submitted papers. To create the reviewer profiles, we collected data from academic resources such as the DBLP Computer Science Bibliography[1], ResearchGate[2], and CiteSeer[3], that provide easy user access. Each reviewer was distinguished based on their name, affiliation, publications, and network. We then manually labeled the dataset to obtain the ground truth.

4.2 Evaluation

Several methods can be used in assessing the performance of a support system. In this work, we found a list of reviewers who are matched to each submitted paper. We then needed to evaluate the relevance of all reviewers to their submitted paper. For this, we used normalized discounted cumulative gain $(nDCG)$ [16] and $Precision@K$ (P@K) [14]. Discounted cumulative gain (DCG) [1] and $nDCG$ are computed as follows:

$$nDCG_{K,p} = \frac{DCG_{K,p}}{Ideal\_DCG_{K,p}} \qquad (8)$$

$$DCG_{K,p} = \sum_{r=1}^{K} \frac{2^{rel_{r_i}} - 1}{log_2(1 + r_i)} \qquad (9)$$

where rel_{r_i} represents the binary relevance of the returned results at the Kth ranking. If a reviewer is fit to review paper p, the value of rel_{r_i} is set to 1;

---

[1] http://dblp.uni-trier.de/xml/.

[2] https://www.researchgate.net/.

[3] http://csxstatic.ist.psu.edu/downloads/data.

otherwise 0. $Ideal\_DCG_{k,p}$ represents the ideal obtained value for the ground truth. A higher value of $nDCG$ corresponds to a higher connection between submitted paper p and reviewer r_i.

We set the number of reviewers for each paper at 2 and 3, and the values of α, β, γ at 0.5. We chose two papers - one by Protasiewicz [13], the other by Hoang et al., [5] as baselines for our support system.

Protasiewicz [13] proposed a method to compute the content similarity between a submitted paper p and a reviewer's profile. Each reviewer's profile was converted to the vector V_{r_i}, and each submitted paper p was represented by the vector V_p. The content similarity between V_p and V_{r_i} was then computed as follows:

$$Similarity(r_i, p) = \frac{|V_p \times V_{r_i}|}{|V_p| \times |V_{r_i}|} \tag{10}$$

The results could be obtained by sorting in descending order according to the values of $Similarity(r_i, p)$.

Hoang et al. [5] proposed a method to find a group of experts. They extracted features from expert profiles and computed the *suitableness*, *diversity*, and *similarity* between query (Q) and expert (e_i).

As shown in Figs. 2 and 3, our support system achieved better results in both evaluation methods than the baselines. This is understandable because the baseline methods depend on the quality of feature vectors to determine the results. A reviewer's profile has many features that can be extracted as structured data. We considered the quality of a reviewer according to the *quantity* and *activity*. Moreover, we considered the referring network of reviewers. The matching degree between a submitted paper and reviewer was then computed based on the *quality* of the reviewers as well as the relevance between the two. These factors make our system more accurate than the baseline methods.

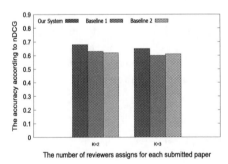

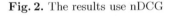

Fig. 2. The results use nDCG

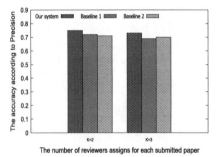

Fig. 3. The results use Precision

5   Conclusion and Future Work

In this work, we developed a support system to automatically assign submitted papers to reviewers. The matching degree between a submitted paper and reviewer was computed according to the *Quality* of a reviewer, as well as the relevance between the two. The *Quality* of a reviewer was determined by their *Quantity* and *Activity* in recent years. The relevance between a submitted paper and a reviewer was then computed based on the content similarity between the reviewer's profile, submitted paper, and referring network. Assigning rules—such as CoI and assignment limit—were then applied for paper assignment. The experimental results proved that our support system achieved better results in comparison to the baseline methods.

In future work, we will consider the experience level of reviewers. For each paper, at least one senior reviewer should be considered in the review process. Additionally, some reviewers are lenient while others are stringent, which could lead to an unfair final decision. These are important factors to consider for further improvement this work.

Acknowledgment. This research was supported by Basic Science Research Program through the National Research Foundation of Korea (NRF) funded by the Ministry of Science, ICT & Future Planning (2017R1A2B4009410). And this work was also supported by the National Research Foundation of Korea (NRF) grant funded by the BK21PLUS Program (22A20130012009).

References

1. Burges, C., et al.: Learning to rank using gradient descent. In: Proceedings of the 22nd International Conference on Machine Learning, pp. 89–96. ACM (2005)
2. Charlin, L., Zemel, R.: The Toronto paper matching system: an automated paper-reviewer assignment system (2013)
3. Conry, D., Koren, Y., Ramakrishnan, N.: Recommender systems for the conference paper assignment problem. In: Proceedings of the Third ACM Conference on Recommender Systems, pp. 357–360. ACM (2009)
4. Fan, Z.P., Chen, Y., Ma, J., Zhu, Y.: Decision support for proposal grouping: a hybrid approach using knowledge rule and genetic algorithm. Expert Syst. Appl. **36**(2), 1004–1013 (2009)
5. Hoang, D.T., Nguyen, N.T., Hwang, D.: A group recommender system for selecting experts to review a specific problem. In: Nguyen, N.T., Pimenidis, E., Khan, Z., Trawiński, B. (eds.) ICCCI 2018. LNCS (LNAI), vol. 11055, pp. 270–280. Springer, Cham (2018). https://doi.org/10.1007/978-3-319-98443-8_25
6. Le, Q., Mikolov, T.: Distributed representations of sentences and documents. In: International Conference on Machine Learning, pp. 1188–1196 (2014)
7. Li, L., Wang, Y., Liu, G., Wang, M., Wu, X.: Context-aware reviewer assignment for trust enhanced peer review. PLoS ONE **10**(6), e0130493 (2015)
8. Li, X., Watanabe, T.: Automatic paper-to-reviewer assignment, based on the matching degree of the reviewers. Procedia Comput. Sci. **22**, 633–642 (2013)

9. Lin, C.-W., Hong, T.-P., Lu, W.-H.: Efficiently mining high average utility itemsets with a tree structure. In: Nguyen, N.T., Le, M.T., Świątek, J. (eds.) ACIIDS 2010. LNCS (LNAI), vol. 5990, pp. 131–139. Springer, Heidelberg (2010). https://doi.org/10.1007/978-3-642-12145-6_14

10. Mori, J., Kajikawa, Y., Kashima, H., Sakata, I.: Machine learning approach for finding business partners and building reciprocal relationships. Expert Syst. Appl. **39**(12), 10402–10407 (2012)

11. Nguyen, J., Sánchez-Hernández, G., Agell, N., Rovira, X., Angulo, C.: A decision support tool using order weighted averaging for conference review assignment. Pattern Recogn. Lett. **105**, 114–120 (2018)

12. Pavlov, M., Ichise, R.: Finding experts by link prediction in co-authorship networks. In: Proceedings of the 2nd International Conference on Finding Experts on the Web with Semantics-Volume 290, pp. 42–55. CEUR-WS.org (2007)

13. Protasiewicz, J.: A support system for selection of reviewers. In: 2014 IEEE International Conference on Systems, Man and Cybernetics (SMC), pp. 3062–3065. IEEE (2014)

14. Sanderson, M., Manning, C.D., Raghavan, P., Schütze, H.: Introduction to Information Retrieval. Cambridge University Press, Cambridge (2008). ISBN 13 978-0-521-86571-5, xxi+ 482 p. Natural Language Engineering 16(1), 100–103 (2010)

15. Tian, Q., Ma, J., Liang, J., Kwok, R.C., Liu, O.: An organizational decision support system for effective R&D project selection. Decis. Support Syst. **39**(3), 403–413 (2005)

16. Wang, Y., Wang, L., Li, Y., He, D., Chen, W., Liu, T.Y.: A theoretical analysis of NDCG ranking measures. In: Proceedings of the 26th Annual Conference on Learning Theory (COLT 2013) (2013)

17. Xu, W., Du, W., Ma, J., Wang, W., Liu, Q.: An integrated decision support model to assess reviewers for research project selection. In: 2012 45th Hawaii International Conference on System Science (HICSS), pp. 1414–1423. IEEE (2012)

Co-evolution Dynamics Between Individual Strategy and Gaming Environment Under the Feedback Control

Siyuan Liu[1] and Jianlei Zhang[1,2(✉)]

[1] Department of Automation, College of Artificial Intelligence, Nankai University,
Tianjin 300071, China
`jianleizhang@nankai.edu.cn`
[2] Tianjin Key Laboratory of Intelligent Robotics, Nankai University,
Tianjin 300071, China

Abstract. A co-evolution between individual strategy and gaming environment in two systems with two strategies is proposed here. Different from the general evolutionary game dynamics, the gaming system developed here is deeply coupled with the strategy choices and the environment state. The game state, payoff matrices and gaming environment of the system will influence each other dynamically. Besides, we employ two typical game models, prisoner's dilemma game and division of labor game as two illustrative examples. In this framework, we derive the sufficient condition under feedback mechanism, under which the state of strategy and environment will evolve periodically. Results provide some inspirations to tackle with the cooperation dilemma and realize the effective division of labor in the real situations.

Keywords: Co-evolution · Evolutionary game · Feedback ·
Cooperation · Division of labor

1 Introduction

In a multi-agent system, the interest conflicts between individual and the group often exist [3,6,9]. From an individual perspective, they want to maximize their own interests. However, in group activities, maximizing group benefits often requires individuals to pay uneven costs. This kind of phenomenon is very common in group activities, and game theory provides an effective mathematical framework for this [16]. Task allocation is an important activity related to the survival and development of groups. In the optimal task allocation results, various tasks are executed, while individuals reap unequal benefits. How to coordinate the decisions of these individuals who pursue interests and ideals is a difficult problem with wide application background [2,4,5].

This work was supported by National Natural Science Foundation of China (Grants Nos. 61603201 and 61603199) and the Tianjin Natural Science Foundation of China (Grant No. 18JCYBJC18600).

N. T. Nguyen et al. (Eds.): ICCCI 2019, LNAI 11683, pp. 451–462, 2019.
https://doi.org/10.1007/978-3-030-28377-3_37

Therefore, the individual decision-making process is the core element related to the stable state of system evolution. The updating rules of strategies play an important guiding role in the evolution process. As for the strategy updating, many studies consider that players imitate or replicate their neighbors' strategy with a certain probability p, which depends on payoff comparison [7,8,14]. The switching probability p could be a linear function of the payoff difference [13] (e.g., $p = \frac{1}{2} + \omega_1 \frac{\pi_f - \pi_r}{\Delta \pi}$), or indicated by non-linear functions, such as Fermi function $p = \frac{1}{1+e^{\omega_2(\pi_f - \pi_r)}}$ [10]. Here, π_f and π_r denote the payoffs of the focal individual and referenced one, respectively, and $\Delta \pi$ is the maximum payoff difference. The parameter ω_1 and ω_2 denote the noise or inverse temperature which control the selection intensity and take values in the range of $[0,1]$ and $(0,\infty)$, respectively. The situation of $\omega_1 \to 0$ or $\omega_2 \to 0$ (weak selection) manifests all information is covered by noise, yet the condition of $\omega_1 \to 1$ or $\omega_2 \to \infty$ (strong selection) signifies decided imitation rules.

Besides, considering the fact that acquiring payoffs is not easy due to individuals' bounded rationality or ability in real social systems, some works based on incomplete information are established [1]. Thus, the rules driving the strategy evolution is a fascinating and meanwhile key topic. Especially, how can individuals update strategies and improve their profits by not requiring the known payoffs? Our previous works have realized it by introducing the willingness that one individual shifts her current strategy to the other one, an intriguing feature of which is the absence of usually required payoff information [15,17].

When considering the individual intelligence, another important direction is to consider the interaction between individual and environment. It is well known that, feedback control can make the output of system run spontaneously according to the predetermined law, is an effective method in the automatic control area. Here, we consider to combine feedback control with evolutionary game in the multi-agent systems to improve the individual intelligence. From the view of control theory, the evolutionary game process can be regarded as a controller. We can establish a game where the factors (individuals or players in the game) influencing the target variables interact (play games) with each other. The variables to be controlled are the game environment which influences the payoffs of players. In such settings, the optimum strategy distribution, and the target game environment, can co-evolve by the self-organization of the involved members.

2   Problem Statement

2.1   Dynamic Payoff Matrices

In the traditional evolutionary game dynamics, each individual in the population updates her strategy according to the fixed payoff matrix. In detail, the player compares her payoff after every game round with her excepted value or others' benefits in terms of the per-determined payoff matrix, and refine her strategy choice at the next time to profit more from the game. Figure 1 depicts this process intuitively.

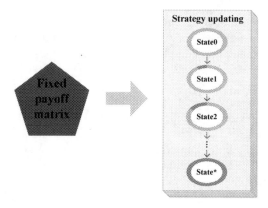

Fig. 1. Schematic of traditional evolutionary game process.

However, payoff matrices vary with surroundings in the practical situation, such as the abundance of social resource in the cooperative dilemma, or the degree of dependence to others in the division of labor game. The current effect of division of labor will directly affect the income of all the members. Hence, the dynamic payoff matrix changing with the environment is reasonable to explore the strategy updating more comprehensively as Fig. 2.

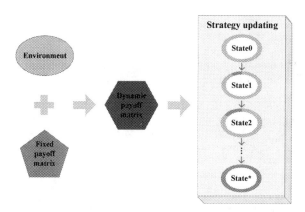

Fig. 2. Schematic of evolutionary game process with feedback.

In a multi-agent system, each player owns a strategy set with m optional strategies $s = \{s_1, \ldots, s_m\}$, thus the dynamic payoff matrix can be described as

$$A(r) = \begin{bmatrix} a_{11}(r) & \cdots & a_{1m}(r) \\ \vdots & \ddots & \vdots \\ a_{m1}(r) & \cdots & a_{mm}(r) \end{bmatrix}, \tag{1}$$

where r is the environment coefficient and the entries of the matrix are the corresponding scalar functions of r. The detailed meaning of r will be explained in the later subsection.

2.2 Strategy Updating Rule

We employ the replicator dynamic equation [9] to describe the evolution of the strategy distribution in a well-mixed system, to motivate our analysis. Given a single system with finite individuals who encounter others with a strategy set $s = \{s_1, \ldots, s_m\}$, and the probability of each strategy being executed is p_i, $i = 1, \ldots, m$. By employing $p = [p_1, \ldots, p_m]^T$ and setting the growth rate $\dot{p}_i$ to be proportional to the difference between the individual benefit of s_i and the average payoff of the whole system, i.e.,

$$\dot{p}_i = p_i[U_i(p) - \bar{U}(p)]. \tag{2}$$

Here, $U_i(p) = (Ap)_i$ is the individual benefit of player i and $\bar{U}(p) = p^T Ap$ is the average payoff, $\sum_i p_i = 1$.

When extending the replicator dynamics from a single population the n-population case, the strategy updating equation can be written as

$$\dot{p}_i^k = p_i^k[U_i^k(\mathbf{p}) - \bar{U}^k(\mathbf{p})], \tag{3}$$

where p_i^k represents the probability to choose strategy s_i in the system k, $k = 1, \ldots, n$; $\mathbf{p} = [p^1, \ldots, p^n]^T$, and p^k depends on the proportions of the individuals with different strategies in the system k.

2.3 Environment Coefficient

The r is a main factor as the feedback variable of the dynamic payoff matrix, which plays a key role in the strategy updating. In turn, r is also affected by the system state $\mathbf{p}$. The interaction of these variables composes a deeply coupled system. The change of environment coefficient r [9] can be represented as

$$\dot{r} = r(1 - r)h(\mathbf{p}). \tag{4}$$

Here, r is limited in the range $[0, 1]$, and $h(\mathbf{p})$ is the feedback equation showing the influence of the system states on the environment. The meaning of r and the form of $h(\mathbf{p})$ are determined by the specific situation, the details of which will be discussed in the next section.

2.4 Model Setting

Without loss of generality, the interaction between two populations ($k = 1, 2$) with two strategies ($s = \{s_1, s_2\}$) is considered here. Two populations are featured by different payoff matrices and each individual just plays game with the agent from the other population. On account of two optional strategies of each population, we define that the state of population 1 is $\mathbf{x} = [x, 1 - x]^T$, where x represents the proportion of players adopting s_1 and $1 - x$ corresponds to s_2. Similarly, the state of population 2 is $\mathbf{y} = [y, 1 - y]^T$.

The dynamic payoff matrices of two populations can be denoted as

$$A(r) = \begin{bmatrix} a_{11}(r) & a_{12}(r) \\ a_{21}(r) & a_{22}(r) \end{bmatrix},$$

$$B(r) = \begin{bmatrix} b_{11}(r) & b_{12}(r) \\ b_{21}(r) & b_{22}(r) \end{bmatrix}.$$

And the utility functions are given by

$$\begin{cases} U_i^1 = (A(r)\mathbf{y})_i \\ U_i^2 = (B(r)\mathbf{x})_i \\ \bar{U}^1 = \mathbf{x}A(r)\mathbf{y} \\ \bar{U}^2 = \mathbf{y}B(r)\mathbf{x} \end{cases} \tag{5}$$

Combining Eqs. 3–5, we can derive a 3-dimensional co-evolutionary system coupled with strategy dynamics and environment state as

$$\begin{cases} \dot{x} = x(1 - x)f(y, r) \\ \dot{y} = y(1 - y)g(x, r) \\ \dot{r} = r(1 - r)h(x, y) \end{cases}, \tag{6}$$

where

$$f(y, r) = (a_{11}(r) - a_{12}(r) - a_{21}(r) + a_{22}(r))y \\ + a_{12}(r) - a_{22}(r), \tag{7}$$

and

$$g(x, r) = (b_{11}(r) - b_{12}(r) - b_{21}(r) + b_{22}(r))x \\ + b_{12}(r) - b_{22}(r). \tag{8}$$

Owing to the fact that x, y and r value in the range $[0, 1]$, the region of the system (6) is the unit cube $[0, 1]^3$. It is easy to find that the eight corners of the cubic domain $(0, 0, 0)$, $(1, 0, 0)$, $(0, 1, 0)$, $(0, 0, 1)$, $(1, 1, 0)$, $(1, 0, 1)$, $(0, 1, 1)$ and $(1, 1, 1)$ are fixed points, on which the evolution will not occur.

3   Analysis and Results

In this section, we focus on two game models. One is the Prisoner Dilemma (PD) game, a typical example for describing the interest conflicts between individuals and group. The other is the division of labor (DOL) game which describes the cooperative dilemma in realizing the maximization of collective interests. Results show that both systems display periodic orbits, which provides the best predictions of long-run behaviors.

3.1   PD Game

Reference [9] has proved that in a modified Prisoner Dilemma (PD) game applied to the system (6), oscillation offers the best predictions of long-run behavior by using reversible system theory, but different influence of defection strategies in two populations on the environment, and how important distinct social resources are to individuals are not taken into account. Here, we improve the model to overcome the limitations and expand its adaptability. Our focus is to verify whether periodic orbits can maintain or not when its applicability is extended.

Each agent in both of the systems has a strategy set $S = \{C, D\}$, in which C represents cooperation and D denotes defection. The dynamic payoff matrices are defined as follows

$$A(r) = (1 - r) \begin{bmatrix} T_1 & P_1 \\ R_1 & S_1 \end{bmatrix} + \alpha r \begin{bmatrix} R_1 & S_1 \\ T_1 & P_1 \end{bmatrix}, \tag{9}$$

$$B(r) = (1 - r) \begin{bmatrix} T_2 & P_2 \\ R_2 & S_2 \end{bmatrix} + \alpha r \begin{bmatrix} R_2 & S_2 \\ T_2 & P_2 \end{bmatrix}, \tag{10}$$

where $P_1 > S_1$, $T_1 > S_1$ and $P_2 > S_2$, $T_2 > S_2$. The environment factor r here represents the richness of the social resource. And its value is related with the strategy distribution of the system. For example, its value increases by the mutual cooperation of the agents, while decreases along with mutual defection of the players. It is understandable that under the condition of abundant resource (i.e. $r \to 1$), individuals tend to defect. The depletion of resources (i.e. $r \to 0$) will bring survival risks to the group, so individuals tend to cooperate. The constant $\alpha > 0$ improves with the importance of the resource to individuals, more precisely, defection is more likely to take place in the case of a larger α.

And we define $h(x, y)$ as

$$h(x, y) = \theta_1 x - (1 - x) + \theta_2 y - \theta_3 (1 - y), \tag{11}$$

where $\theta_1, \theta_2, \theta_3 > 0$ denote different degree of affects which cooperative and defective agents of two populations have on the environment respectively.

In combination with Eqs. 6–11, the system arrives at

$$\begin{cases} \dot{x} = x(1 - x)[\delta_{PS_1} + (\delta_{TR_1} - \delta_{PS_1})y][1 - (1 + \alpha)r] \\ \dot{y} = y(1 - y)[\delta_{PS_1} + (\delta_{TR_1} - \delta_{PS_1})x][1 - (1 + \alpha)r] \\ \dot{r} = r(1 - r)[(1 + \theta_1)x + (\theta_2 + \theta_3)y - (1 + \theta_3)] \end{cases}, \tag{12}$$

where $\delta_{PS_1} = P_1 - S_1 > 0$, $\delta_{TR_1} = T_1 - R_1 > 0$ and $\delta_{PS_2} = P_2 - S_2 > 0$, $\delta_{TR_2} = T_2 - R_2 > 0$. It easy to find that $r > \frac{1}{1+\alpha}$ leads to the advent of defection ($\dot{x}, \dot{y} < 0$).

Let $\theta_1 = 2$, $\theta_2 = 3$, $\theta_3 = 4$, $\alpha = 2$, and thus interior equilibrium point set is $\{(x, y, r) : 3x + 7y - 5 = 0, r = \frac{1}{3}\}$. The trajectories setting out from different initial points (x_0, y_0, r_0) in the interior of the cube $[0, 1]^3$ and not at the fixed points exhibit closed periodic orbits centered at the interior equilibrium points as Fig. 3 shows.

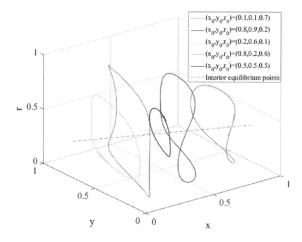

$(x_0, y_0, r_0) = (0.1, 0.1, 0.7)$
$(x_0, y_0, r_0) = (0.8, 0.9, 0.2)$
$(x_0, y_0, r_0) = (0.2, 0.6, 0.1)$
$(x_0, y_0, r_0) = (0.8, 0.2, 0.6)$
$(x_0, y_0, r_0) = (0.5, 0.5, 0.5)$
Interior equilibrium points

Fig. 3. Periodic orbits of PD game with parameters $P_1 = 5$, $S_1 = 1$, $T_1 = 3$, and $R_1 = 2$; $P_2 = 4$, $S_2 = -2$, $T_2 = 6$, and $R_2 = 0$; $\theta_1 = 2$, $\theta_2 = 3$, $\theta_3 = 4$ and $\alpha = 2$.

Figure 4 depicts how parameter α impacts the evolution of the system. We can see that the cooperators tend to decrease in both of the populations as $r > \frac{1}{1+\alpha}$ and on the contrary increase when $r < \frac{1}{1+\alpha}$.

So the system can evolve periodically without the extinction of any strategy when refining the modified PD game in [9] to a wider range of application.

3.2 DOL Game

Division of labor is an attractive phenomenon which can improve the total utility of the society. Here, an example researching co-evolution between import rate and exchange rate is introduced here.

The payoff matrix without feedback can be written as

		W	
		I	E
M	I	(A,D)	(B,C)
	E	(C,B)	(D,A)

M and W represent two countries, each of which is featured by a strategy set $S = \{I, E\}$, where I denotes import and E for export. Division of labor is realized when two countries choose different strategies, which promotes the international trade, so $B, C > A, D$. Assuming that country M is dominated by import in the long-term international market and export is the same for W, so M and W can obtain higher payoff from strategy I and E respectively, making $B > C > A > D$ a reasonable relationship. Here, we use x and y to denote the import rate of M and W respectively, namely the probability to adopt strategy I, while $1 - x$ and $1 - y$ corresponds to export rate.

The environment factor r represents the similarity level of exchange rate movements of the two countries. When exchange rates move in perfect unison,

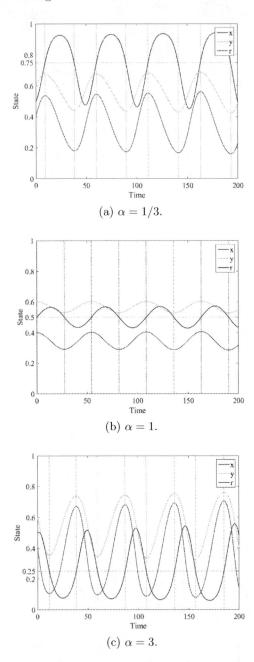

(a) $\alpha = 1/3$.

(b) $\alpha = 1$.

(c) $\alpha = 3$.

Fig. 4. Time evolution of states (x, y, r) under different α with original conditions $(0.4, 0.6, 0.5)$. Parameters setting is $P_1 = 3$, $S_1 = -1$, $T_1 = 4$, and $R_1 = 2$; $P_2 = 2$, $S_2 = 0$, $T_2 = 5$, and $R_2 = 4$; $\theta_1 = 2$, $\theta_2 = 3$ and $\theta_3 = 4$.

r tends to 1, and in turn goes to 0 when they move in exactly the opposite direction. As is known, currency appreciates when exchange rate rises, leading to the preference to import, and vice versa. Thus, two countries trends to adopt opposite strategy as r declines, where division of labor is come true.

We introduce dynamic payoff matrices as

$$M(r) = (1 - r)\begin{bmatrix} A & B \\ C & D \end{bmatrix} + r\begin{bmatrix} C & D \\ A & B \end{bmatrix} \tag{13}$$

$$W(r) = (1 - r)\begin{bmatrix} D & C \\ B & A \end{bmatrix} + r\begin{bmatrix} B & A \\ D & C \end{bmatrix} \tag{14}$$

When $r \to 0$ and two countries are expected to trade with each other, different strategies choice brings a higher payoff. But division of labor can't be realized when $r \to 1$, because both of the populations are in favor of the same strategy in this condition.

Due to that M is an importer in general, we set a parameter $\mu > 1$, limiting x to $[\frac{1}{\mu+1}, 1]$. And the same goes for W, leading to $1 - y$ restricted to $[\frac{1}{\mu+1}, 1]$, namely $y \in [0, \frac{\mu}{\mu+1}]$. The corresponding 3-dimensional co-evolutionary system can be expressed as

$$\begin{cases} \dot{x} = x(1 - x)[(A - B - C + D)y + B - D][1 - 2r] \\ \dot{y} = y(1 - y)[(A - B - C + D)x + C - A][1 - 2r] \\ \dot{r} = r(1 - r)(x - y - \frac{1}{\mu+1}) \end{cases} \tag{15}$$

From Eq. 15, we find that there is a set of fixed points in the interior of the cuboid Θ: $x \in (\frac{1}{\mu+1}, 1)$, $y \in (0, \frac{\mu}{\mu+1})$ and $r \in (0, 1)$, namely $\left\{ (x, y, r) : x - y = \frac{1}{\mu+1}, r = \frac{1}{2} \right\}$, on which the system cannot evolve.

Theorem 1. *For the system (15), if $B - D > \mu(C - A)$, the trajectories initialized with (x_0, y_0, r_0), which are in the interior of the cuboid Θ and not at the fixed points, will exhibit closed periodic orbits and each is centered at an interior equilibrium point.*

Proof. Reference [9] has proved that for a reversible system [11,12], if some three-dimensional open region Ω is an positively invariant set, there will be infinitely many independent periodic orbits which are centered at an interior equilibrium point in Ω. First, it is obviously that $\left\{ (x, y, r) : x - y = \frac{1}{\mu+1}, r = \frac{1}{2} \right\}$ is an interior equilibrium points set for the system (15). Second, the phase space $G : x \to x, y \to y, r \to 1 - r$ is an involution for the system (15), so (15) is a reversible system with respect to the above G. Finally, we will show that Θ is an (positively and negatively) invariant set for the system. For the sake of simplicity, we let $\delta = (A - B - C + D)y + B - D$ and $\sigma = (A - B - C + D)x + C - A$. Owing to $y \in [0, \frac{\mu}{\mu+1}]$ and $A - B - C + D < 0$, δ reaches its minimum when $y = \frac{\mu}{\mu+1}$, so $\delta_{\min} = \frac{1}{\mu+1}[\mu(B - D) - (C - A)] > 0$. Thus, $\delta > 0$ for any $y \in [0, \frac{\mu}{\mu+1}]$. The same method can be used to verify that $\sigma_{\max} = \frac{1}{\mu+1}[(C - A) - \mu(B - D)] < 0$,

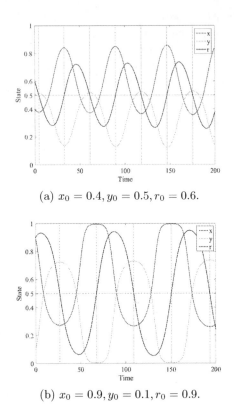

(a) $x_0 = 0.4, y_0 = 0.5, r_0 = 0.6$.

(b) $x_0 = 0.9, y_0 = 0.1, r_0 = 0.9$.

Fig. 5. Time evolution of DOL game with the parameters $A = 3$, $B = 5$, $C = 4$, $D = 1$ and $\mu = 3$.

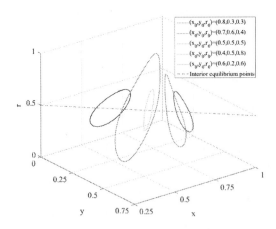

Fig. 6. Periodic orbits of DOL game with the parameters $A = 3$, $B = 5$, $C = 4$, $D = 1$ and $\mu = 3$.

then $\sigma < 0$ for any $x \in [\frac{1}{\mu+1}, 1]$. It can be easily examined in the plane $\left\{x = \frac{1}{\mu+1}\right\}$ the point $(\frac{1}{\mu+1}, \frac{\mu}{\mu+1}, 0)$ is asymptotically stable for (15). Afterwards, mark one trajectory starting from an arbitrary point q in the domain Θ with $\gamma(t, 0, q)$. If it reaches the face $\left\{x = \frac{1}{\mu+1}\right\}$ at some time t_1, it will always converges to the point $(\frac{1}{\mu+1}, \frac{\mu}{\mu+1}, 0)$ as $t \rightarrow \infty$ on account of the continuity of $\dot{x}$ and $\dot{y}$. Consider the deleted neighborhood Q of $(\frac{1}{\mu+1}, \frac{\mu}{\mu+1}, 0)$ in Θ, namely $Q \subset \Theta$. It is simple to check that $\dot{x} > 0$ in Q. Thereafter, the trajectory cannot reach the point $(\frac{1}{\mu+1}, \frac{\mu}{\mu+1}, 0)$. It is analogous to prove that the trajectory $\gamma(t, 0, q)$ cannot approach any other plane. Thus, it has been verified that Θ is the positive invariant area. Above all, closed periodic orbits centered at the interior point in the open region Θ is proved.

It is obvious in Fig. 5 that M and W tend to import and export respectively when $r < \frac{1}{2}$ and they go in the opposite direction when $r > \frac{1}{2}$, which guarantees that the division of labor can be fulfilled no matter how exchange rate varies. Figure 6 shows periodic orbits centered at the interior equilibrium point start from different original points.

4 Conclusion

A 3-dimensional co-evolutionary system amid the states of two populations and environment is studied here. We introduce the PD game and DOL game coupled with environment feedback. And then we verify the property of periodic orbits which can predict long-term behavior of the system. Importantly, results show that the game will go on regularly without the extinction of any strategy, which is meaningful in the realm of the prediction of system performance, the realization of the division of labor and so on. Summarizing, the framework proposed here provides an insightful method to investigate the interaction between individual strategy and gaming environment, which is more relevant to the real system.

References

1. Blume, L.E.: How noise matters. Games Econ. Behav. **44**(2), 251–271 (2003)
2. Caplan, A.J., Ellis, C.J., Silva, E.C.: Winners and losers in a world with global warming: noncooperation, altruism, and social welfare. J. Environ. Econ. Manage. **37**(3), 256–271 (1999)
3. Chang, S., Zhang, Z., Wu, Y., Xie, Y.: Cooperation is enhanced by inhomogeneous inertia in spatial prisoner's dilemma game. Physica A **490**, 419–425 (2018)
4. Du, J., Jia, Y.: Evolutionary game dynamics and risk control in global dilemmas with insurance compensation. IFAC-PapersOnLine **50**(1), 7669–7674 (2017)
5. Du, J., Wu, B., Wang, L.: Climate collective risk dilemma with feedback of real-time temperatures. EPL (Europhys. Lett.) **107**(6), 60005 (2014)
6. Fan, S., Li, Z., Wang, J., Piao, L., Ai, Q.: Cooperative economic scheduling for multiple energy hubs: a bargaining game theoretic perspective. IEEE Access **6**, 27777–27789 (2018)

7. Fosco, C., Mengel, F.: Cooperation through imitation and exclusion in networks. J. Econ. Dyn. Control **35**(5), 641–658 (2011)
8. Galla, T.: Imitation, internal absorption and the reversal of local drift in stochastic evolutionary games. J. Theor. Biol. **269**(1), 46–56 (2011)
9. Gong, L., Gao, J., Cao, M.: Evolutionary game dynamics for two interacting populations in a co-evolving environment. In: 2018 IEEE Conference on Decision and Control (CDC), pp. 3535–3540. IEEE (2018)
10. Hauert, C., Szabó, G.: Game theory and physics. Am. J. Phys. **73**(5), 405–414 (2005)
11. Roberts, J.A., Quispel, G.: Chaos and time-reversal symmetry. Order and chaos in reversible dynamical systems. Phys. Rep. **216**(2–3), 63–177 (1992)
12. Sachs, R.G.: The Physics of Time Reversal. University of Chicago Press, Chicago (1987)
13. Traulsen, A., Claussen, J.C., Hauert, C.: Coevolutionary dynamics: from finite to infinite populations. Phys. Rev. Lett. **95**(23), 238701 (2005)
14. Vilone, D., Ramasco, J.J., Sánchez, A., San Miguel, M.: Social imitation versus strategic choice, or consensus versus cooperation, in the networked prisoner's dilemma. Phys. Rev. E **90**(2), 022810 (2014)
15. Xu, Z., Zhang, J., Zhang, C., Chen, Z.: Fixation of strategies driven by switching probabilities in evolutionary games. EPL (Europhys. Lett.) **116**(5), 58002 (2017)
16. Zhang, C., Li, Q., Xu, Z., Zhang, J.: Stochastic dynamics of division of labor games in finite populations. Knowl.-Based Syst. **155**, 11–21 (2018)
17. Zhang, J., Zhang, C., Cao, M., Weissing, F.J.: Crucial role of strategy updating for coexistence of strategies in interaction networks. Phys. Rev. E **91**(4), 042101 (2015)

Fuzzy Inference Model for Punishing a Perpetrator in a Judicial Process

Michał Lower[1,2](✉) and Monika Lower[1,2]

[1] Wroclaw University of Science and Technology,
ul. Wyb. Wyspianskiego 27, 50-370 Wroclaw, Poland
`michal.lower@pwr.edu.pl`
[2] University of Wrocław, pl. Uniwersytecki 1, 50-137 Wroclaw, Poland
`290088@uwr.edu.pl`

Abstract. Court jurisdiction shows that the infliction of penalty by a judge is his personal decision. In judicial decisions, the judges do not specify clear premises or rules that were the basis for a concrete decision on the size of the penalty. In this paper, we attempt to build a model of inference based on fuzzy logic, allowing to formalize the principles resulting from the act. The logical model was built without a judge, through a detailed study of legal prerequisites contained in the Polish Penal Code. The purpose of this paper is a formal analysis of the rules and principles of the functioning of the law using mathematical tools. The results of our research will show whether the model built by us, based on a profound analysis of the premises contained in the Penal Code can give similar results as judicial decisions. In practical terms, the proposed inference model may also help inexperienced judges to make decisions. Due to the assumed limitations in the model, the reasons for general and special prevention as well as many other special regulations contained in the law code were not taken into account.

Keywords: Fuzzy inference · Logic in law · Expert system

1 Introduction

Legal provisions are laid down by people in many countries. Interpretations and decrees issued by relevant regulatory authorities are complementary to the law. In relation to the application of law, it is socially expected that the result of action based on legal provisions would be repeatable and predictable. In order for this purpose to work, the provisions of the law should be internally coherent, logical and interpretations should be unambiguous. The first step that can contribute to achieving this goal is a formal analysis of the rules and principles of the functioning of the law, using mathematical tools such as logic. However, it turns out that some elements of the legal system are so complex and based on many factors difficult to assess in terms of classical membership in the set, that the authors decided to use fuzzy logic to carry out such an analysis. The authors

© Springer Nature Switzerland AG 2019
N. T. Nguyen et al. (Eds.): ICCCI 2019, LNAI 11683, pp. 463–473, 2019.
https://doi.org/10.1007/978-3-030-28377-3_38

took up the task of building a fuzzy inference model which will determine the complete final assessment of the perpetrator on the basis of premises assessed by the judge. As a template for the developed model Polish criminal law supplemented with doctrinal studies was used. The judge resolving the case issues a verdict in which he decides on the penalty. Because the principle of legalism is adopted in criminal law, the judge is limited by an act and by the catalog of penalties and specific provisions specifying the minimum and maximum limits at which punishment can be imposed. In the Polish law the rules concerning the punishment, i.e. the premises to be a guideline for a judge, are contained in Chapter VI of the Penal Code (KK) in Article 53. Observing judicial decisions, it is easy to notice that in many cases the judges do not justify the size of punishment by referring to particular premises of Article 53 KK but only indicate that "according to the court, the size of the punishment corresponds to the size of the guilt and satisfies the social sense of justice [5]. We are interested in whether the specific size of the punishment corresponds to the size of guilt, where e.g. the adjudged number of years of imprisonment comes from, and next, what factors influence such a size of the punishment. Studying the Penal Code, these factors seem to be clearly defined and mentioned in Article 53, and the role of the judge is to analyze and assess each of them in a given case and then to impose a penalty on this basis. Since in court jurisdiction it is difficult to find a reference to the specific premises of KK it seems that judges impose a penalty by relying on their intuition and a specific number of years of imprisonment does not result from a detailed analysis of the premises in connection with the given case in question. Therefore, in this paper we attempt to build a model of inference based on fuzzy logic, allowing to formalize the principles resulting from the KK. The logical model was built without a judge, through a detailed analysis of the premises contained in the KK. The results of our research will show whether the model built by us, based on a profound analysis of the premises contained in the KK, can give similar results as judicial decisions. In practical terms, the proposed inference model may also help inexperienced judges to make decisions.

Due to the fact that the process of assessing the size of culpability is based on many premises, while the fulfillment of premises is usually ambiguous, fuzzy logic seems to be a tool with which these processes can be described and analyzed.

Fuzzy logic is a helpful tool used to apply in many fields, e.g. urban planning, transport systems, etc. [3,4]. It is particularly useful when a decision has to be taken on the basis of ambiguous and difficult to measure criteria. The discussion on the possibilities and ways of using artificial intelligence and logic in law has long been carried out in scientific literature. The author of [6] notes that classical logic, effectively applied in legal reasoning, is too abstract when there is uncertainty, ambiguity and misunderstanding. Whereas, this is a good moment to use fuzzy logic. The author of [7] points out the fact that what counts as valid inference depends to a large extent on the choices depending on the context. In view of this approach, the paper of authors [2] showing the modeling of the possibility of predicting the behavior of the Supreme Court of the United States is interesting.

2   Assumptions of the Model

The model is based on the interpretation of Article 53 KK which defines the general and specific principles of punishment and applies to all decisions made in the criminal trial. Thus, the model built by us will be a basic model, in which we do not consider cases in which special circumstances occur, for which KK provides for a special change in the size of punishment. Therefore, the basic assumption is that the act is a crime and is punishable, and there are no circumstances excluding guilt or unlawfulness. Another assumption of the model is the majority of the perpetrator and his accountability. Therefore, we assume that an act is a crime, is culpable, unlawful, the perpetrator is of age and compos mentis, there are no indications for extraordinary commutation or strengthening the punishment, conviction in the sequence of offenses and the size of combined punishment.

The model does not specify the type of punishment in cases where the choice of the type of punishment belongs to the judge or when the judge has the option of converting the penalty of imprisonment to fine or restriction of liberty. Moreover, the directive of general and special prevention contained in Article 53 of the KK are not included in the model. First of all, they both are of a follow-up and control nature - they commute or strengthen the punishment. Second, their concept is so difficult to classify that it requires separate work on this subject. Due to the fact that these directives are of a verifying nature, they may be included in the subsequent stages of our research.

3   The Concept of the Fuzzy Inference Model

The concept of the inference model is presented in the block diagram in the Fig. 1. The inference model consists of six fuzzy local models. The input values of the model are determined by means of eight criteria, the values of which are determined by an expert or a judge. The result of the inference are two values defining:

– The proposed penalty (PK), specified in the universal range 0–100%; the actual penalty results from the KK in which the maximum and minimum size of penalties (given in years or months) which the judge can impose for a specific offense are specified.
   PK is determined by the local inference model LMPK.
– Special legal prerequisites (SZ) - may affect the commutation or strenghtening of the proposed penalty, in the range from −80% to +80%. SZ may reduce or increase the size of the proposed penalty in the range of up to 80% of the remaining possible range of PK for increasing (PMZ) or reducing the size of the penalty (OMZ). For example, if the maximum penalty is 10 years and the minimum is 2 years, it means that PK = 0% is 2 years and PK = 100% is 10 years. If the proposed PK penalty is 75% then it will be the result of 8 years $(0.75 * 8 + 2)$. 2 years remain for the increase of the size of the penalty, therefore PMZ = 2, while OMZ = 6. Thus, in this case SZ can maximally reduce

the penalty by 4.8 years $(0.8*6)$ while they can increase it by a maximum of 1.6 years $(0.8*2)$. If SZ is 0% then it is a neutral result which does not reduce or increase the size of penalty.

SZ is determined by the local inference model LMSZ.

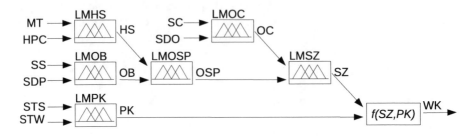

Fig. 1. The fuzzy inference model for punishing a perpetrator

The final result WK determining the size of the penalty (in the range of K_{min} i K_{max}) is calculated with (1), where $K = K_{max} - K_{min}$, $S_Z = SZ/100\%$ and $P_K = PK/100\%$.

$$WK = \begin{cases} S_Z \cdot K_{max} + P_K \cdot K \cdot (S_Z - 1) + (S_Z - 1) \cdot K_{min} & \text{if } P_K \geq 0 \\ -S_Z \cdot K_{min} + P_K \cdot K \cdot (S_Z + 1) + (S_Z + 1) \cdot K_{min} & \text{if } P_K < 0 \end{cases} \quad (1)$$

3.1   The Local Inference Model (LMPK) - The Proposed Penalty

Fuzzy inference model LMPK determines the proposed penalty (PK). In the polish criminal trial two general directives and two justice directives are distinguished. The general directives are special prevention and general prevention. The justice directives are the size of guilt directive (STW) and directive on the level of social harmfulness of an act (STS) [1] In our model the culpability and the social harmfulness of the act are the basis for determining the specific size of punishment, i.e. they have a limiting character.

3.2   The Local Inference Model (LMSZ) - Special Legal Prerequisites

Fuzzy inference model LMSZ determines special legal prerequisites (SZ).

In the process of infliction of punishment, the court should take into consideration legal prerequisites which have been divided into three groups:

– historical prerequisites (HS), because they refer to the time before the crime,
– present prerequisites (OB) refer to the behavior of the perpetrator during the criminal trial, i.e. the period after the commission of the delinquency.

– prerequisites regarding the delinquency (OC) committed by the perpetrator. We have included to them the effects of the delinquency considered as the size of the damage caused by the perpetrator and the relationship of the perpetrator to the obligations incumbent on him at the moment of committing the delinquency.

Due to the fact that the first two prerequisites - HS and OB are directly related to the perpetrator, they are considered together and constitute a common indicator which is determined by the local model of inference (LMOSP). This indicator was marked as an assessment of the perpetrator (OSP). Therefore, the basis for determining the resulting indicator SZ is the local model where OSP and OC are input parameters.

Historical prerequisites (HS) result from motivation of the perpetrator (MT) and the life of the perpetrator before committing a delinquency (HPC).

Present prerequisites (OB) result from repentance of the perpetrator (SS) and the perpetrator's relation to the victim (SDP).

Prerequisites regarding the delinquency (OC) result from the effect of the delinquency (SC) and the perpetrator's relationship to special duties (SDO).

4   Evaluation Criteria - Input Parameters of the Model

The input parameters of the model are the legal prerequisites allowing to assess the perpetrator, the delinquency and the size of guilt and the level of social harmfulness of the delinquency. All these parameters are defined in the range of 0–100%. For each prerequisite, appropriate triangular membership functions of fuzzy sets are assigned, which help the expert to determine the value of the linguistic variable.

4.1   The Size of Guilt (STW)

We have assigned a three-point scale to the criterion of guilt, where the highest criterion would be the full guilt of perpetrator who "had the full subjective ability to match his purposeful behavior to the obligation indicated in the norm" [8]. However, the lowest criterion would be a small guilt. This criterion was constructed in this way, because the guilt is the legal prerequisite of delinquency. The assumption of the model is that the committed act is a crime, so it must be culpable. Therefore, when assessing blame the lowest is the situation where the degree of fault of the perpetrator is small, i.e. where there were such circumstances beyond the perpetrator that made the perpetrator not be able to match the obligation indicated in the norm, and at the same time those circumstances do not exclude guilt.

Linguistic values: Small guilt (0%), Medium guilt (50%), Large guilt (100%).

4.2   The Level of Social Harmfulness of the Act (STS)

The court judges the social harmfulness of an act based on legal prerequisites contained in the KK (Article 115 of the KK). The linguistic values of STS are estimated on a three-point scale: Low (0%), Medium (50%), High (100%).

4.3   Motivation of the Perpetrator (MT)

We present the assessment of the motivation of the perpetrator on a five-point scale, where the lowest percentage (0%) concerns the mildest motivation (the perpetrator had good intentions). i.e. where the perpetrator good intentions affect the mitigation of punishment. Motivation deserving special condemnation is (100%).

The linguistic values are presented in the following way:

- The mitigating motivation - the perpetrator committed a deliberate act, but his motivation was objectively good, he finally had good intentions
- Subjectively mitigating motivation - the perpetrator deliberately committed a prohibited act, and his motivation was good but only according to him, but in the opinion of the man in the street it was meaningless
- Average motivation - the perpetrator commits offense only for its own benefit.
- Motivation consisting in a special action to the disadvantage - concerns the situation when the perpetrator commits an offense specifically to deteriorate the situation of the other person.
- Psychopathic motivation - the perpetrator commits an offense intentionally having the pleasure of the action itself, without committing the act for any specific purpose or having no benefits from it.

4.4   The Life of the Perpetrator Before Committing an Act (HPC)

While assessing the way of life of the perpetrator before the delinquency was committed, three linguistic values were formulated:

- An exemplary citizen - a person who has never been punished before, has a good reputation in his environment, is honest, engaged in various social initiatives
- Ordinary - a person who does not stand out particularly positively or negatively
- Robber - a person with a bad opinion in his environment, involved in many scrimmages, revolving in a criminal environment.

4.5   Repentance of the Perpetrator (SS)

The linguistic variable described as the repentance of the perpetrator includes an assessment of whether the perpetrator regrets his act. whether it is probable that he will commit another offense in the future, an assessment of the behavior of the perpetrator immediately after the commission of the act and its behavior during the trial - whether the perpetrator admits his guilt and provides detailed explanations regarding the crime. The repentance is assessed using the following linguistic values:

- Full repentance - the perpetrator pleads guilty, makes an explanation, regrets the act and does not intend to commit it again
- Lack of a greater or lesser number of prerequisites of full repentance - e.g. the perpetrator pleads guilty but during the action submits incomplete explanations, the perpetrator evaluates his behavior negatively but only because of the regulations and because of the consequences that threaten him,
- Lack of repentance - the perpetrator does not plead guilty (although his guilt is proven conclusively) or thinks he did well and does not regret the act (if he could he would do it again).

4.6   The Perpetrator's Relation to the Victim (SDP)

The perpetrator's relation to the victim includes the relationship between perpetrator and the injured person, reconciliation with the injured person; reparation, apologies, mediation results, the victim's reaction to penitence and apologies. The perpetrator's relation to the victim is assessed using the following linguistic values:

- Full reconciliation - the perpetrator regrets his delinquency, atoned the aggrieved party and the aggrieved party has forgiven him
- Positive - the perpetrator wants to be reconciled, but the injured person does not want to forgive him and demands punishment
- Neutral - the perpetrator does not take a stand, the aggrieved party is indifferent to him but at the same time he does not object in any way to the injunctive remedy
- Negative - the perpetrator does not intend to apologize to the aggrieved party, he does not regret his act, he does not want to atone
- Very negative - the perpetrator hates the victim, wishes him wrong if he could he would commit the act again.

4.7   The Perpetrator's Relation to His Duties (SDO)

The perpetrator attitude to the duties he had at the time of committing the offense. The perpetrator's relation to his duties is assessed using the following linguistic values:

- The perpetrator did not have any special duties
- The perpetrator had special duties but the same as man in the street had
- The perpetrator had special duties individually related to him which he did not fulfill by doing the act.

4.8   The Fallout of the Act (SC)

The fallout of the act is assessed using the following linguistic values:

- A small damage - falls within half of the country's minimum wage
- Average damage - corresponding to several years' income of the average citizen
- Significant damage - life achievement of the average citizen
- Great damage - damage exceeding the possible life achievements of the average citizen, damage involving large losses of a group of people, an enterprise or a state.

Despite qualitative specification of these criteria, one should remember about situations in which it is impossible to determine the value of damage in money or the monetary term does not reflect the actual damage suffered by the aggrieved party. Therefore, all four criteria should also be used when assessing the damage in relation to the victim and the given amounts should only be treated as a support.

5   Inference Results

To show the result of the application of the inference model, the court decrees in real criminal trials were examined. Decrees in which the judge's assessment of the legal prerequisites in the case could be found, was selected for testing. The results obtained were compared to the size of the penalty issued by the judge. In judicial decisions, the perpetrator assessment was carried out in a descriptive manner. In order for it to be used in the model, the expert determined the value of this assessment on a scale of 0–100%.

In order to test the model, several dozen court judgments were analyzed. As a result of the analysis, it was found that the fuzzy penalties determined by the model are much higher than those determined by the judges. The obtained model results were consulted with an expert - experienced lawyer. According to the assessment of the expert, our logical analysis of the model is correct. The discrepancy in the final penalty for the perpetrator results from the lack of taking into account historical cultural changes in the model and general guidelines for judges, which are not widely published. It turns out that criminal law has its several hundred years of tradition and formally the size of the penalty in the act is not modified, despite cultural changes in society and customary norms. This means that the judges do not currently apply the maximum penalty, moreover, the scope of the judgments is within one-third of the maximum scope resulting from the Act. This is confirmed by the analysis of criminal judgments. Therefore, the authors decided to determine on the basis of judicial decisions the maximum penalty imposed on the perpetrators and on the basis of this value, to adjust the obtained results. The results obtained after correction were consulted with an expert. According to an experienced expert, the adjusted results of the model's operation coincide with the intention of the act and such judgments would be considered fair if they were issued by a real human judge. Four types of crime were selected for the study:

- Theft - statutory range is from 3 months to 5 years imprisonment
- Theft with a break-in - the statutory range is prison from 1 to 10 years
- Causing serious health detriment - the statutory range means deprivation of liberty from 1 year to 10 years
- Fraud - the statutory period is deprivation of liberty from 6 months to 8 years

5.1   Theft

The minimum size of penalty is 5 months and the maximum is 60 months. Based on the analysis of court verdicts, the maximum sentence was adjusted to 15 months.

Judgment of the District Court in Walbrzych City in Poland

Convicted criminal demanded a remuneration from the victim, which he did not deserve. Unable to obtain remuneration from the injured person, the offender robbed his car.

The input values of the model determined by the expert:

SC = 10%, SDO = 5%, MT = 60%, HPC = 0%,
SS = 60%, SDP = 80%, STS = 10%, STW = 40%.

The result of fuzzy inference WK = 8 months. The obtained result is higher than the penalty set by the judge. The judge set a penalty of 4 months.

Judgment of the District Court in Bielsko Podlaskie City in Poland

Convicted criminal regularly robbed the store in which he worked.

The input values of the model determined by the expert:

SC = 25%, SDO = 50%, MT = 60%, HPC = 80%,
SS = 40%, SDP = 50%, STS = 70%, STW = 90%.

The result of fuzzy inference WK = 12 months. The obtained result is the same as the penalty set by the judge.

5.2   Theft with a Break-In

The minimum size of penalty is 12 months and the maximum is 120 months. Based on the analysis of court verdicts, the maximum sentence was adjusted to 30 months.

Judgment of the District Court in Legionowo City in Poland

Convicted criminal broke into the car and stole it. The stolen car was noticed by the police, the convicted criminal did not stop at the call of the police. During the escape he caused a collision; after the collision the convicted criminal continued to escape from the police.

The input values of the model determined by the expert:

SC = 45%, SDO = 10%, MT = 50%, HPC = 20%,
SS = 20%, SDP = 30%, STS = 70%, STW = 80%.

The result of fuzzy inference WK = 25 months. The obtained result is higher than the penalty set by the judge. The judge set a penalty of 24 months.

5.3   Causing Serious Health Detriment

The minimum size of penalty is 12 months and the maximum is 120 months. Based on the analysis of court verdicts, the maximum sentence was adjusted to 36 months.

Judgment of the District Court in Slupsk. Convicted criminal struck the victim twice with a knife and walked away without giving him help. As a result of the incident, the victim was left with permanent mutilations. The convicted criminal committed the crime immediately after his release from prison.

The input values of the model determined by the expert:

$SC = 50\%$, $SDO = 10\%$, $MT = 50\%$, $HPC = 80\%$,
$SS = 50\%$, $SDP = 60\%$, $STS = 70\%$, $STW = 70\%$.

The result of fuzzy inference $WK = 29$ months. The obtained result is lower than the penalty set by the judge. The judge set a penalty of 30 months.

5.4   Fraud

The minimum size of penalty is 6 months and the maximum is 96 months. Based on the analysis of court verdicts, the maximum sentence was adjusted to 30 months.

Judgment of the District Court in Wroclaw-Krzyki. On the basis of a false certificate of work convicted criminal obtained a loan from the bank, to buy a car, and then simulated a collision and theft of a car.

The input values of the model determined by the expert:

$SC = 50\%$, $SDO = 50\%$, $MT = 50\%$, $HPC = 20\%$,
$SS = 50\%$, $SDP = 50\%$, $STS = 20\%$, $STW = 50\%$.

The result of fuzzy inference $WK = 15$ months. The obtained result is higher than the penalty set by the judge. The judge set a penalty of 8 months.

Judgment of the District Court in Wroclaw-Fabryczna. Convicted criminal had a managerial function in a brokerage house, cheated a group of investors, significantly and unjustifiably overstating the value of the company, which had little value. The damage of investors exceeded 1 million euros.

The input values of the model determined by the expert:

$SC = 75\%$, $SDO = 50\%$, $MT = 60\%$, $HPC = 20\%$,
$SS = 50\%$, $SDP = 50\%$, $STS = 90\%$, $STW = 60\%$.

The result of fuzzy inference $WK = 24$ months. The obtained result is the same as the penalty set by the judge.

6   Conclusions

The presented model showed logical relations resulting from the Polish KK in relation to the size of the punishment. Due to the assumed limitations, the structure of the model can be extended in further research. First of all, the model can be extended with the rules of inference taking into account the general and special prevention conditions as well as many other special regulations contained in the law code. The next stages of research, however, require going beyond the resources defined in KK. A large part of the rules resulting from the decisions made is a personal decision of the judge. Research work in this area requires direct cooperation with the judges legal profession and an attempt to define rules that are developed by these group of experts and are not explicitly described in the law. In this context, the presented proposal can be used as a voice in the discussion on the justice of the judge's decisions and his impartiality and independence. These features are a constitutional requirement for the judge. Therefore, the question can be asked whether one can speak of a just sentence if there are no clearly established rules for the sentence, and many are left to the judge himself, not only to assess the premises but also to their weight and impact on the final sentence. Meanwhile, the punishment is left to the recognition of the judge himself, who assesses not only the legal prerequisites but also their weight and influence on the final infliction of punishment. Therefore, the question can be asked whether it is possible to speak of a just sentence if there are no clearly established rules for the size of punishment.

References

1. Bojarski, M., Giezek, J., Sienkiewicz, Z.: Prawo karne materialne. Cześć ogólna i szczególna. Material criminal law. General and detailed part. Wolters Kluwer (2004)
2. Katz, D.M., Bommarito II, M.J., Blackman, J.: A general approach for predicting the behavior of the supreme court of the united states. PLOS ONE **12**(4), 1–18 (2017). https://doi.org/10.1371/journal.pone.0174698
3. Lower, M., Lower, A.: Evaluation of the location of the P&R facilities using fuzzy logic rules. In: Zamojski, W., Mazurkiewicz, J., Sugier, J., Walkowiak, T., Kacprzyk, J. (eds.) Theory and Engineering of Complex Systems and Dependability, vol. 365, pp. 255–264. Springer, Cham (2015). https://doi.org/10.1007/978-3-319-19216-1_24
4. Lower, M., Lower, A.: Determining the criteria for setting input parameters of the fuzzy inference model of P&R car parks locating. In: Nguyen, N.T., Iliadis, L., Manolopoulos, Y., Trawiński, B. (eds.) Computational Collective Intelligence, vol. 9875, pp. 239–248. Springer, Cham (2016). https://doi.org/10.1007/978-3-319-45243-2_22
5. Markiewicz, Ł., Markiewicz-Żuchowska, A.: Skłonności poznawcze sedziego wpływające na wysokość wymierzonej kary. Cognitive inclinations of the judge affecting the size of the penalty. Central Eur. J. Soc. Sci. Hum. **18**(3), 49–82 (2012)
6. Prakken, H.: AI & Law, logic and argument schemes. Argumentation **19**(3), 303–320 (2005). https://doi.org/10.1007/s10503-005-4418-7
7. Verheij, B.: Logic, context and valid inference - or: can there be a logic of law? (1999)
8. Zakrzewski, P.: Stopniowanie winy w prawie karnym. Graduation of guilt in criminal law. Wolters Kluwer (2015)

Research Methodology Trending
in Evolutionary Computing

Siti Mariam Shahar, Muhamad Yusnorizam Ma'arif[(✉)],
Mohd Fikri Hafifi Yusof, and Nurhizam Safie Mohd Satar

Research Center for Software Technology and Management (SOFTAM),
Faculty of Information Science and Technology (FTSM),
Universiti Kebangsaan Malaysia, Bangi, Malaysia
{p89063,p89058,p88760}@siswa.ukm.edu.my,
nurhizam@ukm.edu.my

Abstract. This article presents an exhaustive review of these studies and suggests a direction for future studies in the IS domain. Research Methodology Trending in Enterprise Architecture (EA), Information Technology Shared Services (ITSS) and Enterprise Resource Planning System (ERP) fields from 2014 until early 2019 was identified applied from the three research methods; qualitative, quantitative and mixed-method is investigated by a numerical study. The results also show that the IS field research in the past 5 years was not focused on one method, it covers quantitative, qualitative, and even mixed methods. The field of ERP study has matured, but not in the EA and ITSS fields. It was found that most studies in EA and ITSS fields focus on qualitative methods to create relevant theories in this field. A different approach of analysis technique in the IS domain for future research are recommended.

Keywords: Enterprise Resource Planning · Enterprise Architecture ·
Information Technology Shared Services · Information System

1 Introduction

In recent years, there has been an increasing interest in research methodology trending in Information System (IS) system. The knowledge of the research methodology in conducting a study in IS is important to ensure that the research adheres to the right ethics of academic writing. It will be a reference for future researchers. Research can be categorized into three different areas, which is Qualitative, Quantitative and Mixed-Method. Quantitative research is based on the measurement of quantity or amount. It is applicable to phenomena that can be expressed in terms of quantity [1]. The qualitative research approach is normally used where knowledge about the problem domain is rare and rather unstructured [2]. While the mixed-method designs were used to complement the depth of understanding afforded by the qualitative methods with the breadth of understanding afforded by the quantitative methods [3]. The past decade has seen the rapid development of research methods on information systems in many areas. In this paper, the authors have studied the research methodology trending in IS comprises of Enterprise Architecture (EA), Information Technology Shared Services (ITSS) and Enterprise Resource Planning System (ERP).

© Springer Nature Switzerland AG 2019
N. T. Nguyen et al. (Eds.): ICCCI 2019, LNAI 11683, pp. 474–485, 2019.
https://doi.org/10.1007/978-3-030-28377-3_39

2   Review of Literature

There are numerous studies in the literature reporting about the methodology used in conducting IS research using the three methods as stated. Literature review, in any academic field, is considered to be useful to give a good look at the whole research field, to highlight the important studies, and to pinpoint the potential opportunity for future research [4]. During the past 10 years, much more information has become available on the indexed journal database including Scopus, Web of Science (WoS), IEEE, Springer and many more. In recent years, there has been an increasing amount of literature on EA, ITSS, and ERP research that apply a variety of research methods by using more sophisticated research instruments. A number of study analyses have examined the research finding using qualitative/quantitative approach only, sometimes there is a combination of qualitative and quantitative approach or mixed-method that has been used to interpret the research data. Authors provide in-depth analysis of the IS research methodology trending in the field of EA, ITSS, and ERP for the past 5 years as described in Tables 1, 2 and 3 in the next paragraph.

2.1   Enterprise Architecture (EA)

IS defined as a systemic approach that administers and delivers infrastructure, as well as develops and supports applications [5]. IS had been used as how information technology in an organization manages and apply and help management of the organization in making a decision where information was powerful input to make a decision. Since management required information technology to support organization businesses and vice versa, an organization need to align their business and information technology. For that, nowadays many organizations had embarked EA in their organization where EA is a tool that can align business and information technology. Therefore, many researchers had shown interest in the implementation of EA either in the public or private sector. Table 1 of Research Methodology Trending in EA Fields show numerous studies regarding EA from 2014 until early of 2019.

Table 1.   Research Methodology Trending in EA Fields.

Research method	Analysis	Number of papers	Authors
Qualitative	Content/Thematic Analysis	13	[6–18]
	Delphi/Fuzzy Delphi	2	[19, 20]
	Others/Not Mentioned	2	[21, 22]
Quantitative	Others/Not Mentioned	1	[23]
Mixed method	SPSS	1	[24]
	Others	2	[25, 26]

2.2 Information Technology Shared Services (ITSS)

Evolution of ICT from management perspective can be depicted as a change of strategy from standalone, distributed, centralized/decentralized and now towards shared services. Shared services have implemented in public and private sector across the nation. This strategy becomes a prominent decision to achieve cost efficiency and improve service performance motives [27]. Managing of ITSS should not be treated as conventional management and need serious attention from the shared services organization. According to [28], *"There must be real competition for the services, and not simply lip service demands…Real competition for business from outside vendors is the pressure that keeps shared services competitive, forcing management and employees to keep up with best practices, and motivating employees to keep customers delighted, as opposed to simply satisfied".*

Recently, researchers have shown an increased interest in shared services. Research on shared services focuses on human resources, finance, health and Information Technology. We realized that shared services research in IS start getting attention after comprehensive review focusing on shared services in IS by [29]. Literature from 2014 till March 2019 shows that only 13 studies have included ITSS as part of their discussion and 7 papers that study specifically on ITSS. Table 2 summarizes the research methodology and analysis used for ITSS study.

Table 2. Information Technology Shared Services (ITSS).

Research method	Analysis	Number of papers	Authors
Qualitative	Content/Thematic Analysis	10	[29–38]
	Case study analysis	2	[39, 40]
	Others/Not Mentioned	1	[41]
Quantitative	Hierarchical Linear Model	1	[42]

2.3 Enterprise Resource Planning (ERP)

Previous studies have not primarily concentrated on ERP implementation in general, but focuses on ERP in Pre-Implementation, during implementation as well as Post-implementation phase. Researchers have also studied the effect of ERP usage on performance evaluation with other mediator's element like Knowledge Management and Incentives [43]. Numerous studies have attempted to explain the ERP research trending using a different methodology in the past 5 years. The author traces the research of ERP fields and demonstrates the finding in Table 3 of Research Methodology Trending in ERP fields from 2014 until early 2019.

Table 3. Research Methodology Trending in ERP Fields.

Research method	Analysis	Number of papers	Authors
Qualitative	Content/Thematic Analysis	2	[44, 45]
	Delphi/Fuzzy Delphi	1	[46]
	Case study analysis	6	[47–52]
	Others/Not Mentioned	1	[53]
Quantitative	Content/Thematic Analysis	5	[4, 54–57]
	Smart-PLS	6	[58–63]
	SPSS	3	[64–66]
	Others/Not Mentioned	3	[67–69]
Mixed method	Delphi/Fuzzy Delphi	3	[70–72]

3 Methodology

The criteria for choosing journals for the review are as follows. First of all, the journal must have been published in a peer-review and proprietary journal. Second, to avoid never-ending revision of the journal, 24 March 2019 was selected as the cut-off date (Literature start from 2014). Third, only the journal/articles relevance to 'EA', 'ITSS' and 'ERP' were selected. There are restrictions were imposed on the field of the surveyed journal. This should allow a comprehensive set of viewpoints on IS research by the EA, ITSS and ERP fields. According to these criteria, an attempt has been made to collect all the available journal articles. The effort to compile has been carried out through an exhaustive journal database search. However, it is always possible that some of the articles are missing from this list. The complete list of the 65 journals along with the number of articles and proceeding appeared in each journal is found in Tables 1, 2 and 3 in the previous paragraph.

4 Finding and Analysis

The most striking result to emerge from the data is that authors find that the IS field research in the past 5 years is not focused on one method; it covers quantitative, qualitative, and even mixed methods that have been used. It is apparent from the table that very few types of research in EA and ITSS fields were conducted using quantitative and mixed-method approach. The figures shown in the next paragraph Sects. 4.1, 4.2 and 4.3 is quite revealing in several ways. First, unlike the previous tables of literature, the analysis indicates the research finding in graphical views as shown in Figs. 1 and 2 below. Second, the data from these figures can be compared among others from a different perspective of EA, ITSS, and ERP, which shows the research methodology trending, and analysis tools used from 2014 until early 2019.

Figure 1 exhibits research methodology trending in EA, ERP and ITSS from 2014 until early 2019 that includes qualitative, quantitative and mixed-method.

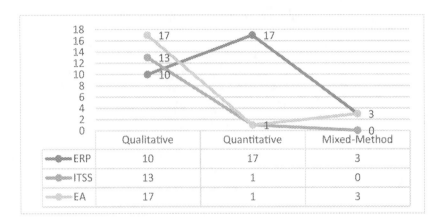

Fig. 1. Research methodology trending in EA, ITSS, and ERP in 2014 until 2019

Figure 2 Exhibits analysis trending in EA, ERP and ITSS from 2014 until early 2019, which includes Content/Thematic Analysis, Delphi/Fuzzy Delphi, Smart-PLS, SPSS, Case Study Analysis, Hierarchical Linear Model and Others/Not Mentioned. The following section discussed finding specifically according to EA, ERP, and ITSS.

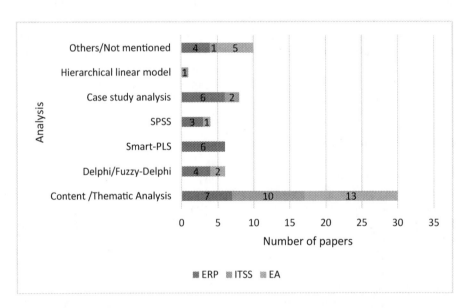

Fig. 2. The analysis used in EA, ITSS and ERP research in 2014 until 2019

4.1   EA Research Trending

From the data that had been analyzed via the literature review as shown in Fig. 1, 17 out of 21 literature implemented qualitative methods in doing their research about the implementation of EA. Qualitative research had been implemented by researchers because they can gain an in-depth understanding about the phenomenon regarding EA implementation where they are able to understand, explain, explore, discover and clarify situations, feelings, perceptions, attitudes, values, beliefs and experience of research subject [9, 20].

For the research analysis by the researcher in the EA study as Fig. 2, it shows that content/thematic analysis are most popular analysis used by the researcher where 13 out of 21 kinds of literature had used content/thematic analysis in their study. Since lots of issues and challenges in implementing EA still be studied by the researchers, by doing the content/thematic analysis, the researchers can identify themes to address the research and highlight the issues.

4.2   ITSS Research Trending

Figure 1 shows that qualitative methods become the popular choice for ITSS study. We can see that only one out of 13 kinds of literature using the quantitative method and none for the mixed method. This is proof that the study in this field still at the early stage [32]. Normally the most frequency methods used in the early stage of new research using exploratory or longitudinal study. Moreover, a case study is the most appropriate method to study in-depth for a new research field. We believe that more qualitative study will come and quantitative/mixed methods study will start extensively in the near future.

Almost all of the ITSS study using the qualitative method, so the content/thematic analysis is the most popular analysis used. Most of the study using a qualitative method by a case study where interviews and observation are the top methods implemented. Furthermore, ITSS research focuses on public education institution. We conclude that research on IT shared services still inadequate and numerous scope needs to be explored in future research using a variety of analysis technique.

4.3   ERP Research Trending

From this data, we can see that the trend of applying qualitative and quantitative methods in ERP study is 10 and 17 kinds of literature respectively. Figure 1, however, shows that only 3 out of 30 works of literature that used mixed-method in their ERP research. This is really unexpected results as the research of ERP systems should involve surveys against ERP users themselves, but the critical ERP expert views are also desirable to be addressed in accordance with unstructured nature of qualitative methods.

The analysis used in ERP research methodology from 2014 until early 2019 are presented in Fig. 2. As shown in the figure, there are several types of research analysis used in the previous study like Content/Thematic Analysis, Delphi/Fuzzy-Delphi, Smart-PLS, SPSS, Case Study Analysis and Others/Not Mentioned. It appears from

Fig. 2 that, other various analysis as not described like the first five analysis also a popular way among the researchers. This kind of analysis indicates 4 times used out of 30 pieces of literature in the past 5 years. The least used analysis in that period was SPSS, which is 3. Content/Thematic Analysis, Smart-PLS, and Case Study Analysis became trending in ERP research, which was 7, 6 and 6 studies out of 30 pieces of literature respectively during the same period.

5   Future Research Direction and Challenges

The single most striking observation to emerge from the data comparison was that the methods choose in IS research on EA, ITSS, and ERP is very limited. Future research in IS for those research should use more on other analysis methods such as Delphi, Fuzzy Delphi, SPSS and Smart-PLS. These findings suggest that most study in IS focusing on one single method, it is time for the new research in IS to adopt more on a mixed method in the study.

The author found that EA is about the architecture consist of alignment of business and IT to achieve organization goals and ITSS are about sharing of IT services such as network infrastructure, data center, and applications for the enterprise business. It is recommended that further research be undertaken in broad areas like how EA can improve ITSS, which both are about services for the enterprise.

This research has thrown up many questions in need of further investigation. Further work needs to be done to establish whether the similarity and differences exist in the research and whether similar challenges appear in its implementation. Other than that, the author also found that ERP is one type of ITSS application but none of the studies on ITSS specifically discusses ERP. The author also found that EA could embark to ERP as a transformation tool to improve ERP as a digital transformation to the businesses.

6   Conclusion and Limitation

This study set out to determine research methodology trending in evolutionary computing from the IS domain. Based on the findings in this paper, we conclude that the field of ERP study has matured, there are many studies in various methods and analyses have been and are in progress, followed by the EA and ITSS fields. The use of quantitative methods has shown that research theories in this field have been developed. The EA and ITSS fields are considered as new fields in evolutionary computing, which are still in the initial stages. Most studies have been conducted qualitatively to create relevant theories.

This study has found that there is a limitation in the IS domain. There are only three areas in the IS domain are studied in this paper. The scope of the study only covers literature from 2014 to early 2019. In this investigation, only a methodology analysis and analytical tools were used to measure the trend resulting from the IS research. These findings provide the following insights for future research; more research opportunities can be further explored especially in EA and ITSS, especially in Asian countries where it still can research more. A different approach of analysis technique in the IS domain should be carried out to find a significant output that emerges from the study in the field of EA, ITSS, and ERP.

Acknowledgment. The study is financially supported by the Public Service Department of Malaysia.

References

1. Kothari, C.R.: Research Methodology - Method and Techniques. New Age International Publishers (2004)
2. Elragal, A., Haddara, M.: The impact of ERP partnership formation regulations on the failure of ERP implementations. Procedia Technol. **9**, 527–535 (2013). https://doi.org/10.1016/j. protcy.2013.12.059
3. Palinkas, L.A., Horwitz, S.M., Green, C.A., Wisdom, J.P., Duan, N., Hoagwood, K.: Purposeful sampling for qualitative data collection and analysis in mixed method implementation research. Adm. Policy Ment. Heal. Ment. Heal. Serv. Res. **42**, 533–544 (2013). https://doi.org/10.1007/s10488-013-0528-y
4. Huang, T., Yasuda, K.: Comprehensive review of literature survey articles on ERP. Bus. Process Manag. J. **22**, 2–32 (2016). https://doi.org/10.1108/BPMJ-12-2014-0122
5. Canada, T.: Enterprise Architecture Transformation Process from a Federal Government Perspective : A Qualitative Case Study (2016)
6. Gong, Y., Janssen, M.: The value of and myths about enterprise architecture. Int. J. Inf. Manag. **46**, 1–9 (2019). https://doi.org/10.1016/j.ijinfomgt.2018.11.006
7. Ansyori, R., Qodarsih, N., Soewito, B.: A systematic literature review: critical success factors to implement enterprise architecture. Procedia Comput. Sci. **135**, 43–51 (2018). https://doi.org/10.1016/j.procs.2018.08.148
8. Hussein, S.S., et al.: Towards designing an EA readiness instrument: a systematic review. In: 2016 4th IEEE International Colloquium on Information Science and Technology, pp. 158–163 (2016). https://doi.org/10.1109/cist.2016.7805034
9. Dang, D., Pekkola, S.: Institutionalising enterprise architecture in the public sector in vietnam (2016)
10. Olsen, D.H., Trelsgård, K.: Enterprise architecture adoption challenges: an exploratory case study of the norwegian higher education sector. Procedia Comput. Sci. **100**, 804–811 (2016). https://doi.org/10.1016/j.procs.2016.09.228
11. Kotusev, S.: Enterprise architecture: a reconceptualization is needed/Kotusev enterprise architecture: a reconceptualization is needed. Pacific Asia J. Assoc. Inf. Syst. **10**, 1–36 (2018). https://doi.org/10.17705/1PAIS.10401
12. Hussein, S.S., Mahrin, M.N., Maarop, N.: Preliminary study of Malaysian Public Sector (MPS) transformation readiness through Enterprise Architecture (EA) establishment. In: 21st Pacific Asia Conference on Information System (PACIS 2017), pp. 1–12 (2017)
13. Dang, D.D., Pekkola, S.: Problems of enterprise architecture adoption in the public sector: root causes and some solutions. In: Rusu, L., Viscusi, G. (eds.) Information Technology Governance in Public Organizations. ISIS, vol. 38, pp. 177–198. Springer, Cham (2017). https://doi.org/10.1007/978-3-319-58978-7_8
14. Abd Rahim, Y., Safie, N.: Enterprise architecture framework: basics and ideas for selection. MALTESAS Multi-Discipl. Res. J. **2**, 37–46 (2017)

15. Bhattacharya, P.: Modelling strategic alignment of business and IT through enterprise architecture: augmenting archimate with BMM. Procedia Comput. Sci. **121**, 80–88 (2017). https://doi.org/10.1016/j.procs.2017.11.012

16. Bakar, N.A.A., Selamat, H., Kama, N.: Investigating enterprise architecture implementation in enterprise public sector organisation investigating architecture implementation in public sector organisation. In: International Conference on Computer and Information Sciences (ICCOINS 2016). pp. 1–6, Kuala Lumpur (2016)

17. Hussein, S.S., Mahrin, M.N., Ismail, Z.: Towards readiness in Enterprise Architecture establishment : a critical success factors. In: Postgraduate Annual Research on Informatics Seminar (2016)

18. Hussein, S.S., Ismail, Z., Mat Taib, M.Z.: Towards sustainability of EA practices: a systematic review. In: First International Conference on ICT for Transformation 2016 (2016)

19. Hussein, S.S., Mahrin, M.N., Maarop, N.: Sustainability through innovations of Enterprise Architecture (EA) in public sector's management: issues & challenges. J. Southeast Asian Res. **2017**, 1–13 (2017). https://doi.org/10.5171/2017.722027

20. Hussein, S.S., Ismail, Z., Mahrin, M.N.: EA innovations in managing public sectors: issues & challenges. Innov. Manag. Educ. Excell. Vis. 2020 From Reg. Dev. Sustain. Glob. Econ. Growth **I–Vi**, 3498–3505 (2016)

21. Julia, K., Kurt, S., Ulf, S.: Challenges in Integrating Product-IT into Enterprise Architecture - a case study. Procedia Comput. Sci. **121**, 525–533 (2017). https://doi.org/10.1016/j.procs.2017.11.070

22. Rijo, R., Martinho, R., Ermida, D.: Developing an enterprise architecture proof of concept in a Portuguese hospital. Procedia Comput. Sci. **64**, 1217–1225 (2015). https://doi.org/10.1016/j.procs.2015.08.511

23. Abd Rahim, Y., Mohamad, M., Safie, N., Rahim@Ab Rasim, Z.: Faktor Kejayaan Kritikal, Cabaran Serta Kebaikan Pelaksanaan Seni Bina Perusahaan (EA) Dalam Agensi Awam Malaysia. MALTESAS Multi-Discipl. Res. J. **3**, 62–71 (2018)

24. Bakar, N.A.A., Selamat, H., Kama, N.: Enterprise architecture implementation model: measurement from experts and practitioner perspectives. In: Colloquium on Information Science and Technology Cist, pp. 1–6 (2016). https://doi.org/10.1109/cist.2016.7804849

25. Hussein, S.S., Ismail, Z., Mahrin, M.N.: EA governance towards sustainability of EA practices in digital government: a systematic review. J. Teknol. (Sci. Eng.) **72**, 1–6 (2015)

26. Bakar, N.A.A., Selamat, H., Kama, N.: Assessment of Enterprise Architecture implementation capability and priority in public sector agency. Procedia Comput. Sci. **100**, 198–206 (2016). https://doi.org/10.1016/j.procs.2016.09.141

27. McIvor, R., McCracken, M., McHugh, M.: Creating outsourced shared services arrangements: Lessons from the public sector. Eur. Manag. J. **29**, 448–461 (2011). https://doi.org/10.1016/j.emj.2011.06.001

28. Bergeron, B.: Essentials of Shared Services. Wiley, Hoboken (2003)

29. Fielt, E., Gable, G.: Exploring shared services from an IS perspective: a literature review and research agenda. Commun. Assoc. Inf. Syst. **34**, 54 (2014)

30. Olsen, T., Welke, R.: Managerial challenges to realizing IT shared services in a public university. Transform. Gov. People Process Policy (2019). https://doi.org/10.1108/tg-04-2018-0030

31. Hashim, N.M., Ali, N.M., Abdullah, N.S., Miskon, S., Huspi, S.H.: Success factors Model for ICT shared services. Int. Conf. Res. Innov. Inf. Syst. ICRIIS (2017). https://doi.org/10.1109/icriis.2017.8002503

32. Richter, P.C., Brühl, R.: Shared service center research: a review of the past, present, and future. Eur. Manag. J. **35**, 26–38 (2017). https://doi.org/10.1016/j.emj.2016.08.004

33. Hafizi, R., Rahman, A.A., Miskon, S., Ali, N.M., Abdullah, N.S., Huspi, S.H.: Transformation of shared service typology arrangement using Watson ans Mundy's E-Government Framework. In: 21st Pacific Asia Conference on Information System (PACIS 2017), pp. 1–14 (2017)

34. Miskon, S., Bandara, W., Fielt, E.: Understanding the benefits of IT shared services: insights from the Higher Education sector. In: Pacific Asia Conference on Information Systems (PACIS 2017), pp. 16–20 (2017)

35. Yusof, A.F., et al.: Drivers influencing shared services adoption. J. Theor. Appl. Inf. Technol. **90**, 93–100 (2016)

36. Paagman, A., Tate, M., Furtmueller, E., De Bloom, J.: An integrative literature review and empirical validation of motives for introducing shared services in government organizations. Int. J. Inf. Manage. **35**, 110–123 (2015). https://doi.org/10.1016/j.ijinfomgt.2014.10.006

37. Knol, A., Janssen, M., Sol, H.: A taxonomy of management challenges for developing shared services arrangements. Eur. Manag. J. **32**, 91–103 (2014). https://doi.org/10.1016/j.emj.2013.02.006

38. Ulbrich, F., Schulz, V.: Seven challenges management must overcome when implementing IT-shared services. Strateg. Outsourcing **7**, 94–106 (2014). https://doi.org/10.1108/SO-12-2013-0024

39. Tammel, K.: Shared services and cost reduction motive in the public sector. Int. J. Public Adm. **40**, 792–804 (2017). https://doi.org/10.1080/01900692.2016.1204617

40. Zilic, T., Cosic, V.: Implementing shared service center in telecom environment as more efficient and more cost effective business model. In: 2016 39th International Convention on Information and Communication Technology, Electronics and Microelectronics MIPRO 2016 – Proceedings, pp. 716–719 (2016). https://doi.org/10.1109/mipro.2016.7522234

41. Elston, T., MacCarthaigh, M.: Sharing services, saving money? Five risks to cost-saving when organizations share services. Public Money Manag. **36**, 349–356 (2016). https://doi.org/10.1080/09540962.2016.1194081

42. Aldag, A.M., Warner, M.: Cooperation, not cost savings: explaining duration of shared service agreements. Local Gov. Stud. **44**, 350–370 (2018). https://doi.org/10.1080/03003930.2017.1411810

43. Ma'arif, M.Y., Mohd Satar, N.S., Valbir Singh, D.S.: A mediating effect on ERP KM model for the performance of oil and gas sector in Klang Valley: a preliminary study. Press, pp. 1–9 (2019)

44. Jayawickrama, U., Liu, S., Hudson Smith, M.: Empirical evidence of an integrative knowledge competence framework for ERP systems implementation in UK industries. Comput. Ind. **82**, 205–223 (2016). https://doi.org/10.1016/j.compind.2016.07.005

45. Chayakonvikom, M., Fuangvut, P., Prinyapol, N.: The incompatibility of end-user learning styles and the current ERP training approach. Int. J. Inf. Educ. Technol. **6**, 481–487 (2016). https://doi.org/10.7763/IJIET.2016.V6.736

46. Parhizkar, M., Comuzzi, M.: Impact analysis of ERP post-implementation modifications: design, tool support and evaluation. Comput. Ind. **84**, 25–38 (2017). https://doi.org/10.1016/j.compind.2016.11.003

47. Phaphoom, N., Qu, J., Kheaksong, A., Saelee, W.: An investigation of ERP implementation: a comparative case study of SME and large enterprises in Thailand. In: 2018 16th International Conference on ICT and Knowledge Engineering (ICT&KE), pp. 1–6. IEEE (2019)

48. de Almeida, A.R., Pelarin, A.L.: Use oral history of in the analysis of the evolution of the ERP system in the manufacturer. Rev. Eletrônica Gestão e Serviços **9**, 2496–2511 (2018). https://doi.org/10.15603/2177-7284/regs.v9n2p2496-2511

49. Maas, J.B., van Fenema, P.C., Soeters, J.: ERP as an organizational innovation: key users and cross-boundary knowledge management. J. Knowl. Manag. **20**, 557–577 (2016). https://doi.org/10.1108/JKM-05-2015-0195

50. Ajer, A.K., Hustad, E.: Enterprise system implementation in a franchise context: an action case study. Procedia Comput. Sci. **64**, 948–956 (2015). https://doi.org/10.1016/j.procs.2015.08.612

51. Haddara, M.: ERP selection: the SMART way. Procedia Technol. **16**, 394–403 (2014). https://doi.org/10.1016/j.protcy.2014.10.105

52. Gajic, G., Stankovski, S., Ostojic, G., Tesic, Z., Miladinovic, L.: Method of evaluating the impact of ERP implementation critical success factors – a case study in oil and gas industries. Enterp. Inf. Syst. **8**, 84–106 (2014). https://doi.org/10.1080/17517575.2012.690105

53. Abdinnour, S., Saeed, K.: User perceptions towards an ERP system: comparing the post-implementation phase to the pre-implementation phase Sue. J. Enterp. Inf. Manag. **28**, 243–259 (2015). https://doi.org/10.1108/mrr-09-2015-0216

54. Motahar, S.M., Mukhtar, M., Safie, N., Ma'arif, M.Y., Mostafavi, S.: Towards a product independent ERP training model: an insight from a literature review. Australas. J. Inf. Syst. **22**, 1–18 (2018). https://doi.org/10.3127/ajis.v22i0.1537

55. Jagoda, K., Samaranayake, P.: An integrated framework for ERP system implementation. Int. J. Account. Inf. Manag. **25**, 91–109 (2017). https://doi.org/10.1108/IJAIM-04-2016-0038

56. Ali, M., Miller, L.: ERP system implementation in large enterprises – a systematic literature review. J. Enterp. Inf. Manag. **30**, 666–692 (2017). https://doi.org/10.1108/JEIM-07-2014-0071

57. Ali, M., Nasr, E.S., Geith, M.: Benefits and challenges of cloud ERP systems - a systematic literature review. Future Comput. Inform. J. **1**, 1–9 (2017). https://doi.org/10.1016/j.fcij.2017.03.003

58. AlBar, A.M., Hoque, M.R.: Factors affecting cloud ERP adoption in Saudi Arabia: an empirical study. Inf. Dev. **35**, 150–164 (2019). https://doi.org/10.1177/0266666917735677

59. Gill, A.A., Shahzad, A., Ramalu, S.S.: Examine the influence of enterprise resource planning quality dimensions on organizational performance mediated through business process change capability. Glob. Bus. Manag. Rev. **10**, 41–57 (2018)

60. Nwankpa, J.K.: ERP system usage and benefit: a model of antecedents and outcomes. Comput. Human Behav. **45**, 335–344 (2015). https://doi.org/10.1016/j.chb.2014.12.019

61. Rajan, C.A., Baral, R.: Adoption of ERP system: an empirical study of factors influencing the usage of ERP and its impact on end user. IIMB Manag. Rev. **27**, 105–117 (2015). https://doi.org/10.1016/j.iimb.2015.04.008

62. Ha, Y.M., Ahn, H.J.: Factors affecting the performance of Enterprise Resource Planning (ERP) systems in the post-implementation stage. Behav. Inf. Technol. **33**, 1065–1081 (2014). https://doi.org/10.1080/0144929X.2013.799229

63. Fatimee, S., Shah, M.U., Hussain, S.: Impact of enterprise resource planning implementation on supply chain efficiencies: a case of telecom sector. J. Basic Appl. Sci. Res. **4**, 20–30 (2014)

64. Ma'arif, M.Y., Motahar, S.M., Mohd Satar, N.S.: A descriptive statistical based analysis on perceptual of ERP training needs. In: Proceedings of 2018 International Conference on Engineering, Science, and Application (ICESA 2018), pp. 46–62 (2018)

65. Jinno, H., Abe, H., Iizuka, K.: Consideration of ERP effectiveness: from the perspective of ERP implementation policy and operational effectiveness. Information **8** (2017). https://doi.org/10.3390/info8010014

66. Khoualdi, K., Basahel, A.: The impact of implementing SAP system on human resource management: application to Saudi Electricity Company. Int. J. Bus. Manag. **9**, 28–34 (2014). https://doi.org/10.5539/ijbm.v9n12p28
67. Harun, A., Mansor, Z.: Individual readiness for change in the pre-implementation phase of campus Enterprise Resource Planning (ERP) project in Malaysian Public University. Int. J. Adv. Comput. Sci. Appl. **10**, 128–134 (2019). https://doi.org/10.14569/ijacsa.2019.0100116
68. Ma'arif, M.Y., Mohd Satar, N.S.: ERP training mechanism for upskilling users and optimization of ERP system. Adv. Sci. Lett. **24**(5), 2908–2912 (2018). https://doi.org/10.1166/asl.2018.11092
69. Almgren, K., Bach, C.: ERP systems and their effects on organizations: a proposed scheme for ERP success. In: ASEE 2014 Zone I Conference, pp. 1–5 (2014)
70. Motahar, S.M., Mukhtar, M., Mohd Satar, N.S., Maarif, M.Y., Mostafavi, S.: Revisiting the diversification on the implementation of open source ERP teaching models. J. Adv. Res. Dyn. Control Syst. **10**, 2379–2385 (2018)
71. Mahendrawathi, E.R., Zayin, S.O., Pamungkas, F.J.: ERP post implementation review with process mining: a case of procurement process. Procedia Comput. Sci. **124**, 216–223 (2017). https://doi.org/10.1016/j.procs.2017.12.149
72. Shen, Y.C., Chen, P.S., Wang, C.H.: A study of enterprise resource planning (ERP) system performance measurement using the quantitative balanced scorecard approach. Comput. Ind. **75**, 127–139 (2016). https://doi.org/10.1016/j.compind.2015.05.006

Dynamic Airspace Configuration: A Short Review of Computational Approaches

Manuel Graña[⊠]

University of the Basque Country (UPV/EHU), Leioa, Spain
manuelgrana@ehu.es

Abstract. Ever growing commercial air traffic forces the development of new generation airspace management policies, computational resources, and avionics tracking and control hardware. The dynamic airspace configuration (DAC) proposes the continuous adaptation of air traffic management (ATM) parameters in order to cope with the changing traffic conditions in a setting of almost saturated control and airspace resources. The DAC has been tackled from simulation and combinatorial optimization points of view. Here we give a review of the literature and some hints about the challenges ahead.

1 Introduction

With the ever increasing density of air traffic, there is a pressing need for improved air traffic control (ATC) and air traffic management (ATM). The estimated growth of *en route* traffic in the European Union is 2.5% in the next seven years. Besides the conventional management of commercial and military airplane flight, new uses or airspace are appearing, such as drone delivery, personal air-transport vehicles in local areas, etcetera. For conventional ATM, a basic management unit is airspace sectorization: the airspace is usually divided into smaller regions referred to as sectors. Each sector is managed by one or several air traffic controllers (ATCo) whose role is to direct the flights to avoid conflict and optimize airspace use. So there is a direct link between sectorization and human workforce. As a consequence of the growing traffic, the existing controllers are working at the limit of their capacity. Hence, the National aeronautics and space administration (NASA) and the European Organization for the Safety of Air Navigation (Eurocontrol) are working on new ATM strategies of airspace dynamical organization and allocation to respond to changing air traffic imposed workload. At the same time, the political definition of airspaces is evolving to accommodate such overwhelming reality. An example of this evolution is the fusion of southwest European airspaces into a single block [16]. This kind of political decisions add even more flexibility to an already fluid situation.

In summary, the need for dynamic airspace configuration (DAC) rises from several fronts:

- The need to solve conflicting situations due to unforecasted events, such as weather, reentry of space objects [29], and others.

© Springer Nature Switzerland AG 2019
N. T. Nguyen et al. (Eds.): ICCCI 2019, LNAI 11683, pp. 486–497, 2019.
https://doi.org/10.1007/978-3-030-28377-3_40

- The steady increase in air traffic, which is also covering regions of the atmosphere previously free of traffic, such as cities and suburbs with the advent of personal air transportation and the proposed goods delivery via drones.
- The distribution of human resources in order to avoid overload and underload of the traffic controllers.

The call for DAC is not new. Linear dynamic modeling for trajectory optimization was proposed in the early 90's [4]. Studies about the feasibility of the dynamic shaping of airspace sectors were on the way by the turn of the century, already testing Genetic Algorithms (GA) [1,5,18], and modeling by Finite Element Methods (FEM) [18], and graph partitioning by evolutionary computation methods [6]. The problem of airspace management was even approached from the philosophical point of view of conflict resolution [8]. We try to summarize here the diverse computational approaches have been published in the following years. A recent review which cover similar topics is [13].

The intended contributions of this paper are the following: Firstly, we focus on the description of the research questions that drive the published works. In other words, we try to state in a consistent way how authors have formulated their motivations and research goals. Secondly, we provide an overview of the diverse computational approaches and algorithms that have been applied to attack these research questions. Thirdly, we extract as much information as possible from the papers regarding their use of available data and to what extent this data is publicly available for confirmation of results. Availability of data is very important, because it is the support for recommendations that, once they reach the political spheres, will have a major impact on the population. Fourthly, we summarize actual challenges and critical view of computational technologies that may be applied to attack them. Finally, we provide some conclusions.

2   Research Questions

There is a basic distinction between *en route* and terminal airspaces. The en route airspace control is concerned with flight trajectories that are straight with little turning points if any, and at constant altitude. On the other hand, terminal airspace contains approximation and departure trajectories at various altitudes and land operations, such as taxi operations. Some research efforts focus on the modeling of terminal airspace interactions, which are very complex in large airports like Beijing [15]. Metroplex areas are big cities served by several airports posing complex interactions between flight trajectories and controller resources [24].

A basic research objective is the minimization of workload differences among air traffic controller sectors [21,23,25,35]. Hence, the focus is on the availability and reliability of human resources. They try to minimize simultaneously the monitoring and coordination workload of the operators based on the dynamic density measure of traffic. Controllers have to monitor flights, avoid conflicts, and communicate with neighboring sectors the flights crossing from one sector to another. Monitoring workload is defined in terms of the number of flights crossing the sector, number of crossing points between flights, and flights with specific features, such as changing direction, altitude, or speed. The coordination workload is proportional to the number of flights departing from the sector towards neighboring sectors per unit of time. The constraints taken into account in the optimization problem are the minimum distance between crossing points and sector boundaries, and the deviation from the average workload across sectors, in an attempt to balance the workload across airspace. This goal is achieved as a minimization problem, where the stated workload goals are transformed into a cost function, sometimes considered as a multi-objective minimization problem. The cost function includes sector overloads, number of sectors, reconfiguration costs, workload imbalance, coordination and communication cost, expected delays, number of short crossings and reentries, and geometric features such as the so-called balconies and the proximity of critical points to a sector boundary. This optimization problem is formulated with some constraints, such as the convexity of the sectors, minimum sector crossing time, compactness and connectivity of the sectors, and bounds on the workload of the controllers. In some studies, the characteristics of the flight trajectories are of interest in order to show reduction of flight time and fuel consumption, which are a main concern of the air companies [16].

When considering that space sectorization is not static, an additional goal is the smooth transition between space sectorizations achieved in short time [9,25,38] in order to cope with the changing of traffic patterns. The time scale of the airspace planning is quite relevant to the computational approaches. The DAC usually refers to short time variations of schedule in response to events such as bad weather [13].

A more specific statement of purpose of the research efforts can be ascertained from the formal specification of the input/output maps defined by the computational algorithm. Inputs are often the time horizon for planning, the periods for reconfiguration, the structure of the airspace with specific detail of the sectors and units, the controller's schedule, while the expected outputs are often the new controller assignments and sector structures. Recent works try to provide individual trajectory specifications [14,21] in a very detailed time frame.

Finally, it is also relevant the dimensionality of the problem, either 2D, 3D or 4D. Planing in 2D contemplates only one plane of flight trajectories, while 3D planning contemplates diverse sector structures at various altitudes, a much tougher problem. 4D planning contemplates individual trajectory variations [17,20].

3   Computational Approaches

The computational issues of DAC have two basic aspects: the chosen representation of the problem and the specific computational algorithm.

3.1   Representation Approaches

The chosen representation is essential to the formulation of the problem. There are three basic approaches in the literature, which may be hybridized:

- Spatial region decomposition into small regular regions, i.e. hexagonal, which are merged into larger regions by clustering algorithms. Sectors are thus formed by aggregation of the basic regions. Quadrangular basic regions are considered in [26]. This is a representation akin to the occupancy maps used in robotics.
- Graph based partitions of the space, often based on Voronoi tessellations [7,35], or the dual Delaunay triangulation graphs. The sectors are obtained as subgraphs by means of graph partitioning algorithms. For instance, graph partitioning is used in [3] as follows. The airspace and the traffic supported is modelled as a weighted undirected graph whose nodes are the airports and waypoints, the weights correspond to the supported traffic in each voronoi region induced by the spatial localization of the nodes. The cuts algorithm provides the partition of the graph into subgraphs, and subsequent load balancing produces the desired optimized airspace configuration.
- Trajectories that model each individual flight path, in a multi-agent simulation approach. Air traffic is treated as a flow problem, defining the highways of the air. Sector controls are defined by aggregations of such individual trajectories [21].

3.2   Algorithmic Approaches

A critical computational tool is the ability to simulate operations at several spatial and temporal resolutions, by means of discrete event models at several granularities: airspace sectors [16] and airport terminal [15]. These models need calibration against real data that is provided by historical archives of the controller organization. The airspace management agencies have developed such general simulation tools, like the Network Strategic Tool (NEST) developed by the Eurocontrol, and the Airspace Concept Evaluation System (ACES)[1][2] developed by NASA. Such tools allow the definition of scenarios and the recording of diverse system performance metrics. ACES allows a very detailed simulation of the entire system based on event driven technology for agent simulation. It is possible to model all kinds of situations, such as the occurrence of weather conditions forcing trajectory changes [36]. An example of commercial simulator is AirTop[3]. Other approaches [33] model the time distributions of the approach trajectories from radar data in order to achieve air traffic flow simulation that they characterize into three states of controllability.

A recent proposed simulation environment [21] allows the detailed optimization of flight 4D trajectories in terms of operating cost, ecological costs, and

---

[1] https://software.nasa.gov/software/ARC-15068-1.

[2] https://ieeexplore.ieee.org/stamp/stamp.jsp?arnumber=5935378.

[3] http://www.airtopsoft.com/.

ATM criteria (separation infringement characteristics, operator workload). The so-called TOMATO system is composed of modules for cost computation, lateral trajectory optimization (using A* algorithm), and vertical profile optimization. It provides various assessments related to the considered costs (flight path characteristics, ecological metrics, key performance metrics) that can be used for decision making.

Another recent proposal of a simulation system that encompasses all aspects of the terminal management, including controller's cognitive issues, is proposed in [34]. The system is a multi-layer network encompassing the Route-based Airspace Network (RAN), Flight Trajectory Network (FTN), Integrated Flow-Driven Network (IFDN), and Interrelated Conflict-Communication Network (ICCN). RAN and FTN are developed to represent critical physical and operational characteristics. The metrics produced include chaotic behavior measures. The system is essentially a network dynamics analysis tool for the identification of critical regions of system operation.

The optimization of metroplex operations considered in [24] involves several components: the first component is a procedure for characterizing dynamic arrival and departure routes based on the spatiotemporal distributions of flights by means of clustering algorithms. The second component is an Analytic Hierarchy Process (AHP) model for the prioritization of the dynamic routes, which takes into account a set of quantitative and qualitative attributes important for MAS operations. It is achieved by greedy lexicographic multi-objective optimization taking into account separation between planes, spatial constraints (airspace restrictions, areas of convective weather), and aircraft performance. The third component is a priority-based method for the positioning of terminal waypoints as well as the design of three- dimensional, conflict-free terminal routes. Similar problem is tackled by [19] performing a multi-layer clustering analysis in order to mine spatial and temporal trends in flight trajectory data for identification of traffic flow patterns. Then, a multiway classification model is trained to generate probabilistic forecasts of the metroplex traffic flow structure for look-ahead times of up to eight hours. Finally, an empirical approach for arrival capacity estimation is proposed based on historical flow pattern behavior.

At the end of the day, DAC is an optimization problem, so much of the research effort is devoted to design and test computational optimization approaches. In some instances, linear programming has been applied [28,37], but the recent works are on the line of stochastic random search approaches, such as simulated annealing [12], swarm intelligence in the form of Particle Swarm Optimization (PSO) [10], and a wide spectrum of evolutionary algorithms. In fact, population based algorithms are the vast majority of approaches taken. Early approaches treated the problem as single-objective problem, with all the cost terms combined into a weighted expression [22,23]. A critical issue when applying genetic algorithms is the solution encoding into the chromosomes. Each approach has some specific encoding, which in turn requires specific definitions of the genetic operators (crossover, mutation, selection). As an example, in [22] each chromosome is composed of two layers of representations: one for the opened controlled sectors and their centers along the time periods, the other for the subsets of connected components *per* time period (a graph representation is used). The genetic operators are defined accordingly. This specificity poses some questions about convergence and operator completeness that are not addressed in the literature.

Recently, multi-objective optimization with constraints is increasingly applied. The classical NSGA-II multi-objective algorithm has been applied by several approaches. In [35] it is applied to the optimization of controller workload using over a Voronoi representation of the problem, where the chromosomes are composed of the Voronoi sites. In [27] it is applied for optimization of terminal airspace with environmental restrictions. Prediction of workload using artificial neural networks has been considered [11], predicted values *per* sector fall into three classes (low, acceptable, excessive). The workload prediction is then feed into a tree search algorithm for the best sectorization. This problem of indexing the traffic complexity has been also tackled using knowledge based representation approaches [2].

Aggregation of sectors has been considered from various perspectives: [30] states it as a traveling salesman problem (TSP), while other carry out clustering approaches. For instance, [22] applies k-means clustering to obtain a good initial state for the genetic algorithm searching. On the other hand, [3] carries out graph partitioning and afterwards relies on heuristic algorithm to obtain the best workload balancing of the aggregated subgraphs. In [31] graph partitioning is carried out by an iterative spectral bipartite method.

Heuristic approaches are proposed when the complexity of the problem can not be coped with traditional integer programming techniques, and the encoding into evolutionary algorithms is discarded. The objective in [37] is the minimization of the departure and arrival delays in a multi-airport system, subjected to flow constraints and the conventional management constraints, such as interference. The links in the network are aggregated in a bottom up process, and this aggregation is then used for the individual planning of trajectories. The variety of heuristic approaches includes the use of Petri Net modeling of the restrictions [17].

4   Validation

Real data is of critical importance for the assessment of the improvements introduced by the proposed approaches. In Europe, a source of data is the EUROCONTROL historical air traffic Data Demand Repository (DDR2) database. The data contains 33816 flights coordinated by the Network Manager Operations Center (NMOC, previously called CFMU) (Online. Available[4]). Beside flights to and from European airports, overflights above the European airspace are also included. The data is given as a SO6 m3 file containing departure and destination airports and an aircraft 4D segmented trajectory (position, altitude,

---

[4] http://www.eurocontrol.int/articles/ddr2-web-portal.

time stamps) synchronized by radar. Speeds are not provided. The vertical discretization of the flight plan amounts to 1000 ft (flight level) and the lateral resolution depends on waypoints and flight phase. The en-route phase resolution can be more than 100 NM but on average is 40 NM. The mean lateral resolution is less than 3 NM during climb and less than 10 NM during descent. Except for the amount between day and night traffic, an analysis of the flight plan yields no significant diurnal variation because of the multiple time zones within Europe spanning from Russia (GMT+5) to Portugal (GMT-1). A high number of short haul flights, namely 9673 (26% of all flights), are shorter than 500 km. This data has been used in recent publications for validation and as a reference value [16,21]. Other agencies provide data for other airspace, such as the Chinese [3,32,35,38] which has experienced the biggest growth in traffic.

The validation issue has been dealt with extensively in the context of machine learning model building, where it has become standard procedure. In the context of DAC it is a methodological question that is solved simplistically. The papers report the results of the simulations or the optimization algorithms, providing comparison with the actual metrics computed from the real data that may serve as validation and tuning reference. For instance, [21] reports results from three scenarios which correspond to different stakeholder interests: airline efficiency considering ecological and operational costs, contrail minimization, and reference scenario. The results are a discussion of the improvements achieved by the optimization. Similarly, in [16] results are mostly referring to operational cost improvements achieved by the new airspace block partition. In [34] results are visualizations of detected network dynamics and identification of some system operating regions which show some critical feature. In the case of automated resectorization, the reported results are the metric variations of the optimized versus the reference state. In [22] the goal is the minimization of the operator workload achieved by dynamic sector adaptation along the operating day. In [24] simulation is the mean to demonstrate the improvements introduced by the intended optimization of metroplex operations over example data from New York area, while in [37] simulation is used to demonstrate the advantages of the proposed heuristic planning.

5   Challenges

Currently, the most important challenge is political. The airspace is an essential part of national sovereignty which encompasses not only commercial value but great security value. Airspace is a military issue that will never be overlooked by the political authorities. It is also a law enforcement (police) issue, because it can be used for criminal purposes. The drug traffic is an outmost example. The tradeoff is therefore of national and social security versus economical development, and the increasing pressure of human and goods motion in a globally connected world. One critical issue is that the aircontrol needs to have accurate and continuously updated (at a resolution of minutes or even seconds) of the localization and state of the flying objects. This can be achieved partially with ground based radar, but increasingly it is the flying object itself that keeps track of its position by GPS sensors broadcasting it to the controllers. Therefore, "legal" flying objects pose a problem quite similar to the Internet of Things, in the broad sense of security. Problems such as identity theft and malware contamination would need to be taken into account in order to allow for secure ATC in a highly dense population of flying objects. Some works are directed nowadays to apply blockchain technology to this problem, allowing for the flying objects to trade automatically airspace concessions, such as securing availability flight trajectories. Secure flying object identity is another challenging issue so far untackled.

If we restrict our view to commercial passenger intercity/intercountry transport, these problems are not so pressing, because the number of planes is locally in the order of some hundred per day at much. Moreover, they use a region of high altitude space, with short corridors for landing and take-off. However, there is an huge number of drones sold for pleasure and gaming which can reach not so low altitudes posing security threads. Besides, internet retailing companies are seriously experimenting with drone delivery of goods at retailer level. That would multiply the presence in our air of unmaned aircrafts of non negligible size and flying capabilities. Finally, there is a high push towards the personalized air transport. Several companies are developing manned/unmaned aircrafts though to fly at moderate altitude, moderate speeds to serve distances up to 100 km, i.e. vehicles up to several hundred kilograms transporting up to five or six persons. These initiatives have not taking into consideration the problem of ATC. Their implementation require to solve ATC problems that are several order of magnitude greater than the currently posed by commercial airlines. In these new scenario the cybersecurity problems also grow to a new level.

Focusing in the pure airspace distribution problem, there are some timid attempts to apply machine learning approaches in this domain. Some lines of research steeming from the works in [11] have identified the following avenues of research on machine learning application to ATC:

1. Climb prediction: the prediction the aircraft climbing trajectory after take-off in order to detect anomalies and provide warnings. The prediction is based on recorded climbing trajectories database and must be stratified by aircraft type and model. It is also highly dependent of the local geography.
2. Detection of non-compliant approaches, again stratified by aircrafts. This problem made the front research interest because of terrorist attack risks, but it also can be justified to detect performing anomalies that pose some kind of risk.
3. Estimated time of arrival prediction for flights en route.
4. Prediction of ATCo workload depending of the airspace configuration, which is of critical importance for the smooth management of the air traffic.

All these approaches have been explored with conventional statistical machine learning techniques, and some with (not-so-deep) artificial neural networks. The three first problems are trajectory prediction problems, the fourth is a configuration prediction. As recognized by the authors, the main problem posed by machine learning approaches is its validity, which is limited to the scope of the data. For example, training our system with data captured in good methereological conditions only would be clearly insufficient to deal with harsh methereological conditions. Even if the formal validation results (cross-validation, etc.) are quite good, the data selection imposes a limitation for the applicability of the system. Therefore, the collection and curation of extensive datasets is the underlying challenge for any machine learning development that may lead to commercial and military application.

Another pressing issue for machine learning approaches is the non-stationary nature of the real data. The datasets used for training and validation would be restricted to some specific dates, however the air traffic is evolving in an explosive manner worldwide. For instance, China and India are developing a large number of airports and airtraffic infrastructure in order to achieve the level of air transport similar to Europe and USA in a short time. New stakeholders appear almost out of the blue depending on economical decisions, such as the hubs developed in the arabic peninsula or Turkey. These changes involve changes in airspace utilization that can be changing dramatically the ATC scenario rendering data obsolete. Therefore, continuous learning a long the life is the appropriate paradigm to tackle air traffic prediction issues. No single work in the literature has taken this issue into consideration.

Machine learning approaches are not explicative, they do not provide insights into the causes for anomalies/troubles and the possible corrections. In this regard their usefulness is limited and can always be questioned by the people in charge of political decisions. Therefore, simulation models with explicative power will be always required. Such simulation models can be based on discrete event modelling, mixed with continuous dynamical processes modeling aspects of the individual agents. In an scenario of high density local airtraffic, with many unmaned aircrafts relying on automated guidance to a large extent, simulation and prediction models must be interwined and run on real time in order to be able to cope with the huge load of real time decisions and planning that must be solved in order to manage securely the large float of aircrafts buzzing across a big city or a megalopolis.

Even after solving the referred simulation and prediction problems, the management of the airspace is an optimization problem that must be solved with enough quality in a limited time. Some of the problems tackled fall in the range of intractable problems, so that they must be solved approximatively. For this reason researchers have been resorting to evolutionary algorithms and other stochastic search algorithms. However, these algorithms are usually highly unstable (repetitions of the same process can provide wildly different results) or in fact are local optimization algorithms highly dependent on initial conditions. Anyway, next generation ATM and ATC control systems need stable minimization algorithms with truly global optimization properties. Moreover they must be able to tackle with large size problems in short real time, because the air traffic conditions would not allow extended response lags in the depicted dense traffic scenarios.

6   Conclusions

The management of airspace has become a highly complex problem due to the almost exponential growth of the number of commercial flights. As developing countries are incorporated to the system, the problem is getting a global dimension as well as local one. Locally, metroplex areas pose highly dynamical and interconnected management problems. At continental scale, i.e. Europe, USA, China, the control of en route flights minimizing a diversity of costs creates the need for dynamic reconfiguration at various spatial and temporal levels. At a global scale, the interoperability of the controlling systems poses an additional issue. Most of the approaches considered in the literature are relatively static, even when considering short time reconfigurations the process is relatively independent from one time period to another. There is a lack of predictive approaches in the literature. Modern predictive techniques, such as those based on deep learning, may open a new area of intense research and practical applications.

Acknowledgments. The work reported in this paper was supported by FEDER funds for the MINECO project TIN2017-85827-P, and projects KK-2018/00071, KK-2018/00082 of the Elkartek 2018 funding program of the Basque Government.

References

1. Alliot, J.-M., Gruber, H., Joly, G., Schoenauer, M.: Genetic algorithms for solving air traffic control conflicts. In: Proceedings of 9th IEEE Conference on Artificial Intelligence for Applications, pp. 0–6 (1993)
2. Cao, X., Zhu, X., Tian, Z., Chen, J., Dapeng, W., Wenbo, D.: A knowledge-transfer-based learning framework for airspace operation complexity evaluation. Transp. Res. Part C: Emerg. Technol. **95**, 61–81 (2018)
3. Chen, Y., Zhang, D.: Dynamic airspace configuration method based on a weighted graph model. Chin. J. Aeronaut. **27**(4), 903–912 (2014)
4. Crouch, P.E., Jackson, J.W.: Dynamic interpolation for linear systems (air traffic control). In: 29th IEEE Conference on Decision and Control, vol. 4, pp. 2312–2314, December 1990
5. Delahaye, D., Alliot, J.-M., Schoenauer, M., Farges, J.-L.: Genetic algorithms for partitioning air space. In: Proceedings of the Tenth Conference on Artificial Intelligence for Applications, pp. 291–297 (1994)
6. Delahaye, D., Schoenauer, M., Alliot, J.-M.: Airspace sectoring by evolutionary computation. In: 1998 International Conference on Evolutionary Computation, pp. 218–223. IEEE (1998)
7. Feng, X., Murray, A.T.: Allocation using a heterogeneous space Voronoi diagram. J. Geogr. Syst. **20**, 207–226 (2018)
8. Fulton, N.L.: Airspace design: towards a rigorous specification of conflict complexity based on computational geometry. Aeronaut. J. **103**(1020), 75–84 (1999)
9. Gerdes, I., Temme, A., Schultz, M.: Dynamic airspace sectorisation for flight-centric operations. Transp. Res. Part C: Emerg. Technol. **95**, 460–480 (2018)
10. Ghorpade, S.: Airspace configuration model using swarm intelligence based graph partitioning. In: 2016 IEEE Canadian Conference on Electrical and Computer Engineering (CCECE), pp. 1–5, May 2016

11. Gianazza, D.: Forecasting workload and airspace configuration with neural networks and tree search methods. Artif. Intell. **174**(7), 530–549 (2010)

12. Han, S.C., Zhang, M.: The optimization method of the sector partition based on metamorphic Voronoi polygon. Chin. J. Aeronaut. **17**(1), 7–12 (2004)

13. Hind, H., El Omri, A., Abghour, N., Moussaid, K., Rida, M.: Dynamic airspace configuration: review and open research issues. In: 2018 4th International Conference on Logistics Operations Management (GOL), pp. 1–7, April 2018

14. Hossain, M.M., Alam, S., Delahaye, D.: An evolutionary computational framework for capacity-safety trade-off in an air transportation network. Chin. J. Aeronaut. **32**, 999–1010 (2019)

15. Li, M.Z., Ryerson, M.S.: A data-driven approach to modeling high-density terminal areas: a scenario analysis of the new Beijing, China airspace. Chin. J. Aeronaut. **30**(2), 538–553 (2017)

16. Nava-Gaxiola, C.A., Barrado, C.: Performance measures of the sesar southwest functional airspace block. J. Air Transp. Manag. **50**, 21–29 (2016)

17. Nosedal, J., Piera, M.A., Solis, A.O., Ferrer, C.: An optimization model to fit airspace demand considering a spatio-temporal analysis of airspace capacity. Transp. Res. Part C: Emerg. Technol. **61**, 11–28 (2015)

18. Pawlak, W., Goel, V., Rothenberg, D., Brinton, C.: Comparison of algorithms for the dynamic resectorization of airspace. American Institute of Aeronautics and Astronautics, 08 April 2019 (1998)

19. Rocha-Murca, M.C., Hansman, R.J.: Identification, characterization, and prediction of traffic flow patterns in multi-airport systems. IEEE Trans. Intell. Transp. Syst. **20**, 1–14 (2018)

20. Rosenow, J., Fricke, H., Schultz, M.: Air traffic simulation with 4D multi-criteria optimized trajectories. In: 2017 Winter Simulation Conference (WSC), pp. 2589–2600, December 2017

21. Rosenow, J., Fricke, H.: Impact of multi-criteria optimized trajectories on European airline efficiency, safety and airspace demand. J. Air Transp. Manag. (2019, in press)

22. Sergeeva, M., Delahaye, D., Mancel, C., Vidosavljevic, A.: Dynamic airspace configuration by genetic algorithm. J. Traffic Transp. Eng. (Engl. Ed.) **4**(3), 300–314 (2017)

23. Sergeeva, M., Delahaye, D., Mancel, C., Zerrouki, L., Schede, N.: 3D sectors design by genetic algorithm towards automated sectorisation (2015)

24. Sidiropoulos, S., Majumdar, A., Han, K.: A framework for the optimization of terminal airspace operations in multi-airport systems. Transp. Res. Part B: Methodol. **110**, 160–187 (2018)

25. Standfuß, T., Gerdes, I., Temme, A., Schultz, M.: Dynamic airspace optimisation. CEAS Aeronaut. J. **9**(3), 517–531 (2018)

26. Temizkan, S., Sipahioglu, A.: A mathematical model suggestion for airspace sector design. J. Fac. Eng. Arch. Gazi Univ. **31**, 913–920 (2016)

27. Tian, Y., Wan, L., Han, K., Ye, B.: Optimization of terminal airspace operation with environmental considerations. Transp. Res. Part D: Transp. Environ. **63**, 872–889 (2018)

28. Trandac, H., Duong, V., Baptiste, P.: Optimized sectorization of airspace with constraints. In: 5th Europe/USA Air Traffic Management Research and Development (ATM R&D) Seminar, pp. 1–11 (2003)

29. Wargo, C.A., Hunter, G., Leiden, K., Glaneuski, J., Van Acker, B., Hatton, K.: New entrants (RPA/space vehicles) operational impacts upon NAS ATM and ATC. In: 2015 IEEE/AIAA 34th Digital Avionics Systems Conference (DASC), pp. 5B2-1–5B2-13, September 2015

30. Wei, G., Ting-Yu, G., Zhi-Jian, Y.: Airspace sector dividing method to balance dynamic control workload, April 2015
31. Wei, J.: Dynamic airspace configuration algorithms for next generation air transportation system. Ph.D. thesis (2014)
32. Wei, J., Sciandra, V., Hwang, I., Hall, W.D.: Design and evaluation of a dynamic sectorization algorithm for terminal airspace. J. Guid. Control. Dyn. **37**, 1539–1555 (2014)
33. Yan, X., Zhang, H., Liao, Z., Yang, L.: A dynamic air traffic model for analyzing relationship patterns of traffic flow parameters in terminal airspace. Aerosp. Sci. Technol. **55**, 10–23 (2016)
34. Yang, L., Yin, S., Minghua, H., Han, K., Zhang, H.: Empirical exploration of air traffic and human dynamics in terminal airspaces. Transp. Res. Part C: Emerg. Technol. **84**, 219–244 (2017)
35. Yin, C.W.S., Venugopalan, T.K., Suresh, S.: A multi-objective approach for 3D airspace sectorization: a study on Singapore regional airspace. In: 2016 IEEE Symposium Series on Computational Intelligence, SSCI 2016, pp. 1–8. IEEE, December 2017
36. Yousefi, A., Myers, T., Mitchell, J.S.B., Kostitsyna, I., Sharma, R.: Robust airspace design methods for uncertain traffic and weather. In: 2013 IEEE/AIAA 32nd Digital Avionics Systems Conference (DASC), pp. 1D2-1–1D2-11, October 2013
37. Zhang, Y., Su, R., Sandamali, G.G.N., Zhang, Y., Cassandras, C.G., Xie, L.: A hierarchical heuristic approach for solving air traffic scheduling and routing problem with a novel air traffic model. IEEE Trans. Intell. Transp. Syst. **PP**(October), 1–14 (2018)
38. Zou, X., Cheng, P., An, B., Song, J.: Sectorization and configuration transition in airspace design. Math. Probl. Eng. **2016**, 21 (2016)

Comparison of Heuristic Algorithms for Path Planning in 3D Printing with Multistage Experimentation System

Martyna Poslednik, Iwona Pozniak-Koszalka$^{(\boxtimes)}$, Leszek Koszalka, and Andrzej Kasprzak

Department of Systems and Computer Networks,
Wroclaw University of Science and Technology, Wroclaw, Poland
martynaposlednik@gmail.com, {iwona.pozniak-koszalka,
leszek.koszalka,andrzej.kasprzak}@pwr.edu.pl

Abstract. The objective of this work is to present the implemented algorithms to solving path planning in 3D printing problem. The algorithms have been compared on the basis of the obtained results of simulation experiments. As the indices of algorithm's performance the total distance, the energy cost, and the time cost are taken into account. The designed and implemented two-stage experimentation system is described. The simulation experiments have been carried on along with own experiment design. Short analysis of the obtained results allowed for recommendation of the most promising algorithms.

Keywords: Algorithm · 3D printing · Experimentation system · Simulation

1 Introduction

Nowadays, 3D printing is undoubtedly one of the breakthrough technologies that may strongly impact today's world of science. It can be treated as the revolutionary approach to additive manufacturing by its main advantages: competitive lead-time, possibility to design whatever the creator wants and the cost which is getting lower and lower because the technology is becoming widely available [1]. Almost everything can be created with 3D printing. It is widely used in areas like: automotive architecture, education, fashion industry, art, military and defense, jewelry and many more [2]. Particularly special place holds 3D printing in medicine. Printing pills that contain personalized doses of medications or bio-printed organs are nothing unusual these days and is very helpful in healthcare. 3D printing is used for orthopedic implants, prosthetics, for creating of patient-specific replicas of bones, organs and blood vessels. A compendium of knowledge at this aspect can be found in [3].

3D can be improved by the efficient algorithms created for solving optimization problems. This work particularly focuses on problem of path planning in one layer, as the problem was formulated in our works [4] and [5]. In this paper, we focus on presenting the results of the studies on the implemented heuristic and meta-heuristic algorithms, including Left-to-Right, Snake, Edge Following, Greedy, 2 opt, Greedy 2 opt, Harmony Search, Greedy Harmony, Simulated Annealing, and Greedy Annealing.

The aim of this work is to compare properties of these algorithms when they are used to optimize 3D printing.

The rest of the paper is organized as follows. In Sect. 2, the mathematical model of the considered problem is formulated. In Sect. 3, the related works are presented. Section 4 contains a brief description of the implemented heuristic and meta-heuristic algorithms for solving the path planning problem. The created experimentation system is described in Sect. 5. The investigation focus on properties of algorithms and the comparison. The selected results of research have been presented in Sect. 6. The conclusion and plans for the further work appear in Sect. 7.

2 Problem Statement

The main objective is to find (generate) the path which fulfil the printing area. In this paper, following our work [4] we concentrate on the single layer of the whole 3D model. The layer can be described as an array of binary points with size (n × m), where n is the length of the printing layer, and m is the width of the printing layer. A point can have a value equal to 1, when point is to be printed, or equal to 0, otherwise. The problem can be formulated - in convention: *given-to find- such that* –as follows.

Given:
Printing layer as an array (size n × m) of binary points where

$$X_{i,j} = \begin{cases} 1 \text{ if printing point} \\ 0 \text{ otherwise} \end{cases} \quad i \in n, \ j \in m$$

To find:
The path denoted by the order of visiting points $V = [v_1, v_2, ..., v_p]$, where p is the total number of points to be printed in a layer.

Such that:
To minimize the total cost of printing expressed by (1):

$$L = \sum_{k=2}^{p} \left(L_{v_{k-1}, v_k} \right) \tag{1}$$

It is taken into account that the cost for move between two points can be calculated in one of three possible ways introduced as minimum time problem, minimum distance problem, and minimum energy problem, expressed by (2), (3), and (4), respectively.
Minimum time

$$L_{P_{a,b}, P_{c,d}} = \max(|a - c|, |b - d|) \tag{2}$$

Minimum distance

$$L_{P_{a,b},P_{c,d}} = \sqrt{(a-c)^2 + (b-d)^2} \tag{3}$$

Minimum energy (sum of movements, due to separate engines)

$$L_{P_{a,b},P_{c,d}} = |a-c| + |b-d| \tag{4}$$

where $a, c \in n$ and $b, d \in m$.

Subject to constraints:

Each point can be visited only once.

Remark: Most likely, it is impossible to find one continuous path. Therefore, usually, the resulting path consists of the sub-paths found by the path planning algorithm. In such a case the final path is created as the connection of these sub-paths [4]. Therefore, instead of (3) the final total cost is formulated as the sum of two lengths: $L = L_F = L_{paths} + L_{switch\,path}$. The first part of the sum is the length between the points in the sub-paths. The second is the sum of lengths between last point in the given sub-path and first point in the connected sub-path.

3 Related Work

The considered problem is strongly connected with the practice. Many interesting industrial applications are studied in literature, including the first 3D printed prosthetic leg [6], the first 3D bio-printer to print the blood vessel [7], and 3D printed thermo-plastic material used to manufacture a rocket [8]. The review of recent methods is available in [9].

The authors of the report [10] states that in this year 3D printing will concern on featuring block-chain technology, the Internet of Things, high-speed 3D printers and trends in metal 3D printing.

After paths generating phase, which is made using the algorithm presented in our work [4], the optimization algorithms have to be used to choose the final path. The main goal of optimization is to find the best permutation of sub-paths. The authors of [11] successfully modified TSP to the considered problem, pointing on some important differences, including the fact that the toolpath cells are not points (like in standard TSP we have cities), but polygons with a number of possible entries and exit points for each cell. The efficiency of their procedure depends on paths shape. If path got closed circuit like in contour paths, there are many entries and exit points. In paths without closed circuit, there is just one entry point and one exit point. This problem was also studied in [12] where two genetic algorithms to solve the problem are described. The paper [13] showed that the neural network self-organizing map (SOM) can be also used in path planning of pocket milling machine. Authors of this approach proposed also algorithm which is based on ant colony optimization.

In this paper, we concentrate on implementations of heuristic and meta-heuristic optimization algorithms, which are presented in the next section.

4   Algorithms

In this section, the ten implemented algorithms are briefly described:

Left-To-Right. This algorithm starts in top-left corner and processes line-by-line from left to right, adding to route all points on its way. And because of the reason that only point to print are on the found route, printer will go straight from last point in one line, to first in next one containing any point.

Snake. The idea behind snake algorithm is to find path which contains points on a closer end. This on the contrary to previous algorithm not necessarily can be obtained from going from left end to right. To obtain this, distances in both directions are calculated and the shortest one is chosen. Then the path goes to another end of it instead of going always from left to right.

Edge Following. The main idea of edge following strategy is to create a boundary and successively reduce it by changing the margin. Basically, this algorithm goes from the boundary to the middle of it. Finding edges and neighbours depend on chosen cost function. For example, diagonal neighbours exist only for time cost type.

Greedy. A greedy algorithm always makes the choice that seems to be the best at that moment. After choosing the first point to start, the algorithm iterates over the rest of the points and searches for next points to add into the route. The first point to start is taken randomly. Greedy algorithm is well-described in [14].

2-Opt. The algorithm removes two connections between points and establishes new shorter one. It continues removing and reconnecting the tour until no improvements found. Two versions of 2-opt algorithm were implemented: first, that swaps vertex when the first possible swap is found; second, that find best swap from all of the vertices. More detailed description of the algorithm can be accessed in [15].

Greedy 2-Opt. Greedy two opt is a composition of two algorithms (Greedy and 2-Opt). Such a composition helps to improve path which itself is close to optimal. Theoretically, less iteration will be needed and computation time, distance or energy parameters will be optimised. The details can be found in [16].

Harmony Search. Harmony search algorithm just like in the process of composing a piece of music aims for a perfection and harmony while searching for an optimal solution. It acts like a musician improvising: play from the memory piece of music, play something similar to it or to compose completely new song. The algorithm chooses the best path using these three ways. If a new solution is generated it is compared to the solutions stored in the memory. If found solution is better than the worst in the memory, the one is replaced with the better one. More information about this algorithm can be found in [17].

Greedy Harmony. The algorithm is a combination of Greedy and Harmony Search. Input parameters are from both. At first, Greedy algorithm is executed and then the result is passed to Harmony Search as its initial solution. The potential aim of this combination is to obtain possibly the most optimal result as harmony search is said to be easily operated thanks to its robustness.

Simulated Annealing. This algorithm helps to avoid local minima while searching for solution in path finding in graph [18]. It acts, analogically to the annealing in solids; it relies on the cooling of the initial temperature to find the optimal solution. Heating solid past melting point and then cooling it makes the structural properties dependent on the rate of cooling.

Greedy Annealing. This algorithm is a composition of two previously described algorithms which are called one by one. Simulated annealing gives a large spectrum of parameters to be tuned. As the first point to start of Greedy algorithm, the solution found by Simulated Annealing is taken. Details concerning this algorithm can be found in [19].

5   Experimentation System

The experimentation system was designed and implemented following the rules described in our paper [20]. The general flow of experiments was regarded as an input–output system, which ensures fixing by the user problem's parameters and algorithm's parameters at the input, and obtaining the solution (path to be printed) as well as the values of the indices of performance at the output. The model of the system is shown in Fig. 1.

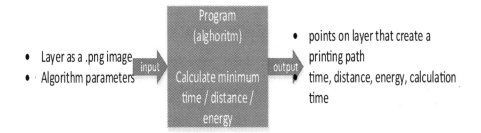

Fig. 1. The model of the system.

Input parameters of the system are: the layer (recognized as an image in .png. format) and inner parameters for the chosen algorithm. For instance, if simulated annealing is chosen, the input parameters are: minimal temperature, cooling rate, number of iterations on temperature and maximal number of iterations with no improvement. Given .png. image is denoted as an array of binary points of size n × m. The cost for move between two points is calculated in one of three possible ways described in Sect. 2, i.e., to ensure: minimum distance, minimum time, or minimum energy. At the output, there are produced points included in the resulting path found by a given algorithm.

The main idea is that the system allows making two-stage experiments following the ideas presented in [20]. At the first stage, a given algorithm can be tuned for a particular image. At the second stage, the tuned algorithms (with properly adjusted parameters) can be compared.

For the purposes of this paper, the system was activated for a set of 3 layers in .png. format, including star, ellipse, and apple. The program loaded these images and after choosing the algorithm, it processed the resulting path. The obtained results have been saved to a file to be analysed. The area, which was assumed to simulate the print, was a square with an area sufficient for a .png. layer of size 95 × 73 pixels.

Experiments were taken on the following setup:

- Intel Core i5-3230M CPU 2.60 GHz.
- Software written in Java- developed in IntelliJ IDEA 14.1.6.

6 Research

6.1 Experiments on the First Stage: Tuning Algorithms

The goal was tuning all implemented algorithms, i.e., adjusting their inner parameters.

The exemplary result of tuning is presented for harmony search algorithm. Parameters to be set are: memory size, number of iterations, memory probability. Table 1 shows the results of an experiment due memory probability when the other parameters were fixed. The last column of the table contains the time (in *ms*) that a given algorithm took to found the solution.

Table 1. Memory probability parameter for harmony search algorithm.

Memory probability	Memory size	Iterations number	Time cost	Distance cost	Energy cost	Computing time
0.95	10	100000	213864	237273	301506	144297
0.90	10	100000	267634	297381	378455	131128
0.80	10	100000	268133	297582	377933	133665
0.50	10	100000	268900	298596	379662	84340

It may be observed that the greater the value of this parameter, then, the better solution of the optimization problem (for each criterion formulated in Sect. 2). Thus, the reasonable value of memory probability is 0.95. Based on such experiments, the inner parameters of all algorithms have been adjusted for all algorithms.

6.2 Experiments on the Second Stage: Algorithms Comparison

Experiment #1 – Star. Table 2 shows the best results produced by the tuned algorithms for the object (picture) *star.png.*, when the problem of minimizing time was solved.

Table 2. Time minimization: the results of experiments for the layer *star.png*.

Algorithm	Time cost	Distance	Energy	Comp. time
Greedy	**2374**	2504	2688	553
Greedy 2 opt	**2374**	2543	2783	1044
Greedy Harmony	**2374**	2513	2710	30135
Greedy Annealing	**2375**	2509	2701	30659
2 opt	**2379**	2551	2798	14465
Edge Following	**2504**	2541	2619	375
Left-to-Right	**2696**	5176	5246	175
Simulated Annealing	**2702**	3011	3529	106682
Snake	**5174**	2710	2733	401
Harmony Search	**5543**	6147	7822	20629

It may be observed that for the relatively simple object (star) to be printed, the less complicated algorithms, like belonging to the greedy family, got the better results. The range of the computing time used by the algorithms was large. As expected, the sophisticated algorithms, like Simulated Annealing or Harmony Search, need more time for finding a solution. The highest computing time of Simulated Annealing gives an immense effort before even starting to print.

In Fig. 2. The results of performing the paths by two exemplary algorithms are shown. On the left picture, one can see the connections between sub-paths.

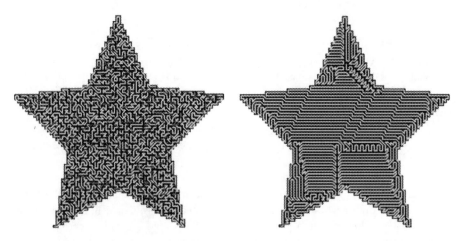

Fig. 2. The paths found by Simulated Annealing (on the left) and Greedy Annealing (on the right) when solving time optimization problem.

Table 3 shows the best results produced by the considered algorithms for object (picture) *star.png.*, when the problem of minimizing distance was solved.

Table 3. Distance minimization: the results of experiments for the layer *star.png*.

Algorithm	Time cost	Distance	Energy	Comp. time
Greedy	2374	**2353**	2763	607
Greedy 2 opt	2374	**2521**	2728	6182
Greedy Harmony	2504	**1005**	2688	2374
Greedy Annealing	2599	**1079**	2848	2427
2 opt	2382	**2545**	2780	59703
Edge Following	2459	**2484**	2528	342
Left-to-Right	4933	**4936**	5008	17
Simulated Annealing	2976	**2465**	3467	2682
Snake	2969	**2710**	2733	2136
Harmony Search	5635	**6266**	7985	2729

It may be observed that Greedy Harmony produced the best result. Other greedy algorithms were also among these which got well results. Harmony Search performed rather weak.

Experiment #2 – Ellipse. Table 4 shows the results of experiments for picture *ellipse. png* in distance domain. The best result again was obtained with a use of Greedy Harmony algorithm. Surprisingly, because Harmony Search itself got the worst result. However, the algorithms based on greedy approach gave promising results for almost all experiments, and the combination of these two algorithms seems to be very promising.

Table 4. Distance minimization: the results of experiments for the layer *ellipse.png*.

Algorithm	Time cost	Distance	Energy	Comp. time
Greedy	4429	**4159**	4813	2218
Greedy 2 opt	4156	**4401**	4747	41280
Greedy Harmony	4159	**3390**	4775	4413
Greedy Annealing	4181	**4431**	4791	545
2 opt	15244	**13831**	19251	1593
Edge Following	4153	**4287**	4348	86
Left-to-Right	9556	**9556**	9644	1
Simulated Annealing	7695	**6858**	9447	34861
Snake	4914	**4900**	4944	1
Harmony Search	13054	**14461**	18337	94454

While finding path with the use of 2 opt and Harmony Search in distance domain the paths generated weren't effective enough which means that while 3D printing process the printing nozzle would jump plenty of times from one point to another at long distance. Figure 3 shows the obtained paths with connections between sub-paths (red marks). Greedy Harmony (on the left), which performed better, utilized less of them than Greedy (on the right).

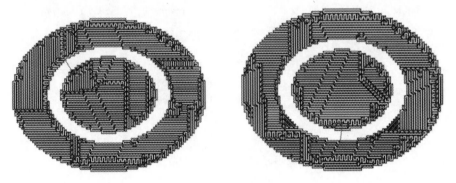

Fig. 3. The paths found by Greedy Harmony (on the left) and Greedy (on the right) when solving distance optimization problem for *ellipse.png*.

Experiment #3 – Apple. Table 5 presents the results for energy optimization for picture *apple.png*. Three algorithms that obtained best results are: left to right, snake and edge following algorithm. Algorithms that generate path without special tactic to optimize it occurred to be the most energy saving. Just after them stands Greedy algorithm with much more higher computing time. Simulated annealing took a lot of time and wasn't very effective. The worst results were obtained for Greedy Annealing.

Table 5. Energy minimization: the results of experiments for the layer *apple.png*.

Algorithm	Time cost	Distance	Energy	Comp. time
Greedy	4072	3864	**4371**	1876
Greedy 2 opt	4036	43854	**4298**	43978
Greedy Harmony	4046	3864	**4309**	2758
Greedy Annealing	4077	3874	**4371**	545
2 opt	12419	11166	**15815**	1912
Edge Following	3947	3934	**3979**	62
Left-to-Right	7968	7968	**8042**	1
Simulated Annealing	5996	6676	**8101**	7403484
Snake	3975	3961	**4004**	1
Harmony Search	10644	11799	**15014**	6974335

Figure 4 allows for the visual comparison of eight algorithms. Because of no good results, two algorithms namely 2opt and Harmony Search are eliminated.

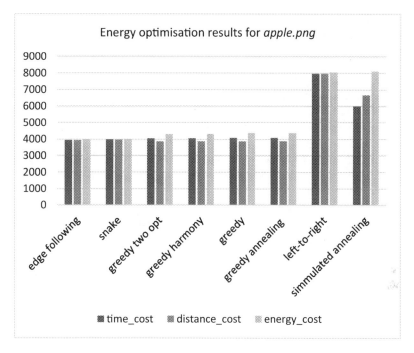

Fig. 4. Comparison of algorithms.

Greedy and its hybrids weren't so successful in this case when it goes for values of time cost. However, looking at the pictures of the paths generated they seem to be really promising. There are only two switches (connections), what can be seen in Fig. 5 (on the right).

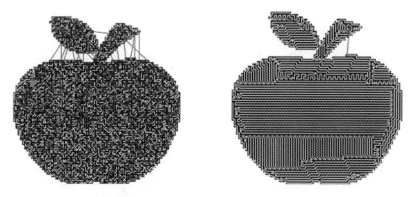

Fig. 5. The paths found by Simulated Annealing (on the left) and Greedy (on the right) when solving energy optimization problem for *apple.png*.

7   Final Remarks

7.1   Conclusion

This paper focused on path finding in designing processes of 3D printing. The optimization problem was formulated. The selected heuristic and metaheuristic algorithms for solving the problem were implemented. The authors of this paper decided to take into account ten algorithms. In order to check the properties of these algorithms simulation experiments were carried out using the created and implemented experimentation system. The system allows two-stage experiments – adjusting algorithm's inner parameters at the first stage, and the comparison between tuned algorithms at the second stage. In this paper, three complex experiments were made taking into account three different testing sets for three objects to be printed. It gave the overall view on how the algorithms work in different conditions depending on factors like layer shape or cost type. The efficiency of algorithms was discussed on the basis of the obtained results.

The comparison led to the main conclusion that there is a strong need to look on the obtained results with the holistic way as the results depend on many factors. We pointed our attention on the algorithms based on harmony search approach, and greedy algorithms. It was observed that these algorithms can give satisfactory results (Greedy Harmony produced often very good results) but they are not always the best. Thus, the answer to the question which algorithm is performing as the best requires knowledge about user's priority concerned the chosen criterion, i.e., minimization of time, or minimization of distance, or minimization of energy defined by (2), (3), or (4), respectively. Moreover, if the computing time is important for the user, then, it is worth to consider this fact and modified the criterion introduced by the formula (1).

The experimentation system, presented in this paper, is serving at the Wroclaw University of Science and Technology, Faculty of Electronics, as a tool to support teaching and preparing research projects by the master students in the area of Advanced Informatics and Control, in particular on Research Skills and Methodologies courses.

7.2   Plans for Further Research

The research done gave answers to some questions concerning the optimization of path for 3D printing in some aspects, however, there still are a lot of fields where further work can be conducted.

First of all, some improvements should be made to extend potential opportunities of Harmony Search algorithm. Additionally, after accurate comparison of all recently implemented algorithms, there is a need for implementing new algorithms and make a challenge with the algorithms presented in this work. In the further development, the evolutionary strategies should be considered.

We also plan a development of the experimentation system to ensure the opportunity of carried on complex multistage experiments in the automatic way.

Acknowledgement. This work was supported by the statutory funds of the Department of Systems and Computer Networks, Wroclaw University of Science and Technology, Wroclaw, Poland.

References

1. Campbell, T., Williams, Ch., Ivanova, O, Garrett, B.: Could 3D printing change the world? Technologies, potential, and implications of additive manufacturing, Strategic Foresight Report, The Atlantic Council 2011(1) (2011)
2. Gebhardt, A., Fateri, M.: 3D printing and its applications. RTE J. Forum Rapid Technol. (2013)
3. Rybicki, F.J., Grant, G.T.: 3D Printing in Medicine: A Practical Guide for Medical Professionals. Springer, AG (2017). https://doi.org/10.1007/978-3-319-61924-8
4. Wojcik, M., Koszalka, L., Pozniak-Koszalka, I., Kasprzak, A.: MZZ-GA algorithm for solving path optimization in 3D printing. In: Proceedings of the Tenth International Conference on Systems (ICONS), pp. 30–35 (2015)
5. Lechowicz, P., Koszalka, L., Pozniak-Koszalka, L., Kasprzak, A.: Path optimization in 3D printer: algorithms and experimentation system. In: Proceedings of the 4th International Symposium on Computational and Business Intelligence (ISCBI), pp. 137–142 (2016)
6. https://en.org/wiki/RepRap_Project. Accessed Nov 2018
7. https://en.org/wiki/MakerBot. Accessed Nov 2018
8. https://www.engineering.com/3DPrinting/3DPrintingArticles/ArticleID/11847/Atlas-V-Rocket-Soars-from-Earth-with-3D-Printed-Plastic-Parts.aspx. Accessed Nov 2018
9. Ngo, T.D., Kashani, A., Imbalzano, G., Nguyen, K.T.Q., Hui, D.: Additive manufacturing (3D printing): a review of materials, methods, applications and challenges. Compos. Part B Eng. **143**, 172–196 (2018)
10. https://3dprintingindustry.com/news/whats-next-3d-printing-2018-additive-manufacturing-expert-perspective-126680/. Accessed Dec 2018
11. Castelino, K., D'Souza, R., Wright, P.K.: Toolpath optimization for minimizing airtime during machining. J. Manuf. Syst. **22**(3), 173–180 (2003)
12. Wah, P.K., Murty, K.G., Joneja, A., Chiu, L.C.: Tool path optimization in layered manufacturing. IIE Trans. **34**(4), 335–347 (2002)
13. Suh, S.-H., Shin, Y.-S.: Neural network modeling for tool path planning of the rough cut in complex pocket milling. J. Manuf. Syst. **15**(5), 295–304 (1996)
14. Cormen, T.H., Leiserson, C.E., Rivest, L., Stein, C.: Introduction to Algorithms, 3rd edn. The MIT Press, Cambridge (2009)
15. Engels, C., Manthey, B.: Average-case approximation ratio of the 2-opt algorithm for the TSP. Oper. Res. Lett. **37**(2), 83–84 (2009)
16. McGovern, S.M., Gupta, S.M.: Disassembly Line: Balancing and Modeling with Greedy 2-Opt Hybrid. McGraw-Hill, New York (2011)
17. Yadav, A., Yadav, N., Kim, J.H.: A study of harmony search algorithms: exploration and convergence ability. In: Kim, J.H., Geem, Z.W. (eds.) Harmony Search Algorithm. AISC, vol. 382, pp. 53–62. Springer, Heidelberg (2016). https://doi.org/10.1007/978-3-662-47926-1_6

18. Dowsland, K., Thompson, J.: Simulated annealing. In: Rozenberg, G., Back, T., Kok, J.N. (eds.) Handbook of Natural Computing, pp. 1623–1655. Springer, Heidelberg (2012). https://doi.org/10.1007/978-3-540-92910-9_49
19. Geng, X., Chen, Z., Yang, W., Shi, D., Zhao, K.: Solving the traveling salesman problem based on an adaptive simulated annealing algorithm with greedy search. Appl. Soft Comput. **11**, 3680–3689 (2011)
20. Hudziak, M., Pozniak-Koszalka, I., Koszalka, L., Kasprzak, A.: Multi-agent pathfinding in the crowded environment with obstacles: algorithms and experimentation system. J. Intell. Fuzzy Syst. **32**(2), 1561–1573 (2017)

An Integer Programming Model
for the Capacitated Vehicle Routing Problem
with Drones

Jarosław Wikarek, Paweł Sitek[✉], and Łukasz Zawarczyński

Department of Information Systems, Kielce University of Technology,
Al. 1000-lecia PP 7, 25-314 Kielce, Poland
{j.wikarek,sitek,l.zawarczynski}@tu.kielce.pl

Abstract. The Capacitated Vehicle Routing Problem with Drones (CVRPD) is caused by the increasing interest in commercial drone delivery by many logistic companies (Amazon, DHL, etc.). Our proposition is a binary integer linear programming (BILP) model with objective function which minimizes the distance covered by drones. In our model, we consider the parcel delivery by a truck that transports/has a certain number of drones. Each drone can take off from the truck and deliver a parcel to the customer. It can also pick up a parcel from the customer. Drones have a specific range and payload. We assume that for each delivery area there are several points – so-called mobile distribution centers – where a drone can be launched/retrieved from the truck. The question that arises for such a problem is the selection of drone launch/retrieval locations to minimize the cost of delivery. The paper presents also the implementation of the model in the mathematical programming environment. An author's own iterative algorithm using mathematical programming methods was proposed to solve the problem.

Keywords: Integer programming · Capacitated Vehicle Routing Problem · Optimization · Drones

1 Introduction

The Unmanned Aerial Vehicles (UAVs), i.e. drones, have in recent years drawn increased interest from researchers and practitioners, particularly in terms of their use in logistics. Their use as a complimentary way of delivering parcels to customers within the so-called last mile delivery (Amazon, UPS, etc.), inspecting difficult to reach technical equipment, measuring pollution, etc. is considered. The most promising and universal field of application for drones seems to be intermodal transport, i.e. one that uses more than one type of transport in the distribution process.

An unquestionable advantage of using drones in the above mentioned fields is the lack of restrictions related to the road network, railway network, traffic volume, etc. Usually, drone delivery of a parcel between two points, especially in urban areas, is much faster compared to other means of transport. Unfortunately, the use of drones has also numerous limitations, such as those related to their payload, range, etc. Drones usually can only deliver a certain number of parcels or packages, require replacement

N. T. Nguyen et al. (Eds.): ICCCI 2019, LNAI 11683, pp. 511–520, 2019.
https://doi.org/10.1007/978-3-030-28377-3_42

or charging of batteries, etc. One of the key problems that must be solved in the distribution process using drones is the appropriate VRP (Vehicle Routing Problem) variant. The VRP is one of the most well-known problems in the field of operational research, which is derived from the TSP (Traveling Salesman Problem). In its simplest version, it is defined as follows – for a given fleet of vehicles and a set of customers, an optimal set of routes in order to deliver shipments to customers should be found. Detailed studies on the VRPs are presented in [1].

In the literature there are models of problems where deliveries are made by drones and other means of transport in an integrated way [2, 3]. These include for example the FSTSP (Flying Sidekick Traveling Salesman Problem) [3], where a drone travels along with a vehicle, both of which start from a distribution center (DC) and must return to the same DC at the end of their travel. It is assumed that each customer awaiting a parcel is located within the range of a drone starting from DC. Another version of this problem is the PDSTSP (Parallel Drone Scheduling Traveling Salesman Problem). It assumes that DCs are close to the customers, making them independent of other means of transport. Both problems adopt the minimal delivery and return time of drones to DC as an objective function. In [4] the VRPD (Vehicle Routing Problem with Drones) was presented, where deliveries are carried out by a fleet of trucks, each equipped with drones. The VRPD can be classified as a variant of the Distance-Constrained Capac-itated Vehicle Routing Problem (DCVRP) with a set of different types of vehicles. Also other versions of VRPs can be considered in the context of drone use, e.g. CVRP, VRPTW, 2E-CVRP [5] etc.

Our proposal is to build a Binary Integer Linear Programing (BILP) model [6, 7] for the CVRP variant with the use of drones and iterative solution method, including the problem of location of mobile distribution centers (MDCs). We also consider increasing the functionality of the model, which includes not only the delivery of parcels, but also their pick-up from the customer.

Section 1 presents the description and formalization of the CVRPD in the form of a BILP model. Section 2 discusses the method of its solution together with implemen-tation aspects. Section 3 describes computational experiments verifying the correctness of the model and the proposed iterative method. The last chapter consists of conclu-sions and directions of future research.

2 The Capacitated Vehicle Routing Problem with Drones – Problem Statement and Formalization

The problem examined is the delivery of a set of parcels to customers using intermodal transport [8], consisting of a truck loaded with drones. At the same time, drones are loaded with parcels. Both trucks and drones are characterized by a specific capacity/payload. When formalizing the problem, the following additional assumptions were adopted:

- Given is a set of so-called mobile distribution centers (MDCs);
- Drones can be launched/retrieved from the truck only in specific locations (i.e. in MDCs);

- The launch location of a drone may be different than its landing location (these are different MDCs);
- Drones may vary in range, payload and number of parcels carried;
- Drones can not only deliver but also pick up parcels from customers.

The key to this problem is the answer to the question: *From which mobile distribution centers should drones be launched in order to keep the cost/distance/of delivery to the customers as low as possible?* This question can also be more general if we are not looking for an optimal solution. It will then be: *From which mobile distribution centers should drones be launched to guarantee delivery of parcels to customers?* An example of a diagram illustrating the above problem with the use of two MDCs and five drones is shown in Fig. 1. To address this type of problem, the BILP (Binary Integer Linear Programming) [7] model was proposed. The objective (1) function was the distance covered by drones, which is minimized. Of course, it is possible to adopt other objective functions, e.g. related to the number of drones used, taking into account not only the distance covered by the drones, but also the distance covered by the truck, etc. The proposed model has a set of constraints (2) … (12), which defines the space for feasible solutions. Some of these constraints are characteristic for VRP variants, while others result from the specificity of drone use. The description of individual model constraints is presented in Table 2. The model is characterized by binary decision variables. The decision variable X_{cpj} determines whether the drone c travels from point p to point j. At the same time the decision variable Y_{cpji} additionally determines whether the drone travels with the parcel i. The detailed description and significance of decision variables, indices and model parameters are presented in Table 1.

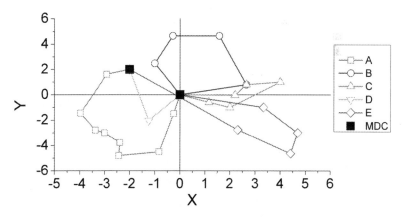

Fig. 1. Diagram illustrating the realization of deliveries by 5 drones from two mobile distribution centers (MDCs).

Table 1. Indices, sets, parameters and decision variables

Symbol	Description
Indices and sets	
P	A set of delivery points (customers)
I	A set of all items
C	A set of all drones
p,j	Delivery point index $(p, j \in P)$
i	Item index $(i \in I)$
c	Drone index $(c \in C)$
d	Mobile distribution center (MDC)
Parameters	
vi_i	Item volume (volumetric weight) $i(i \in I)$
vc_c	Drone's c payload $(c \in C)$
de_{ip}	If item i mast be delivered to delivery point p then $de_{ip} = 1$, otherwise $de_{ip} = 0 (i \in I, p \in P)$
di_{pj}	Distance between delivery points $p, j(p, j \in P \cup d)$
ti_{pj}	Transfer time between points $p, j(p, j \in P \cup d)$
dr_i	If item i is delivered from the MDC to the delivery point then $dr_i = 1$ otherwise $dr_i = 0(i \in I)$
Decision variables	
X_{cpj}	If drone c travels from point p to point j, then $X_{cpj} = 1$, otherwise $X_{cpj} = 0$, $(c \in C, p, j \in P \cup d)$
Y_{cpji}	If drone c travels from delivery point p to delivery point j carrying item i, then $Y_{cpji} = 1$, otherwise $Y_{cpji} = 0$, $(c \in C, p, j \in P \cup d)$

Table 2. Description of the constraints

Constraints	Description
(2)	Arrival and departure of the drone at/from delivery point (customer)
(3)	If no items are to be carried on the route, the drone does not travel that route
(4)	If the drone does not travel along a route, no items are to be carried on that route
(5)	At no route segment drone carries more items than payload
(6)	Items are delivered to/from delivery points
(7)	Single run of the drone
(8)	Items picked up/delivered to a delivery point
(9)	Runs executed within the required time
(10)	Each courier picks up/delivers items from/to a source (MDC)
(11)	Binarity

$$\sum_{c\in C}\sum_{p\in P\cup d}\sum_{j\in P\cup d} di_{pj} \cdot X_{cpj} \tag{1}$$

$$\sum_{j\in P\cup d} X_{cpj} = \sum_{j\in P\cup d} X_{cjp} \, \forall c \in C, p \in P\cup d \tag{2}$$

$$X_{cpj} \leq \sum_{i\in I} Y_{cpji} \, \forall c \in C, p \in P, j \in P \tag{3}$$

$$Y_{cpji} \leq X_{cpj} \, \forall c \in C, p \in P\cup d, j \in P\cup d, i \in I \tag{4}$$

$$\sum_{i\in I} vi_i \cdot Y_{cpji} \leq vc_c \, \forall c \in C, p \in P\cup d, j \in P\cup d \tag{5}$$

$$\sum_{c\in C}\sum_{p\in P\cup d} Y_{cpji} = de_{ip} \, \forall j \in P, i \in I : de_{ip} = 1, dr_i = 1$$
$$\sum_{c\in C}\sum_{p\in P\cup d} Y_{cjpi} = de_{ip} \, \forall j \in P, i \in I : de_{ip} = 1, dr_i = 0 \tag{6}$$

$$\sum_{j\in P} X_{cdj} \leq 1 \, \forall c \in C \tag{7}$$

$$\sum_{j\in P}\sum_{c\in C} Y_{cjpi} - \sum_{j\in O}\sum_{c\in C} Y_{cpji} = de_{ip} \, \forall p \in P, i \in I : dr_i = 1$$
$$\sum_{j\in P}\sum_{c\in C} Y_{cjpi} - \sum_{j\in P}\sum_{c\in C} Y_{cpji} = -de_{ip} \, \forall p \in P, i \in I : dr_i = 0 \tag{8}$$

$$\sum_{p\in P\cup d}\sum_{j\in P\cup d} ti_{pj} \cdot X_{cpj} \leq T \forall c \in C \tag{9}$$

$$\sum_{c\in C}\sum_{p\in P} Y_{cdpi} = 1 \, \forall i \in I : dr_i = 1$$
$$\sum_{c\in C}\sum_{p\in P} Y_{cdpi} = 1 \, \forall i \in I : dr_i = 0 \tag{10}$$

$$Y_{cpji} = \{0, 1\} \, \forall c \in C, p \in P\cup d, j \in P\cup d, i \in I$$
$$X_{cpj} = \{0, 1\} \, \forall c \in C, p \in P\cup d, j \in P\cup d \tag{11}$$

3   Iterative Algorithm for the CVRPD

An original iterative algorithm (Fig. 2) has been proposed for solving and verifying the proposed CVRPD model. The algorithm based on mathematical programming methods [6, 7]. Its idea is to iteratively solve the CVRPD model for each mobile distribution center (MCD). These iterations are little in number, as there are usually several MCDs in the parcel delivery area under consideration. An alternative to this approach is to expand the BILP model (Sect. 2) with a set of MCDs. This increases the number of decision variables, constraints and model indices. This, in turn, results in the need to search a larger space for feasible solutions, which translates into longer search times. Such a model will be proposed in subsequent studies. We will also present comparative analyses of the size of both models, their complexity and, most importantly, the time needed to find a solution for the same data instances in future research.

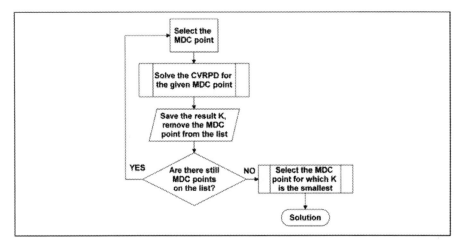

Fig. 2. Schematic diagram of the iterative algorithm-iterations of the algorithm are performed for subsequent MDC points.

For the proposed model (1) … (12) a number of computational experiments (N01 … N24) were carried out. The aim of these experiments was to verify the correctness of the model and the original iterative algorithm. The data for location and customer demand calculations were taken from [9]. Two types of data instances *6.10.1.TXT* (six customers) for N01 … N12 and *20.10.1.TXT* (twenty customers) for N13 … N24 were used. For both instances of data, experiments were carried out with different number of available drones C and various payload vc_c thereof. Additionally, two more drone parameters were taken into account: drone range K and number of drone handles L, i.e. the maximum number of parcels that can be taken. The test data were also supplemented with starting points for drones, i.e. MDCs. It was assumed that there are three mobile distribution centers in the delivery area in question: $MDC(A) = S_A$ (coordinates 0,0), $MDC(B) = S_B$ (coordinates 5,5) and $MDC(C) = S_C$ (coordinates −3,−3). Some simplifying assumptions were also adopted when carrying out the experiments, i.e. drones are launched from and return to the same MDC and are used only to deliver parcels (no pickup option) to the customer. These experiments can also be carried out without simplifications for the same model (1) … (12). To do so, only the values of some model parameters in the data instances need to be changed.

The results of the experiments are presented in Table 3. Additionally, the results of experiments N04(6), N05(6), N06(6) and N13(20) are presented as drone routes in Fig. 3, 4, 5, 6 respectively. The computation time for the first series of experiments (N01 ... N12) ranged from 2 to 6 s and for the second series of experiments (N13 ... N24) from 30 to 1200 s respectively. For experiments N01, N02 and N03 the results of computations for individual iterations of the algorithm, i.e. for individual starting points (S_A, S_B, S_C) are presented in Table 4. The gray color indicates optimal solutions characterized by the lowest value of the objective function (Fc).

Table 3. Results of computational experiments

Parameters								Results	
No	Instances	C	C'	v	K	L	L'	MDC	Fc
N01	6.10.1.TXT	3	2	20	3800	20	4	S_A	2464
N02	6.10.1.TXT	3	2	20	1800	20	4	S_A	2464
N03	6.10.1.TXT	3	3	20	3800	2	2	S_A	3128
N04	6.10.1.TXT	3	1	60	3800	20	6	S_A	2377
N05	6.10.1.TXT	3	2	60	1800	20	4	S_A	2464
N06	6.10.1.TXT	3	3	60	3800	2	2	S_A	3128
N07	6.10.1.TXT	6	2	20	3800	20	4	S_A	2464
N08	6.10.1.TXT	6	2	20	1800	20	4	S_A	2464
N09	6.10.1.TXT	6	3	20	3800	2	2	S_A	3128
N10	6.10.1.TXT	6	1	60	3800	20	6	S_A	2377
N11	6.10.1.TXT	6	2	60	1800	20	4	S_A	2464
N12	6.10.1.TXT	6	3	60	3800	2	2	S_A	3128
N13	20.10.1.TXT	6	4	20	3800	20	6	S_A	5697
N14	20.10.1.TXT	6	4	20	1800	20	10	S_A	6019
N15	20.10.1.TXT	6	5	20	3800	4	4	S_A	6151
N16	20.10.1.TXT	6	3	60	3800	20	12	S_A	5688
N17	20.10.1.TXT	6	4	60	1800	20	9	S_A	5927
N18	20.10.1.TXT	6	5	60	3800	4	4	S_A	6100
N19	20.10.1.TXT	9	4	20	3800	20	6	S_A	5697
N20	20.10.1.TXT	9	4	20	1800	20	10	S_A	6002
N21	20.10.1.TXT	9	5	20	3800	4	4	S_A	6151
N22	20.10.1.TXT	9	3	60	3800	20	12	S_A	5688
N23	20.10.1.TXT	9	4	60	1800	20	10	S_C	5915
N24	20.10.1.TXT	9	5	60	3800	4	4	S_A	6100

C' - The number of drones required in the delivery process
L' - The number of used and free slots
Fc - The total distance covered by drones

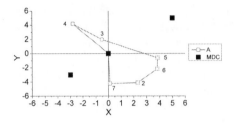

Fig. 3. Drone routes for the example N04

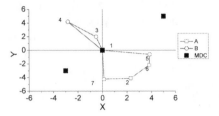

Fig. 4. Drone routes for the example N05

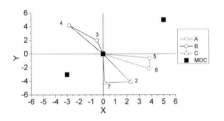

Fig. 5. Drone routes for the example N06

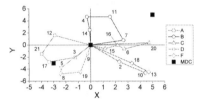

Fig. 6. Drone routes for the example N15

Table 4. Results of subsequent iterations of the algorithm for selected examples

Parameters									Results
No	Instancja	C	C'	vc	K	L	L'	MDC	Fc
N01	6.10.1.TXT	3	2	20	3800	10	4	S_A	2464
	6.10.1.TXT	3	2	20	3800	10	4	S_B	3972
	6.10.1.TXT	3	2	20	3800	10	4	S_C	3279
N02	6.10.1.TXT	3	2	20	1800	10	4	S_A	2464
	6.10.1.TXT	3	-	20	1800	10	-	S_B	NFSF
	6.10.1.TXT	3	2	20	1800	10	4	S_C	3279
N03	6.10.1.TXT	3	3	20	3800	2	2	S_A	3128
	6.10.1.TXT	3	-	20	3800	2	-	S_B	NFSF
	6.10.1.TXT	3	3	20	3800	2	2	S_C	4261

4   Conclusions

The proposed model allows for optimization of deliveries by means of intermodal transport with drones. The total distance covered by drones is minimized. Moreover, as a result of solving the model for optimal Fc value, we obtain information that allows for multi-faceted decision support during the delivery process. This is because it is possible to determine the optimal route for drones, the number and type of drones required in the delivery process (C'), the number of used and free slots (L') and drones launch delivery points. In further studies it is planned to expand the model, which will take into account the weather conditions, e.g. the impact of wind on the drone range, dependence of the drone range on the weight of the transported load, etc. Comparative analyses of the model presented (Sect. 2) with the model containing the MDC selection are also planned. Due to the high computational complexity of the larger problems, it is planned to use heuristics, metaheuristics [10–14] and original hybrid methods to solve the problem [15–17].

References

1. Toth, P., Vigo, D.: Vehicle Routing: Problems, Methods, and Applications, 2nd edn. Society for Industrial and Applied Mathematics and the Mathematical Optimization Society, Philadelphia (2014)
2. Mourelo, F.S., Harbison, T., Weber, T., Sturges, R., Rich, R.: Optimization of a truck-drone in tandem delivery network using k-means and genetic algorithm. J. Ind. Eng. Manag. 9(2), 374–388 (2016)
3. Murray, C.C., Chu, A.G.: The flying sidekick traveling salesman problem: optimization of drone-assisted parcel delivery. Transp. Res. Part C Emerg. Technol. 54, 86–109 (2015)
4. Poikonen, S., Wang, X., Golden, B.: The vehicle routing problem with drones: extended models and connections. Networks 70(1), 34–43 (2017)
5. Wang, X., Poikonen, S., Golden, B.: The vehicle routing problem with drones: several worst-case results. Optim. Lett. 11(4), 679–697 (2016)
6. Sitek, P., Wikarek, J.: A hybrid approach to the optimization of multiechelon systems. Math. Probl. Eng. 2015, 12 (2015). https://doi.org/10.1155/2015/925675. Article ID 925675
7. Sinha, S.M.: Mathematical Programming, Theory and Methods (2005). eBook ISBN: 9780080535937
8. Lun, Y.H.V., Lai, K.H., Cheng, T.C.E.: Shipping and Logistics Management, 1st edn. Springer, London (2010). https://doi.org/10.1007/978-1-84882-997-8
9. Zenodo. https://zenodo.org/record/1403150?fbclid=IwAR366Ezt5p-ax3Yf5P7uKHXkjh9p-zdD4U-g8UKZI4gMprN6VKhFfFUpvIpA#.XJYfXdR6St9. Accessed 20 Apr 2019
10. Crawford, B., Soto, R., Peña, C., Palma, W., Johnson, F., Paredes, F.: Solving the set covering problem with a shuffled frog leaping algorithm. In: Nguyen, N.T., Trawiński, B., Kosala, R. (eds.) ACIIDS 2015. LNCS (LNAI), vol. 9012, pp. 41–50. Springer, Cham (2015). https://doi.org/10.1007/978-3-319-15705-4_5
11. Li, C., Chiang, T.-W.: Complex fuzzy computing to time series prediction a multi-swarm PSO learning approach. In: Nguyen, N.T., Kim, C.-G., Janiak, A. (eds.) ACIIDS 2011. LNCS (LNAI), vol. 6592, pp. 242–251. Springer, Heidelberg (2011). https://doi.org/10.1007/978-3-642-20042-7_25
12. Gola, A., Kłosowski, G.: Application of fuzzy logic and genetic algorithms in automated works transport organization. In: Omatu, S., Rodríguez, S., Villarrubia, G., Faria, P., Sitek, P., Prieto, J. (eds.) Distributed Computing and Artificial Intelligence, 14th International Conference. AISC, vol. 620, pp. 29–36. Springer, Cham (2018). https://doi.org/10.1007/978-3-319-62410-5_4
13. Rutczyńska-Wdowiak, K.: Replacement strategies of genetic algorithm in parametric identification of induction motor. In: 22nd International Conference on Methods and Models in Automation and Robotics, MMAR 2017, pp. 971–975 (2017). https://doi.org/10.1109/mmar.2017.8046961

14. Dang, Q.V., Nielsen, I.E., Bocewicz, G.: A genetic algorithm-based heuristic for part-feeding mobile robot scheduling problem. In: Rodríguez, J., Pérez, J., Golinska, P., Giroux, S., Corchuelo, R. (eds.) Trends in Practical Applications of Agents and Multiagent Systems. AINSC, vol. 157, pp. 85–92. Springer, Heidelberg (2012). https://doi.org/10.1007/978-3-642-28795-4_10

15. Sitek, P., Wikarek, J.: Capacitated vehicle routing problem with pick-up and alternative delivery (CVRPPAD): model and implementation using hybrid approach. Ann. Oper. Res. **273**, 1–21 (2019). https://doi.org/10.1007/s10479-017-2722-x

16. Sitek, P., Wikarek, J., Nielsen, P.: A constraint-driven approach to food supply chain management. In: Industrial Management & Data Systems, vol. 117, pp. 2115–2138 (2017). https://doi.org/10.1108/imds-10-2016-0465

17. Wikarek, J.: Implementation aspects of hybrid solution framework. In: Szewczyk, R., Zieliński, C., Kaliczyńska, M. (eds.) Recent Advances in Automation, Robotics and Measuring Techniques. AISC, vol. 267, pp. 317–328. Springer, Heidelberg (2014). https://doi.org/10.1007/978-3-319-05353-0_31

Cooperative Strategies for Decision Making and Optimization

Current Trends
in the Population-Based Optimization

Piotr Jedrzejowicz[(✉)]

Gdynia Maritime University, Gdynia, Poland
p.jedrzejowicz@umg.edu.pl

Abstract. Population-based methods are used to deal with computationally difficult optimization problems. The outcome of the current research effort in the field of the population-based optimization can be broadly categorized as a new, stand-alone, P-B metaheuristics, ensemble P-B metaheuristics including multi-population and multi-agent approaches, new hybrid approaches involving P-B metaheuristics, and improvements and successful modifications of the earlier known P-B metaheuristics. Research results obtained during the last few years in each of the above categories are briefly discussed. The last part of the paper includes comments on directions of future research in the population-based optimization.

Keywords: Population-based methods · Metaheuristics · Algorithms

1 Introduction

Population-based (P-B) methods belong to the wider class of metaheuristics. Metaheuristics are algorithms producing approximate solutions to a wide range of optimization problems. In fact, metaheuristics are not problem-specific, although their parameters, as a rule, have to be fitted to particular problems.

Population-based methods are nowadays commonly used to deal with computationally difficult optimization problems. Population in this context represents possible solutions, parts of solutions or some constructs that can be easily transformed into solutions. Population-based algorithms are designed to carry out various operations on populations, sub-populations or individuals (population members) aiming at finding the best solution.

Pioneering work in the area of the population-based methods included genetic programming – (GP) [33], genetic algorithms (GA) [17], evolutionary computations - EC [15, 39], ant colony optimization (ACO) [13], particle swarm optimization (PSO) [30] and bee colony algorithms (BCA) [53]. Since the nineties, research interest in population-based optimization has been constantly growing. In this paper, we review and analyze developments in the area of the population-based optimization taking place more recently. The paper is organized as follows. Section 2 contains an overview of the recent research effort in the area of the population-based metaheuristics. In Sect. 3, some promising and recently proposed approaches are reviewed. Finally, Sect. 4 offers some insights into future directions of research in population-based optimization.

© Springer Nature Switzerland AG 2019
N. T. Nguyen et al. (Eds.): ICCCI 2019, LNAI 11683, pp. 523–534, 2019.
https://doi.org/10.1007/978-3-030-28377-3_43

2 Overview of the Recent Research Effort

Optimization algorithms can be classified into one of the two main classes – deterministic and stochastic. Population-based metaheuristics belong to the second class even if some of their sub-procedures might be deterministic. P-B metaheuristics, like all other optimization methods, are constrained by the no-free-lunch (NFL) theorem of Wolpert and Macready [64]. This makes P-B metaheuristics difficult to evaluate and comparisons between competing metaheuristics are valid with respect to the set of problems selected as the benchmark.

Two major worries of anyone involved in designing P-B metaheuristics are being trapped at local optima and not achieving convergence to the optimality. To avoid a disaster with respect to either of the above, two strategies are used in practically all P-B metaheuristic algorithms. These are intensification and diversification also referred to as exploitation and exploration. According to [65], the randomized diversification means generating diverse solutions to explore the search space on a global scale, and intensification means to focus on the search in a local region by exploiting the information that a current good solution is found in this region. Because of the usual huge size of the solution space, there is a need for selection. Iterative selection of the best-fitted individuals is a strategy expected to assure convergence to the optimality.

During the whole period of the P-B metaheuristics development, that is during the last 30 years, the focus of research in the field of the population-based metaheuristics has been centered on improving and designing procedures of diversification, intensification, and selection. Ultimate goals of these efforts are more effective methods assuring a better balance between exploitation and exploration and quicker convergence towards the optimality. Achieving convergence and speeding-up its pace has been the focus of research aiming at constructing effective or even "intelligent" selection procedures. All these efforts have been and still are inspired by a variety of phenomena, historically, in the beginning, from nature only and recently also from physics, astrophysics, geometry, geography, and social behavior. Another direction of research is applying the emerging ICT technologies to scale-up and speed-up search for the optimum solution through parallelization and distribution of the computational effort. As expected, new methods and approaches cannot reach beyond the NFL theorem. Hence, the best what a researcher in the field of population-based metaheuristics can get is proving that the proposed approach is, in some aspects better than earlier approaches aiming at solving a particular problem or particular class of problems.

In their survey published in 2013, Boussaï et al. [6] proposed the classification of the population-based metaheuristics and grouped them into two broad classes. The first is evolutionary computation with subclasses including genetic algorithms, evolution strategy, evolutionary programming, genetic programming, estimation of distribution algorithms, differential evolution, coevolutionary algorithms, cultural algorithms and scatter search and path relinking. The second class is swarm intelligence with subclasses including ant colony optimization, particle swarm optimization, bacterial foraging optimization, bee colony optimization, artificial immune systems and biogeography-based optimization. Since 2013, more subclasses have appeared and gained recognition as shown in Table 1.

Nearly all of the above-listed approaches have been inspired by various natural phenomena. The spectrum of the natural phenomena inspiring researchers have substantially grown during the last few years. The outcome of the current research effort in the field of population-based optimization can be broadly categorized as follows:

- New, generic P-B metaheuristics
- Ensemble P-B metaheuristics including multi-population and multi-agent approaches
- New hybrid approaches involving P-B metaheuristics
- Improvements and successful modifications of the earlier known P-B metaheuristics

Following the above taxonomy Tables 1, 2, 3 and 4 list recently published new P-B metaheuristics, ensemble P-B metaheuristics and multi-population/multi-agent approaches, hybrid metaheuristics and major improvements of the P-B metaheuristics, respectively.

Table 1. Recently published new generic P-B metaheuristics

Metaheuristic name	Inspiring phenomenon	Source	Year
Black Hole Algorithm	Black hole phenomenon in the space	[20]	2013
Backtracking Search Optimization Algorithm	Evolutionary process	[11]	2013
Dolphin Echolocation Algorithm	Strategies used by dolphins for their hunting process	[28]	2013
Mine blast Algorithm	Mine bomb explosion	[51]	2013
League Championship Algorithm	Championship environment wherein teams play in a league for several weeks	[27]	2014
Grey Wolf Optimizer	Leadership hierarchy and hunting mechanism of grey wolfs		
Ions motion Algorithm	Physical processes	[25]	2015
Ant Lion Algorithm	Hunting mechanism of ant lions in nature	[40]	2015
Invasive Tumor Growth Optimization Algorithm	Invasive behaviors of proliferative cells and quiescent cells	[61]	2015
Moth-flame Optimization Algorithm	Navigation method of moths in nature	[41]	2015
Optics-inspired Optimizer	Optical phenomena (a physical process)	[26]	2015
Lightning Search Algorithm	The natural phenomenon of lightning	[56]	2015
Dragonfly algorithm	Static and dynamic swarming behaviors of dragonflies	[42]	2015
Artificial Algae Algorithm	Living behaviors of microalgae	[62]	2015
Sine Cosine Algorithm	Trigonometric functions	[43]	2016
Lion Optimization Algorithm	Lion's behavior and social organization	[66]	2016

(continued)

Table 1. (*continued*)

Metaheuristic name	Inspiring phenomenon	Source	Year
Crow Search Algorithm	Intelligent behavior of crows	[4]	2016
Dolphin Swarm Optimization Algorithm	Mechanism of dolphins in detecting, chasing and preying on swarms of sardines	[69]	2016
Virulence Optimization Algorithm	Special mechanism and function of viruses which includes the recognition of fittest viruses to infect body cells	[22]	2016
Virus Colony Search Algorithm	Diffusion and infection strategies for the host cells adopted by a virus to survive and propagate in the cell environment	[35]	2016
Shark Smell Optimization	The behavior of sharks finding its prey using smell sense	[1]	2016
Multi-Verse Optimizer	Astrophysical phenomena	[45]	2016
Selfish Herd Optimizer	Selfish-herd behavior manifested by individuals within a herd of animals subjected to some form of predation risk	[14]	2017
Salp Swarm Algorithm	Swarming behavior of salps during navigating and foraging in oceans	[46]	2017
Grasshopper Optimization Algorithm	Swarming behavior of grasshoppers	[54]	2017
Electro-Search Algorithm	Orbital movement of the electrons around the atomic nucleus	[60]	2017
Thermal Exchange Optimization	Newton's law of cooling	[28]	2017
Weighted Superposition Attraction	Superposition principle	[5]	2017
Spotted Hyena Optimizer	Natural hyena behavior	[12]	2017
Butterfly-Inspired Algorithm	Mate searching behavior of the butterfly	[52]	2017
Lightning Attachment Procedure Optimization	Physical phenomenon	[49]	2017
Mouth Brooding Fish Optimizer	Behavior and the distance of movement and dispersion of children around the mother's mouth	[23]	2018
Queuing Search Algorithm	Human activities in queuing	[71]	2018
Volleyball Premier League Algorithm	Competition and interaction among volleyball teams during a season	[47]	2018
Squirrel Search Algorithm	Dynamic foraging behavior of southern flying squirrels and their efficient way of locomotion known as gliding	[24]	2019

Table 2. Ensemble P-B metaheuristics and multi-population/multi-agent approaches

Metaheuristic name	Inspiring phenomenon	Source	Year
Artificial Cooperative Search Algorithm	Social behavior	[10]	2013
Cooperative Differential Evolution with Multiple Populations	Evolutionary process	[63]	2016
Competitive Optimization Algorithm	Competitive behavior in nature	[57]	2016
Collective Information Differential Evolution	Evolutionary process	[73]	2017
Collective decision optimization algorithm	Social behavior	[70]	2017
Multi-swarm Particle Swarm Optimization	Natural phenomenon	[67]	2017
Ensemble Differential Evolution	Evolutionary process	[19]	2018
Coevolutionary Multiobjective Evolutionary Algorithms	Evolutionary process	[3]	2018
Multi-Agent Simulated Annealing Algorithm	Physical process	[36]	2018
Majority-Voting Algorithm	Social interactions	[38]	2019
Ensemble Strategies for P-B Optimization	Evolutionary process	[18]	2019
Multi-Population Algorithms	Evolutionary process	[38]	2019
Raccoon Optimization Algorithm	Rummaging behaviors of real raccoons for food	[31]	2019
Quantum Firefly Swarms	Multi-population swarm behavior	[50]	2019
Island-Based Differential Evolution	Evolutionary process	[59]	2019

Table 3. Recently published hybrid metaheuristics

Main components	Inspiring phenomena	Source	Year
Hybrid GWO-SCA	Hunting mechanism of grey wolves in nature + sine and cosine functions	[58]	2017
Brainstorm Optimization with Chaotic Local Search	Social behavior	[68]	2017
Hybrid Particle Swarm Optimizer with Sine Cosine Algorithm	Swarm behavior + sine and cosine functions	[7]	2018
Island Bat Algorithm	Island GA + bat algorithm	[2]	2018
Hybrid Clonal Selection Algorithm with Combinatorial Recombination	Immune system + evolutionary computation	[72]	2019
Hybrid sine cosine algorithm with differential evolution	Sine and cosine functions + evolutionary computation	[48]	2019

Table 4. Recently published major improvements of the P-B metaheuristics

Metaheuristic name	Inspiring phenomenon	Source	Year
Bare Bones Fireworks Optimizer	Imitation of fireworks explosion (a physical process)	[34]	2018
Ameliorated Particle Swarm Optimizer	Social behaviors of the individuals in bird flocking and fish schooling	[8]	2018
New Bat Algorithm	Nature behavior of bats	[16]	2018
β-Chaotic Map Enabled Grey Wolf Optimizer	Leadership hierarchy and hunting mechanism of grey wolves in nature	[55]	2019
Modified Gravitational Search	Newton's laws of gravity and motion	[21]	2019
Improved fireworks algorithm	Explosion process of fireworks	[9]	2019

3   Interesting New Results

3.1   Ensemble P-B Metaheuristics Including Multi-population and Multi-agent Approaches

The idea of the ensemble population-based metaheuristics covers approaches characterized by multiple search operators, parameters, constraint handling, neighborhood structures, and computation controlling procedures. The above diversity is expected to support dealing with hard optimization problems. The main assumption behind the ensemble methods is that different search trajectories brought about by the ensemble may help to avoid getting trapped in a local optimum and achieve quicker convergence.

According to [18] P-B ensembles can be classified into the low-level ensemble and high-level ensemble. The low-level ensemble is the ensemble of multiple algorithmic components like search operators, parameter values, neighborhood structures, etc. The high-level ensemble covers different P-B metaheuristic variants in the form of islands, agents or independent solutions dealing with a given optimization problem.

Among recent advances in constructing the ensemble metaheuristics on can mention new cooperative and co-evolutionary algorithms. Civicioglu in [10] proposed the Artificial Cooperative Search (ACS) algorithm. In [57] the authors proposed a novel optimization algorithm based on a competitive behavior of various creatures. In the proposed method a competition takes place between competing algorithms solving the problem. The rules of competition are based on the, so called, imperialist competitive algorithm deciding which of the algorithms can survive.

Collective computational intelligence stands behind two interesting approaches - Collective Information Differential Evolution [72] and Collective Decision Optimization algorithm [68]. Both approaches are inspired by human information exchange and decision-making processes including the experience phase, group thinking phase, leader-based phase, and innovation phase. Another interesting approach is the Multi-Swarm Particle Swarm Optimization algorithm [67] where information exchange among sub-swarms is possible. The idea proposed in [36] is based on a multi-agent system paradigm where a multi-agent simulated annealing (MASA) algorithm with parallel adaptive multiple sampling (MASA-PAMS) that features better search ability is proposed. Mahdavi with co-authors [38] proposes the majority voting scheme for discrete population-based optimization algorithms which uses the information of all candidate solutions in the current generation to create a new trial candidate solution.

3.2 Hybrid Metaheuristics

Hybrid P-B metaheuristics are expected to profit from the synergetic effect of integrating at least two optimization algorithm of which at least one belongs to the P-B algorithms class. Hybrid algorithms are designed with a view to cover deficiencies of the participating methods, thus making the application area of the hybrid wider than such area for the stand-alone solutions. In the paper by [58] a hybrid Grey Wolf Optimizer (GWO) – Sine Cosine Algorithm (SCA) is proposed. Substantial improvement is also expected through merging Brain Storm Optimization (BSO) with the chaotic local search proposed by [68]. The incorporation of chaotic search can help to avoid stagnation and to assure population's diversity, thus resulting in a better balance between exploration and exploitation. Another successful marriage is a hybridization of the Particle Swarm Optimization (PSO) with the SCA, as proposed in [7]. It is well known that PSO tends to converge prematurely or stops being trapped at a local optimum. To overcome the shortcomings of PSO, a hybrid particle swarm optimizer with sine cosine acceleration coefficients was proposed.

Yet another hybridization of the SCA, this time with the differential evolution method, was proposed by [48]. When solving complex multimodal optimization problems SCA often converges to a local minimum quickly, missing better opportunities [32]. To prevent premature convergence of SCA, differential evolution algorithm is used as a local search operator.

Integrating an artificial immune system with evolutionary computation is the idea put forward in [72]. They propose a well-known and widely used clonal selection algorithm (CSA) with modified combinatorial recombination to diversify the population and avoid the premature convergence. The approach is a remedy for diversity loss, poor searchability, premature convergence, and stagnation. To address the problem, modified combinatorial recombination and the success-history based adaptive mutation strategy are introduced to form a success-history based adaptive mutation based clonal selection algorithm.

4   Conclusions

P-B metaheuristics remain a vivid and still growing area of research. Because of the constraints posed by the NFL theorem, it is very likely that search for a better, more effective and more universal metaheuristics will be opened for the years to come. There is a lot of possible directions to be followed in attempts to build new stand-alone, ensemble, and hybrid P-B metaheuristics. Researchers will also continue working on improvements to the existing solutions.

Search for inspirations from nature, social processes, physics, mechanics and various other scientific disciplines will certainly remain an effective way to publish. Some of the yet to be discovered inspirations may also bring worthy, stand-alone solutions to problems belonging to some specific problem classes. Another direction of research will focus on alleviating some of the typical P-B metaheuristics deficiencies such as high demand for computation resources, slow convergence, and tendency to be trapped in local optima.

Advances of the ICT technology will support the construction of the ensemble metaheuristics including parallelized algorithms, agent-based solutions, and algorithms that can be executed within a distributed environment. Ensemble solutions will bring the possibility to explore wider search spaces without dramatically increasing computation time. In effect, more complex and bigger problems would yield to optimization efforts and a new branch of optimization methods that can be named as the "big data optimization" will appear. Big data optimization will require solution able to deal with the dynamic situations through adaptation and self-tuning.

Another important research direction in the area of P-B metaheuristics will remain hybridization. There is a lot of research options to conceive solutions where integration of different approaches will result in a synergetic effect offering new quality solutions. Similarly, even in well-established methods there might be still a room for improvements through redesigning computation control processes.

References

1. Abedinia, O., Amjady, N., Ghasemi, A.: A new metaheuristic algorithm based on shark smell optimization. Complexity **21**(5), 97–116 (2016). https://doi.org/10.1002/cplx.21634
2. Al-Betar, M.A., Awadallah, M.A.: Island bat algorithm for optimization. Expert Syst. Appl. **107**, 126–145 (2018). https://doi.org/10.1016/j.eswa.2018.04.024
3. Antonio, L.M., CoelloCoello, C.A.: Coevolutionary multiobjective evolutionary algorithms: survey of the state-of-the-art. IEEE Trans. Evol. Comput. **22**(6), 851–865 (2018). https://doi.org/10.1109/TEVC.2017.2767023
4. Askarzadeh, A.: A novel metaheuristic method for solving constrained engineering optimization problems: crow search algorithm. Comput. Struct. **169**, 1–12 (2016). https://doi.org/10.1016/j.compstruc.2016.03.001
5. Baykasoglu, A., Akpinar, S.: Weighted superposition attraction (WSA): a swarm intelligence algorithm for optimization problems–part 1: unconstrained optimization. Appl. Soft Comput. **56**, 520–540 (2017). https://doi.org/10.1016/j.asoc.2015.10.036
6. Boussaï, I., Lepagnot, D.J., Siarry, P.: A survey on optimization metaheuristics. Inf. Sci. **237**, 82–117 (2013). https://doi.org/10.1016/j.ins.2013.02.041
7. Chen, K., Zhou, F., Yin, L., Wang, S., Wang, Y., Wan, F.: A hybrid particle swarm optimizer with sine cosine acceleration coefficients. Inf. Sci. **422**, 218–241 (2018). https://doi.org/10.1016/j.ins.2017.09.015
8. Chen, K., Zhou, F., Wang, Y., Yin, L.: An ameliorated particle swarm optimizer for solving numerical optimization problems. Appl. Soft Comput. J. **73**, 482–496 (2018). https://doi.org/10.1016/j.asoc.2018.09.007

9. Cheng, R., Bai, Y., Zhao, Y., Tan, X., Xu, T.: Improved fireworks algorithm with information exchange for function optimization. Knowl.-Based Syst. **163**, 82–90 (2019). https://doi.org/10.1016/j.knosys.2018.08.016

10. Civicioglu, P.: Artificial cooperative search algorithm for numerical optimization problems. Inf. Sci. **229**, 58–76 (2013). https://doi.org/10.1016/j.ins.2012.11.013

11. Civicioglu, P.: Backtracking search optimization algorithm for numerical optimization problems. Appl. Math. Comput. **219**, 8121–8144 (2013). https://doi.org/10.1016/j.amc.2013.02.017

12. Dhiman, G., Kumar, V.: Spotted hyena optimizer: a novel bio-inspired based metaheuristic technique for engineering applications. Adv. Eng. Softw. **114**, 48–70 (2017). https://doi.org/10.1016/j.advengsoft.2017.05.014

13. Dorigo, M., Maniezzo, V., Colorni, A.: Ant system: optimization by a colony of cooperating agents. IEEE Trans. Syst. Man Cybern. Part B (Cybern.) **26**(1), 29–41 (1996). https://doi.org/10.1109/3477.484436

14. Fausto, F., Cuevas, E., Valdivia, A., González, A.: A global optimization algorithm inspired in the behavior of selfish herds. Biosystems **160**, 39–55 (2017). https://doi.org/10.1016/j.biosystems.2017.07.010

15. Fogel, D.B.: Evolutionary Computation: Toward a New Philosophy of Machine Intelligence. IEEE Press, Piscataway (1995)

16. Gan, C., Cao, W., Wu, M., Chen, X.: A new bat algorithm based on iterative local search and stochastic inertia weight. Expert Syst. Appl. **104**, 202–212 (2018). https://doi.org/10.1016/j.eswa.2018.03.015

17. Goldberg, D.E.: Genetic Algorithms in Search, Optimization and Machine Learning. Addison-Wesley Longman Publishing Co., Inc., Boston (1989)

18. Guohua, W., Shen, X., Li, H., Chen, H., Lin, A., Suganthan, P.: Ensemble of differential evolution variants. Inf. Sci. **423**, 172–186 (2018). https://doi.org/10.1016/j.ins.2017.09.053

19. Guohua, W., Mallipeddi, R., Suganthan, P.N.: Ensemble strategies for population-based optimization algorithms – a survey. Swarm Evol. Comput. **44**, 695–711 (2019). https://doi.org/10.1016/j.swevo.2018.08.015

20. Hatamlou, A.: Black hole: a new heuristic optimization approach for data clustering. Inf. Sci. **222**, 175–184 (2013). https://doi.org/10.1016/j.ins.2012.08.023

21. He, S., Zhu, L., Wang, L., Yu, L., Yao, C.: A modified gravitational search algorithm for function optimization. IEEE Access **7**, 5984–5993 (2019). https://doi.org/10.1109/ACCESS.2018.2889854

22. Jaderyan, M., Khotanlou, H.: Virulence optimization algorithm. Appl. Soft Comput. **43**, 596–618 (2016). https://doi.org/10.1016/j.asoc.2016.02.038

23. Jahani, E., Chizari, M.: Tackling global optimization problems with a novel algorithm–mouth Brooding Fish algorithm. Appl. Soft Comput. **62**, 987–1002 (2018). https://doi.org/10.1016/j.asoc.2017.09.035

24. Jain, M., Singh, V., Rani, A.: A novel nature-inspired algorithm for optimization: squirrel search algorithm. Swarm Evol. Comput. **44**, 148–175 (2019). https://doi.org/10.1016/j.swevo.2018.02.013

25. Javidy, B., Hatamlou, A., Mirjalili, S.: Ions motion algorithm for solving optimization problems. Appl. Soft Comput. **32**, 72–79 (2015). https://doi.org/10.1016/j.asoc.2015.03.035

26. Kashan, A.H.: League championship algorithm (LCA): an algorithm for global optimization inspired by sport championships. Appl. Soft Comput. **16**, 171–200 (2014). https://doi.org/10.1016/j.asoc.2013.12.005

27. Kashan, A.H.: A new metaheuristic for optimization: optics inspired optimization (OIO). Comput. Oper. Res. **55**, 99–125 (2015). https://doi.org/10.1016/j.cor.2014.10.011

28. Kaveh, A., Farhoudi, N.: A new optimization method: dolphin echolocation. Adv. Eng. Softw. **59**, 53–70 (2013). https://doi.org/10.1016/j.advengsoft.2013.03.004

29. Kaveh, A., Dadras, A.: A novel meta-heuristic optimization algorithm: thermal exchange optimization. Adv. Eng. Softw. **110**, 69–84 (2017). https://doi.org/10.1016/j.advengsoft.2017.03.014

30. Kennedy, J., Eberhart, R.: Particle swarm optimization. In: Proceedings of ICNN 1995 - International Conference on Neural Networks. IEEE Xplore (1995). https://doi.org/10.1109/icnn.1995.488968

31. Koohi, S.Z., Hamid, N.A.W.A., Othman, M., Ibragimov, G.: Raccoon optimization algorithm. IEEE Access **7**, 5383–5399 (2019). https://doi.org/10.1109/ACCESS.2018.2882568

32. Kommadath, R., Dondeti, J., Kotecha, P.: Benchmarking JAYA and sine cosine algorithm on real parameter bound constrained single objective optimization problems (CEC2016). In: ISMSI 2017, Proceedings of the 2017 International Conference on Intelligent Systems, Metaheuristics & Swarm Intelligence, Hong Kong, pp. 31–34 (2017). https://doi.org/10.1145/3059336.3059363

33. Koza, J.R.: Genetic Programming: On the Programming of Computers by Means of Natural Selection. MIT Press, Boston (1992)

34. Li, J., Tan, Y.: The bare bones fireworks algorithm: a minimalist global optimizer. Appl. Soft Comput. **62**, 454–462 (2018). https://doi.org/10.1016/j.asoc.2017.10.046

35. Li, M.D., Zhao, H., Weng, X.W., Han, T.: A novel nature-inspired algorithm for optimization: virus colony search. Adv. Eng. Softw. **92**, 65–88 (2016). https://doi.org/10.1016/j.advengsoft.2015.11.004

36. Lin, J., Zhonga, Y., Li, E., Lina, X., Zhang, H.: Multi-agent simulated annealing algorithm with parallel adaptive multiple sampling for protein structure prediction in AB off-lattice model. Appl. Soft Comput. **62**, 491–503 (2018). https://doi.org/10.1016/j.asoc.2017.09.037

37. Ma, H., Shen, S., Yu, M., Yang, Z., Fei, M., Zhou, H.: Multi-population techniques in nature inspired optimization algorithms: a comprehensive survey. Swarm Evol. Comput. **44**, 365–387 (2019). https://doi.org/10.1016/j.swevo.2018.04.011

38. Mahdavi, S., Rahnamayan, S., Mahdavi, A.: Majority voting for discrete population-based optimization algorithms. Soft Comput. **23**, 1–18 (2019). https://doi.org/10.1007/s00500-018-3530-1

39. Michalewicz, Z.: Genetic Algorithms + Data Structures = Evolution Programs, 3rd edn. Springer, Heidelberg (1996). https://doi.org/10.1007/978-3-662-03315-9

40. Mirjalili, S.: The ant lion optimizer. Adv. Eng. Softw. **83**, 80–98 (2015). https://doi.org/10.1016/j.advengsoft.2015.01.010

41. Mirjalili, S.: Moth-flame optimization algorithm: a novel nature-inspired heuristic paradigm. Knowl.-Based Syst. **89**, 228–249 (2015). https://doi.org/10.1016/j.knosys.2015.07.006

42. Mirjalili, S.: Dragonfly algorithm: a new meta-heuristic optimization technique for solving single-objective, discrete, and multi-objective problems. Neural Comput. Appl. **27**(4), 1053–1073 (2016). https://doi.org/10.1007/s00521-015-1920-1

43. Mirjalili, S.: SCA: a sine cosine algorithm for solving optimization problems. Knowl.-Based Syst. **96**, 120–133 (2016). https://doi.org/10.1016/j.knosys.2015.12.022

44. Mirjalili, S., Mirjalili, S.M., Lewis, A.: Grey wolf optimizer. Adv. Eng. Softw. **69**, 46–61 (2014). https://doi.org/10.1016/j.advengsoft.2013.12.007

45. Mirjalili, S., Mirjalili, S.M., Hatamlou, A.: Multi-verse optimizer: a nature-inspired algorithm for global optimization. Neural Comput. Appl. **27**(2), 495–513 (2016). https://doi.org/10.1007/s00521-015-1870-7

46. Mirjalili, S., Gandomi, A.H., Mirjalili, S.Z., Saremi, S., Faris, H., Mirjalili, S.M.: Salp swarm algorithm: a bio-inspired optimizer for engineering design problems. Adv. Eng. Softw. **114**, 163–191 (2017). https://doi.org/10.1016/j.advengsoft.2017.07.002

47. Moghdani, R., Salimifard, K.: Volleyball premier league algorithm. Appl. Soft Comput. **64**, 161–185 (2018). https://doi.org/10.1016/j.asoc.2017.11.043

48. Nenavath, H., Jatoth, R.K.: Hybridizing sine cosine algorithm with differential evolution for global optimization and object tracking. Appl. Soft Comput. **62**, 1019–1043 (2018). https://doi.org/10.1016/j.asoc.2017.09.039

49. Nematollahi, A.F., Rahiminejad, A., Vahidi, B.: A novel physical based meta-heuristic optimization method known as lightning attachment procedure optimization. Appl. Soft Comput. **59**, 596–621 (2017). https://doi.org/10.1016/j.asoc.2017.06.033

50. Ozsoydan, F.B., Baykasoglu, A.: Quantum firefly swarms for multimodal dynamic optimization problems. Expert Syst. Appl. **115**, 189–199 (2019). https://doi.org/10.1016/j.eswa.2018.08.007

51. Sadollah, A., Bahreininejad, A., Eskandar, H., Hamdi, M.: Mine blast algorithm: a new population based algorithm for solving constrained engineering optimization problems. Appl. Soft Comput. **13**(5), 2592–2612 (2013). https://doi.org/10.1016/j.asoc.2012.11.026

52. Qi, X., Zhu, Y., Zhang, H.: A new meta-heuristic butterfly-inspired algorithm. J. Comput. Sci. **23**, 226–239 (2017). https://doi.org/10.1016/j.jocs.2017.06.003

53. Sato, T., Hagiwara, M.: Bee system: finding solution by a concentrated search. In: Proceedings of the IEEE International Conference on Systems, Man, and Cybernetics, Computational Cybernetics and Simulation, Orlando, FL, pp. 3954–3959 (1997)

54. Saremi, S., Mirjalili, S., Lewis, A.: Grasshopper optimization algorithm: theory and application. Adv. Eng. Softw. **105**, 30–47 (2017). https://doi.org/10.1016/j.advengsoft.2017.01.004

55. Saxena, A., Kumar, R., Das, S.: β-chaotic map enabled grey wolf optimizer. Appl. Soft Comput. J. **75**, 84–85 (2019). https://doi.org/10.1016/j.asoc.2018.10.044

56. Shareef, H., Ibrahim, A.A., Mutlag, A.H.: Lightning search algorithm. Appl. Soft Comput. **36**, 315–333 (2015). https://doi.org/10.1016/j.asoc.2015.07.028

57. Sharafi, Y., Khanesar, M.A., Teshnehlab, M.: COOA: competitive optimization algorithm. Swarm Evol. Comput. **30**, 39–63 (2016). https://doi.org/10.1016/j.swevo.2016.04.002

58. Singh, N., Singh, S.B.: A novel hybrid GWO-SCA approach for optimization problems. Eng. Sci. Technol. Int. J. **20**, 1586–1601 (2017). https://doi.org/10.1016/j.jestch.2017.11.001

59. Skakovski, A., Jedrzejowicz, P.: An Island-based differential evolution algorithm with the multi-size populations. Expert Syst. Appl. (2019) https://doi.org/10.1016/j.eswa.2019.02.027

60. Tabari, A., Ahmad, A.: A new optimization method: electro-search algorithm. Comput. Chem. Eng. **103**, 1–11 (2017). https://doi.org/10.1016/j.compchemeng.2017.01.046

61. Tang, D., Dong, S., Jiang, Y., Li, H., Huang, Y.: ITGO: invasive tumor growth optimization algorithm. Appl. Soft Comput. **36**, 670–698 (2015). https://doi.org/10.1016/j.asoc.2015.07.045

62. Uymaz, S.A., Tezel, G., Yel, E.: Artificial algae algorithm (AAA) for nonlinear global optimization. Appl. Soft Comput. **31**, 153–171 (2015). https://doi.org/10.1016/j.asoc.2015.03.003

63. Wang, J., Zhang, W., Zhang, J.: Cooperative differential evolution with multiple populations for multiobjective optimization. IEEE Trans. Cybern. **46**(12), 2848–2861 (2016). https://doi.org/10.1109/tcyb.2015.2490669

64. Wolpert, D.H., Macready, W.G.: No free lunch theorems for optimization. IEEE Trans. Evol. Comput. **1**(1), 67–82 (1997). https://doi.org/10.1109/4235.585893
65. Yang, X.S.: Nature-Inspired Optimization Algorithms. Elsevier, Amsterdam (2014)
66. Yazdani, M., Jolai, F.: Lion optimization algorithm (LOA): a nature-inspired metaheuristic algorithm. J. Comput. Des. Eng. **3**, 24–36 (2016). https://doi.org/10.1016/j.jcde.2015.06.003
67. Ye, W., Feng, W., Fan, S.: A novel multi-swarm particle swarm optimization with dynamic learning strategy. Appl. Soft Comput. **61**, 832–843 (2017). https://doi.org/10.1016/j.asoc.2017.08.051
68. Yu, Y., Gao, S., Cheng, S., Wang, Y., Song, S., Yuan, F.: CBSO: a memetic brain storm optimization with chaotic local search. Memetic Comput. **10**, 353–367 (2018). https://doi.org/10.1007/s12293-017-0247-0
69. Yong, W., Tao, W., Cheng-Zhi, Z., Hua-Juan, H.: A new stochastic optimization approach dolphin swarm optimization algorithm. Int. J. Comput. Intell. Appl. **15**(2), 1650011 (2016). https://doi.org/10.1142/S1469026816500115
70. Zhang, Q., Wang, R., Yang, J., Ding, K., Li, Y., Hu, J.: Collective decision optimization algorithm: a new heuristic optimization method. Neurocomputing **221**, 123–137 (2017). https://doi.org/10.1016/j.neucom.2016.09.068
71. Zhang, J., Xiao, M., Gao, L., Pan, Q.: Queuing search algorithm: a novel metaheuristic algorithm for solving engineering optimization problems. Appl. Math. Model. **63**, 464–490 (2018). https://doi.org/10.1016/j.apm.2018.06.036
72. Zhang, W., Gao, K., Zhang, W., Wang, X., Zhang, Q., Wang, H.: A hybrid clonal selection algorithm with modified combinatorial recombination and success-history based adaptive mutation for numerical optimization. Appl. Intell. **49**, 819–836 (2019). https://doi.org/10.1007/s10489-018-1291-2
73. Zheng, L.M., Zhang, S.X., Tang, K.S., Zheng, S.Y.: Differential evolution powered by collective information. Inf. Sci. **399**, 13–29 (2017). https://doi.org/10.1016/j.ins.2017.02.055

Fuzzy Shapley Value-Based Solution for Communication Network

Barbara Gładysz[1] ⓘ, Jacek Mercik[2(✉)] ⓘ, and Izabella Stach[3] ⓘ

[1] Faculty of Computer Science and Management, Wroclaw University
of Science and Technology, Wyb. Wyspianskiego 27, 50-360 Wroclaw, Poland
barbara.gladysz@pwr.edu.pl
[2] WSB University in Wroclaw, Fabryczna 29/31, 53-609 Wroclaw, Poland
jacek.mercik@wsb.wroclaw.pl
[3] AGH University of Science and Technology, Al. Mickiewicza 30,
30-059 Krakow, Poland
istach@zarz.agh.edu.pl

Abstract. The paper presents a solution to the problem of cost allocation for a communication network in which the connection values between two nodes are defined by a fuzzy utility function. The utility function can refer to both existing communication nodes and new node proposals. For the allocation mechanism, the authors used the fuzzy Shapley value built on a complete coalition of all paths connecting the root of the tree with all nodes of the given network.

Keywords: Tree network game · Shapley value · Utility function ·
Communication problem

1 Introduction

We deal with the problem of finding cost allocations in dendrites, i.e. in such networks where there is only one way to determine paths from a selected vertex to any other vertex of the network. Depending on what parameter is used to describe the arcs present in the dendrite (e.g. time or cost) such an approach can be used to describe the problems of determining the optimal solution associated with communication in a given dendrite. Such problems occur, for example, in determining effective development of various networks (transport, computer, logistics, etc.). For example, Littlechild and Owen (1973) present a so-called airport game, Rosenthal (2013) presents the problem of underground development in an urban agglomeration, or in the work of Algaba et al. (2019) Metropolitan Consortium of Seville. If we additionally allow a fuzzy description of the network parameters, which is a very rational assumption in relation to real network problems, we face the problem of determining the fuzzy Shapley value and fuzzy path utility in dendrites.

Generally, we approach the problem of allocating certain services (transport, logistics, telecommunications, etc.) as follows. Let an area M which consists of $N = \{1, \ldots, n\}$ separate subareas (e.g., each of the subareas $i \in N$ describes the population of inhabitants in a geographically separated area). Each of the sub-areas is shown as a vertex in the network describing the area M and relations between areas are presented

© Springer Nature Switzerland AG 2019
N. T. Nguyen et al. (Eds.): ICCCI 2019, LNAI 11683, pp. 535–544, 2019.
https://doi.org/10.1007/978-3-030-28377-3_44

as arcs connecting the vertices. In such a graph, we can always distinguish one of the vertices $s \in M$ as so-called source or final stop (terminal).

Let the community represented by the given vertex $i \in M$ maintains communication (a graph arc) with the vertex $s \in M$. Such a connection (relation, relationship, etc.) can be a direct or indirect connection passing through other vertices from M. Each such connection can be described using the utility function. For example, if we consider travel time, the utility function increases while the travel time decreases, and vice versa.

Another component of the utility function may be the cost of building infrastructure for such connections. The cost of building an additional node or extending an existing node has an inverse proportion to the utility function being built.

The optimization task in this case consists in optimizing the utility functions for all possible paths connecting two any network nodes when certain conditions are met. For example, the natural conditions (Rosenthal 2013) for the network describing the network of connections of the municipal communication network were formulated as follows:

Condition 1. Utility for each user is inversely related to their travel time from given node.
Condition 2. The optimal network for a subset of communities should minimize the weighted travel times of their joint user population from the source.
Condition 3. No subset of communities should pay more, in the final cost allocation, than they would on their own.

The solution for such a network model can be a solution analogous to looking for Shapley values (Shapley 1953) in a cooperative game[1], in which "players" are the vertices of the network and critical paths found in dendrites possible to build on a given network describe possible and impossible coalitions. This is a special case of a cooperative game in which the assumption of equal probability of all possible coalitions was rejected[2].

Because the values of the cost allocation model parameters are related to the economic values that mostly refer to the future, it is reasonable to present the time and cost in the model in the form of fuzzy values, as they are imprecisely defined. They can depend on the conditions in which a given investment is carried out, while travel times are also non-deterministic in real-life conditions - they depend, for example, on the intensity of traffic at a given hour, as well as on weather conditions and other factors. This fact is taken into account in the model, assuming that the travel and station construction costs are set as interval-valued fuzzy triangular numbers.

---

[1] A broader look at the value of Shapley in such situations can be found, for example, in the work of Gladysz and Mercik (2018).

[2] It is worth noting that there are many possible solutions related to rejection of the same probability of coalition implementation and modification of Shapley value (e.g. Gambarelli and Owen (1994); Mercik (2015, 2016) or Forlicz et al. (2018).

2 Preliminary Definitions

Fuzzy set $\tilde{A}$ in space X (Zadeh 1965) is a collection ordered pairs $\{(x, \mu_A(x)): x \in X)$ where $\mu_A: X \rightarrow [0, 1]$ is a function of belonging to a fuzzy set.

If we have two fuzzy sets $\tilde{A}$ and $\tilde{B}$ it is the degree of belonging of a given element x to a set $\tilde{A} \cap \tilde{B}$ is equal to:

$$\mu_{A \cap B}(x) = min\{\mu_A(x), \mu_B(x)\}. \tag{1}$$

An interval-valued fuzzy number $\tilde{X}$ we call a family of real closed intervals $[\tilde{X}]_\lambda$ where $\lambda \in [0, 1]$ such that: $\lambda_1 < \lambda_2 \Rightarrow [\tilde{X}]_{\lambda_1} \subset [\tilde{X}]_{\lambda_2}$ and $I \subseteq [0, 1] \Rightarrow [\tilde{X}]_{sup I} = \bigcap_{\lambda \in I} [\tilde{X}]_\lambda$. Interval $[\tilde{X}]_\lambda$ for a fixed $\lambda \in [0, 1]$ is called λ-level of fuzzy number $\tilde{X}$. We will mark it as $[\tilde{X}]_\lambda = [\underline{x}(\lambda), \bar{x}(\lambda)]$.

Carrier (Support) $supp(\tilde{X})$ of interval-valued fuzzy number $\tilde{X}$ we call the set $\{x : \mu_X(x) > 0\}$. A fuzzy number $(\tilde{X})$ is a positive fuzzy number when $supp(\tilde{X}) \subset \mathcal{R}^+$.

An interval-valued fuzzy number $(\tilde{X})$ is called an L-R fuzzy number if its affiliation function takes the form of (Dubois and Prade 1978):

$$\mu_X(x) = \begin{cases} L\left(\frac{m-x}{\alpha}\right) & for & x < \underline{m} \\ 1 & for & \underline{m} \le x \le \overline{m} \\ R\left(\frac{x-\overline{m}}{\beta}\right) & for & x > \overline{m} \end{cases} \tag{2}$$

where: $L(x)$. $R(x)$ - continuous non-increasing functions x; $\alpha, \beta > 0$.

Functions $L(x)$. $R(x)$ are called shape functions of a fuzzy number. The most commonly used shape functions are: $max\{0, 1 - x^p\}$ and $exp(-x^p)$. $x \in [0, +\infty)$. $p \ge 1$. An interval-valued fuzzy number for which $L(x)$. $R(x) = max\{0, 1 - x^p\}$ and $\underline{m} = \overline{m} = m$. $p = 1$ is called a triangular fuzzy number, which we denote as (m, α, β).

Let $\tilde{X}, \tilde{Y}$ be two fuzzy numbers with membership functions, respectively $\mu_X(x), \mu_Y(y)$ and let $z = f(x, y)$ be a real function. Then, according to the Zadeh's extension principle (1965), the function of belonging to a fuzzy number $\tilde{Z} = f(\tilde{X}, \tilde{Y})$ takes the form:

$$\mu_Z(z) = sup_{z=f(x,y)}(min(\mu_X(x), \mu_Y(y))) \tag{3}$$

According to formula (3), the sum of two triangular fuzzy numbers $\tilde{X} = (m_X, \alpha_X, \beta_X)$ and $\tilde{Y} = (m_Y, \alpha_Y, \beta_Y)$ is a triangular fuzzy number $\tilde{X} + \tilde{Y} = (m_X + m_Y, \alpha_X + \alpha_Y, \beta_X + \beta_Y)$. The product of the fuzzy number $\tilde{X} + \tilde{Y}$ and a positive constant $c \in \mathcal{R}^+$ is a triangular fuzzy number $c \cdot \tilde{X} = (c \cdot m_X, c \cdot \alpha_X, c \cdot \beta_X)$.

If we want to compare two fuzzy numbers, that is, to determine the possibility that the realization $\tilde{X}$ will be greater than, or greater or equal to the realization $\tilde{Y}$ then we can use the indexes proposed by Dubois and Prade (1988):

$$Pos(X > Y) = sup_x \inf_{y \geq x}(min(\mu_X(x), 1 - \mu_Y(y)))$$ (4)

3   Problem of Fuzzy Critical Path in Dendrites

Let the graph $T = \{N \cup \{s\}, A\}$ will be a tree in which the vertex s is a source or mouth. N is a set of vertices representing communication nodes. In graph theory, a tree is called an undirected graph in which any two vertices are connected by exactly one path. So in the tree T for each vertex $i \in N$ there is exactly one path connecting it to the vertex s.

Each vertex $i \in N$ is connected to a non-empty set of U_i users of the transport network. The power of the set U_i is given by the weights $w_i > 0$ for each $i \in N$. Let $U = \bigcup_{i \in N} U_i$. We assume that all users of the communication network are identical; they are only differentiated by belonging to particular communities.

In addition, each vertex $i \in N \cup \{s\}$ is connected to a cost $\tilde{F}_i$ of construction of the station in i. A is a set of unrecorded edges (i,j) specifying connections between vertices $i,j \in N \cup \{s\}; i \neq j$. Each edge has a specific time or distance $\tilde{A}(i,j)$ representing the travel time between the station i and station j. Users of the i-th station are residents of the i-th area. Other users only pass through this station or completely bypass it. Both times $\tilde{A}(i,j)$ and the construction of the station $\tilde{F}_i$ are triangular positive fuzzy numbers.

Let the user set U in the tree T be a set of players. For any subset $S \subset U$ let $N(S)$ be a set of vertices in N such that a vertex is an element $N(S)$ only if it has at least one vertex in S with which it has a connection (path). Thus, the construction costs of the station $\tilde{F}_i$ in point i are incurred only by S coalitions, for which: $N(S) \cap \{i\} \neq \varnothing$. On the other hand, the costs of building the station at a point s are incurred by all users $i \in N$. The construction costs of the station in s is shared among all the users. The game defined in this way fulfills the conditions 1–3 provided above (Rosenthal 2013).

A classic cooperative game is defined (Owen 1995) by a set of players $P = \{1, \ldots, n\}$ and the characteristic function $c : 2^n \to \mathcal{R}$.

The characteristic function $c(S)$ - is the minimum cost in the tree T which must be incurred to connect all vertices in $N(S)$ with the tip s, for everyone $S \subseteq U$. For specific realizations of times $a(i,j) \in supp(\tilde{A}(i,j))$, $f_i \in supp(\tilde{F}_i)$ the characteristic function meets the conditions:

$$c(\varnothing) = 0$$ (5)

$$c(S \cup T) \leq c(S) + c(T) \text{ for } S, T \subseteq P,$$ (6)

The possibility that a given system of times and costs of building a station will be realised is respectively $\lambda_{S,T} = \min\limits_{i \in S \cup T} \{\mu^{-1}(a(i,j))\}$ and $\lambda_{S,T} = \left\{ \min\limits_{i \in S \cup T} \mu^{-1}((f_i)) \right\}$.

Proposition 1. The Shapley value for arc costs in fuzzy path game on a tree networks defined on tree networks is given by

$$\tilde{\Phi}_i = \sum_{k=1}^{m_i} \frac{\tilde{A}_{i_k}}{n'_{i_k}} \tag{7}$$

where:

$\tilde{A}_{i_k}$ – fuzzy cost (time) of the k-th edge on the path leading from s to the vertex i $(k = 1, \ldots, m_i)$

m_i – number of nodes on the path (s, i).

$n'_{i_k} = \sum_{j \in N} w_j$ for j being on the path (s, j).

Proof. Proposition 1 is a generalization of Rosenthal's theorem (2013) for Shapley's value for shortest path games for fuzzy costs. According to this statement, fixed cost realizations $a_{i_k} \in supp(\tilde{A}_{i_k})$ correspond to the Shapley value for i-th player

$$\varphi_i = \sum_{k=1}^{m} \frac{a_{i_k}}{n'_{i_k}} \tag{8}$$

where:

a_{i_k} – cost (time) of the k-th edge on the path leading from s to the vertex i $(k = 1, \ldots, m_i)$

Let us now apply the extension principle of Zadeh (1965) to the function $\varphi_i = \sum_{k=1}^{m_i} \frac{a_{i_k}}{n'_{ik}}$. According to the formula (3), the fuzzy Shapley value is:

$$\tilde{\Phi}_i = \sum_{k=1}^{m_i} \frac{\tilde{A}_{i_k}}{n'_{i_k}} \tag{9}$$

where $\tilde{A}_{i_k}$ is fuzzy time (cost) with the membership function $\mu_{A_{i_k}}(a_{i_k})$ for k-th edge on the path leading from s to the vertex i $(k = 1, \ldots, m_i)$.

The fuzzy Shapley value (9) is a triangular Shapley fuzzy number $\tilde{\Phi}_i$ of the membership function

$$\mu_{\Phi_i}(\varphi) = \sup_{\varphi = \sum_{k=1}^{m_i} \frac{\tilde{A}_{i_k}}{n'_{i_k}}} \min_{k=1,\ldots,m_i} \mu_{A_{ik}}(a_{i_k}) \tag{10}$$

The membership function (10) determines the possibility of realization of a given cost arrangement a_{i_k} and thus the possibility that the Shapley value of i-th player $\tilde{\Phi}_i$ will be equal φ. QED.

To determine which player has the smallest Shapley value, and thus the largest utility function value in the fuzzy shortest path game, we can use the Pos index (4). Namely, the possibility that the i-th player has the smallest value is:

$$Pos\left(\tilde{\Phi}_i \geq \tilde{\Phi}_j \text{ for all } j \in N, j \neq i\right) = \min_{j \in N, j \neq i} Pos\left(\tilde{\Phi}_i \geq \tilde{\Phi}_j\right) \tag{11}$$

Now, let's adjust the Shapley value $\tilde{\Phi}_i$ for the costs of constructing local stations and the construction costs of the station in the hub s. The station costs are added on as follows. The Shapley value will allocate the station cost s equally among all users. Then, since user i is the sole user of station $i \in U$, the Shapley value must allocate the entire cost of station i to user i.

So the final Shapley value for i-th user is:

$$\tilde{\Psi}_i = \tilde{\Phi}_i + \tilde{F}_i + \frac{1}{\sum_{i \in N} w_i} \tilde{F}_s \tag{12}$$

The Shapley values $\tilde{\Psi}_i$, $i = 1, \ldots, n$ as linear combinations of triangular fuzzy numbers are triangular fuzzy numbers.

Let us now define the possibility that the i-th player will have the smallest Shapley value Ψ (greatest utility), as follows:

$$Pos\left(\tilde{\Psi}_i \geq \tilde{\Psi}_j \text{ for all } j \in N, j \neq i\right) = \min_{j \in N, j \neq i} Pos\left(\tilde{\Psi}_i \geq \tilde{\Psi}_j\right) \tag{13}$$

4 Example

Consider the example from Rosenthal (2013). Figure 1 shows the communication system for five areas $N = \{1, 2, 3, 4, 5\}$. In each area there is one user $w_i = 1$ for $i = 1, \ldots 5$. Let us assume that transport times and station construction costs are not determined quantities but triangular fuzzy numbers, where the values of times (costs) given in the example are the most possible values here (Fig. 1).

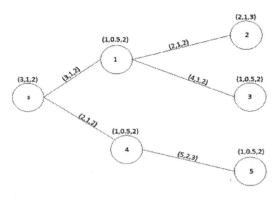

Fig. 1. The fuzzy shortest path game on a tree network.

Two coalitions $A = \{1, 2, 3\}$ and $B = \{3, 4\}$ comprise two subtrees. Let us set Shapley values $\tilde{\Phi}_i$ ($i = 1, \ldots, 5$) for transport times for individual users of the transport network.

Using Proposition 1 for the arc cost component, we obtain the Shapley Value. In the Shapley value allocation, Player 3, for example, pays all (4, 1, 2) for the link (1, 3) while the link $(s, 1)$ is shared equally among players 1, 2, and 3. Thus Player 3's total arc cost share is (4, 1, 2) + 1/3*(3, 1, 2) = (5, 1.33, 2.67), and the other players' allocations are computed similarly.

For all five players, we'll get the following Shapley values:

$\tilde{\Phi}_1 = (1, 0.33, 0.67)$, $\tilde{\Phi}_2 = (3, 1.33, 2.67)$, $\tilde{\Phi}_3 = (5, 1.33, 2.67)$, $\tilde{\Phi}_4 = (1, 0.5, 1)$ and $\tilde{\Phi}_5 = (6, 3, 4)$

Let's now consider the costs of building user stations $i = 1, \ldots, 5$ and the cost of building the station at the interchange s.

The station costs are added on as follows. The Shapley value will allocate the station cost s equally among all users. Thus, all five users are allocated a cost of (3, 1, 2)/5 = (0.6, 0.2, 0.4). Then, since user i is the sole user of station i, for all $1 = 1, \ldots, 5$ the Shapley value must allocate the entire cost of station i to user i. For player 3, for example, these costs are equal (5, 1.33, 2.67) + (0.6, 0.2, 0.4) + (1, 0.5, 2) = (6.6, 2.03, 5.07).

By analogy, for all five players, we'll get the following Shapley values: $\tilde{\Psi}_1 = (2.6, 1.03, 3.06)$, $\tilde{\Psi}_2 = (5.6, 2.53, 6.06)$, $\tilde{\Psi}_3 = (6.6, 2.03, 5.06)$, $\tilde{\Psi}_4 = (2.6, 1.2, 4.4)$, $\tilde{\Psi}_5 = (7. 6, 3.7, 6.4)$.

Let's now determine the possibility that player 3 is the winner (has the most usability, i.e. the lowest costs) we set out as follows:

$\text{Pos}(\tilde{\Psi}_1 > \tilde{\Psi}_3 \text{ and } \tilde{\Psi}_2 > \tilde{\Psi}_3 \text{ and } \tilde{\Psi}_4 > \tilde{\Psi}_3, \text{ and } \tilde{\Psi}_5 > \tilde{\Psi}_3) = 0.00$,

Finally, the possibility that individual players are the winning players is given in Table 1.

Table 1. The probability that a player will have the smallest Shapley value

Player (i)	1	2	3	4	5
$\text{Pos}(\tilde{\Psi}_j > \tilde{\Psi}_i \text{ for } i \neq j)$	0.59	0.01	0.00	0.41	0.00

In other words, there is no player who would be the winning player in any of the variants of possible transport times and building costs.

In the proposed model, depending on the conditions of investment (weather, construction, etc.), the player (node) who would not have built the station would always have a minimum Shapley value. Which player is the winner in terms of maximizing usability depends on the actual travel times and construction costs of the stations, which are inherently unknown (Fig. 2).

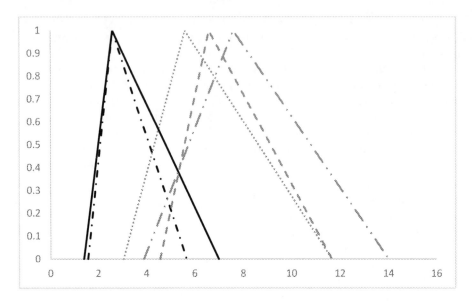

Fig. 2. Membership function of fuzzy Shapley value of the combined costs for each of the five players (vertices).

Possible scenarios of transport times and station construction costs for different levels of possibilities λ shown in Table 2.

Table 2. Total transport times and station construction costs for various scenarios

Time/Cost	a(s,1)	a(s,4)	a(1,2)	a(1,3)	a(4,5)	fs	f1	f2	f3	f4	f5
Scenario 1 ($\lambda = 1$)	3	2	2	4	5	3	1	2	1	1	1
Scenario 2 ($\lambda = 0.5$)	4	3	3	5	6.5	4	2	3	2	3	2
Scenario 3 ($\lambda = 0.25$)	2.5	1.25	1.5	3.5	3.5	2.5	0.75	1.5	0.75	0.75	0.75

Table 3. Shapley values Ψ for different scenarios

Player	1	2	3	4	5
Scenario1 ($\lambda = 1$)	2.60	5.60	6.60	2.60	7.60
Scenario 2 ($\lambda = 0.5$)	2.13	5.13	7.13	2.3	8.8
Scenario 3 ($\lambda = 0.25$)	1.33	2.83	4.83	1.25	5.25

And so, in the most possible Scenario 1, players 1 and 4 have the greatest utility = 2.6. In Scenario 2, which is possible in the ½ degree, the player 1 has the greatest utility = 2.13, and in Scenario 3 (possible in the degree ¼) player 4 has the maximum usability = 1.25.

The model proposed in the work allows to determine the possibility that the usefulness of communication connecting a given region (1, 2, 3, 4, 5) from the centre of the metropolis (top s) will be the highest. The measure of usefulness here is the time of travel from a given area to the center and the investment costs of constructing communication connections. In the analysed example, the inhabitants of the region 1 have the maximum possibility that their communication system will be equal to 0.59 (on a scale of 0–1) Table 1. The inhabitants of the region 4 place second. It should be noted that both regions have a direct connection to the centre.

In specific real-life conditions, both communication systems $(1, s)$ and $(4, s)$ can have the same maximum usability equal to 2.6 (Table 3). In other situations, when the travel times and/ or investment costs change due to the non-deterministic nature of travel conditions or construction, the communication network $(1, s)$ (Scenario 2) or communication network $(4, s)$ (Scenario 3) may have the greatest utility. The possibility that communication systems $(2, s)$, $(3, s)$ and $(5, s)$ will have the highest utility is equal, or almost equal to zero.

At the end of the analysis of the example, we would like to emphasize that the parameters used in the model are fuzzy. It allows to capture the basic problem which affects all models of real situations - the lack of determinism of parameters describing particular quantities. In particular, this applies to all types of economic or demographic parameters, but also technical parameters, due to the range tolerances, are in this sense blurred.

5 Concluding Remarks

The subject of the work is the issue of cooperative games derived from the issue of the shortest (cheapest) paths from a specific vertex of the network to the remaining vertices. This is a very important problem, which is widely used in communication networks. The paper proposes a solution to the problem of cost allocation for a communication network in which the connection values between two nodes are described by a fuzzy utility function and cost of investment. In practice, both transport time and investment costs are not deterministic. In transport networks, they depend on the intensity of traffic at particular times of the day, season, weather conditions and many other factors. In generalized communication networks the factors depend on analogous parameters describing the transmissions occurring in them. In our opinion, the model taking into account the uncertainty occurring in transport networks and describing real situations well should include fuzzy parameters, as in the proposed transport model fuzzy numbers were proposed to describe the uncertainty of transport times and investment costs.

Another issue requiring further research is the impact of the choice of a given class of fuzzy numbers on the results obtained. However, it must be remembered that the basic criterion is the practicality of the solutions used and the proposed fuzzy numbers should be adjusted to match the natural measures applied in optimization issues.

Acknowledgements. The research is partially supported by the Polish Ministry of Science and Higher Education for Faculty of Computer Science and Management, Wroclaw University of Science and Technology (No 0401/0193/18), by AGH University of Science and Technology funds (No. 16.16.200.396) and by WSB University in Wroclaw.

References

Algaba, E., Fragnelli, V., Llorca, N., Sanchez-Soriano, J.: Labeled network allocation problems. an application to transport systems. Trans. Comput. Collect. Intell. (2019, forthcoming)

Dubois, D., Prade, H.: Algorithmes de plus courts Chemins pour traiter des donnes floues. RAIRO Recherche Operationnelle/Oper. Res. **12**, 213–227 (1978)

Dubois, D., Prade, H.: Possibility Theory: An Approach to Computerized Processing of Uncertainty. Plenum Press, New York (1988)

Forlicz, S., Mercik, J., Stach, I., Ramsey, D.: The shapley value for multigraphs. In: Nguyen, N., Pimenidis, E., Khan, Z., Trawiński, B. (eds.) Computational Collective Intelligence. Lecture Notes in Computer Science, vol. 11056. Springer, Cham (2018). https://doi.org/10.1007/978-3-319-98446-9_20

Gładysz, B., Mercik, J.: The shapley value in fuzzy simple cooperative games. In: Nguyen, N.T., Hoang, D.H., Hong, T.P., Pham, H., Trawiński, B. (eds.) ACIIDS 2018. LNCS (LNAI), vol. 10751, pp. 410–418. Springer, Cham (2018). https://doi.org/10.1007/978-3-319-75417-8_39

Gambarelli, G., Owen, G.: Indirect control of corporations, International. J. Game Theory **23**, 287–302 (1994)

Littlechild, S.C., Owen, G.: A simple expression for the Shapley value in special case. Manag. Sci. **20**(3), 370–372 (1973)

Mercik, J.: Classification of committees with vetoes and conditions for the stability of power indices. Neurocomputing **149**, 1143–1148 (2015)

Mercik, J.: Formal a priori power analysis of elements of a communication graph. In: Nguyen, N. T., Trawiński, B., Fujita, H., Hong, T.-P. (eds.) ACIIDS 2016. LNCS (LNAI), vol. 9621, pp. 410–419. Springer, Heidelberg (2016). https://doi.org/10.1007/978-3-662-49381-6_39

Owen, G.: Game Theory, 3rd edn. Academic Press, San Diego (1995)

Rosenthal, E.C.: Shortest path games. Eur. J. Oper. Res. **224**, 132–140 (2013)

Shapley, L.S.: A value for n-person games. In: Kuhn, H.W., Tucker, A.W. (eds.) Contributions to the Theory of Games volume II. Annals of Mathematical Studies, vol. 28, pp. 307–317. Princeton University Press, Princeton (1953)

Zadeh, L.A.: Fuzzy sets. Inf. Control **8**, 338–353 (1965)

New Optimization Algorithm Based on Free Dynamic Schema

Radhwan Yousif Al-Jawadi[1]([⊠]), Marcin Studniarski[2]([⊠]) [iD],
and Aisha Azeez Younus[2]([⊠])

[1] Engineering Technical College of Mosul, Northern Technical University,
Kirkuk, Iraq
radwanyousif@yahoo.com, radwan.aljawadi@ntu.edu.iq
[2] Faculty of Mathematics and Computer Science, University of Łódź,
Banacha 22, 90-238 Łódź, Poland
marcin.studniarski@wmii.uni.lodz.pl,
azeezzena74@yahoo.com

Abstract. In this paper, we describe and test a new evolutionary algorithm based on the notion of a schema, which is designed to solve global optimization problems. We call it Free Dynamic Schema (FDS). It is a more refined variant of our previous DSC, DSDSC and MDSDSC algorithms. FDS processes two populations which are partially composed of the same chromosomes. The algorithm divides each population into several groups to which various genetic operators are applied: free dynamic schema, dissimilarity, similarity, and dynamic dissimilarity. Also, some new chromosomes are regenerated randomly. The FDS algorithm is applied to 22 test functions in 2, 4 and 10 dimensions. It is also compared with the classical GA, CMA-ES and DE algorithms. Moreover, the FDS algorithm is compared with the BA and PSA algorithms for some functions. In most cases, we have found the FDS algorithm to be superior to the classical GA and BA.

Keywords: Free dynamic schema · Dynamic schema ·
Similarity and dissimilarity · Dynamic dissimilarity

1 Introduction

The multi-population idea in evolutionary algorithms is used to increase diversity of the population, and also to improve searching for optimal solution. For optimization problems, the authors of [1] used a double population in the Swarm Optimization Algorithm. Also, a genetic algorithm with dual population was presented in [2], where the first population was used to find a good solutions to the problem, then the second population was used to evolve and provide the control of diversity of the first one. In [3] the authors introduced a new approach with double population called "Double Bee Population Evolutionary Genetic Algorithm with Filtering Operation", where one population is produced by the algorithm itself, and the other population is generated randomly.

This research presents a new global optimization method: the Free Dynamic Schema algorithm (FDS). This algorithm is a modification of our previous algorithms called Multi-Dynamic Schema with Dissimilarity and Similarity of Chromosomes

© Springer Nature Switzerland AG 2019
N. T. Nguyen et al. (Eds.): ICCCI 2019, LNAI 11683, pp. 545–555, 2019.
https://doi.org/10.1007/978-3-030-28377-3_45

(MDSDSC) [4], Dynamic Schema with Dissimilarity and Similarity of Chromosomes (DSDSC) [5] and Dissimilarity and Similarity of Chromosomes (DSC) [6].

The algorithm presented here is very similar to MDSDSC. The difference is that in FDS one replaces the dynamic schema operator with the free dynamic schema operator. In the FDS algorithm a double population of chromosomes technique is used. In this technique the first population is the original one and a part of the second population is copied from the first one, but with various types of genetic operators are applied to them.

Briefly, FDS aims to find an optimal solution for a given problem by fixing the most significant bits of each variable in the chromosome (i.e., the most significant bits of all variables $(x_1, \ldots, x_n)$, which are represented in the chromosome) and at the same time changing the less significant bits completely. The free dynamic schema operator in the algorithm searches for the optimal solution near the best chromosome in the population of each iteration.

2 Methodology

The FDS begins with a random population (P0) of M chromosomes which represent some solutions to a given optimization problem. Next, a new population (P1) is created, which is partially a copy of some subpopulation of (P0). Each population (P0, P1) is divided into several equal groups to which various operators are applied (see Table 1).

Table 1. Seven groups of chromosomes in populations (P0), (P1).

Original groups of chromosomes (P0)		Copy groups of chromosomes (P1)	
Ch_1	G1: In this group the dynamic dissimilarity operator is used	Ch_1	G5: In this group the dissimilarity operator is used
Ch_2		Ch_2	
Ch. ...		Ch. ...	
$Ch_{M/4}$		$Ch_{M/4}$	
$Ch_{M/4+1}$	G2: In this group the similarity operator is used	$Ch_{M/4+1}$	G6: In this group the dynamic dissimilarity operator is used
$Ch_{M/4+2}$		$Ch_{M/4+2}$	
Ch. ...		Ch. ...	
$Ch_{M/2}$		$Ch_{M/2}$	
$Ch_{M/2+1}$	G3: In this group the free dynamic schema operator is used	$Ch_{M/2+1}$	G7: In this group the free dynamic schema operator is used
$Ch_{M/2+2}$		$Ch_{M/2+2}$	
Ch. ...		Ch. ...	
$Ch_{M/2+ M/4}$		$Ch_{M/2+ M/4}$	
$Ch_{M/2+ M/4+1}$	G4: The fourth group is generated randomly		
$Ch_{M/2+ M/4+2}$			
Ch. ...			
Ch_M			

Briefly, the FDS generates new chromosomes by exploring similarity, dissimilarity, dynamic dissimilarity and free dynamic schema. These operators are defined as follows:

2.1 Dissimilarity Operator

In the group of dissimilarity (G5), compare the first two chromosomes (A, B) by comparing all corresponding bits. Compare each two bits in (A, B) chromosomes, if they are equal, put a star (*) in the second chromosome (B); otherwise keep the bit in the chromosome (B) without any change. Then replace the bits having stars (*) by 1 or 0 randomly in the chromosome (B). Then, compare this new chromosome (B) with the next chromosome in the group, and so on (see Table 2).

Table 2. The dissimilarity operator.

Before change:										
Chromosome A	1	1	1	0	0	1	0	1	1
Chromosome B	1	0	0	1	1	0	0	0	1
Check: Putting (*) in the second chromosome										
Chromosome A	1	1	1	0	0	1	0	1	1
Chromosome B	*	0	0	1	1	0	*	0	*
After change: put randomly 0 or 1 in (*) bits										
Chromosome A	1	1	1	0	0	1	0	1	1
Chromosome B	1	0	0	1	1	0	0	0	0

2.2 Similarity Operator

In the group of similarity (G2), compare the first two chromosomes (A, B) by comparing all corresponding bits. Compare each two bits in (A, B) chromosomes, if they are not equal, put a star (*) in the second chromosome (B); otherwise keep the bit in the chromosome (B) without any change. Then replace the bits having stars (*) by 1 or 0 randomly in the chromosome (B). Then, compare the new chromosome (B) with the next chromosome in the group, and so on (see Table 3).

Table 3. The similarity operator.

Before change:										
Chromosome A	1	1	1	0	0	1	0	1	1
Chromosome B	1	0	0	1	1	0	0	0	1
Check: Putting (*) in the second chromosome										
Chromosome A	1	1	1	0	0	1	0	1	1
Chromosome B	1	*	*	*	*	*	0	*	1
After change: put randomly 0 or 1 in (*) bits										
Chromosome A	1	1	1	0	0	1	0	1	1
Chromosome B	1	1	0	0	1	0	0	1	1

2.3   Free Dynamic Schema Operator

This operator obtains a schema from the first chromosome Ch_1 in each of the populations (P0, P1). This fixes the higher bits of each x_i and changes the rest of the bits for each x_i. It works the following way:

First, each chromosome is divided into n segments corresponding to n variables $(x_1, \ldots, x_n)$, the i-th segment having length m_i, where m_i represents the number of bits for x_i. Then, for each variable x_i, the number of fixed higher bits R_i is chosen randomly from the set $\{3, \ldots, m_i/2\}$. Next, we divide the string corresponding to x_i into two parts: the "gray" part of x_i containing the fixed R_i bits and the "white" part of x_i containing the remaining $m_i - R_i$ bits (see Table 4).

Table 4. The free dynamic schema operator.

Ch. No.	m_1							m_2				
	R_1			$m_1 - R_1$				R_2		$m_2 - R_2$		
Before change: an example for finding schema from the first chromosome. Here shadow bits are not destroyed.												
Ch_1	1	1	0	0	0	1	0	1	1	0	1	0
Schema	1	1	0	*	*	*	*	1	1	*	*	*
After finding the schema: put it in $M/2+1$ .... $M/2+M/4$ positions.												
$Ch_{M/2+1}$	1	1	0	*	*	*	*	1	1	*	*	*
$Ch_{M/2+2}$	1	1	0	*	*	*	*	1	1	*	*	*
Ch ...	1	1	0	*	*	*	*	1	1	*	*	*
Ch ...	1	1	0	*	*	*	*	1	1	*	*	*
$Ch_{M/2+M/4}$	1	1	0	*	*	*	*	1	1	*	*	*
After change: put randomly 0 or 1 in (*) bits.												
$Ch_{M/2+1}$	1	1	0	1	1	1	0	1	1	0	0	1
$Ch_{M/2+2}$	1	1	0	1	0	0	0	1	1	1	1	1
Ch ...	1	1	0	0	1	1	0	1	1	1	1	0
Ch ...	1	1	0	0	1	0	1	1	1	0	0	0
$Ch_{M/2+M/4}$	1	1	0	1	0	1	1	1	1	0	1	1

For the "white" segment of chromosomes, put a star (*) to find a schema. Then, copy this schema $K = M/4$ times and put it in group (G3), then in the positions with (*), put 0 or 1 randomly. The "gray" positions are kept without any change. Repeat the same procedure for group (G7).

Note. The lengths of "white" and "gray" parts of chromosomes may be different in different iterations. This explains the name "free dynamic schema operator".

2.4   Dynamic Dissimilarity Operator

This operator is applied onto each two subsequent chromosomes (A, B) in groups (G1, G6). It starts with finding the "gray" and "white" segments corresponding to variables $(x_1, \ldots, x_n)$ the same way as the free dynamic schema operator does. Here the "gray" segment of x_i is left unchanged, while "white" part of x_i is transformed as follows: if two corresponding bits in (A) and (B) are the same, we put a star (*) in the second (B) chromosome; if they are different, we leave this bit without change in (B). Then we place randomly 0 or 1 in the positions having stars (*) in (B). This procedure is repeated for this new second chromosome, which is compared with the third one, and so on (see Table 5).

Table 5. The dynamic dissimilarity operator.

	m_1							m_2				
	R_1			$m_1 - R_1$				R_2		$m_2 - R_2$		
Before change: an example for the chromosomes (A, B). Here shadow bits are not destroyed.												
Ch. A	1	1	1	0	0	1	0	1	0	0	1	0
Ch. B	1	0	1	1	0	0	1	0	0	0	1	1
Ch. A	1	1	1	0	0	1	0	1	0	0	1	0
Ch. B	1	0	1	1	*	0	1	0	0	*	*	1
After change: put randomly 0 or 1 in (*) bits												
Ch. A	1	1	1	0	0	1	0	1	0	0	1	0
Ch. B	1	0	1	1	1	0	1	0	0	1	0	1

3   The FDS Algorithm

The following optimization problem is considered:

$$\text{minimize|maximize } f(x_1, \ldots, x_n) \text{ subject to}$$
$$x_i \in [a_i, b_i], i = 1, \ldots, n,$$

where $f : \mathbb{R}^n \to \mathbb{R}$ is a real-valued function of n variables.

The FDS algorithm uses a standard encoding of real numbers as described in the book of Michalewicz [7]. In particular, we use the following formula to transform a bit string into a real number $x_i \in [a_i, b_i]$:

$$x_i = a_i + \text{decimal}(1001..001) * \frac{b_i - a_i}{2^{m_i} - 1}$$

where m_i is the length of the string corresponding to variable x_i and "decimal" is used to denote the decimal value of this string. For each coordinate x_i, the value of m_i

(length in bits) depends on the interval $[a_i, b_i]$. A decimal string of length $m = \sum_{i=1}^{n} m_i$ is used for encode a point $(x_1, \ldots, x_n)$. Suppose that M is a positive integer. For technical reasons, we assume that M is divisible by 8.

The following steps describe the FDS algorithm:

1. Generate $2M$-$M/4$ chromosomes, where each chromosome represents one point $(x_1, \ldots, x_n)$. Divide the chromosomes into seven groups, each group having $M/4$ chromosomes. Combine these groups in two populations (P0) and (P1), where the first population (P0) includes four groups (G1, G2, G3, G4), and the second population (P1) includes three groups (G5, G6, G7).
2. Compute the fitness function values of f for all chromosomes in the populations (G1, ..., G7).
3. Sort the chromosomes in (G1, ..., G7) in ascending order (for minimization problems) or in descending order (for maximization problems), according to the fitness function values.
4. Copy the groups (G1, G2) onto groups (G5, G6) to replace the original chromosomes.
5. For $C = M/8$, produce C copies of the first chromosome (with the best fitness) and put them in C randomly selected positions in groups (G1, G2); they replace the original chromosomes.
6. Apply the free dynamic schema operator two times for chromosome $A = Ch_1$ in populations (P0, P1). First, copy the obtained schema $M/4$ times, put it in (G3) for population (P0), and fill the "white" parts with randomly chosen digits. Next, repeat this procedure with another schema, group (G7) and population (P1).
7. Apply the dynamic dissimilarity operator to group (G1) and the similarity operator to group (G2) in population (P0). Apply the dissimilarity operator to group (G5) and the dynamic dissimilarity operator to group (G6) in population (P1).
8. Generate randomly chromosomes for group (G4) in population (P0).
9. Go to Step 2, then repeat steps 2–8 until a stopping criterion is satisfied.

Notes:

- The stopping criteria for the FDS algorithm may be different for different examples, see Tables 7 and 8.
- The authors of [8] proposed a "fixpoint injection" concept to preserve the diversity of a population. This was a method to introduce new randomly generated chromosomes to certain selected generations. In the FDS algorithm, a similar strategy was applied by generating the last quarter (G4) of population (P0) randomly in each iteration.
- The chromosomes created in steps 6 and 7 replace the original chromosomes in positions from 2 to $3M/4$, in the groups (G1, G2, G3, G5, G6, G7).

4 Experimental Results

In this section, the results of computational tests of the FDS algorithm are presented (by using a computer having 8 GB RAM and CPU core i5 with 2.4 MHz, also, Matlab software R2015b) on 5 test functions of 10 dimensions, one test function of 4 dimensions and 18 test functions of 2 dimensions. The result of FDS algorithm has been compared with the known global optimum and with the result of a CGA taken from our experimental result (see Table 7 for 2-dimensional functions and Table 8 for 4- and 10-dimensional functions).

To prove the efficiency of the FDS algorithm, the algorithm was applied on 22 tested function. The 20 tested functions with optimal solutions are described in Table 6 in [4], and two new functions are added in Table 6 of this paper. The FDS algorithm with 80 chromosomes in (P0) was applied to the 2 and 4 dimensions functions, while 160 chromosomes in (P0) were used for 10 dimensions functions. The stopping criterion was that the difference between the known optimal solution and our best solution is less than or equal to the threshold given in Tables 7 and 8.

The FDS algorithm has the ability to find the optimum solutions for some optimization problems (like Schaffer N.2, Beale's, Schwefel's, ...) that the CGA can not reach with 100% success rate with double vector or bit string, as shown in Table 7. For FDS, the success rates are 100% for all test functions with 80 chromosomes in (P0), here the success rate means that the algorithm reaches to a solution which falls below the given threshold (see Tables 7 and 8).

In Table 9 the success rate and average number of function evaluations have been compared among the algorithms CMA-ES (Covariance Matrix Adaptation Evolution Strategy) [9], DE (Differential Evolution) [10] and FDS by using 50 runs, 80 chromosomes in (P0) and the maximum number of iterations 2500. It is clear that the FDS algorithm has the best results in success rate for most tested functions. Furthermore, Table 10 contains a comparison of the number of functions evaluations and success rate of Bees Algorithm (BA) and Particle Swarm Optimization (PSO) (see [11]) for two dimensions functions with FDS. It is clear that the FDS algorithm is better than PSO and BA in success rate.

In each iteration, the FDS algorithm keeps the best solution found so far at the first position until it is replaced by another solution with better fitness.

Table 6. Test functions.

Function name	Interval	Function	Global optimum Min/max
Ackley $D = 4$	$x_i \in [-32.768, 32.768]$	$f(x) = -a.exp\left(-b.\sqrt{\dfrac{1}{n}\sum_{i=1}^{n} x_i^2}\right)$ $- exp\left(\dfrac{1}{n}\sum_{i=1}^{n} cos(c.x_i)\right) + a + exp(1)$	$f(0,0,0,0) = 0,$ min
Zakharov	$x_i \in [-5, 10]$	$f(x) = \sum_{i=1}^{d} x_i^2 + \left(\sum_{i=1}^{d} 0.5 \cdot x_i\right)^2$ $+ \left(\sum_{i=1}^{d} 0.5 \cdot x_i\right)^4$	$f(x^*) = 0$ at $(0,...,0)$

Table 7. The results for 50 runs of the FDS algorithm.

Function name	Threshold	Min number of iteration/ Min time in seconds	Max number of iterations/ Max time in seconds	Mean no. of iterations for all successful runs/Average time	Std. Dev. of mean no. of Iter.	Mean of the best solution fitness from all successful runs	Success rate of FDS	Success rate of GA
Easom	0.001	24 0.02824	241 0.26588	89 0.1024	51.9	−0.99936	100%	100% DV
Matyas	0.001	2 0.00542	14 0.01726	6 0.0101	2.6	0.00047	100%	100% DV
Beale's	0.001	2 0.00555	18 0.02215	8 0.0123	4	0.00049	100%	70% DV
Booth's	0.001	3 0.00672	37 0.03861	12 0.0152	6.7	0.00053	100%	100% DV
Goldstein– Price	0.001	10 0.01423	115 0.12671	35 0.0409	21.6	3.00050	100%	100% DV
Schaffer N.2	0.001	2 0.00588	58 0.06565	16 0.0204	11.7	0.00036	100%	70% DV
Schwefel's	0.001	11 0.01554	130 0.13659	39 0.046	27.5	0.00066	100%	0% BS
Branins's rcos	0.001	2 0.00496	89 0.12197	11 0.0171	15.8	0.39842	100%	100% DV
Six–hump camel back	0.001	2 0.00550	27 0.03045	7 0.0110	5.3	−1.03111	100%	100% DV
Shubert	0.01	3 0.00445	134 0.15403	45 0.0562	50.4	−186.717	100%	100% DV
Martin and Gaddy	0.001	2 0.00171	12 0.01534	5 0.0093	2.5	0.00047	100%	40% DV
Michalewicz	0.04	3 0.00902	166 0.17056	55 0.0605	37.8	38.8153	100%	80% DV
Holder table	0.001	4 0.007824	55 0.062127	19 0.0239	12.5	−19.208	100%	80% DV
Drop–wave	0.001	7 0.011624	111 0.122926	45 0.0502	23.5	−0.99952	100%	100% BS
Levy N. 13	0.001	4 0.007922	63 0.066639	19 0.0235	11.2	0.00054	100%	100% BS
Rastrigin's	0.001	11 0.0199	131 0.1079	58 0.0555	31.4	0.00039	100%	100% BS
Sphere	0.001	2 0.0069	15 0.0222	7 0.0161	3.5	0.0004	100%	100% BS
Rosenbrock's valley	0.001	4 0.0088	56 0.0538	18 0.0255	13.2	0.0006	100%	100% BS

DV means double vector and BS means bit string parameters of population type in Genetic Algorithm toolbox, Std.Dev. means standard deviation.

Table 8. The results for 25 runs of the FDS algorithm for 10-dimensional functions with run time.

Function name	Threshold	Min number of iterations/Min time in seconds	Max number of iterations/Max time in seconds	Mean no. of iterations for all successful runs/Average time	Std.Dev. of mean no. of Iter.	Mean of the best solution fitness from all successful runs	Success rate of FDS	Success rate of GA
Sum Squares d = 10	0.1	164 0.3055	634 1.1877	320 0.6115	141	0.08291	100%	100% BS
Sphere d = 10	0.1	29 0.0534	102 0.1781	51 0.0928	17	0.08303	100%	100% BS
Sum of different powers d = 10	0.1	2 0.0032	9 0.0599	4 0.0115	2.1	0.03835	100%	100% BS
Zakharov d = 10	0.1	180 0.4853	1711 4.4823	581 1.5508	395	0.08719	100%	100% BS
Rastrigin d = 10	0.1	680 2.1410	1953 6.1124	1159 3.9758	454.4	1.49088	32% 84%*	100% BS
Ackley d = 4	0.001	111 0.1133	1334 2.4283	536 1.3704	465	0.00140	86%	100% BS

- DV means double vector and BS means bit string parameters of population type in Genetic Algorithm toolbox, Std.Dev. means standard deviation.

- *This result found by changing the size of R_i to a random number from {0, 1, .., m_i}, with 200 chromosomes in (P0) and 2000 iterations.

Table 9. Comparing the average number of function evaluations and success rate for the CMA-ES, DE and FDS algorithms with (50 runs, max 2500 iterations, 80 chromosomes).

Function name	CMA-ES success rate	Function evaluations of CMA-ES	DE success rate	Function evaluations of DE	FDS success rate	Function evaluations of FDS
Easom	70%	17053	100%	3240	100%	12460
Matyas	100%	500	100%	2700	100%	840
Beale	100%	460	100%	3060	100%	1120
Booth's	100%	492	100%	2820	100%	1680
Goldstein–Price	100%	1812	100%	1620	100%	4900
Schaffer N.2	90%	6726	100%	5016	100%	2240
Schwefel's	0%	——	0%	——	100%	5460
Branins's rcos	100%	6876	100%	840	100%	1540
Six-hump camel	100%	780	100%	2160	100%	980
Shubert	90%	2220	100%	8160	100%	6300
Martin and Gaddy	100%	1660	100%	2400	100%	700
Michalewicz	100%	1848	0%	—	100%	7700
Drop-wave	50%	26470	94%	9048	100%	6300
Levy N. 13	100%	606	100%	1958	100%	2660
Rastrigin's	80%	13134	100%	2388	100%	8120
Sphere	100%	720	100%	1800	100%	980
Ackley d = 4	100%	2240	100%	3480	86%	85760
Rosenbrock's	100%	1644	100%	4560	100%	2520

Table 10. Comparison of BA, PSO and FDS algorithms in terms of success rate and average number of functions evaluations.

Function name	BA	Fun. Eval. of BA	PSO	Fun. Eval. of PSO	FDS	Fun. Eval. of FDS
Easom	72%	5868	100%	2094	100%	12460
Shubert	0%	—	100%	3046	100%	6300
Schwefel's	85%	5385	86%	3622	100%	5460
Goldstein–Price	7%	9628	100%	1465	100%	4900
Martin and Gaddy	100%	1448	3%	9707	100%	700
Rosenbrock	46%	7197	100%	1407	100%	2520

5 Conclusion

FDS is a new evolutionary algorithm that uses double populations and different operators to find the optimal solution. It applies the new free dynamic schema operator to find the best area of solutions and to search within that area in each iteration, after detects the free dynamic schema from the best solution in the population. Moreover, the dynamic dissimilarity operator searches in a wide range of solutions in (G1) and (G6), where the higher bits are kept unchanged and the lower bits can be changed. The similarity operator and dissimilarity operator have the ability to search in the whole search space because any bit of a chromosome may be modified. Finally, the random generation of chromosomes in (G4) helps to increase the diversity of a population and to not stick in a local optimum solution.

In this research, the FDS, GA, CMA-ES and DE algorithms are applied on 22 test function with 2, 4 and 10 dimensions. The outcome shows that the FDS algorithm is superior to the GA, CMA-ES, DE algorithms for most functions. Also, on 2-dimensional functions, the FDS is better than BA and PSO for some test functions.

For the future work, we plan to apply free dynamic schema and dynamic schema operators simultaneously to multiple groups of chromosomes, to make the algorithm still more effective.

Acknowledgments. The first author wishes to thank the Ministry of Higher Education and Scientific Research (MOHESR), Iraq.

References

1. Wu, Y., et al.: Dynamic self-adaptive double population particle swarm optimization algorithm based on Lorenz equation. J. Comput. Commun. **5**(13), 9–20 (2017)
2. Park, T., Ryu, K.R.: A dual-population genetic algorithm for adaptive diversity control. IEEE Trans. Evol. Comput. **14**(6), 865–884 (2010)
3. Mei, J., Wu, H.: Double bee population evolutionary genetic algorithm with filtering operation. In: Wen, Z., Li, T. (eds.) Foundations of Intelligent Systems. AISC, vol. 277, pp. 693–700. Springer, Heidelberg (2014). https://doi.org/10.1007/978-3-642-54924-3_65

4. Al-Jawadi, R., Studniarski, M.: An optimization algorithm based on multi-dynamic schema of chromosomes. In: Rutkowski, L., Scherer, R., Korytkowski, M., Pedrycz, W., Tadeusiewicz, R., Zurada, J.M. (eds.) ICAISC 2018, Part I. LNCS (LNAI), vol. 10841, pp. 279–289. Springer, Cham (2018). https://doi.org/10.1007/978-3-319-91253-0_27
5. Al-Jawadi, R.: An optimization algorithm based on dynamic schema with dissimilarities and similarities of chromosomes. Int. J. Comput. Electr. Autom. Control Inf. Eng. 7(8), 1278–1285 (2016)
6. Al-Jawadi, R., Studniarski, M., Younus, A.: New genetic algorithm based on dissimilaries and similarities. Comput. Sci. J. AGH Univ. Sci. Technol. Pol. 19(1), 19 (2018)
7. Michalewicz, Z.: Genetic Algorithms + Data Structures = Evolution Programs, 3rd edn. Springer, Heidelberg (1996). https://doi.org/10.1007/978-3-662-03315-9
8. Sultan, A.B.M., Mahmod, R., Sukaiman, M.N., Abu Bakar, M.R.: Maintaining diversity for genetic algorithm: a case of timetabling problem. J. Teknol. Malaysia 44(D), 123–130 (2006)
9. CMA-ES. Matlab program. https://www.mathworks.com/matlabcentral/fileexchange/52898-cma-es-in-matlab
10. Price, K.V.: Differential Evolution, pp. 187–214 (2013). http://www.dii.unipd.it/~alotto/didattica/corsi/Elettrotecnica%20computazionale/DE.pdf
11. Eesa, A.S., Brifcani, A.M.A., Orman, Z.: A new tool for global optimization problems-cuttlefish algorithm. Int. J. Comput. Electr. Autom. Control Inf. Eng. 8(9), 1198–1202 (2014)

VNS-Based Multi-agent Approach to the Dynamic Vehicle Routing Problem

Dariusz Barbucha[✉]

Department of Information Systems, Gdynia Maritime University,
Morska 83, 81-225 Gdynia, Poland
d.barbucha@wpit.umg.edu.pl

Abstract. The paper focuses on Dynamic Vehicle Routing Problem (DVRP), where customers' requests arrive dynamically while the process of planning and execution of the routing plan is running. Typically, the dynamic problem increases the complexity of the problem and introduces new challenges while finding the optimal route plan. The main contribution of the paper is to propose a multi-agent approach to the DVRP with efficient VNS-based procedure to periodic re-optimization of static subproblems, including requests, which have already arrived to the system. The results of evaluation of the proposed approach confirmed its practical ability do simulate and efficient solve the DVRP.

Keywords: Dynamic Vehicle Routing Problem · Multi-agent system · Variable Neighborhood Search

1 Introduction

The term Dynamic Vehicle Routing refers to a wide range of transportation problems where a set of vehicles have to deliver (or pickup) goods or persons to (from) locations situated in a given area. While customer requests can either be known in advance or appear dynamically during the day, requests have to be dispatched and routed in the real time, possibly, by taking into account uncertain demands, varying service times, or changing traffic conditions [16]. The goal of such process is to provide the required transportation and, at the same time, minimize service cost subject to various constraints including vehicle and fleet capacities.

Practical importance of the Dynamic Vehicle Routing Problems (DVRP) supported by recent advances in ICT (Geographic Information Systems, Global Positioning Systems or cellular technologies) implies that different real-world applications of them have been reported in the literature last years. They can be divided into several categories focusing on *services* (for example maintenance operations), *transport of goods* (fleet management, courier services), and *transport of persons* (dial-a-ride problems, taxi services, transport of children from their home to schools) [16].

© Springer Nature Switzerland AG 2019
N. T. Nguyen et al. (Eds.): ICCCI 2019, LNAI 11683, pp. 556–565, 2019.
https://doi.org/10.1007/978-3-030-28377-3_46

Focusing on methods dedicated to solve DVRPs, definitely less advances have been proposed for dynamic versions of vehicle routing problems than for their static counterparts. Among dedicated methods to solve different versions of DVRP dominant position have heuristics, such as a genetic algorithm [10], parallel tabu search heuristic with an adaptive memory mechanism [8], ant colony system [15], and others. In context of the paper, it is also worth to mention an interesting and efficient group of approaches to simulate and solve different variants of DVRP based on *multi-agent* paradigm proposed. They have been presented in several papers, for example [1,19]. The reader can find broader studies on different variants of static and dynamic VRPs, methods of solving them and examples of practical applications in several review papers [6,13,16–18].

The goal of this paper is to propose a new multi-agent approach to the Dynamic Vehicle Routing Problem. It extends the multi-agent environment proposed by author in his previous papers for solving DVRP and its version with time windows [2–5]. The main contribution of the paper is to propose an effective procedure of improvement of partial solution including already received requests. It is based on Variable Neighborhood Search (VNS) procedure [9,14] and implemented within the multi-agent system (MAS).

A general idea of VNS is a systematic exploration of the set of predefined neighborhoods $N_1, N_2, \ldots, N_{k_{max}}$ while the search process is performed. The main reason of changing between neighborhoods is to diversify the search and to avoid getting trapped in a local optima with poor quality solutions. Using various neighborhoods in a local search may generate different local optima and the global optimum can be seen as a local optimum for a given neighborhood.

Apart from the defining the form of neighborhoods, a major challenge in designing an effective VNS algorithm is to define the order in which the neighborhoods should be explored. The natural strategy is to explore neighborhoods at random order. Another one is to order the neighborhoods according to the neighborhood size and/or complexity of exploring them, such that one starts with the simplest neighborhood, and gradually covers the more complex and expensive. And finally, the order of selecting neighborhoods may also be defined by considering one neighborhood, but with variable depth, forming a set of variable depth neighborhoods. Whenever the algorithm reaches a local minimum using one of the neighborhoods, it proceeds with a larger one belonging to the set of neighborhoods.

The paper is organized as follows. Section 2 presents a formal definition of the DVRP. Section 3 presents a multi-agent approach to the DVRP, its architecture and details of the process of simulating and solving the problem using dedicated VNS procedure. Goal, assumptions and results of the computational experiment which has been carried out to evaluate the proposed approach are presented in Sect. 4. Finally, Sect. 5 includes conclusions and directions of the future work.

2   Problem Formulation

Dynamic Vehicle Routing Problem is derived from the *static* version of it, which can be formulated as an undirected graph $G = (V, E)$, where $V = \{0, 1, \ldots, N\}$ is a set of nodes and $E = \{(i, j)|i, j \in V\}$ is a set of edges. Node 0 is a central depot with K identical vehicles of capacity W. Each node $i \in V \setminus \{0\}$ denotes a customer characterized by demand d_i and service time s_i. Each edge $(i, j) \in E$ denotes the path between customers i to j and is described by the cost c_{ij} of travel from i to j by shortest path $(i, j \in V)$.

The goal is to minimize the vehicle fleet size and the total distance needed to pass by vehicles in order to supply all customers. The following constraints have to be also satisfied: each route starts and ends at the depot, each customer $i \in V \setminus \{0\}$ is serviced exactly once by a single vehicle, the total load on any vehicle associated with a given route does not exceed vehicle capacity, each route must start and finish within the time window associated with the depot.

The most common source of dynamism in Vehicle Routing Problem, also considered in the paper, is the online arrival of customer's requests while the process of execution of already arrived requests is running. By assuming that the planning horizon starts at time 0 and ends at time T, and let $t_i \in [0, T]$ $(i = 1, \ldots, N)$ denotes the time when the i-th customer's request is submitted (disclosure time), the problem considered in the paper is fully dynamic, which means that all $t_i > 0$.

3   Multi-agent Approach to DVRP

3.1   Architecture of the System

Process of simulating and solving DVRP is performed by several agents which are responsible for:

- initialization of all agents - **GlobalManager (GM)**,
- generating (or reading from a file) new customers' requests - **RequestGenerator (RG)**,
- serving the customers' requests - **Vehicle (Vh)** agents,
- management of the list of customers' requests and allocation of them to the available **Vh** agents - **RequestManager (RM)**,
- solving the partial static problem including requests which have been already arrived - **Optimizing (OPT)** agent,

Communication between the agents includes many different messages but in order to increase the readability of the paper, only messages strictly related to simulation and solving the DVRP have been emphasized in the paper.

3.2   Simulation and Solving Process

The process of simulating and solving the DVRP mainly focuses on managing dynamically arriving requests and dispatching them to the available vehicles. Two general models are typically used by authors. The first one assumes that each new request is dispatched to the available vehicles as soon as it has been received (see for example [2,8]). The second one, used also in the proposed approach, is based on the idea of dividing the working day into several discrete time slices (see for example [5,11,12]). Within each such time slice, newly received requests are cumulated, and next, at the end of each time slice, they are dispatched to the available vehicles.

The process starts with initialization of all agents engaged in the process of simulating and solving the DVRP. At first, the **GM** agent is created, which next initializes all other agents (**RG**, **RM**, **OPT**, and **Vh**). After receiving answers from all agents about their readiness to act, the system is ready to simulate and solve the problem.

Let T be a length of the working day, and n_{ts} be a number of time slices of equal length $T_{ts} = T/n_{ts}$. Let T_t be a beginning of time slice t ($t = 0, ..., n_{ts} - 1$). It means that $T_0 = 0$, $T_{n_{ts}} = T$. When simulation time starts, the first time slice is initialized and the process of simulating and solving DVRP is starting.

Within each time slice $[T_t, T_{t+1}]$, where $t = 0, ..., n_{ts} - 1$, the following subprocesses are performed:

1. Receiving and collecting newly arriving requests.
2. Solving the static subproblem of DVRP consisting of the requests which have been already received.
3. Allocating cumulated requests to the available vehicles whenever the end of the time slice has been reached.

The process is repeated for each time slice and finishes when T has been reached.

Algorithm 1 (MAS-DVRP) presents the above main steps by focusing on communication between **RM** and **Vh** and between **RM** and **OPT** agents and actions performed by each of them as a reaction on the received message. They are presented in details below.

Receiving and Collecting Newly Arriving Requests

During the whole process of simulating and solving the DVRP, the new requests arrive to the system. Whenever such request has been registered in the system, the **RG** agent sends to the **RM** agent the ::newRequest message. Let *CRequests* be a set of cumulated requests which have arrived at the time slice t but have not been sent yet to available **Vh** agents. Initially, the set is empty, but after receiving the ::newRequest message by the **RM** agent, it updates *CRequests* by adding the newly received request to this set. As a consequence, at any moment of time, requests cumulated in the *CRequests* form a static subproblem of the DVRP - $P_{DVRP}(t)$, which has to be solved.

Algorithm 1. MAS-DVRP

1: Initialize all agents: **GM**, **RG**, **RM**, **OPT**, and **Vh**
2: Let T be a length of the working day
3: Divide T into n_{ts} time slices of equal length $T_{ts} = T/n_{ts}$
4: Let T_t be a start of time slice t $(t = 0...n_{ts} - 1)$
5: Let $CRequests$ be a set of cumulated requests which have arrived but have not been sent yet to vehicles
6: Let P_{DVRP} be a static subproblem of DVRP including requests belonging to the $CRequests$ set
7: Let s be a solution of P_{DVRP}, and let $R_s(t) = [R_s^{v(1)}(t), R_s^{v(2)}(t), \ldots, R_s^{v(K)}(t)]$ be a global plan formed by s at time slice t, where each $R_s^{v(k)}(t)$ is a route associated with vehicle $v(k)$ $(k = 1, \ldots, K)$ in solution s at time slice t
8: $T_0 \leftarrow 0$
9: $T_{n_{ts}} \leftarrow T$
10: $CRequests \leftarrow \emptyset$
11: $iter \leftarrow 0$
12: **while** $(iter < n_{ts})$ **do**
13:     $event = getEvent()$
14:     {Receiving and collecting newly arriving requests}
15:     **if** $(event = $ **::newRequest**$)$ **then**
16:         {message with a new request o received by **RM** from **RG** agent}
17:         $CRequests \leftarrow CRequests \cup \{o\}$ {cumulate newly arrived requests}
18:         {Re-solve the static subproblem of DVRP - P_{DVRP} taking into account the requests belonging to $CRequests$ set}
19:         $s \leftarrow VNS\_DVRP(s)$
20:         Update the routing plan $R_s(t)$, where s is a new solution of P_{DVRP}.
21:     **end if**
22:     **if** $(event = $ **::endOfTimeSlice**$)$ **then**
23:         {Allocate cumulated requests to the available vehicles basing on global routing plan}
24:         **for** $k = 1, \ldots, K$ **do**
25:             Send $R_s^{v(k)}(t)$ to vehicle $v(k)$
26:         **end for**
27:         $CRequests \leftarrow \emptyset$
28:     **end if**
29:     $iter + +$
30: **end while**

Solving the Static Subproblem of DVRP

Subproblem $P_{DVRP}(t)$ is (re-)solved by the **RM** agent whenever ::newRequest message has been received by it. To do this, it first inserts the newly arrived requests to one of the route using the *cheapest insertion* heuristic, and next uses dedicated VNS procedure to improve the current best solution of $P_{DVRP}(t)$ at the time slice t. It is presented in Algorithm 2 as VNS-DVRP.

Let **OPT** agent represents VNS heuristic with three groups of methods exploring six neighborhoods using the following moves:

Algorithm 2. VNS_DVRP(s)

Input: s - current solution
1: $k \leftarrow 1$
2: $k_{max} \leftarrow 3$
3: **while** $(k \leq k_{max})$ **do**
4:    Select the group of neighborhoods N_k
5:    Explore N_k using a predefined family of still deeper neighborhoods: N_{k1}, and next N_{k2} to find the most improving neighbor s' of s in N_k
6:    **if** $(f(s') < f(s))$ **then**
7:       $s \leftarrow s'$
8:       $k \leftarrow 1$
9:    **else**
10:      $k \leftarrow k + 1$
11:   **end if**
12: **end while**
Output: s - improved solution

- relocate one or two customers, respectively, from their original positions to another ones (two methods $relocate(v), v = 1, 2$ exploring two neighborhoods $N_1 = \{N_{11}, N_{12}\}$).
- choose one or two pairs of customers, respectively, and swap customers within each pair (two methods $swap(v), v = 1, 2$ exploring two neighborhoods $N_2 = \{N_{21}, N_{22}\}$).
- remove two or three edges, respectively (each edge includes two successive customers) forming two or three, respectively, disconnected segments and next reconnect these segments in all possible ways (two methods $opt(v), v = 2, 3$ exploring two neighborhoods $N_3 = \{N_{31}, N_{32}\}$).

VNS-DVRP starts from the first group of neighborhoods N_1 and explores it by using a family of still deeper neighborhoods: N_{11}, and next N_{12}. If current best solution has not been improved, it selects the second group of neighborhoods N_2 and explores N_{21} and N_{22}, otherwise it goes back to the first group of neighborhoods, and the process of its exploration is repeated, etc. The general idea is that if the local search leads to a new best solution then the process starts from the first neighborhood, otherwise it goes to the next neighborhood. The process stops where no improvement is observed for all neighborhoods.

Assume that s is a *solution* of $P_{DVRP}(t)$ and $R_s(t)$ is a *global routing plan* formed by s at the time slice t:

$$R_s(t) = [R_s^{v(1)}(t), R_s^{v(2)}(t), \ldots, R_s^{v(K)}(t)].$$

Each $R_s^{v(k)}(t)$ is a route associated with vehicle $v(k)$ $(k = 1, \ldots, K)$ in solution s at the time slice t:

$$R_s^{v(k)}(t) = [r_1^{v(k)}(t), r_2^{v(k)}(t), \ldots, r_p^{v(k)}(t), \ldots, r_{length(R^{v(k)})}^{v(k)}(t)],$$

where $r_j^{v(k)}(t)$ are customers already assigned to the route of vehicle $v(k)$ ($j = 1, \ldots, length(R^{v(k)})$, $k = 1, \ldots, K$).

It is easy to see that each $R_s^{v(k)}(t)$ consists of two parts. The first part - $[r_1^{v(k)}(t), r_2^{v(k)}(t), \ldots, r_p^{v(k)}(t)]$ is constructed in time slices $0, 1, \ldots, t-1$, and the second one - $[r_{p+1}^{v(k)}(t), \ldots, r_{length(R^{v(k)})}^{v(k)}(t)]$ is constructed in the current time slice t. It means, that the first part is fixed (it includes customers' requests received in time slices $0, \ldots, t-1$ which have been already sent to the **Vh** agents), and the process of assigning a new request to the existing route (and improvement of the solution) is possible only on position $p+1, \ldots, length(R^{v(k)}), \ldots$ of the route of $v(k)$.

Allocating Cumulated Requests to the Available Vehicles

Whenever the end of the current time slice has been reached (**::endOfTimeSlice** message received by the **RM** from the **GM**), the **RM** agent gradually incorporates the requests to the available **Vh** agents basing on the global routing plan available at the end of current time slice t. It means that each **Vh** agent $v(k)$, $k = 1, \ldots, K$ receives requests defined by $R_s^{v(k)}(t)$ available on positions $p+1, \ldots, length(R^{v(k)}), \ldots$ of the route of $v(k)$ in solution s of the static sub-problem $P_{DVRP}(t)$. Next, all **Vh** agents start servicing the requests assigned to them.

When all requests from the current time slice have been dispatched, the next time slice starts, and the process of collecting newly arrived requests and allocating them to the **Vh** agents is repeated. In the same time, all **Vh** agents start servicing the requests assigned to them. After reaching a location of the last customer to be served in current time slice, the **Vehicle** agent $v(k)$ informs the **RM** agent about readiness for serving next requests.

4   Computational Experiment

The performance of the proposed multi-agent approach to the DVRP has been evaluated in the computational experiment. Classical 14 instances of Christofides et al. [7] (named *vrpnc01-vrpnc14*) containing 50–199 customers and transformed into its dynamic versions have been chosen for testing. All tested instances have capacity constraints, and some of them (*vrpnc06-vrpnc10*, *vrpnc13-vrpnc14*) - additionally maximum length route constraints.

Quality of the results has been measured as the percentage increase of cost of allocating all dynamic requests as compared to the best known solution of the static instance. It has been also assumed that requests may arrive with various frequencies. For the purpose of the experiment, arrivals of the requests have been generated using the Poisson distribution with λ parameter (mean number of requests occurring in the unit of time - 1 h in the experiment) set to 5, 10, and 20. It has been also assumed that the vehicle speed was 60 km/h and all requests have to be served.

Table 1. Results obtained by the proposed MAS-DVRP

Instance	Customers	Best known (static)	MAS $\lambda = 5$	MAS $\lambda = 10$	MAS $\lambda = 20$	MAS (static)
vrpnc01	50	524,61	603,63	606,34	546,90	528,21
			15,06%	15,58%	4,25%	0,69%
vrpnc02	75	835,26	1145,75	946,74	936,22	860,16
			37,17%	13,35%	12,09%	2,98%
vrpnc03	100	826,14	1065,12	975,97	920,14	850,61
			28,93%	18,14%	11,38%	2,96%
vrpnc04	150	1028,42	1284,21	1129,78	1168,21	1033,69
			24,87%	9,86%	13,59%	0,51%
vrpnc05	199	1291,29	1578,62	1516,81	1370,03	1327,44
			22,25%	17,46%	6,10%	2,80%
vrpnc06	50	555,43	761,93	633,15	630,85	556,07
			37,18%	13,99%	13,58%	0,12%
vrpnc07	75	909,68	1132,57	1062,22	990,07	921,17
			24,50%	16,77%	8,84%	1,26%
vrpnc08	100	865,94	1031,98	1011,89	977,83	891,03
			19,17%	16,85%	12,92%	2,90%
vrpnc09	150	1162,55	1427,53	1399,14	1277,10	1194,63
			22,79%	20,35%	9,85%	2,76%
vrpnc10	199	1395,85	1788,55	1609,83	1551,90	1425,45
			28,13%	15,33%	11,18%	2,12%
vrpnc11	120	1042,11	1231,14	1205,71	1119,05	1070,44
			18,14%	15,70%	7,38%	2,72%
vrpnc12	100	819,56	1124,45	896,76	932,30	841,13
			37,20%	9,42%	13,76%	2,63%
vrpnc13	120	1541,14	1786,36	1790,04	1651,51	1583,49
			15,91%	16,15%	7,16%	2,75%
vrpnc14	100	866,37	1195,26	977,61	978,32	882,55
			37,96%	12,84%	12,92%	1,87%

Each instance was repeatedly solved five times and mean results from these runs were recorded. All simulations have been carried out on PC Intel Core i5-2540M CPU 2.60 GHz with 8 GB RAM running under MS Windows 7.

The experiment results are presented in Table 1. It includes the following columns: the name of the instance, the best known solution for the static version of the instance, and the results of the experiment averaged over all runs (total cost and the percentage increase of cost of allocating all requests of dynamic instance as compared to the best known solution of static instance) for dynamic instances with $\lambda = 5, 10, 20$. It has been also decided to test the proposed approach for instances where all requests have been known in advance. The last column of the table presents the results obtained for that case.

Analysis of the results presented in the table allows one to observe that dynamization of the problem goes to the deterioration of obtained results when compare them to the best known results for their static counterparts. Although deterioration has been observed for all tested instances, its level was not the same for different instances and for different frequencies of arrival of requests. Generally, the worst values of the goal function have been observed when the mean number of requests per hour has been set to 5, the best one - for instances with dynamic requests relatively often arriving to the system ($\lambda = 20$). It can be argued that low frequency of new requests arrivals causes that possibility of re-optimization of the routes may be limited. On the other hand, arriving many requests in the unit of time increases the probability of obtaining better results.

By comparing the results for instances with two groups of constraints (only capacity and both, capacity and max route constraints) it has not been observed significant differences in results obtained for these cases.

By focusing observation on results obtained by proposed MAS-DVRP for static instances, one can conclude that although the routing cost obtained for this case is worse than the best solutions produced by state-of-the art algorithms such as tabu search, it still remains competitive to other approaches to solve the Vehicle Routing Problem. Mean relative error from the best known solution does not exceed 3% for all tested instances.

5   Conclusions

The paper proposes a multi-agent approach to solve the Dynamic Vehicle Routing Problem, where new customer requests arrive continuously arrive over time, while the system is running. It means that at any moment of time, there may exist customers already under servicing and new customers which need to be serviced. As a consequence, each newly arriving dynamic request, needs to be incorporated into the existing vehicles tours and the current solution may need to be reconfigured to minimize the goal functions. An efficient dedicated VNS procedure has been used to periodic re-optimization of the subproblems including requests which have already arrived. Computational experiment confirmed effectiveness of the proposed approach.

Future research will aim at extension of the proposed multi-agent platform by adding other efficient methods of periodic re-optimization and adapt them to solve different variants of DVRP.

References

1. Badeig, F., Balbo, F., Scemama, G., Zargayouna, M.: Agent-based coordination model for designing transportation applications. In: Proceedings of the 11th International IEEE Conference on Intelligent Transportation Systems (ITSC 2008), pp. 402–407. IEEE Press, New York (2008)

2. Barbucha, D., Jędrzejowicz, P.: Agent-based approach to the Dynamic Vehicle Routing Problem. In: Demazeau, Y., Pavon, J., Corchado, J.M., Bajo, J. (eds.) PAAMS 2009. Advances in Intelligent and Soft Computing, vol. 55. Springer, Heidelberg (2009). https://doi.org/10.1007/978-3-642-00487-2_18
3. Barbucha, D.: A multi-agent approach to the Dynamic Vehicle Routing Problem with time windows. In: Bădică, C., Nguyen, N.T., Brezovan, M. (eds.) ICCCI 2013. LNCS (LNAI), vol. 8083, pp. 467–476. Springer, Heidelberg (2013). https://doi.org/10.1007/978-3-642-40495-5_47
4. Barbucha, D.: An improved agent-based approach to the dynamic vehicle routing problem. In: Czarnowski, I., Caballero, A.M., Howlett, R.J., Jain, L.C. (eds.) Intelligent Decision Technologies 2016. SIST, vol. 56, pp. 361–370. Springer, Cham (2016). https://doi.org/10.1007/978-3-319-39630-9_30
5. Barbucha, D.: Solving DVRPTW by a multi-agent system with vertical and horizontal cooperation. In: Nguyen, N.T., Pimenidis, E., Khan, Z., Trawiński, B. (eds.) ICCCI 2018. LNCS (LNAI), vol. 11056, pp. 181–190. Springer, Cham (2018). https://doi.org/10.1007/978-3-319-98446-9_17
6. Braekers, K., Ramaekers, K., van Nieuwenhuyse, I.: The vehicle routing problem: state of the art classification and review. Comput. Ind. Eng. **99**, 300–313 (2016)
7. Christofides, N., Mingozzi, A., Toth, P., Sandi, C. (eds.): Combinatorial Optimization. Wiley, Chichester (1979)
8. Gendreau, M., Guertin, F., Potvin, J.-Y., Taillard, E.: Parallel tabu search for real-time vehicle routing and dispatching. Transp. Sci. **33**(4), 381–390 (1999)
9. Hansen, P., Mladenovic, N., Brimberg, J., Moreno Perez, J.A.: Variable neighborhood search. In: Gendreau, M., Potvin, J.-Y. (eds.) Handbook of Metaheuristics. International Series in Operations Research & Management Science, vol. 146, pp. 61–86. Springer, New York (2010). https://doi.org/10.1007/978-1-4419-1665-5_3
10. Hanshar, F.T., Ombuki-Berman, B.M.: Dynamic vehicle routing using genetic algorithms. Appl. Intell. **27**, 89–99 (2007)
11. Khouadjia, M.R.: Solving dynamic vehicle routing problems: from single-solution based metaheuristics to parallel population based metaheuristics. Ph.D. Thesis, Lille University, France (2011)
12. Kilby, P., Prosser, P., Shaw, P.: Dynamic VRPs: a study of scenarios. Technical Report APES-06-1998, University of Strathclyde, Glasgow, Scotland (1998)
13. Laporte, G.: Fifty years of vehicle routing. Transp. Sci. **43**(4), 408416 (2009)
14. Mladenovic, N., Hansen, P.: Variable neighborhood search. Comput. Oper. Res. **24**, 1097–1100 (1997)
15. Montemanni, R., Gambardella, L.M., Rizzoli, A.E., Donati, A.V.: Ant colony system for a dynamic vehicle routing problem. J. Comb. Optim. **10**(4), 327–343 (2005)
16. Pillac, V., Gendreau, M., Guret, C., Medaglia, A.L.: A review of dynamic vehicle routing problems. Eur. J. Oper. Res. **225**, 1–11 (2013)
17. Psaraftis, H.N., Wen, M., Kontovas, C.A.: Dynamic vehicle routing problems: three decades and counting. Networks **67**(1), 3–31 (2016)
18. Toth, P., Vigo, D. (eds.): Vehicle Routing: Problems, Methods, and Applications, 2nd edn. Society for Industrial and Applied Mathematics, Philadelphia (2014)
19. Vokrinek, J., Komenda, A., Pechoucek, M.: Agents towards vehicle routing problems. In: Proceedings of the 9th International Conference on Autonomous Agents and Multiagent Systems (AAMAS 2010), pp. 773–780 (2010)

Refining the Imprecise
Meaning of Non-determinism in the Web
by Strategic Games

Jorge Castro$^{(\boxtimes)}$ ⓘ, Joaquim Gabarro$^{(\boxtimes)}$ ⓘ, and Maria Serna ⓘ

Computer Science Department, Universitat Politècnica de Catalunya,
Barcelona, Spain
{castro,gabarro,mjserna}@cs.upc.edu

Abstract. Nowadays interactions with the World Wide Web are ubiquitous. Users interact through a number of steps consisting of site calls and handling results that can be automatized as orchestrations. Orchestration results have an inherent degree of uncertainty due to incomplete Web knowledge and orchestration semantics are characterized in terms of imprecise probabilistic choices. We consider two aspects in this imprecise semantic characterization. First, when local knowledge (even imprecise) of some part of the Web increases, this knowledge goes smoothly through the whole orchestration. We deal formally with this aspect introducing orchestration refinements. Second, we analyze refinement under uncertainty in the case of parallel composition. Uncertain knowledge is modeled by an uncertainty profile. Such profiles allow us to look at the uncertainty through a zero-sum game, called angel/daemon-game, or $ɑ/ð$-game. We propose to use the structure of the Nash equilibria to refine uncertainty. In this case the information improves not through cooperation but through the $ɑ$ and $ð$ competition.

Keywords: Web · Orchestrations · Refinement ·
Non-deterministic choice · Probabilistic and uncertain reasoning ·
$ɑ/ð$-games

1 Introduction

Users interact with the Web through services. In our view an interaction involves a number of steps, each step consisting of some site or basic service calls and the handling of the results of the call. Often, this type of interactions can be automatized as orchestrations. In a real scenario where only a partial knowledge on the Web behaviour can be assumed, orchestration results have some uncertainty degree. The inherent uncertainty of an orchestration is reflected in the semantic characterization in terms of imprecise probabilistic choices proposed in [2].

J. Castro was partially supported by MINECO and FEDER grant TIN2017- 89244-R and AGAUR grant 2017 SGR-856. J. Gabarro and M. Serna were partially supported by MINECO and FEDER grant TIN2017-86727-C2-1-R and AGAUR 2017 SGR 786. M. Serna was also supported by MINECO grant MDM-2014-044.

ⓒ Springer Nature Switzerland AG 2019
N. T. Nguyen et al. (Eds.): ICCCI 2019, LNAI 11683, pp. 566–578, 2019.
https://doi.org/10.1007/978-3-030-28377-3_47

We analyse how a better Web knowledge affects orchestration imprecise semantics. We introduce a partial order [1] on orchestration semantics and we show that, as expected, a decrease on Web uncertainty is transferred to a better (less imprecise) characterization.

Delays on delivering site call answers have a crucial role on the orchestration output. Frequently our knowledge about delays is imprecise. Even having tight bounds on time delays it is difficult to provide an orchestration assessment. A way to deal with this problem is to look at the uncertainty through an strategic situation with two antagonistic players the angel a and the daemon $\eth$ [3]. The angel a tries to force the best possible scenario while the daemon $\eth$ tries to worsen it. This strategic approach provides an scenario in between the optimistic and the pessimistic ones. We apply this point of view and we show that it allows to refine orchestration semantics.

The paper is organized as follows. In Sect. 2, we introduce basic concepts concerning orchestrations and Web uncertainty. In particular, we introduce the notion of *knowledge framework* to deal with imprecise return times of site calls. In Sect. 3, we introduce a partial order on orchestration semantics and we show a refinement result. In Sect. 4, we adapt *uncertainty profiles* and $a/\eth$-games to develop the idea of *forget-refinement*. In Sect. 5, we summarize the work and consider some possible extensions.

2   Web Under Stress: Imprecision

An *orchestration* is a user-defined program that uses services on the Web. An orchestrator may utilize any service that is available on the Web. Although a concrete language is not necessary to present the problem under investigation, our results rely in a precise semantics characterization of the Orc language [11,13]. In particular, Orc will allow us to develop the interplay between non-determinism and imprecise probabilities in a mathematical setting. As we will see, the analysis of the Orc expressions strongly guide the mathematical approach.

In the Orc language services are modelled by sites having predefined semantics A site is *silent* if it does not publish any result. A site call publishes *at most one response*. An orchestration which composes a number of site calls into a complex computation can be represented by an Orc expression.

We only deal with orchestrations generating a finite number of results. Two Orc expressions E and F can be combined using the following operators [11,13]. The *symmetric parallelism* $E \mid F$: E and F are evaluated in parallel. $E \mid F$ publishes some interleaving of the streams published by E and F. The *asymmetric parallelism* $E(x) < x < F$: E and F are evaluated in parallel. Some subexpressions in E may become blocked by a dependency on x. The first result published by F is bound to x, the remainder of F's evaluation is terminated and the evaluation of the blocked residue of E is resumed. Finally, the *sequence* $E > x > F(x)$: E is evaluated and, for each value v published by E, an instance $F(v)$ is executed. Given an orchestration E we denote by $\mathsf{sites}(E)$ the set of sites in the definition of E. Information on delays is given by an *evaluation function* δ providing the return time of each orchestration site.

Example 1. In *MaryNews* orchestration sites *CNN* and *BBC*[1] are called in parallel and the result of the first one to answer is emailed to Mary. This procedure can be described in Orc as: *MaryNews* = *Mary*(x) < x < *TwoNews* where *TwoNews* = *CNN* | *BBC*. Orchestration sites are *CNN* and *BBC* in *TwoNews* and site *Mary*(x) providing an email service to Mary. Roughly, the information received by Mary depends on the response times (the delays) of *CNN* and *BBC*, denoted as $\delta(CNN)$ and $\delta(BBC)$. Depending on the delays several cases can arise as we will see in the examples below. □

In order to characterize ex-ante the execution of an orchestration E, we introduced in [5] the meaning or *semantics* of E, denoted by $[\![E]\!]$. When there is no information about return times but we know that orchestration results are $m_1, \ldots, m_k$, semantics $[\![E]\!]$ is given by the multiset $\lfloor\!\lfloor m_1, \ldots, m_k \rfloor\!\rfloor$ abstracting away any time order[2], and we write $[\![E]\!] = \lfloor\!\lfloor m_1, \ldots, m_k \rfloor\!\rfloor$. As we will see later, a non-deterministic choice[3] of multisets M_i may be necessary to express the semantics of an orchestration. We write in this case $[\![E]\!] = \sqcap_i M_i$. First of all, we consider an example with no information about delays. When delay time δ is used to analyze semantics of E we write $[\![E]\!]_\delta$.

Example 2. Let consider Example 1 under lack of information about delays. Suppose $[\![CNN]\!] = \lfloor\!\lfloor \mathsf{cnn} \rfloor\!\rfloor$ and $[\![BBC]\!] = \lfloor\!\lfloor \mathsf{bbc} \rfloor\!\rfloor$. Then $[\![TwoNews]\!] = \lfloor\!\lfloor \mathsf{cnn}, \mathsf{bbc} \rfloor\!\rfloor$. Assume that both delays are unknown, encoded as $\delta(CNN) = \bot$ and $\delta(BBC) = \bot$. Parameter x in *MaryNews* = *Mary*(x) < x < *TwoNews* will get either cnn or bbc, in fact the first one to arrive. As we do not have any prior knowledge of the first arrival we assume $[\![x]\!]_\delta = \lfloor\!\lfloor \mathsf{cnn} \rfloor\!\rfloor \sqcap \lfloor\!\lfloor \mathsf{bbc} \rfloor\!\rfloor$, i.e. a non-deterministic choice of two small multisets. Then $[\![MaryNews]\!]_\delta = \lfloor\!\lfloor \mathsf{mary\_cnn} \rfloor\!\rfloor \sqcap \lfloor\!\lfloor \mathsf{mary\_bbc} \rfloor\!\rfloor$ pointing out that Mary gets an email with news provided by either *CNN* or *BBC*. □

Having full knowledge means that the delay function δ is known and it is defined on each orchestration site. We take from [9] the notation $P \lhd Q \rhd R$. It should be read: P if Q else R.

Example 3. We assume true values $\delta(CNN)$ and $\delta(BBC)$ are known. Under the hypothesis $\delta(CNN) \neq \delta(BBC)$ we have

$$[\![MaryNews]\!]_\delta = \lfloor\!\lfloor \mathsf{mary\_cnn} \rfloor\!\rfloor \lhd \delta(CNN) < \delta(BBC) \rhd \lfloor\!\lfloor \mathsf{mary\_bbc} \rfloor\!\rfloor.$$

For function $\delta(CNN) = 5$ and $\delta(BBC) = 6$, $[\![x]\!]_\delta = \lfloor\!\lfloor \mathsf{cnn} \rfloor\!\rfloor$ and $[\![MaryNews]\!]_\delta = \lfloor\!\lfloor \mathsf{mary\_cnn} \rfloor\!\rfloor$. □

When (consistent) information increases the imprecision reduces. However, it is impossible to avoid completely the non-determinism.

---

[1] A call to *CNN* or *BBC* can be interpreted as a call to https://edition.cnn.com/ or https://www.bbc.com/news.

[2] Notations are taken from [12].

[3] We take from [10] the non-determinism $P \sqcap Q$ (called daemonic choice).

Example 4. Assume that $\delta(CNN)$ and $\delta(BBC)$ could have the same value, a case that assuming discrete time is feasible. Here, a race condition give us

$$[\![MaryNews]\!]_\delta = \lfloor\!\lfloor\mathtt{mary\_cnn}\rfloor\!\rfloor \sqcap \lfloor\!\lfloor\mathtt{mary\_bbc}\rfloor\!\rfloor \lhd \delta(CNN) = \delta(BBC) \rhd$$
$$(\lfloor\!\lfloor\mathtt{mary\_cnn}\rfloor\!\rfloor \lhd \delta(CNN) < \delta(BBC) \rhd \lfloor\!\lfloor\mathtt{mary\_bbc}\rfloor\!\rfloor).$$

$\square$

When a site S is *under stress*, information about delay is uncertain. Uncertainty refers here to response time, as a natural feature of network searches. As opposed to risk, we assume *lack of data on distributions*. To deal with this lack of probabilistic information, we adopt here a two antagonistic approach. When site S is overloaded, the stress can be exerted by the angel $\mathfrak{a}$ or the daemon $\mathfrak{d}$ or both. We denote by $\delta_\mathfrak{a}(S)$, $\delta_\mathfrak{d}(S)$ the corresponding level of stress. We assume that $\delta_\mathfrak{d}(S) \geq 0$, $\delta_\mathfrak{a}(S) \leq 0$. We denote by $S_\mathfrak{d}$ site S under *daemonic stress*, in such a case $\delta(S_\mathfrak{d}) = \delta(S) + \delta_\mathfrak{d}(S)$. Similarly, $S_\mathfrak{a}$ denotes S under *angelic stress*; here delay decreases to $\delta(S_\mathfrak{a}) = \delta(S) + \delta_\mathfrak{a}(S)$. It could happen that S is under the joint action of $\mathfrak{a}$ and $\mathfrak{d}$ denoted as $S_{\mathfrak{a},\mathfrak{d}}$ and $\delta(S_{\mathfrak{a},\mathfrak{d}}) = \delta(S) + \delta_\mathfrak{a}(S) + \delta_\mathfrak{d}(S)$.

Definition 1. *A knowledge framework is a tuple* $\mathcal{K} = \langle E, \delta, \delta_\mathfrak{a}, \delta_\mathfrak{d}\rangle$ *where δ is the delay function and $\delta_\mathfrak{a}$ and $\delta_\mathfrak{d}$ provide the delay bounds under stress. Let $(a, d) \subseteq \mathsf{sites}(E) \times \mathsf{sites}(E)$ be a pair of site subsets under respectively $\mathfrak{a}$ stress (subset a) and $\mathfrak{d}$ stress (subset d). We evaluate $S[a, d]$, under risk conditions, as follows.*

$$S[a, d] = \begin{cases} S & \text{if } S \notin a \cup d \\ S_\mathfrak{a} & \text{if } S \in a \setminus d \\ S_\mathfrak{d} & \text{if } S \in d \setminus a \\ S_{\mathfrak{a},\mathfrak{d}} & \text{if } S \in a \cap d \end{cases}$$

We denote $E[a, d]$ the orchestration under stress where each $S \in \mathsf{sites}(E)$ has been replaced by $S[a, d]$.

When we want to emphasize $\mathcal{K}$, we write $S_\mathcal{K}[a, d]$ and $E_\mathcal{K}[a, d]$. The delay cost function $\mathcal{D}(E_\mathcal{K}[a, d])$ is the delay of the first return based on $\delta(S_\mathcal{K}[a, d])$. Next example borrows many ideas from a typical fuzzy approach.

Example 5. Consider the following knowledge framework $\mathcal{K}$ for *MaryNews*.

	δ	$\delta_\mathfrak{a}$	$\delta_\mathfrak{d}$		δ	$\delta_\mathfrak{a}$	$\delta_\mathfrak{d}$
CNN	5	-2	3	BBC	6	-4	2

Take $(a, d) = (\{CNN, BBC\}, \{\})$. Then $TwoNews_\mathcal{K}[a, d] = (CNN_\mathfrak{a} \mid BBC_\mathfrak{a})$ and $MaryNews_\mathcal{K}[a, d] = Mary(x) < x < TwoNews_\mathcal{K}[a, d]$.

Then $\mathcal{D}(TwoNews_{\mathcal{K}}[a,d]) = \min\{5-2, 6-4\} = 2$. As BBC_a returns before than CNN_a the result of the orchestration is $\llbracket MaryNews_{\mathcal{K}}[a,d] \rrbracket = \lfloor\lfloor\texttt{mary\_bbc}\rfloor\rfloor$. Other results are also possible depending on (a,d), for instance $\llbracket MaryNews_{\mathcal{K}}[\{CNN\}, \{\}] \rrbracket = \lfloor\lfloor\texttt{mary\_cnn}\rfloor\rfloor$. $\qquad\square$

3   Imprecise Probability and Refinement

A semantics for orchestrations where non-determinism is modeled with imprecise probabilities was proposed in [2]. We adapt this approach to deal with delays. Let $\Delta_k = \{(p_1, \ldots, p_k) \mid \forall i : p_i \geq 0 \text{ and } \sum_i p_i = 1\}$ be a k probabilistic space with $k-1$ degrees of freedom.

Example 6. Let us revisit Example 2 where $\delta(CNN) = \delta(BBC) = \bot$. We encode $\llbracket x \rrbracket_\delta = \lfloor\lfloor\texttt{cnn}\rfloor\rfloor \sqcap \lfloor\lfloor\texttt{bbc}\rfloor\rfloor$ through imprecise probabilities, *ip* for short, into

$$\llbracket x \rrbracket_{ip} = \lfloor\lfloor\texttt{cnn}\rfloor\rfloor @\mu_1 \parallel \lfloor\lfloor\texttt{bbc}\rfloor\rfloor @\mu_2.$$

for some indefinite probability vector (μ_1, μ_2) in Δ_2. Last expressions show that semantics of parameter x is the result of a probabilistic choice between two multisets with imprecise weights μ_1 and μ_2. Therefore,

$$\llbracket MaryNews \rrbracket_{ip} = \lfloor\lfloor\texttt{mary\_cnn}\rfloor\rfloor @\mu_1 \parallel \lfloor\lfloor\texttt{mary\_bbc}\rfloor\rfloor @\mu_2.$$

In the case we need to emphasize the set structure in the probabilistic choices we write

$$
\begin{aligned}
\llbracket x \rrbracket_{ip} &= \{\lfloor\lfloor\texttt{cnn}\rfloor\rfloor @\mu_1 \parallel \lfloor\lfloor\texttt{bbc}\rfloor\rfloor @\mu_2 \mid (\mu_1, \mu_2) \in \Delta_2\} \\
&= \{\lfloor\lfloor\texttt{cnn}\rfloor\rfloor @\mu_1 \parallel \lfloor\lfloor\texttt{bbc}\rfloor\rfloor @\mu_2 \mid \mu_1, \mu_2 \geq 0 \text{ and } \mu_1 + \mu_2 = 1\}.
\end{aligned}
$$

Therefore, $\llbracket MaryNews \rrbracket_{ip}$ is represented by

$$\{\lfloor\lfloor\texttt{mary\_cnn}\rfloor\rfloor @\mu_1 \parallel \lfloor\lfloor\texttt{mary\_bbc}\rfloor\rfloor @\mu_2 \mid \mu_1, \mu_2 \geq 0 \text{ and } \mu_1 + \mu_2 = 1\}.$$

$\qquad\square$

We adapt from Theorem 3 in [2] the definition of *multiset probabilistic choice* to our setting. Given ℓ multisets $M_1, \ldots, M_\ell$ and a Cartesian product of probability spaces $\Delta = \Delta_{m_1} \times \cdots \times \Delta_{m_k}$, we introduce the imprecise probabilistic choice of multisets $M = \parallel_{1 \leq i \leq \ell} M_i @ P_i(\mu)$ where multiset M_i is chosen with probability $P_i(\mu)$; here μ is any element of Δ and P_i's are arithmetic expressions on μ adding up one. Imprecision comes from the fact that value of μ is indefinite. In set notation

$$M = \{\parallel_{1 \leq i \leq \ell} M_i @ P_i(\mu) \mid \mu \in \Delta \text{ and } \sum_{1 \leq i \leq \ell} P_i(\mu) = 1\}.$$

We isolate the different probabilities arising at M as

$$\texttt{prbs}(M) = \{(P_1(\mu), \ldots, P_\ell(\mu)) \mid \mu \in \Delta\}.$$

We consider some examples.

Example 7. From Example 3, we have $[\![x]\!]_\delta = \lfloor\!\lfloor\mathtt{cnn}\rfloor\!\rfloor = (\lfloor\!\lfloor\mathtt{cnn}\rfloor\!\rfloor@1 \parallel \lfloor\!\lfloor\mathtt{bbc}\rfloor\!\rfloor@0)$. Therefore $P_1 = 1$, $P_2 = 0$ and then $\mathtt{prbs}([\![x]\!]_\delta) = \{(1,0)\}$. From Example 6, we have $\mathtt{prbs}([\![x]\!]_{ip}) = \{(\mu_1,\mu_2) \mid \mu_1 + \mu_2 = 1\} \subseteq [0,1] \times [0,1]$. Also we have that $\mathtt{prbs}([\![MaryNews]\!]_{ip}) = \mathtt{prbs}([\![x]\!]_{ip})$. Now, consider another possible meaning (see Example 12 below for details).

$$[\![x]\!]_{\mathtt{rf}} = \lfloor\!\lfloor\mathtt{cnn}\rfloor\!\rfloor@\Big(\frac{8}{25} + \mu_1\frac{2}{25}\Big) \parallel \lfloor\!\lfloor\mathtt{bbc}\rfloor\!\rfloor@\Big(\frac{3}{5} + \mu_2\frac{2}{25}\Big),$$

where (μ_1,μ_2) is an indefinite pair in Δ_2. In this case $\mu = (\mu_1,\mu_2)$ and, writing

$$P_1(\mu) = \frac{8}{25} + \mu_1\frac{2}{25}, \ P_2(\mu) = \frac{3}{5} + \mu_2\frac{2}{25},$$

we get $[\![x]\!]_{\mathtt{rf}} = \lfloor\!\lfloor\mathtt{cnn}\rfloor\!\rfloor@P_1(\mu) \parallel \lfloor\!\lfloor\mathtt{bbc}\rfloor\!\rfloor@P_2(\mu)$, for indefinite $\mu \in \Delta_2$. Probabilities are

$$\mathtt{prbs}([\![x]\!]_{\mathtt{rf}}) = \{\Big(\frac{8}{25} + \mu_1\frac{2}{25}, \frac{3}{5} + \mu_2\frac{2}{25}\Big) \mid \mu_1 + \mu_2 = 1\}.$$

Note that $\mathtt{prbs}([\![x]\!]_{\mathtt{rf}}) \subseteq [0.32, 0.4] \times [0.4, 0.6]$. Also

$$[\![MaryNews]\!]_{\mathtt{rf}} = \lfloor\!\lfloor\mathtt{mary\_cnn}\rfloor\!\rfloor@P_1(\mu) \parallel \lfloor\!\lfloor\mathtt{mary\_bbc}\rfloor\!\rfloor@P_2(\mu)$$

and $\mathtt{prbs}([\![MaryNews]\!]_{\mathtt{rf}}) = \mathtt{prbs}([\![x]\!]_{\mathtt{rf}})$. $\qquad\square$

In order to compare $[\![x]\!]_{ip}$ and $[\![x]\!]_{\mathtt{rf}}$, we introduce *refinements* in the case of multiset probabilistic choice. This needs some careful considerations. For probability distributions, standard deviation is mostly accepted as a measure of being "more precise". Following [8], we consider a different approach.

Given ℓ multisets $(M_1, \ldots, M_\ell)$ and a Cartesian product of probability spaces Δ we would like to compare probabilistic multisets over the M_i and Δ. Given $(F_1(\mu), \ldots F_\ell(\mu))$ and $(G_1(\mu'), \ldots G_\ell(\mu'))$ for $\mu, \mu' \in \Delta$ such that $\sum_i F_i(\mu) = \sum_j G_j(\mu) = 1$, consider the probabilistic multisets

$$M = \{ \parallel_{1 \le i \le \ell} M_i@F_i(\mu) \mid \mu \in \Delta\}, \ M' = \{ \parallel_{1 \le j \le \ell} M_j@G_j(\mu') \mid \mu' \in \Delta\}.$$

The *set of probability distributions* are,

$$\mathtt{prbs}(M) = \{(F_1(\mu), \ldots F_\ell(\mu)) \mid \mu \in \Delta\}$$
$$\mathtt{prbs}(M') = \{(G_1(\mu'), \ldots G_\ell(\mu')) \mid \mu' \in \Delta\}$$

We say that M is more imprecise than M' (or M' is more precise than M), denoted as $M \sqsubseteq M'$ if probabilities in M' are less spread than in M, formally iff $\mathtt{prbs}(M') \subseteq \mathtt{prbs}(M)$. This approach makes sense because,

- any choice in M' is also a choice in M,
- moreover, both choices appear with the same probability distribution.

As in M' there are less possible choices than in M, uncertainty increases from M' to M. In this framework, *increasing the imprecision means increasing the number of probabilistic choices*. We summarize this point of view in the following definition.

Definition 2. *Given ℓ multisets $M_1, \ldots, M_\ell$ and two multiset choices with imprecise weights $M = \|_{1 \leq i \leq \ell} M_i @ F_i(\mu)$ and $M' = \|_{1 \leq i \leq \ell} M_i @ G_i(\mu')$ for, respectively, indefinite elements μ and μ' in Δ. We say that M is more imprecise than M' (or M' is more precise than M), denoted as $M \sqsubseteq M'$ iff $prbs(M') \subseteq prbs(M)$.*

Example 8. Let us continue with Example 7. As $\mathtt{prbs}(\llbracket x \rrbracket_\delta) \subseteq \mathtt{prbs}(\llbracket x \rrbracket_{ip})$, according to Definition 2, we have $\llbracket x \rrbracket_{ip} \sqsubseteq \llbracket x \rrbracket_\delta$. As $\mathtt{prbs}(\llbracket x \rrbracket_{rf}) \subseteq \mathtt{prbs}(\llbracket x \rrbracket_{ip})$, we have $\llbracket x \rrbracket_{ip} \sqsubseteq \llbracket x \rrbracket_{rf}$. Observe that $\llbracket x \rrbracket_{rf}$ and $\llbracket x \rrbracket_\delta$ are not comparable, as $\mathtt{prbs}(\llbracket x \rrbracket_\delta) \not\subseteq \mathtt{prbs}(\llbracket x \rrbracket_{rf})$ and $\mathtt{prbs}(\llbracket x \rrbracket_{rf}) \not\subseteq \mathtt{prbs}(\llbracket x \rrbracket_\delta)$. □

Theorem 1. *Let F be a sub-orchestration of $E = E(F)$. Suppose that our knowledge $\llbracket F \rrbracket$ improves into $\llbracket F' \rrbracket$, i.e., $\llbracket F \rrbracket \sqsubseteq \llbracket F' \rrbracket$. Then, the increase of knowledge goes smoothly through the whole orchestration; $\llbracket E(F) \rrbracket \sqsubseteq \llbracket E(F') \rrbracket$.*

	∂			∂	
	$\{CNN\}$	$\{BBC\}$		$\{CNN\}$	$\{BBC\}$
a $\{CNN\}$	6	3	a $\{CNN\}$	$CNN_{a,\partial} \sqcap BBC$	CNN_a
$\{BBC\}$	2	4	$\{BBC\}$	BBC_a	$BBC_{a,\partial}$

Fig. 1. Take $\mathcal{U} = \langle \mathcal{K}, \mathsf{sites}(TwoNews), \mathsf{sites}(TwoNews), 1, 1, \Delta(E_\mathcal{K}[a, d]) \rangle$. The left table corresponds to $\Gamma(\mathcal{U})$ and the right table to the values of the indicator function.

Proof (Sketch). We proceed by structural induction showing that refinement is monotone through Orc operators. As an illustration, let us consider the parallel composition case. Take $E = F \mid G$ where

$$\llbracket F \rrbracket = \|_{1 \leq i \leq \ell} M_i @ P_i(\mu), \quad \llbracket G \rrbracket = \|_{1 \leq j \leq m} N_j @ Q_j(\gamma),$$

for imprecise μ and γ in Δ. According to [2], $\llbracket F \mid G \rrbracket = \|_{i,j}(M_i + N_j) @ (P_i(\mu) Q_j(\gamma))$. We write $\mathtt{prbs}(F \mid G)$ when $\ell = m = 2$,

$$\{(P_1(\mu) Q_1(\gamma), P_1(\mu) Q_2(\gamma), F_2(\mu) G_1(\gamma), F_2(\mu) G_2(\gamma)) \mid \mu, \gamma \in \Delta\}.$$

Suppose $\llbracket G \rrbracket \sqsubseteq \llbracket H \rrbracket$ with $\llbracket H \rrbracket = \|_{1 \leq j \leq m} N_j @ R_j(\tau)$ for imprecise τ in Δ, so $\mathtt{prbs}(\llbracket H \rrbracket) \subseteq \mathtt{prbs}(\llbracket G \rrbracket)$. For $m = 2$ this inclusion can be written as,

$$\{(R_1(\tau), R_2(\tau) \mid \tau \in \Delta\} \subseteq \{(Q_1(\gamma), Q_2(\gamma) \mid \gamma \in \Delta\}.$$

For each value $P_i(\mu)$, it holds that $\{(P_i(\mu) R_1(\tau), P_i(\mu) R_2(\tau) \mid \tau \in \Delta\}$ is contained into $\{(P_i(\mu) Q_1(\gamma), P_i(\mu) G_2(\gamma) \mid \gamma \in \Delta\}$. Therefore $\mathtt{prbs}(\llbracket F \mid H \rrbracket) \subseteq \mathtt{prbs}(\llbracket F \mid G \rrbracket)$ and $\llbracket F \mid G \rrbracket \sqsubseteq \llbracket F \mid H \rrbracket$ holds. With the definitions given in [2], we prove similar results for the asymmetric parallelism and sequence operators. □

Example 9. From Example 7, we get $\mathtt{prbs}(\llbracket MaryNews \rrbracket_{ip}) = \mathtt{prbs}(\llbracket x \rrbracket_{ip})$ and also $\mathtt{prbs}(\llbracket MaryNews \rrbracket_{rf}) = \mathtt{prbs}(\llbracket x \rrbracket_{rf})$. Therefore $\llbracket x \rrbracket_{ip} \sqsubseteq \llbracket x \rrbracket_{rf}$ translates directly into $\llbracket MaryNews \rrbracket_{ip} \sqsubseteq \llbracket MaryNews \rrbracket_{rf}$. $\square$

4   Uncertainty Profiles and Refinement

Stressed orchestrations can deliver different results depending on the location of the stress, see for instance Example 5 above. If we bound the spread of the stress but it is not possible to locate it, what can be said about the delay? To give an answer to this question we adapt *uncertainty profiles* to this framework [3].

A uncertainty profile $\mathcal{U}$ takes a closer look to a knowledge profile $\mathcal{K} = \langle E, \delta, \delta_a, \delta_\eth \rangle$ providing bounds to the spread and intensity of the stress. The stress effects are measured through a cost (or utility) function. Formally $\mathcal{U} = \langle \mathcal{K}, \mathcal{A}, \mathcal{D}, b_a, b_\eth, \mathcal{D}(E_\mathcal{K}[a, d]) \rangle$ where agents (or players) a and $\eth$ have the capability to act on subsets of sites $\mathcal{A}$ and $\mathcal{D}$ of the orchestration E from $\mathcal{K}$. Parameters b_a and $b_\eth$ give the number of sites that a or $\eth$ can stress. The effects of the joint interaction of a and $\eth$ is measured by $\mathcal{D}(E_\mathcal{K}[a, d])$.

As in [3], we associate to $\mathcal{U}$ a zero-sum $a/\eth$-game $\Gamma(\mathcal{U}) = \langle A_a, A_\eth, \mathcal{D}(E_\mathcal{K}[a, d]) \rangle$ with two antagonistic players the angel a and the daemon $\eth$. The actions of a and $\eth$ are given by the sets $A_a = \{a \subseteq \mathcal{A} \mid \#a = b_a\}$ and $A_\eth = \{d \subseteq \mathcal{D} \mid \#d = b_\eth\}$. The delay $\mathcal{D}(E_\mathcal{K}[a, d])$ becomes a *cost* function. Angel a tries to minimize the delay and $\eth$ to maximize it. The set of strategy profiles is $A_a \times A_\eth$. Choices for a and $\eth$ can be defined probabilistically. Mixed strategies for a and $\eth$ are probability distributions $\alpha : A_a \to [0, 1]$ and $\beta : A_\eth \to [0, 1]$ respectively. Delay of the mixed strategy (α, β) is $\mathcal{D}(E_\mathcal{K}[\alpha, \beta]) = \sum_{(a,d) \in A_a \times A_\eth} \alpha(a) \mathcal{D}(E_\mathcal{K}[a, d]) \beta(d)$. Let Δ_a and $\Delta_\eth$ denote the set of mixed strategies for a and $\eth$, respectively. A pure strategy profile (a, d) is a special case of mixed strategy (α, β) in which $\alpha(a) = 1$ and $\beta(d) = 1$. A mixed strategy profile (α, β) is a *Nash equilibrium* if, for any $\alpha' \in \Delta_a$, it holds $\mathcal{D}(E_\mathcal{K}[\alpha, \beta]) \leq \mathcal{D}(E_\mathcal{K}[\alpha', \beta])$ (a tries to minimize the delay as possible; going out of the Nash cannot reduce delay) and, for any $\beta' \in \Delta_\eth$, it holds $\mathcal{D}(E_\mathcal{K}[\alpha, \beta]) \geq \mathcal{D}(E_\mathcal{K}[\alpha, \beta'])$ ($\eth$ tries to maximize the delay; going out of the Nash cannot increase delay). A *pure Nash equilibrium*, PNE, is a Nash equilibrium (a, d) with pure strategies.

It holds that all Nash equilibrium (pure and mixed) of a zero-sum game Γ have the same value $\nu(\Gamma)$ corresponding to the cost of the row player [14]. For an $a/\eth$ game $\Gamma(\mathcal{U})$ we have:

$$\nu(\Gamma(\mathcal{U})) = \min_{\alpha \in \Delta_a} \max_{\beta \in \Delta_\eth} \mathcal{D}(E_\mathcal{K}[\alpha, \beta]) = \max_{\beta \in \Delta_\eth} \min_{\alpha \in \Delta_a} \mathcal{D}(E_\mathcal{K}[\alpha, \beta]).$$

This observation is important because it allows us to associate a delay to an uncertain situation looking at it as a zero-sum game. We take this value as the result of the strategic approach to uncertainty.

Definition 3. *The delay associated to $\mathcal{U}$ is $\mathcal{D}(\mathcal{U}) = \nu(\Gamma(\mathcal{U}))$.*

When (α, β) is a Nash equilibrium it holds $\mathcal{D}(\mathcal{U}) = \mathcal{D}(E_{\mathcal{K}}[\alpha, \beta])$.

Example 10. We consider for orchestration $TwoNews = CNN \mid BBC$ the knowledge profile $\mathcal{K}$ in Example 5. We examine the uncertainty profile $\mathcal{U}$ defined as

$$\langle \mathcal{K}, \mathsf{sites}(TwoNews), \mathsf{sites}(TwoNews), 1, 1, \mathcal{D}(E_{\mathcal{K}}[a, d]) \rangle,$$

where both sites can be stressed but the angel (respectively, the daemon) affects only to one site. Along this example we shorten $\mathcal{D}(E_{\mathcal{K}}[a, d])$ as $\mathcal{D}(a, d)$. Actions of $\mathfrak{a}$ in $\Gamma(\mathcal{U})$ are given by $A_{\mathfrak{a}} = \{a \subseteq \mathsf{sites}(TwoNews) \mid \#a = 1\} = \{\{CNN\}, \{BBC\}\}$. As $A_{\mathfrak{d}} = A_{\mathfrak{a}}$, the set of strategy profiles $A_{\mathfrak{a}} \times A_{\mathfrak{d}}$ is

$$\{(\{CNN\}, \{CNN\}), (\{CNN\}, \{BBC\}), (\{BBC\}, \{CNN\}), (\{BBC\}, \{BBC\})\}.$$

It holds

$$\mathcal{D}(\{CNN\}, \{CNN\}) = \min\{\delta(CNN) + \delta_{\mathfrak{a}}(CNN) + \delta_{\mathfrak{d}}(CNN), \delta(BBC)\} = 6.$$

Other cases are computed similarly. The $\mathfrak{a}/\mathfrak{d}$-game is shown on the left table in the Fig. 1. A strategy giving the Nash equilibrium for $\mathfrak{a}$, $\alpha = (\alpha(\{CNN\}), \alpha(\{BBC\}))$, can be found solving the equation $\mathcal{D}(\alpha, \{CNN\}) = \mathcal{D}(\alpha, \{BBC\})$. Similarly, to get β for $\mathfrak{d}$ we solve $\mathcal{D}(\{CNN\}, \beta) = \mathcal{D}(\{BBC\}, \beta)$. Then $\alpha = (2/5, 3/5)$ and $\beta = (1/5, 4/5)$. Thus, the expected return time on the first output of $TwoNews$ in equilibrium is

$$\mathcal{D}(\mathcal{U}) = \frac{2}{5} \times 6 \times \frac{1}{5} + \frac{2}{5} \times 3 \times \frac{4}{5} + \frac{3}{5} \times 2 \times \frac{1}{5} + \frac{3}{5} \times 4 \times \frac{4}{5} = \frac{18}{5}.$$

$\square$

We are interested in modelling how the $\mathfrak{a}/\mathfrak{d}$-games are able to refine the imprecise knowledge on asymmetric parallelism. Consider $E(x) < x < F$ where F is a parallel composition of sites $S_1 \mid \cdots \mid S_k$. Assume $[\![S_i]\!] = \lfloor\!\lfloor \mathsf{s}_i \rfloor\!\rfloor$, then $[\![F]\!] = \lfloor\!\lfloor \mathsf{s}_1, \ldots, \mathsf{s}_k \rfloor\!\rfloor$, and, with no delay time information ($\delta = \bot$), we can only infer that parameter x will hold any of the values in $[\![F]\!]$. So, $[\![x]\!] = \lfloor\!\lfloor \mathsf{s}_1 \rfloor\!\rfloor \sqcap \cdots \sqcap \lfloor\!\lfloor \mathsf{s}_k \rfloor\!\rfloor$. The imprecise probabilistic model gives

$$[\![x]\!]_{ip} = \lfloor\!\lfloor \mathsf{s}_1 \rfloor\!\rfloor @\mu_1 \parallel \cdots \parallel \lfloor\!\lfloor \mathsf{s}_k \rfloor\!\rfloor @\mu_k,$$

for an indefinite probability vector $(\mu_1, \ldots, \mu_k)$ in Δ_k, and so

$$[\![E(x) < x < F]\!]_{ip} = \parallel_{1 \leq k \leq k} [\![E(\mathsf{s}_i)]\!] @\mu_i.$$

In order to provide an expression for the refinement of $[\![x]\!]_{ip}$ through $\mathfrak{a}/\mathfrak{d}$-games, we introduce some additional concepts.

Definition 4. *Let* $\mathcal{U} = \langle \mathcal{K}, \mathcal{A}, \mathcal{D}, b_{\mathfrak{a}}, b_{\mathfrak{d}}, \mathcal{D}(E_{\mathcal{K}}[a, d]) \rangle$, *where* $\mathcal{K} = \langle F, \delta, \delta_{\mathfrak{a}}, \delta_{\mathfrak{d}} \rangle$ *and* F *is a parallel composition of sites* $S_1 \mid \cdots \mid S_k$. *For each strategy profile* (a, d) *we consider* $F[a, d] = T_1 \mid \cdots \mid T_k$ *where* $T_{\ell} = S_{\ell}[a, d]$, *for* $1 \leq \ell \leq k$. *The indicator function of strategy profile* (a, d) *in* $\Gamma(\mathcal{U})$ *is the set consisting of all* S_{ℓ} *sites such that* $\delta(T_{\ell})$ *is minimum among* $\{\delta(T_1), \ldots, \delta(T_k)\}$. *Formally,*

$$I_{\mathcal{U}}(a, d) = \{S_{\ell} \mid \delta(T_{\ell}) = \mathcal{D}(F[a, d])\}.$$

Proposition 1. *Let (α, β) be a Nash equilibrium in $\Gamma(\mathcal{U})$. For any $S \in I_{\mathcal{U}}(a, d)$ it holds:*

$$\mathcal{D}(\mathcal{U}) = \sum_{a,d} \alpha(a)\delta(S[a, d])\beta(d).$$

Proof. By definition, $\mathcal{D}(\mathcal{U}) = \sum_{a,d} \alpha(a)\mathcal{D}(F[a, d])\beta(d)$. As $S \in I_{\mathcal{U}}(a, d)$, it holds $\delta(S[a, d]) = \mathcal{D}(F[a, d])$ and we get the result.   □

Let us introduce refinements $[\![x]\!]_{\mathcal{U}}$, provided by $\Gamma(\mathcal{U})$ game , on the $[\![x]\!]_{ip}$ semantics.

Example 11. We continue with the Example 10 emphasizing the stress suffered by the sites, see the right table in Fig. 1. This table points out the sites giving minimum return time in $(CNN \mid BBC)[a, d]$. For instance, when $(a, d) = (\{CNN\}, \{CNN\})$, the table value is a non-deterministic choice between $CNN_{\mathfrak{a,\eth}}$ and BBC representing that $I_{\mathcal{U}}(CNN, CNN)$ is $\{CNN, BBC\}$. The following refinement of $[\![x]\!]_{ip}$ can be introduced from a Nash equilibrium and the indicators functions of $\Gamma(\mathcal{U})$. First consider a version where the $\mathfrak{a}/\mathfrak{d}$ stress over the sites is explicitly added when needed to improve readability,

$$\left(([\![CNN_{\mathfrak{a,\eth}}]\!] \sqcap [\![BBC]\!]) @ \frac{2}{5} \times \frac{1}{5} \; [\![CNN_{\mathfrak{a}}]\!] @ \frac{2}{5} \times \frac{4}{5} \; [\![BBC_{\mathfrak{a}}]\!] @ \frac{3}{5} \times \frac{1}{5} \; [\![BBC_{\mathfrak{a,\eth}}]\!] @ \frac{3}{5} \times \frac{4}{5} \right).$$

Finally $[\![x]\!]_{ip}$ is

$$\left(([\![CNN]\!] \sqcap [\![BBC]\!]) @ \frac{2}{5} \times \frac{1}{5} \; [\![CNN]\!] @ \frac{2}{5} \times \frac{4}{5} \; [\![BBC]\!] @ \frac{3}{5} \times \frac{1}{5} \; [\![BBC]\!] @ \frac{3}{5} \times \frac{4}{5} \right).$$

Note that in this case $\mathcal{D}(\mathcal{U})$ is 18/5.   □

The formal definition of the $\mathcal{U}$ refinements that fixes stress exerted by $\mathfrak{a}$ and $\mathfrak{d}$ over the sites according to weighted strategy profiles in $\Gamma(\mathcal{U})$ in a Nash equilibrium is as follows

Definition 5. *The $\mathcal{U}$ refinements of $[\![x]\!]_{ip}$ is given by*

$$[\![x]\!]_{\mathcal{U}} = \; |_{a,d}(\sqcap_{S \in I_{\mathcal{U}}(a,d)}[\![S]\!]) @ \alpha(a) \times \beta(d),$$

where (α, β) is a Nash equilibrium of $\Gamma(\mathcal{U})$.

Example 12. For the Nash equilibrium in Example 10, the $\mathcal{U}$ refinement for $[\![x]\!]_{ip}$ is

$$[\![x]\!]_{\mathcal{U}} = ([\![CNN]\!] \sqcap [\![BBC]\!]) @ \frac{2}{5} \times \frac{1}{5} \; [\![CNN]\!] @ \frac{2}{5} \times \frac{4}{5} \; [\![BBC]\!] @ \frac{3}{5} \times \frac{1}{5} \; [\![BBC]\!] @ \frac{3}{5} \times \frac{4}{5}$$

$$= (\lfloor\!\lfloor cnn \rfloor\!\rfloor \sqcap \lfloor\!\lfloor bbc \rfloor\!\rfloor) @ \frac{2}{5} \times \frac{1}{5} \; \lfloor\!\lfloor cnn \rfloor\!\rfloor @ \frac{2}{5} \times \frac{4}{5} \; \lfloor\!\lfloor bbc \rfloor\!\rfloor @ \frac{3}{5}.$$

Replacing the daemonic choice ⊓ by imprecise probabilities and regrouping, we have

$$\lfloor\!\lfloor\text{cnn}\rfloor\!\rfloor@\left(\frac{2}{5}\times\frac{4}{5}+\mu_1\times\frac{2}{5}\times\frac{1}{5}\right) \text{\textup{\char"0A6}} \lfloor\!\lfloor\text{bbc}\rfloor\!\rfloor@\left(\frac{3}{5}+\mu_2\times\frac{2}{5}\times\frac{1}{5}\right),$$

for some indefinite probability vector (μ_1,μ_2) in Δ_2. Using $\mathcal{U}$, from Example 6, we get the meaning into

$$[\![x]\!]_{\mathcal{U}} = \lfloor\!\lfloor\text{cnn}\rfloor\!\rfloor@\left(\frac{8}{25}+\mu_1\frac{2}{25}\right) \text{\textup{\char"0A6}} \lfloor\!\lfloor\text{bbc}\rfloor\!\rfloor@\left(\frac{3}{5}+\mu_2\frac{2}{25}\right),$$

where probability vector (μ_1,μ_2) is indefinite. Then, we have the following meaning for *MaryNews*, $[\![MaryNews]\!]_{\mathcal{U}}$

$$\lfloor\!\lfloor\text{mary\_cnn}\rfloor\!\rfloor@\left(\frac{8}{25}+\mu_1\frac{2}{25}\right) \text{\textup{\char"0A6}} \lfloor\!\lfloor\text{mary\_bbc}\rfloor\!\rfloor@\left(\frac{3}{5}+\mu_2\frac{2}{25}\right).$$

$\square$

As $[\![x]\!]_{ip}$ is described by any probability distribution, $\texttt{prbs}([\![x]\!]_{\mathcal{U}}) \subseteq \texttt{prbs}([\![x]\!]_{ip})$. Moreover, if we assume that the environment behaves as predicted by $\mathcal{U}$, a more precise behaviour can be announced.

Theorem 2. *Given $E(x) < x < F$ where $F = (S_1 \mid \cdots \mid S_k)$ and an uncertainty profile $\mathcal{U}$ on F we have $[\![x]\!]_{ip} \sqsubseteq [\![x]\!]_{\mathcal{U}}$ and $[\![E(x) < x < F]\!]_{ip} \sqsubseteq [\![E(x) < x < F]\!]_{\mathcal{U}}$. Assuming that F behaves as predicted by $\Gamma(\mathcal{U})$, the arrival times to x of the different possible values follow the $[\![x]\!]_{\mathcal{U}}$ distribution. Moreover, assuming that the execution of E is triggered by x, $\mathbb{E}(\mathcal{D}(E(x) < x < F)) = \mathcal{D}(E) + \mathcal{D}(\mathcal{U})$.*

In this way, using induction and additional rules for more complex composition, we can associate a meaning to any E under uncertainty profile $\mathcal{U}$, $[\![E]\!]_{\mathcal{U}}$ which is a refinement on $[\![E]\!]_{ip}$.

5   Conclusions

Although cooperation is the usual model to improve situations, in real scenarios it is more likely to find some sort of competition. We have shown a way to use the competition between agents, ɑ and ɒ, to improve our knowledge of the environment. Our approach allows to consider more realistic scenarios and provides an additional analysis tool to support the decisions of the system managers. Here, we have continued the work in [2] considering the relation between imprecise probability semantics and the ɑ/ɒ-approach. In particular, we have shown that the structure of Nash equilibria due to ɑ/ɒ-games can be used to refine the imprecise meaning of $E(x) < x < F$ which is the unique composition rule that inserts additional non-determinism in the behaviour of an orchestration. Our results also show a monotonic behaviour of imprecise meaning versus the level of knowledge. We are working towards understanding better the framework, in particular, monotonicity properties with respect to different uncertainty profiles in general orchestrations.

Nash equilibria and the value of the $\mathfrak{a}/\mathfrak{d}$-game is a natural solution for refinement, however finding Nash equilibria in $\mathfrak{a}/\mathfrak{d}$-games can be computationally difficult, in fact it is an EXP-complete problem [4]. As $\mathfrak{a}/\mathfrak{d}$-games are zero-sum games, it might also be possible to find the game values through iterative methods [16]. Furthermore, the approach through mixed strategies, appearing in the Nash equilibria, seems also to suggest the possibility to develop algorithms based Monte Carlo techniques, that could be more efficient. It will be of interest to explore these approaches.

It will also be of interest to analyse whether the $\mathfrak{a}/\mathfrak{d}$-refinement applies to other settings in particular to short-term economic systems like the IS-LM or IS-MP models [6] or other decision support models. Finally it could be interesting to apply this approach to more applied problems like real politics [7] or climate change [15].

References

1. Allison, L.: A Practical Introduction to Denotational Semantics. Cambridge University Press, New York (1986)
2. Castro, J., Gabarro, J., Serna, M.: Web apps and imprecise probabilitites. In: Medina, J.S., et al. (eds.) IPMU 2018, Part II. CCIS, vol. 854, pp. 226–238. Springer, Cham (2018). https://doi.org/10.1007/978-3-319-91476-3_19
3. Gabarro, J., Serna, M., Stewart, A.: Analysing web-orchestrations under stress using uncertainty profiles. Comput. J. **57**(11), 1591–1615 (2014)
4. Gabarro, J., Garcia, A., Serna, M.: Computational aspects of uncertainty profiles and angel-daemon games. Theory Comput. Syst. **54**(1), 83–110 (2014)
5. Gabarro, J., Leon-Gaixas, S., Serna, M.: The computational complexity of QoS measures for orchestrations. J. Comb. Optim. **34**(4), 1265–1301 (2017)
6. Gabarro, J., Serna, M.: Uncertainty in basic short-term macroeconomic models with angel-daemon games. IJDATS **9**(4), 314–330 (2017). https://doi.org/10.1504/IJDATS.2017.10009422
7. García-Sanz, M.D., Llamazares, I., Manrique, M.A.: Ideal and real party positions in the 2015–2016 Spanish general elections. In: Medina, J., Ojeda-Aciego, M., Verdegay, J.L., Perfilieva, I., Bouchon-Meunier, B., Yager, R.R. (eds.) IPMU 2018, Part III. CCIS, vol. 855, pp. 52–62. Springer, Cham (2018). https://doi.org/10.1007/978-3-319-91479-4_5
8. He, J., Seidel, K., McIver, A.: Probabilistic models for the guarded command language. Sci. Comput. Program. **28**(2–3), 171–192 (1997). https://doi.org/10.1016/S0167-6423(96)00019-6
9. Hoare, C.A.R.: A couple of novelties in the propositional calculus. Math. Log. Q. **31**(9–12), 173–178 (1985). https://doi.org/10.1002/malq.19850310905
10. Hoare, C.: Communicating Sequential Processes. Prentice-Hall, London (1985)
11. Kitchin, D., Quark, A., Cook, W., Misra, J.: The Orc programming language. In: Lee, D., Lopes, A., Poetzsch-Heffter, A. (eds.) FMOODS/FORTE-2009. LNCS, vol. 5522, pp. 1–25. Springer, Heidelberg (2009). https://doi.org/10.1007/978-3-642-02138-1_1

12. McIver, A., Morgan, C.C.: Abstraction, Refinement and Proof for Probabilistic Systems. Monographs in Computer Science. Springer, New York (2005). https://doi.org/10.1007/b138392
13. Misra, J., Cook, W.: Computation orchestration: a basis for wide-area computing. Softw. Syst. Model. **6**(1), 83–110 (2007)
14. von Neumann, J., Morgenstern, O.: Theory of Games and Economic Behavior, 60th Anniversary Commemorative Edition, Commemorative edn. Princeton University Press, Princeton (1953)
15. Nordhaus, W.: Climate Casino: Risk, Uncertainty, and Economics for a Warming World. Yale, New Haven (2013)
16. Robinson, J.: An iterative method of solving a game. Annal. Math. **54**(2), 296–301 (1951). Second Series

Imprecise Data Handling with MTE

Włodzimierz Filipowicz$^{(\boxtimes)}$ ⓘ

Gdynia Maritime University, Gdynia, Poland
w.filipowicz@wpit.umg.edu.pl

Abstract. Measurements, indications and forecasts are randomly and very often systematically corrupted. The distribution of stochastic distortions is empirically evaluated; an estimate is usually given by histogram. Empirical distributions available from various sources differ. Discrepancies are due to testing methodology, conditions of experiments etc. Whatever the reason they introduce some kind of doubtfulness. In many modern applications propagation of uncertainty is an important issue. The ability to model and process uncertainty through traditional approaches is rather limited. To propose new solutions, one should start with an alternative approach towards modelling and processing uncertainty. Mathematical Theory of Evidence might be useful provided supporting measures on representing the true value by any location in the neighborhood of observation are available. Theoretical Gaussian density distribution as well as histograms are exploited. In recent paper by the author transformation from probability density to probability distribution with fuzzy sets was presented. In order to obtain most probable forecast various height histogram bins are converted to fuzzy limited ones. Necessary membership functions are proposed. Paper concludes with example calculations results.

Keywords: Belief functions · Uncertainty · Empirical data

1 Introduction

Mathematical Theory of Evidence (MTE for short) delivers unique opportunity of evaluating hypothesis truth based on related evidence at hand. Observation facts and knowledge are the evidence main constituents. Widely known information on taken observation is that it represents instance of random variable governed by some sort of density distribution. Adaptation of the theory for metrology and nautical science requires supporting measure on representing the true value by any location in the neighborhood of observation. In recent paper by the author transformation from probability density to probability distribution with fuzzy sets was presented. Adopted method involved theoretical Gaussian density distribution. Hereafter empirical data are considered.

To introduce fuzzy systems to metrology and nautical science requires definition of uncertain probability sets on representing the true measurement. Family of fuzzy sets are introduced in the vicinity of observation. Given Gaussian density function one can use confidence intervals with the width of single standard deviation value. Any point that falls within this range represent the true measurement with the same probability. It is also known that mentioned range has rather interval than crisp valued limits.

© Springer Nature Switzerland AG 2019
N. T. Nguyen et al. (Eds.): ICCCI 2019, LNAI 11683, pp. 579–588, 2019.
https://doi.org/10.1007/978-3-030-28377-3_48

Publications devoted to practical aspects of metrology introduce standard deviation of a mean observation as a sort of metrological uncertainty measure. It is widely assumed that any point out of a discernment frame belonging to this range is governed by sigmoidal membership function. Therefore, any confidence range has interval valued limits and requires membership function to evaluate possibility of considered point being located within the range. Probabilistic and possibilistic way of approach proved to be practical for discussed scope of applications [2, 7]. Set of necessary items required when dealing with uncertainty in metrology are presented in Fig. 1. Given density distribution confidence intervals are to be establish in the vicinity of taken measurement. Each interval has assigned probability on true observation being located within its imprecise limits. One may perceive introduced ranges as fuzzy probability sets, which require membership functions. Given geometric location may be considered to be the true measurement with likelihood attributed to particular set taking into account possibility of its belonging to the set.

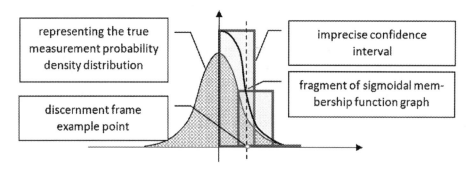

Fig. 1. Basic items required when dealing with uncertainty and theoretical distribution in metrology and nautical science.

2   Basic Uncertainty Model for Imprecise Data

Popular basic uncertainty model includes proposition and associated range of probabilities also called as belief interval [4]. Given proposition z and range of real values $[p_{min}; p_{max}]$ one can write the model in the form of expression (1).

$$Z : [p_{min}; p_{max}], \ p_{min}, p_{max} \in [0; 1], \ and \ p_{min} \leq p_{max} \tag{1}$$

where:

p_{min}	upper limit of probability that proposition z is true
$p_{max} - p_{min}$	range of uncertainty, possibility of the truth of z is defined by a descending part of diagram (see Fig. 2)
p_{max}	lower limit of probability that proposition z is false

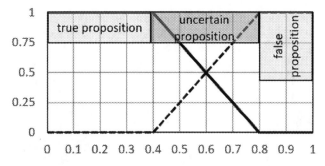

Fig. 2. Interval uncertainty representation.

The uncertainty for z can be transferred into belief assignment shown in Table 1. The assignment engages two elements hypothesis space Θ that is truth (true or false) of considered proposition z and its negation. Thus one of the items is marked with z and another with ¬z. Within probability assignment all elements of power set of the considered frame might appear, consequently one more multiple item $\{z, ¬z, \Theta\}$ is usually considered. The last item expresses uncertainty. Range-valued uncertainty is relevant while seeking solution in erroneous data condition. Possibility of various geographic/geometric locations, observations belonging to a fuzzy probability sets is to be defined. Thus possibility and probability can be used jointly in order to include uncertainty into the defined mathematical model. In order to introduce the concept appropriate fuzzy sets are to be defined regarding random distortions of all observations at hand.

3   Gathering and Modelling Evidence

Uncertainty, which is related to random and systematic measurement deflections, is present in all measurements and any kind of prediction. A forecast is randomly deflected and can be treated as an instance of a random variable, governed by some kind of distribution. Professionals, along with most of end users know much about the unavoidable random nature of measurements or predictions. This sort of doubtfulness can be referred to as aleatory uncertainty. Hereafter it is assumed that randomness is governed by empirical or theoretical distribution. Usually there are various estimations of dispersion parameters available. Two dispersions for single bin, one of which can be considered optimistic with p_{max} and the second one assumed as pessimistic with p_{min} as interval valued probability estimations are shown at Fig. 2. The measured value is considered to be located somewhere within presented rectangle in accordance with basic uncertainty model. Given the above mentioned data, one can seek for the truth of the proposition "is the true observation represented by a point close to any of selected abscissa".

In order to reasoning on forecast weather parameter one has to gather evidence related to each of prediction systems credibility. Simplest case is a histogram displaying evidence, meant as notified discrepancies between predicted and observed data.

Then relationship between considered predicted value and its support by a piece of evidence at hand is to be established. Finally considering all systems, most credible value for given weather parameter is to be found.

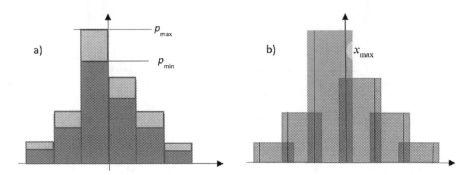

Fig. 3. Empirical random error distribution (a) and its alternative fuzzy limited bins version (b)

For given weather parameter such as speed or direction of wind one has to collect adequate evidence. Expected evidence may take form presented at part a) of Fig. 3. In order to obtain the diagram, forecast and real values are to be compared in order to upgrade histogram. Collection of relative discrepancies are included within the diagram. Histograms are widely used as graphical representation of empirical probabilities. It shows a diagram of the distribution of observed data. A histogram consists of adjacent rectangles, primarily erected over non-overlapping intervals or bins. The histogram is usually normalized and displays relative frequencies considered as empirical probabilities. It shows the proportion of cases that fall into each of bins The intervals are usually chosen to be of the same width, for example 20% of the forecast value. It is assumed that family of sets of relative frequencies are given as a result of long term observations. For given set of observations and particular bin interval $[p_{min}, p_{max}]$ can be obtained and treated as uncertainty regarding given deflection. In order to establish relation with before mentioned approach histograms with uncertainty are to be transferred to fuzzy limited bins version as shown at part b) of Fig. 3. Plotted x_{max} indicates extension of a bin width due to uncertainty.

3.1 Nautical Observations and Uncertain Data

In nautical practice an observation made with a navigational aid can be treated as an instance of a random variable governed by some kind of distribution. The Gaussian bell function is often used in order to represent density of locations to be considered as true measurements. Discrepancies in estimated parameters of such distributions frequently occur. Two of the density dispersions, one of which is named dd_1 with a standard deviation σ_{min}, and the second one dd_2 with deflection σ_{max}, are presented in Fig. 4. Given various diagrams leads to overlapping ranges while selecting confidence intervals. Having value of σ_{min}, related value of $|\sigma_{max} - \sigma_{min}|$ can be attributed to uncertainty of the observation. The difference is an overlap range that can be perceived as a doubtfulness level.

Above mentioned approach is valid for many applications it is also presented in [1, 2]. It enables evaluation of the question "what is the truth that the true observation is represented by point x". For each x_i out of considered frame of discernment value of appropriate support is to be obtained. Concept of fuzzy probability sets can be useful to establish adequate relation.

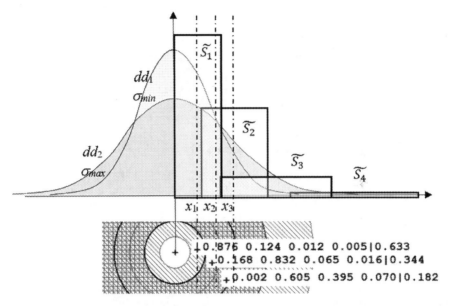

Fig. 4. Observation's adjacent confidence intervals with fuzzy limits and membership grades for example points.

Four fuzzy cumulated probability sets were introduced in the right vicinity of given observation. Possibility of various values of measurement belonging to each of fuzzy probability sets are returned by sigmoidal membership functions. Example sets of figures refereeing to plotted points are presented in included insertion. Each of the sets contains four figures meaning particular point inclusion grades within each of probability sets. The latest number refers to sought support. It estimates probability that given point represents the true observation.

Two probability assignments for example points are included in Table 1. Collected data response to the propositions involving particular points and their representation of the true measurement. For the first point considered support is calculated as 0.68. With the second option support figure is much lower and it is evaluated as 0.31. Uncertainty of 0.20 is the same for both cases. Presented data are meaningful while processing uncertain and erroneous data.

Belief function defined over certain domain in practical application represent evidence and its encoded relationship with propositions as defined by Formula (2). It refers to established fuzzy probability sets and involved uncertainty. Fuzzy sets may be associated with cumulated probability calculated for specified intervals while theoretical density distribution is considered. They can be related to bins when empirical distribution is involved. Fuzzy sets are defined by membership functions.

$$m(e_i) = \left\{ \left(z_x, m(z_x)_i \right), \left(\neg z_x, m(\neg z_x)_i \right), \left(\Theta, m(\Theta)_i \right) \right\}$$
$$m(z_x)_i = f \left(\mu(x)|_{\tilde{S}_k}, \Theta \right)_i \tag{2}$$
$$m(\Theta)_i = g(\Theta, s_i)$$

where:

z_x proposition stating truth of location x to represent: true observation, true prediction, fixed position, etc.);

$m(z_x)_i$ supporting mass of the proposition imbedded within i-th piece of evidence;

s_i subjective evaluation of i-th piece of evidence

Table 1. Two probability assignments for example selected points

	x_1	x_2
$m(z)$	0.68	0.31
$m(\neg z)$	0.12	0.49
$m(\Theta)$	0.20	0.20

3.2 Empirical Distribution Handling

In order to explore basic uncertainty model and its practical application appropriate fuzzy sets are to be defined in the neighborhood of an instance of random variable that is a distorted nautical observation or considered predictions. This way one can reason on true ship's location, distance to reference object [1] or most probable weather condition. Uncertainty in empirical distributions are expressed by variety of cases falling within selected ranges. That makes differences in histogram bins heights. In order to follow concept proposed by the author for, as example, position fixing various widths of bins might also express uncertainty. Two approaches are presented at Fig. 3, that illustrates empirical uncertain random error distribution (a) and its alternative fuzzy limited bins version (b). Proposal of the way of transformation between the two versions, aimed at their equivalency, are presented below. Definition of sigmoidal membership functions are also included.

Possibility and probability can be used jointly in order to include uncertainty into the defined mathematical model. Figure 5 shows example of observation result and diagram including six bins in its vicinity. Heights of bins are related to frequency that the true result can be located within each of them. Uncertainty of available data is emphasized by included extra rectangle in second bin. Three adjacent unary width intervals $\tilde{S}_1$, $\tilde{S}_2$ and $\tilde{S}_3$ are depicted in exploded insertion. Probability density within each of the bins are estimated respectively as: 0.57, 0.25 and 0.18. Drawn graphs represent functions that return membership grades within second and third bin. Note that pairs of sigmoidal functions reflect different level of uncertainty. Narrow based ones refer to doubtfulness close to zero, wider were calculated for about 0.5 uncertainty.

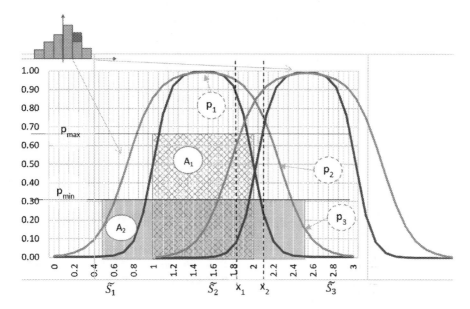

Fig. 5. Selected widened bins with membership functions.

In order to establish probability of elsewhere location of true measurement one has to explore proximity of the observation at hand. In case of none or low doubtfulness one should concentrate on defined bins width. Otherwise wider ranges covered by membership sigmoidal functions are to be used to obtain satisfactory solution. Thus a bin can be treated as fuzzy set with belonging grades governed by pairs of functions for which $f(k) = 0.5$ for $k = (1, 2, 3, ..)$ as shown in Fig. 5 (see also Formula(3)). For the sake of considering higher uncertainty one should widen exploring area in order to deal with the same cumulated probability. Figure 5, where considered probability range is $[p_{min}; p_{max}]$ with degree of doubtfulness $1 - p_{min}/p_{max} \approx 0.5$, displays areas A_1 and A_2. Both of them satisfy equality $A_1 = A_2$ since $1*p_{max} = w*p_{min}$. From the latest relation one can calculate width w of the expanded bin. Note that modified histogram contains overlapping bins, width of overlapped ranges express uncertainty. Respective pairs of functions for estimated uncertainty close to 0.5 and $f(k) = 0.5$ where $k = (0.75, 2.25, 1.75, 3.25)$ are also displayed at the figure.

Algorithms that enable to define membership function are to be presented. Similar cases designated for theoretical distributions were discussed in the author previous papers [2, 3]. Proposed algorithm engage characteristic points p_1, p_2 and p_3 as marked at Fig. 5 (see also Table 2 for their basic features). Mentioned procedure calculates necessary coefficients to obtain smallest/largest descending rate (max/min ordinate of point p_3) of the sigmoidal function regarding given bin range and its center location.

Formulas of two sigmoidal complementary functions are specified by expression (3) [6]. For given fuzzy probability set descending upper function specifies grade of x belonging to the set at the left hand side. At the same time lower formula returns the same point degree of being included within the same set at its right hand side.

Table 2. Sigmoidal functions characteristic points features

Point	Abscissa	Ordinate
p_1	Bin's centre	1
p_2	Mean of A_1 and A_2 rightmost	0.5
p_3	A_2 rightmost	Min/max

$$\mu_i(x) = \frac{1}{1 + e^{-a_{mi} \cdot (x - (i + r_{mi}))}}$$
$$\mu_i'(x) = 1 - \frac{1}{1 + e^{-a_{mi} \cdot (x - (i-1 + r_{mi}))}}$$

(3)

where:

r_{mi} abscissa of point p_2 related to uncertainty range regarding i-th bin and m-th source of data,

i number of the bin,

a_{mi} membership diagram steepness (close to point p_2) factor related to uncertainty range (assigned to i-th bin and m-th source of data), to be calculated with algorithm I.

Algorithm I calculates membership function steepness factor. It engages points related to right fuzzy extension of the second bin marked at Fig. 5. Sigmoidal functions characteristic points features were presented in Table 1. Procedure calculates coefficient am to obtain smallest descending rate (at ordinate equal to 0.5) of the sigmoidal function regarding given uncertainty range and centre of considered set. Note that smallest steepness factor stipulates highest ordinate of point p_3. At the same time point p_1 should be situated at ordinate close to one. In presented algorithm this value is expected to be greater than 0.999. Algorithm starts with calculation of variable rm which is related to uncertainty ranges located at both sides of a bin.

```
Algorithm I
if (p_min>0)  rm := (p_max/p_min-1)/2 else exit
assign y_of_point_p3 := 0.05; step := 0.01
repeat
am:= -ln(1/ y_of_point_p3 - 1)/(2.5 -(2 + rm))
y_of_point_p1:=1/(1 + exp(-am·(1.5 - (2 - rm))
y_of_point_p3 := y_of_point_p3 + step
until y_of_point_p1 < 0.999
```

Table 3 contains features of two points named as x_1 and x_2 marked at Fig. 5. Their locations within second and third bins were calculated with functions defined by presented algorithm. The data are shown in columns entitled $\mu(x_1)$ and $\mu(x_2)$ in Table 3. There are two pairs of such columns included. First one refer to close to zero uncertainty, which value for second case is close to 0.5. Bins' probability values are also degraded due to doubtfulness (see second last row of Table 3). Based on mentioned values likelihood on representation of the true measurement by selected points were calculated. Support values are strictly related to particular bins probability once uncertainty is low. Appropriate figures are more or less the same while doubtfulness is high. This expresses popular in metrology or nautical science proposition that uncertainty means that the true location/prediction can be located everywhere.

Table 3. Two example selected points features along with selected bins, probability and uncertainty.

Fuzzy sets	Bins' probability	$\mu(x_1)$	$\mu(x_2)$	Bins' probability	$\mu(x_1)$	$\mu(x_2)$
$\widetilde{S}_1$	0.57	0.00	0.00	0.37	0.00	0.00
$\widetilde{S}_2$	0.25	0.89	0.28	0.16	0.94	0.78
$\widetilde{S}_3$	0.18	0.10	0.67	0.12	0.60	0.90
Uncertainty	0.00	0.00	0.00	0.35	0.35	0.35
Support(..)		0.232	0.130		0.188	0.179

4 Combining Evidence

In the latest chapter two points were considered in order to depict their membership grades under various uncertainty conditions. Their supports of representing the true measurement, with reference to the taken one, were also calculated. Two separate cases with respect to different accuracy factor were considered. Important practical remarks were introduced. Their most crucial issue is they bring ability to transform density distributions to probability dispersions with respect to uncertainty level.

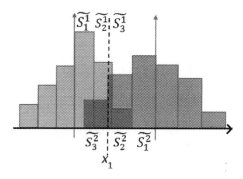

Fig. 6. Two observations with histograms depicting their accuracy, with single point of interest.

In nautical science and metrology more interesting is the case where single point is engaged with reference to different observations. Various quality factors are assumed regarding each of them. Appropriate scheme is presented at Fig. 6. Proposition that could be considered is "what is a support that given point represents true observation given two (all) measurements at hand".

5 Summary

Method of handling randomly distorted data was presented. Two different ways of representing measurement uncertainty were introduced at first. Variety arises while dealing with various forms of density distributions. Direct transformation between concepts was depicted.

The approach can be exploited while modelling and processing uncertainty encountered in weather predictions. Knowledge related to random deflections of forecasts is included within histograms. Histograms display variety of relative frequencies considered as empirical probabilities. Proportion of cases that fall into each of bins fits into basic uncertainty model. Presented approach is intended for a fuzzy environment. Modelling doubtfulness always involves fuzzy probability sets, that could be directly related to bins of empirical distributions. Membership functions are exploited to decide on location of the true measurements taking into account all predictions available. Sigmoidal functions are used very often. Fuzzy sets may be associated with cumulated probability calculated for specified intervals.

Acknowledgements. This research was supported by The National Centre for Research and Development in Poland under grant on ROUTING research project (MARTERA-1/ROUTING/3/2018) in ERA-NET COFUND MarTERA-1 programme (2018-2021).

References

1. Filipowicz, W.: On nautical observation errors evaluation. TransNav 9(4), 545–550 (2015)
2. Filipowicz, W.: A logical device for processing nautical data. Sci. J. SMU Szczecin 52(124), 65–73 (2017)
3. Filipowicz, W.: Mathematical theory of evidence in navigation. In: Cuzzolin, F. (ed.) BELIEF 2014. LNCS (LNAI), vol. 8764, pp. 199–208. Springer, Cham (2014). https://doi.org/10.1007/978-3-319-11191-9_22
4. Lee, E.S., Zhu, Q.: Fuzzy and Evidence Reasoning. Physica-Verlag, Heidelberg (1995)
5. Liu, W., Hughes, J.G., McTear, M.F.: Representing heuristic knowledge and propagating beliefs in Dempster-Shafer theory of evidence. In: Federizzi, M., Kacprzyk, J., Yager, R.R. (eds.) Advances in the Dempster-Shafer Theory of Evidence. Willey, New York (1992)
6. Piegat, A.: Fuzzy Modelling and Control. AOW Exit, Warsaw (2003)
7. Yen, J.: Generalizing the Dempster–Shafer theory to fuzzy sets. IEEE Trans. Syst. Man Cybern. 20(3), 559–570 (1990)

The Relationship Between Collective Intelligence and One Model of General Collective Intelligence

Andy E. Williams[✉]

Nobeah Foundation, Nairobi, Kenya
awilliams@nobeahfoundation.org

Abstract. A recently developed model of collective intelligence (CI) has been proposed to have the capacity for general collective intelligence (GCI), that is, the capacity for general problem-solving ability that can be reapplied across any domain. This paper explores the relationship between this model of GCI and a model proposed to describe existing CI solutions that are conventional in the sense of accomplishing a single function. The properties required for GCI in this model, and how they make this model unique from other approaches to CI, as well as the implications of these differences, are also explored. In addition, the implications of GCI are explored in terms of the capacity to drive societal impact at transformative scale, where that impact is suggested not to be reliably possible with other approaches to CI.

Keywords: General collective intelligence · Collective intelligence · Functional model · Functional decomposition · Functional fitness

1   A Model for Collective Intelligence as a Component of Collective Consciousness

A functional model of human consciousness has recently been proposed [1]. Where other approaches attempt to define the physical implementation of consciousness according to theories that are as yet incomplete, this new approach borrows the concept of functional modeling from software and systems engineering, and borrows aspects of functionalism [11] from the philosophy of consciousness, to define what is suggested to be the most complete model of the functions of consciousness to date. This approach focuses on modeling the functions consciousness is observed to have, including conscious self-awareness, where consistency with these observations can be validated. This functional model is proposed to be applicable to different physical implementations including not only human, but also to artificial, and Nth order collective consciousness [2]. In practice this flexibility has enabled this model to be used to design collective intelligence based social impact programs with the potential to vastly increase capacity for collective social impact [4]. This model of collective consciousness consists of four functional systems, the collective body, the collective emotions, the collective mind, and the collective consciousness. The collective body obeys principles enabling functionality to be decomposed into objectively defined

© Springer Nature Switzerland AG 2019
N. T. Nguyen et al. (Eds.): ICCCI 2019, LNAI 11683, pp. 589–600, 2019.
https://doi.org/10.1007/978-3-030-28377-3_49

building blocks so the collective can self-assemble physical or virtual (software) products to interact with the world without centralized control. The collective emotions focus on the motivations most highly prioritized by the group. The collective mind (the collective intelligence of the collective consciousness) creates a single cognitive model of the world and identifies interventions that maximize a given collective outcome. And the collective consciousness switches attention between these systems to maximize collective well-being.

2   A Model for General Collective Intelligence

Though groups have been suggested to have some degree of general collective intelligence [12] inherently, and despite the existence of general CI algorithms [13] to enhance that intelligence, the complexity of applying such algorithms may encourage each CI solution to target a specific problem. While Salminen and others point out a number of properties of CI [3] in addition to decision-making, from the functional modeling perspective CI solutions in general are represented here as systems of decision-making that function to maximize some outcome for the group. Considering the initial state and desired final state to be points in a "conceptual space", any solution can potentially be modeled as a function providing a path between those two points. A single conventional CI solution is represented in Fig. 1 as a function tracing a path through this "problem space".

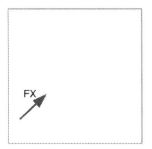

Fig. 1. Conventional CI solutions are represented as achieving a single function.

GCI is defined here as a system of decision-making that functions in any way required to continually maximize collective well-being for the group. To do so this model of GCI aims to model all other CI solutions as functions, and add those functions to a library so it becomes possible to select the intervention with the greatest projected fitness in mapping from the initial state to the final state. The resulting sequence of functions is represented in Fig. 2 as a sequence of lines tracing a path through the problem space. In this model the choice of function, results in its dynamics being locally chaotic and therefore non-deterministic, but globally stable in terms of keeping the collective's state of well-being within a bounded region [1]. This well-being function is defined with the assistance of a Universal Impact Metrics Framework [7] that enables all interventions to be objectively compared according to their capacity to achieve any targeted outcome, and a Semantic Metrics Framework [6] that enables the outcomes to be compared in terms of their impact on the well-being function, which is defined in terms of the collective's capacity to execute all its capabilities (capacity to execute all available functions). Setting aside the issue of validating these frameworks (to be addressed elsewhere [6, 7]), defining them as functional components in the model enables these approaches to assessing fitness to be continually honed across all problems.

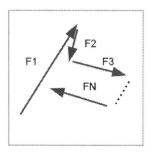

Fig. 2. GCI executes whatever sequence of functions is available to navigate problems.

In psychology individual intelligence is accepted to be defined as general problem-solving ability. The fact that this problem solving is fundamentally aligned with the well-being of the individual distinguishes the intelligence of one individual from that of another. By analogy, in this model, GCI is problem solving ability fundamentally aligned with achieving collective well-being, as opposed to the intelligence of individual members of the group, which is problem solving ability fundamentally aligned with their own individual well-being.

From this point of view GCI requires collectively navigating the problem space (collectively reasoning) according to collective well-being. In addition to modeling each CI solution so that it can potentially be used in a library, gaining the capacity to navigate the problem space in a globally stable way requires the problem space itself, that is the problems to be solved, to be modeled as well. In this approach problems are modeled in a consistent way using a semantic modeling framework (the eXtensible Domain Modeling Framework or XDMF [9]), so that the models of each problem can over time be combined into a single functional model of the world the collective can navigate. Again setting aside validation (to be addressed elsewhere [9]), defining the framework as a functional components in the model enables the modeling approach to be continually honed across all problems.

The ability to maximize collective outcomes per unit of resources increases the capacity of the collective to maintain well-being until the problem of making more resources available can be solved, so that well-being becomes self-sustaining. If a problem is the lack of a path from an initial state to a final state, the ability to sustainably construct a path of interventions to get from any initial state to any final state enables a decision-making system to potentially compose a series of interventions (a solution) to solve any problem. In other words, it potentially creates general problem-solving ability that can be transferred to any domain, that is, true GCI.

From the functional modeling perspective, a reasoning process is a potential solution to a reasoning problem. As a functional system, the GCI (collective mind) is a set of processes that "chooses" one reasoning process over another targeting the same outcome. To do so it must model the function the reasoning process is trying to achieve and must assign a metric of "fitness" according to the degree the function successfully achieves the targeted output. To have the capacity to be consciously chosen, all conscious reasoning processes must have some fitness metric.

In this model the collective mind being globally stable in terms of being constrained to a bounded region in the property "well-being" means that the projected impact of the reasoning process on well-being is assessed and continually compared to the actual impact achieved with the resources invested, so that projections can be updated. Conclusions (the output of reasoning) that decrease well-being sufficiently in this model direct investment of more mental resources to solving the current problem. And conclusions that increase well-being sufficiently direct reasoning elsewhere to shift investment of mental resources to the next problem. This flow between focus on the current problem and focus on the next problem moves with a convection that follows a pattern of dynamical stability in which the key metric is well-being. The model represents this convection using the Lorenz equations governing atmospheric convection, so that the dynamics follow a strange attractor providing the locally chaotic (and therefore non-deterministic) and globally stable behavior predicted as being required [1] (Fig. 3).

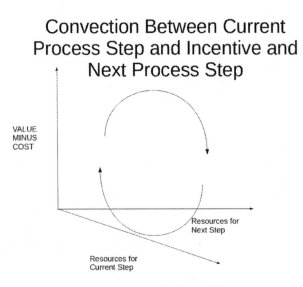

Fig. 3. Convection in the GCI

Since this GCI also contains "basic life processes" providing functional adaptation (the capacity to evolve and otherwise adapt any functional component to become more fit [3]), the initial choice to base global stability on the Lorenz model of convection is less important than the fact that global stability is the targeted outcome, that all functional components can be decomposed into their most basic building blocks, and that these processes can adapt each functional building block independently to achieve this targeted outcome through replacement by one that is more fit. Having a mechanism to measure actual results of implementing the selected solution and having a mechanism to use those results to continuously improve the predictions enables every aspect of the system to gain the capabilities required for GCI even if the initial proposed implementation lacks those capabilities.

Another goal of having a mechanism to objectively project the effectiveness of any solution in mapping from the initial state to the final state is to enable the collective to reliably converge on a choice between any set of proposed solutions.

3   Validation of the Model

If GCI is general problem solving ability then a GCI must have the ability to target any outcome. If problems can be defined as a lack of a path between an initial point and a final point in a problem space, then problem solving ability is related to the volume of problem space that can be navigated in a given time. Using impact on the volume of collective outcomes as a measure of this ability, ways to increase this impact are increasing the probability of achieving targeted outcomes, increasing the magnitude of targeted outcomes, and increasing the duration of the outcome by making it self-sustaining. As validation of the potential for the functional modeling, functional decomposition, and functional fitness aspects of this approach to significantly increase collective impact, these aspects of the approach were used to design an Agricultural Livelihoods Program. Using only a few of the many patterns of collectively intelligent cooperation available, the increase in impact on agricultural livelihoods was projected to be up to seven hundred and fifty times per dollar spent. This program was designed to be phase I of a proposed ten phase Collective Intelligence based Program to Accelerate Achievement of the Sustainable Development Goals (CIPAA-SDGs) [4] targeting a wide variety of SDGs, thereby validating the ability of this approach to be used to target a range of outcomes. This agricultural livelihoods program leverages CI to increase projected impact per program dollar to the point that the program is projected to become essentially self-funding so deployment at massive scale is reliably possible, thereby validating the potential to become self-sustaining. The pilot of this program is of sufficiently small scale that it can reliably be deployed, while the scale of cooperation targeted long-term is large enough to create sufficient value that it is projected to create sufficient competitive advantage for local businesses to ensure their participation. A functional model for a collective intelligence platform called the Social Impact Marketplace has been defined to orchestrate this cooperation between the pilot governments, donors, impact investors, entrepreneurs, and services providers leveraging patterns of cooperation that use this competitive advantage to incentivize participation by significantly increasing projected benefits for all participants, thereby validating the potential to increase the probability of achieving targeted outcomes.

In this Agricultural Livelihoods program a number of agricultural value chains have been proposed, each with a functional model allowing the fitness of that value chain in achieving outcomes for each role to be projected, so the value chain can be added to a library of functions the GCI can use to achieve collective impact. This enables the value chain with the best collective outcomes to be selected. For example, for governments and donors the projected fitness in increasing agricultural livelihoods of farmers per unit of program dollar is assessed. While for impact investors the fitness in increasing returns and decreasing risk is assessed. The volume of outcomes for all participants is measured on a universal scale so the total combined volume of outcomes for all participants (collective outcomes) can be maximized.

4 Differences with Other Models of Collective Intelligence

Though they might not be explicitly named, many perspectives on collective intelligence currently exist, and single purpose CI solutions have been defined from a number of those different perspectives [3]. In this GCI each of those CI solutions might be added to a library used to increase problem solving ability. Since multiple different functions in this library might serve the same purpose, in order to use the library effectively there must be some mechanism for the GCI to select the best one for a given purpose and a given set of conditions (a given context). This mechanism must be general enough to enable the choice of function to be optimized for any purpose and context.

From the perspective of whether the decision or the decision-maker is the focus, there are two approaches to using collective intelligence. One is optimizing selection of the decision, the other is optimizing selection of the decision-maker itself (any entity that makes decisions, whether an individual, or an algorithm or other process) [10]. Each of these approaches is suggested [10] to have a tendency to be used in certain domains, with selection of the decision-maker suggested to predominate in the structured problems often the focus of computer science approaches to CI, and with selection of the optimal decision proposed to predominate in the unstructured problems often the focus of social science approaches to CI. Assigning a weight that stores the projected or actual measured fitness of each function for each of the two domains enables both sets of solutions to be used so intelligence grows.

This approach can be generalized to use such weights to bridge larger sets of solutions, each of which is optimal in one or more of an arbitrary and potentially much larger number of domains (functional domain bridging).

In summary, a unique set of elements combine to steadily increase CI so it can converge on GCI. Functional modeling of any problem in terms of reusable building blocks (functional decomposition) is used to collaboratively find the best solution according to functional fitness. Functional domain bridging connects different problem domains into a single larger one. The GCI navigates through the problem space (functional stability) with a path that imitates human intelligence in its global stability. The GCI continually improves each functional component (functional adaptation). Of course using this GCI in any domain requires building up a library of collective reasoning processes and a set of functional models representing that domain.

5   The Principles of Collectively Intelligent Cooperation and Functional Modeling of Problems and Solutions

If collective decomposition of the world into functional models is to be achieved in a way that maximizes outcomes for all, it must be achieved through several layers of decentralization at the physical, virtual, and other levels. This decentralization requires adherence to principles of collectively intelligent cooperation [5]. If functional decomposition is essential for GCI in this model, and these principles are critical to functional decomposition, then these principles in this model are also required to have the capacity for GCI, which again is maximizing collective outcomes.

The "Operation" principles of collectively intelligent cooperation are that activities operate in a way that is:

- Decentralized in that activities don't belong to any given entity and instead are executed by the best candidate. The interaction can't be co-opted by any centralized interests.
- Peer to Peer in that all roles interact directly so no middle-man can insert their interests. A process may consist of many steps involving many participants, but each step can be considered as a direct interaction between two participants.
- Node-centric in that other than the input, no other role defines the information required for the interaction, so no third party can insert their interests. All the definitions required for interactions are stored by each participant. In groups this can be interpreted as the need to retrieve definitions from any third party can't be used to insert that third party's subjective judgment about what those definitions are, and in doing so enable them to co-opt the interaction to serve their interests.
- Massively collaborative in removing the limits to which collaboration can be scaled. In groups this can be interpreted as the interaction removing any subjectivity that makes a single decision-maker a bottleneck, removing any monopolization of roles that would make a single role a bottleneck, and removing any other factors that introduce bottlenecks limiting massive collaboration.

The "Ownership" principles of collectively intelligent cooperation are that entities are owned in a way that permits:

- Open exchange of information (open but not necessarily free). Such sharing is also important to increasing the scope and scale of cooperation.

The "Participation" principles of collectively intelligent cooperation are that each activity has their own metric of performance that permits:

- Each activity (and each solution consisting of chains of activities) to be replaced by better ones, and enables new modes of cooperation to be introduced over time through the hierarchy of processes of life (homeostasis, autopoiesis, etc.) represented within this model.

Leveraging these principles to open participation in collaborative processes to all prospects, functional modeling can be used to define a semantic model of each user's data, identities, and applications, to "open" them as well, so they are available for use in those processes. Functional decomposition breaks those models into objectively defined functions that any participant with the required role can potentially cooperate to execute. And semantic modeling enables outcomes of interactions within those collaborative processes to be stored in a common way. This functional decomposition and semantic modeling enable parts of processes to run in parallel, so a GCI can orchestrate execution of those functions collaboratively at far greater speed and scale. By creating a private intelligent agent for each user that provides access to the user's data on the user's behalf according to policies they specify, where interactions follow processes that can be modeled, if an individual's responses follow policies that can be implemented by a trusted intelligent agent that responds far more quickly on the individual's behalf, then the number of those agents can be multiplied, and the rate of interactions can be further scaled. Most or all of the required components for such agents already exist. By defining a metric for fitness in implementing each component GCI can enable vendors to collectively self-assemble them. In a model in which each entity owns their own data, GCI can coordinate massive decentralized queries to provide access to large datasets. By enabling users or intelligent user-agents to spontaneously self-assemble into communities GCI can potentially enable collaboration with this data to achieve any outcome. Without scaling collective reasoning through the assistance of intelligent agents in this way, there is a limit to the scale and speed at which a group can cooperate to find and evaluate solutions, e.g. resulting in the capacity to evaluate perhaps tens or hundreds of options where a GCI might evaluate trillions. Without the capacity to consider sufficient solutions to do so, maximizing impact on collective outcomes (such as the sustainable development goals) cannot be reliably achievable.

6   The Collective Body in Practice

Since the principles of collectively intelligent cooperation [5] must govern all interactions, whether human-human or human-machine in order to achieve the capacity to maximize collective outcomes, then they also must govern all design of all products or services in this model of GCI. Therefore, unlike any other model of CI, this model defines principles of collectively intelligent cooperation [5] that must be applied to the design and use of physical products, software, processes, or anything else, in order to gain the ability to reliably achieve massive increases in impact by decoupling elements into discrete units of functionality that can be manipulated at computational rather than human scales.

A functional model of all the components of a physical or software solution and a metric for projecting the fitness of each prospective solution provider's component in achieving that function, combined with applying the principles of decentralized cooperation required for functional decomposition, together allows providers to self-assemble into solutions, even where providers don't understand or know about each other's offerings.

Phase III of the CIPAA-SDGs program is intended to deploy a collective intelligence platform (a Collaborative Design Platform) with the goal of providing competitive advantage for groups of businesses that cooperate to increase the re-use of materials through sustainable circular business practices. This planned Collaborative

Design Platform is intended to enable businesses to algorithmically search for opportunities to share designs of components and materials to lower costs and increase reuse, to algorithmically search for opportunities for consumers and users to share use, and other opportunities for cooperation that create value for the end user. Then to combine businesses into value chains that cooperate to share that benefit.

For example, an auto manufacturer could create value for the consumer if they designed their vehicles in a more modular way that enabled greater reuse, and if they created programs that facilitated reutilization of parts and materials after first use, so that parts were cheaper and cars lasted much longer. But currently this isn't feasible because a business can't compete by making cars last longer and therefore reducing revenue. However by finding a great many of these opportunities, a GCI could increase the value until it creates unbeatable competitive advantage for the group, and could spread the cost of this "subsidy" (i.e. the loss in revenue due to reducing use) across a larger and larger chain of cooperating businesses so that the portion of the subsidy paid by the auto manufacturer alone decreases until the increase in competitive advantage due to this subsidy outweighs their cost in offering the subsidy.

Finding these potentially thousands or even millions of opportunities to cooperate, and therefore achieving this increased material reutilization, is too complex without computational CI. And though increasing the size of the chain of cooperating businesses can potentially increase competitive advantage until it's sufficient for the group to dominate any market, this cooperation is unstable without GCI [5]. Furthermore, this cooperation must follow the previously mentioned well-defined principles for algorithmic searches for opportunities to cooperate to be possible. But where the dollar value of cooperation is greater than zero such algorithmic approaches enable cooperation to reliably be scaled until it can subsidize or pay for achieving the targeted social, economic, environmental or other collective impact.

The collective emotions and other features have not been implemented in the current design of the Agricultural Livelihoods Program that is phase I of the CIPAA-SDGs program. However, eventually it is required to ensure a decentralized process for deciding which goals the collective will target.

7 Algorithmically Maximizing Collective Outcomes

Optimizing processes through use of a fitness function to select optimal components, enables processes to be redesigned algorithmically to follow a more optimal path through this state space that minimizes cost of execution while maximizing value of the outcome achieved (Fig. 4).

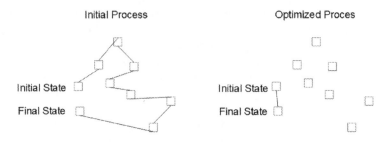

Fig. 4. Optimizing processes.

This GCI approach firstly optimizes processes through "functional fitness". A solution is modeled as a process consisting of a series of activities. Optimization theory, a large area of applied mathematics, concerns finding best available values of some objective function given a defined domain (or input) [8]. In the case of maximizing collective outcomes, this requirement of optimization can be satisfied by assigning a metric of an entity's "performance" in terms of its impact on collective well-being (the collective's capacity to execute its capabilities [6]).

The approach then optimizes processes through "functional decomposition". Algorithms can increase the rate of outcomes by finding opportunities to execute functions in parallel. Functions can be executed in parallel when they are decomposed into building blocks according to the previously mentioned principles so that execution of one instance can be decoupled from that of another. Algorithms can increase the magnitude of outcomes, or can transform outcomes to more optimal ones, by executing additional functions in series. Functions can be executed in series when inputs and outputs are modeled so one function can be set to act on the outputs of another, in this way execution of functions can be coupled together. The resources available to execute functions can be increased by cooperating through sharing functionality. That is, by finding all other processes where the same function is used, and creating value through cooperating to save costs in creating and using these functions.

Functional modeling of both problems and solutions enables reuse and sharing of both. Each individual in the collective is a piece of the jigsaw puzzle that may have the capacity to execute some unique function, that is, may have some functionality others don't have. Each individual also may have some unique information others don't have. Each individual has a finite capacity for information. That is, there are limits to the volume of information an individual can navigate. And each individual has a finite capacity to learn and execute processes. That is, there are limits to the volume of processes that an individual can navigate. It's also important to have the ability to navigate all the domains of expertise of the group rather than being limited to the domains of expertise of a few decision-makers. Furthermore, its important to have the ability to harness the resources of the group, rather than being limited to the resources controlled by a limited sub-set of decision-makers. A GCI platform however might orchestrate cooperation according to functional models of problems and solutions to address these challenges (Fig. 5).

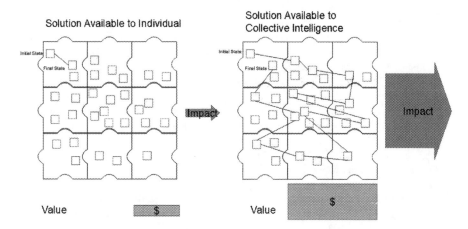

Fig. 5. Far more solutions (more paths) are available to the collective with a GCI.

Without GCI (including with conventional CI) outcomes can become aligned with individual interests, and individuals who don't compete to further their own interests rather than serving the collective well-being gradually lose access to resources and therefore gradually lose decision-making power [5]. With GCI outcomes are aligned with collective interests, and individuals who don't cooperate to further collective interests are the ones who gradually lose decision-making power [5].

8   Conclusion

Existing conventional CI solutions have be modeled here as single functions. An approach to GCI has been modeled as using a library of such functions to potentially gain vastly greater general problem solving ability. This creates opportunity for each other CI project to become a function in a much larger and much more powerful GCI. Reusable functional building blocks in turn create the potential to enable construction of far more powerful and comprehensive CI functionality far more quickly.

By combining individuals into a single potentially vastly greater intelligence, this model of GCI creates the potential to reliably address collective challenges where they are not reliably solvable with existing approaches to CI that don't adhere to the required principles [5]. This includes the SDGs [5]. With the United Nations estimating a $23 trillion USD gap in funding to achieve the SDGs, the potential to reliably address such issues is of profound global importance. This potential importance provides motivation to take next steps, such as conducting a survey of domain experts to validate claims regarding some of the required functional components.

References

1. Williams, A.E.: A Model for Human, Artificial and Collective Consciousness, under review
2. Williams, A.E.: A Model for General Collective Intelligence, under review
3. Salminen, J.: Collective intelligence in humans: a literature review. In: Proceedings, CI2012 (2012)
4. Williams, A.E.: Case Study: Job Creation in Phase I of the Collective Intelligence based Plan to Accelerate Achievement of the Sustainable Development Goals (CIPAA-SDGs), working paper
5. Williams, A.E.: The Principles Enabling Cooperation within Conscious Organisms and Collectives, working paper
6. Williams, A.E.: The Semantic Metrics Framework, working paper
7. Williams, A.E.: The Universal Impact Metrics Framework, working paper
8. Intriligator, M.D.: Mathematical Optimization and Economic Theory. Prentice-Hall, Englewood Cliffs (1971)
9. Williams, A.E.: The eXtensible Domain Modeling Framework (XDMF), working paper
10. Williams, A.E.: A Bridge Between Computer Science and Social Innovation Approaches to Collective Intelligence, under review
11. Ned Block, Consciousness, Function, and Representation: Collected Papers, Bradford (2007)
12. Woolley, A.W., Chabris, C.F., Pentland, A., Hashmi, N., Malone, T.: Evidence for a collective intelligence factor in the performance of human groups. Science **330**, 686–688 (2010)
13. De Vincenzo, I., Massari, G.F., Giannoccaro, I., Carbone, G., Grigolini, P.: Mimicking the collective intelligence of human groups as an optimization tool for complex problems. Chaos Solitons Fractals **110**, 259–266 (2018)

An Approach to Imbalanced Data Classification Based on Instance Selection and Over-Sampling

Ireneusz Czarnowski$^{(\boxtimes)}$ ⓘ and Piotr Jędrzejowicz ⓘ

Department of Information Systems, Gdynia Maritime University,
Morska 83, 81-225 Gdynia, Poland
{i.czarnowski,p.jedrzejowicz}@umg.edu.pl

Abstract. The paper referees to a problem of learning from class-imbalanced data. The class imbalance problem arises when the number of instances from different classes differs substantially. Instance selection aims at deciding which instances from the training set should be retained and used during the learning process. Over-sampling is an approach dedicated to duplicate minority class instances. In the paper, a hybrid approach for the imbalanced data learning using the over-sampling and instance selection techniques is proposed. Instances are selected to reduce the number of instances belonging to the majority class, while the number of instances belonging to the minority class is expanded. The process of instance selection is based on clustering, where the authors' approach to clustering and instance selection using an agent-based population learning algorithm is applied. As a result a more balanced distribution of instances belonging to different classes is obtained and a dataset size is reduced. The proposed approach is validated experimentally using several benchmark datasets.

Keywords: Instance selection · Clustering · Imbalanced data ·
Over-sampling · Under-sampling

1 Introduction

In the real world, there are many problems for which available data are class imbalanced. Class imbalance means that the number of instances in classes is not equally distributed. In the case of the imbalanced data, *the distribution of the data in the feature space is usually skewed in class imbalanced datasets* [1]. The imbalanced data have to be dealt with in numerous practical applications, like for example text classification, medical diagnosing, financial decision making, discovering network intrusions, and others.

When the available data set has a skewed distribution one faces a data sample overlap, small sample size, and small disjoints. From the point of view of the traditional machine learning process, examples in the majority class will have a greater influence on the induced classifier, causing its classification weight to be in favor of the majority class. Conventional machine learning algorithms which are focused on optimizing the overall classification accuracy, in the class imbalanced situations, tend to achieve poor classification performance, especially for the minority class, which might be of special

N. T. Nguyen et al. (Eds.): ICCCI 2019, LNAI 11683, pp. 601–610, 2019.
https://doi.org/10.1007/978-3-030-28377-3_50

interest to the user [2, 3]. This is due to the fact, that classifiers try, in the first place, to correctly predict the majority class labels. The minority class in such a process might be ignored in favors of the majority one. However, in many real-life problems, the correct minority predictions are crucial, like for example in case of the medical diagnostics or software fault prediction. In the machine learning literature, class imbalance is recognized as one of the most challenging problems in data mining [4].

Research work in the field of imbalanced data classification has resulted in the development of numerous approaches and algorithms. Among them the most successful are the bagging ensemble methods, cost-sensitive methods, approaches based on sampling techniques [6] and methods based on the so-called, data level [7]. The data level methods aim to transform original data into a more balanced dataset, thus reducing the imbalance ratio between the majority and minority classes.

In general, data level techniques transform a dataset with a view to reducing the imbalance ratio between the majority and minority classes [9]. Such transformation takes place at the pre-processing stage and the resulting dataset can be further processed using standard machine learning methods. In the literature, three main types of the data level approaches have been, so far, proposed. These are over-sampling, under-sampling and a hybrid of over and under-sampling [5].

The aim of the under-sampling technique is balancing the distribution of data classes. In practice, under-sampling techniques just remove instances from the majority class. The strength of this approach depends, however, on what kind of rules for instance removal have been implemented [9]. Many methods belonging to this group base on clustering and instance selection. They are referred to as the cluster-based sampling group (see for example [19, 20]). These methods group instances from a majority class into clusters. Next, some instances, representing clusters are selected from each cluster. Main drawbacks of the cluster-based sampling include difficulty to decide on the optimal number of clusters and the lack of rules telling which instances should be selected as cluster representatives [9].

An improved approach for under-sampling based on clustering has been proposed in [12]. The algorithm reduces the number of instances in the majority classes by grouping instances and next selecting only the representative instances. Finally, the majority class set of instances is reduced and the required balance between the minority and the majority class instances is achieved. The clustering algorithm was based on the similarity coefficient calculations, originally proposed in [13]. The instance selection has been carried out using an agent-based population learning implementation. The main feature of the approach is that the number of clusters from which the instances are selected and the process of instance selection are carried out automatically. In this approach, the earlier described drawbacks of the cluster-based sampling reduced or, at least partly, eliminated.

Over-sampling techniques are dealing with expanding the number of minority class instances to balance the classes' distribution. The approach includes techniques providing for the artificial synthesis of the required number of new examples in the minority class. The most simple of the discussed approaches involve simple duplication of the minority class instances. More advanced approaches duplicate or synthesize instances from areas deemed as most promising [10].

Random over-sampling algorithms duplicate minority class instances until the balance between minority and majority class instances will be achieved. Their simplicity makes such an approach practicable. There is, however, a drawback. It is not clear which instances from the minority class should be duplicated. This makes looking for a more effective way of duplicating the minority class instances and, at the same time, avoiding problems with the random duplication, worth a research effort.

SMOTE is the most popular over-sampling method, proposed originally to improve random over-sampling [11]. SMOTE interpolates existing instances to generate new instances. However, the algorithm is not free from weaknesses. One of them is the assumption that all minority class instances are of equal importance. From a practical point of view, it means that each one instance of the minority class can be chosen to over-sample with uniform probability and the duplication may include instances which do not provide any useful information for identification of boundaries between classes.

To eliminate SMOTE's disadvantages numerous extensions of the basic algorithm have been, so far, proposed. These algorithms aim to emphasize certain minority class regions, others intend to reduce the within-class imbalance or attempt to avoid the generation of noise [10]. Example approaches include borderline-SMOTE [14], self-level-SMOTE [18], cluster-SMOTE [16], CURE-SMOTE [15], k-means SMOTE [10] and others (see for example [10] and [17]).

In this paper, a hybrid algorithm for the imbalanced data learning is proposed. The main idea of the proposed algorithm is based on balancing of the minority and majority classes by over-sampling and instance selection. The instance selection is carried out in the majority class. The process is based on clustering using the similarity coefficient as the criterion for grouping instances. The process of clustering is carried-out independently for instances from all classes. Next, the prototypes are selected from the induced clusters. The process of instance selection is integrated with the learning phase executed by the team of agents. In some cases to achieve the balanced distribution of instances between different classes requires an over-sampling. However, the process of over-sampling is run only when the instance selection does not assure the required balance.

The paper is organized as follows. Section 3 contains problem formulation and a detailed description of the proposed method. Section 4 provides details on the computational experiment setup and discusses experiment results. Conclusions and suggestions for future research are included in the final section.

2 An Approach to Imbalanced Learning

In this section, the imbalanced data classification problem is formulated and the details of the proposed approach are discussed.

2.1   Problem Formulation

The aim of learning from data is to output the hypothesis $h \in H$ optimizing performance criterion F using dataset D, where D is the multiclass data set $D = D_1 \cup D_2 \dots \cup D_d$ and d is the number of different classes.

In case of the imbalanced training set, $D_{minority}$ is the subset of D which contains the minority class dataset. It is assumed that the cardinality of $D_{minority}$ is definitely smaller than the cardinality of each of the remaining subsets of D representing the remaining classes. Among these remaining subsets, there is the majority class subset containing the majority class instances. Data level methods aim at transforming an imbalanced dataset into a better-balanced one by reducing the imbalance ration between the majority and minority classes. The reduction can be carried out by over-sampling or under-sampling.

The data level approach involves two stages. First, cardinalities of all classes including the minority class are identified. Next, the instance selection process aiming at reducing the cardinality of all datasets representing classes other than the minority one is carried out. Ideally, the reduction process should produce datasets with cardinalities not exceeding cardinality of the dataset representing the minority class. Formally, the number of instances from each subset $\forall_{i \in \{1,\dots,d\} \setminus \{minority\}} D_i$ is reduced and the resulting subsets are denoted as $\forall_{i \in \{1,\dots,d\} \setminus \{minority\}} S_i$, that also means that $\forall_{i \in \{1,\dots,d\} \setminus \{minority\}} S_i \subset D_i$.

In case when the reduction process cannot guarantee the required balance, i.e. $\exists_i |S_i| > |D_{minority}|$, then the second stage with the over-sampling process on $D_{minority}$ has to be entered. The process produces dataset obtained by duplication of instances from $D_{minority}$ and denoted as $S_{minority}$. In the ideal case the following holds:

$$\forall_{i \in \{1,\dots,d\} \setminus \{minority\}} |S_i| \cong |S_{minority}| \text{ and} \tag{1}$$

$$\forall_{i \in \{1,\dots,d\}} |S_i| < |D_i| \text{ and} \tag{2}$$

$$\bigcup_{i=1}^{d} |S_i| < |D| \tag{3}$$

In case of the imbalanced data, when the over and under-sampling processes have been carried out, the task of the learner L is to output the hypothesis $h \in H$ optimizing performance criterion F using datasets $S_1, \dots, S_d$, which are subsets of D containing instances obtained by the over and under-sampling processes, and where the condition (1) is satisfied.

2.2   The Proposed Approach

After the instance selection has been carried out with respect to subsets representing all classes except the minority one, we suggest the following procedure: :

– when the number of considered classes in D is equal to 2 (i.e. $d = 2$), then the over-sampling process is run on the minority class subset,

– when the number of considered classes in D is greater than 2 (i.e. $d > 2$), then at first, the reduced subset of instances containing the maximum number of instances is identified, and on all remaining subsets, the over-sampling procedure is run.

In all cases, under-sampling is based on the instance selection approach where instances are selected from clusters grouping similar instances, that is carried-out under umbrella of the instance selection procedure. The process of clustering is carried-out independently for each of the considered classes without the minority class. It is also assumed that only a single instance, as a reference instance, is selected from each cluster. Thus, the number of clusters produced at the clustering stage has a direct influence on the size of the reduced dataset. Reference instances are selected from the clusters during the learning process executed by the team of agents, as described in a detailed manner in [8], forming the reduced dataset.

The similarity-based clustering algorithm (SCA) produces clusters, where the similarity coefficients are calculated as shown in [8]. The SCA induces clusters with an identical similarity coefficient, and the number of clusters is determined by the value of this coefficient across all instances belonging to the considered class. Clusters are initialized automatically and without any user intervention.

In the paper, the population-based metaheuristics known as the population-learning algorithm (PLA) originally proposed in [21] has been applied for instance selection. The population-learning algorithm is an implementation of the set of agents and different optimization procedures executed by the agents within the asynchronous team of agents (A-Team). These agents cooperate and exchange information. Agents working in the A-Team achieve implicit cooperation by sharing the population of current solutions to the problem to be solved. The A-Team can be also defined as a set of agents and a set of memories, forming a network in which every agent remains in a closed loop [22]. The framework for the agent-based instance selection has been adopted from earlier papers of the authors including [12, 23–25] and [13]. In the [13] the cluster-based instance selection, as a tool for under-sampling has been proposed.

In case when the instance reduction in majority class datasets does not guarantee the required balance, that is $\exists_i |S_i| > |D_{minority}|$, then the over-sampling procedure is activated on all subsets of instances representing classes other than the majority one. The over-sampling procedure starts with identifying for each two closest clusters from the same class their neighbors. The closeness of neighbors is measured using the Euclidean measure. The number of neighbors k is a parameter of the approach and should be set by the user.

The pseudo-code explaining how a new (artificial) instance for the minority class is generated is shown as Algorithm 1. Algorithm 2 shows the pseudo-code of the agent-based population learning algorithm (PLA) where individuals (solutions) represent the selected instances. The pseudo-code covering the proposed method of the imbalanced data classification is shown as Algorithm 3.

Algorithm 1 Generation of an artificial instance (GAI)

 Input: x_1, x_2 – reference instances for the minority class; S – a subset of instances; k - number of neighbors;
 Output: x_a – an artificial instance;

Begin

 For x_1 and x_2 find its k-nearest neighbor instances, which belong to S and where N contains the neighbor instances;
 Generate randomly an artificial instance x_a located between instances from N;
 Return x_a;
End

Algorithm 2 Agent-based population learning algorithm

 Generate initial population P of individuals randomly;
 Activate optimizing agents;
 While (*stopping criterion is not met*) **do** {*in parallel*}
 Read the individual from the common memory;
 Execute the instance selection procedure;
 Send an improved individual back to the common memory;
 Evaluate the fitness of the newly arriving individual and update the common memory;
 End while

Algorithm 3 Generation of the balanced instances set

 Input: D - training set; k - number of neighbors; d - the number of classes;
 Output: $S=S_1 \cup S_2 .... \cup S_d$ - sets of balanced instances forming a training set.

Begin

 Set *minority* = minority class number.
 Set $S_{minority}$ = subset of D contains of instances belong to the minority class;
 For $i:=1,...,(d\text{-}1)$ **and** $i \neq minority$ **do**
 Run the SCA procedure and map instances from D_i into clusters;
 Run the PLA on the instances from obtained clusters within D_i and return the reduced subsets of instances S_i contains references instances;
 End for
 Set *majority* = number of class for which the cardinality of the reduced subset is maximum;
 If d=2 **then**
 While $\dfrac{|S_{minority}|}{|S_{majority}|} ! \cong 1$ **do**
 For each cluster from $S_{majority}$ select its closest cluster and return their reference instances x_1, x_2;
 $S_{minority} = S_{minority} \cup \{GAI(x_1, x_2, k, S_{minority})\}$;
 End while
 Else
 For $i:=1,...,(d\text{-}1)$ **and** $i \neq majority$ **do**
 While $\dfrac{|S_i|}{|S_{majority}|} ! \cong 1$ **do**
 For each cluster from $\bigcup_{j:j \in \{1,...d\} \setminus \{i\}} S_j$ select their closest clusters and return their reference instances x_1, x_2;
 $S_i = S_i \cup \{GAI(x_1, x_2, k, S_i)\}$;
 End while
 Return $S_1,...,S_d$;
End

3 Computational Experiment

The proposed approach has been validated experimentally. The main research question was whether the proposed approach performs better than the traditional approach where machine learning algorithms are used for learning from the original imbalanced data.

Classification accuracy of the classifier obtained using the proposed approach, denoted as AOUSID - **A**gent-based **O**ver and **U**nder-**S**ampling for the **I**mbalanced **D**ata, has been compared with the accuracy of:

- *AISAID* – the algorithm originally introduced in [12] assuring balance between minority and majority classes by applying instance selection and a special merging procedure to reduce the cardinality of the majority class instances to the level comparable to the cardinality of the minority class.
- *ALP* - the procedure originally proposed in [25] for data reduction carried-out only in the majority class. The procedure produces clusters of instances in the majority classes using k-means. Next, these clusters are merged to obtain the reduced number of clusters equal to the cardinality of the minority class.
- k-means - in this case, the *k*-means clustering has been implemented using data from the majority class, and next, from thus obtained clusters, prototypes are selected using the agent-based population learning algorithm as in [8].
- C4.5, CART, CNN, 10NN – traditional ML algorithms.

Datasets used in the reported experiment have been obtained from the KEEL dataset repository [25]. Details of these datasets are shown in Table 1. It has been decided to use the 10-cross-validation scheme, and each benchmarking problem has been solved 30 times. The reported values of the quality measure have been averaged over all runs. Classification accuracy has been used as the performance criterion. In the 10-cross-validation scheme, for each fold, the training dataset was reduced using the proposed approach. The learning tool used was the C4.5 algorithm [26]. Details of the parameter settings are shown in Table 2. Values of these parameters included in Table 2 have been set arbitrarily.

Based on the results shown in Table 3, it can be observed that the AOUSID approach assures competitive results in comparison to other algorithms. In several cases, the algorithm performs best including the multi-class imbalanced data sets (wine and balance) and abalone19 and glass2 datasets. One can also observe that the AOUSID outperforms traditional machine learning tools (C4.5, kNN, CART, and CNN - Convolutional Neural Network) when the algorithms have been used on imbalanced datasets.

Table 1. Datasets used in the reported experiment (column IR informs about the ratio of the number of instances of the majority class per instance of the minority class).

Dataset	Number of instances	Number of attributes	Number of classes	IR – the imbalance radio
abalone19	4174	8	2	129.44
shuttle-c0-vs-c4	1829	9	2	13.87
vowel0	988	13	2	9.98

(*continued*)

Table 1. (*continued*)

Dataset	Number of instances	Number of attributes	Number of classes	IR – the imbalance radio
yeast5	1484	8	2	32.73
glass2	214	9	2	11.59
ecoli-0-1-4-6_vs_5	280	6	2	13
glass0	214	9	2	2.06
yeast2	514	8	2	9.08
vehicle2	846	18	2	2.88
wine	178	13	3	1.5
balance	625	4	3	5.88

Table 2. Parameter settings in the reported experiment

Parameter	Value
Number of neighbours k	2
Population size	40
Number of iterations without improvement until the search is stopped	100

Table 3. Results obtained for the AOUSID algorithm and other algorithms on imbalanced datasets and their comparison based on the accuracy (in %)

Dataset	Reduced datasets				Non-reduced datasets			
	AOUSID	AISAID	k-means	ALP	C4.5	CART	CNN	10NN
abalone19	**82,04**	81,42	74,26	72,45	82,02	–	58,1	48,05
shuttle-c0-vs-c4	97,62	**98,01**	84,25	87,08	97,17	–	84,12	90
vowel0	93,72	91,05	89,21	92,45	94,94	84,67	48,83	**100**
yeast5	88,4	**89,12**	84,45	86,2	87,50	71,45	41,32	79,42
glass2	**71,69**	71,2	54,21	65,45	60,08	43,84	58,24	33,4
ecoli-0-1-4-6_vs_5	80,21	77,13	62,41	77,34	81,36	79,28	82,16	**83,9**
glass0	77,45	**79,24**	72,61	72,14	78,13	74,59	71,61	70,57
yeast2	79,81	68,49	57,82	55,54	62,82	53,96	60,14	**81,63**
vehicle2	94,06	93,67	84,25	82,61	**94,85**	93,51	49,64	88,31
wine	**94,87**	93,04	91,8	92,14	91,42	90,54	89,34	90,71
balance	**73,48**	71,05	68,45	69,33	70,5	67,21	68,06	69,78

4   Conclusions

In the paper a hybrid approach for the imbalanced data learning based on over-sampling and instance selection, is proposed. Both discussed techniques have been integrated and implemented with a view to deal with classifying the imbalanced data by reducing the imbalance ration between minority and majority classes. Over sampling has been used as a tool for instance duplication in the minority class. Instance selection has been used as a procedure for reducing the number of instances in the majority class. Selection of instances starts with data clustering using the similarity coefficient technique. In the next step, instances are selected from clusters by the team of agents. The proposed approach has been validated experimentally on two and multi-class imbalanced data sets. Based on the results of the computational experiment, one may conclude that the proposed approach can be considered as a promising one with respect to solving the machine learning tasks in case of the imbalanced data.

Future research will focus on studying the influence of different parameters on the performance of the proposed approach as, for example, the number of neighbours in GAI. It is also planned to extend the experiments using additional datasets, as well as to carry out a deeper statistical analysis of the obtained results.

References

1. Chawla, N.V., Japkowicz, N., Drive, P.: Editorial: special issue on learning from imbalanced data sets. ACM SIGKDD Explor. Newsl. **6**(1), 1–6 (2004)
2. Sun, B., Chen, H., Wang, J., Xie, H.: Evolutionary under-sampling based bagging ensemble method for imbalanced data classification. Front. Comput. Sci. **12**(2), 331–350 (2018)
3. Fernandez, A., del Jesus, M.J., Herrera, F.: Hierarchical fuzzy rule based classification systems with genetic rule selection for imbalanced data-sets. Int. J. Approximate Reasoning **50**, 561–577 (2009). https://doi.org/10.1016/j.ijar.2008.11.004
4. Galar, M., Fernandez, A., Barrenechea, E., Bustince, H., Herrera, F.: A review on ensembles for the class imbalance problem: bagging-, boosting-, and hybrid-based approaches. IEEE Trans. Syst. Man Cybern. Part C Appl. Rev. **42**(4), 463–484 (2012)
5. Lin, W.-C., Chih-Fong, T., Hu, Y.-H., Jhang, J.-S.: Clustering-based undersampling in class-imbalanced data. Inf. Sci. **409** (2017). http://doi.org/10.1016/j.ins.2017.05.008
6. Kim, S.-W., Oommen, B.J.: A brief taxonomy and ranking of creative prototype reduction schemes. Pattern Anal. Appl. **6**, 232–244 (2003)
7. Bhanu, B., Peng, J.: Adaptive integration image segmentation and object recognition. IEEE Trans. Syst. Man Cybern. **30**(4), 427–441 (2000)
8. Czarnowski, I., Jędrzejowicz, P.: A new cluster-based instance selection algorithm. In: O'Shea, J., Nguyen, N.T., Crockett, K., Howlett, Robert J., Jain, Lakhmi C. (eds.) KES-AMSTA 2011. LNCS (LNAI), vol. 6682, pp. 436–445. Springer, Heidelberg (2011). https://doi.org/10.1007/978-3-642-22000-5_45
9. Tsai, C.-F., Lin, W.-C., Hu, Y.-H., Ya, G.-T.: Under-sampling class imbalanced datasets by combining clustering analysis and instance selection. Inf. Sci. **477**, 47–54 (2019). https://doi.org/10.1016/j.ins.2018.10.029
10. Last, F., Douzas, G., Bacao, F., Oversampling for Imbalanced Learning Based on K-means and SMOTE, p. 19. CoRR abs/1711.00837 (2017)
11. Chawla, N.V., Bowyer, K.W., Hall, L.O., Kegelmeyer, W.P.: Smote: synthetic minority over-sampling technique. J. Artif. Intell. Res. **16**(16), 321–357 (2002)
12. Czarnowski, I., Jędrzejowicz, P.: Cluster-based instance selection for the imbalanced data classification. In: Nguyen, N.T., Pimenidis, E., Khan, Z., Trawiński, B. (eds.) ICCCI 2018. LNCS (LNAI), vol. 11056, pp. 191–200. Springer, Cham (2018). https://doi.org/10.1007/978-3-319-98446-9_18

13. Czarnowski, I.: Cluster-based instance selection for machine classification. Knowl. Inf. Syst. **30**(1), 113–133 (2012)
14. Han, H., Wang, W.-Y., Mao, B.-H.: Borderline-smote: a new over-sampling method in imbalanced data sets learning. Adv. Intell. Comput. **17**(12), 878–887 (2005)
15. Ma, L., Fan, S.: Cure-smote algorithm and hybrid algorithm for feature selection and parameter optimization based on random forests. BMC Bioinf. **18**(1), 169 (2017)
16. Cieslak, D.A., Chawla, N.V., Striegel, A.: Combating imbalance in network intrusion datasets. In: Proceedings of the 2006 IEEE International Conference on Granular Computing, 2006, pp. 732–737. IEEE (2006)
17. Skryjomski, P., Krawczyk, B.: Influence of minority class instance types on SMOTE imbalanced data oversampling. In: Proceedings of the First International Workshop on Learning with Imbalanced Domains: Theory and Applications, PMLR, vol. 74, pp. 7–21 (2017)
18. Bunkhumpornpat, C., Sinapiromsaran, K., Lursinsap, C.: Safe-Level-SMOTE: safe-level-synthetic minority over-sampling TEchnique for handling the class imbalanced problem. In: Theeramunkong, T., Kijsirikul, B., Cercone, N., Ho, T.-B. (eds.) PAKDD 2009. LNCS (LNAI), vol. 5476, pp. 475–482. Springer, Heidelberg (2009). https://doi.org/10.1007/978-3-642-01307-2_43
19. Nejatian, S., Parvin, H., Faraji, E.: Using sub-sampling and ensemble clustering techniques to improve performance of imbalanced classification. Neurocomputing **276**(7), 55–66 (2018)
20. Sowah, R.A., Agebure, M.A., Mills, G.A., Koumadi, K.M., Fiawoo, S.Y.: New cluster undersampling technique for class imbalance learning. Int. J. Mach. Learn. Comput. **6**(3), 205–214 (2016). https://doi.org/10.18178/ijmlc.2016.6.3.599
21. Jędrzejowicz, P.: Social learning algorithm as a tool for solving some difficult scheduling problems. Found. Comput. Decis. Sci. **24**, 51–66 (1999)
22. Talukdar, S., Baerentzen, L., Gove, A., de Souza, P.: Asynchronous teams: co-operation schemes for autonomous, computer-based agents. Technical report EDRC 18-59-96, Carnegie Mellon University, Pittsburgh (1996)
23. Czarnowski, I., Jędrzejowicz, P.: An approach to data reduction and integrated machine classification. New Gener. Comput. **28**(1), 21–40 (2010)
24. Czarnowski, I., Jędrzejowicz, P.: Cluster integration for the cluster-based instance selection. In: Pan, J.-S., Chen, S.-M., Nguyen, N.T. (eds.) ICCCI 2010. LNCS (LNAI), vol. 6421, pp. 353–362. Springer, Heidelberg (2010). https://doi.org/10.1007/978-3-642-16693-8_37
25. Alcalá-Fdez, J., Fernández, A., Luengo, J., Derrac, J., García, S., Sánchez, L., Herrera, F.: KEEL data-mining software tool: data set repository, integration of algorithms and experimental analysis framework. J. Multiple Valued Logic Soft Comput. **17**(2–3), 255–287 (2011). Last accessed to the repository 2018/04/10
26. Quinlan, J.R.: C4.5: Programs for Machine Learning. Morgan Kaufmann Publishers, SanMateo (1993)

Intelligent Modeling and Simulation
Approaches for Real World Systems

Gender-based Insights into the Fundamental Diagram of Pedestrian Dynamics

Rudina Subaih[1,3], Mohammed Maree[2(✉)], Mohcine Chraibi[3(✉)],
Sami Awad[4], and Tareq Zanoon[4]

[1] Faculty of Engineering and Information Technology,
Computer Science Department, Arab American University, Jenin, Palestine
rudina.subaih@aaup.edu
[2] Faculty of Engineering and Information Technology,
Information Technology Department, Arab American University, Jenin, Palestine
mohammed.maree@aaup.edu
[3] Institute for Advanced Simulation,
Forschungszentrum Jülich, 52425 Jülich, Germany
{m.chraibi, r.subaih}@fz-juelich.de
[4] Faculty of Engineering and Information Technology,
Computer Systems Engineering Department,
Arab American University, Jenin, Palestine
{sami.awad, tareq.zanoon}@aaup.edu

Abstract. Over the past few years, several experimental studies have been conducted to explore the diversity in pedestrian dynamics with respect to several factors like culture and motivation. However less attention has been payed to the influence of gender on a crowd. One of the most fundamental experiments in this context aims at investigating the differences of pedestrian dynamics in narrow corridors with closed boundary conditions. The main advantage of this simplified set-up is the ease to control the density, which enables studying the so-called Fundamental Diagram (density-velocity relationship, FD) in a controlled and consistent manner. In this paper, we investigate the main characteristics of pedestrian dynamics observed in laboratory experiments conducted in Palestine, using single-file pedestrian flow information. Furthermore, we conduct a comparative analysis among the gender-based FDs for different cultures, in an attempt to study the different characteristics and factors that may influence their dynamics and motion flows.

Keywords: Pedestrian dynamics · Fundamental Diagram ·
Single-file movement · Experiment · Gender

1 Introduction

Understanding and predicting the properties of pedestrians in the surrounding environment is important in various application domains, such as in buildings and stations design [1], planning and designing mass gathering facilities [2], developing socially-aware robots [3] and building autonomous vehicle navigation systems [4]. Many researches have studied the different dynamic characteristics – both microscopic and

© Springer Nature Switzerland AG 2019
N. T. Nguyen et al. (Eds.): ICCCI 2019, LNAI 11683, pp. 613–624, 2019.
https://doi.org/10.1007/978-3-030-28377-3_51

macroscopic characteristics [5] - to describe the dynamics of pedestrians. One of the basic characteristics is the relation between density and velocity or density and flow a.k.a. Fundamental Diagram (FD). Several factors including cultural differences [6], psychological factors [7], uni- and multi-directional flow [8, 9], and different boundary conditions [10] influence the dynamics of pedestrians resulting in a deviation among several fundamental diagrams.

To study these factors and collect movement parameters in a controlled way, many experiments - under laboratory conditions - have been performed. For instance, Chattaraj et al. [11] studied the impact of obstacles inside corridors at a fundamental level and also understand how different geometric features impact the motion of pedestrians. On the other hand, Lian et al. [1] studied the pedestrian merging behavior using a merging channel (corridor with branches) where the branch flow joins the main corridor flow at a junction point in an attempt to understand the complete pedestrian flow (Macroscopic characteristic) during traffic. As reported in [12] more experiments for difference cultures are still needed. Accordingly, it's important to focus more on experiments that investigate the influence of the cultural difference on pedestrian dynamics. To figure out these factors and their impact on pedestrian dynamics, earlier studies and experiments have been performed in Germany [13], China [14] and India [13]. In the experiments that were carried out in Indian and Germany, the minimum personal space, distance headway, and free flow speed were measured. While in the experiments of China [12], the authors have discovered that there exist cultural differences that are caused due to the physical body size and the personal-space habit that may influence the movement behavior of the pedestrians.

Starting from this position, in this paper, we investigate the impact of one of these cultural factors (gender) on the pedestrian's FD, namely in the Palestinian culture. To do this, we carry out - in the same manner as in [13, 15] - single-file movement experiments under laboratory condition in Palestine. In addition, we compare the produced diagrams against other diagrams that have been produced during experiments in Germany, India, and China. The intention is to analyze the trajectory data extracted from Palestinian experiments and compare pedestrian dynamic characteristics such as velocity, free flow speed, and velocity changes with different densities, and see how these vary between different cultures and gender groups (male, female).

The remainder of this paper is organized as follows. In Sect. 2, we introduce the related work. Section 3 describes our experiments and the data extraction methodology. Section 4 discusses the results of our experiments and provides a comparative analysis across various culture-based diagrams. In Sect. 5, we draw the conclusions and discuss the future work.

2 Related Work

Several experimental studies have been conducted to study the characteristics of pedestrian dynamics [1, 11, 16, 17]. However, few experiments have been carried out to study the influence of cultural factors on the dynamics of pedestrians. For instance, the study conducted in [18] aimed to understand the cultural differences between Canada and Sri Lanka through measuring the dynamic characteristics including density, velocity, flow using different widths of sidewalks. However, this study didn't incorporate high-density pedestrians, and the velocities and other quantities were determined via manual observations using time-lapse photography. Another study was performed by Chattaraj el al. [13] using two single-file movement laboratory experiments in different countries (Germany, India). Both experiments were conducted using the same experimental set-up and the results have indicated that the obtained FDs varied where each culture has its own characteristics that controlled the dynamics of pedestrians. For instance, the authors found that Indian pedestrians are less concerned about the comfort zone because the minimum personal space of Indians is less than the personal space of Germans. Also, the Indians walk a bit faster than Germans and their velocity is less sensitive to the increase in density compared to Germans. However, this study didn't consider the gender factor during the experiments where in the Indian experiments only male pedestrians were involved, but in the German experiments both male and female were involved. This bias may affect the results observed. In addition, the analysis of the obtained results was performed using classical measurement methods which showed strong fluctuations in density results compared with Voronoi measurement methodology that have been used in other studies.

Cao et al. [14] studied the dynamics of pedestrians in China. The authors focused on investigating the stepping behavior of different age compositions of pedestrians. They conducted a single-file movement experiment under laboratory conditions using an oval set-up with different compositions of pedestrian (different ages, mixed gender) in Tianshui Health School in China to analyze the relationship between velocity-step length, velocity-step width for different age groups (young, old) male and female. For precise data extraction, they used PeTrack software to extract pedestrian trajectories. Additionally; they investigated the effect of height and gender on the velocity-density relationship. The authors found that gender and height have no obvious influence on the density-velocity relationship for both old and young people. Another research studied the single-file movement in China [12, 19]. The authors investigated the microscopic characteristics of pedestrian dynamics, including, velocity, density, and lateral sway. The experiments were conducted using the same set-up as in [13]. The position data of each pedestrian over time was extracted using image processing techniques based on the mean-shift algorithm. The authors compared the obtained FD with the German FD [15]. The results showed that Chinese people show larger velocities than German in the experiments due to the different body size (physiological) and psychological differences in terms of the need for personal space. In this research work, we aim to study the characteristics that control the dynamics of pedestrians in Arab countries, namely in Palestine and compare the obtained FD results to other FDs of different cultures (Germany, Indian, China).

3   Experiments

In this section, we first present the set-up of our experiments and discuss the experimental details. Then, we describe the data collection methodology used to extract pedestrian trajectories using PeTrack [20]. After that, we discuss the observations that we deduce after analyzing the video footage recordings using PeTrack.

3.1   Experimental Set-Up

In our experiments and in an aim to replicate the experiments conducted in [12, 13] and [15], we have created an oval corridor which includes two 3.15 m length by 0.6 m width straight parts and two semicircles with an inner and outer radius of 1.45 m and 2.05 m respectively. The width of the pathway prevents the pedestrians from over-taking and enforces the single-file movement. The length of the measurement section (straight part) is l_m = 3.15 m and the length of the whole corridor is l_c = 17.3 m. The dimensions of the set-up are shown in Fig. 1.

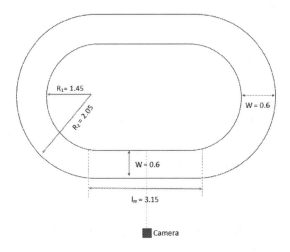

Fig. 1. Experimental set-up sketch for Palestine experiment

We used two set-ups A and B with the same dimensions to perform the runs in parallel (one for the male and the second for the female participants). In addition, we used a separation board - located at the middle area of the set-ups - to separate the participants walking in straight lines and to only focus on the measurement section. To capture the pedestrians' motion in the measurement section two different cameras were used at each set-up: Nikon D610 and Nikon D3300, with settings: 25 fps, 1600 ISO, 5.6 F-stop, 125 Shutter speed, and 1280 * 720 resolution. The cameras at set-up A (Nikon D610) and B (Nikon D3300) were set at a sufficient distance of 3.23 m and 3.44 m, and height from the floor 0.86 m and 0.95 m, respectively. Both cameras were set at a side view along the perpendicular bisector of the measurement section. Figure 2 shows sample frames extracted from one of the runs with N = 14 persons.

Fig. 2. Sample frames extracted from one of the runs with $N = 14$ persons.

3.2 Experiment Details

A series of controlled experiments were conducted at the Arab American University in Palestine. The total number of participants was 47 pedestrians (26 female and 21 male students) from different faculties and departments of the university. Their heights ranged from 1.52 to 1.84 m and their ages ranged from 18 to 23 years old. Table 1 provides a summary of the participants' attributes. All pedestrians moved normally without overtaking in a relaxed manner to help studying the normal movement of pedestrians. We conducted a series of experiments (runs) with different pedestrian compositions. Male runs and Female runs were performed to study and compare the dynamic characteristics of different gender compositions.

Table 1. Summary of participants' attributes

Gender	Mean age	Mean height (m)	Number of participants (%)
Male	19	175.38	45%
Female	19	161.26	55%

Each run was repeated from two to three times wherein each pedestrian walks for two to three cycles along the corridor at each experiment in order to increase the trajectory data available for measurements. During the runs, the pedestrians were distributed uniformly along the corridor. Table 2 shows the details of the runs: Run Index, Name, Repetitions, Number of Participant (Male, Female), Density, Remarks.

Table 2. Description of runs for different compositions of participants

Run index	Name	Repetitions	Number of participants Female	Male	Density (m^{-1})	Remarks
01	UF_1	7	1	–	–	Measure the free flow speed of Female participants
02	UM_1	7	–	1	–	Measure the free flow speed of Male participants
03	UF_14	3	14	–	0.81	
04	UM_14	3	–	14	0.81	
05	UF_20	3	20	–	1.16	
06	UM_20	3	–	20	1.16	

As shown in Table 2, there are two types of runs: UM, (Unidirectional Flow Male experiments) and UF, (Unidirectional Flow Female experiments). At the first two runs, UF_1 and UM_1, seven pedestrians moved inside the corridor alone one after the other to calculate the average free flow speed. After these runs, we started increasing the number of participants to realize the different densities that will be used in our FDs. To maximize the data used to calculate the mean speed, we repeated the same run for several times, as shown under Repetition column in Table 2.

3.3   Data Collection

The trajectories for each pedestrian at different time points are automatically extracted from the captured video footage using PeTrack software package [20]. First, we correct the lens distortion and perspective views automatically through the calibration step using the captured chessboard pattern. After that, we position the 2-D coordination system as precisely as possible starting from the beginning of the measurement section to the end. Then, to make PeTrack recognize our participant's we detect pedestrian head positions in video recordings manually and then PeTrack automatically tracks them to extract their 2-D coordinates. Figure 3 shows a snapshot captured from PeTrack with the 4 main Tabs: *calibration, recognition, tracking,* and *analysis.* These Tabs correspond to the steps of the processing pipeline. For more information about PeTrack, please refer to [16].

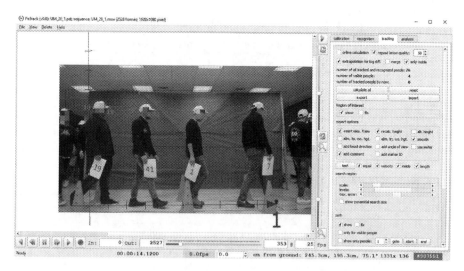

Fig. 3. Snapshot of PeTrack during extraction of trajectories from video recording

4   Comparative Analysis

There are different measurement methodologies that are used to analyze the pedestrian dynamics [8]. These methodologies lead to different FDs [21, 22] based on how they reduce the fluctuation of the measured densities and velocities to improve the quality of the results. According to the previous studies [8–10, 21], the best method that has proved to outperform other conventional methods for the FD analysis is the Voronoi method [23]. This method shows small fluctuations in the measured densities and high precision in 2-D and 1-D pedestrian flow. In 1-D flow, the Voronoi space for each pedestrian i is determined by the sum of the half distance between the pedestrian and his/her neighbors. Each pedestrian has two neighbors: the predecessor $i - 1$, and successor $i + 1$. So, to calculate the individual mean Voronoi density, and individual mean Voronoi velocity at time t in the measurement section, we used the definition:

$$\rho(i) = \frac{1}{d(i)} \quad \text{and} \quad v_i(t) = \frac{x_i(t + \Delta t') - x_i(t - \Delta t')}{\Delta t'}, \tag{1}$$

where:

- $\rho(i)$ is the individual mean Voronoi density of pedestrian i at time t.
- $v_i(t)$ is the individual mean Voronoi velocity of pedestrian i at time t.
- $d(i)$ is the Voronoi space of pedestrian i.
- $x_i(t)$ the x-coordinate of pedestrian position at time t.
- $\Delta t'$ short time interval around t.

For our analysis, we implemented python scripts to analyze pedestrian data using Voronoi method. The short time interval $\Delta t'$ used to calculate the velocity is 10 frames (0.4 s). Also, we calculate the individual mean velocity and density every 200 frames (4 s) to reduce the data points used to draw the fundamental diagrams shown in Fig. 4.

4.1   Studying the Free Flow Speed

The data for free flow speed was extracted for each pedestrian walking in the corridor. 14 pedestrians (male, female) moved inside the corridor one at each round to calculate the mean free flow speed. The mean free flow speeds from female and male data were 1.15($\pm$0.25) ms^{-1} and 1.20($\pm$0.28) ms^{-1}, respectively.

For hypothesis testing, we use the Kolmogorov-Smirnov statistical test (k-s 2-sample test). Here, independent samples of data points were obtained, so the k-s test is appropriate for hypothesis testing. The Null hypothesis H_0 is that the distribution of the free flow speed of female v_0^f and that from male v_0^m are the same, and the alternate hypothesis H_0 is that the two free flow speeds don't come from the same distribution.

We compared the two empirical distribution functions of female and male free flow speed data points using the stats.ks_2samp() method from Scipy python library. If the Kolmogrov-smirnov value that is obtained from the stats.ks_2samp() method is greater than the D-Critical value of the expression:

$$D_\alpha = c(\alpha)\sqrt{\frac{n_1 + n_2}{n_1 * n_2}}, \tag{2}$$

where:

- $c(\alpha)$ is the coefficient (0.05).
- n_1 is the number of female free flow speed data points.
- n_2 is the number of male free flow speed data points.

The Null hypothesis can be rejected saying that there is a difference in the free flow speed between male data and female data, otherwise not (H_a is accepted). The D_α value come out from the previous expression is equal to 0.066, and the Kolmogrov-Smirnov value is 0.0, so we accept the null hypothesis.

The conclusion is that the female and male free flow speeds do statistically have the same distribution. This indicates that the Palestinian female and male pedestrians walk in the same speed if the number of successor and predecessor pedestrians does not hinder their free flow speed.

4.2   Fundamental Diagram (Density-Velocity Relationship)

The velocity (ρ) – density (v) data obtained from the Palestinian experiments for both male and female pedestrians are plotted in Fig. 4.

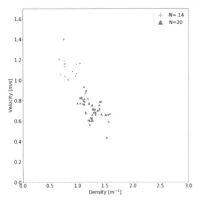 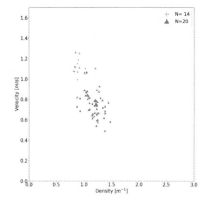

a) Velocity–Density relationship for female run N=14, 20   b) Velocity-Density relationship for male run N=14, 20

Fig. 4.   Velocity-Density data from different gender with different densities

By looking at the data presented in the scatter diagrams, we can conclude the following subjective observations. First, with increasing densities, the velocity decreases for both male and female experiments. This negative correlation between density and velocity is consistent with common fundamental diagrams [24]. Second, for different density groups, the female and male walk at a similar velocity. E.g. the mean velocities of female and male when N = 14 are $1.10(\pm0.08)$ ms^{-1} and 1.12 (±0.07) ms^{-1} respectively. Also, in N = 20 runs the females walk with a mean velocity equal to $0.71(\pm0.11)$ ms^{-1} and the males walk with mean velocity $0.72(\pm0.10)$ ms^{-1}. In ordered to confirm these observations a hypothesis is tested using Kolmogrov-Smirnov (2-sample test) to see if the FDs of females and males are similar. After measuring the D-Statistics = 0.0 and D-Critical = 0.016 we accept the Null hypothesis. So, the distribution of female and male data points on the FD are similar which means that they walk approximately the same.

Table 3. Descriptive statistics for male and female runs for Palestinian pedestrians

Run	Mean velocity	Velocity standard deviation
UF_1	1.15	0.25
UF_14_1	1.16	0.08
UF_14_2	1.15	0.09
UF_14_3	1.08	0.06
UF_20_1	0.70	0.09
UF_20_2	0.70	0.09
UF_20_3	0.64	0.10
UM_1	1.20	0.28
UM_14_1	1.09	0.07
UM_14_2	1.14	0.06
UM_14_3	1.12	0.07
UM_20_1	0.70	0.11
UM_20_2	0.72	0.08
UM_20_2	0.76	0.11

Table 3 provides detailed descriptive statistics for the runs of Palestine experiments. By looking at Table 3, we can see that there are no significant differences between the velocities of each run for different genders. After reviewing the literature in [12, 13] and [15], we present in Table 4 the information about these experiments compared to our experiments.

Table 4. Information about the Palestinian, Indian, German, and Chinese experiments

	Palestine	India	Germany	China A	China B
Place	Rhythm Hall at the Arab American University	Indian Institute of Technology, Kanpur	Central Institute for Applied Mathematics (ZAM) of the Research Centre Jülich	Hefei, China	Baoji, China
Participants	Students from different departments of Arab American University	Graduate students, technical staff of Indian Institute of Technology, Kanpur and local residents of Kanpur city	Students and staff of the Institute	College students	College students
Gender	Male, female	Male	Male, female	Male, female (mostly male)	Male, female (mostly female)
Length of the corridor (m)	17.3	17.3	17.3	17.3	17.3
Width of the corridor (m)	0.6	0.8	0.8	0.8	0.6, 0.7
Length of the measurement area (m)	3	2	2	2	3.2
Width of the curve (m)	0.6	1.2	1.2	1.2	1.2
Number of participants in each run	1, 14, 20	1, 15, 20, 25, 30, 34	1, 15, 20, 25, 30, 34	1, 15, 20, 25, 30, 34	1, 10, 20, 30, 40, 50, 60

By comparing the mean flow speed of our experiments with other cultures as shown in Table 5, we find that the mean free flow speed of Palestinian (male) experiment is a bit greater than the mean free flow speed of Indian (male) experiment.

Table 5. Free flow speed of different cultures

	Palestine (male)	Palestine (female)	India (male)	Germany (mixed)	China A (mixed)	China B (mixed)
Free flow speed (ms^{-1})	1.20	1.15	1.27	1.24	1.72	1.41

Also, when we compared the mean free flow speed of Palestinian (female) experiment with China B (mostly female) experiment we found that the Chinese pedestrians walk faster than the Palestinian. Furthermore, the mean velocity also varied between different cultures, e.g. when N = 20 in China A and China B [12], Germany [15] and Palestine experiments the velocity equal to 0.91 m, 1.06 m, 0.56 m, and 0.7, respectively. As a result, there is a difference between the free flow speed and mean velocities of different cultures.

5   Conclusions and Future Work

In this paper, a unidirectional single-file movement experiments for Palestinian culture is presented in details. Various experiments were conducted with different gender pedestrian compositions to investigate their dynamic characteristics especially velocity and free flow speed. The fundamental diagrams of different experiments are plotted and statistically analyzed. The pedestrians' trajectory data from the video recordings for the conducted experiments were extracted using the PeTrack software package and then used to calculate the velocity-density quantities using Voronoi diagram methodology. The results of the gender-based fundamental diagrams indicate that the differences were insignificant between velocity and free flow speed of different gender composition in Palestine. However, differences are found to be between different cultures, and this confirms that different types of pedestrians have different dynamic behaviors.

In the future work, we plan to carry out more experiments to investigate the factors that control the dynamics of pedestrians from the trajectory data of Palestinian culture and compare the results with other studies with respect to additional cultural differences. In addition, we plan to investigate the impact on the currently obtained findings on the FD of pedestrians in open and real-world scenarios. To do this, we plan to explore various machine learning and neural networks based techniques that can assist in anticipating future pedestrians' behavior based on the currently acquired observations.

References

1. Lian, L., et al.: Pedestrian merging behavior analysis: an experimental study. Fire Saf. J. **91**, 918–925 (2017)
2. Gulhare, S., Verma, A., Chakroborty, P.: Comparison of pedestrian data of single file movement collected from controlled pedestrian experiment and from field in mass religious gathering. Collective Dynam. **3**, 1–14 (2018)
3. Luber, M., et al.: People tracking with human motion predictions from social forces. In: 2010 IEEE International Conference on Robotics and Automation (ICRA). IEEE (2010)
4. Rasouli, A., Tsotsos, J.K.: Autonomous vehicles that interact with pedestrians: a survey of theory and practice. arXiv preprint arXiv:1805.11773 (2018)
5. Chraibi, M., et al.: Modelling of pedestrian and evacuation dynamics. In: Meyers, R. (ed.) Encyclopedia of Complexity and Systems Science, pp. 1–22. Springer, Heidelberg (2018). https://doi.org/10.1007/978-3-642-27737-5

6. Biswal, M.K.: Comparison of Pedestrian Fundamental Diagram: A Cultural and Gender Aspect (2014)
7. Sieben, A., Schumann, J., Seyfried, A.: Collective phenomena in crowds—where pedestrian dynamics need social psychology. PLoS ONE **12**(6), e0177328 (2017)
8. Zhang, J.: Pedestrian fundamental diagrams: comparative analysis of experiments in different geometries, vol. 14. Forschungszentrum Jülich (2012)
9. Zhang, J., Seyfried, A.: Comparison of intersecting pedestrian flows based on experiments. Physica A **405**, 316–325 (2014)
10. Zhang, J., Tordeux, A., Seyfried, A.: Effects of boundary conditions on single-file pedestrian flow. In: Wąs, J., Sirakoulis, G.Ch., Bandini, S. (eds.) ACRI 2014. LNCS, vol. 8751, pp. 462–469. Springer, Cham (2014). https://doi.org/10.1007/978-3-319-11520-7_48
11. Chattaraj, U., Chakroborty, P., Subhashini, A.: Empirical studies on impacts of obstacle inside corridor on pedestrian flow. Procedia Soc. Behav. Sci. **104**, 668–677 (2013)
12. Song, W., Lv, W., Fang, Z.: Experiment and modeling of microscopic movement characteristic of pedestrians. Procedia Eng. **62**, 56–70 (2013)
13. Chattaraj, U., Seyfried, A., Chakroborty, P.: Comparison of pedestrian fundamental diagram across cultures. Adv. Complex Syst. **12**(03), 393–405 (2009)
14. Cao, S., et al.: The stepping behavior analysis of pedestrians from different age groups via a single-file experiment. J. Stat. Mech. Theory Exp. **2018**(3), 033402 (2018)
15. Seyfried, A., et al.: The fundamental diagram of pedestrian movement revisited. J. Stat. Mech. Theory Exp. **2005**(10), P10002 (2005)
16. Boltes, M., Schumann, J., Salden, D.: Gathering of data under laboratory conditions for the deep analysis of pedestrian dynamics in crowds. In: 2017 14th IEEE International Conference on Advanced Video and Signal Based Surveillance (AVSS). IEEE (2017)
17. Zhang, J., Seyfried, A.: Experimental studies of pedestrian flows under different boundary conditions. In: 17th International IEEE Conference on Intelligent Transportation Systems (ITSC). IEEE (2014)
18. Morrall, J.F., Ratnayake, L., Seneviratne, P.: Comparison of central business district pedestrian characteristics in Canada and Sri Lanka. Transportation Research Record, 1991 (1294)
19. Liu, X., Song, W., Zhang, J.: Extraction and quantitative analysis of microscopic evacuation characteristics based on digital image processing. Physica A **388**(13), 2717–2726 (2009)
20. Boltes, M.: Software PeTrack. http://www.fz-juelich.de/jsc/petrack/
21. Zhang, J., et al.: Transitions in pedestrian fundamental diagrams of straight corridors and T-junctions. J. Stat. Mech Theory Exp. **2011**(06), P06004 (2011)
22. Kerner, B.S.: The Physics of Traffic—Empirical Freeway Pattern Features, Engineering Applications, and Theory, Understanding Complex Systems, 1st edn. Springer, Heidelberg (2004). https://doi.org/10.1007/978-3-540-40986-1
23. Liddle, J., Seyfried, A., Steffen, B.: Analysis of bottleneck motion using Voronoi diagrams. In: Peacock, R., Kuligowski, E., Averill, J. (eds.) Pedestrian and Evacuation Dynamics, pp. 833–836. Springer, Boston (2011). https://doi.org/10.1007/978-1-4419-9725-8_83
24. Hurley, M.J., et al.: SFPE Handbook of Fire Protection Engineering, 5th edn. Springer, New York (2016). https://doi.org/10.1007/978-1-4939-2565-0

Active Redundancy Allocation in Complex Systems by Using Different Optimization Methods

Petru Caşcaval and Florin Leon[(✉)]

Department of Computer Science and Engineering,
"Gheorghe Asachi" Technical University of Iaşi, Iaşi, Romania
{cascaval,florin.leon}@tuiasi.ro

Abstract. This paper addresses the issue of optimal allocation of spare modules in complex series-parallel redundant systems in order to obtain a required reliability under cost constraints. To solve this optimization problem, an analytical method based on the Lagrange multipliers technique is first applied. Then the results are improved by using other optimization methods such as an evolutionary algorithm and an original fine tuning algorithm based on the idea of hill climbing. The numerical results highlight the advantage of combining analytical approaches with fine tuning algorithms in case of very large systems. By using such a combined technique, better solutions are obtained than those given by classic heuristic search algorithms.

Keywords: Reliability allocation · Series-parallel reliability models ·
Lagrange multipliers · Evolutionary algorithms · Pairwise Hill Climbing

1 Introduction

The reliability design of a complex system is one of the most studied topics in the literature. The problems mainly refer to the kind of solution (reliability allocation and/or redundancy allocation), the kind of redundancy (active, standby, etc.), the type of the system (binary or multi-state), the levels of the redundancy (multi-level system or multiple component choice) etc. All these issues have practical applications and provide a good sphere for further research. An excellent overview of all these problems can be found in [1–4].

According to the decision variables [3, 4], a reliability optimization problem may belong to the following types: (a) reliability allocation, when the decision variables are component reliabilities, (b) redundancy allocation, when the variable is the number of component units, and (c) reliability-redundancy allocation, when the decision variables include both the component reliabilities and the redundancies.

In this paper we address the problem of redundancy allocation in which the number of redundant units in a series-parallel reliability model is the only decision variable. Unfortunately, as presented in [5], this is a problem that falls into the NP-hard category.

© Springer Nature Switzerland AG 2019
N. T. Nguyen et al. (Eds.): ICCCI 2019, LNAI 11683, pp. 625–637, 2019.
https://doi.org/10.1007/978-3-030-28377-3_52

We have limited ourselves to the binary systems in which each component is either operational or failed and, regarding the kind of redundancy, we focus only on the active spares.

To solve this optimization problem of redundancy allocation, more methods or techniques can be applied, such as intuitive engineering methods [6], heuristic search algorithms [7–10], analytical methods based on Lagrange multipliers [11–13], or dynamic programming [14]. Other metaheuristic methods based on genetic algorithms are also appropriate [15–18].

2 Notations and Preliminary Considerations

Reliability is the probability that a component or a system works successfully within a given period of time. A s*eries-parallel model* is a reliability model corresponding to a redundant system consisting of basic components and other active spare components.

The following notations are used throughout the paper: n is number of components in the non-redundant system or number of subsystems in the redundant system, as the case; r_i is the reliability of a component of type i, $i \in \{1, 2, ..., n\}$, for a given period of time; c_i is the cost of a component of type i; R_{ns} is the reliability of the non-redundant system (system with series reliability model); k_i is the number of components that compose the redundant subsystem i, $i \in \{1, 2, ..., n\}$; R_i is the reliability of subsystem i (subsystem with parallel reliability model); C_i is the cost of subsystem i; R_{rs} is the reliability of the redundant system (system with series-parallel reliability model); C_{rs} is the cost of the redundant system; R^* is the required reliability level for the system; C^* is the maximum accepted cost for the system.

It is assumed that: each component in the system is either operational or failed, i.e. a binary system, a spare is identical with the basic component, and the events of failure that affect the components of the system are stochastically independent.

3 Problem Description

Let us consider a non-redundant system composed of n basic components for which the reliability model is a series one as presented in Fig. 1. For complex systems with a large number of components, the reliability of the system without redundancy is often quite low. To reach a required reliability, spare components are added so that the reliability model for this redundant system is a series-parallel one as presented in Fig. 2.

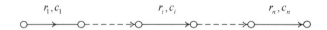

Fig. 1. Series reliability model for a non-redundant system

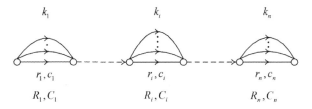

Fig. 2. Series-parallel reliability model for a redundant system with spare components

Typically, in this allocation process the criterion is reliability, cost, weight or volume. One or more criteria can be considered in an objective function, while the others may be considered as constraints [3, 4, 19]. From a mathematical point of view, one must solved an optimization problem of an objective function with constraints.

In this work, we address the issue of maximizing system reliability within the cost constraint. Thus, one must maximize the reliability function $R_{rs} = \prod_{i=1}^{n} R_i$, with the restriction of cost $\sum_{i=1}^{n} C_i \leq C^*$.

In case of large systems, to master the complexity of the problem, we choose to first apply an analytical method based on Lagrange multipliers in order to quickly obtain an approximate solution, and then, this approximate solution is improved by using other optimization methods such as an evolutionary algorithm and an original fine tuning algorithm. To check the results, we have also implemented some heuristic algorithms, as presented in the following section.

4   Heuristic Search Algorithms

For the reliability model presented in Fig. 2, the following equation is valid: $R_{rs}(t) = \prod_{i=1}^{n} R_i(t) \leq \min_{i}\{R_i(t)\}$. Starting from this observation, the following two heuristic methods are applied to solve this optimal allocation problem.

Algorithm 1: This is a greedy algorithm given by Misra [7] that tries to make an optimal choice at each step. Thus, starting with the minimum system design presented in Fig. 1 ($k_i, i \in \{1, 2, \ldots, n\}$), the system reliability is increased by adding one component to the subsystem with the lowest reliability. This process is repeated as long as the cost constraint is met.

Algorithm 2: This algorithm given by Rajendra Prasad, Nair, and Aneja [9] ensures an acceleration of the allocation process. The basic idea is that the subsystem with the highest reliability will have the smallest number of components, and the least reliable subsystem, the greatest number of components. Thus, starting with the system in a non-redundant form, the reliability is increased by adding one component to each subsystem (a row allocation) as long as the cost constraint is met. For the most reliable subsystem, this is the final allocation. The process of allocation continues in the same manner with the other subsystems, until no allocation is possible any longer.

As presented in Sect. 8, these heuristic algorithms are useful in many cases, but sometimes they do not give good solutions. Therefore, we choose to apply first an analytical method based on Lagrange multipliers as presented in the following section.

5   Analytical Approach

As the spares are identical with the basic component, for the series-parallel reliability model presented in Fig. 2, the reliability function can be expressed by the equation:

$$R_{rs} = \prod_{i=1}^{n} \left(1 - (1 - r_i)^{k_i} \right). \tag{1}$$

We have to determine the values k_i that maximize the function R_{rs} with the cost constraint:

$$\sum_{i=1}^{n} c_i k_i \leq C^*. \tag{2}$$

Based on (1) and (2), the following Lagrangian function results:

$$L(k_1, k_2, \ldots, k_n, \lambda) = \prod_{i=1}^{n} \left(1 - (1 - r_i)^{k_i} \right) + \lambda \left(\sum_{i=1}^{n} c_i k_i - C^* \right), \tag{3}$$

where λ is the Lagrange multiplier.

Thus, instead of maximizing the function R_{rs} given by (1) within the cost restriction (2), we have to maximize the Lagrange function given by (3) without constraints. For this propose, a system with partial derivatives must be solved, where $\partial L / \partial k_i = 0$, $i \in \{1, 2, \ldots, n\}$, and $\partial L / \partial \lambda = 0$. But the resulting system of algebraic equations is very difficult to solve because of the products that appear. For this reason, we use another way of expressing the reliability of the system, as presented as follows.

The reliability of a system can be expressed by the reliability function (R) or the non-reliability function ($F = 1 - R$), that means, by a point within the unit segment [0, 1]. As presented in Fig. 3, this value can be uniquely identified by a point on the diagonal of a square with the side length equal to the unit (denoted by P).

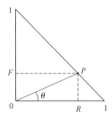

Fig. 3. Another way of expressing the reliability

The point P in Fig. 3 is uniquely identified by the angle θ, and thus by $x = \tan(\theta)$. Related to the two reliability indicators, R and x, the following equations are valid: $x = (1 - R)/R = 1/R - 1$, and $R = 1/(x + 1)$. Notice that, if $R \to 1$ then $x \to 0$, and if $R \to 0$ then $x \to \infty$.

Let us now consider a system with a series reliability model, composed of n modules of reliability given by x_i. The system reliability, denoted by $x_{S(n)}$, can be expressed by the following equation:

$$x_{S(n)} = \frac{1}{R_{S(n)}} - 1 = \frac{1}{\prod\limits_{i=1}^{n} \frac{1}{x_i + 1}} - 1 = \prod_{i=1}^{n} (x_i + 1) - 1. \tag{4}$$

This relationship is rather complicated, but for the values $x_i \ll 1$, $i \in \{1, 2, \ldots, n\}$, the products that are formed can be neglected and the reliability of the system can be approximated with good accuracy by the equation $x_{S(n)} \approx \sum\limits_{i=1}^{n} x_i$. In the same manner, one show that for a parallel reliability model with n components, when $x_i \ll 1$, $i \in \{1, 2, \ldots, n\}$ the reliability of the redundant system denoted by $x_{P(n)}$ can be approximated with good accuracy by $x_{P(n)} \approx \prod\limits_{i=1}^{n} x_i$.

In this form of representation for the system reliability, the optimization problem assumes the maximization of the reliability function $x_{rs} = \sum\limits_{i=1}^{n} x_i^{k_i}$ with the cost constraint (2). In this case, the Lagrangian function is:

$$L(k_1, k_2, \ldots k_n, \lambda) = \sum_{i=1}^{n} x_i^{k_i} + \lambda \left(\sum_{i=1}^{n} c_i k_i - C^* \right). \tag{5}$$

By applying the partial derivatives, and using the notations $\alpha_i = 1/\ln x_i$ and $\beta_i = \alpha_i(\ln c_i + \ln(-\alpha_i))$, $i \in \{1, 2, \ldots, n\}$, the system solution of algebraic equations is:

$$\lambda = e^{\gamma}, \text{ where } \gamma = \left(C^* - \sum_{i=1}^{n} c_i \beta_i \right) \Big/ \sum_{i=1}^{n} c_i \alpha_i, \text{ and } k_i = \alpha_i \ln \lambda + \beta_i,$$
$$i = 1, 2, \ldots, n \tag{6}$$

Note that, this analytical result is valid only if $\alpha_i < 0$ (i.e. $r_i > 0.5$).

The only impediment for solving the problem remains that the values k_i obtained by applying (6) are real values, and the allocation is, by its nature, a discrete problem. Therefore, it is necessary to determine the optimal allocation in integer numbers starting from the actual solution.

An approximate solution results by adopting the integers closest to the real values. But, in this case, it is possible that the new solutions for k_i, $i \in \{1, 2, \ldots, n\}$, not longer satisfy the cost constraint. Starting from the value of the Lagrange multiplier λ

given by (6), a searching process is carried out in a neighborhood of this value in order to obtain a better approximate solution for k_i, $i \in \{1, 2, \ldots, n\}$, while satisfying the cost constraint. Unfortunately, this approximate solution is not accurate enough. Consequently, this approximate solution is further improved by applying other methods of refining the search process, as shown in the following sections.

As mentioned in Sect. 1, regarding the kind of redundancy, in this work we have limited ourselves to the active spares, because for the case of passive spares the Lagrangian function is more complicated and the system of partial derivatives is very difficult to solve. But the following optimization methods may be tailored to cover this case as well, or better, to cover the most general case in which some subsystems may have active spares and the others, passive spares.

6   Evolutionary Algorithm

Evolutionary algorithms are optimization methods inspired by natural selection. The search is made in parallel, with a population of potential solutions, also known as individuals or chromosomes, which are randomly initialized. Each chromosome is associated with a value determined by the fitness function that describes the problem to be solved. The evolution of the population is based on the successive application of genetic operators such as selection, which gives the better individuals more changes to reproduce, crossover, which combines the genetic information of two parents and creates offspring, and mutation, which may slightly change a newly generated child in order to introduce new genetic information into the population. The search progresses until a stopping criterion is met.

In our case, the encoding of the problem is real-valued, and each chromosome has n real genes, corresponding to k_i. The domain of the genes $[1, k_{max}]$ depends on the problem. k_{max} is the maximum estimated value for any k_i.

The fitness function is the expression in (1). Since the genes are real-values and k_i are integer numbers, the gene values are rounded in order to convert them into integers.

Since we have a constraint, one method of handling it is to add a penalty to the fitness function of the chromosomes that do not satisfy the constraint. However, this can have a very negative impact on the quality of the solution, because, especially in the beginning, very few or no individuals may satisfy the cost constraint. This can likely lead to very poor local optima, or may cause the algorithm to fail altogether in finding any solution.

The method adopted in the present work was to repair the chromosomes that violate the cost constraint, i.e. randomly removing one redundant component at a time, until the remaining components satisfy the constraint. Each subsystem must have at least one component, so only redundant components may be removed.

The selection method is tournament selection with two individuals. We use arithmetic crossover and mutation by gene resetting. As a stopping criterion, both fitness convergence and a fixed number of generation were tried. It was found that after a small number of generation, the values of all the fitness functions become very close, but these small differences actually make a big difference for the quality of the final result. Thus, a fixed number of generations was chosen as a stopping criterion.

Several variants of genetic evolution were evaluated:

- the typical method that generates offspring from parents, creates a complete new generation and then the new generation replaces the old one;
- elitism, where the best individual of a generation is directly copied into the next one, and that guarantees that the best solution at one time is never lost;
- steady state evolution, where from the current population of size s a new population of size s is generated by regular selection, crossover and mutation, but the new population does not directly replace the old one; instead, the two populations are merged, and from the resulting population of size $2s$, the best s individuals are selected to form the next generation;
- optimized offspring generation, where after a child has been created by regular selection, crossover and mutation, it is not directly inserted into the next generation; instead the individual with the best fitness out of the mother, the father and the child is inserted into the next generation.

From the experiments conducted for large problem instances, it was found that the optimized offspring generation combined with elitism provided the best results.

7 Pairwise Hill Climbing

An evolutionary algorithm has a good chance of find the global optimum, but it often finds a solution within the neighborhood of the optimum. On the other hand, the analytical method presented in Sect. 5 provides an approximate solution because of the conversion of the real solution into an integer one. In both situations, it is important to fine tune the initial approximation, it order to find a better solution, closer or equal to the actual optimum.

The typical hill climbing procedure starts from an initial solution and generates its neighbors in the problem space. The best neighbor is identified and if the value of its objective function is better than the one of the initial solution, the neighbor becomes the current solution and the same process is repeated until no neighbor is better that the current (and final) solution.

However, for the problems we study, the above algorithm cannot be applied because of the existence of the constraint. The approximate solvers usually find good, but sub-optimal solutions, which all have a cost very close or equal to C^*. Therefore, the classic hill climbing procedure cannot increase reliability further by adding, for example, an additional component, because the cost constraint would be violated.

In order to increase reliability at fairly the same total cost, a few, e.g. usually 1–2, components need to be removed from one or a few redundant subsystems, while simultaneously a few components need to be added to other few redundant subsystems.

Therefore, beside the addition of a component, a swap operation must also be considered when generating the neighbors of an allocation.

In some situations, the initial solution may not be in a direct neighborhood of the optimum, and thus solely relying on the addition of new components, which is the only way to increase reliability, in not sufficient.

Consequently, we propose an original fine tuning algorithm, Pairwise Hill Climbing, presented in Pseudocode 1, based on the main idea of hill climbing, but with several heuristics that make it more appropriate for our class of problems.

Pairwise Hill Climbing(initial)	Refine(current)

solutionList.Add(initial)
 	
for i **in** [1..n] **do**
  initial2 ← initial
  initial2.k[i] ← *max*(1, initial2.k[i] - 1)
  solutionList.Add(initial2)
 	
initial3 ← initial
for i **in** [1..n] **do**
  initial3.k[i] ← *max*(1, initial3.k[i] - 1)
  solutionList.Add(initial3)
 	
best ← initial
while solutionList *is not empty* **do**
  bestSoFar ← solutionList[bi] **where**
  solutionList[bi].reliability *is the largest*
  solutionList.Remove(bestSoFar)
  Refine(bestSoFar)
 	
return best
	for each pair (i, j) **in** ([1.. n], [1.. n]) **and** i ≠ j **do**
	  next ← current **with** (next.k[i], next.k[j]) += (1, 0)
	  and then += (1, -1)
	  next.reliability ← ComputeReliability ()
	
	  if IsFeasible(next) **and** next.reliability >
	  current.reliability **then**
	  solutionList.Add(next)
	
	if current.reliability > best.reliability **then**
	  best ← current

Pseudocode 1. Pairwise Hill Climbing

As the pseudocode shows, the successive allocations, starting from $n + 2$ initial points, are added to a priority queue, which helps to first expand the most promising solution. However, if the corresponding subtree yields a suboptimal solution, other parts of the tree can be used to find a better one. From the practical point of view, the search may be limited to a maximum number of levels in the tree l_{max} and to a maximum number of solutions taken from the queue s_{max}.

8   Experimental Results

In this section, we present the results of the previously described methods for three problems, designed in such a way as to make the optimization more difficult. Thus, for some components, we have chosen values so that, for a very similar reliability, the cost is very different. For example, in Problem 3, as highlighted by bold face in Table 1, the components with order number 4 and 43 have quite similar reliabilities (0.74 and 0.75, respectively), but very different cost values (49 and 4, respectively). The same remark holds for components with order number 39 and 44. The parameters of the components are presented in Table 1. For all three problems, $n = 50$.

The obtained results are presented in Table 2.

Methods 1 and 2 are the heuristic methods presented in Sect. 4.

Method 3 is the analytical method from Sect. 5 where the real-valued coefficients are converted into integers by rounding them down, i.e. $k_i = \lfloor k_i^r \rfloor$. This method obviously provides suboptimal results, but it can be a good starting point for solution improvement, because its solution has a good chance of being in the neighborhood of the optimal one.

Table 1. The optimization problems considered in the experimental study

	Component reliability $(r_1, r_2, \ldots, r_n)$	Component cost $(c_1, c_2, \ldots, c_n)$	C^*
Problem 1	0.59, 0.70, 0.84, 0.99, 0.81, 0.69, 0.88, 0.68, 0.65, 0.92, 0.67, 0.73, 0.68, 0.87, 0.71, 0.51, 0.66, 0.98, 0.73, 0.88, 0.87, 0.55, 0.73, 0.55, 0.59, 0.83, 0.76, 0.58, 0.77, 0.52, 0.87, 0.76, 0.77, 0.71, 0.63, 0.96, 0.97, 0.96, 0.79, 0.63, 0.61, 0.88, 0.86, 0.71, 0.91, 0.91, 0.93, 0.82, 0.72, 0.93	14, 5, 21, 21, 9, 9, 44, 35, 27, 30, 16, 22, 28, 22, 7, 15, 33, 47, 13, 38, 37, 34, 11, 41, 9, 45, 35, 48, 34, 41, 7, 17, 21, 10, 2, 33, 9, 40, 23, 38, 4, 34, 32, 20, 17, 40, 26, 48, 4, 32	6240
Problem 2	0.83, 0.91, 0.88, 0.99, 0.93, 0.73, 0.89, 0.96, 0.80, 0.95, 0.60, 0.88, 0.64, 0.83, 0.70, 0.86, 0.95, 0.70, 0.85, 0.80, 0.66, 0.86, 0.86, 0.84, 0.72, 0.91, 0.62, 0.69, 0.78, 0.70, 0.83, 0.86, 0.92, 0.53, 0.58, 0.65, 0.77, 0.57, 0.93, 0.79, 0.78, 0.67, 0.75, 0.94, 0.72, 0.70, 0.91, 0.97, 0.63, 0.80	47, 25, 21, 49, 20, 13, 44, 28, 8, 23, 45, 44, 34, 7, 14, 15, 42, 25, 42, 29, 23, 44, 2, 22, 7, 17, 18, 28, 20, 26, 48, 21, 8, 5, 17, 2, 6, 32, 49, 50, 26, 22, 4, 4, 42, 31, 44, 10, 45, 26	6370
Problem 3	0.83, 0.91, 0.88, **0.74**, 0.93, 0.73, 0.89, 0.96, 0.80, 0.95, 0.60, 0.88, 0.64, 0.83, 0.70, 0.86, 0.95, 0.70, 0.85, 0.80, 0.66, 0.86, 0.61, 0.84, 0.72, 0.91, 0.62, 0.69, 0.78, 0.70, 0.83, 0.86, 0.92, 0.53, 0.58, 0.56, 0.77, 0.57, **0.89**, 0.79, 0.78, 0.67, **0.75**, **0.90**, 0.72, 0.70, 0.91, 0.97, 0.55, 0.80	47, 25, 21, **49**, 20, 13, 44, 28, 8, 23, 45, 44, 34, 7, 14, 15, 42, 25, 42, 29, 23, 44, 2, 22, 7, 17, 18, 28, 20, 26, 48, 21, 8, 5, 17, 2, 6, 32, **49**, 50, 26, 22, **4**, **4**, 42, 31, 44, 10, 45, 26	6370

Method 4 involves an additional heuristic search starting from the initial estimates of the analytical method.

Method 5 uses the same estimates given by the analytical method, but employs the Pairwise Hill Climbing (PHC) search presented in Sect. 7. For PHC, the parameters used are $l_{max} = 20$ and $s_{max} = 1000$.

Method 6 only uses the Evolutionary Algorithm (EA) described in Sect. 6 with a large number of generations, i.e. 10000. In all cases, the other parameters of the EA are the following: the population size is 100, the crossover rate is 0.9, the mutation rate is 0.1. The search range for this method is 1–15 for each gene, i.e. k_i. Since the EA is nondeterministic, 10 runs for each configuration were performed and the best result was reported.

Method 7 uses the EA with a smaller number of generations, i.e. 1000, and its solution is used as the initial point for the PHC search.

Finally, method 8 uses the solution of the analytical method to define the search range for the EA genes. The range of a gene is the suboptimal $k_i \pm 2$, but ensuring that the lower limit remains at least 1.

Beside the actual reliability value of the redundant system R_{rs}, we included an additional, more intuitive measure of the results, namely the redundancy efficiency defined as: $Ef = (1 - R_{ns})/(1 - R_{rs})$. The efficiency shows how many times the risk of a failure decreases for the redundant system, compared to the baseline, non-redundant one. For example, at the first glance, it may not seem to be a big difference between two reliability values of 0.88 and 0.98, e.g. for Problem 2. However, the efficiency shows us that the risk of a failure decreases almost 6 times.

Table 2. The results obtained (R_{rs}, Ef, C_{rs}) with different optimization methods

Method	Problem 1	Problem 2	Problem 3
1. Heuristic 1	0.8242, 5.69, 6239	0.9803, 50.76, 6369	0.9701, 33.44, 6370
2. Heuristic 2	0.9628, 26.88, 6240	0.8882, 8.94, 6370	0.8591, 7.10, 6370
3. Analytical method with k_i rounded down	0.9678, 31.06, 6204	0.9830, 58.82, 6344	0.9755, 40.82, 6351
4. Analytical method followed by heuristics	0.9685, 31.75, 6239	0.9831, 59.17, 6369	0.9757, 41.15, 6369
5. Analytical method followed by pairwise hill climbing	0.9690, 32.26, 6239	0.9835, 60.77, 6370	0.9759, 41.50, 6370
6. Evolutionary algorithm with long search	0.9687, 31.99, 6239	0.9819, 55.42, 6370	0.9742, 38.82, 6370
7. Evolutionary algorithm followed by pairwise hill climbing	0.9668, 30.19, 6240	0.9825, 57.41, 6370	0.9751, 40.27, 6369
8. Analytical method followed by evolutionary algorithm with reduced search range	0.9686, 31.87, 6239	0.9834, 60.28, 6370	0.9755, 40.89, 6370

As one can notice, the first two heuristic methods give very different results for all the three problems. This highlights the difficulty of the optimization problems we considered.

The first observation is that in all three cases, the best results are obtained by the hybrid Method 5. The results of the analytical method are a very good starting point for the PHC, because the component allocation is likely less than the optimal one and a procedure based on the hill climbing idea can easily add new components and thus improve the objective function.

Conversely, it is more difficult for the PHC to improve more extensively the EA solution, because that is already near the maximum cost, and therefore some components need to be removed in order to add others, while keeping the solution in the feasibility region, i.e. satisfying the cost constraint. As it was seen, such refining does not only address simple component swaps, but sometime, more components should be removed from or added to a subsystem, and the changes to be made involve not only two subsystems, but often more.

It is somewhat surprising that the EA does not seem capable of finding the optimum, even with a very large number of generations and even starting from an estimated neighborhood of the optimal solution. This is because the problem has many local optima with the maximum cost, and the genetic search procedure is also affected by the fact that infeasible solutions are repaired, i.e. modified outside the influence of the genetic operators, by randomly removing components until the cost constraint is met. This repairing procedure is however critical to the convergence of the EA; if one uses penalties for constraint violation, usually the EA does not find a solution at all, or finds a very poor one. Thus, a different repairing procedure may be needed, where components are not removed at random, but some problem specific information is used in order to find the most appropriate change that can help the optimization process.

It is also important to discuss the execution times of these methods. The first four techniques are very fast, because they are based on the application of formulas or a linear search in a very limited range, comparable with n. The average execution times for ten runs for each problem using a computer with a 4-core 2 GHz Intel processor and 8 GB of RAM are given as follows: Method 5 – 1061.98 ms, Method 6 – 45,603.83 ms, Method 7 – 6,877.77 ms, Method 8 – 4252.38 ms.

Therefore, Method 5, which gives the best results, is also the fastest.

In Table 3, the best solutions are presented for each of the three problems under study.

Table 3. The best solutions found, i.e. the k_i values and total cost for the best R_{rs}

	Optimal allocation: k_1, k_2, ..., k_n	C_{rs}
Problem 1	8, 7, 4, 2, 5, 7, 3, 6, 7, 3, 7, 6, 6, 4, 7, 10, 6, 2, 6, 4, 4, 8, 6, 8, 9, 4, 5, 7, 5, 8, 5, 5, 5, 6, 9, 3, 3, 3, 5, 7, 9, 4, 4, 6, 4, 3, 3, 4, 7, 3	6239
Problem 2	4, 4, 4, 2, 3, 7, 4, 3, 6, 3, 8, 4, 7, 5, 7, 5, 3, 6, 4, 5, 7, 4, 6, 5, 7, 4, 8, 7, 6, 6, 4, 4, 4, 12, 9, 10, 7, 8, 3, 5, 5, 7, 7, 4, 6, 6, 3, 3, 7, 5	6370
Problem 3	4, 4, 4, 5, 3, 6, 3, 3, 5, 3, 7, 4, 7, 5, 7, 4, 3, 6, 4, 5, 7, 4, 11, 4, 7, 4, 8, 6, 5, 6, 4, 4, 4, 11, 9, 12, 6, 8, 3, 5, 5, 7, 7, 4, 6, 6, 3, 3, 8, 5	6370

9 Conclusions

In this paper several optimization methods where presented for the problem of maximizing the reliability of a redundant system, with a series-parallel reliability model, in the presence of cost-related constraints. Beside domain-specific heuristics and an analytical solution based on Lagrange multipliers, other general techniques were applied: an evolutionary algorithm with chromosome repairs meant to satisfy the constraint and an optimized offspring generation, and also a original algorithm based on the hill-climbing idea, but using swaps and a priority queue in addition to the incremental greedy improvements, in order to fine tune the approximate solutions found by other methods.

Our study shows that the hybrid methods provided the best results, especially the combination of the analytical method with the original Pairwise Hill Climbing algorithm, which is also the fastest.

As future directions of investigation, other optimization methods will be tried, and other variants of the problem will be addressed, for example, the issue of passive redundancy allocation and the converse problem of minimizing the cost while having a minimum imposed reliability, as a means to further verify the optimality of the solutions.

References

1. Tillman, F.A., Hwang, C.L., Kuo, W.: Optimization techniques for system reliability with redundancy. A review. IEEE Trans. Reliab. **26**, 148–155 (1977)
2. Tillman, F.A., Hwang, C.L., Kuo, W.: Optimization of System Reliability. Marcel Dekker, New York (1980)
3. Shooman, M.: Reliability of Computer Systems and Networks, pp. 331–383. Wiley, New York (2002)
4. Misra, K.B. (ed.): Handbook of Performability Engineering, pp. 499–532. Springer, London (2008). https://doi.org/10.1007/978-1-84800-131-2
5. Chern, M.: On the computational complexity of reliability redundancy allocation in series system. Oper. Res. Lett. **11**, 309–315 (1992)
6. Albert, A.A.: A measure of the effort required to increase reliability. Technical report No. 43, Stanford University, Applied Mathematics and Statistics Laboratory (1958)
7. Misra, K.B.: A simple approach for constrained redundancy optimization problems. IEEE Trans. Reliab. **R-20**(3), 117–120 (1971)
8. Agarwal, K.K., Gupta, J.S.: On minimizing the cost of reliable systems. IEEE Trans. Reliab. **R-24**, 205–206 (1975)
9. Rajendra Prasad, V., Nair, K.P.K., Aneja, Y.P.: A heuristic approach to optimal assignment of components to parallel-series network. IEEE Trans. Reliab. **40**(5), 555–558 (1992)
10. El-Neweihi, E., Proschan, F., Sethuraman, J.: Optimal allocation of components in parallel-series and series-parallel systems. J. Appl. Probab. **23**(3), 770–777 (1986)
11. Everett, H.: Generalized Lagrange multiplier method of solving problems of optimal allocation of resources. Oper. Res. **11**, 399–417 (1963)

12. Misra, K.B.: Reliability optimization of a series-parallel system, part I: Lagrangian multipliers approach, part II: maximum principle approach. IEEE Trans. Reliab. **R-21**, 230–238 (1972)
13. Blischke, W.R., Prabhakar, D.N.: Reliability: Modelling, Prediction, and Optimization. Wiley, New York (2000)
14. Belmann, R., Dreyfus, S.: Dynamic programming and the reliability of multi-component devices. Oper. Res. **6**(2), 200–206 (1958)
15. Coit, D.W., Smith, A.E.: Reliability optimization of series-parallel systems using a genetic algorithm. IEEE Trans. Reliab. **45**, 254–260 (1996)
16. Marseguerra, M., Zio, E.: System design optimization by genetic algorithms. In: Proceedings of the Annual Reliability and Maintainability Symposium, Los Angeles, CA, pp. 222–227. IEEE (2000)
17. Agarwal, M., Gupta, R.: Genetic search for redundancy optimization in complex systems. J. Qual. Maintenance Eng. **12**(4), 338–353 (2006)
18. Romera, R., Valdes, J.E., Zequeira, R.I.: Active redundancy allocation in systems. IEEE Trans. Reliab. **53**(3), 313–318 (2004)
19. Shooman, M.L., Marshall, C.: A mathematical formulation of reliability optimized design. In: Henry, J., Yvon, J.P. (eds.) System Modelling and Optimization. LNCIS, vol. 197, pp. 941–950. Springer, Heidelberg (1994). https://doi.org/10.1007/BFb0035543

Mining Stock Market Time Series and Modeling Stock Price Crash Using a Pretopological Framework

Ngoc Kim Khanh Nguyen[1,3]([✉]), Quang Nguyen[2], and Marc Bui[3]

[1] Van Lang University, Ho Chi Minh City, Viet Nam
nguyenngockimkhanh@vanlanguni.edu.vn
[2] Hong Bang International University, Ho Chi Minh City, Viet Nam
[3] EPHE-PSL Research University and Energisme R&D, Paris, France

Abstract. We introduce a computational framework, namely a pretopological construct, for mining time series of stock prices in a financial market in order to expand a set of stocks by adding outside stocks whose average correlations with the inside are above a threshold. The threshold is considered as a function of the set's size to verify the effect of group impact in a financial crisis. The efficiency of this approach is tested by a consecutive expansion process started from a single stock of Merrill Lynch & Co., which had a large influence in the United State market during the studying time. We found that the ability to imitate the real diffusion process can be classified into three cases according to the value of θ - a scaling constant of the threshold function. Finally, the process using pretopological framework is compared to a classical one, the minimum spanning tree of the corresponding stock network, showing its pertinence.

Keywords: Pretopology theory · Modeling of a stock market crash · Computational intelligence

1 Introduction

Complex systems is a well-established science. A system can be defined as complex if it is composed of many components interacting with each other and has chaotic behavior and/or collective behavior, among other properties [1–4]. As this point of view, a stock market can be considered as a complex system with the interactions among stock prices and their collective behavior observed many times, especially in crises. A complex system can be modeled as a graph whose nodes represent its components and edges represent the interactions between each pair of nodes, which is called a complex network. Many networks, both modeled and real-world networks, are demonstrated to be fragile under an intentional attack [5–8]. However, the system can be damaged if there is a failure in one or several components that may imply its cascading failures and prevent it from properly working [9, 10]. Unlike intentional attacks where nodes are removed sequentially (rely on their structural characters such as degrees, betweenness…) by external intervention, the failures happen by itself due to the strong relationships between the system's components. In order to study the failures, we need a method that examines the evolution of a complex system in each

© Springer Nature Switzerland AG 2019
N. T. Nguyen et al. (Eds.): ICCCI 2019, LNAI 11683, pp. 638–649, 2019.
https://doi.org/10.1007/978-3-030-28377-3_53

individual step and is able to reflect the relationships of the system's subgroups. Therefore, we introduce pretopology theory as a good method. As given in [11], let E be a nonempty set and $\mathcal{P}(E)$ be the set of all its subsets, we define:

Definition 1. A pretopological space is a pair (E, a) where a, called the pseudoclosure, is a map from $\mathcal{P}(E)$ into $\mathcal{P}(E)$ such that:

$$a(\emptyset) = \emptyset,$$
$$\forall A \subset E, \quad A \subset a(A) \tag{1}$$

Definition 2. Given a pretopological space (E, a), we call the closure of any subset A of E, when it exists, the smallest subset of (E, a) which contains A and is a fixed-point of the map a. The closure of A is denoted by $\mathbf{F}(A)$.

For any subset A of E, we have $A \subset a(A) \subset a^2(A) \subset \ldots \subset \mathbf{F}(A)$. This is similar to a dilation process from A to $\mathbf{F}(A)$. In a certain problem, with a suitable pseudoclosure, we can model the proximity concept to follow the transformation process step by step instead of going directly to the closure $\mathbf{F}(A)$ as in topology [12]. There are many theoretical and practical works about this theory such as pollution modeling [13, 14], macroeconomics [15], images analysis [16], Smart Grid model [17, 18]. In those works, pretopology was used to model complex systems as an extension because graph or even hyper-graph is just its special case [12]. While we need to construct each graph for each relation, pseudoclosure can process multiple relations among components as well as relationships among groups. Sometimes, a connection between a pair of nodes cannot reflect relationships between a node and a group. For example, with a system of five components labeled "*cat*", "*horse*", "*mouse*", "*tail*", "*grass*", the following pseudoclosure is defined by the appearance and eating habit of the animals: $a(\{tail\}) = \{tail, cat, horse, mouse\}$, $a(\{grass\}) = \{grass, horse\}$, $a(\{mouse\}) = \{mouse, cat\}$, $a(\{tail, grass\}) = \{tail, grass, horse\}$, $a(\{tail, mouse\}) = \{tail, mouse, cat\}$ and other combinations are unchanged with map a. Obviously, we can get "*cat*" from "*tail*" but, from both "*tail*" and "*grass*", we get "*horse*". Any graph constructed on the components cannot describe this situation exactly.

Although pretopology and its applications have been studied many years, there are little works in financial markets where the group impact cannot be ignored. In this work, we construct a pretopological space of stocks in a financial market and study its behavior following a price crash from a stock and see how others are affected. This problem has been widely studied, especially after the financial crisis in 2007–2008. The answer can be helpful for market managers, investors as well as corporations.

2   Pretopological Space of Stocks

Let E be the set of all listed stocks in a stock market. For considering the market as a system, the correlation coefficients of the returns calculated from stock prices are often used to get the relationships between pairs of stocks. Then, a graph whose nodes are stocks and edges defined from the node relationships are built. Since this graph is completed with many nodes and edges, scientists tend to consider its subgraphs such as its minimum spanning tree (MST) [19–22] or ones constructed by using a threshold of the node correlations [8, 22–24]. While MST is not good enough to reflect nodes relationships because of its constructing conditions, the latter is just a special case of our method using pretopology theory with a pseudoclosure defined as follow:

Definition 3. Given a positive constant θ and a nonincreasing concave function f from $\mathbb{N}^+$ into $\mathbb{R}^+ \cup \{0\}$, we define a function a from $\mathcal{P}(E)$ into $\mathcal{P}(E)$ such that:

$$a(\varnothing) = \varnothing,$$

$$\forall V \subset \mathcal{P}(E) \backslash \{\emptyset\}, \quad a(V) = V \cup \left\{ i \notin V \middle| \frac{1}{\|V\|} \sum_{j \in V} c_{ij} \geq \theta.f(\|V\|) \right\} \tag{2}$$

where c_{ij} is the correlation coefficient between returns of stock i and stock j; $\|V\|$ is the size of V, i.e. the number of stocks in V.

By Definition 1, (E, a) is a pretopological space. The pseudoclosure a helps to expand V by adding stocks whose the average of correlations between their returns and returns of stocks in V must not be smaller than the threshold relied on θ and $\|V\|$.

About the role of the function f, we can see that the effect of a group to an individual is often stronger than that of a smaller group. For example, in medicine, measles must be more dangerous if it is accompanied by bronchitis and diarrhea; in computer networks, the more computers send signals to a hub, the more likely the connection's quality decrease; in social science, because of the crowd effect, people normally act or think similarly to a group and the probability of this phenomena almost increases with the crowd size. Especially, in the literature of financial markets worldwide, we saw many times that more and more investors, governed by greed and fear, engaged buying or selling stocks frantically and consequently create economic bubbles or stock market crash. Thus, to construct influenced stocks of a stock group, we propose to consider the group's size as a factor which increases the group's influence on others. It means that the threshold decreases when the size of V increases. By contrast, if the size has no influence, f must be a constant function. Moreover, a change of the size of V must make more impact if its present size is large enough, so f should be concave.

On the other hand, since θ is a constant, it is a scaled factor for f. Thus, f can be assumed to get values between 0 and 1 without loss of generality, so $f(1)$ is equal to 1. Then, for any stock i_0, we have:

$$a(\{i_0\}) = \{i_0\} \cup \{k \neq i_0 | c_{ki_0} \geq \theta\} \tag{3}$$

As a result, if we start by a set of only one stock i_0, θ is expected to be the threshold helping to discover stocks whose returns are correlated most with the return of i_0 so that their price trends can be similar as much as possible. Naturally, the higher θ is, the better its function performs. However, with a too large θ, we may skip stocks having close relationships with i_0. In this work, we would like to follow the diffusion of the price fall from a given stock i_0 to the whole or a part of a market by observing the expanding process from $\{i_0\}$ to its closure. In the process, θ also takes an important role which is shown in Sect. 4. Obviously, we want to focus on a stock i_0 which has a great relationship with others. It is wondered whether the closure gives meaningful information about the sphere of influence of i_0 and how the infection spreads throughout the market.

3 Data and Method

3.1 Case Study: Merrill Lynch & Co.

The efficiency of the pseudoclosure in Definition 3 is tested with the stock Merrill Lynch & Co. as i_0. This stock, which traded under the symbol MER on the New York Stock Exchange (NYSE), is a common stock of an American investment bank existing independently from 1914 until January 2009. Its brokerage network was so remarkable that it had the ability to move stocks, securities and bonds based on its interests and that of its clients. However, from the second half of 2007, its serious losses were announced in the ongoing mortgage crisis. Its stock price also declined significantly during that time. On September 14, 2008, it was announced to be purchased by Bank of America. Its last trading day before the acquisition's completion is December 31, 2008. We can find the company's history when it was an independent one from this link: en. wikipedia.org/wiki/Merrill_Lynch_%26_Co.

3.2 Database

In order to investigate the infection of the price fall of MER, we consider its closing price time series and find the time when it declined seriously. In fact, it is generally seen that relation of stocks in developed markets is relatively close, especially among stocks in the same sector. Hence, a negative price motion of a stock whose influence was not small like MER must be already observed, and when it had fallen significantly, the market could be affected even long before its consolidated day. During one year before the day, its price peaked at 58.4 dollars on February 1, 2008, and quickly fell more than 70% since September 12, 2008 (see Fig. 1). The significantly fallen day is used as a milestone to see serious down trends in other stocks which are highly correlated with MER. However, we consider only stocks being components of the S&P 500 index at that time. This index is the most popular ones of the U.S market which tracks 500 large-cap companies. Other stocks on NYSE are not mentioned because of not only their large number and their less important role in the U.S market but also the difficulty to get their historical prices before mergers, acquisitions, bankruptcies and removal decisions from the committee. Due to the difficulty of getting historical prices of delisted or consolidated stocks, our database contains just $N = 489$ stocks with their adjusted closing prices from September 12, 2006, to March 12, 2009.

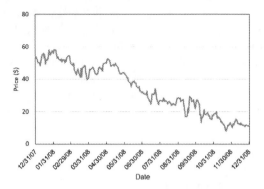

Fig. 1. Adjusted closing price (dollars) of MER from 12/31/2007 to 12/31/2008 (Source: Investorpoint.com)

3.3   Method

We investigate 6 months after the milestone day to find out the set H of risky stocks whose prices fall down more than 70% after this day. The stocks delisted or consolidated in this period are still examined until their last trading days. As a result, there are 101 stocks (without MER) in our database belonging to H. We use H to validate the pseudoclosure in Definition 3. As mentioned in Sect. 2, the pseudoclosure of $\{i_0\}$ is expected to be able to predict stocks most affected by i_0 and vice versa. Moreover, applying the pseudoclosure map many times until no expansion can occur to get $F(\{i_0\})$ may give opportunities to track the path that the extreme decline of MER's price spreads throughout the market (see the below algorithm).

Require: set of all stocks E, seed stock i_0, positive constant θ, nonincreasing concave function f
procedure Finding_Closure(E, i_0, θ, f)
$t \leftarrow 0$, $V \leftarrow \varnothing$, $a(V) \leftarrow i_0$
  while $a(V) \neq V$ **do**
    $t \leftarrow t + 1$, $V \leftarrow a(V)$

$$a(V) \leftarrow V \cup \left\{ i \in E \setminus V \,\middle|\, \frac{1}{\|V\|} \sum_{j \in V} c_{ij} \geq \theta.f\left(\|V\|\right) \right\}$$

  end while
  return $a(V)$
end procedure

We use the following measures to evaluate this method:

• *Precision*: Precision of a set is the fraction of the number of really risky stocks belonging to the set. This is an important measure used to define the probability of right predict when applying our pseudoclosure.

- *Recall*: Recall of a set is the ratio of the number of really risky stocks detected from the set to the size of H. Someone such as market managers may take care of this measure since it provides the capacity that the risky set H can be predicted.

In order to run the algorithm, firstly, we estimate the correlation coefficients of stock returns on the milestone day. Generally, a too long historical period cannot capture the short-term stock prices' relation, especially in a crisis. By contrast, a too short period may increase the estimate's error. In this study, we use the adjusted closing prices in two years before the milestone day.

Secondly, we select a suitable value for parameter θ. As mentioned in Sect. 2, θ should be large enough to expand the initial set $\{i_0\}$ with the most related risky stocks. The precision of $a(\{i_0\})$ as a function of θ is demonstrated in Fig. 2. We can see that if θ is larger or equal 0.768, i.e. 99.84%-quantile of correlation coefficients between pairs of stock returns in our database, only 3 or fewer stocks are added to $a(\{i_0\})$ but all of them belong to H. However, let be careful with a too large θ because it seems difficult to continue expanding $a(\{i_0\})$. Further details are given in Sect. 4.

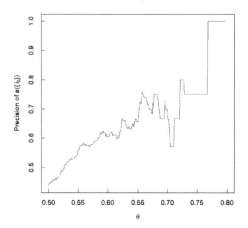

Fig. 2. Precision of the pseudoclosure of MER

Finally, we choose a function f which defined on $\overline{1,N}$, nondecreasing, concave and get values from 0 to 1. One of the simple functions that we look forward to satisfying the conditions is the inverse function. So, we try on constructing the pseudoclosure in Definition 3 as following: let N be the size of E and γ be a nonnegative constant then

$$f(x) = \left(\frac{N}{N-1}\right)^{\gamma}\left(\frac{1}{x-N-1}+1\right)^{\gamma}, \quad x = \overline{1,N} \tag{4}$$

The parameter γ is used to adjust flexure of the curve suiting with the market's behavior because the change's rate of function f can vary in different markets and timeline. Indeed, the curve is less concave if γ is larger (see Fig. 3). Hence, the larger γ is, the more impact of risky stock number is supposed to affect others.

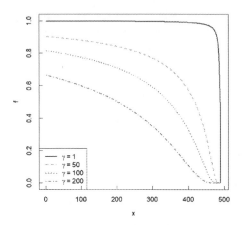

Fig. 3. Graph of function f with different values of γ

4 Results

Figure 4 shows that the recall of $\mathbf{F}(\{i_0\})$ is a decreasing function of θ and an increasing ones of γ (since a larger θ or lower γ makes the threshold higher) but the precision of $\mathbf{F}(\{i_0\})$ has different behaviors in each case of value of θ including (i) small ($\theta < 0.65$), (ii) medium ($0.65 \leq \theta \leq 0.72$) and (iii) large ($\theta > 0.72$). In the following, γ is changed from 1 to 200 if there is no further information.

In case (i), the precision of $\mathbf{F}(\{i_0\})$ is close to an increasing function of θ and a decreasing function of γ whose maximum value is found at $\gamma = 0$. Thus, it is unnecessary to decrease the threshold when the size increases. Besides, for any γ and small θ, the precision decreases gradually through expanding steps while the recall changes hardly. Figure 5 shows an example of this observation in the case when γ equals to 0, where the expanding process is stopped after only two or three steps.

In case (ii), the precision of $\mathbf{F}(\{i_0\})$ is almost higher than that in case (i) and also higher than that of $a(\{i_0\})$ with a suitable γ. Figure 6 shows an example of $\theta = 0.72$, both precision and recall of $\mathbf{F}(\{i_0\})$ found in the last step are higher than those of $a(\{i_0\})$.

Finally, in case (iii), we found that the precision of $\mathbf{F}(\{i_0\})$ is significantly high (larger or equal than 75%) for all γ but the recall is just about 3% (red area on top of Fig. 4(b)). It means that only 3 risky stocks in a total of 101 ones are discovered by $\mathbf{F}(\{i_0\})$ which coincides with $a(\{i_0\})$ for all γ.

In the following paragraphs, we propose some interpretation of the above results.

Firstly, when θ is small, many stocks, which are not affected much by i_0, still belongs to $a(\{i_0\})$ since θ is the threshold of correlation between i_0 and another stock so that the latter can be added into $a(\{i_0\})$ according to (3). Consequently, in the next expanding steps, more and more such stocks are added because of the threshold's decline. A larger γ makes this problem more serious because it results in a larger change's rate of f as discussed in Sect. 3.3.

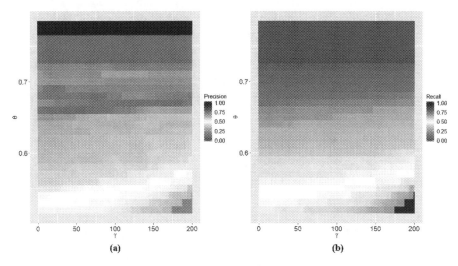

Fig. 4. Precision (a) and recall (b) of $F(\{i_0\})$ as a function of θ and γ (Color figure online)

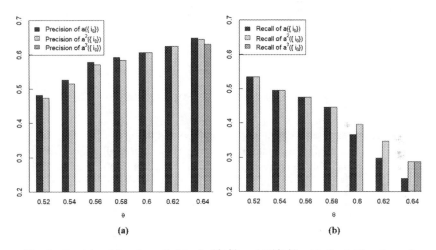

Fig. 5. Precision (a) and recall (b) of $a(\{i_0\})$ and $F(\{i_0\})$ with $\theta < 0.65$ and $\gamma = 0$

By contrast, if θ is large, we found high precision but extremely low recall because it is too difficult to get more risky stocks related to i_0 since the threshold is too high. Apparently, for a given function f, such large θ helps to find risky stocks related most to i_0 but we can neglect stocks whose returns are also correlated highly enough to be influenced by i_0. The price of those neglected stocks might not decline enough to be considered as risky ones because the influence of i_0 on the corresponding companies can be weakened due to their better business, larger market capitals, longer operation... However, although a crash happening at stock i_0 may have a smaller impact at a robust stock k but can cause a large decline in stock j which are related tightly enough with both i_0 and k. It is similar to the existence of some viruses in a person's body without causing any serious illnesses because of his resistance or treatment. Unluckily, other people contacting closely to that man could be infected and have dangerous symptoms.

Consequently, a medium θ may not skip not only other risky stocks most related to i_0 but also intermediate stocks in the infected process of the price crash. Thus, both precision and recall of $\mathbf{F}(\{i_0\})$ are higher than those of $a(\{i_0\})$ as seen in Fig. 6.

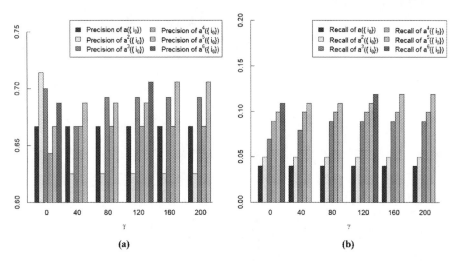

Fig. 6. Precision (a) and recall (b) in each expanding step from $\{i_0\}$ to $\mathbf{F}(\{i_0\})$ with $\theta = 0.72$

In summary, θ is selected to satisfy the prediction's purpose. If we only care about the precision of the prediction, θ should be large but if the recall is also important, a smaller θ is more suitable. However, a too small θ implies a low precision. Figure 7 gives details about the measures in some special cases of θ when γ changes.

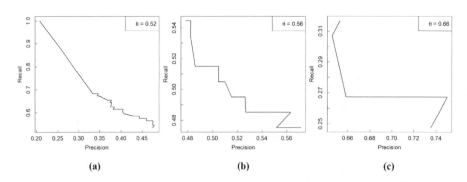

Fig. 7. Precision and recall of $\mathbf{F}(\{i_0\})$ when γ changes and (a) $\theta = 0.52$, (b) $\theta = 0.56$, (c) $\theta = 0.66$

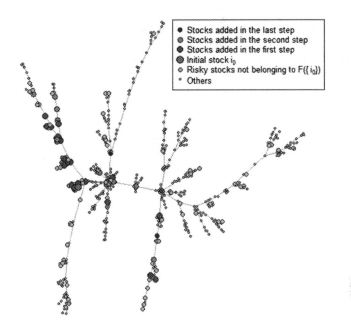

Fig. 8. MST of the stock network and the expanding process from $\{i_0\}$ with $\theta = 0.66$, $\gamma = 50$

Finally, let's observe stocks added in each individual step of the dilation process from $\{i_0\}$ to $\mathbf{F}(\{i_0\})$ in order to get the diffusion process of the price crash from i_0. We consider $\theta = 0.66$ and $42.5 \leq \gamma \leq 62.5$. In this case, the precision of $\mathbf{F}(\{i_0\})$ is 75%, the recall is 26.73% and the stocks added in each step are shown in Fig. 8. We found that the diffusion usually goes through MST of the corresponding stock network but sometimes it can reach a distanced stock. We suppose that this difference is due to the way the MST is constructed, with which some largely weighted connections could be ignored. Moreover, our method studies the relationship between each stock and a certain group instead of focus on the relationship of every pair of stocks. Therefore, our pretopological approach can be an improvement in which all stocks, as well as relationships between all pairs of stocks, are not ignored.

5 Conclusion

In this work, we propose a pretopological space to model the diffusion of distress stocks in the market. We define a pseudoclosure a with two main parameters θ and γ as an expansion of a given set by adding outside stocks whose returns have high enough correlation in average with stocks in the set. The threshold is lower if the size of the given set is larger. For checking the model's efficiency, we study the case of stock MER. The moment when this stock dropped 70% is considered as a sign of a potential alarm. Then, we study how our model reflects the diffusion and evaluate the results by two measures: precision and recall. After applying a many times for the set of single stock MER until getting its closure, we found that the diffusion process could be distinguished into three cases of value of parameter θ: large, medium and small. A suitable θ depends on the prediction's purpose. Lastly, if we are relatively interested in the precision, we propose an "optimal" parameter set $\theta = 0.66$, $42.5 \leq \gamma \leq 62.5$ and visualize the pretopological percolation. We found that our approach can capture stocks that are not directly linked by MST of the corresponding stock network. In conclusion, pretopology theory can be an efficient tool to study dynamic processes in stock markets. It allows us to take into account all stocks' relationships and to follow a diffusion of a stock's price crash with less computation as in graph theory. In the next studies, we may consider not only the pseudoclosure but also the interior of the pretopological space to give another vision of diffusion from the receiver's side. With such improvement, one can continue by considering other pretopological pseudoclosure functions and parameters, as well as other markets in the future.

Acknowledgement. This research is funded by Vietnam National University Ho Chi Minh City (VNU-HCM), Ho Chi Minh city, Vietnam under grant number B2018-42-01.

References

1. Whitesides, G.M., Ismagilov, R.F.: Complexity in chemistry. Science **284**, 89–92 (1999). https://doi.org/10.1126/science.284.5411.89
2. Parrish, J.K., Edelstein-Keshet, L.: Complexity, pattern, and evolutionary trade-offs in animal aggregation. Science **284**, 99–101 (1999). https://doi.org/10.1126/science.284.5411.99
3. Foote, R.: Mathematics and complex systems. Science **318**, 410–412 (2007). https://doi.org/10.1126/science.1141754
4. Newman, M.E.J.: Complex systems: a survey. Am. J. Phys. **79**, 800–810 (2011). https://doi.org/10.1119/1.3590372
5. Albert, R., Jeong, H., Barabasi, A.L.: Error and attack tolerance of complex networks. Nature **406**, 378–382 (2000). https://doi.org/10.1038/35019019
6. Cohen, R., Erez, K., Ben-Avraham, D., Havlin, S.: Breakdown of the Internet under intentional attack. Phys. Rev. Lett. **86**, 3682–3685 (2001). https://doi.org/10.1103/PhysRevLett.86.3682
7. Nie, T., Guo, Z., Zhao, K., Lu, Z.-M.: New attack strategies for complex networks. Physica A **424**, 248–253 (2015). https://doi.org/10.1016/j.physa.2015.01.004
8. Nguyen, N.K.K., Nguyen, Q.: Resilience of stock cross-correlation network to random breakdown and intentional attack. In: Anh, L.H., Dong, L.S., Kreinovich, V., Thach, N.N. (eds.) ECONVN 2018. SCI, vol. 760, pp. 553–561. Springer, Cham (2018). https://doi.org/10.1007/978-3-319-73150-6_44
9. Buldyrev, S.V., Parshani, R., Paul, G., Stanley, H.E., Havlin, S.: Catastrophic cascade of failures in interdependent networks. Nature **464**, 1025–1028 (2010). https://doi.org/10.1038/nature08932
10. Berezin, Y., Bashan, A., Danziger, M.M., Li, D., Havlin, S.: Localized attacks on spatially embedded networks with dependencies. Sci. Rep. **5**, 8934 (2015). https://doi.org/10.1038/srep08934
11. Belmandt, Z.: Basics of Pretopology. Hermann, Paris (2011)

12. Levorato, V., Bui, M.: Modeling the complex dynamics of distributed communities of the web with pretopology. In: Proceedings of the 7th International Workshop on Innovative Internet Community Systems (I2CS), Munich, Germany, p. 2 (2007)

13. Lamure, M., Bonnevay, S., Bui, M., Amor, S.B.: A stochastic and pretopological modeling aerial pollution of an urban area. Stud. Inform. Uni. **7**, 410–426 (2009)

14. Amor, S.B., Bui, M., Lamure, M.: Modeling urban aerial pollution using stochastic pretopology. Afr. Math. Ann. J. Afr. Math. Uni. **1**, 7–19 (2010)

15. Auray, J.-P., Duru, G., Mougeot, M.: A pretopological analysis of the input-output model. Eco. Lett. **2**, 343–347 (1979). https://doi.org/10.1016/0165-1765(79)90048-X

16. Bonnevay, S.: Pretopological operators for gray-level image analysis. Stud. Inform. Univ. **7**, 175–195 (2009)

17. Petermann, C., Amor, S.B., Bui, A.: A pretopological multi-agents based model for an efficient and reliable Smart Grid simulation. In: 14th International Conference on Artificial Intelligence (ICAI), USA, pp. 354–360. CSREA Press (2012)

18. Guérard, G., Amor, S.B., Bui, A.: A context-free Smart Grid model using pretopologic structure. In: 14th International Conference on Smart Cities and Green ICT Systems, Lisbon, Portugal, vol. 1, pp. 335–341. SciTePress (2015). https://doi.org/10.5220/0005409203350341

19. Mantegna, R.N.: Hierarchical structure in financial markets. Eur. Phys. J. B **11**, 193–197 (1999). https://doi.org/10.1007/s100510050929

20. Vandewalle, N., Brisbois, F., Tordoir, X.: Non-random topology of stock markets. Quant. Fi. **1**, 372–374 (2001). https://doi.org/10.1088/1469-7688/1/3/308

21. Bonanno, G., Caldarelli, G., Lillo, F., Micciche, S., Vandewalle, N., Mantegna, R.N.: Networks of equities in financial markets. Eur. Phys. J. B **38**, 363–371 (2004). https://doi.org/10.1140/epjb/e2004-00129-6

22. Nguyen, Q., Nguyen, N.K.K., Nguyen, L.H.N.: Dynamic topology and allometric scaling behavior on the Vietnamese stock market. Physica A **514**, 235–243 (2019). https://doi.org/10.1016/j.physa.2018.09.061

23. Onnela, J.-P., Kaski, K., Kertsz, J.: Clustering and information in correlation based financial networks. Eur. Phys. J. B **38**, 353–362 (2004). https://doi.org/10.1140/epjb/e2004-00128-7

24. Garas, A., Argyrakis, P., Havlin, S.: The structural role of weak and strong links in a financial market network. Eur. Phys. J. B **63**, 265–271 (2008). https://doi.org/10.1140/epjb/e2008-00237-3

A Cognitive Temporal-Causal Network Model of Hormone Therapy

S. Sahand Mohammadi Ziabari[(⊠)] [ID]

Social AI Group, Vrije Universiteit Amsterdam, De Boelelaan 1105,
Amsterdam, The Netherlands
sahandmohammadiziabari@gmail.com

Abstract. In this paper, the effect of using sex hormones such as estrogen and producing this hormone in the body using cognitive, biological temporal-causal network model is presented. Reviewing neuroscience pieces of literature about hormone therapy shows the effect of estrogen on some brain components such as basolateral Amygdala, ventromedial Prefrontal Cortex, Hippocampus and resulting in decreasing the extreme emotion. This finding shows that for post-natal depression transdermal estrogen is an effective treatment. Moreover, the presented model integrates the cognitive, biological and effective principle of neuroscience.

Keywords: Cognitive temporal-causal network model · Extreme emotion · Hormone therapy · Hebbian learning

1 Introduction

During recent years many studies have been done on how the amount of generating hormones can affect the stress level of women and vice versa. These can be seen in women than men [11]. These sex hormones in women most of the time synthesized by the ovaries and testes in women and adrenal glands in both men and women. These sex hormones are called neuro-steroids. Many studies concentrated on fluctuations of sex hormones in women such as estrogen and their impacts on brain and behavioral changes [17]. There are some previous works in temporal-causal modeling via network-oriented modeling on the cognitive behavior of the patient in a stressful condition [23, 25–38].

The paper is organized as follows. In Sect. 2 the neurological principles of the brain components involved in stress and are discussed. In Sect. 3 the integrative temporal-causal network model is defined. In Sect. 4 the results of the simulation model are presented, and finally in Sect. 5 the conclusion is presented.

2 Underlying Neurological Principles

The role of response to the stress in both physical and mental threats is remarkable as it emerges from the evolutionary aspect of human being and necessary for being alive in dangerous situations such as accident, natural disasters. There are two categories of

© Springer Nature Switzerland AG 2019
N. T. Nguyen et al. (Eds.): ICCCI 2019, LNAI 11683, pp. 650–660, 2019.
https://doi.org/10.1007/978-3-030-28377-3_54

responses to the stress and tough situations for different genders, fight or flight for males, and tend and be-friend for females [23].

The cognitive view of the model presented in Sect. 3 is based on the book published by Damasio [6]. The sensory optical cortex of brain components acts as the sensory representation of the model. Then the perceive of the stimulus, here stressful condition, and feeling of the phenomena works in the brain and it brings the feeling state in the brain and availability for responding and preparation for the stress comes later.

In many recent pieces of research literature, the effect of sex hormone on the brain components has been discovered. Brain parts involved in fear and extreme emotion extinction are namely amygdala, hippocampus, and medial prefrontal cortex [13]. Literatures in [16, 19, 21] concluded that these brain parts contain a vast major level of estrogen. These shreds of evidences are in line with the temporal-causal model which is presented in the paper.

Like females, males also experience fluctuations in sex hormone levels depending on season and days but few investigations have been done on this topic [18]. There is also a study on which how hormone therapy can affect women. This finding shows that for postnatal depression transdermal estrogen is an effective treatment [9].

There is a large body of literature about the influence of sex hormones such as estrogen on regulating neural plasticity of the hippocampus in fear extinction. The next brain components involved in extreme emotion extinction is amygdala, basolateral amygdala more specifically, and the intercalated GABAergic neurons within the amygdala as it has been mentioned in [1, 2, 14]. Moreover, in [15, 20] the major role of the amygdala is discussed.

Another component in the brain which is involved in modulating called ventro-medial prefrontal cortex (vmPFC). It also plays an important role in consolidation.

In order to make a precise conceptual cognitive and biological temporal causal network going deep into neuroscientific literature was necessary and based on the findings in [12] there is a connection via neurons from thalamus into amygdala and based on [7, 8] manipulations of hippocampal inputs to IL. Another brain part involved in extreme emotion extinction is hippocampus. Based on studies [3, 5] hippocampus can learn about the context in which extreme emotion and fear is happening and manage to learn to do extinction. The accurate connection activation among hippocampus and either amygdala or vmPFC has been mentioned in [4]. In the extinction condition, based on the situation, the hippocampus can activate neurons to amygdala or IL neurons. In [Gupta] the role of increase estrogen level on decreasing of contextual conditioning.

3   The Temporal-Causal Network Model

In the first part the Network-Oriented Modelling approach used to model the integrative overall process is thoroughly explained. As discussed in detail in [22, Ch 2] this approach is constructed on temporal-causal network models which can be defined at two levels: firstly, representing by a conceptual representation and secondly, by a numerical representation.

A conceptual representation of a model in the first step contains presenting in a explainable manner states and connections between them that illustrate (causal) influences of states on each other.

The states are assumed to have (triggering) levels that alters over time. In reality, not all causal relations are equally strong, so some notion of *strength of a connection* is used. Furthermore, when more than one causal relation influences a state, some way to *aggregate multiple causal impacts* on a state is applied. Furthermore, a notion of *speed of change* of a state is used for timing of the processes. These three notions form the defining part of a conceptual representation of a temporal-causal network model:

- **Strength of a connection** $\omega_{X,Y}$ The *connection weight value* $\omega_{X,Y}$ representing the strength of the connection, usually between 0 and 1, but sometimes also below 0 (negative effect) or above 1.
- **Combining multiple impacts on a state** $c_Y(..)$ The *combination function* $c_Y(..)$ is chosen to combine the causal impacts of other states on state Y for each state.
- **Speed of change of a state** η_Y Representing a *speed factor* η_Y For each state means how fast a state is altering during a time and upon causal impact.

Figure 1 illustrates the conceptual representation of the temporal-causal network mode. The components of the conceptual representation shown in Fig. 1 are explained here. The state ws_c shows the world state of the contextual stimulus c. The states ss_c and ss_{ee} are the sensor state for the context c and sensor state of the body state ee for the extreme emotion. The states srs_c and srs_{ee} are the sensory representation of the contextual stimulus c and the extreme emotion, respectively. The state srs_{ee} is a stimulus influencing the activation level of the preparation state. Furthermore, ps_{ee} is the preparation state of an extreme emotional response to the sensory representation srs_c of the context c, and fs_{ee} shows the feeling state associated to this extreme emotion. The state es_{ee} indicates the execution of the body state for the extreme emotion. All these relate to the affective processes. The (cognitive) goal state shows the goal for using hormone (estrogen here) in the body. The (cognitive) state ps_H is the preparation state of using (here estrogen). The state es_H is the execution state of using hormone (estrogen). The other states relate to biological brain components (Estrogen produced in the body, Thalamus, Amygdala, Hypothalamus, Hippocampus, ventromedial Prefrontal Cortex) which are involved in the extreme emotion condition, and in the influence of the estrogen applied.

The connection weights ω_i in Fig. 1 are presented as follows. The sensor states ss_{ee}, ss_{cc} have two incoming connections from ws_{ee} (weights ω_1). The world state of extreme emotion ws_{ee} has one incoming connection from es_{ee}, with a weight ω_{11}. The sensory representation state of an extreme emotion srs_{ee} has two arriving connection weights ω_8 and ω_3 from state preparation state of an extreme emotion ps_{ee} and sensory representation state of extreme emotion, respectively. The feeling state fs_{ee} has one incoming connection weight ω_5 from srs_{ee}. The preparation state of an extreme emotion ps_{ee} has five arriving connection weights ω_6, ω_7, ω_{27}, ω_{25}, ω_{26} from states srs_c, fs_{ee}, vmPFC, Hypothalamus, and Hippocampus, respectively. The preparation state of an extreme emotion ps_{ee} has two outgoing connection weights, es_{ee}, and srs_c, (ω_{10}, ω_7), respectively (Table 1).

Table 1. Explanation of the states in the model

X_1	ws_{ee}	World (body) state of extreme emotion ee
X_2	ss_{ee}	Sensor state of extreme emotion ee
X_3	ws_c	World state for context c
X_4	ss_c	Sensor state for context c
X_5	srs_{ee}	Sensory representation state of extreme emotion ee
X_6	srs_c	Sensory representation state of context c
X_7	fs_{ee}	Feeling state for extreme emotion ee
X_8	ps_{ee}	Preparation state for extreme emotion ee
X_9	es_{ee}	Execution state (bodily expression) of extreme emotion ee
X_{10}	goal	Goal of using hormone (estrogen)
X_{11}	ps_H	Preparation state of using hormone (estrogen)
X_{12}	es_H	Execution of using hormone (estrogen)
X_{13}	Estrogen	Hormone
X_{14}	Thalamus	Brain part
X_{15}	Amygdala	Brain part
X_{16}	Hypothalamus	Brain part
X_{17}	Hippocampus	Brain part
X_{18}	vmPFC	Brain part

The goal has one arriving connection weight from the sensory representation srs_{ee} (ω_{12}) and preparation state ps_H an entering connection from the goal with weight ω_{11}. The execution of using hormone (here estrogen) is named es_H, and has an entering connection weight ω_{21} from preparation state of using hormone ps_H. The state Thalamus has an incoming connection weight ω_{13} from sensory representation state of extreme emotion srs_{ee}. The Estrogen hormone has two entering connection weights ω_{17} from es_H and ω_{14} from Thalamus. The Hippocampus in brain has one incoming connection weight ω_{16} from Estrogen. The Hypothalamus in brain has one incoming connection weight ω_{15} from estrogen. The Amygdala has three entering connection weights ω_{18}, ω_{20}, ω_{22} from Estrogen, Thalamus, and vmPFC, respectively. Note that the connection weight between states vmPFC and Amygdala is adaptive and using Hebbian learning means through time will be changed. The vmPFC has only one entering connection weight ω_{23} from Amygdala.

The aforementioned conceptual representation was presented into a numerical representation as follows [21, Ch 2]:

- Each state Y in the model has a real number value in the interval [0, 1] at each time point t, represented by $Y(t)$
- The effect of one state X connected to state Y with having an effect on Y At each time point t, defined as **impact**$_{X,Y}(t) = \omega_{X,Y} X(t)$ where $\omega_{X,Y}$ is the weight of the connection from X to Y

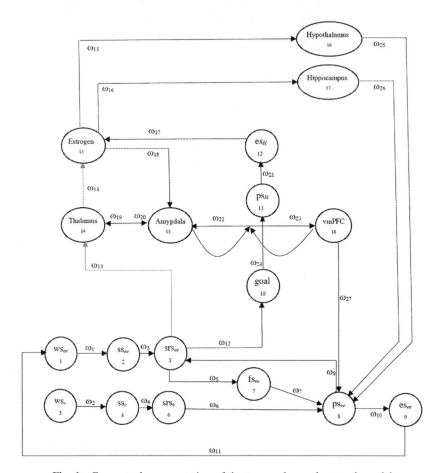

Fig. 1. Conceptual representation of the temporal-causal network model

- The *aggregated impact* of multiple states X_i on Y at t is determined using a *combination function* $c_Y(..)$:

$$\mathbf{aggimpact}_Y(t) = \mathbf{c}_Y(\mathbf{impact}_{X_1, Y}(t), ..., \mathbf{impact}_{X_k, Y}(t))$$
$$= \mathbf{c}_Y(\omega_{X_1, Y} X_1(t), ..., \omega_{X_k, Y} X_k(t))$$

where X_i are the states with connections to state Y

- The effect of $\mathbf{aggimpact}_Y(t)$ on Y is exerted over time gradually, depending on speed factor η_Y:

$$Y(t+\Delta t) = Y(t) + \eta_Y [\mathbf{aggimpact}_Y(t) - Y(t)] \Delta t$$
or $$dY(t)/dt = \eta_Y [\mathbf{aggimpact} Y(t) - Y(t)]$$

- Thus, the following *difference* and *differential equation* for Y are obtained:

$$Y(t+\Delta t) = Y(t) + \eta_Y [\mathbf{c}_Y(\omega_{X_1,Y}X_1(t), \ldots, \omega_{X_k,Y}X_k(t)) - Y(t)] \Delta t$$
$$\mathbf{d}Y(t)/\mathbf{d}t = \eta_Y [\mathbf{c}_Y(\omega_{X_1,Y}X_1(t), \ldots, \omega_{X_k,Y}X_k(t)) - Y(t)]$$

For each state the upcoming combination functions $\mathbf{c}_Y(\ldots)$ were used, the identity function **id**(.) for states with impact from only one other state, and for states with multiple impacts the scaled sum function $\mathbf{ssum}_\lambda(\ldots)$ with scaling factor λ, and the advanced logistic sum function $\mathbf{alogistic}_{\sigma,\tau}(\ldots)$ with steepness σ and threshold τ.

$$\mathbf{id}(V) = V$$
$$\mathbf{ssum}_\lambda(V_1, \ldots, V_k) = (V_1 + \ldots + V_k)/\lambda$$
$$\mathbf{alogistic}_{\sigma,\tau}(V_1, \ldots, V_k) = [(1/(1+e^{-\sigma(V_1+\ldots+V_k-\tau)})) - 1/(1+e^{\sigma\tau})] (1+e^{-\sigma\tau})$$

4 Example Simulation

The simulation results of the cognitive temporal causal network model, which was constructed based on the neurological science which contains qualitative empirical information (such as fMRI) both for the mechanism by which the brain components work and for emerging result of the processes, has been shown in Fig. 2.

Therefore, one can imply that the best option for declining the stress level has been chosen, given the usage of fluoxetine. The model used the Matlab codes which have been implemented in [24]. Using appropriate connections weights make the model numerical and adapted to qualitative empirical information. Table 2 illustrates the connection weights that has been used, where the values for are initial values as these weights are adapted over time. The time step was $\Delta t = 1$. The scaling factors λ_i for the nodes with more than one arriving connection weights are mentioned in Table 2. At first, an external world state of an extreme emotion-stimuli context c (represented by ws_c) will influence

Table 2. Connection weights and scaling factors for the example simulation

Connection weight	ω_1	ω_2	ω_3	ω_4	ω_5	ω_6	ω_7	ω_8	ω_{10}	ω_{11}	ω_{12}	ω_{13}
Value	1	1	1	1	1	1	1	1	1	1	1	-0.01
Connection Weight	ω_{14}	ω_{15}	ω_{16}	ω_{17}	ω_{18}	ω_{19}	ω_{20}	ω_{21}	ω_{22}	ω_{23}	ω_{24}	ω_{25}
Value	-0.01	1	1	1	1	1	1	1	0.2	0.2	-0.9	-0.9
Connection Weight	ω_{26}											
Value	-0.9											

state	X_5	X_8	X_{13}	X_{15}
λ_i	2	3	2	1

the affective internal states of the individual by influencing the emotional response es_{ee} (via ss_c, srs_c, and ps_{ee}) conducted to manifest the extreme emotion by body state ws_{ee}. As a consequence, the stressed individual senses the extreme emotion (and at the same time all the biological brain components increased over time), so as a cognitive process, as a next step the goal becomes active to decrease this stress level by using hormone at time around 100.

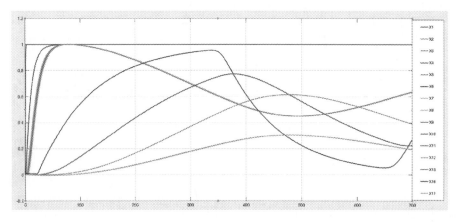

Fig. 2. Simulation results for temporal-causal network modeling of the hormone therapy

As a biological process, the goal and in further steps, execution of using hormone stimulates the changes and suppression of execution of stress at the first state and this affects other brain components to be less active around time 100 and continues until time around 500. However, this effect is just temporary, and as the stressful context c still is present all the time, after a while the stress level goes up again, which in turn again leads to activation of the goal and performing another desire or prescription of using hormone, and so on and on repeatedly until the person or the doctor decides to stop taking hormone. The fluctuation in Fig. 2 shows how in real life the repeated usage of hormone (here estrogen) decreases the stress level over each intake. It is worth to tell that all of this fluctuation is produced internally by the model; the environment is constant, external input for the model is only the constant world state ws_c. Therefore, based on the simulation results it is shown that the model for hormone therapy (estrogen) works as expected. The model has been implemented in [24].

In Fig. 3, the equilibrium situation where there is not an active goal (intake) has been shown. Based on this figure, when there is no intake, not using hormone, (the goal is blocked in an artificial manner here), the stress level and activity of brain parts go up and stay high.

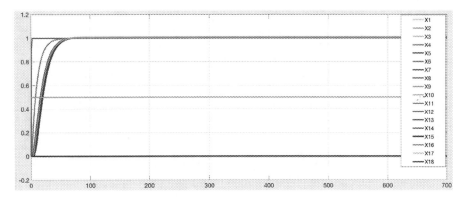

Fig. 3. Simulation results for equilibrium state without using hormone

5 Conclusion

In this paper, a cognitive temporal causal network-oriented model of therapy by using hormone (estrogen) for individuals under stress is introduced in which usage of hormone is done. The proposed model can be used to test the different hypothesis and neurological principles about the impacts of the brain and the effects that different brain areas have the extinction of stress, but also on other processes.

In the current paper stress was modelled as mental stress, without taking the physical effects hormone (estrogen) and the effect on stress into account. Especially with higher doses of the hormone, physical effects can become more noticeable. These physical effects of hormone might cause subjective feelings of stress or nervousness (e.g. due to tremor or increased heart-rate), future research could determine this further. Thereby, is a different modelling approach useful in the future, taking hormone doses and hormone tolerance into account since this enhances dopamine levels and its effects. Finally, evidence has been found that there are age differences in stress response and hormone consumption and uptake. Therefore, future modelling approaches could take this into account as well.

Some simulations have been implemented, one of which was presented in the paper. This model can be considered as a basis of a cognitive model to get insight in such processes and to conclude a certain therapy or treatment of people to perform the treatments of extreme emotions for post-traumatic disorder individuals.

References

1. Arnano, T., Unal, C.T., Pare, D.: Synaptic correlates of fear extinction in the amygdala. Nat. Neurosci. **13**, 489–494 (2010)
2. Arnir, A., Anano, T., Pare, D.: Physiological identification and infralimbic responsiveness of rat intercalated amygdala neurons. J. Neurophysiol. **105**, 3054–3066 (2011)

3. Bouton, M.E., Westbrrok, R.F., Corcoran, K.A., Maren, S.: Contextual and temporal modulation of extinction: behavioral and biological mechanisms. Biol. Psychiatry **60**, 352–360 (2006)
4. Corcoran, K.A., Maren, S.: Factors regulating the effects of hippocampal inactivation on renewal of conditional fear after extinction. Learn Mem. **11**, 598–603 (2004)
5. Corcoran, K.A., Quirk, G.J.: Recalling safety: cooperative functions of the ventromedial prefrontal cortex and the hippocampus in extinction. CNS Spectr. **12**, 200–206 (2007)
6. Damasio, A.: Self Comes to Mind: Constructing the Conscious Brain. Panthon Books, New York (2010)
7. Deschaux, O., Thevenet, A., Spennato, G., Arnaud, C., Moreau, J.L., Garcia, R.: Low-frequency stimulation of the hippocampus following fear extinction impairs both restoration of rapid eye movement sleep and retrieval of extinction memory. Neuroscience **170**, 92–98 (2010)
8. Deschaux, O., Motanis, H., Spennato, G., Moreau, J.L., Garcia, R.: Re-emergemnce of extinguished auditory-cued conditioned fear following a sub-conditioning procedure: effects of hippocampal and prefrontal tetanic simulations. Neurobiol. Learn. Mem. **95**, 510–518 (2011)
9. Gregoire, A.J.P., Kumar, R., Everitt, B., Henderson, A.F., Studd, J.W.W.: Transdermal oestrogen for treatment of severe postnatal depression. Lancet **347**(9006), 930–933 (1996)
10. Gupta, R.R., Sen, S., Diepenhorst, L.L., Rudick, C.N., Maren, S.: Estrogen modulates sexually dimorphic contextual fear conditioning and hippocampal long-term potentiation (LTP) in rats (1). Brain Res. **888**, 356–365 (2001)
11. Hausmann, M.: Why sex hormones matter for neuroscience: a very short review on sex, sex hormones, and functional brain asymmetries. J. Neurosci. Res. **95**, 40–49 (2017)
12. Herry, C., Garcia, R.: Behavioral and paired-pulse facilitation analyses of long-lasting depression at excitatory synapses in the medial prefrontal cortex in mice. Behav. Brain Res. **146**, 89–96 (2003)
13. Lebron-Milad, K., Milad, M.R.: Sex differences, gonadal hormones and the fear extinction network: implications for anxiety disorders. Biol. Mood Anxiety Disord. **2**, 3 (2012)
14. Likhtik, E., Popa, D., Apergis-Schoute, J., Fidacaro, G.A., Pare, D.: Amygdala intercalated neurons are required for expression of fear extinction. Nature **454**, 642–645 (2008)
15. Myers, K.M., Davis, M.: Mechanisms of fear extinction. Mol Psychiatry **12**, 120–150 (2007)
16. Montague, D., Weickert, C.S., Tomaskovic-Crook, E., Rothmond, D.A., Kleinman, J.E., Rubinow, D.R.: Oestrogen receptor alpha localization in prefrontal cortex of three mammalian species. J. Neuroendocrinol. **29**, 219–237 (2008)
17. Rupprecht, R.: Neuroactive steroids: mechanisms of action and neuropharmacological properties. Psychoneuroendocrinology **28**, 139–168
18. Smith, R.P., Coward, R.M., Kovac, J.R., Lipshultz, L.I.: The evidence for seasonal variations of testosterone in men. Maturitas **74**, 208–212
19. Spencer, J.L., Waters, E.M., Romeo, R.D., Wood, G.E., Milner, T.A., McEwen, B.S.: Uncovering the mechanisms of estrogen effects on hippocampal function. Front Neuroendocrinal **29**, 219–237 (2019)
20. Sortes-Bayon, F., Quirk, G.J.: Prefrontal control of fear: more than just extinction. Curr. Opin. Neurobiol. **20**, 231–235 (2010)
21. Walf, A.A., Frye, C.A.: A review and update of mechanisms of estrogen in the hippocampus and amygdala for anxiety and depression behavior. Neuropsychopharmachology **31**, 1097–1111 (2006)
22. Treur, J.: Network-Oriented Modeling: Addressing Complexity of Cognitive, Affective and Social Interactions. Springer, Cham (2016). https://doi.org/10.1007/978-3-319-45213-5

23. Mohammadi Ziabari, S.S., Treur, J.: Computational analysis of gender differences in coping with extreme stressful emotions. In: Proceedings of the 9th International Conference on Biologically Inspired Cognitive Architecture (BICA 2018). Elsevier, Czech Republic (2018)

24. Mohammadi Ziabari, S.S., Treur, J.: A modeling environment for dynamic and adaptive network models implemented in Matlab. In: Proceedings of the 4th International Congress on Information and Communication Technology (ICICT 2019), 25–26 February. Springer, London (2019)

25. Treur, J., Mohammadi Ziabari, S.S.: An adaptive temporal-causal network model for decision making under acute stress. In: Nguyen, N.T., Pimenidis, E., Khan, Z., Trawiński, B. (eds.) ICCCI 2018. LNCS (LNAI), vol. 11056, pp. 13–25. Springer, Cham (2018). https://doi.org/10.1007/978-3-319-98446-9_2

26. Mohammadi Ziabari, S.S., Treur, J.: Decision making under acute stress modeled by an adaptive temporal causal network model. Vietnam J. Comput. Sci. (2019, submitted)

27. Mohammadi-Ziabari, S.S., Treur, J.: Integrative biological, cognitive and affective modeling of a drug-therapy for a post-traumatic stress disorder. In: Fagan, D., Martín-Vide, C., O'Neill, M., Vega-Rodríguez, M.A. (eds.) TPNC 2018. LNCS, vol. 11324, pp. 292–304. Springer, Cham (2018). https://doi.org/10.1007/978-3-030-04070-3_23

28. Mohammadi Ziabari, S.S., Treur, J.: An adaptive cognitive temporal-causal network model of a mindfulness therapy based on music. In: Tiwary, U.S. (ed.) IHCI 2018. LNCS, vol. 11278, pp. 180–193. Springer, Cham (2018). https://doi.org/10.1007/978-3-030-04021-5_17

29. Mohammadi Ziabari, S.S., Treur, J.: Cognitive modeling of mindfulness therapy by autogenic training. In: Satapathy, S.C., Bhateja, V., Somanah, R., Yang, X.-S., Senkerik, R. (eds.) Information Systems Design and Intelligent Applications. AISC, vol. 863, pp. 53–66. Springer, Singapore (2019). https://doi.org/10.1007/978-981-13-3338-5_6

30. Lelieveld, I., Storre, G., Mohammadi Ziabari, S.S.: A temporal cognitive model of the influence of methylphenidate (Ritalin) on test anxiety. In: Proceedings of the 4th International Congress on Information and Communication Technology (ICICT 2019), 25–26 February. Springer, London (2019)

31. Mohammadi Ziabari, S.S., Treur, J.: An adaptive cognitive temporal-causal network model of a mindfulness therapy based on humor. NeuroIS Retreat, 4–6 June, Vienna, Austria (2019)

32. Mohammadi Ziabari, S.S.: Integrative cognitive and affective modeling of deep brain stimulation. In: Wotawa, F., Friedrich, G., Pill, I., Koitz-Hristov, R., Ali, M. (eds.) Advances and Trends in Artificial Intelligence. From Theory to Practice. LNCS, vol. 11606, pp. 608–615. Springer, Cham (2019). https://doi.org/10.1007/978-3-030-22999-3_52

33. Andrianov, A., Guerriero, E., Mohammadi Ziabari, S.S.: Cognitive modeling of mindfulness therapy: effects of yoga on overcoming stress. In: Herrera, F., Matsui, K., Rodríguez-González, S. (eds.) Distributed Computing and Artificial Intelligence. AISC, vol. 1003, pp. 79–86. Springer, Cham (2019). https://doi.org/10.1007/978-3-030-23887-2_10

34. de Haan, R.E., Blankert, M., Mohammadi Ziabari, S.S.: Integrative biological, cognitive and affective modeling of caffeine use on stress. In: Herrera, F., Matsui, K., Rodríguez-González, S. (eds.) Distributed Computing and Artificial Intelligence. AISC, vol. 1003, pp. 71–78. Springer, Cham (2019). https://doi.org/10.1007/978-3-030-23887-2_9

35. Mohammadi Ziabari, S.S.: An adaptive temporal-causal network model for stress extinction using fluoxetine. In: MacIntyre, J., Maglogiannis, I., Iliadis, L., Pimenidis, E. (eds.) AIAI 2019. IAICT, vol. 559, pp. 107–119. Springer, Cham (2019). https://doi.org/10.1007/978-3-030-19823-7_8

36. Mohammadi Ziabari, S.S., Gerritsen, C.: An adaptive temporal-causal network model using electroconvulsive therapy (ECT) for PTSD patients. In: 12th International Conference on Brain Informatics, BI (2019, submitted)

37. Langbroek, J., Treur, J., Mohammadi Ziabari, S.S.: A computational model of the influence of myelin excess for patients with post-traumatic stress disorder. In: Proceedings of the 18th International Conference on Artificial Intelligence and Soft Computing. Lecture in Notes in AI, Springer, June 16–20, Zakopane, Poland (2019)
38. Mohammadi Ziabari, S.S., Treur, J.: An adaptive cognitive temporal-causal model for extreme emotion extinction using psilocybin. In: International Conference on Hybrid Artificial Intelligent Systems (HAIS), 4–6 September, Leon, Spain (2019)

Innovations in Intelligent Systems

An Ontology-Based Approach for Preventing Incompatibility Problems of Quality Requirements During Cloud SLA Establishment

Taher Labidi[1,2(✉)], Zaineb Sakhrawi[1,3], Asma Sellami[1,3], and Achraf Mtibaa[1,2]

[1] Miracl Laboratory, University of Sfax, Sfax, Tunisia
[2] National School of Electronic and Telecommunications,
University of Sfax, Sfax, Tunisia
taherlabidi@gmail.com, achraf.mtibaa@enetcom.usf.tn
[3] Higher Institute of Computing and Multimedia, University of Sfax, Sfax, Tunisia
zaynebsakhraoui40@gmail.com, asma.sellami@isims.usf.tn

Abstract. Cloud computing paradigm has emerged as response to challenges of managing and delivering on-demand services, in which provider and customer are willing to sign a Service Level Agreement (SLA). Even though the SLA is used to specify the level of services provided and the guarantee where negotiated conditions are specified, customers are not always satisfied. In order to promote the use of SLA without any ambiguities in quality requirements definitions, it is useful to develop an ontology-based support tool that automate the process of generating SLA regarding the interaction among the ISO 25010 quality characteristics. We propose an approach that uses ontology to semantically classify the quality requirements into the quality characteristics such as described by ISO 25010 and define their relationships. Taking into account customer requirements and considering their interactions before using cloud service is one of the most important and difficult tasks of SLA establishment. Ontology is used to semantically define diverging quality requirements and their relationships. In order to show the applicability of our approach, a tool for SLA generation is implemented and tested.

Keywords: Cloud computing · Service Level Agreement · Ontology ·
ISO 25010 · NFR interaction · Quality requirements

1 Introduction

Cloud computing is used as the paradigm for enabling ubiquitous, convenient, on-demand network access to a shared pool of configurable cloud resources accessed through services. Companies offering this computing services/utility are called cloud providers to a cloud customer via Internet. With the integration of cloud services as a business solution in many software organizations, the Quality of Service (QoS) is becoming the main concern of both service providers and customers. QoS requirements are recorded as part of the Service Level Agreement

© Springer Nature Switzerland AG 2019
N. T. Nguyen et al. (Eds.): ICCCI 2019, LNAI 11683, pp. 663–675, 2019.
https://doi.org/10.1007/978-3-030-28377-3_55

(SLA). The SLA contains the negotiated conditions between service providers and customers [6]. It acts as a guarantee where the set of terms governs the executions of the specified services. SLA also states the penalties to be applied upon the violation of such terms [14].

It is therefore important to keep attention on the consequences derived from the internal elements of an SLA guarantee term violations. Establishing a successful SLA need to a system that takes into account the customer requirements and considers their relations before using a cloud service. In this research, we focus on identifying the Non-Functional Requirements (NFR) needed to be described in SLA establishment. Representing NFR must be in enough detail that providers have a clear description of the final service to be delivered. It is important to understand the customer's quality requirements (NFR) and to support their relations before the beginning of design or building a computer-based solution. Generally speaking, requirements establish the basis for an agreement between customers and contractors or providers on what the system will do as well as what it is not expected to do. Clarifying quality requirements and identifying their interactions before preparing the software design create the opportunity for software organization to prevent software project failure. Requirement is a first phase in the software life-cycle. To avoid any misunderstandings of software requirements, interaction among software quality characteristics should be identified first; then their sub characteristics should be analyzed. In this paper, we propose (i) an ISO-based Cloud SLA Ontology; (ii) a Quality Interaction Reference Model including the interaction among ISO 25010 quality characteristics; and (iii) a Practical System to Generate SLAs.

The rest of the paper is structured as follows. Section 2 explains the motivation, which consists of two parts. The need for ontology representation and the need for NFR interactions. Section 3 presents our ontology based approach in which four phases are described and refined. Section 4 describes the implementation of the proposed approach through a tool. The usefulness behind this tool is illustrated through an example. Section 5 outlines the related work. Finally, Sect. 6 summarizes the presented work and outlines some of its extensions.

2   Motivation

2.1   Common Terminology Throughout Ontologies

An ontology is a "formal and explicit specification of shared conceptualization" [9]. It formally describes a domain of interest via an abstract model, providing a common terminology shared by a Web community [5]. Bhatia [4] presented the advantages of collaborating semantic techniques with software engineering in order to detect ambiguities in software requirements specification. The different types of ambiguity are identified here: lexical, syntactic, semantic, pragmatic, vagueness and generality, and language error [4]. In addition, software requirements may include Non-Functional Requirements (NFR) that describe not what the software will do but how the software will do it. As an example of NFR, the "Scalability" and "changeability" are different terminologies having the same meaning. Using ontology, NFR is defined formally as:

"F: I − > O" where, I is the input and O is the output.

If I is valued as "Scalability" and O is valued as "changeability" then an "equivalent to" relationship is created between I and O in the ontology. Any execution on I will be automatically transferred to O.

Furthermore, the lack of a common terminologies in SLAs may lead to the ambiguity and redundancy in the quality requirements. Consequently, there is a need for a well-defined and standardized quality concepts to ensure consistency and allow SLA comparison among customers and across providers. The ISO 25010 presents a standardized software quality model with different levels: characteristics and sub characteristics, and quality measures related to sub characteristics and characteristics. For instance, the quality characteristic "security" is decomposed into sub-characteristics "Integrity, Authenticity, Confidentiality, Non-Repudiation and Accountability". To provide for these concepts, we used the ISO 25010 quality model as a reference to provide a common terminology in the SLA. Thus, to avoid any ambiguity in the customer/provider definitions of quality requirements, the use of ontology is required.

2.2 Interactions Between Quality Concepts

The QoS concepts are becoming the main concern of both service providers and customers. These concepts are recorded as part of the SLA in cloud computing. Satisfying all quality requirements at the same time is not feasible. Therefore prioritizing NFR according to customers needs is required. In addition, instead of taking into account each element of a guaranty term individually in SLA, we focus on how relevant quality concepts collectively interact to provide the required result without ambiguity. More precisely, how can the provider prove that one or two NFRs can be achieved at a certain level simultaneously? Therefore, identifying interactions between quality requirements is paramount. Many researchers proposed models for identifying conflict and cooperation among requirements [7,15,17]. However, none of these researches consider these interactions in the establishment of the SLA in cloud computing. The most effective SLA appropriately takes into account the requested customer NFR and analyzes their interactions before using a cloud service.

3   A Proposed Ontology-Based Approach

An ontology-based approach for automated SLA establishment in cloud-services environment is crucial for business success. Our contribution is to generate an effective SLA that takes into account the interaction among customer's requirements (i.e., NFR). NFRs are represented by ontology including the Quality Interaction Rules. This approach is composed of four phases named respectively Ontology-based Models, Corresponding Terms Detection, Quality Interaction Reference Model and SLA Generation (Fig. 1). Ontology-based Models is divided into two sub-steps. (i) The definition of SLA ontology representing the provider offering services and (ii) the ISO 25010 ontology describing the customer expecting quality requirements. WS-Agreement [1] is used to define the provider offer and ISO 25010 is used as a baseline to represent the customer quality requirements. Corresponding Terms Detection includes a customized database for classifying synonym terms. The objective here is to extract the similarity between the ISO 25010 quality characteristics (NFR) and the guarantee terms expressed in cloud SLA. Quality Interaction Reference Model consists of identifying the relationships among quality characteristics. We define a set of interaction indicators among the quality characteristics as described in ISO 25010. Thus, we translate the quality interactions into semantic rules. The test result of our approach is a set of SLAs that will be used by the customer, which is the output of the SLA Generation phase of our approach.

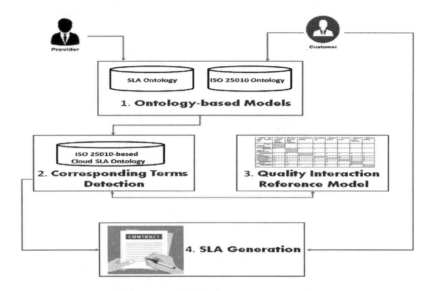

Fig. 1. Ontology-based SLA establishment approach

3.1   Ontology-Based Models

The representation and the management of quality requirements are problematic not only in Software Engineering (SE) but also in the context of cloud SLA. Quality requirements are mostly based on NFRs which can be an important issue to characterize a service by the quality it provides. Requirements are often ambiguous, incomplete and redundant where the goal of using ontology in our approach is to minimize the heterogeneity among provider offers and customer requirements. Ontology-based Models phase is divided into two sub-steps.

The first sub-step involves the formulation of SLA concepts representing the provider offer description. It is based on a semantic meaning for drawing up an SLA agreement model using ontology. This model takes into consideration the QoS concepts presented in Service Level Objectives (SLO). Often, the SLO concept is a guarantee term expressed as an assertion over service attributes and/or external factors such as date, time. We choose to use the most known standard WS-Agreement [1] which is an SLA specification proposed by the Open Grid Forum[1]. As shown in Fig. 2, the SLA includes the "Name", the "Context" and the "Terms". Each term contains "Service Terms" and "Guarantee Terms" composed of a set of SLO.

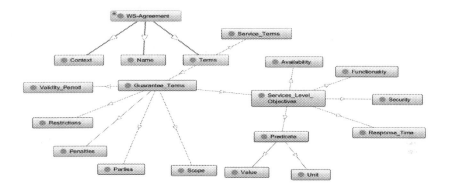

Fig. 2. SLA ontological model

The second sub-step takes into account the ISO 25010 quality characteristics to represent the customer requirements using ontology. To reach agreement on the QoS, an early consensus should be developed between providers and customers about the quality requirements (NFR). We select the ISO 25010 standard as a means to specify NFR since it provides the relationships between software product quality and its quality in use. In ISO 25010, it is stated that the software product quality influences the software quality in use (i.e. the QoS). Figure 3 presents the ISO 25010 quality characteristic ontology.

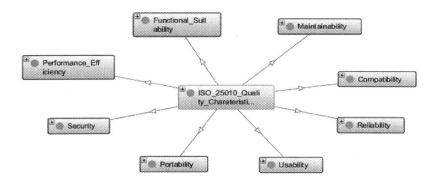

Fig. 3. ISO 25010 ontological model

---

[1] www.ogf.org.

3.2   Corresponding Terms Detection

The major goal of the SLA definition is to clearly point out the requirements between the providers and the customers. According to ISO 25010, there are eight software quality characteristics that are defined as internal and external quality of software product. These characteristics will influence on the quality in use and consequently on the QoS specified in the SLA. To evaluate a cloud service, we need a consistent terminology. Indeed, characteristics and sub characteristics illustrated by the ISO 25010 international standard provide this consistency where QoS have been simulated to NFR. In order to align the concepts of SLA with those of ISO 25010, the use of ontology is useful. It allows detecting the similarity between guarantee terms presented in SLA and NFR as described in ISO 25010.

Table 1. Mapping between ISO 25010 and SLA concepts

ISO 25010		WS-Agreement [1]
Characteristics	Sub characteristics	QoS clause
Functional suitability	Functional compliance	Functionality
	Functional correctness	
	Functional appropriateness	
Performance-efficiency	Time behavior	Response time
	Resources utilization	
	Capacity	
Compatibility	Co-existence	–
	Interoperability	
Usability	Accessibility	–
	Learn ability	
	Operability	
	User interface aesthetic	
	Use error protection	
Reliability	Maturity	Availability
	Availability	
	Recoverability	
	Fault tolerance	
Security	Confidentiality	Security
	Authenticity	
	Integrity	
	Non-repudiation	
	Accountability	
Maintainability	Modularity	–
	Analyzability	
	Testability	
	Modifiability	
	Reusability	
Portability	Adaptability	–
	Install ability	
	Replace ability	

Table 1 presents the ISO 25010 characteristics and sub characteristics and their corresponding SLA concepts. Note that some ISO 25010 quality characteristics are used with the same terminology in the WS-agreement such as "Security". However, other sub characteristics in the ISO 25010 are used as quality concepts in WS-agreement. For instance, the "Availability" concept in SLA corresponds to a sub characteristic belonging to the "Reliability" characteristic in the ISO 25010 model. To identify common interests and ensure the non ambiguity of the used quality characteristics, the stated NFR (i.e., quality characteristics) in the SLA should be aligned with characteristics and sub characteristics of ISO 25010.

Figure 4 presents the result of this alignment between the SLA concepts and the ISO 25010 quality characteristics concepts using ontology. We noticed that only four characteristics from the ISO 25010 (Functional-Suitability, Performance Efficiency, Reliability and Security) tend to be concerned with WS-Agreement. However, the software quality characteristics "Compatibility", "Usability", "Maintainability" and "Portability" are not specified in WS-Agreement. These quality requirements are evident in cloud computing. Thus, the ISO-25010 based Ontology should be integrated into the SLA based Ontology to early predict the QoS.

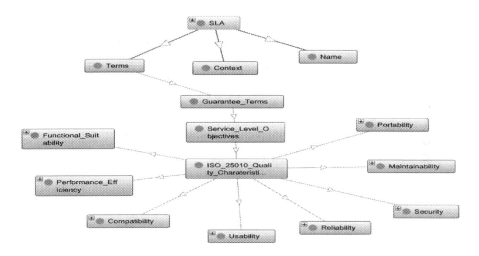

Fig. 4. ISO-based Cloud SLA Ontology

3.3 Quality Interaction Reference Model

Identifying the interaction among the ISO 25010 quality characteristics is required to illustrate which characteristics are compatible and which are not compatible. In fact, many researchers identified the importance of deriving the relationships between the quality characteristics [7,8,15,17]. Table 2 represents the NFR interaction matrix proposed by Egyed and Grunbacher [7]. Recall that in the scope of this paper, we will explain how this matrix is used to establish the SLA document. "0" indicates that QR might be indifferent to one another, cooperation represented by "+" and conflict represented by "−". The rows represent the characteristic and the columns represent their effects on the other characteristics. For instance, a requirement that increases Functional-Suitability likely has a negative effect on Performance-Efficiency (−).

Table 2. Interaction among NFR [7]

	Functional-Suitability	Performance-Efficiency	Compatibility	Usability	Reliability	Security	Maintainability	Portability
Functional-Suitability		-	+	+	-	-	-	+
Performance-Efficiency	0		0	+	-	-	-	-
Compatibility	+	0		+	+	0	+	+
Usability	+	+	+		+	0	0	0
Reliability	0	0	+	+		0	0	0
Security	0	-	0	-	+		0	0
Maintainability	0	0	+	0	0	+		+
Portability	+	0	0	+	+	0	0	

3.4 SLA Generation

Recall that our main goal is to prevent incompatibility among quality requirements during SLA establishment in cloud computing. Thus, we exploit the reasoning features of the ontology specified in the Web Language-Description Logics (OWL-DL) [2]. Particularly, using semantic reasoning, we translate the proposed Quality Interaction Reference Model (Table 2) to a set of rules. Moreover, these rules should express the essential and the optional quality characteristic. Typically, we cannot find a software product that can satisfy all QR at the same time. There the need of priority matrix is required, which allows customer identifying the essentially quality characteristic and those optional. Thus, the "Essential" value is attributed to requirements having high priority. However, the "Optional" value is attributed to requirements having weak priority.

An example of analyzing customer NFR where Functional-Suitability and Security are selected as "Essential" is provided. In practice, this case is impossible and our quality interactions matrix do not allow it. We can prove to the customer that Functional-Suitability has a negative effect on Security. In other words, Functional-Suitability and security cannot be totally satisfied at the same time. So, the customer has two choices. The first one consists to increase the Functional-Suitability where Security must be automatically decreased. However, the second choice consists to increase Security where Functional-Suitability must be automatically decreased. The first choice is illustrated using DL Query with a set of conditions that must be respected for attributing the increased and the decreased states to the selected NFR. Then we use the semantic rules to analyze the possible cases of interactions. The first choice is defined as follow:

$$increasedFun(?f), decreasedSec(?S)- > negativeFunction(?S)$$

This rule means that the effect of increasing Functional-Suitability on Security is negative. So we can deduce an SLA having the effect of Functional-Suitability on the others NFR. More precisely, if "Functional-Suitability" is checked as "Essential", our Quality Interaction Reference Model detects the possible interactions of this requirement with the eight quality characteristics based on Table 2. This condition repeat until satisfied the entire checked quality characteristic. The test result of our approach is a set of SLAs that will be used by the customer, which is the output of the SLA Generation phase of our approach.

4   Example Implementation

In this section, we present our prototype and its applicability in the Azure Media Services[2] as an example. Azure Media Services allow user downloading, storing, processing, browsing, controlling, selecting and publishing media. We use the Microsoft Azure SLA[3] to show the feasibility of our prototype in the SLA establishment and representation. In fact, the major issue of SLAs available on the net is that they are complex and not detailed enough. Our prototype aims to avoid this complexity using the ontology as explained in the motivation section. Moreover, it gives more detail on SLO to satisfy the customers needs. Precisely, our prototype allows to extend the SLA and especially the SLO terms with the eight ISO 25010 quality characteristics. Each quality characteristic has a threshold that should not be exceeded, otherwise, a penalty must be applied. The main characteristic of our proposed prototype is its ability to automatically determine the threshold of each SLO using the interaction among the quality requirements.

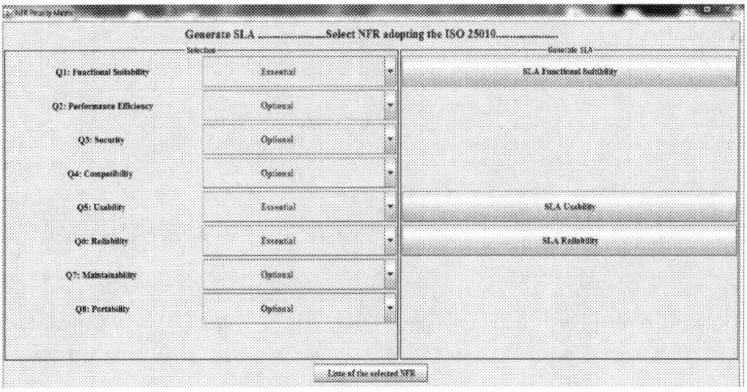

Fig. 5. Customer Priority NFRs Interface

---

[2] https://msdn.microsoft.com/en-us/library/dn735911.aspx.

[3] https://azure.microsoft.com/fr-fr/support/legal/sla/.

First, our prototype allows to populate the ISO 25010-based Cloud SLA Ontology with instances from Azure Media Services. This ontology is created using "Protege"[4] framework in a semi-automatic manner and populated by the Apache Jena API. ISO 25010-based Cloud SLA Ontology contains the mains SLA concepts defined by the OWL language[5]. These concepts include the guarantee terms that are deduced after executing the Corresponding Terms Detection. Then, the Quality Interaction Reference Model is integrated into our prototype as a set of inference rules executed with the Pellet[6] reasoner. These rules are executed on instances from Azure Media Services. Thus, the positive and the negative interactions between the Functional-Suitability and the other quality characteristics instances are generated.

Figure 5 presents the generic interface of our prototype. Regarding the first part named "Selection", there are eight quality characteristics defined in the ISO 25010 quality model. Therefore, the customer is in front of two choices "Essential" or "Optional". We take the example where the customer selects Functional-Suitability, Usability and Reliability as "Essential" and the other NFRs are selected as "Optional". The second part of the interface consists of generating one SLA for each NFR selected as "Essential". In this example, three SLAs are provided. Each one represents the interactions between the "Essential" NFR and the other NFRs as presented in Table 3.

Table 3. Example of NFRs interactions

	SLA1:Functional-Suitability	SLA2:Usability	SLA3:Reliability
Functional-Suitability	+	+	0
Performance-Efficiency	−	+	0
Compatibility	+	+	+
Usability	+	+	+
Reliability	−	+	+
Security	−	0	0
Maintainability	−	0	0
Portability	+	0	0

Each quality requirement having positive interaction (+) is presented in the SLA with a threshold equal to "99.95%". However, the negative interaction (−) implies a threshold equal to "99%". (0) expresses the relationship of independence between two quality requirements. In this case, attributes might be indifferent to one another and the threshold could be "99%" or "99.95%". Our prototype provides a front-end tool from the client side to choose one SLA among the proposed ones.

---

[4] http://protege.stanford.edu/.
[5] http://www.w3.org/TR/owl-ref/.
[6] http://pellet.owldl.com/.

5   Related Work

Research on SLA establishment is limited despite its necessity to define the QoS. Andrieux et al. [1] proposed WS-Agreement, a formal language for the representation of SLA in Web service. Keller and Ludwig [11] proposed a framework for defining and monitoring SLAs in the Web service environment. This Framework provides a flexible and extensible XML-based language, named WSLA, for representing SLAs in a formal way. Tata et al. [18] proposed rSLA, a language for managing SLA in cloud computing. It allows defining the basic metrics and how they will be aggregated to composite ones. In addition, it defines and evaluates the SLO in order to detect violations and subsequently change the system configuration. Chhetri et al. [3] proposed a policy-based framework for the automated establishment of SLAs in open, diverse and dynamic cloud environments. This framework allows entities to specify their requirements and capabilities, and preferences over them in a flexible and expressive manner. Kahina et al. [10] proposed an SLA ontology that introduces key concepts, such as service, QoS requirements, role, actor and feedback which are connected with SLA. The authors focused on their work on how the objective and subjective feedback could provide input to a cloud service. Rady [16] figure out which NFRs should be included as SLA parameters in cloud computing. She compared different NFRs from the consumer's point of view in order to generate SLA.

   In our previous work, we proposed a cloud SLA ontology to describe the main concepts of SLA. We introduced the elasticity strategies and their different methods used in order to maintain the QoS [12,13]. However, we have not introduced neither the customers requirements nor their interactions. The idea of using ISO-25010 to represent customers requirements and analyze their interactions in order to establish an SLA for the cloud is the originality of this work. The benefits of the ontology, such as the semantic representation and the reasoning techniques improve the SLA generation.

6   Conclusion

In this work, we presented an ontology-based approach for SLA establishment in cloud computing. Exploiting the semantic richness of ontology, we developed a comprehensible SLA model that detects correspondence among the NFRs and the QoS. Thus, the reasoning techniques and the power of the inference rules presented in the ontology allowed us to create interaction's rules to prove the relationship among the NFRs. The interaction among quality requirements during SLA establishment can be clarified to both provider/customer. Providers can classify each SLA and the customer can choose the preferred one. The findings of this study fills up the literature gap presented by the proposal of a single SLA document satisfying only the providers requirements. Through this study, we also solve the problems of quality requirements ambiguity and propose new approach to handle their interactions. Our solution helps to automatically establish and generate SLAs that satisfy customer needs.

As prospects for this work, we intend to put our tools into practice by taking into account not only quality characteristics but also quality sub characteristics. Using our model, we have addressed the establishment life-cycle phase of SLA. We also aim to handle the SLA monitoring phase while testing the importance of the interactions among NFR.

References

1. Andrieux, A., et al.: Web services agreement specification (WS-Agreement). Global Grid Forum, Grid Resource Allocation Agreement Protocol (2011)
2. Baader, F., Calvanese, D., McGuinness, D.L., Nardi, D., Patel-Schneider, P.F. (eds.): The Description Logic Handbook: Theory, Implementation, and Applications. Cambridge University Press, Cambridge (2003)
3. Baruwal Chhetri, M., Bao Vo, Q., Kowalczyk, R.: AutoSLAM: a policy-based framework for automated SLA establishment in cloud environments. Concurr. Comput.: Pract. Exp. **27**(9), 2413–2442 (2015)
4. Bhatia, M., Kumar, A., Beniwal, R.: Ontology based framework for detecting ambiguities in software requirements specification. IEEE (2016)
5. Drozdowicz, M., Ganzha, M., Wasielewska, K., Paprzycki, M., Szmeja, P.: Using ontologies to manage resources in grid computing: practical aspects. In: Ossowski, S. (ed.) Agreement Technologies, vol. 8, pp. 149–168. Springer, Dordrecht (2013). https://doi.org/10.1007/978-94-007-5583-3_9
6. Drozdowicz, M., et al.: Ontology for contract negotiations in an agent-based grid resource management system. Trends Parallel Distrib. Grid Cloud Comput. Eng. 335–354 (2011)
7. Egyed, A., Grunbacher, P.: Identifying requirements conflicts and cooperation: how quality attributes and automated traceability can help. IEEE Softw. **21**(6), 50–58 (2004)
8. Fernando, P.: Improving software applications quality by considering the contribution relationship among quality attributes. Elsevier (2016)
9. Gruber, T.R.: A translation approach to portable ontology specifications. Knowl. Acquis. **5**(2), 199–220 (1993)
10. Hamadache, K., Rizou, S.: Holistic SLA ontology for cloud service evaluation. In: 2013 International Conference on Advanced Cloud and Big Data, pp. 32–39 (2013)
11. Keller, A., Ludwig, H.: The WSLA framework: specifying and monitoring service level agreements for web services. J. Netw. Syst. Manag. **11**(1), 57–81 (2003)
12. Labidi, T., Mtibaa, A., Brabra, H.: CSLAOnto: a comprehensive ontological SLA model in cloud computing. J. Data Semant. **5**(3), 179–193 (2016)
13. Labidi, T., Mtibaa, A., Gaaloul, W., Tata, S., Gargouri, F.: Cloud SLA modeling and monitoring. In: 2017 IEEE International Conference on Services Computing (SCC), pp. 338–345 (2017)
14. Palacios, M., Garcia-Fanjul, J., Tuya, J., Spanoudakis, G.: Identifying test requirements by analyzing SLA guarantee terms. IEEE Computer Society (2012)
15. Márquez, G., Astudillo, H.: Selecting components assemblies from non-functional requirements through tactics and scenarios. In: 2016 35th International Conference of the Chilean Computer Science Society (SCCC), pp. 1–11 (2016)

16. Rady, M.: Parameters for service level agreements generation in cloud computing. In: Castano, S., Vassiliadis, P., Lakshmanan, L.V., Lee, M.L. (eds.) ER 2012. LNCS, vol. 7518, pp. 13–22. Springer, Heidelberg (2012). https://doi.org/10.1007/978-3-642-33999-8_3

17. Tabassum, M.R., Siddik, M.S., Shoyaib, M., Khaled, S.M.: Determining interdependency among non-functional requirements to reduce conflict. IEEE (2014)

18. Tata, S., Mohamed, M., Sakairi, T., Mandagere, N., Anya, O., Ludwig, H.: rSLA: a service level agreement language for cloud services. In: IEEE International Conference on Cloud Computing, pp. 415–422 (2016)

American Sign Language Recognition: Algorithm and Experimentation System

Martyna Lagozna, Milosz Bialczak, Iwona Pozniak-Koszalka,
Leszek Koszalka[✉], and Andrzej Kasprzak

Department of Systems and Computer Networks,
Wroclaw University of Science and Technology, Wroclaw, Poland
m.lagozna@gmail.com, milosz.bialczak@gmail.com,
{iwona.pozniak-koszalka, leszek.koszalka,
andrzej.kasprzak}@pwr.edu.pl

Abstract. The objective of this paper is an attempt to take part in the fast development of computer science, especially machine learning, in the field of finding the tools for supporting the disabled people. Speech-and–hearing impaired people are the part of our society and it would be a great convenience both for them and for speaking people, who would have an opportunity for a better communication using computer technology. In this paper, the results of the research concerning recognition of sign language have been provided. The research includes experimenting with the images transformations and the usage of different learning and feature detecting algorithms to obtain the best quality of signs recognition. In addition, the recommendations based on results of experiments can be applied in practical issues, for example, in determining hands rotations used in sign language, which can improve the accuracy of recognition.

Keywords: Sign language · Recognition · Machine learning · Algorithm · Experimentation system

1 Introduction

Nowadays, using computer technology in solving medical issues became a common practice. Fast development and the growing popularity of machine learning approach allowed for creating technologically advanced applications and complex algorithms, which are aimed at helping people. Sign language recognition is an interesting and a significant issue strictly connected with both machine learning and medical technology. People with disability hearing loss account for 5% of the whole society [1]. In the past, these people had no technical possibilities to facilitate their lives and communication ways. Now, it is still challenging but more possible, so our motivation is the contribution in solving this issue.

In this work, we concentrate on experiments with different features extraction and learning algorithms, paying a particular attention to image processing. Moreover, the scope of this work includes also checking the impact of background and hands rotation on the received accuracy basing on the usage of two completely different data sets.

© Springer Nature Switzerland AG 2019
N. T. Nguyen et al. (Eds.): ICCCI 2019, LNAI 11683, pp. 676–685, 2019.
https://doi.org/10.1007/978-3-030-28377-3_56

The main objective is implementing an own algorithm taking into account that at the current stage of research we concentrate on single letters from American Sign Language (ASL) alphabet. One of the crucial assumptions, considered in this work, is recognition of images taken with average-quality camera. The algorithm, which has been implemented, might be available for everyone, for example, by a build-in camera in mobile phone or computer. The algorithm should be given an image on input and the result should be returned as recognized letter on string type. Therefore, we consider the following problems:

- Finding crucial features on the picture.
- Emphasizing hand features.
- Finding satisfying way of learning the algorithm.

The paper is organized as follows. Section 2 is devoted to related work. The problem is formulated in Sect. 3. The proposed algorithm is described in Sect. 4. This section is divided on four subsections: preprocessing, features extraction, post-processing, and learning. The experimentation system is presented in Sect. 5, including experiment design with data sets used. The obtained results of experiments and comments are presented in Sect. 6. In Sect. 7, appear the conclusion and plans for further research in the area.

2   Related Work

In the last decade there were many of researches in the field of sign language recognition. In very important work [2] was shown that gesture recognition gives an opportunity for interacting with machine without any mechanical devices. The authors of this paper have proposed the recognition system, which understands human gestures. Another interesting method for the recognition of human gesture is presented in [3]. The method is based on neural network and stochastic computing. However, the authors confirmed that most of the technologies in the area of human gesture recognition was power consuming.

In the last years, Microsoft Kinect sensors give the possibility for lower cost of Human-Computer-Interaction (HCI). It allows for proposing a new sensible solutions, e.g., in [4], a novel multi-sensor fusion framework was proposed; in [5] a Novel CNNs with multiview and fusion for American Sign Language recognition; in [6], an attempt of hand gesture recognition, using the SIFT algorithm is described. The authors of this paper showed that SIFT algorithm is working good with the standard ASL database but also with home-made database.

The paper [7] has reported the interesting idea of three - stage translation system. The first stage is responsible for the communication with the neuromorphic camera DVS sensors. The second stage regards feature extraction of the events generated by the DVS – it gives the opportunity for a presentation of the digital image processing algorithms developed in software. The third stage consists in the classification of the ASL alphabet basing on the implemented artificial neural network.

The very important work [8], in our opinion, is focused on the recognition of single letters of American alphabet. The authors of this paper used a hierarchical mode-seeking method for localization hand joint positions under kinematic constraints. They also used special Microsoft Kinect camera what allowed them to achieve high accuracy.

3   Problem Formulation

The objective of this work is to create an algorithm, which can recognize static gestures of single letters from American Sign Language alphabet. The single task is a classification of hand's photos:

Given: the images of gestures on photos.

To find: the recognized letters on string type.

Such that: the index of performance defined by (1) is of the highest possible accuracy. The accuracy is the index of performance expressed by the formula (1).

$$\text{Accuracy} = (N_c)/(N) \tag{1}$$

where Nc is the number of the corrected recognitions, N is the total number of recognitions.

For a single classification task the Support Vector Machine - a set of methods for supervised learning [9] has been used. In this case, the decision function is defined by the following formula:

$$sgn\left(\sum_{i=1}^{n} y_i \alpha_i K(x_i, x) + \rho \right)$$

where x and y are training vectors, $x_i \in R^p, i = 1, 2 \ldots, n, y \in \{1, -1\}^n$ and $K(x_i, x_j)$ is the kernel [10].

4   Algorithm

As it was mentioned, creating an algorithm requires taking into consideration the following tasks: (i) Finding crucial features on the picture; (ii) Emphasizing of hand features; (iii) Finding satisfying way of learning the algorithm.

The structure of the recognition algorithm concerns step by step performing. In Fig. 1, the proposed model in the form of the general data flow scheme is presented.

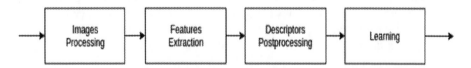

Fig. 1. Data flow model.

4.1 Preprocessing

In the first step, the appropriate preparation of the images should be made. We have applied two methods of the image modification, including Gaussian Blur for reducing image noise and Anisotropic Filtering for sharpening the main shape of the gesture. These methods and their properties are presented in [11] and [12], respectively. Using of these methods allows avoiding recognition of excess points and enhancing quality of the considered image. These methods and their properties are presented in [11] and [12], respectively.

In Fig. 2, the pre-processing data flow is shown in the form of block-scheme.

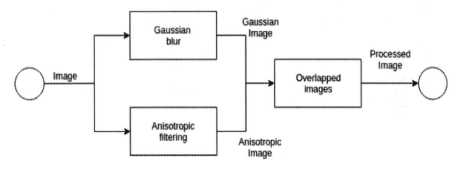

Fig. 2. Model of preprocessing.

4.2 Features Extraction

The following tree different features extractors (available in *ski-image* library [10]) have been utilized.

- CENSURE (The Center Surround Extrema) extractor, which is characterized by fast computing time [13]. However, this extractor is able to find usually only key points but not descriptors [14].
- BRIEF (The Binary Robust Independent Elementary Features) extractor is an efficient feature point descriptor [15]. Unfortunately, it is unable to sensible dealing with images rotation.
- ORB (The Oriented FAST and Rotated BRIEF) extractor is a combination of the modified BRIEF extractor (presented in [16]) and FAST key point feature detector (described in [17]). This extractor allows for images rotation and possesses ability to fast computing.

4.3 Post-processing

Between steps of features extraction and classifier learning, the extracted data are processed and improved to become more reliable. This step, called post-processing, is presented in the form of the block-scheme in Fig. 3.

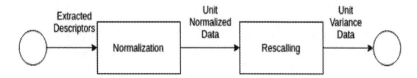

Fig. 3. Model of post-processing data flow.

Two processes have been implemented:

- NORMALIZE, which rescales the vector for each sample to ensure the unit norm, independently of the distribution of the samples [18].
- STANDARD SCALER, which can remove mean and scale the data to unit variance.

However, the outliers have an influence when computing the empirical mean and standard deviation which shrink the range of the feature values. Standard Scaler unfortunately cannot guarantee balanced feature scales in the presence of outliers [18].

4.4   Learning

Support Vector Machines (SVMs) are a set of related methods for supervised learning, applicable to both classification and regression problems. A SVM classifiers create a maximum-margin hyperplane that lies in a transformed input space and splits the example classes, while maximizing the distance to the nearest cleanly split examples. The parameters of the solution hyperplane are derived from a quadratic programming optimization problem [9]. In the paper, the following methods are used:

- VECTOR – CLASSIFIER, which learns with use of vector of descriptors retrieved from the picture and the information about the correct letter on the image. This method has a significant disadvantage. Vectors received by the classifier must have exactly the same length which as a consequence, extorts cutting the longer ones and ignoring the ones that are too short.
- POINTS – CLASSIFIER, which learns by processing descriptor after descriptor and the information about related letter from the picture. This way of learning makes the algorithm independent from the data vector length.
- COMBINED - CLASSIFIER, when the outputs from both vector and points classifiers are taken into consideration. This classifier learns by taking those outputs and the information about correct answer.

5   Experimentation System

The input of the experimentation system is an image. The output states the result returned as recognized letter on string type.

5.1   Datasets

Two different data sets have been used. The first one has been downloaded from the website of Silesian University of Technology [19]. An example of data base element is shown in Fig. 4.

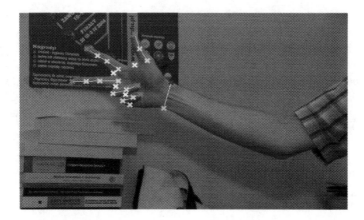

Fig. 4. An element of database with hand gestures [19].

The data base consists of 899 images of gestures from American alphabet from A to Y excluding J. Letters 'Z' and 'J' are moving gestures and it is impossible to show them on a single picture. This data set contains images with uncontrolled background and lightning conditions, different angle of hand rotations form observer perspective and different resolution. Images are oriented both vertically and horizontally.

The second data set used in the experiment is a self-made set of images which has been created in possibly similar lightning condition. On each image only hands at uniform, plain background has been shown. An example is shown in Fig. 5.

Fig. 5. An element of our own database with hand gestures.

Each image has exactly the same height, resolution and all of them are oriented horizontally. The set contains images of gestures of all American sign alphabet also with 'J' and 'Z' excluded.

5.2   Process of Experiment

During the research the successive steps have been added to the algorithm. At first the model has been learned by pure descriptors. Next anisotropic filtering has been added. Then Standard Scaler and Gaussian Blur have been implemented. The last step was adding normalization to the output.

The above described steps have been applied to three different features extractors: BRIEF, CENSURE and ORB. On each extractor three methods of learning has been tested: by points, vectors and combined. As a metric for evaluation of classification the accuracy defined by Eq. (1) has been used.

6   Research

6.1   Complex Experiment

Table 1 contains the results of the accuracy (the percentage values of correct recognition) at every step of the algorithm. These results were obtained for the complex experiment composed of single experiments. For simple experiment we fixed the considered various elements of preprocessing, features extraction, learning, and postprocessing. In some cases, we decided to abandon taking into account some features extractors because of their unsatisfying accuracy in comparison to the others (see elements in Table 1 with "no data").

Table 1.   Results when adding next steps to the algorithm.

Features extractions	Learning	Descriptors	Anisotropic filtering	Standard Scaler	Gaussian blur	Normalize
ORB	Points	51.72%	60.34%	91.38%	94.84%	96.55%
ORB	Combined	13.79%	13.79%	12.07%	13.79%	12.07%
ORB	Vector	13.79%	13.79%	13.79%	22.41%	25.86%
CENSURE	Points	20.69%	22.41%	15.52%	12.07%	–
CENSURE	Combined	13.79%	18.97%	15.52%	5.17%	–
CENSURE	Vector	8.61%	1.72%	0.00%	1.72%	–
BRIEF	Points	15.52%	–	–	–	–
BRIEF	Combined	15.52%	–	–	–	–
BRIEF	Vector	0.00%	–	–	–	–

It can be observed in Table 1, that among all used features extractors ORB occurred to be the most effective for the considered problem. Probably, its ability to dealing with rotations had a big impact on the obtained results.

Therefore, the aim of the next experiments has been collecting more detailed information about elements (versions of preprocessing, learning and post-processing) connected with ORB features extraction.

6.2   Experiment for ORB Testing

In Fig. 6, the detailed results of experiments for ORB features extraction are shown.

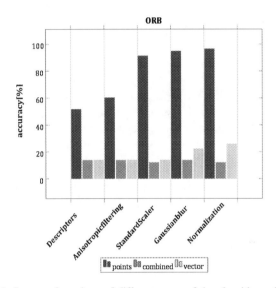

Fig. 6. Influence of versions of different steps of the algorithm with ORB.

The best method of learning the classifier occurred to be learning by points. Furthermore, successively added algorithms at following steps significantly improved the result. Adding Standard Scaler was a crucial step and had considerable impact on the final accuracy.

We can be satisfied with the performance of the algorithm for gestures on the plain background. In case of adding distorting background, e.g., check shirt (we tested some cases), the performing of algorithm should be improved.

In Table 2, are shown the results produced by the final (all steps) version of the algorithm tested on three different data sets (mentioned in Sect. 5.1):

Set #1 - The set of the numbers (digits) prepared by us.

Set #2 – The set of the letters prepared by us.

Set #3 - The set of images of gestures regarding alphabet taken from [19].

Table 2. Results when adding next steps to the algorithm

Dataset	ORB		
	Points	Combined	Vector
Set #1	96.55%	12.07%	25.86%
Set #2	72.90%	3.23%	12.26%
Set #3	27.36%	3.48%	2.49%

It may be observed once more that learning by using points classifier leads to better accuracy of the recognition.

7 Final Remarks

7.1 Conclusion

In the version, presented in this paper, the recognition of static gestures on plain background seems to work fine. To sum up, we managed to implement an algorithm which can pose a good basis to continue extended research.

7.2 Plans for Further Research

In the nearest future we plan to focus on further developing the algorithm to reach the improvement of accuracy. Our main goal is to ensure the possibilities of experiments:

- For recognition of moving signs.
- For recognition with special classifier only for mistaken gestures.

We should also concentrate on designing and implementing the extended experimentation system which allows making multi-stage experiments in automatic manners, following the rules described in our works [20] and [21].

Acknowledgement. This work was supported by the statutory funds of the Department of Systems and Computer Networks, Wroclaw University of Science and Technology, Wroclaw, Poland.

References

1. Deafness and hearing loss. World Health Organization. http://www.who.int/newsroom/fact-sheets/detail/deafness-and-hearing-loss. Accessed Nov 2018
2. Sridevj, K., Sundarambal, M., Muralidharan, K., Rathinadurai, J.L.: FPGA implementation of hand gesture recognition system using neural networks. In: 2017 11th International Conference on Intelligent Systems and Control (ISCO), January 2017
3. Wang, X., Chen, W., Ji, Y., Ran, F.: Gesture recognition based on parallel hardware neural network implemented with stochastic logics. In: 2016 International Conference on Audio, Language and Image Processing, July 2016

4. Kumar, P., Gauba, H., Roy, P., Dogra, D.P.: Coupled HMM-based multi-sensor data fusion for sign language recognition. Pattern Recogn. Lett. **86**, 1–8 (2017)
5. Tao, W., Leu, M.C., Yin, Z.: American sign language alphabet recognition using convolutional neural networks with multi-view augmentation and inference fusion. Eng. Appl. Artif. Intell. **76**, 202–213 (2018)
6. Nicholai, M.: Alphabet recognition of ASL: a hand gesture recognition approach using SIFT algorithm. Int. J. Artif. Intell. Appl. **4**(1), 105–115 (2013)
7. Rivera-Acosta, M., Ortega-Cisneros, S., Dominguez, J.R., Sandoval, F.: American sign language alphabet recognition using a neuromorphic sensor and an artificial network. Sensors **17**(10), 2176 (2014)
8. Dong, C., Leu, M.C., Yin, Z.: American sign language alphabet recognition using microsoft kinect. In: IEEE Conference on Computer Vision and Pattern Recognition Workshops (CVPRW), pp. 44–52 (2015)
9. Shmilovici, A.: Data Mining and Knowledge Discovery Handbook, pp. 231–247. Springer, USA (2005)
10. https://scikitlearn.org/stable/modules/svm.html. Accessed Jan 2019
11. Flusser, J., Farokhi, S., Hoschl, C., Zitova, B., Pedone, M.: Recognition of images degraded by Gaussian blur. IEEE Trans. Image Process. **25**(2), 790–806 (2016)
12. Yang, G.Z., Burger, P., Firmin, D.N., Underwood, S.R.: Structure adaptive anisotropic image filtering (1995)
13. Schmidt, A., Kraft, M., Fularz, M., Domagala, Z.: Comparative assessment of point feature detectors and descriptors in the context of robot navigation. J. Autom. Mob. Rob. Intell. Syst. **7**, 11–20 (2013)
14. Lee, P., Timmaraju, A.S.: Learning binary descriptors from images (2012)
15. Calonder, M., Lepetit, V., Strecha, C., Fua, P.: BRIEF: binary robust independent elementary features. In: Daniilidis, K., Maragos, P., Paragios, N. (eds.) ECCV 2010. LNCS, vol. 6314, pp. 778–792. Springer, Heidelberg (2010). https://doi.org/10.1007/978-3-642-15561-1_56
16. Rublee, E., Rabaud, V., Konolige, K., Bradski, G.: ORB: an efficient alternative to SIFT or SURF, November 2011
17. Rosten, E., Drummond, T.: Machine Learning for High-Speed Corner Detection. In: Leonardis, A., Bischof, H., Pinz, A. (eds.) ECCV 2006. LNCS, vol. 3951, pp. 430–443. Springer, Heidelberg (2006). https://doi.org/10.1007/11744023_34
18. http://scikitlearn.org/stable/auto_examples/preprocessing/plot_all_scaling.html. Accessed Dec 2018
19. http://sun.aei.polsl.pl/~mkawulok/gestures/. Accessed Jan 2019
20. Bogalinski, P., Davies, D., Koszalka, L., Pozniak-Koszalka, I., Kasprzak, A.: Evaluation of strip nesting algorithms: an experimentation system for the practical users. J. Intell. Fuzzy Syst. **27**(2), 611–623 (2014)
21. Hudziak, M., Pozniak-Koszalka, I., Koszalka, L., Kasprzak, A.: Multi-agent pathfinding in the crowded environment with obstacles: algorithms and experimentation system. J. Intell. Fuzzy Syst. **32**(2), 1561–1578 (2017)

SEADer: A Social Engineering Attack Detection Method Based on Natural Language Processing and Artificial Neural Networks

Merton Lansley, Nikolaos Polatidis$^{(\boxtimes)}$, and Stelios Kapetanakis

School of Computing, Engineering and Mathematics,
University of Brighton, Brighton BN2 4GJ, UK
{M.Lansley,N.Polatidis,S.Kapetanakis}@Brighton.ac.uk

Abstract. Social engineering attacks are one of the most well-known and easiest to apply attacks in the cybersecurity domain. Research has shown that the majority of attacks against computer systems was based on the use of social engineering methods. Considering the importance of emerging fields such as machine learning and cybersecurity we have developed a method that detects social engineering attacks that is based on natural language processing and artificial neural networks. This method can be applied in offline texts or online environments and flag a conversation as a social engineering attack or not. Initially, the conversation text is parsed and checked for grammatical errors using natural language processing techniques and then an artificial neural network is used to classify possible attacks. The proposed method has been evaluated using a real dataset and a semi-synthetic dataset with very high accuracy results. Furthermore, alternative classification methods have been used for comparisons in both datasets.

Keywords: Social engineering · Attack detection · Online chat environments · Natural language processing · Neural networks · Cybersecurity

1 Introduction

There have been various research projects demonstrating the need for an automated system to recognize SE attacks. Many of these projects show proof of concept models using a variety of different techniques, most commonly Natural Language Processing (NLP) and Machine Learning (ML) methods like Artificial Neural Networks. Whilst these exist, there is a lack of evidence that the theory has been implemented and proved working, with very little evidence of the rate of success [1–4].

Human Psychology plays a large part in the creation of NLP software as it is important to understand how people socialize and behave with others. A common and well-regarded psychologist, Dr. Robert Cialdini proposed the 6 principles of persuasion [5]: Authority, Scarcity, Liking/Similarity, Reciprocation, Social Proof and Commitment/Consistency. Further studies by psychologists also follow a similar consensus that these are the key factors in defining a persuasive person. Using these key features as a base, Computer Scientists theorized and attempted to build systems that recognized these traits.

© Springer Nature Switzerland AG 2019
N. T. Nguyen et al. (Eds.): ICCCI 2019, LNAI 11683, pp. 686–696, 2019.
https://doi.org/10.1007/978-3-030-28377-3_57

The research projects on this area can be loosely broken down into three stages, Data Pre-Processing, Feature Extraction and Aggregation of Results as shown in Fig. 1.

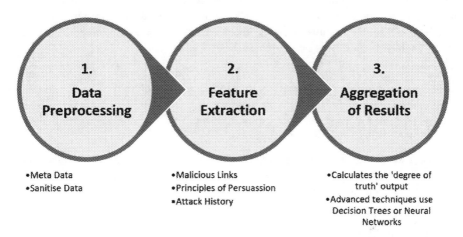

1. Data Preprocessing	2. Feature Extraction	3. Aggregation of Results
•Meta Data •Sanitise Data	•Malicious Links •Principles of Persuassion •Attack History	•Calculates the 'degree of truth' output •Advanced techniques use Decision Trees or Neural Networks

Fig. 1. Data pre-processing and feature extraction.

Most research approaches into this problem domain have some relevant data and these data are usually pre-processed. The method of pre-processing differs per system, but generally involves the same goal; preparing the data for classification. The contextual, or meta data, such as time, date and IP addresses are captured in a relationship with the original data. This can be used for correlating different dialogues with one another, one by matching the IP as an internal or external agent and secondly by highlighting potential reoccurring adversaries that may persist under different aliases. The dialogues are sanitized to remove any erroneous content such as HTML tags or corrupt texts. The data can then be parsed using a Natural Language Processing (NLP) parser such as the Stanford CoreNLP [6]. NLP parsers provide a vast array of tools that are able to dissect the human language into dependency trees, define grammatical relations and their Parts of Speech (POS) to name a few common uses. Using these libraries, it allows programmers to create algorithms which are able to classify conversations based on the linguistic features the parser extracts.

This paper is based on the concept that a dialogue is taking place in an online chat environment. To determine if a dialog between two interlocutors is a Social Engineering attack, certain criteria, or else known as features, need to be chosen, a process known as feature selection. The features are selected before the three stages and are commonly based on the principles of persuasion, common phishing tactics like malicious links and the history of the attacker. We can then classify the data based on these features and produce a 'score' of how strongly the selected dialog matches the criteria. Each implementation designed to detect each feature will use a variety of classification techniques, such as: Fuzzy Logic, Topic Blacklists, Decision Trees, Random Forest and Neural Networks depending on what needs to be extracted. Furthermore, an automated system requires the output of a clear decision, albeit a probabilistic decision, this can be done by aggregating the outputs from the Feature Extraction process. The results of each feature are weighted by importance, and at basic level can be averaged to give a Fuzzy logic prediction. By using more advanced techniques such as decision trees or neural networks, the weight of each feature can be calculated programmatically to determine which features carry the most importance regarding whether or not a social engineering attack is taking place.

The following contributions are delivered:

1. A method for detecting social engineering attack in online chat environments is proposed.
2. The proposed method has been evaluated using a real and a semi-synthetic dataset with the results validating our approach.

The rest of the paper is organized as follows: Sect. 2 presents the related work, Sect. 3 delivers the proposed method, Sect. 4 contains the experimental evaluation and Sect. 5 is the conclusions part.

2   Related Work

An early implementation of SE detection in real-time telephone systems is SEDA (Social Engineering Defense Architecture) [7]. The researchers mainly focused on identifying repeat callers using their voice signatures. Later a proof of concept model of SEDA [8] was produced being able to correctly identify all attacks in their dataset. A method of detection used by [1] is to identify the questions requesting private information and commands requesting that the user perform tasks they are not authorized to perform. This technique uses a manually derived topic blacklist of verb-noun pairs for which they state should be built around security policies associated with a system. This work is taken further in [2] by identifying 4 main attack; the urgency of the dialog, negative commands and questions, whether the message is likely automated identified by a generic greeting. Finally, they use a reputable cyber security service, Netcraft, to check the safety of a URL. Instead of manual blacklist creation, they use a large corpus of phishing emails to generate a topic blacklist using a Naive Bayes classier. Some approaches like SEADMv2 [3] and MPMPA [9] use complex state machines in order to map out the pathways that can be followed as a checklist-type system to mitigate an attack. This proposal is suited where there are multiple authorization layers that might prevent a request from being carried out. These two separate machines provide some overlap, but the explicit state definition required could be limiting to where these can be applied. The nature of SE attacks is unpredictable meaning that new methods of attacks are always being introduced. The SEADM versions state machines still rely on the user input for changing state, which means the chance for user error and naivety is still present. The works of [4] covers an extensive overview of the existing systems and provide a comprehensive recognition of sub-systems for their detection architecture; in influence, deception, personality, speech act and past experiences. The work of [10] provides a semantic based approach of dialogues to detect social engineering attacks. In [11] the authors show that the human factor is the weakest link in social engineering attacks and based on a human study the prove that. In [12] and [13] the authors provide a theoretical foundation that potentially could be used in real systems to detect attacks., In the works of [14] it is explained how social engineering attacks can potentially be detected, whereas in [15] and [16] different examples of attacks with scenarios are presented. In addition to the works mentioned, there are numerous other articles from relevant domains that can be useful such as the one in [17] where the authors performed an influence analysis of the number of members on the quality of knowledge in a collective, the work in [18] where a neural network is used along with harmony for searching, the one in [19] where nature inspired optimization algorithms for fuzzy control servo systems are discussed and the one found in [20] where an Island-based cuckoo search algorithm with highly disruptive polynomial mutation is proposed.

3   Proposed Method

The proposed method consists of several steps to preprocess the dialogs into a dataset for classification. The last steps are applying the classifier. All the steps explained below, have been written in the Python programming language. The SymSpellpy library (a Python port of SymSpell) was used for spelling, the Web of Trust (WOT) Application Programming Interface (API) was used to check any links and finally the SciKit library for the MLP classifier.

In more particular, steps 1 to 5 check for malicious links, steps 6 and 7 determine the spelling quality, and steps 8 to 11 determine the intent of the text, using a predefined blacklist. The score of each feature can be given by: Link score, S_L, Spelling score, S_{sp}, and Intent score, S_I. Each score is then scaled down to between 0 and 1. After the pre-processing of the dialogues (steps 1–11), the classification dataset has the following 4 labels: (1) Intent, (2) Spelling, (3) Link and (4) attack or no attack. The final steps use these as inputs for the MLP classifier.

The steps are as follows:

1. Extract all URLs from the dialog text using a regex pattern matcher.
2. If the text contains URLs, send the link/s to the WOT API to evaluate if the web link is malicious.
3. The WOT API returns the reputation of the site (value between 0–100), the confidence of the given reputation (value between 0–100) and the identifying categories (17 in total) that identify the nature of the website. The broad categories and example subcategories are as follows:

   - 1XX Negative (101 Malware, 103 Phishing, 104 Scam, 105 Potentially illegal etc.)
   - 2XX Questionable (201 Misleading claims or unethical, 205 spam, 207 ads/popups etc.)
   - 3XX Neutral (301 Online tracking, 302 controversial, 303 political etc.)
   - 5XX Positive (501 A good site)

4. If the returned category is of group 1XX or 2XX, then $S_L = 1$.
5. Otherwise, divide the reputation by 100 and take it away from 1 as shown in Eq. 1.

$$S_L = 1 - \frac{reputation\ value}{100} \tag{1}$$

6. Check for spelling using the SymSpellpy library.
7. Using the best suggested spelling correction, determine the number of misspelled words, given by x. This number is then scaled between 0 and 1 by applying Eq. 2. The value of S_{SP} represents the spelling quality, where higher values represents poorer spelling. Rather than a linear function, an exponential function is used to rate a higher number of spelling mistakes more severely. To adjust the rate at which the score tends towards 1, the constant a can be varied to affect how harsh you want to be on spelling errors. After extensive testing it was identified that 0.5 allowed the text to contain a small number of mistakes without creating a high score. For example, if a is set to 0.5 and $x = 1$ then $S_{SP} = 0.39$, if $x = 5$ then $S_{SP} = 0.92$.

$$S_{SP} = 1 - e^{-ax} \tag{2}$$

8. The next step uses the corrected spelling of the dialog, and checks it against a blacklist, derived from 48 security policy style words. This can be easily populated with company or environment related words such as: credentials, passwords, database etc. The number of blacklist matched words is given by M_B.
9. The algorithm at this step checks for intent verbs and adjectives such as need, must, urgent etc. This value is given by M_I
10. To tune the results, values M_B and M_I are multiplied by the weights W_B and W_I, weighted at values of 2 and 1 retrospectively. This step has been added as an equation in case someone wants to change the weight of this step, if it is considered more important. The value x can hence be given by Eq. 3.

$$x = (M_B \times W_B) + (M_I \times W_I) \tag{3}$$

11. Then, the value of x is normalized in Eq. 4, using the same exponential function as Eq. 2. Where $a = 0.4$ to give the best output. A higher value of S_I indicates a higher concentration of blacklisted words in the text.

$$S_I = 1 - e^{-ax} \tag{4}$$

12. At this step the original dialogue dataset is being checked to identify which dialogue was indeed an attack and assign the true (1) or false (0) value to the new dataset used for classification.

13. The dataset is populated and the MLP classifier is applied. If the output is high, then it is considered an attack otherwise it is not considered an attack. Initially, we define an activation function as: $g(z)$ with x input values and w weights as input. The activation function is shown in Eq. 7.

$$z = w_1x_1 + w_2x_2 + \ldots + w_mx_m \tag{7}$$

If $g(z)$ is greater than a given threshold theta, the output is 1 or -1 otherwise, as shown in Eq. 8.

$$g(z) = \begin{cases} 1 & \text{if } z > \text{theta} \\ -1 & \text{otherwise} \end{cases} \tag{8}$$

Where $z = w_1x_1 + w_2x_2 + \ldots + w_mx_m = \sum_{j=1}^{m} x_jw_j = w^Tx$

At the next step, we use Rosenblatt's perceptron rule to update the weights as follows: (a) Each weight was initialized with small random numbers and (b) for each iterative training step for each input x the output value was calculated, and the weights were updated.

The output update is defined in Eq. 9, with $\Delta w_j = e(target(i) - output(i))x_j^i$ and e is the learning rate, *target* the actual (true) class label and *output* the predicted label. Weight updates were iterative, and updates were performed simultaneously.

$$w_j^+ = w_j + \Delta w_j \tag{9}$$

4   Experimental Evaluation

The experimental evaluation took place in an offline environment using a real dataset and a semi-synthetic dataset, which we call the standard dataset and the compound dataset. Following from Sect. 3, we have built both datasets using a social engineering attack dataset with 147 entries classified as an attack or not. After the preprocessing steps followed in section three, we derived the following four classification labels: (a) intent (b) spelling (c) link (d) is attack[1]. Furthermore, the standard dataset contains 147 entries obtained from [12], while the compound dataset is based on the 147 entries plus 600 entries from customer support-based tweets from Twitter, none of which are classified as attacks. Both dataset text entries have been converted to numerical based classification datasets with four entries each. Three labels for the respective data and one with a yes or no (1 or 0) value of a conversation being a social engineering attack or not. To both datasets a small number of links to websites have been added, with some being malicious.

The accuracy metric has been used for the evaluating the classification models. The metric calculates the fraction of the prediction that each model got right. Equation 10

---

[1] The datasets can be found at https://github.com/npolatidis/seader.

represents the accuracy where TP stands for true positives, TN for true negatives, FP for false positives and FN for false negatives.

$$Accuracy = \frac{TP + TN}{TP + TN + FP + FN} \tag{10}$$

The results of the evaluation as shown in Tables 1, 2, 3, 4, 5, 6, and 7 are based on the standard and compound datasets respectively and a 5-fold cross-validation approach has been used. In Tables 1, 2, 3, 4, 5, 6 the MAX and MIN values represent the maximum and minimum values of the 5-fold returned after each time the algorithm ran and the MEAN is the median value. Each algorithm was executed 10 times and at the end of each table the value is the mean value of 10 iterations for each of the three table labels. Table 7 however, presents the average mean results for the standard and compound datasets respectively.

Three algorithms from the SciKit machine learning library have been used for comparison purposes: Decision Tree, Random Forest and Neural Network multi-layer perceptron. The settings used for the algorithms were the following:

Decision Tree: SciKit learn settings with default settings which included unlimited leaf nodes.

Random Forest: SciKit Random Forest classifier with 50 Estimators.

Neural Network: SciKit MLP classifier with lbfgs solver, alpha = 1e-5 and hidden layer size = (15,15,15).

Table 1. Decision Tree results for the standard dataset

MEAN	MAX	MIN
0.736231884	0.826086957	0.583333333
0.692885375	0.782608696	0.625
0.68442029	0.833333333	0.458333333
0.650362319	0.695652174	0.583333333
0.656347826	0.76	0.608695652
0.659914361	0.826086957	0.5
0.694762846	0.826086957	0.416666667
0.647463768	0.791666667	0.5
0.65	0.695652174	0.583333333
0.741798419	0.833333333	0.652173913
0.681	**0.787**	**0.551**

Table 2. Random Forest results for the standard dataset

MEAN	MAX	MIN
0.683333333	0.791666667	0.608695652
0.631521739	0.708333333	0.565217391
0.691304348	0.791666667	0.608695652
0.657608696	0.75	0.565217391
0.651811594	0.782608696	0.333333333
0.700724638	0.75	0.666666667
0.647826087	0.75	0.5
0.736067194	0.782608696	0.708333333
0.699130435	0.8	0.608695652
0.72826087	0.826086957	0.583333333
0.683	**0.773**	**0.575**

Table 3. Multi-Layer Perceptron results for the standard dataset

MEAN	MAX	MIN
0.709057971	0.75	0.652173913
0.74384058	0.826086957	0.652173913
0.673043478	0.8	0.565217391
0.640217391	0.782608696	0.47826087
0.75273386	0.833333333	0.625
0.65085639	0.739130435	0.541666667
0.751449275	0.826086957	0.565217391
0.659826087	0.739130435	0.56
0.68173913	0.8	0.52173913
0.65	0.695652174	0.583333333
0.691	**0.779**	**0.574**

Table 4. Decision Tree results for the compound dataset

MEAN	MAX	MIN
0.908050847	0.916666667	0.9
0.921481816	0.957983193	0.900826446
0.921386555	0.941176471	0.890756303
0.923023127	0.95	0.890756303
0.921470588	0.957983193	0.9
0.923120703	0.941176471	0.909090909
0.909774011	0.93220339	0.891666667
0.919747899	0.9327773109	0.908333333
0.913009121	0.925619835	0.899159664
0.914705882	0.933333333	0.890756303
0.918	**0.939**	**0.898**

Table 5. Random Forest results for the compound dataset

MEAN	MAX	MIN
0.902910619	0.95	0.857142857
0.919787138	0.941176471	0.900826446
0.909703336	0.924369748	0.899159664
0.92640056	0.941666667	0.915966387
0.921414566	0.95	0.883333333
0.919803922	0.941176471	0.891666667
0.916468927	0.940677966	0.883333333
0.911358543	0.933333333	0.883333333
0.931468273	0.941666667	0.917355372
0.911372549	0.916666667	0.907563025
0.917	**0.938**	**0.894**

Table 6. Multi-layer perceptron results for the compound dataset

MEAN	MAX	MIN
0.929803922	0.949579832	0.908333333
0.921442577	0.932773109	0.908333333
0.926414566	0.941666667	0.915966387
0.923107345	0.933333333	0.908333333
0.936442577	0.949579832	0.915966387
0.919789916	0.949579832	0.891666667
0.923120934	0.949579832	0.899159664
0.924733894	0.941176471	0.899159664
0.924747899	0.941666667	0.907563025
0.921398477	0.949579832	0.907563025
0.925	**0.944**	**0.906**

Table 7. Comparison of algorithms for the standard and the compound datasets

<table>
<tr><td colspan="2" align="center">(a)</td><td colspan="2" align="center">(b)</td></tr>
<tr><td>ALGORITHM</td><td>RESULT</td><td>ALGORITHM</td><td>RESULT</td></tr>
<tr><td>Decision Tree</td><td>0.681</td><td>Decision Tree</td><td>0.918</td></tr>
<tr><td>Random Forest</td><td>0.683</td><td>Random Forest</td><td>0.917</td></tr>
<tr><td>Multi-Layer Perceptron</td><td>0.691</td><td>Multi-Layer Perceptron</td><td>0.925</td></tr>
</table>

5 Conclusions

In this paper we presented a novel method for social engineering attack detection based on natural language processing and artificial neural networks. The method initially processes a dialogue and then creates a dataset that can be used for classification purposes. The proposed method has been evaluated using a real and a semi-synthetic dataset and can detect social engineering attacks with very high accuracy. Furthermore, alternative classification methods have been used for comparison in order to show the effectiveness of our method.

Although the accuracy results are high, we believe that there is still room for improvement, thus in the future we plan investigate the possibility of adding more features to the dataset and to apply a deep neural network for the classification process. In addition to that we aim to investigation performance and optimization issues.

References

1. Sawa, Y., Bhakta, R., Harris, I.G., Hadnagy, C.: Detection of social engineering attacks through natural language processing of conversations. In: 2016 IEEE Tenth International Conference on Semantic Computing (ICSC), pp. 262–265. IEEE (2016)
2. Peng, T., Harris, I., Sawa, Y.: Detecting phishing attacks using natural language processing and machine learning. In: 2018 IEEE 12th International Conference on Semantic Computing (ICSC). IEEE (2018)
3. Mouton, F., Nottingham, A., Leenen, L., Venter, H.S.: Finite state machine for the social engineering attack detection model: SEADM. SAIEE Afr. Res. J. **109**(2), 133–148 (2018)
4. Tsinganos, N., Sakellariou, G., Fouliras, P., Mavridis, I.: Towards an automated recognition system for chat-based social engineering attacks in enterprise environments. In: Proceedings of the 13th International Conference on Availability, Reliability and Security, p. 53. ACM (2018)
5. Cialdini, R.B.: The science of persuasion. Sci. Am. **284**(2), 76–81 (2001)
6. Manning, C., Surdeanu, M., Bauer, J., Finkel, J., Bethard, S., McClosky, D.: The stanford CoreNLP natural language processing toolkit. In: Proceedings of 52nd Annual Meeting of the Association for Computational Linguistics: System Demonstrations, pp. 55–60 (2014)
7. Hoeschele, M., Rogers, M.: Detecting social engineering. In: Pollitt, M., Shenoi, S. (eds.) DigitalForensics 2005. ITIFIP, vol. 194, pp. 67–77. Springer, Boston, MA (2006). https://doi.org/10.1007/0-387-31163-7_6
8. Hoeschele, M.: CERIAS Technical report 2006–15 DETECTING SOCIAL ENGINEERING (2006)
9. Jamil, A., Asif, K., Ghulam, Z., Nazir, M.K., Alam, S.M., Ashraf, R.: MPMPA: a mitigation and prevention model for social engineering based phishing attacks on facebook. In: 2018 IEEE International Conference on Big Data (Big Data), pp. 5040–5048. IEEE (2018)
10. Bhakta, R., Harris, I.G.: Semantic analysis of dialogs to detect social engineering attacks. In: Proceedings of the 2015 IEEE 9th International Conference on Semantic Computing (IEEE ICSC 2015). IEEE (2015)
11. Heartfield, R., Loukas, G.: Detecting semantic social engineering attacks with the weakest link: Implementation and empirical evaluation of a human-as-a-security-sensor framework. Comput. Secur. **76**, 101–127 (2018)

12. Bezuidenhout, M., Mouton, F., Venter, H.S.: Social engineering attack detection model: SEADM. In: 2010 Information Security for South Africa. IEEE (2010)
13. Mouton, F., Leenen, L., Venter, H.S.: Social engineering attack detection model: SEADMv2. In: 2015 International Conference on Cyberworlds (CW). IEEE (2015)
14. Nicholson, J., Coventry, L., Briggs, P.: Can we fight social engineering attacks by social means? Assessing social salience as a means to improve phish detection. In: Thirteenth Symposium on Usable Privacy and Security ({SOUPS} 2017) (2017)
15. Krombholz, K., Hobel, H., Huber, M., Weippl, E.: Advanced social engineering attacks. J. Inf. Secur. Appl. **22**, 113–122 (2015)
16. Mouton, F., Leenen, L., Venter, H.S.: Social engineering attack examples, templates and scenarios. Comput. Secur. **59**, 186–209 (2016)
17. Nguyen, N.T., Nguyen, V.D., Hwang, D.: An influence analysis of the number of members on the quality of knowledge in a collective. J. Intell. Fuzzy Syst. **32**(2), 1217–1228 (2017)
18. Saadat, J., Moallem, P., Koofigar, H.: Training echo state neural network using harmony search algorithm. Int. J. Artif. Intell. **15**(1), 163–179 (2017)
19. Precup, R.-E., David, R.-C.: Nature-Inspired Optimization Algorithms for Fuzzy Controlled Servo Systems. Butterworth-Heinemann, Oxford (2019)
20. Abed-Alguni, B.H.: Island-based cuckoo search with highly disruptive polynomial mutation. Int. J. Artif. Intell. **17**(1), 57–82 (2019)

Usability Testing of Data Entry Patterns Implemented According to Material Design Guidelines for the Web

Marcin Drygielski[1], Agnieszka Indyka-Piasecka[1] (ID),
Mateusz Piwowarczyk[1] (ID), Zbigniew Telec[1] (ID),
Bogdan Trawiński[1(✉)] (ID), and Trong Hai Duong[2] (ID)

[1] Faculty of Computer Science and Management,
Wrocław University of Science and Technology, Wrocław, Poland
{agnieszka.indyka-piasecka,mateusz.piwowarczyk,
zbigniew.telec,bogdan.trawinski}@pwr.edu.pl
[2] Faculty of Information Technology, Nguyen Tat Thanh University,
Ho Chi Minh City, Vietnam
haiduongtrong@gmail.com

Abstract. Analysis of data entry design patterns in web application was presented in the paper. 22 design patterns were tested with different sets of input data. In order to facilitate the process of conducting usability tests, a web application was developed according to the Google's Material Design principles. It contained all tested data entry design patters. Due to automating test results collection it was possible to perform the test with a larger number users. Usability tests were carried out with a group of 49 people. The group of participants consisted of people in different age, having different education, occupation and experience in using web applications. Based on the analysis of results a set of recommendations was formulated on the usage of selected data entry design patterns in web applications.

Keywords: Usability testing · Data entry · Design patterns ·
Web applications · Material design

1 Introduction

Usability testing is designed to assess a product or service in terms of usability. Real users take part in the tests to measure the intuitiveness and usability of the solution and how easy it is for users to achieve their goals. By collecting qualitative and quantitative data they allow for assessing the difficulty of use, detecting problems with usability and determining the satisfaction from the usage. Typically, the tests involve the participants performing previously prepared tasks, while the person conducting the test collects data on the behaviour of users. The main difference between usability tests and other tests in the software development process (e.g. integration and acceptance tests) is the fact that real users of the system participate in them. They cannot be replaced by software development team members as they could be biased providing unreliable test results.

© Springer Nature Switzerland AG 2019
N. T. Nguyen et al. (Eds.): ICCCI 2019, LNAI 11683, pp. 697–711, 2019.
https://doi.org/10.1007/978-3-030-28377-3_58

The introduction of new technologies and software development methods contributes to a significant increase in the number of new applications and modernization of the existing ones. One of the most important elements of any system is the way in which data are entered. Each encountered difficulty or unnecessary action discourages the users from using the application. For this reason, the key role is played by the awareness of the needs, possibilities and limitations of the users who are to be recipients of a software product. This allows for designing and implementing user friendly applications.

Usability models, methods, and metrics have been intensively studied for three decades. ISO 9241-11 introduces the usability model composed of three attributes: effectiveness, efficiency and satisfaction [1]. In turn, Nielsen's model of usability comprises five following attributes: efficiency, satisfaction, learnability, memorability, and errors [2]. Harrison et al. [3] proposed the PACMAD usability model for mobile applications which embraces seven attributes effectiveness, efficiency, satisfaction, learnability, memorability, errors and cognitive load. A large number of works addresses challenges and problems of usability and report the evaluation of web applications and systems with different approaches [4–7].

The aim of this paper is to examine the usability of selected data entry patterns in web applications that form the basis of interaction with the user. Conducting tests with users and then analysing the collected results allowed to formulate conclusions and recommendations for the usage of individual patterns. The usability metrics such as task completion time, number of errors, user assessment of task difficulty were collected. Moreover users' attitude towards individual patterns was analysed based on their opinions and comments. User satisfaction was assessed employing the Single Ease Question (SEQ) questionnaire administered after completion of each task.

Up to date the authors have tested a responsive conference website developed to assist with the organization of a scientific conference [8, 9] and a responsive web application for a school for disabled children [10]. Moreover, they conducted comparative analysis of usability of data entry design patterns devoted to mobile applications [11].

For the purpose of testing the usability of the data entry patterns, a web application has been prepared, which made it possible to carry out research along with data collection and analysis. To ensure the consistency of the graphical interface, a simple yet readable style of Material Design created by Google was used [12, 13]. The main argument in favour of using this approach is its popularity. In 2014, it was announced as the official style of applications produced by Google, e.g. Gmail, Google Drive and Google Docs. Numerous developers began to use this style, thus contributing to its widespread recognition among the web application users. Three exemplary pages of the web application developed according to the Material Design guidelines to carry out research are depicted in Figs. 1, 2 and 3. The workflow of the scenario to enter dates is shown in Fig. 1. In turn, Fig. 2 presents the Single Ease Question (SEQ) questionnaire to measure users' satisfaction, and finally, the input of a complex text using voice typing is illustrated in Fig. 3.

The tests were carried out with the use of equipment currently used by the participants, i.e. computers located in a computer lab, a company or in their private homes. The use of equipment that was not foreign to the subjects allowed for the minimization of factors not related to the use of data entry patterns, for example a different arrangement of keys on the keyboard or the use of a touch panel for people using mainly mice.

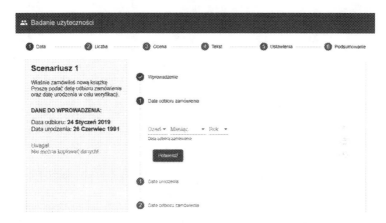

Fig. 1. The workflow of the scenario to enter dates

Fig. 2. Single Ease Question (SEQ) questionnaire to measure users' satisfaction

Fig. 3. The input of a complex text using voice typing

2 Setup of Usability Tests

The study aimed at gathering information on the use of selected data entry patterns, and then analysing their usability in terms of their application and types of values entered in web services. In total 22 design patterns were implemented and tested with different sets of input data. The following metrics were collected during the tests: task completion time, number of errors, user assessment of task difficulty. Moreover users' opinions were gathered to analyse their attitude towards individual patterns.

We recruited 49 participants to take part in our study. Their basic characteristics are depicted in Fig. 4. Vast majority of them were young people, 43% were under 20 years of age and the other 43% were between 20 and 35. Only 14% were over 35. Women constituted 22% and men 78% of the users. 39% of the participants were the students of a technical secondary school; this means that they attained lower secondary level education (LSE). In turn, 18% of the users had the General Certificate of Secondary Education (GCSE) and 12% finished study at the bachelor's level. Finally, 31% of them received master's degree from a university. The majority of the participants, namely 57%, declared that they use computers very frequently (VF), i.e. they spent on the computer more than 2 h a day. In turn, 14% spent on the computer up to 2 h a day; this was denoted as F – frequent usage. 19% of participants used computers occasionally (O), i.e. several times a week. The remaining 4% and 6% participants used computers rarely (R) and very rarely (VR), namely several times a month and several times a year, respectively.

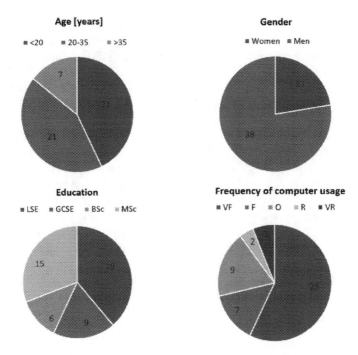

Fig. 4. Descriptive characteristics of the participants of the usability study

3   Results of Experiment

The results of usability testing for entering dates, numbers, ratings and selecting one out of two options as well as inputting text are depicted in Figs. 5, 6, 7, 8, 9, 10, 11, 12, 13 14, 15 and 16. Mean and median time of completion individual tasks was presented in the form of bar charts. The difference between the values of corresponding means and medians indicates performance variability among the participants.

The satisfaction was measured using a questionnaire based on the Single Ease Question (SEQ) which was administered after the users had completed each task. Compared to the standard SEQ [14] the rating scale in our questionnaire was reversed. Our version of SEQ contained one item based on the seven-point Likert scale ranging from 1 – *very easy* to 7 – *very difficult*. Thus, the average SEQ score after entering data with individual design patterns presented in Figs. 7, 10, 13, and 16 should be interpreted in the following way: the smaller value if the SEQ score the easier a given design pattern was perceived by the users.

Entering Dates
The goal of this scenario was to examine the usefulness of design patterns for date entry. At the beginning, the participant was informed about the situation in which he/she ordered a new book. His/her tasks was to give the date of receipt of the parcel with the book and the date of his/her birth. The first date was to investigate the efficiency of entering near dates (NDT) that represent the day in the same month.

The motivation for choosing this value was the popularity of applications which contain planning or supplementing information about near events. The second value was chosen in order to analyse entering a distant date (DDT) because it is the most common case in the forms.

Six following design patterns for date entering were tested: NDT1, DDT1 – two numeric fields to input a day and year with a numeric keyboard and the drop-down list of months between them, NDT2, DDT2 – the text field to input date with the dd/mm/yyyy mask, NDT3, DDT3 – the editable text field with a date picker, NDT4, DDT4 – three drop-down lists to select a day, month and year, NDT5, DDT5 – three scrollers to input a day, month and year, NDT6, DDT6 – selecting a date with the standard date picker. The task of each person was to introduce a near and distant date three times using three different data entry patterns. The evaluation for this type of data was carried out in two variants, thus examining 6 different patterns.

It is clearly seen in Fig. 5 that the date picker (NDT6) is the most efficient pattern to enter a near date. On the other hand, the three scrollers (NDT5) took the longest time to input a near date. A comparison of the number of errors made during the test indicates that the text field with the date mask (NDT2) can lead to the largest amount of incorrect data entered by users. In turn, no error was observed when subjects used the date picker (NDT6). Regarding satisfaction questionnaire the date picker (NDT6) obtained the best score whereas the numeric fields with the drop-down list of months (NDT1) were rated the lowest.

The shortest times to enter a distant date (see Fig. 6) were obtained by using three scrollers (DDT5), the text field with the date mask (DDT2), and two numeric fields with the drop-down list of months (DDT1). The patterns using the calendar pickers (DDT6 and DDT3) provided the worst performance. The only design pattern which did not lead to an attempt to introduce incorrect values was the date picker (DDT6). The best SEQ (see Fig. 7) score was obtained by using the drop-down lists (DDT4) and numeric fields with the drop-down list of months (DDT1). The worst assessed were the patterns using the calendar (DDT3 and DDT6).

Entering Numbers

This scenario was applied to test the usefulness of design patterns for the input of small and large numbers. It continued the book purchase scenario. The participants were asked to enter numerical values regarding the cost of the book delivery and the EAN-13 barcode of the book. The former was a small amount of 8 PLN and the latter was the long 13-digit number of 9788375780635. Four following design patterns for entering small and large numbers were assessed: SNB1 – the numeric field to input a one-digit integer number, SNB2 – the spinner to input a one-digit integer number. LNB1 – the numeric field to enter a 13-digit integer number using a numeric keyboard, and LNB2 – input of a 13-digit number using voice typing.

The means and medians of completion time for the small number for two consecutive iterations one after the other are shown in Fig. 8. It can be easily noticed that utilizing the numeric field (SNB1) outperformed the spinner (SNB2) in both iterations. None of the users made a mistake when entering a simple amount with the spinner (SNB2) whereas two participants attempted to enter incorrect values into the numeric field (SNB1). No significant difference between SEQ scores for both input methods could be observed.

Looking at the graph in Fig. 9, it is clear that the use of the numeric field to input the 13-digit integer number (LNB1) yielded significantly better results. The second iteration did not show any improvement in the results for the use of voice typing (LNB2). Nine out of eleven cases in which number input errors occurred were due to the use of speech recognition. The SEQ scores (see Fig. 10) indicated that the use of the numeric field was considered more difficult than the use of voice input in the case of a large number.

Entering Ratings

The next scenario aimed at investigating the patterns for inputting customers' ratings. The participants were requested to rate the book (4 out of 6) and the book vendor (8 out of 10). Four following design patterns for rating were tested: RAT1 – star rating, RAT2 – the spinner, RAT3 – radio buttons, RAT4 – the slider.

From Fig. 11 it is clear that the spinner (RAT1) was the least effective way to enter an assessment. Better results were obtained with the slider (RAT4). The radio buttons (RAT3) provided the lowest times during the first iteration of the test whereas the star rating surpassed the other methods during the second iteration. Familiarization with the patterns led to a significant reduction in the task completion time. It could be observed that the most errors were due to the use of the radio buttons (RAT3). The use of the spinner (RAT2) led to an attempt to enter incorrect data in two cases. In one of the tests, validation of the incorrect value occurred using the slider (RAT4). The use of stars (RAT1) did not caused any error during the whole test. According to the participants, as the chart for SEQ scores in Fig. 13 shows, the easiest ways to enter the rating were the radio buttons (RAT3) and stars (RAT1). The slider (RAT4) was considered the most difficult.

Selecting One Out of Two Options

This scenario refers to a common situation in which the users agree to receive notifications in a web application or by e-mail. The task of the participants was to accept obtaining notifications about promotions and change the status of an order. At the same time, they had to resign from notifications about new products and unfinished transactions. Six following design patterns for selecting one out of two options were examined: SEL1 – checkbox, SEL2 – drop-down list, SEL3 – slide toggle, SEL4 – toggle buttons, SEL5 – radio buttons, SEL6 – text buttons. The text button could take two states: "on" and "off". The change of a state is made by clicking on the button.

The check box (SEL1) turned out to be the most effective pattern for selecting one out of two options (see Fig. 12). In turn, the participants had a problem with the correct use of the text button (SEL6) due to lacking any additional element which could show its current state, e.g. using a colour or displaying an alternative value. During the second iteration all task completion times were significantly shorter because the users became familiar with how the patterns work. The use of the drop-down list (SEL2), radio buttons (SEL5), and toggle buttons (SEL4) resulted in the smallest number of errors. In turn, the largest number of mistakes was caused by the use of the text button (SEL6), which indicates problems with understanding and using this pattern. The best SEQ score (see Fig. 13) was obtained by using checkboxes (SEL1) and radio buttons (SEL5). Utilizing the toggle buttons (SEL4) was rated as quite difficult, while the worst score was achieved by using the text buttons (SEL6).

Entering Text

This scenario focused on the design patterns for inputting text. The participants were asked to enter a comment containing a simple text without punctuation marks and a message to the book vendor representing the official complaint. The simple text was: *"despite some negative reviews i can honestly recommend this book all readers especially for long autumn evenings".* The complex text included the following complaint: *"Hello, I am writing about the order number 543854. Unfortunately, after receiving the package, it turned out that one book is missing. I am looking forward to your earliest response."* Following two design patterns were employed: STX1, CTX1 – the text field to enter the simple and complex text respectively with a keyboard, STX2, CTX2 – input of the simple and complex text respectively using voice typing.

Figure 14 clearly illustrates the advantage of voice typing (STX2) as a form of entering the simple text. The input of the simple text using the keyboard (STX1) required twice as much time in both iterations of the study. Errors occurred more frequently when entering text using the keyboard. The participants rated the voice input as an easier way to enter simple text, as reported in Fig. 16.

Completely different results were obtained when entering the complex text as illustrated in Fig. 15. It can be observed that in the first iteration of the study, the design pattern for entering complex text using the keyboard (CTX1) outperformed significantly voice typing (CTX2). The median and mean times needed to enter data using the first method did not change considerably in the second iteration. The difference is noticeable in the case of voice input (CTX2). The re-use of this method allowed for a nearly two-fold reduction in the average time needed to enter the complex text, thus resulting in a better result. The median in the second iteration still indicates the advantage of using the keyboard, but the difference was almost halved. When entering the complex text with the keyboard the users made a smaller number of mistakes. The SEQ score (see Fig. 16) indicates that voice input was assessed as an easier way to input the complex text. The pattern of text input using only the keyboard was considered more difficult, but the difference was not relatively great.

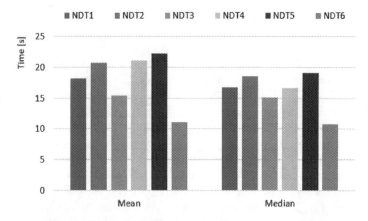

Fig. 5. Mean and median input time for a near date (NDT)

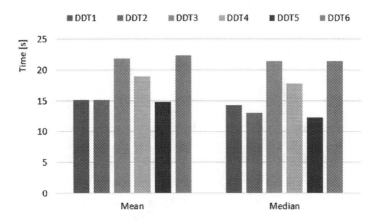

Fig. 6. Mean and median input time for a distant date (DDT)

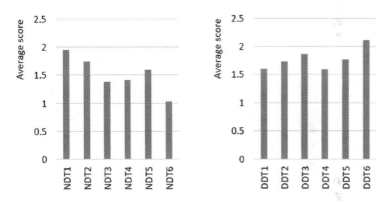

Fig. 7. Average SEQ score after inputting near (NDT) and distant dates (DDT)

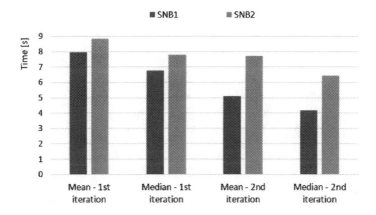

Fig. 8. Mean and median input time for a small integer number (SNB)

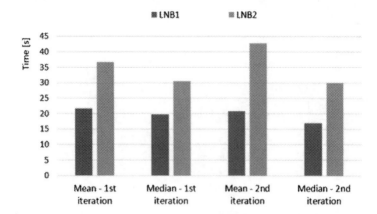

Fig. 9. Mean and median input time for a large integer number (LNB)

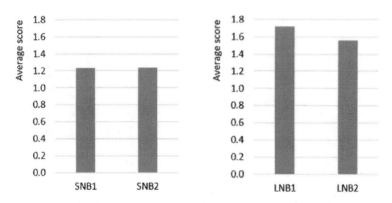

Fig. 10. Average SEQ score after inputting small and large integer numbers

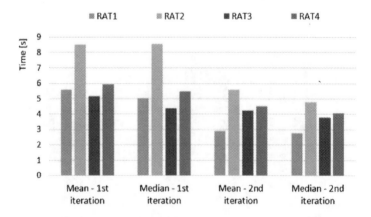

Fig. 11. Mean and median input time for rating (RAT)

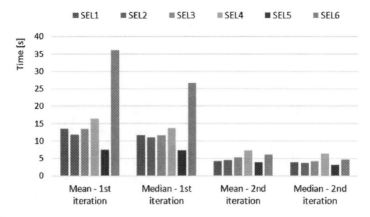

Fig. 12. Mean and median input time for selection one out of two options (SEL)

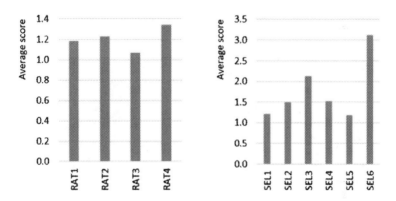

Fig. 13. Average SEQ score after inputting ratings (RAT) and selection (SEL)

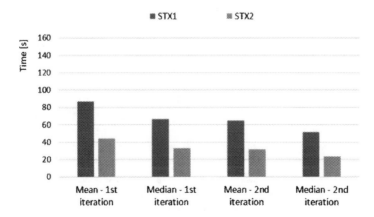

Fig. 14. Mean and median input time for a simple text (STX)

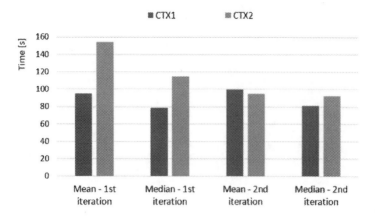

Fig. 15. Mean and median input time for a complex text (CTX)

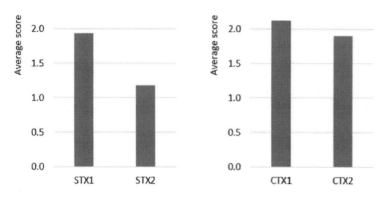

Fig. 16. Average SEQ score after inputting simple (STX) and complex text (CTX)

4 Recommendations on the Usage and Conclusions

Based on the results obtained from the reported research some recommendations regarding the use of the data entry design patterns in web applications were formulated.

Entering Dates

The date picker (NDT6) can be recommended for applications where entering a date is important and should be done without any error. The standard date picker, which does not allow for entering any value, guarantees correctness of the date input. It attracts the users' attention thereby minimizing the risk of mistakes. The date picker turns out to be the most effective if the expected date is in the near future or past, for example if it is used for scheduling tasks or making reservations. In this case, it is likely that it will be a near date. However, the date picker is not recommended for entering distant dates with the date picker which requires a large number of clicks in this case. This adversely affects the users' satisfaction and the effectiveness of this action. For inputting distant dates, such as a date of birth, the use of numeric fields to enter the day and year and a drop-down list to select a month from the list (NDT1) seems to be the best. It may also be useful to use a text field with an input mask (NDT2), but it increases the risk of problems when entering the date. It may be concluded that the possibility of editing facilitated the input of a distant date.

Entering Numbers

Both the classic numeric field (SNB1) and the spinner (SNB1) can be recommended to input one-digit numbers. As the matter of fact the first way took less time but the second one produced no errors. The users' satisfaction level was almost the same. In the case of large numbers, the classic numeric field (LNB1), which allows for entering data using the keyboard, turned out to be the best. Extending it with the possibility of entering using the voice (LNB2), despite a positive assessment among the participants, resulted in a significant increase in the time of data entry and enlarged the number of errors.

Entering Ratings

In the case when entering a rating in a web application occurs very rarely, the best solution is to use radio buttons (RAT3) as values representing the assessment. This is the most familiar solution among users, which will provide the highest usability. When introducing the assessment in the application is not an exceptional event, the recommended solution is to use rating stars (RAT1). This allows the users to quickly identify the purpose and how to enter values. This is the most natural for users among all the surveyed ways of entering ratings. However, we do not recommend the use of numeric spinners (RAT2) and sliders (RAT4), as they unnecessarily require users to focus too much on the introduction of the assessment. They also increase the chance of users entering incorrect values.

Selecting One Out of Two Options

The most recommended design patterns for selecting one out of two options are the use of radio buttons (SEL5) and check boxes (SEL1). The results of entering data using these methods indicate their advantage compared to other ways. A good solution may also be to use switches (SEL3). The use of a drop-down list (SEL2) is recommended when the data input is very important for the application or user. Applying the drop-down list causes people to focus more attention on the current activity. An important factor related to the usability of this type of design patterns is to enable users to select an option with a single click of the mouse. Another important factor is the need for clear displaying the current state, because negligence in this area can lead to a drastic decline in the usability of the solution.

Entering Text

In the situation when the application requires entering a large amount of text, it is recommended to supplement the text field with the possibility of using voice input. This solution allows for faster data entry, which directly translates into increased user satisfaction. The use of voice typing is well received by a large number of users. However, it should be noted that many people may not be able to use this method of entering data due to technical limitations. Some users could not be willing to use this type of text input.

The factors acting to the disadvantage of voice input is the noise caused by dictation of the text and other sound coming from the environment, which also limit the environment in which this pattern can be used. Application developers must also keep in mind technological limitations. The mechanism used to convert speech to text used in the study did not allow for the interpretation of whole sentences, which resulted in the lack of punctuation in the introduced text. The use of a data entry design pattern using voice-to-text conversions should at least be considered by the developers of web applications, since the implementation of this pattern might bring many benefits.

The usability study of 22 design patterns for data input in web applications was reported. The research was conducted with a group of 49 people, differing in their age, education, profession and experience in the use of web applications. The obtained results allowed for the assessment of design patterns in various aspects that make up the usability of the whole application. Based on the knowledge gained recommendations were formulated for usage of data entry design patterns depending on their purpose and the type of values entered in web applications.

References

1. ISO 9241-11: Ergonomic requirements for office work with visual display terminals (VDTs) - Part 11: Guidance on usability (1998)
2. Nielsen, J., Budiu, R.: Mobile Usability. New Riders Press, Berkeley (2012)
3. Harrison, R., Flood, D., Duce, D.: Usability of mobile applications: literature review and rationale for a new usability model. J. Interact. Sci. 1, 1 (2013). https://doi.org/10.1186/2194-0827-1-1
4. Lew, P., Olsina, L., Zhang, L.: Quality, quality in use, actual usability and user experience as key drivers for web application evaluation. In: Benatallah, B., Casati, F., Kappel, G., Rossi, G. (eds.) ICWE 2010. LNCS, vol. 6189, pp. 218–232. Springer, Heidelberg (2010). https://doi.org/10.1007/978-3-642-13911-6_15
5. EL-firjani, N.F.M., Elberkawi, E.K., Maatuk, A.M.: A method for website usability evaluation: a comparative analysis. Int. J. Web Semant. Technol. (IJWesT) 8, 3 (2017). https://doi.org/10.5121/ijwest.2017.8301
6. Bastien, J.: Usability testing: A review of some methodological and technical aspects of the method. Int. J. Med. Inf. 79(4), e18–e23 (2009). https://doi.org/10.1016/j.ijmedinf.2008.12.004
7. Matera, M., Rizzo, F., Carughi, G.T.: Web usability: principles and evaluation methods. In: Mendes, E., Mosley, N. (eds.) Web Engineering, pp. 143–180. Springer, Heidelberg (2006). https://doi.org/10.1007/3-540-28218-1
8. Bernacki, J., Błażejczyk, I., Indyka-Piasecka, A., Kopel, M., Kukla, E., Trawiński, B.: Responsive web design: testing usability of mobile web applications. In: Nguyen, N.T., Trawiński, B., Fujita, H., Hong, T.-P. (eds.) ACIIDS 2016. LNCS (LNAI), vol. 9621, pp. 257–269. Springer, Heidelberg (2016). https://doi.org/10.1007/978-3-662-49381-6_25
9. Błażejczyk, I., Trawiński, B., Indyka-Piasecka, A., Kopel, M., Kukla, E., Bernacki, J.: Usability testing of a mobile friendly web conference service. In: Nguyen, N.-T., Manolopoulos, Y., Iliadis, L., Trawiński, B. (eds.) ICCCI 2016. LNCS (LNAI), vol. 9875, pp. 565–579. Springer, Cham (2016). https://doi.org/10.1007/978-3-319-45243-2_52

10. Krzewińska, J., Indyka-Piasecka, A., Kopel, M., Kukla, E., Telec, Z., Trawiński, B.: Usability testing of a responsive web system for a school for disabled children. In: Nguyen, N.T., Hoang, D.H., Hong, T.-P., Pham, H., Trawiński, B. (eds.) ACIIDS 2018. LNCS (LNAI), vol. 10751, pp. 705–716. Springer, Cham (2018). https://doi.org/10.1007/978-3-319-75417-8_66
11. Myka, J., Indyka-Piasecka, A., Telec, Z., Trawiński, B., Dac, H.C.: Comparative analysis of usability of data entry design patterns for mobile applications. In: Nguyen, N.T., Gaol, F.L., Hong, T.-P., Trawiński, B. (eds.) ACIIDS 2019. LNCS (LNAI), vol. 11431, pp. 737–750. Springer, Cham (2019). https://doi.org/10.1007/978-3-030-14799-0_63
12. Material Design webpage. https://material.io/. Accessed 20 June 2019)
13. Patel, P.: A Guide to Material Design, a Modern Software Design Language. Open Source for You, pp. 64–66 (2016). www.OpenSourceForU.com
14. Sauro, J., Lewis, J.R.: Quantifying the User Experience. Practical Statistics for User Research. Morgan Kaufmann, Boston (2012)

Author Index

Printed in the United States
By Bookmasters